Maritime Security

Maritime Security

An Introduction

Second Edition

Michael A. McNicholas

AMSTERDAM • BOSTON • HEIDELBERG • LONDON
NEW YORK • OXFORD • PARIS • SAN DIEGO
SAN FRANCISCO • SINGAPORE • SYDNEY • TOKYO

Butterworth-Heinemann is an imprint of Elsevier

Butterworth-Heinemann is an imprint of Elsevier
The Boulevard, Langford Lane, Kidlington, Oxford OX5 1GB, UK
50 Hampshire Street, 5th Floor, Cambridge, MA 02139, USA

Notices
Knowledge and best practice in this field are constantly changing. As new research and experience broaden our understanding, changes in research methods, professional practices, or medical treatment may become necessary.

Practitioners and researchers must always rely on their own experience and knowledge in evaluating and using any information, methods, compounds, or experiments described herein. In using such information or methods they should be mindful of their own safety and the safety of others, including parties for whom they have a professional responsibility.

To the fullest extent of the law, neither the Publisher nor the authors, contributors, or editors, assume any liability for any injury and/or damage to persons or property as a matter of products liability, negligence or otherwise, or from any use or operation of any methods, products, instructions, or ideas contained in the material herein

British Library Cataloguing in Publication Data
A catalogue record for this book is available from the British Library

Library of Congress Cataloging-in-Publication Data
A catalog record for this book is available from the Library of Congress

ISBN: 978-0-12-803672-3

For information on all Butterworth-Heinemann publications visit our website at https://www.elsevier.com/

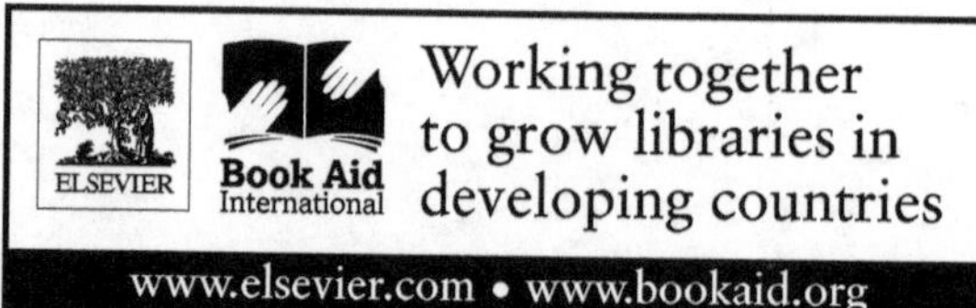

Publisher: Candice G. Janco
Acquisition Editor: Sara Scott
Editorial Project Manager: Hilary Carr
Production Project Manager: Mohanapriyan Rajendran
Designer: Mark Rogers

Transferred to Digital Printing in 2016

Dedication

This book is dedicated to my parents, Francis and Virginia McNicholas, for their never-ending love and support, and to my children, Alexandra, Julian, and Maria, and my granddaughter, Mia; all who are the sunshine in my life.

Dedication

Table of Contents

About the Author

Michael A. McNicholas

Mr. McNicholas is the Managing Director of Phoenix Group in Panama and Costa Rica and Pathfinder Consulting, LLC, in the United States. Michael has over 14 years of distinguished and progressive law enforcement, military, and intelligence experience and, most recently, 20+ years as founder/cofounder of several successful professional security corporations in Latin America and the United States. A former noncommissioned and commissioned officer (presidential direct appointment) in the U.S. Army, he served for 9 years in Airborne Infantry, Military Police, and Military Intelligence units and also is a former sworn police officer. Mr. McNicholas held a *top secret* security clearance in the Central Intelligence Agency, where he specialized in counter-narcotics trafficking and international terrorism and served on the Vice President's Narcotics Interdiction Task Force and as the CIA Liaison to U.S. Coast Guard Intelligence.

Michael designed, implemented, and directed the internationally acclaimed seaport security program at Manzanillo International Terminal—Panama, the largest container port in Latin America, and currently deploys a 200+ man force (security officers, K-9, intelligence, and management) at the seaport. Mr. McNicholas spearheaded the successful efforts to have Phoenix Group designated as the first "Recognized Security Organization" (United Nations IMO classification) by the Republic of Panama Registry and the Dominican Republic. Mr. McNicholas is credited with co-pioneering the Maritime Security Team (antipiracy/stowaway/drug trafficking/terrorist) concept in commercial cargo shipping in Latin America. Phoenix Group deploys security personnel onboard over 500 ships per month in 11 ports in Latin America, and McNicholas' personnel have captured 600+ stowaways and drug couriers, seized over 10,000 kilos of cocaine and heroin, repelled armed pirates in combat on two occasions and denied access in a dozen other pirate attempts, and mitigated two terrorist operations. Mr. McNicholas and his staff have conducted security surveys and training in every major seaport in Latin America and the Caribbean and has been a Sole Source contractor for a U.S. Intelligence agency.

In mid-2001, Mr. McNicholas was contracted by RAND Corporation, under funding by the Defense Intelligence Agency and the U.S. Joint Chiefs of Staff, to provide an intelligence analysis of the "origins and routes of arms procured by Colombian Guerrilla, Para-Military, and terrorist groups." From 2002 to 2004, Mr. McNicholas served as a special advisor to the Congress of the Republic of Panama for Counter-Narcotics, Terrorism, and Intelligence issues and has briefed multiple presidents of Panama. In June 2008, Michael was selected by the Office of the U.S. Secretary of Defense (OSD) as a Maritime Security SME for multiple maritime security-related projects and later that year trained the USCG's International Port Security Assessment Command. In 2009, he was a speaker/panelist at a multiday conference on Somali piracy at the JFK School of Government at Harvard University and in 2010/2011 he conducted presentations at NATO's "Centre of Excellence—Defence Against Terrorism" in Turkey.

In 2012, Mr. McNicholas Chaired/lectured at the inaugural conference of the "Multinational Maritime Security Centre of Excellence" (MARSEC COE) in Turkey and currently he is a member of the Centre's Academic Advisory Board and continues to lecture there on an annual basis. In December 2012, Mr. McNicholas lectured at a joint U.S. ODNI-Naval Intelligence conference on Commercial Maritime Drug Trafficking and in 2013 he was selected by the U.S. Maritime Administration/USMMA/USCG to be a member of a five-person Subject Matter Expert team to develop the new Facility Security Officer Course Instructor Manual and Guidelines (ISPS/MTSA). In 2015 and 2016, Mr. McNicholas was the senior security advisory overseeing the design, development, and implementation of the port security program at the newly constructed seaport, Tuxpan Port Terminal, in Mexico.

Mr. McNicholas has lectured at Harvard University, Johns Hopkins University, the Pentagon, DIA, NATO, USMMA King's Point, British Border Forces, and at numerous conferences sponsored by the Office of the U.S. Secretary of Defense, U.S. Department of Homeland Security, the Office of the Director of National Intelligence, and the Shipping Industry. Mr. McNicholas is the author of *Maritime Security: An Introduction* (McNicholas, 2008; Elsevier, Inc./Butterworth-Heinemann), published in English and Chinese; "Port Security" (chapter ", A Networked Response to Maritime Threats: Interagency Coordination") of *Port Engineering: Planning, Construction, Maintenance, and Security* (Tsinker, Gregory, 2004; Wiley and Sons, Inc.,); *Terrorism and Commercial Transportation: Use of Ships, Cargoes, and Containers to Transport Terrorists and Material* (NATO Science for Peace and Security Series, Vol. 98, 2012); and *Use of Commercial Shipping by Terrorist Groups and Their Cooperation with Other Terrorists Groups and Transnational Criminal Organizations* (MARSEC COE, Global Maritime Security: New Horizons, 2014, Turkish Naval Forces Printing Office); Mr. McNicholas graduated from the University of Baltimore with a Bachelor of Science degree and a Master of Science degree in Criminal Justice.

Contributors to This Edition

Captain Scott D. Genovese, U.S. Coast Guard (Retired), assumed his present position as Director, Global Maritime Operational Threat Response Coordination Center in April 2014. The Global Maritime Operational Threat Response Coordination Center serves as the Department of Homeland Security's Executive Secretariat for maritime operational threat response coordination and is directly responsible to the Departments of Defense and the National Security Council Staff to ensure timely and appropriate implementation of the President's Maritime Operational Threat Response Plan. The Maritime Operational Threat Response Plan (MOTR) is the coordinating process for federal agency actions in response to threats to the United States and its interests in the maritime approaches and maritime domain. Mr. Genovese retired from active duty in the U.S. Coast Guard in 2009. During his service he commanded U.S. Coast Guard Cutters in support of Operation Allied Force (Kosovo) and Operation Iraqi Freedom.

Captain Brian Wilson, U.S. Navy (Retired), is the Deputy Director, U.S. Global Maritime Operational Threat Response Coordination Center (GMCC) and is a visiting professor at the United States Naval Academy (Piracy, Maritime Terrorism, and Law of the Sea). The GMCC coordinates the U.S. Government's interagency response to maritime threats, including drug trafficking, migrant smuggling, and piracy. He has participated in bilateral and multilateral discussions on maritime security and whole-of-government coordination frameworks and previously served in the Pentagon developing maritime security policy for the Office of the Under Secretary of Defense (Policy).

Robi Sen has 20+ years of experience in computer and internet security. As a subject matter expert, he has innovated, designed, and built numerous novel security systems, sensors, electronic warfare platforms, and communication systems, for commercial corporations, DARPA, DOD, TSWG, SOCOM, and elements of the U.S. intelligence community. Some of Robi's most notable Cyber Security efforts include developing the first security enhanced version of Android, developing a large-scale passive wireless monitoring system, and developing a new type of Electronic Warfare/Cyber-Warfare platform focused on commercial-off-the-shelf devices that makes use of protocol exploitation. Robi also is a sought after lecturer and recently lectured on Cyber Security to the Naval Post Graduate Homeland Security 2014 Master Cohort. Robi is a prolific author and has written numerous papers, articles, and technical books on technology in general and security in particular. He is also a well-established inventor who has filed or contributed to numerous patents and currently has been awarded a patent for an innovative electronic warfare and cybersecurity platform. Robi currently holds a Top Secret Security Clearance with the U.S. Government.

Lieutenant Commander Cara Condit, currently serves as the Deputy of the Environmental Law Division within the Office of Maritime and International Law. She is primarily responsible for providing advice on Environmental Crimes cases, including the enforcement of the Act to Prevent Pollution from Ships and the Federal Water Pollution Control Act. Prior to this assignment, Lieutenant Commander Condit served as appellate defense counsel at the Washington Navy Yard in Washington, D.C. Alongside her Navy and Marine Corps counterparts, she provided legal counsel to members entitled to an automatic appeal as a result of a court-marital sentence that included a punitive discharge from the service or over one year confinement. From 2011 to 2013, Lieutenant Commander Condit served as counsel for members in the Physical Disability Evaluation System process as well as those facing administrative separation boards. In addition, Lieutenant Commander Condit served as counsel for courts-martial, Boards of Inquiry and Reliefs for Cause. On a daily basis, she provided legal advice to Coast Guard members on their rights during investigations, adverse evaluations, and non-judicial punishments. Before becoming a judge advocate, Lieutenant Commander Condit served as the Executive Officer of USCGC BLOCK ISLAND in Fort Macon, North Carolina from June 2006 to August 2008 and as a Deck Watch Officer on USCGC TAMPA in Portsmouth, Virginia from May 2004 to June 2006. Lieutenant Commander Condit graduated from the Coast Guard Academy in 2004 with a Government Degree in International Affairs and Public Policy. Through the funded legal education program, she received a Juris Doctor from Suffolk University Law School in Boston, Massachusetts. She is a member of the Massachusetts Bar. Lieutenant Commander Condit also holds a Master of Law in National Security and Foreign Relations Law from George Washington University Law School in Washington, D.C. Individual military awards include the Coast Guard Commendation Medal with the Operational Distinguishing Device and the Coast Guard Achievement Medal.

Lieutenant Rebecca L. Castaneda, currently serves as a staff attorney in the Response Law Division. She is responsible for providing legal support to the Coast Guard's Office of International Affairs (DCO-I). LT Castaneda also is a duty attorney and provides real-time legal and policy advice to senior decision-makers to facilitate Coast Guard maritime law enforcement operations, including advising on domestic law enforcement authorities, international law, and interagency coordination requirements. Prior to joining the Coast Guard, LT Castaneda practiced law in Massachusetts as both a trial and disability attorney. Lieutenant Castaneda graduated from the University of California at Davis with a B.A. in English and a minor in Philosophy. She received a Juris Doctor from New England School of Law in Boston, Massachusetts, and is a member of the Massachusetts Bar. In law school, she was an associate editor for the *New England Journal of International and Comparative Law* and served as the editor-in-chief of *Due Process*. She joined the Coast Guard as a Direct Commission Lawyer in 2012. Individual military awards include the Commandant's Letter of Commendation.

Gerard R. Draughon has over 30 years experience in U.S. law enforcement, with 25 years with U.S. Customs and Border Protection and focused on seaport law enforcement. Gerry started his law enforcement career as a police officer in the Panama Canal Zone, where he was born and raised. After 5 years, Gerry was selected for employment with U.S. Customs and in 1979 started as a Customs Inspector at the Miami Seaport and Miami International Airport. In 1983, Gerry was promoted to Senior Customs Inspector and spearheaded various special operations at the seaports and airports in Miami, Fort Lauderdale, West Palm Beach, and Key West, Florida. Most notable, Senior Inspector Draughon was a "founding member" of the Miami Contraband Enforcement Team (CET), which was U.S. Customs' flagship interdiction task force and became the model implemented at all U.S. Customs' Points of Entry nationwide. Gerry's photo and successes are recorded in the *New York Times* best seller *The Kings of Cocaine*, and he received an award personally from then President George H.W. Bush. In 1990, Gerry was promoted to Supervisory Customs Inspector and tasked with managing the field operations in Miami, Fort Lauderdale, Orlando, West Palm Beach seaports and international airports, as well as the U.S. Customs Preclearance Operation in Nassau, Bahamas. In recognition of his vast experience and successes, and his native Spanish language capability, SCI Draughon was frequently tasked by U.S. Customs' Office of International Affairs and the U.S. Department of State to conduct training classes in Latin America. From 1990 to 2004, Gerry provided seaport and airport security training to police, military, and customs officers in Colombia, Panama, Costa Rica, Nicaragua, Guatemala, Ecuador, Bahamas, Brazil, Jamaica, and Venezuela. After retiring from U.S. CBP, Mr. Draughon continued to share his expertise, as an on-site trainer to Afghan Customs in Kandahar, Afghanistan, and, most recently, for several years as a U.S. Department of State–contracted trainer in seaport security and ISPS Code topics in dozens of ports in Latin America.

Ed Piper has over 30 years of diversified experience in law enforcement, security, intelligence, education, and training. Ed served as a commissioned officer in U.S. Naval Intelligence, the Military Police Corps, and as a police officer in the Baltimore City Police Department. Mr. Piper was a Primary Instructor at the Maritime Institute of Technology and Graduate Studies (MITAGS) for the CSO/SSO/PFSO Courses and has taught numerous police and security management courses and seminars in Africa and Latin America. He is a veteran professor at teaching security, management, leadership, and contingency planning courses at Johns Hopkins University and also serves as the Dean of Homeland Security Studies at Canyon College. Mr. Piper currently is the Director of Security and Emergency Planning at Georgetown University School of Law.

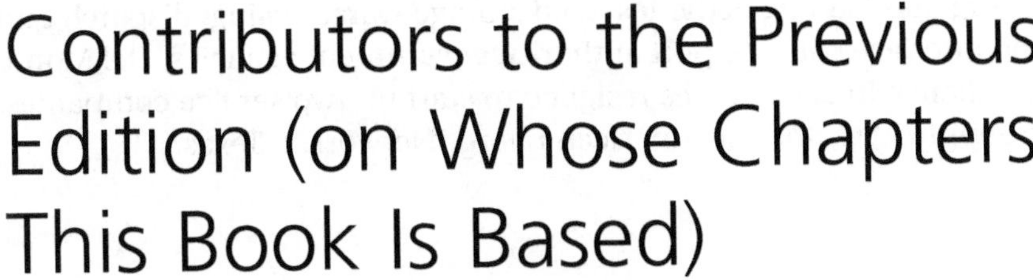

Contributors to the Previous Edition (on Whose Chapters This Book Is Based)

Captain Frederick (Fred) Allen holds an Unlimited Master and First Class Pilot license issued by the U.S. Coast Guard and during the past 30 years he commanded seven containerships and held senior officer positions on several dozen other cargo ships operating in worldwide services. A graduate of West Virginia University, Fred was awarded a direct commission in the U.S. Navy Reserve and during the 1988 Seoul Olympics commanded the U.S. Navy task force in charge of ensuring the security of Korean waters. Today he continues to serve and holds the rank of Captain in the U.S. Navy Reserve. Since 2004, Captain Allen has worked as a consultant for Phoenix Vessel Services, an RSO for the Panamanian government, evaluating and approving/denying Ship Security Plans of vessels in the Panamanian Registry.

Donna Friscia has over 30 years of experience in the maritime industry working for several Shipping Lines trading in Europe, the Far East, the Americas, and the Caribbean, holding a variety of management positions in the Pricing and Documentation Department, Customer Service, and Auditing. Donna started her career working for an NVOCC and then later at Tropical Shipping and Barber Steamship Company, where she learned cargo booking, import-export documentation preparation and filing, vessel chartering, and contract negotiations from the ground-floor up. Ms. Friscia also worked as a Senior Auditor for Tariff Compliance International (TCI), an industry watchdog which audits the rates, agreements, and all documentation of the Latin American operations of Maersk Lines, Crowley Liner Services, Seaboard Marine Line, King Ocean, Tropical Shipping, and the former Sea-Land Service.

James Stapleton is a graduate of the U.S. Merchant Marine Academy in Kings Point, New York. Following graduation, James sailed for 3 years as an officer onboard several U.S. Flag cargo, container, and bulk vessels. In 1999, Mr. Stapleton accepted a position with Del Monte Fresh Produce in Miami, as the Shipping Operations Coordinator. In this position, James was charged with coordinating and scheduling vessel operations (sailing routes and travel times, maintenance, and port activities and cargo stowage issues). Shortly after, in 2000, James was promoted to Port Manager of Del Monte Fresh Produce's operation in the Port of Galveston, Texas. As Port Manager, Mr. Stapleton was responsible for directing all aspects of the port operations, including terminal planning; stevedoring and trucking issues; cargo discharging and loading activities; cold storage warehousing; dispatch and drayage to clients; and interface with the port authority, government agencies, Del Monte foreign sites, and U.S. clients. In 2006, James resigned to start up two service companies: Dolphin Chemical & Supply, LLC, and the American Energy Network in Texas.

Preface

This book provides a thorough introduction to the topic of *maritime security*, as seen through the eyes of practitioners who have decades of on-the-ground, experience-based knowledge in seaport security, vessel security, commercial maritime transport, port operations, cyber security, and maritime law. This book is directed to the academic student, government Homeland Security official or policymaker, and private sector maritime security professional. Specifically for these readers, the book details the fundamentals of commercial shipping and how the business functions; the threats and vulnerabilities to the links in the cargo supply chain; strategies, policies, procedures, and practical measures which have proven to be effective in mitigating terrorist incidents, narcotics smuggling, pilferage, stowaways, and piracy; the laws and international Conventions which codify maritime crime and the legal authority for response; and a window into how the U.S. government provides a coordinated, whole-of-government response to international maritime incidents.

It wasn't until after I left my position as a CIA Counternarcotics Analyst, which included stints as the CIA Liaison to U.S. Coast Guard Intelligence and as a member of the Vice President's Narcotics Interdiction Task Force, and working in the field for several shipping lines, did I realize the critical value of learning the "business" of commercial maritime transport and how seaports and ships actually function. During my first few years in the private sector, I rode many cargo ships through the Atlantic and Pacific Oceans and worked side by side with seaport and shipping line employees in most countries of Latin America and the islands in the Caribbean. Gaining insight from these experiences, learning the native language, and understanding the culture provided me with a somewhat unique perspective on maritime security, one which was key to the development and directing of highly successful maritime security programs for the top 20 shipping lines in the world and several of the largest seaports in Latin America. Working on the "front lines"—or, more appropriately, "behind the lines"—of the War on Drugs, I learned that successes could be achieved when effective and comprehensive security policies, plans, and procedures were implemented at key initial links in the cargo supply chain and focus was placed at the first primary "choke point"—the load seaports and their ships. In these post 9-11 times, with the commercial maritime sector as a highly vulnerable target for terrorist attack, it is important that private sector maritime security professionals and government officials and policymakers have access to the knowledge, experience, and "lessons learned" of practitioners who have successfully operated in the highest risk ports in this hemisphere. This is the reason I wrote this book.

This book provides the reader with a solid familiarization with, and appreciation of, the key tenets of seaport and vessel security and commercial maritime transport, cyber security, and maritime law, and will serve as a practical guide for those private and public sector persons involved in maritime security.

Michael A. McNicholas

Acknowledgments

I would like to recognize and thank the many true maritime security professionals whose hard work, loyalty, dedication, and camaraderie over the past 20+years provided me with the critical support necessary to design, implement, and direct world-class security programs and operations in numerous high-threat seaports in Latin America and the Caribbean. First though, I would like to thank my clients, who have provided invaluable opportunities and support over the years. Gratitude and special thanks to Port Director Stacy Hatfield, Security Manager Gilda Soto, and Superintendent Rigoberto Small of Manzanillo International Terminal, Panama; Port Director John Bressi of Tuxpan Port Terminal, Mexico; Edward Dempster, Captain Doug Spooner, and Captain Adam Wolski of STAR Reefers UK, Ltd; Bill DeWitt, CPP, Vice President of Security and Compliance at SSA Marine/Carrix; Dean Faina, Safety Director, SSA International; Edward Gonzalez, President of Seaboard Marine Line; the late George Weldon, former Security Manager of Crowley American Transport; Ian Pull, past Vice President of Fleet Operations of Dole Fresh Fruit International; and Helmuth Lutty, Vice President Del Monte Fresh Produce. And from one "tire kicker" to another, a debt of thanks to Dave Michou, President, Stevedoring Services of America International, for your support and dedication to building a world-class seaport security program.

I'd like to give a warm thanks to Jerry Peterson and Dave Herring, friends and former business partners, for teaching me the critical business skills necessary to becoming a successful entrepreneur. Also, thanks to my first business partner, Rafael Martinez, for his friendship and helping me expand into Latin America and close friend Gerry Draughon for sharing his many years of unique experience and wisdom.

Special recognition and a hearty military salute to mis compañeros Wilberth Gutierrez, Jose Barrows, Dennis Vargas, Kemly Miller (for keeping the guys in line), Gustavo Ramirez, Jimy Jimenez, Simon Brown, Carlos Wolfe Jackson, Rodolfo Aguilera, Aristides Cortez, Eleuterio Ciel and Jovito Mora for their many years of joining me boarding barges and ships at sea to search for stowaways, pirates, and drug shipments; trudging through banana plantations and container yards; training hundreds of military and port police officers; and passing many, many sleepless nights ensuring the port and vessel security officers were always on their toes. My hat is off to you guys—and gal!

Sincere gratitude goes to Gary Greco for teaching me how to shoot and watching my back on my first trips to Colombia, Peru, and Nicaragua many years ago; Keith Herrington for teaching me to drive; Ed Piper for his expertise in training, leadership, and inspirational motivation; and to Geoffrey Walker for working with the folks on the Miami River.

My sincere appreciation goes to Hilary Carr and Dr. Pamela Chester of Elsevier for their support, hard work, patience, and belief in the book, both editions.

Last, and most importantly, I'd like to give thanks to our Lord for the good health, safe travels, answered prayers, innumerable blessings, and delivered protections of Psalm 91 during the past 25 years working in the field as a practitioner in maritime security.

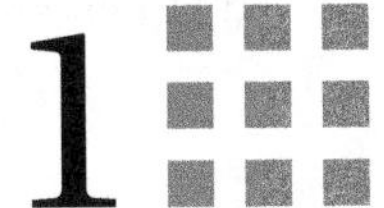

Commercial Seaports and Strategic Maritime Passages in Transformation

OBJECTIVES

After studying this chapter, you will be familiar with

1. The functioning and operations of and equipment utilized in container terminals, bulk cargo terminals, cruise terminals, and nontraditional terminals;
2. The roles and activities of key private-sector stakeholders, including terminal owners, terminal operators, stevedore companies, and longshoremen;
3. The impact and role of the development of the container and intermodalism;
4. Changes to shipping and seaports due to the expansions of the world's two key Canals—the Panama Canal and the Suez Canal;
5. The impact of the transformation of the Polar Passages—and potential benefits and challenges.

Introduction

The human love affair with the ocean is one that has existed since man first laid eyes on the waters that lay before him. The great seas provided man with mystery and intrigue. The oceans presented a backdrop for stories that served as entertainment and the foundations of religions. The conveyances used to cross first the rivers and then the oceans facilitated international trade and commerce, connected cultures and peoples, and made the world a smaller planet.

The evolution of what we now call the modern *shipping industry* began small like all things in this world do. The first seagoing traders did no more than cross rivers and float with the flow of the waters. However, with this foundation, man began to thrive. One small village may have possessed an item that another village needed. This prompted traders to bring their goods to different locations along the river in order to trade their items for the items of others. These villages soon became popular trading spots and attracted people from far-away places. The travelers often brought items that had never before been seen in that particular region. These towns became the foundations of our modern ports. Underneath some of the world's busiest and most modern seaports lie the ruins of these simple yet effective cradles of capitalism.

As oceangoing technology increased, seafarers became more and more bold. They went further and faster in the race to bring trade to the far corners of the world. Each new vessel arrival brought new languages, merchandise, and products. This often led to conflicts and man's ability to use oceangoing vessels as machines of war increased. As the need for protection against military vessels increased, seaports became bases of operations rather than simply trading posts. As technology grew and time marched on, these "bases" became a part of a network of commerce with trade lanes that radiated from ports like the spokes of a wheel. An infrastructure was established and fortunes were made via this ever-expanding spider web of trade.

This chapter focuses on the development, operations, and functioning of the primary variations of the modern commercial seaports, as well the equipment utilized, and changes in the world's two key Canals and the Polar Passages.

Commercial Seaports

If you compared modern commerce to the human body, the shipping lanes would be arteries and veins; ships and intermodal vehicles, the blood; their cargo, the nutrients; and the seaports, the all-important organs. The shipping industry operates in many of the same ways as the human body. There are some periods of rest, but very rarely does the flow of cargo stop. Vessels arrive into ports at all hours of the night, which requires many people to be awake and ready to service the vessel. The seaport's support to the vessels and preparations for cargo operations in the port begin many hours prior to the vessel's arrival dockside.

Approximately 6 hours from arriving at the *sea buoy* (also known as the *pilot station*), a vessel's captain will begin to initiate contact via VHF radio (contact is made on channel 16, and the pilot dispatcher will switch to the local working frequency). Notice of arrival is given, and the dispatcher provides the vessel with boarding information, including appropriate speed and the side of the ship that the ladder is to be located. The position of the pilot ladder is determined by the wind, tide, and direction of the swell. Pilots are taken onboard via special-platform boats simply referred to as *pilot boats.* A *harbor pilot* is a specially trained navigator. He is tested on the local characteristics of the many different factors and variables required to properly navigate from the sea buoy to a safe berth. Once the pilot is onboard, he assumes "the con," or control of the vessel. The captain of the vessel gives up control but does not relinquish overall responsibility of the vessel during this time. As the pilot carefully guides the vessel to the berth, he is in constant communication with tugboats, which provide the vessel with additional steerage capability by connecting to the vessel with large ropes or lines called *hawsers.* Once the vessel nears the berth, the crew connects the ship's mooring lines to smaller lines which are thrown down to *line handlers.* The line handlers physically maneuver the lines to bollards attached to the dock which are used to secure and hold the vessel in place. Typical mooring patterns include a total of eight lines, but the patterns will vary according to currents and tidal fluctuations. Once the ship's crew lowers the gangway, vessel agents employed by the vessel charterer or owner will come aboard with customs and immigration officials in order to clear the vessel to go to work. Vessel security personnel hustle into place to prepare for the identification and search procedures of individuals boarding the vessel. While this process takes place, stevedores, longshoremen, and company representatives stand by for clearance to begin the arduous process of discharging the vessel.

This whole sequence takes place in a very limited amount of time, and the plasma TV sitting in a container at the bottom of a stack of containers on board the vessel has not even been moved toward its final destination: your living room. Countless hours of preparation and planning have gone into this process. Millions of dollars' worth of equipment and man-hours are expended with each and every arrival of every product from orange juice to jet fuel. All of this began with just a simple phone call, purchase order, or Internet search. It is hard for many to comprehend the vast number of resources that are poured into this venture in order to keep the supply chain flowing and further expand the network of commerce. The key component in this process is the *commercial seaport*, which serves as a launching point for the advancement of supply and demand.

Container Terminals

The development of the modern container—the most efficient, safe, and flexible method to transport cargo across the ocean and land—was a watershed event in maritime transportation and served as a catalyst for the evolution of seaports from only handling breakbulk and bulk cargoes and vessels to also—or exclusively—receiving and loading cargo containers. Today, the majority of cargo transported around the world is via containers, and major ports have dedicated berths and terminals for container handling and staging. And, like the ships that arrive, terminals continue to grow in size and complexity. The largest container ports in the world are a reflection of where goods are produced and key gateways of the consumers. So, it should not be surprising that of the largest (measured by container throughput) 14 container ports in the world, 8 are located in Asia—with the port of Shanghai being the largest (35 million containers per year in 2014), as shown in Fig. 1.1.

Key benefits for the shipper utilizing a container include the ability to compartmentalize and segregate different kinds of cargoes and, importantly, the container offers protection from adverse weather and water and handling damages. For example, toys for children can be housed in boxes at the front of the container and radios in the back of the container. Also, multiple shippers with small loads can consolidate the cargo into a single container.

While there are several versions of the shipping container, most commonly they either are 20 or 40 feet long, 8 feet wide, and 8 feet 6 inches in height. Containers are loaded on and off the vessel via a crane, either a shore-based or ship crane (also known as a *Morgan crane*), which is mounted on the vessel deck and moves atop rails running the length of the ship. Trailers are containers that have a chassis affixed and are unloaded/loaded onboard a *roll-on/roll-off* (RO/RO) ship via a terminal tractor. The port may have a special berth to accommodate these vessels and their operations. Some ships carry both containers and trailers, and container terminals generally also service RO/RO ships.

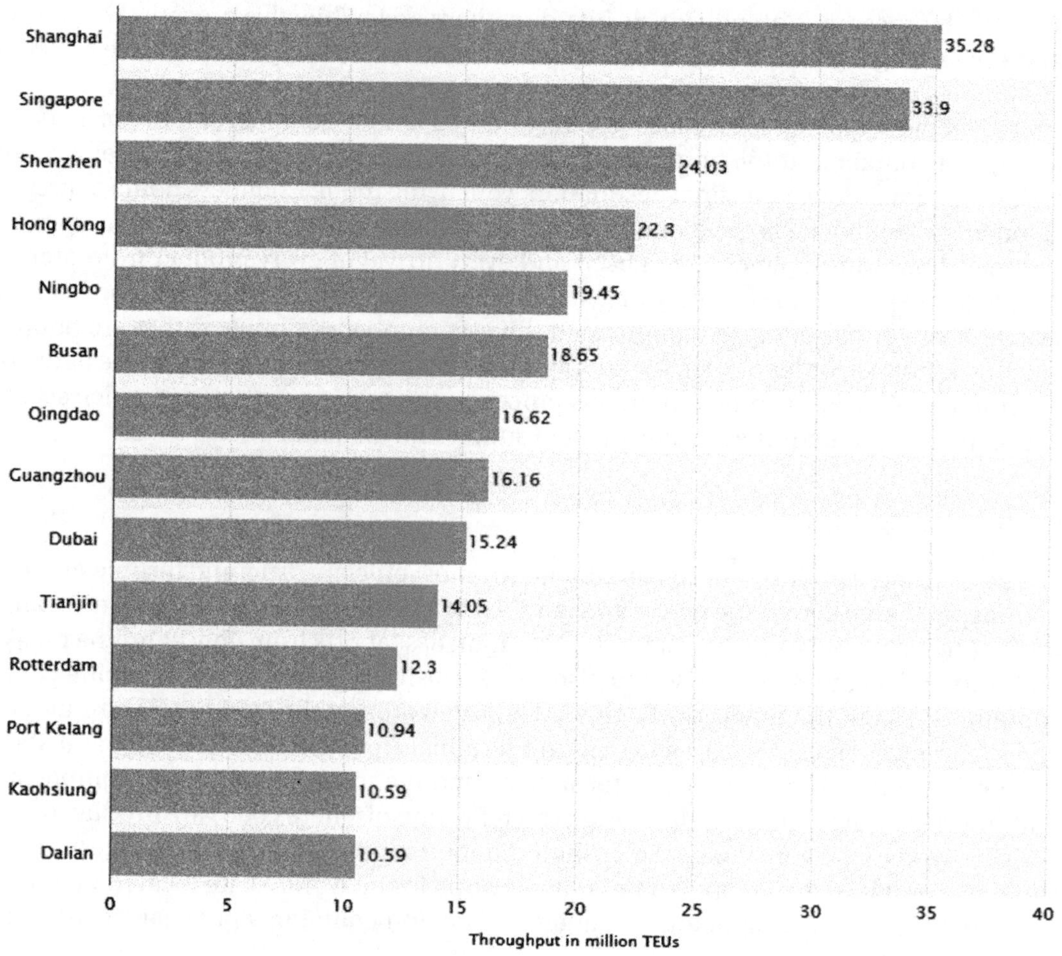

FIGURE 1.1 The world's busiest seaports in 2014.

Prior to the advent of containers, cargo such as fruit, textiles, coffee, etc., was boxed or stacked loose or on pallets in hatches below decks and loaded and unloaded via conveyor belts, physical manpower, ship cranes, or nets. This work was especially dangerous, cargo was frequently damaged, and operations were very slow. The discharging and loading of a break-bulk cargo vessel may have taken from 3 to 5 days, but today the same quantity of cargo in containers can be handled in about 12 hours. The efficiencies and reductions in manpower and damages represent a significant savings for both the port and the shipping line.

Container vessels require the port to offer ample space for staging, specialized types of equipment, skilled manpower, and efficient organizational and logistical management. As you can see in Figs. 1.2 and 1.3, a significant amount of space is needed to stage containers

FIGURE 1.2 The port of Manzanillo International Terminal—Panama.

FIGURE 1.3 The port of Shanghai in China. *Photo credit:* Shutterstock.com.

in the port. Large container ports, such as Shanghai, Shenzhen, Hong Kong, and Ningbo, China; Rotterdam, Netherlands; Antwerp, Belgium; Freeport, Bahamas; and Manzanillo International Terminal, Panama, generally manage a ratio of about 75% or more transshipment containers and 25% or less local containers. This means that only 25% or less of the containers originate in or are destined for the country where the port is located. These ports, located along major trade lanes, function as *collection points* for manufacturing regions or *transfer points*—much like a rail hub or bus depot—for containers that will then be distributed throughout the region or hemisphere. Large containers ships, such as the M/V MSC OSCAR (the world's largest container ship as of September 2015), carrying up to 19,224 *20-foot equivalent unit* (TEU) containers will arrive at the port, discharge a portion of their containers, and reload as planned. At transshipment ports, the intransit containers are then loaded onto smaller ships—called *feeder vessels*—which then transport the containers to smaller ports throughout the region.

In general, the larger vessels (functioning as "mother ships") operate in an east-west, pendulum movement through the oceans of the world, from Asia to the United States and back and from Europe to the United States and back, as well as Asia to Europe and vice versa. The trade lanes of feeder vessels tend to run north-south. For example, a primary feeder trade lane on the west coast of the Americas runs from Panama (the transshipment hub) south to Chile and north to Los Angeles/Long Beach and Seattle. A typical major container transshipment port or terminal will have at least 1 million TEU container movements (unloading/loading) per year and receive at least 200+ ships per month. The Port of Rotterdam, Europe's busiest port, posted a record of 6.3 million TEU containers moved during just the first quarter of 2015, which is more than double the amount moved during the same time period in 2007.[1]

At a major container port, from 2 to 10 *gantry cranes* may be assigned to unload and load a single container ship, depending on the length of the ship, number and location of the cargo hatches to be worked, and the number of container movements. Gantry cranes are computer automated and highly precise; a single crane has the capability to unload or load upward of 75 containers per hour, if the terminal operations personnel can keep up with the pace! In smaller or multipurpose terminals, mobile and portal cranes—sometimes referred to as *stick cranes*—are utilized. In some cases, the ship may have efficient shipboard cranes or the port doesn't have land-based cranes available, so the ship will discharge and reload using its own cranes.

The lading of the container onto the ship via a crane is the end of what is commonly called the *string-piece*. The string-piece is the actual strip of concrete/asphalt/block that runs along the water and extends to the backreach of the crane; however, the term also applies to the final process dockside of container loading. In the string-piece, vehicles, chassis, and bomb carts are staged in line and lurch forward in succession until under the crane, to receive or unload a container. It is important to the speed of the process that there are no obstructions to slow down this movement. Prior to the string-piece, there is a well-choreographed and coordinated movement of the container from where it is "stacked" or staged in the yard or located atop a rail car, to its loading onto a bomb cart or chassis, and then transported through the terminal to the waiting line dockside (beginning of the string-piece). The distance from the rail or stack to the string-piece may vary from 100 feet to a mile and depends on how far away the container stacks/staging areas are from the dock and the layout of the terminal.

For the most part, container vessels are discharged and loaded simultaneously and utilize the same terminal equipment (terminal tractors, top-picks, rubber tire gantry cranes, straddle carriers, gantry cranes, etc.). To add a further level of complexity for the yard planners and vessel planners (the persons in the port who track each container in the port, plan its movement, and coordinate its load position in the ship), each specific container is loaded to a specific position in the ship, so a high level of coordination is required between yard management, equipment operators (who actually sort and move the containers), and the vessel operations (terminal/ship officers).

The equipment most commonly used in container terminals include

- *Gantry Crane* (Fig. 1.4): This large ship-to-shore (STS) crane has a boom that is capable of extending over the beam of the vessel in order to load/unload containers from the cargo hatch or deck. Typically, these cranes are mounted on rails, for horizontal movement along the dock.
- *Mobile Crane* (Fig. 1.5): Also known as a type of *stick crane*, this crane has tracks or wheels and can be moved from location to location for the loading or discharge of containers and other cargoes.

FIGURE 1.4 Gantry cranes in operation.

FIGURE 1.5 Mobile harbor crane. *Photo credit: g0d4ather/*Shutterstock.com.

Continued

—cont'd

FIGURE 1.6 Rubber tire gantry crane.

FIGURE 1.7 Straddle crane. *Photo credit: VanderWolf Images*/Shutterstock.com.

FIGURE 1.8 Top-Pick.

- *Rubber Tire Gantry Crane* (Fig. 1.6): Also called by its initials—*RTG*—this crane is used to lift containers on or off a chassis or bomb cart and place them in stack. It is also used for shifting containers within the stack.
- *Straddle Crane* (Fig. 1.7): A small but more mobile version of the RTG, this crane is capable of working in stacks of up to three containers high.
- *Shuttle Carrier*: Designed to interface between the RTG and the ship crane, this carrier moves containers directly from the stack to shipside and replaces the use of the terminal tractor.
- *Top-Pick* (Fig. 1.8): This large lifting device is used in container yards to lift a loaded container off the chassis and place it either onto the ground, onto another chassis, or to stack it onto another container.
- *Side-Pick* (Fig. 1.9): This equipment is used to rapidly move and shift empty containers.
- *Reachstacker*: This equipment is similar to a top-pick in function but has the ability to extend out on a diagonal angle.
- *Terminal Tractor*: Also called a *yard hustler, Ottawa* (made in Ottawa, Kansas), or *mula*, this tractor is used to hook up to a chassis or bomb cart to transport containers in the terminal and satellite yards.
- *Container Flat-Bed Chassis* (Fig. 1.10): This device has a chassis with a wood or metal bed and locking pins for transport of containers in the terminal.
- *Bomb cart* (Fig. 1.11): This piece of equipment resembles a container chassis but sits lower to the ground and has angled corner and side guides (in lieu of locking pins) to facilitate more rapid lift-off/drop-in of containers.

Continued

—cont'd

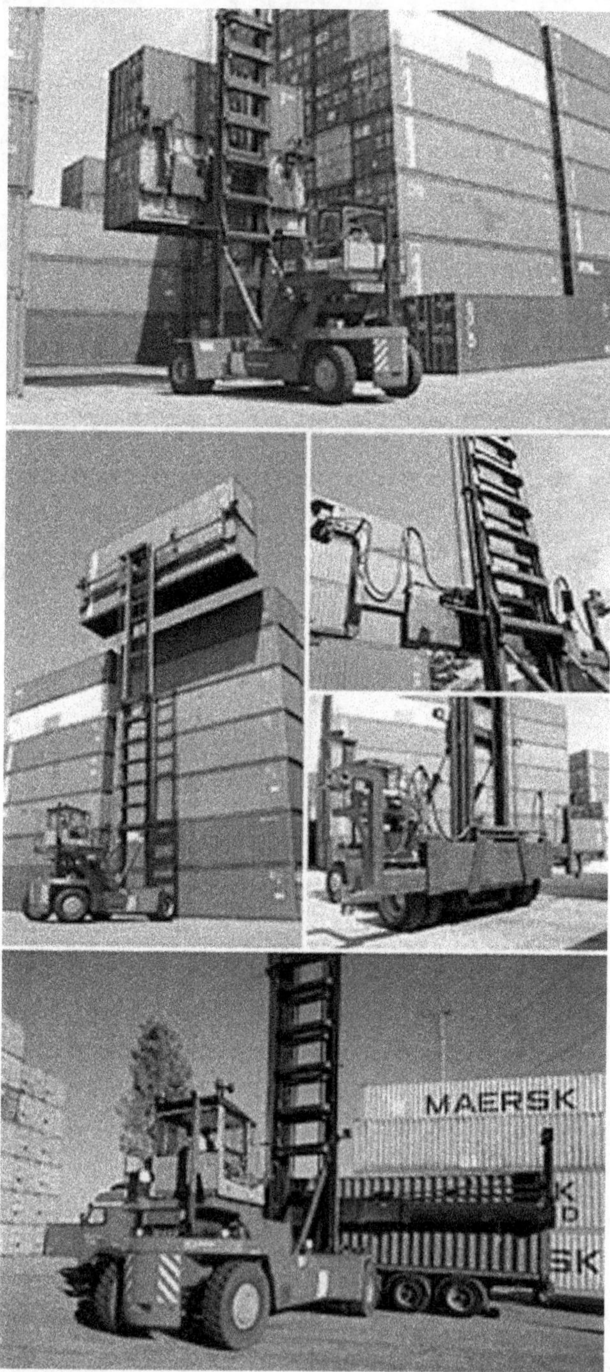

FIGURE 1.9 Side-Pick is used to rapidly shift empty containers.

FIGURE 1.10 Flat-bed chassis.

FIGURE 1.11 Bomb Cart.

It is important to appreciate that "productivity" is measured by the port's number of container moves per hour and the time it takes to turnaround a ship, and these statistics are how a port is rated and success is measured. In a select few ports in the world, automation technology has sought to further reduce manpower, enhance safety, decrease CO_2 emissions and energy consumption, and increase efficiency. The *automated ground vehicle* (AGV) is an unmanned vehicle powered by diesel or diesel-electric engines and carries up to two 20-foot containers. At the Europe Container Terminal in the Port of Rotterdam (the 12th largest port in the world in 2014), 280 AGVs have been in operation for the past 22 years. Another AGV system is installed at the Container Terminal Altenwerder in the Port of Hamburg, Germany. The AGV is controlled by a vehicle navigation system which constantly "reads" passive transponders embedded in the terminal and adjusts its speed and direction. An integrated communication system that can process up to 250 messages simultaneously also provides nonstop communication between the AGV and the fleet management system. The *automated stacking crane* (ASC), deployed at the P&O Terminal at the Port of Antwerp, Belgium, and at other high-tech terminals worldwide, is an unmanned portal crane which runs atop rails and can straddle nine containers wide and five containers high. It is generally used to preshift containers for near-term vessel operations and to reorganize the stacks in the yard, both tasks designed to increase productivity when interfacing with the yard management system.

"APM Terminals" and "SSA Marine" are two terminal operators which are pushing the envelope of software and hardware technology development interface to increase production. In late April 2015, APM Terminals formally opened its ultrahigh-tech and environmentally "green" Maasvlakte II container terminal in Rotterdam, heralded by the APM Terminals CEO Kim Fejer as "...clearly a gamer-changer port in the shipping industry." This APM terminal is constructed on land fully reclaimed from the North Sea and is a zero-emissions facility; with buildings, systems, and equipment powered by wind-generated electricity and battery sources. The terminal introduces a level of automation which significantly reduces manpower—making it inherently safer for workers—and much more productive than a traditional port terminal. According to the APM Terminals' press release, "the facility launches the world's first container terminal to utilize remotely-controlled STS gantry cranes. The cranes move containers between vessels and the landside fleet of 62 battery-powered Lift-Automated Guided Vehicles (Lift-AGVs) which transport containers between the quay and the container yard, including barge and on-dock rail facilities. The Lift-AGVs also represent the world's first series of AGVs that can actually lift and stack a container. A fleet of 54 Automated Rail-Mounted Gantry Cranes (ARMGs) then positions containers in the yard in a high-density stacking system. The terminal's power requirements are provided by wind-generated electricity, enabling terminal operations, which produce no CO_2, emissions or pollutants, and which are also considerably quieter than conventional diesel-powered facilities. The 86 hectare (212 acre) deep-water terminal features 1000 meters of quay, on-dock rail, and eight fully-automated electric-powered Ship-to-Shore (STS) cranes, with an annual throughput capacity of 2.7 million TEUs, representing an APM Terminals investment of EUR 500 million. At planned full build-out, the terminal will cover 180 hectares (445 acres) and offer 2800 meters of deep-sea quay (19.65 meters/64.5 feet depth), with an annual throughput capacity of 4.5 million TEUs."

Another example of the marrying of high technology port hardware equipment and software cargo handling systems to further enhance production is US-based SSA Marine's Tuxpan Port Terminal, located on the Caribbean coast of Mexico and set to come online in March 2016. At full buildout, the port will be capable of handling 710,000 YEUs and 350,000 cars a year. However, what makes the terminal unique is that it will be *the first fully automated terminal in Mexico and Central America.* Tuxpan will boast 4 super post-Panama cranes, 8 ASCs, and 30 automated port trailers, all connected to and operated via Tideworks' terminal operating system software by operators located outside the terminal yard. Like APM Terminals' Maasvlakte II container terminal in Rotterdam, the ASCs in Tuxpan function "intelligently," constantly moving and shifting containers in stacks in the Terminal to optimize the efficiency of container movements for the next vessels docking and to reduce the number of times the containers need to be repositioned. At both of these fully automated terminals, very few humans work inside the yards, and the primary goals are to maximize the terminal's productivity and limit the environmental impact.

Most container ports have some type of computerized yard management system, and there are several very good products in the marketplace. One such system, Mainsail Terminal Management System, was developed by Tideworks Technology, a sister company to SSA Marine (the largest U.S.-owned seaport operator). Mainsail is a browser-based interface for gate, yard, and vessel inventory management. Mainsail records all shipping, gate interchange, and dispatch information real time at the entrance and exit gates (integrating optical character recognition, security cameras, truck scales, voice collection, and information kiosks) and initiates a tracking record of each movement of the container. If the container is shifted from the third to the fifth level in the stack, this information is fully recorded (who, what, when, where, and why). This system also functions with rail operations and relay containers (discharged from one ship and immediately reloaded to a waiting ship).

Tideworks' Spinnaker Planning Management System is a supplemental system which interfaces with Mainsail and enables the yard and vessel planners to quickly direct real-time container information into orders for gate, rail, yard, and vessel moves. The system assists in maximizing efficiency in selection of containers for movement, assigns the moves, communicates with yard equipment operators (cranes, RTGs, top-picks, etc.), and defines the plan for loading of the vessel. The Traffic Control module of Spinnaker replaces radio communications and paper instructions with real-time, electronic dispatching of work instructions to equipment operators, speeding up the process and reducing errors. The Spinnaker system also integrates real-time data and information from differential GPS, handheld devices, and mounted mobile display units. Computer-based systems such as Tideworks' Mainsail and Spinnaker greatly enhance the efficiency of gate, rail, yard, and vessel operations and reduce the time and expenses of servicing the large container vessels.

When a loaded export container arrives at the port for processing for loading onto a vessel, several sequential steps occur, which refer to what is commonly known as the *gate operation* (see Fig. 1.12). The term *gate* does not necessarily refer to a physical structure. It can simply refer to the paperwork process through which the container and/or cargo must flow to be cleared for entrance or exit (in the case of import cargo). The gate operation occurs for both import and export cargo and is somewhat different from country to country—because of local customs requirements and commerce practices—but the general process steps are similar from port to port. In the case of an export container, first the container is staged outside the gate (and outside the port), while the driver takes the customs clearance documentation, the bill of lading, the equipment interchange report, and relevant agriculture/health department certificates to a *pregate office* for processing and information recording in the computerized

Continued

—cont'd

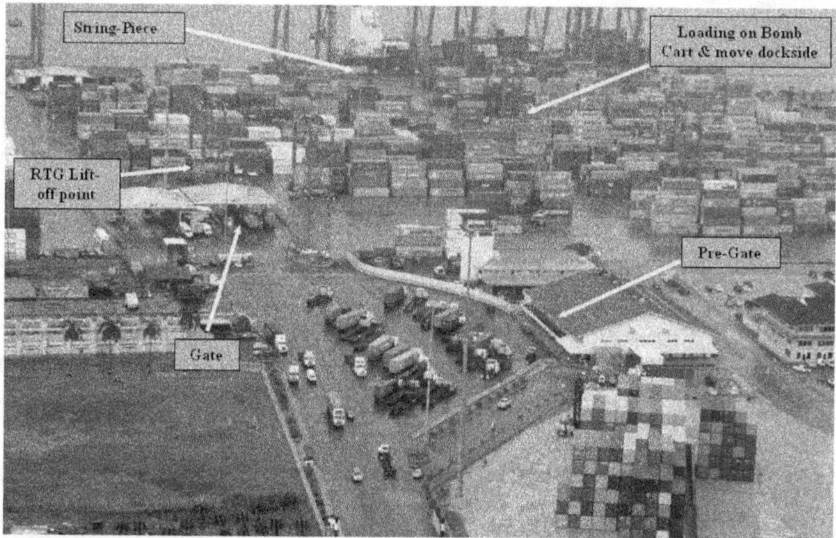

FIGURE 1.12 The process and movement of a container entering the port gate, staging in the terminal, and then loading on a ship.

yard management system. Next, the driver enters the main vehicle gate and proceeds forward to the *gate inspection and interchange point* and stops atop a scale. Here, the container is weighed; all driver, container, and seal information is verified/recorded on an interchange; and possibly security checks are conducted (explosives, narcotics, WMDs, etc.) by K-9 teams and/or nonintrusive inspection equipment. A *checker* makes a physical inspection of the condition of the container (holes, damages, reefer functioning, and temperature check) and records his observations on the interchange. At this same time, the designated equipment (RTG, top-pick, etc.) operator is informed electronically or via radio of the job assignment. Next, the driver proceeds to the preassigned location in the yard for the container to be lifted off and placed in the stack. The RTG records the exact location of the container, time, date, etc., and this information is transmitted real time to the yard management system. When the yard and vessel planners program the container for preparation for loading on a vessel, the equipment (RTG, top-pick, etc.) operator is informed electronically or via radio of the job assignment, and he lifts the container from the stack and places it on a chassis or bomb cart. The terminal tractor driver transports the container to the string-piece and awaits his turn to move under the crane, for lifting of the container onto the vessel.

The processing of pickup and delivery of import cargo/containers to the consignee is somewhat the reverse of the process for the export container. Essentially, when import cargo is scheduled for pickup at a port terminal, a contracted truck driver arrives at what is typically called the port *gate dispatch office* (pregate) and presents one or more reference documents (dock receipt and/or equipment interchange receipt, bill of lading, pickup order) to the terminal operator—demonstrating that he has been contracted by the importer or shipping line to dray the container or cargo to the consignee. Once the documentation is processed, the driver will be given a *load order* or *load document*, instructed to enter the port gate (if the office is located outside the port), and go to the yard location where the cargo/container is to be picked up. The driver will then proceed into the cargo/container/trailer staging area, as per the instructions, and provide the load document to the clerk or foreman working with the loading gang. The truck will be loaded according to the driver's instructions. Once the cargo or container is loaded and inspected/recorded by the checker, the driver will return to the dispatch or clerk's office and retrieve the bill of lading and new equipment interchange receipt. The driver signs the bill of lading and interchange, which is proof that he is authorized to transport the container to the consignee. Once this step is completed, the driver is usually free to begin his journey to the consignee. On some occasions this process actually takes place at the exit point or the gate, but it is not necessary as long as the appropriate steps are taken. This brief process is a small part of a much larger system called the *cargo supply chain*.

Most container terminals also are capable of receiving break-bulk vessels and their cargoes. An example of this type of vessel and cargo would be a *reefer ship* and its cargo of fresh fruit (bananas, pineapple, mangos, melons, etc.). The cargo bays in these ships are refrigerated to keep the boxed fruit cold. The boxes either are loaded loose (individually) or are palletized. Loose boxes are loaded on/off the ship via a conveyor belt, whereas palletized fruit boxes are hoisted on/off the vessel via stick cranes or ships' cranes. In the latter case, the pallets are moved into a metal frame, as in Fig. 1.13, via a forklift or hand truck. The cargo is shuttled from the vessel to cold-storage warehouses via forklifts or trucks. Both of these cargo operations are laborious, time-consuming, and frequently impacted by inclement weather. The unloading of a reefer vessel, such as the ones seen in the figures,

FIGURE 1.13 Palletized boxes of fruit are loaded via ship's gear into the temperature-control led cargo bay of a reefer ship.

FIGURE 1.14 Very large crude carrier unloading crude oil at a port. *Photo credit:* Shutterstock.com.

may take from 24 to 48 hours. Ports providing services to reefer ships usually have large cold-storage facilities and warehouses located inside the terminal.

Bulk Cargo Terminals

Bulk cargo can be classified in two ways: liquid bulk cargo and dry bulk cargo. The terminals that receive, house, and ship bulk cargo are fairly simple in nature but are diverse in structure. This diversity is strictly dependent on the type of cargo being handled at the facility. For the purposes of this discussion, we focus on petroleum/LNG terminals, grain/mineral/cement terminals, and dry bulk facilities.

Petroleum or oil port terminals can vary in size and design, depending on the location of the facility, its services, and the needs of the company which owns it. Typically, there is a refinery or storage facility in close proximity to the dock area (see Figs. 1.14 and 1.15). LNG terminals are designed only for the transfer of LNG product, and the terminals are self-contained and self-sustaining. In the case of a petroleum products facility, it is connected to the dock area by a series of long pipes that lead to multiple holding tanks. These pipes can reach miles inland, their length depending on the final destination of the product being delivered. Oil tankers will carry either refined or unrefined product in multiple cargo holds. The dock area contains a large manifold with load/discharge hoses attached that feed the pipelines leading back to the refinery or storage tanks. The vessel will also have a manifold onboard, and each manifold has valves that can be opened and closed to control the flow of the liquid. There are also a series of pumps both onboard and at the terminal which moves the liquid cargo through the system. If the vessel is discharging the product from its tanks to the facility, then the chief mate (cargo officer) will arrange the

FIGURE 1.15 Storage tank area for petroleum products. *Photo credit:* Shutterstock.com.

FIGURE 1.16 Liquefied natural gas facility.

manifold in the proper setup and will control the starting and stopping of the necessary pumps to move the cargo through the onboard pipelines to the manifold and then to the hoses which link the vessel's manifold to the shore-side manifold. Onboard personnel and shore-side personnel stay in constant communication to make sure that the flow rates and tank volumes maintain the proper safe levels. If the vessel has arrived empty and is scheduled to load product, the process is reversed, utilizing the pumps located within the terminal. The unloading of LNG is similar, with the pipes carrying the supercold liquefied product to a large storage tank set within a spill containment area (see Figs. 1.16 and 1.17).

FIGURE 1.17 Vessel docking berth and product transfer point at liquefied natural gas port terminal.

FIGURE 1.18 Bulk Cargo Port in Poland. *Photo credit: Pawel Szczepanski*/Shutterstock.com.

Grain, mineral, and cement terminals are specialized facilities for a particular type of cargo (see Fig. 1.18). These facilities can be identified by the large conveyor belts, load chutes, and storage silos that are integral to the loading or discharge process. Grains and minerals can come in a variety of sizes and shapes, but most of these cargoes are the size of pebbles or pellets. Vessels that carry this type of cargo typically utilize large cargo holds that hold multiple tons of cargo. These vessels may or may not have cranes on board in order to load directly to trucks or rail cars if a conveyor-type dock facility is not available. When a conveyor-type facility is used, the discharging gear will extend from the shore to the cargo hold of the vessel. The cargo is either vacuumed or scooped up and placed onto a conveyor belt that will transport the cargo from the hold of the vessel across the dock and into a storage silo. The conveyor belt is elevated off the dock so that the cargo is gravity fed into the silo or even directly to trucks or rail cars. These facilities do not require a great deal of land or dock space at their respective ports. Belts and hoses can be extended along the length of the dock in order to allow multiple vessels to work at the same time. Cargo operations within these terminals must be watched very closely due to the rapid movement of large amounts of cargo. Vessel trim and stability measurements must be closely monitored to ensure that the vessel does not have too much stress placed on its structure or that too much weight is loaded to one area of the vessel. Improper loading or discharge of these vessels can result in vessels flipping or even breaking up. Another danger at these terminals is the dust that is generated during cargo operations. Grain dust and mineral dust can not only be bad to breathe in but can also be highly explosive in nature. Grain dust in particular is extremely explosive and must be very closely monitored during discharge or loading. Any ignition source must be removed from the area in which cargo operations are taking place.

Dry bulk facilities are the most simple of the bulk terminals. Dry bulk cargoes are also the most diverse in type. Dry bulk can be palletized or simply loaded into the holds. Examples of dry bulk cargoes are steel, cotton, paper, wood, lumber, and palletized food products. The terminal itself could be as simple as a paved lot that connects to the dock. In some cases, the cargo does not require a warehouse, such as with steel. Wood and lumber products are housed in a standard warehouse or shed. These terminals are typically accessible by rail and truck, depending on the type of cargo being discharged or loaded.

Equipment commonly used in bulk cargo terminals includes, but is not limited to, the following:

- *Mobile Portal Crane*: Also known as a type of stick crane, this crane has tracks or wheels and can be moved from location to location for the loading or discharge of bulk cargoes.
- *Pontoon Crane*: This type of crane is used when the vessel cannot dock against the quay.
- *Flat-Bed Chassis*: This equipment is used to transport the dry bulk products. Typically, heavy tie-downs and chocks are used to secure the cargo.
- *Dump Truck*: This truck has a hydraulic lift and swinging gate and is typically used to haul dirt, grains, or other loose-type cargo.
- *Forklift*: This wheeled machine has two large metal "forks" used for lifting palletized cargo and other items that can't be lifted by hand. Forklifts can be propelled by diesel, propane, and even electricity. Forklifts also come in various sizes, and the size of a forklift is related to its lifting capacity.

Cruise Ship Terminals

Cruise vacations are rapidly becoming one of the most popular ways to relax and see different countries. As the market increases, cruise ship companies have to find ways to compete in a rapidly expanding market. This competition will often affect the terminals that receive the passengers boarding the vessel. This type of terminal is the most aesthetically pleasing of all the terminals since people are the cargo; therefore, the boarding areas must be presentable (see Fig. 1.19). Some cruise ship terminals mimic airport terminals and provide coffee shops, restaurants, and souvenir shops.

FIGURE 1.19 Port of Miami Cruise ship terminal. *Photo credit: mariakraynova/*Shutterstock.com.

Cruise ship terminals are not isolated in industrial areas but are often in the heart of town in order to be easily accessible, such as the Port of Miami—the largest cruise port in the world. Cruise ship terminals must have vehicle access so that passengers can drive up and drop off luggage before moving on to the parking areas. While the external areas of the terminal are designed to please and attract passengers, the internal areas must be able to handle other operations that are hidden from the public. Baggage screening areas are set up in order to make sure that illegal or improper items are not being loaded in passenger baggage. Since a cruise ship is essentially a floating hotel, many supplies and food items must be delivered to the vessel. Therefore, the terminal must be accessible by truck or delivery van. There must also be sufficient space to house the equipment that is going to take the supplies off the trucks. Forklifts, pallet jacks, and dollies are used for this purpose. Ideally, all of this activity is done out of the sight of the passengers in order to maintain the clean look and feel in the terminal. These terminals are expensive to build and operate but contribute greatly to local economies by creating a location that people travel to in order to board a vessel prepared for fun and relaxation.

Nontraditional Ports

It is important to appreciate that not all—not even the majority—of the ports worldwide have a movement of 1 million containers per year or discharge/load millions of tons of bulk materials annually. Likewise, while the vast majority of ports of the world have berths and quays, in some locations there is a significant amount of regional and international maritime commerce but no formal port. The reasons for this generally tend to be environmental issues (silt buildup so that large ships cannot get to the shoreline, insufficient economic incentives, and/or political instability). For example, Turbo, Colombia—where dozens of ships per week load hundreds of thousands of boxes of bananas—does not have a "port." Turbo is a small town in a somewhat remote area in northwest Colombia, on the

FIGURE 1.20 In the Gulf of Uraba, Colombia, a tugboat pulls a line of "bongo barges" holding pallets of bananas and containers from river load points to ships.

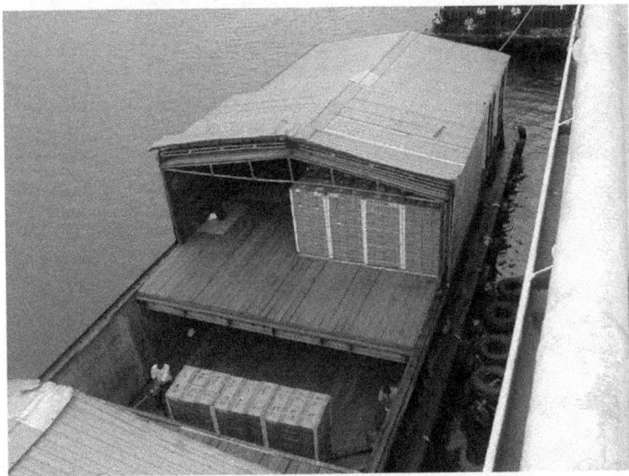

FIGURE 1.21 Pallets hold boxes of bananas and other fruit.

south rim of the Gulf of Uraba. Turbo is a stronghold of former para-militaries, who now are transnational narcotics traffickers. Nevertheless, this location is an excellent growing region for bananas and a significant fruit source for Dole Fresh Fruit, Chiquita Brands, Del Monte, Turbana, and other fruit companies. The ships anchor offshore and ship loading occurs there. The bananas are cut and boxed at hundreds of farms and transported by trucks to central warehouses/port facilities along the rivers flowing into the Gulf for palletizing and or loading into containers. The palletized bananas are loaded into *bongo barges*, which are hooked together like train cars and pulled by a tug. The tug collects the barges (both full of fruit pallets and containers) and transports them into the bay and alongside a ship. When the bongo barges arrive alongside, the laborers slide back the roof on the pallet barges, allowing access to the pallets. The pallets and containers are lifted from the barges using the ship's cranes and loaded into the cargo bays. Once unloaded, the tug returns the bongo barges to the load points for restocking. Because the cargo operation is very long, 36–48 hours in duration, additional maintenance and stevedore housing barges (where the stevedores sleep and eat) are also brought alongside the ship. As you would imagine, these break-bulk operations require a large number of stevedores, from 25 to 40 per work shift, as shown in Figs. 1.20–1.24.

FIGURE 1.22 Ships use their gear (cranes) to load the banana pallets from the bongo barges.

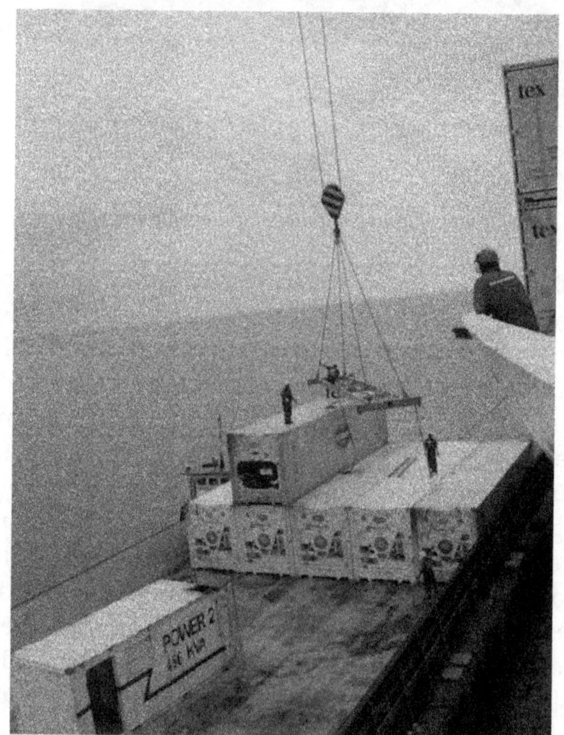

FIGURE 1.23 Barges also transport containers loaded with all types of cargos to the ship.

FIGURE 1.24 View of the ship ringed with barges in loading operations.

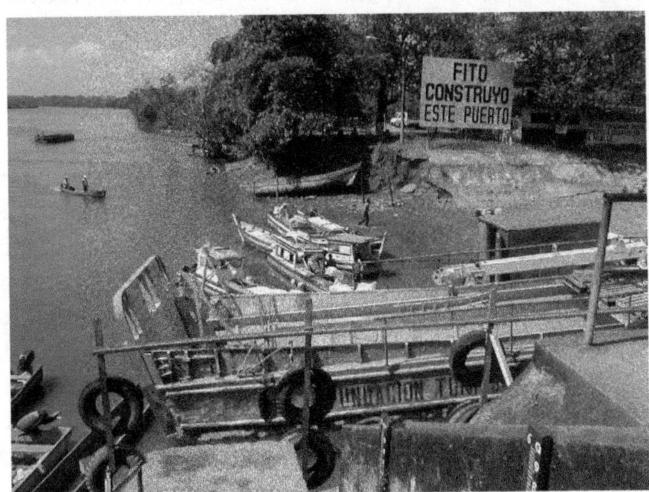

FIGURE 1.25 The river port of Chepo, Panama.

There are also ports where cargo ships tie up to anchored barges and other ports where coastal freighters simply float up onto small boat launches. In the latter case, the port of Chepo, Panama, shown in Fig. 1.25, serves as a good example. Chepo is a river port in Panama with direct access to the Pacific Ocean and is close to the border of Colombia. Chepo serves as a maritime commerce point for tens of small towns and villages in the region, as well as a transshipment point for narcotics from Colombia and arms and supplies going to the narco-guerrillas in Colombia. Again, there is no formal port. Small craft and even costal freighters load and discharge all types of merchandise—even shipping containers and trailers. In other river and bay-loading locations, containers are transported shipside in long boats. Similarly, but for other reasons, bulk ships on the Mississippi River anchor and use cranes from barges to transfer cargo, as shown in Fig. 1.26.

FIGURE 1.26 A bulk ship unloading to river barges on the Mississippi River. *Photo credit:* Shutterstock.com.

Stakeholders at Seaports

Terminal Owners

Terminal owners can be private, or they may be public entities. A public entity such as the group that operates the Port of Houston is controlled by a board of directors whose members are appointed by a city official, most commonly the mayor of that city. The board will hire a *port director* who manages the overall function of the port and provides the board with updates on the progress of the organization. A privately held port is owned and operated just as any other company. Whether privately or publicly owned, the port always has a staff that includes operations, accounting, sales and marketing, and personnel. There may be variations of this business design, but they all follow a similar concept. It is the responsibility of the sales force to attract business to the port in order to ensure revenue and cover the costs of operation. Many times the port will make long-term deals with a company (shipping line or terminal operator) and will lease the space at the port to that company for its exclusive use. In other instances, the port will operate the terminal and charge fees to the shipping companies that bring in cargo. Fees that are charged are typically assessed by length of the vessel, duration of stay, tonnage of the vessel, and weight of the cargo that is discharged. Ports will also charge for the use of other services, such as providing potable water, truck weigh scales, or even security services. With all companies battling to reduce cost and increase profit, terminal owners must often think outside the industry common practices in order to draw in as much revenue as possible. Increased revenue means that there will be money available to maintain and update the port infrastructure (cranes, RTGs, roadways, etc.), which in turn means a greater ability to lure customers to the port.

Terminal Operators

As previously mentioned, sometimes the terminal is operated by the terminal owners themselves. However, in most cases, a company will lease space from the port in order to conduct business. The companies that lease the facilities are considered to be the *terminal operators,* and may be shipping lines or companies which specialize in the functioning of a port for multiple users. The terminal operators will staff their facility with a variety of personnel and deploy a number of assets and equipment to handle the day-to-day business. The principal role the operator plays is to provide a plan for and coordinate the discharging/loading of cargo to the terminal or vessel and the movement of the discharged cargo into a warehouse or to its consignee. The operator will also act as a liaison between the crew of the vessel, the vessel managers (who direct the activities and schedule the fleet for the shipping line or ship owner), the terminal owners, and the workers who handle the cargo. The duties of the terminal operator also may include clearing of the cargo with local customs agents, overseeing the work of vessel agents, supervising cargo operations, preparing all necessary load and discharge documents, and developing and implementing safety practices and procedures.

Stevedore Company

A *stevedoring company* is a company that is hired by the terminal operator to provide the machinery, hire the laborers to work the vessel, move the cargo within the terminal, and handle the execution of the loading of cargo that is to leave the terminal. There is typically a superintendent of stevedores who is the company representative for the stevedoring company. The superintendent will supervise all aspects of the operations within the port and will act according to the plan that has been provided by the terminal operators. The superintendent will ensure that all equipment that is in use is in good working order and is safe to operate. There will be a maintenance staff that executes a preventative maintenance plan and handles any emergency repairs. The stevedoring company will handle all aspects of the payroll for the cargo workers. The stevedore will then bill the terminal operator for services. Perhaps the most valuable role that the stevedore plays is as a buffer between the laborers and the management of the terminal operator. The labor may or may not be members of a labor union. It is often beneficial to have that layer of insulation that the stevedore company provides in order to make the operation move more smoothly.

The stevedore company will also lend valuable expertise to the terminal owner/operator in the area of cargo operations. The superintendent is experienced in the loading and discharge of vessels and has valuable knowledge about manpower requirements that will maximize the efficiency of operations and decrease the cost associated with the operations. The stevedore company not only provides a layer of insulation from the labor but also alleviates the liabilities that are associated with working in this hazardous work environment. Since the employees are actually employed by the stevedore company (full-time or day labor), the stevedore company is responsible for paying workman's compensation and also indemnifying the terminal operator/owner in the event of a lawsuit from a longshoreman.

Longshoremen

Longshoremen are the actual laborers who handle the equipment and discharge or load the equipment. It is important at this juncture to clarify that *longshoremen* is a term used in the United States and in some European countries. In all Latin American countries and many other parts of the world, longshoremen are called *stevedores.* Most longshoremen are hired on a daily basis, and they are often hired through a local union hall. The longshoremen are divided into *gangs* and assigned to *hatches* (also referred to as *cargo bays*). There is a *gang foreman* for each gang, and it is his job to ensure that the men in his gang are working according to plan and in a safe manner. The gang foreman will also report the hourly count to the *clerk in charge.* This information is used to calculate finishing times, which helps plan for the departure time of the vessel. Crane operators are specialized longshoremen who have experience in the operation of all the different types of cranes, including ship cranes. The remainder of the gang is divided up according to seniority and ability. Gang size is dictated by the type of work and the kind of contract that is used when working the vessel. When labor unions are involved, contracts are negotiated based on what type of cargo is being worked. Labor start times, hours, wages, and other work rules are included in these contracts. These laborers are an integral part of the overall process in port operations.

Intermodalism

Intermodalism, propelled forward by the advent of and explosion in the use of cargo containers, represents several of the links in the cargo supply chain and has revolutionized the way ports and ships are designed and function. The use of two or more modes of transport in a shipment from origin to destination is referred to as *intermodalism.* The most common modes of transportation are via sea, air, and over land (trucks and rail). In fact, nearly all door-to-door cargo/container shipments—which are by far the most common type of shipment—use the intermodal transport system. In a door-to-door shipment, the cargo is picked up at the *exporter* (factory, manufacturer, plant, etc.) and transported all the way to the consignee (Wal-Mart distribution center, private residence, etc.). Portions of these links in the supply chain may be controlled by the exporter, the importer, an agent or broker, or the shipping company or airline. However, the exporter and/or the importer determine their level of involvement in the transport and can make certain decisions. For example, Victoria's Secret in the United States places an order for 50,000 bathrobes with its factory coordinator in Colombia. The purchase order is executed, bathrobes made, and either the exporter (factory), the consignee (Victoria's Secret), or an agent/broker coordinates the shipment. The decision of which mode to be used at each transport link on the supply chain (from the factory in Colombia to Victoria Secret's distribution warehouse) may be based on cost, time frame, and/or the type and size of the cargo. The first decision is whether to use sea or air for the international leg of the journey. In this scenario, it most likely would be maritime transport—due to volume and cost—from the closest seaport in Colombia. So, a contracted trucker (first mode of transport) will dray the container(s) from the factory to the seaport. The container(s) will be loaded on a ship (second mode of transport) to the destination port. Once in the U.S. port, the container either will be drayed directly to the Victoria Secret's distribution warehouse or loaded on a cargo train (third mode of transport) and sent via rail to the rail hub closest to the warehouse. If rail is chosen, once at the rail hub, a local trucker will dray the container to the warehouse. As you can see, in this scenario there are at least three links in the transport portion of this supply chain and a minimum of two modes of transport.

Malcom McLean's invention of the large, modern shipping container[2] and its rapid acceptance as the primary method of shipping nonbulk cargo has driven the intermodal transportation system to be the primary way cargo is moved worldwide. Later in this chapter we review in detail Malcom McLean's invention of the container. For now, let's discuss its benefits and impact on intermodalism. What was new about McLean's innovation was the idea of using large containers that were never opened in transit between shipper and consignee and that were transferable on an intermodal basis between trucks, ships, and railroad cars. The reduction in loading time (about 1/20 of the time used for the same quantity of break-bulk cargo) and the reduction in overall port/shipping costs (about 1/50 of the cost of loading and shipping the same quantity of break-bulk cargo) had a huge financial impact on the cost of the operation. These benefits, combined with McLean's freely releasing his patent on the container to the International Standards Organization, ushered in the creation of the standardized container and the development of *container terminals* and *container ships* to support these shipping operations.

Strategic Maritime Passages in Transformation

The Panama and Suez Canals

The Panama Canal and the Suez Canal are heavily transited, key passages which permit ships to significantly reduce the length of sailing time and costs by connecting the Atlantic Ocean to the Pacific Ocean (Panama Canal) and the Mediterranean Sea to the Red Sea (Suez Canal), thereby avoiding a long voyage around either Africa's Cape of Good Hope or South America's Chilean/Argentina's remote tip. The two canals are integral links in the world's maritime cargo supply chains and each just are completing major expansions to increase their capacity—which is resulting in changes to trade lanes and planning at mega seaports worldwide.

The Suez Canal, first opened in 1869, is a 120-mile-long artificial "sea-level" waterway, through which some 17,000 ships passed in 2014, as shown in Fig. 1.27. According to the

FIGURE 1.27 The Suez Canal. *Photo credit:* Shutterstock.com.

Suez Canal Authority, these 47 ships transiting daily carry onboard about 8% of the world's cargo. The canal reduces by 42% the sailing distance from the Persian Gulf to Rotterdam by avoiding the loop around the Cape of Good Hope. For practical purposes, at this point, size restrictions for container ships to transit the Suez Canal is not an issue and the newly ordered 20,000 TEU container ships will be able to transit. In August 2015, the Egyptian government proudly opened the 30 mile long, $8.2 billion canal corridor. This corridor parallels an existing portion of the waterway, specifically a segment which was a problematic chokepoint. The new corridor permits two-way lane traffic, cuts the total transit time from 18 h to 11 h, and eventually will allow up to 97 ships to cross per day. This expansion project initially was estimated to be completed in 3 years; however, so as to beat the expansion of the Panama Canal (their competition), it was completed in only 1 year. While this project is a huge success for the recently elected government of President El-Sisi, the touted return on investment is less than clear. Currently, there is little to no bottleneck of ships waiting to transit the Suez Canal and the number of vessels using the canal remains 20% below its 2008 level and just 2% higher than a decade ago. Not deterred by speculation or critics, the Suez Canal Authority's next proposed phases include construction of new ports and logistical services facilities, which the government anticipates will result in an increase in revenue from $5.5 billion in 2014 to $13 billion by 2023.[3] For the clients (shipping lines), this expansion project does increase the safety in transiting and decrease the transit time.

The Panama Canal, originally completed on August 15, 1914, is a 50-mile long, north-south waterway which crosses the Isthmus of Panama. This key passage is heavily utilized and currently has between 35 and 40 ship transits per day, with consistently between 30 and 50 ships anchored off each of the Pacific and Atlantic coasts awaiting their reserved transit time slot, as shown in Fig. 1.28. The canal uses a system of three separate locks (two on the Pacific side and one on the Atlantic side) to lift ships 85 feet above sea level, with the ships then tiering down and exiting at "sea-level" on the other side—this taking into consideration that the Pacific Ocean is almost 8 inches higher than the Atlantic and the Pacific side of the Canal has a 10–15 foot tide variation. Unlike the Suez Canal, the Panama Canal is handicapped by restrictions on the size of ships permitted to enter the canal—currently a maximum of 5000 TEUs for container ships. And, this restriction has major implications as the majority of new build ships exceed this limit. Moreover, according to the United Nations' 2014 Review of

FIGURE 1.28 The Panama Canal.

Maritime Transport, 57% of the total vessels of the top 50 shipping lines are over 5000 TEUs.[4] This percentage of "Post-Panamax" ships is consistent across the total global fleet of all types of ships. This vessel restriction is a huge disadvantage for the Panama Canal and ships frequently must discharge sufficient containers at one side of the Canal, send them across to the other side via truck drayage or via the Panama Canal Railway (which likewise is fully booked), and then have the containers reloaded on the ship. This process is costly and a factor in a Shipping Line deciding whether the trade route should be via the Suez or Panama Canal or intra-ocean loop services. In 2007, Panama addressed these two disadvantages—size restrictions and long waiting times—with the initiation of a $5.2 billion expansion project. Upon completion, the expansion will permit the passage of ships more than twice the current size and increase the total volume of transits by an estimated 40%. The expansion project, currently in its final test phase and due open in May 2016, involves the construction of a third set of locks both on the Pacific and Atlantic sides of the Canal. These new locks are vastly larger than the existing ones and will permit the transit of 13,000 TEU container ships. These dual enhancements, both in the size and the number of ships transiting, have major implications for world trade lanes and, especially, U.S. seaports. According to a June 2015 research study by the Boston Consulting Group and C.H. Robinson, one impact of the Panama Canal expansion is that up to 10% of the container traffic from East Asia to the United States could shift from the West Coast to the East Coast by 2020. This shift would boost the overall percentage of the East Asia to the U.S. cargo for East and Gulf Coasts port to a full 50% of the total trade.[5] The ports of New York/New Jersey, Norfolk, Savannah, Charleston, Houston, New Orleans, and Gulfport are best positioned to benefit from the larger ships and increased traffic through the Panama Canal.[6] Strategic decisions by major U.S. seaports and shipping lines have been underway in anticipation of the opening of the Panama Canal's larger locks. Port-related improvements at U.S. seaport, due to the Panama Canal expansion, are in excess of $46 billion and focuses on deepening harbors and expanding marine terminals to accommodate the larger ships. Simultaneously, shipping lines are designing their new routes and realigning existing trade routes to reflect the Canal expansion. Currently, there are a total of 25 weekly Asia to U.S. East Coast services, of which 16 go through the Panama Canal and 9 use the Suez Canal. As an indication of the impact of the Panama Canal expansion, during the first half of 2015, there have been six new trade services created between Asia and the U.S. East Coast—with five using the Panama Canal versus only one using the Suez Canal.[7] As of September 2015, the Panama Canal Authority is actively evaluating the next expansion, a *fourth* set of locks. The fourth set of locks would be even larger than the third and would allow the newly ordered 20,000 TEU ships (now classed as ultralarge container ships—ULCS) to transit the canal; thereby competing directly with the Suez Canal. According to the Panama Canal Authority, the cost of the next set of locks is estimated to be approximately $17 billion and could be constructed within 15 years.[8]

The Polar Passages—Future Major Trade Lanes?

The increased velocity of the melting of Arctic ice, combined with rapid developments in ice-classed ships and ice breaking technology, may well lead the Northwest Passage, Northern Sea Route (also referred to as the Northeast Passage), and the Transpolar Sea Passage to near year-round commercial shipping by or before 2040, offering great benefits—but with some lingering challenges and complexities. It is important to note that 80% of the world's industrial production occurs north of the 30th parallel north, which makes the lure of quicker and more cost-effective shipping between the northern regions all the more inviting. A snapshot of the three passages and their time and cost savings as trade routes and challenges are as follows:

- **The Northern Sea Route** (also referred to as the **Northeast Passage**), the majority of which is claimed by Russia, runs through some 58 straits along the Arctic coast of Russia. The shallowness of the straits in some areas affects the size, volume, and drafts of ships that will be able to transit this Passage, however, the sailing season for the entire Northeast Passage has been extended to 6 months a year and this will continue to grow.[9] This Passage offers high significant savings in time and operational costs. For example, the transit from Shanghai to Rotterdam is 10,557 nautical miles via the Suez Canal, but only 8056 via the Northeast Passage, a 24% reduction in distance and more than 10 days in time.[10] From northern China, the savings are even greater. In August 2013, a COSCO ship (China's largest shipping line) traveled from the northern Chinese port of Dalian to Rotterdam using the Northern Sea Route—slicing a full 2 weeks off of the route via Suez Canal. In late 2013, the Polar Research Institute of China reported their estimation that by 2020 between 5% and 15% of China's international trade would be via the Northern Sea Route, which even the midpoint amount to in excess of $700 billion in commerce.[11] The Northern Sea Route already has begun to be used as a route to China for Russian natural gas reserves, oil, coal, and minerals—all of which China needs for its bustling industries and manufacturing—and these bulk cargos (on bulk carrying ships) are expected to continue increasing in the near term.[12] The Northern Sea Route likely could be a financial boon for Russia as by staking claim and managing the route it will decree fees and other regulatory and operational considerations and control which ships are permitted to transit, all which yield new income and have additional political/military/economic implications.

- **The Northwest Passage** runs through one of the largest archipelagoes of the world, crossing Canada's Arctic Ocean, and researchers from the National Academy of Sciences and UCLA using multiple climate models believe it holds the best promise for the most near-term route across the Arctic Ocean.[13] Ice conditions within the Northwest Passage vary dramatically from year to year, and it tends to melt seasonal less quickly than the other Passages/Routes. Nevertheless, the benefits are substantial. In September, 2014, the bulk cargo ship, the M/V Nunavik, carrying 23,000 tons of nickel ore, completed the first solo trip—*no icebreaker used*—via the Northwest Passage. The cargo ship traveled from Canada's Deception Bay via the Passage to the port of Bayuquan, China in *40% less time than using the standard route through the Panama Canal*, resulting in huge savings in fuel and time, as well as significant reductions in greenhouse gas emissions.[14] While the M/V Nunavik is a Polar-classed vessel, the Shipping Line (Fednav) reported that it never encountered any thick ice or chokepoints that hindered the crossing.[15] Using the Northwest Passage to travel between East Asia and Western Europe would yield about the same 40% savings in nautical miles, so in less than 20 years this Passage could be a viable alternative to the Russian-claimed Northern Sea Route for bulk, break-bulk, and container ships operating between the heavy manufacturing regions of East Asia (ports in northern China, Korea, and Japan) and the major destination ports of Northern Europe (Rotterdam and Antwerp).
- **The Transpolar Passage** runs through the Arctic Ocean, in an almost straight line, between the Atlantic Ocean and the Bering Sea, in a zone where up to now multiyear ice is the most frequent. Ice cover of the Arctic Ocean is not a static and is constantly in motion, so this provides additional challenges to commercial shipping. However, this too is beginning to change with the melting of Arctic ice. According to reporting by the Norwegian Scientific Academy for Polar Research, in the 1960s, only 15% of the total area of the Arctic Ocean was open during the summer months. However, since 1970, sea ice thickness in the Central Arctic Ocean has decreased by 42%, and recent model experiments predict a *totally ice-free Arctic Ocean during the summer by the year 2040*.[16] As this Passage is clearly the most direct, at certain times of the year, it will be the quickest route crossing the Arctic Ocean. Again, as container lines run schedules which are "year-round" and with limited flexibility, this Passage is unlikely to be a usage platform for them, however, usage by Polar-classed bulk carriers is a more realistic scenario.

In addition to the before-mentioned challenges for the Arctic Passages to become major trade lanes, there are other technical, human, and support complexities—many of which are addressed and regulated in the International Maritime Organization's Polar

Code, entering into force on January 1, 2017. The unique and harsh weather conditions in the Arctic, which include dense fog, extreme cold, high swells, floating ice, and violent storms, can create additional risks for crews, ice damage to ships, and rapid deterioration and breakdown of unprotected machinery.[17] Furthermore, the limited seaports and assistance capabilities in the Arctic Ocean rim to respond to vessel grounding or a fire onboard is a cause for concern. In 2014, in anticipation of increased usage of the Polar Passages, the UN's International Maritime Organization adopted the "Polar Code" and related Amendments to SOLAS and MARPOL. The Code and SOLAS/MARPOL Amendments address ship design, construction, equipment, operational and crew training issues, search and rescue, and environmental and ecosystem protections. Effective 2017, the Polar Code will require all ships intending to operate in Arctic/Antarctic waters to obtain a Polar Ship Certificate for one of the three classes and full meet the requirements of the Polar Code and SOLAS/MARPOL Amendments.[18]

Summary

The shipping industry is an integral and vital part of our society and culture. Every facet of life is greatly affected by the cargo operations that occur within shipping terminals on a daily basis. Security, commerce, and defense are directly linked with shipping terminals and ships around the world. A nation that has strong commercial shipping capabilities is capable of creating more revenue than a land-locked country. Equally important, ports provide a platform for a strong sea-based military navy. A naval vessel leaving its home port and taking up station off a foreign cost is called *power projection.* That naval vessel then becomes a platform of operation and an extension of the country it represents. As technology improves our way of life and the way we do business, terminal operations will become more and more specialized. The race to improve efficiency of operations and the speed with which cargo is handled will create new and improved ways to get cargo from one point to another. The need for new terminals and vessels is a direct reflection of the laws of supply and demand. As demand for certain items changes, so do the means by which they are delivered. History has shown that maritime commerce is a key factor in the success of a nation's economy.

End Notes

1. https://www.portofrotterdam.com/en/news-and-press-releases/very-strong-first-quarter-for-port-of-rotterdam
2. Levinson, Marc. 2006. *The Box,* Princeton University Press.
3. http://gcaptain.com/did-the-world-actually-need-a-new-suez-canal/#.VdVVj5cYM20
4. http://unctad.org/en/PublicationsLibrary/rmt2014_en.pdf
5. http://www.americanshipper.com/Main/News/Expanded_Panama_Canal_could_cause_coastal_cargo_sh_60607.aspx?source=MostPopular#hide
6. Ibid.

7. http://ciw.drewry.co.uk/features/jockeying-for-panama-position/#.Vda0cpcYM20
8. http://www.inquisitr.com/1958639/17-billion-on-expanding-panama-canal-will-open-up-new-trade-oppertunities/
9. https://people.hofstra.edu/geotrans/eng/ch1en/conc1en/polarroutes.html; http://www.worldpolicy.org/blog/2015/04/08/future-shipping-trade-arctic-waters; http://news.discovery.com/earth/oceans/north-pole-a-major-shipping-lane-by-2040-130305.htm
10. http://www.tandfonline.com/doi/pdf/10.1080/1088937X.2014.965769
11. http://www.theglobeandmail.com/news/national/the-north/for-china-north-is-a-new-way-to-go-west/article16402962/
12. http://www.maritime-executive.com/features/arctic-promising-for-bulk-shipping; http://www.thestar.com.my/News/Regional/2013/08/17/Shipping-firm-starts-using-new-Arctic-route-Northeast-Passage-saves-time-and-cuts-fuel-costs/
13. http://news.discovery.com/earth/oceans/north-pole-a-major-shipping-lane-by-2040-130305.htm
14. http://news.discovery.com/earth/oceans/cargo-ship-is-first-to-solo-the-northwest-passage-141002.htm; http://gcaptain.com/first-arctic-cargo-shipped-through-northwest-passage-fednav/#.VdtmbZerFoN
15. Ibid.
16. http://www.worldpolicy.org/blog/2015/04/08/future-shipping-trade-arctic-waters
17. http://www.brinknews.com/few-ships-or-insurers-are-ready-to-carry-risk-of-arctic-passage/
18. http://www.imo.org/en/MediaCentre/HotTopics/polar/Documents/POLAR%20CODE%20TEXT%20AS%20ADOPTED%20BY%20MSC%20AND%20MEPC.pdf

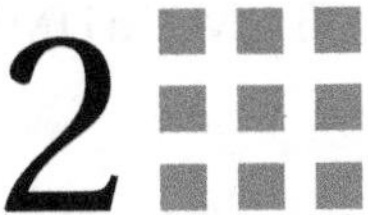

Modes of Maritime Transport

OBJECTIVES

After studying this chapter, you will be familiar with

1. The origins and development of modern commercial ships and shipping;
2. The types and functioning of modern commercial ships, including bulk carriers, tankers, container ships, freighters, oceangoing tugboats, and cruise ships;
3. The emergence of "greener" ships and the factors driving this development;
4. The race for building bigger ships and the reasons why bigger is perceived to be better;
5. Why orders for Polar class ships are on rise.

Introduction

Suppose you are driving along one of the many U.S. interstate highways with a young and inquisitive companion. As you begin passing multiple semitractor trailers, the questioning begins. A Wal-Mart truck passes by, and your guest asks about its contents. You logically assume that it is carrying furniture, toys, or even clothing. Next in line is a silver tank trailer being towed by a Peterbilt with red diamond-shaped placards on the sides and rear panel. He again asks what is being carried, and although unsure, you surmise that the trailer contains a flammable liquid of some sort, perhaps gasoline. This satisfies your companion until a large brown truck comes into view. After seeing the initials "UPS" on the side, you safely answer that many packages are on their way to be delivered. As you can see, the cargoes being carried on our highways vary greatly, and similarly, the vehicles carrying such items are just as diverse in their designs.

The same type of truck is not used to carry both household items and flammable liquids. Therefore, different designs are imperative for a particular use or mission. The same can be said for vessels engaged in ocean transport. Upon our oceans, sounds, bays, rivers, and harbors, you may observe a multitude of different types of ships, boats, watercraft, and occasionally aircraft. In this section of the chapter, we discuss the various types of merchant and commercial vessels, occasionally also referencing military or public vessels. However, the discussion of military vessels, which can also be considered emergency vehicles, is for identification and comparison purposes alone, and instead the unique challenges posed by commercial and pleasure vessels, as well as their own security options, are the main focus.

The merchant or commercial vessels tend to complete their passage as efficiently as possible when proceeding from point A to point B. The military mission is often varied and does not follow the most expedient route when sailing due to specified requirements.

Maritime Security.

Research vessels may head into the ocean only to conduct experiments and then must return to the original port of call. Pleasure crafts are not required to follow such plans and may return to a port only after exhausting their fuel or if passenger needs require a stop.

There are many ways to categorize *merchant* or *commercial vessels.* Size and type are the most common categories. To fully understand this, you need to be familiar with the units of measurement used in the maritime world. With truck trailers, carrying capacity and length are two common measures. When we refer to ships, the units of measurement differ and consist of *gross tons, net tons, deadweight tons, displacement tons, long tons, metric tons,* and *short tons.* Each of these units of measurement has a unique meaning. Gross ton is a volume measurement of 100 cubic feet equaling one gross ton. Net tonnage is also a volume measure indicating the area available to earn revenue. A long ton equals 2240 pounds. A metric ton equals 2204.6 pounds. A short ton equals 2000 pounds. The long and metric tons are commonly used when describing cargo ships. A short ton is used only when referring to the cargo weight. It has been replaced by the long or metric ton in most cases. Gross tonnage is used when bragging about how large a cruise or passenger ship has been built. A ship displaces water in direct relation to its total weight. A large oceangoing ship may easily displace 80,000 long tons or, stated on the metric scale, 81,280 metric tons. The cargo-carrying capacity is known as the deadweight tonnage. It also can be stated in both long tons and metric tons. The deadweight capacity is most easily remembered as the "earning capacity of a ship." After you subtract out the actual weight of the empty ship and the fuel, lubricants, water, and the crew and provisions needed to operate the ship, the remaining lifting capacity is the *deadweight.* Deadweight listing is often used when comparing tankers and bulk-carrying ships. Deadweight is abbreviated as *dwt.* Since most of the world has switched to the metric system, you can assume each dwt is 1000 kg or 2204.6 lbs.

By international treaty, ships can be loaded only to a predetermined limit noted on the side of the hull by an *international load line* or *Plimsoll Mark.* A certain amount of the hull must remain out of the water. If this Plimsoll Mark (a horizontal line inside a circle on the side of the ship) is submerged, local authorities can easily recognize the ship is overloaded. If the voyage is relatively short, the master or owner may decide to carry less fuel and more cargo. But if the fuel price is very low at the departure port and the freight rates are not all that high on this voyage, it may be decided to fill all the fuel tanks and "cut" or reduce the cargo loaded. As you can see, deadweight is very important when deciding to charter a vessel.

Samuel Plimsoll of Bristol, England, as a Member of Parliament in the middle 1800s, campaigned for legislation to protect merchant seamen. Being aware ship owners often overloaded ships, he proposed the marking of the ship's hull with a line, which would disappear below the waterline if the ship were overloaded (see Fig. 2.1). To this day, most seamen know the international load line as the *Plimsoll Mark.*

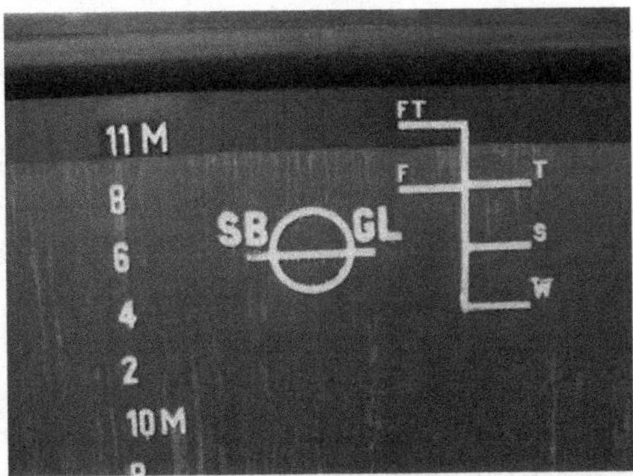

FIGURE 2.1 *Plimsoll Mark* is a marker used to identify if the ship is overloaded.

A cruise ship's enormous appearance is a result of large volumes of air and lightweight fixtures. Cruise ships are seldom loaded down to their Plimsoll Mark. To compare the size of these popular vessels, gross tonnage is used. The word *gross* is nearly always dropped. The net tonnage would actually provide a truer measure. When you subtract from the gross tonnage, the area consumed by the engine room spaces, crew's quarters, control rooms, fan rooms, and navigation spaces, the result is the net tonnage or "revenue-generating space."

These maritime measurements can then be used to understand the next classification of commercial vessels. These two categories include those vessels on a scheduled, published service and those vessels in a tramp service. You could think of *scheduled service* similar to FedEx, which lists on its website all the cities it serves regularly. All you have to do is call and request a pickup location. The *tramp service* closely resembles a moving company similar to North American Van Lines. The tramp service does not necessarily have the destination port determined at the beginning of the voyage. For example, when a family quickly sells their home, they must move out, but without their next location in mind, they may be forced to store their belongings until they can relocate. With shipping, you may ask how this routine could be possible or practical. The answer is simpler than you would think. Tramp service allows for a charterer to stow its commodities onboard until it can find a buyer. A time charterer may load a ship with 50,000 tons of coal and instruct the master to sail to the Panama Canal. The charterer knows this particular ship will take 10 days to reach the Canal. So, during the next 10 days, the charterer will advertise and arrange for a buyer for the 50,000 tons of coal. The master will be advised either before or after he transits the Canal as to his next port of call. If the charterer cannot find a buyer at his desired price, he may order the ship to stop and drift or proceed to anchor and wait. This is somewhat like the family putting their furniture in storage at North American Van Lines. The vessel owner is being paid for every day the time charterer has his vessel hired, so he doesn't mind if the ship must remain at anchor for weeks at a time. The tramp vessel may never have called at the ports it is currently sailing and after this voyage may not ever return again. Those vessels on scheduled runs tend to call at the same ports over and over again until market conditions dictate a change. The security assessments will be quite different for a scheduled liner service vessel and a tramp vessel. A terrorist likely would not or could not as easily plan an attack using a tramp vessel, since he has no certainty it will even reach the desired target country or the desired port.

The type of cargo being hauled further categorizes these oceangoing commercial vessels. Ships that carry large quantities of liquid cargo are called *tankers.* Those that haul their cargo in standard-sized shipping containers are termed *container ships,* or as a class *load on/load off* (LO/LO). Ships that have their cargo broken into smaller quantities and are usually more specialized are termed *freighters.* Bulk carriers or *bulkers* carry large, homogeneous cargoes. Ships that are designed for the cargo to be driven onboard are called *roll on/roll off* (RO/RO) vessels. Other specialized vessels being discussed include oceangoing tugboats, cruise ships, passenger ships, as well as research and hydrographic survey vessels. Smaller versions of each of these types of vessels are often called *coastwise* or *coastal vessels.* Even though these smaller vessels may be seaworthy enough to cross the ocean, it is generally not economically feasible for them to do so. Frequently, small coastal tankers, container-feeder ships, and tugs with barges are seen operating up and down the coast of any country. Within harbors, bays, and sounds, ferries and water-taxi service vessels are often utilized. In this setting, tugboats and other support vessels are engaged in commerce. Though one- or two-person rowboats and sailboats have been known to cross the world's oceans, commercial interests usually support much larger crafts. During colonial times in America, the clipper sailing ships spirited across the Atlantic in weeks rather than the months it took square-rigged barques to make the same passage. These clippers did not have a great deal of cargo capacity but were able to deliver the mail, spirits, and other goods from England to the settlers in America. For the purpose of our discussion, oceangoing vessels will be more than 300 feet long and displace more than 2000 tons.

Going back to the interstate highway analogy, local delivery trucks share the highways with the long-haul truckers just as the coastal vessels sail alongside the huge liner service container ships. The smaller coastal vessels are able to pull into ports that will not or cannot handle the larger oceangoing ships. Large oceangoing ships may at times be ordered into small roadstead ports, especially those located on distant islands and other remote locations. However, this would be more of an exception than a rule for economic reasons. On American highways, special freight may be transported over great distances in a small delivery truck so that additional handling can be avoided. In the same way, smaller ships often are engaged to haul some unique or valuable cargoes across the ocean.

Transporting people and cargo over water has been accomplished for centuries. The rafts, boats, and ships have evolved over the years. With very few exceptions, there have not been tremendous technological innovations during the past 100 years. Nearly all ships and boats are propelled through the water by a submerged propeller. Most ships and boats displace 1 ton of water for each ton the vessel actually weighs. In the commercial world, the internal combustion diesel engine is the standard means of driving this propeller. For a period of time, the steam turbine engine was the power plant of choice. Since the steam was generated from boilers, any fuel could be used. Coal and oil were the most common. In the 1960s, nuclear power was experimented with, but it never gained commercial acceptance. Marine gas turbine engines, which are larger versions of jet airplane engines, are widely used in military vessels but have found only limited applications with merchant ships. Some engines are configured to directly drive the propeller(s), while others make use of reduction gears or may use the engine to generate electricity, which, in turn, powers a large motor that drives the propeller. In most circumstances, it is the internal combustion engine that prevails in the shipping world.

For the past 30 years, the slow-speed diesel engine has been gaining wide acceptance in marine applications. The engine is mounted so that the crankshaft is directly in line with the tail shaft and propeller hub. A direct connection is made between the crankshaft and tail shaft without the use of a reduction gear. The crankshaft is turning at the same speed as the propeller. Top speed may be 125 rpm. To go into reverse, the engine is stopped and the firing order of the pistons is changed; the propeller then turns in the opposite direction. This type of engine tends to run most efficiently at 90% of rated horsepower.

The Panama Canal itself is used when classifying oceangoing ships. As discussed earlier, the third set of locks, set for inauguration in May 2016, will permit more twice the current size (the new limit to be 13,000 TEU container ships) to transit the Canal. Currently, however, the Canal's locks limit transit to ships less than 1000 feet long and 106 feet in beam or width (5000 TEUs for container ships). Because the Canal was constructed in the early 1900s, most shipbuilders have restricted their ship designs in order to meet these requirements. Ships barely able to fit through the canal were known as *Panamax*. In the late 1960s, tankers were the first commercial vessels constructed in excess of these design restrictions and are now referred to as *post-Panamax* vessels. These huge tankers were first classified as *very large crude carriers* or *VLCCs*. When the world's demand for oil increased even more, it became economical to build even larger tankers known as *ultra-large crude carriers* or *ULCCs*. These vessels, as their names imply, carry only crude oil as cargo. Smaller product tankers are used to transport refined petroleum products such as jet fuel, diesel fuel, heating oil, and gasoline. Over the years, these product tankers have so greatly grown in size that many of them can no longer transit the Panama Canal.

Another specialized type of tanker is the chemical ship. Some of these ships may carry 25 or more unique products. They are often constructed with stainless steel tanks and separate pumping and plumbing systems that prevent comingling of the cargoes. The variety of chemicals is overwhelming. It is not unusual for a ship to have liquid acids in some tanks and caustic products in others. Dry-cleaning fluids and chemicals used in the ink-printing business may also be onboard.

A final specialized type of tanker is known as the *fleet oiler*. It is normally a military vessel used to refuel other military vessels while underway at sea.

Containerization may go down in history as one of the most significant events in ocean shipping commerce. Historians will likely rank it up there with the advent of the clipper ships and the evolution to steam-powered ocean liners. In 1956, a trucking company entrepreneur named Malcom McLean decided to load 58 containers onboard a converted tanker and sailed them from Newark, New Jersey, to Houston, Texas. This was the humble beginning to what was to become the world's premier container shipping line, Sea-Land Service, Inc. But McLean was not the first to attempt intermodal shipping. In the 1920s, SeaTrain Lines carried railcars from the East Coast of the United States to Cuba and later to other destinations until the 1970s. In spite of McLean's innovations, the major shipping lines of the day were slow to embrace or adopt containerized shipping. Most of the European and American steamship lines continued to operate exclusively conventional freighters until the late 1960s. However, from time to time, containers would be stowed on their decks.

The longshoremen also resisted handling containers. They were concerned about the loss of jobs and perks (benefits). Since containers were loaded great distances from the ports and not opened until they reached the final destination, the longshoremen were prevented from actually handling or seeing the cargo. It was widely known along the waterfront that some of the longshoremen's unreported income was from an "occasional damaged" case of cargo that had fallen off a pallet. In ports that received Scotch whiskey, for instance, one unopened case was routinely "set aside" for the longshore boss, thus guaranteeing the remaining cargo would be safely unloaded.

In the early years of containerization, there was not any standardization. McLean's company, Sea-Land Service, adopted 35-foot containers. Matson Lines, which sailed between the West Coast of the United States and Hawaii, decided on 24-foot long containers. During the next few years, dozens of container sizes appeared in America and Europe. Finally in 1970, at the urging of McLean, some standards were proposed and adopted by the International Standards Organization, with the 20 and 40 footers becoming the basic units. As we have seen with the eight-track audio players and the Betamax videocassettes, the initial innovators are not always the standard bearers. Sea-Land was forced to change its entire fleet in the 1970s from a 35-foot standard to the internationally adopted norm. By 1985, all Sea-Land ships were capable of handling 20s and 40s. Sea-Land had either purchased or converted its vessels to accommodate the standard container sizes.

FIGURE 2.2 The interior view of a standard reefer (refrigerated) container.

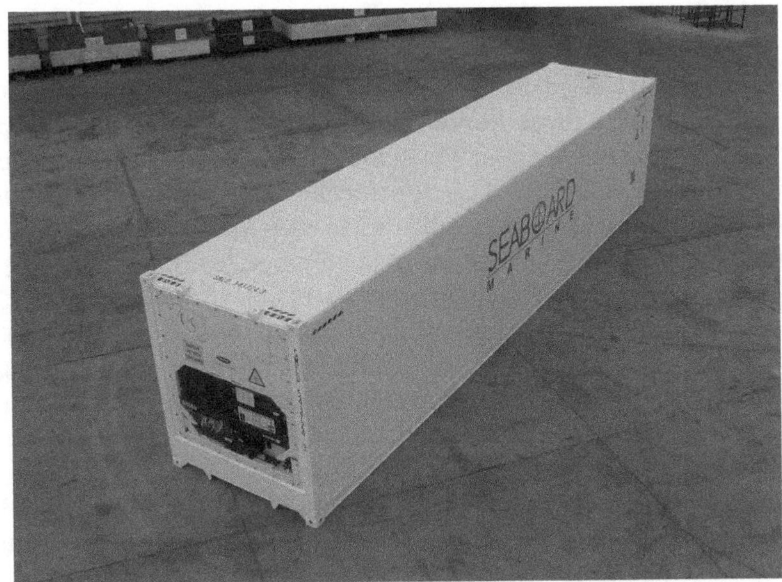

FIGURE 2.3 The exterior of a reefer container, with a view of the cooling unit.

FIGURE 2.4 Containers, 20 foot and 40 foot, loaded on the deck of a ship.

Containerization has truly revolutionized cargo shipping. Specialty containers have been constructed to handle nearly all cargoes from toxic chemicals, to airplane parts, to automobiles, to hanging garments, bagged sugar and grains, case lots, as well as a huge variety of refrigerated and frozen products (see Figs. 2.2–2.4). Today, between 90% and 95% of all nonbulk goods are shipped in containers. The U.S. military has also adopted container shipping for a major portion of its deployment logistics.

Container ships have increased in numbers and size since first invented in the late 1950s. From a security perspective, they pose perhaps the greatest threat because the majority of them maintain an advertised, published, and tight schedule—and most containers are door-to-door, so there is a known destination. This schedule is a major marketing feature of the container shipping industry, on which many clients and customers depend in order to run their businesses smoothly. This specifically refers to the *just-in-time* inventory approach that many manufacturers are utilizing to keep their costs low. The largest of these container ships, the M/V MSC OSCAR (as of September 2015), can carrying up to 19,224 *20-foot equivalent unit* (TEU) containers—almost 10,000 40-foot containers. The average liner service container ship holds approximately 3500 containers. Undoubtedly, you have seen these containers being pulled behind semitractor rigs on our nation's highways. They range in size from 20 feet long to 53 feet long. The larger container ships tend to load at only a few ports on one side of the ocean and then quickly cross and discharge at a few ports on the opposite shore. Liner service container ships usually do not have their own cranes or any other means to load or discharge the containers. They depend on shore-based gantry cranes to handle this task. A good crane operator can handle 40–45 containers per hour. The containers normally weigh 10–25 tons, but these cranes are often able to lift 50-ton containers. A container can be handled multiple times without harm or inspection coming to the cargo. Networks of trucks, rails, and in some cases smaller feeder ships collect containers from various nearby ports and deliver them to their destination or another port where a liner service ship can reload them. Earlier, we discussed the different means used when describing the size of a ship. For charterers, the net carrying capacity is an important consideration—whether it is determined by weight or volume. Another measure used in the container ship industry is the *TEU*, capacity. A 20-foot container is counted as 1 TEU. A 40-foot container is counted as 2 TEUs. A 45-foot container would be counted as 2.25 TEUs. So, a container ship is defined—and measured—by how many TEUs it holds.

Freighter is a general term encompassing a wide variety of oceangoing ships. Until the end of World War II, freighters usually had their own booms (ship cranes) and rigging to load and discharge cargo. Most of the cargo was in boxes or bags stacked on pallets. Loading and unloading was a very slow and tedious job. In some cases, the ship remained in port for weeks at a time only to load 6000–8000 tons of cargo. Today, it is possible for a container ship to load 4000 or more tons of cargo in an hour.

Currently, few of the conventional freighters remain in service. Instead, specialized ships are built for particular trades. A ship needed to sail to Third World or developing countries may be fitted with one or two cranes to load and discharge 20-foot containers and perhaps have a ramp that allows for automobiles and farm equipment to be driven off the vessel. The importing and exporting of automobiles has become a huge global business, and as a result, specialized freighters called *car carriers* have been built during the past 25 years. These vessels have ramps that allow automobiles to be driven directly onboard. Decks are equipped with hydraulic rams that facilitate the raising and lowering of the individual decks in order to maximize the number of vehicles carried. Thousands of automobiles are often carried onboard one of these ships. It is not unusual for hundreds of longshoremen to be employed during the cargo operations. The longshoremen drivers are then loaded into a bus and returned to the main parking area to drive more cars back to the ship. This goes on for hours at a time. These ships tend to maintain a fairly set schedule and operate often between only a few ports. For instance, one automobile manufacturer has a final assembly plant in Nagoya, Japan, and several times a week ships sail to Oakland, California. From a security standpoint, this ship could be more at risk than a bulk carrier or an oil tanker whose schedule has not been finalized until it has sailed from the loading port.

Bulk carriers, or *bulkers*, are designed and built to usually carry but one type of cargo at a time. The products include fertilizers, iron ore, coal, gypsum, and grain, to name just a few. Most of these ships do not have the capability to load and discharge the cargo without the assistance of shore-based cranes, conveyers, or suction devices. It takes very few individuals to load and discharge one of these ships. An independent inspector and a ship's officer examine the cargo holds prior to and after the completion of cargo operations. Since these are commodities traded on the open market, the cargo may be bought and sold several times during a voyage. The destination port often changes throughout the voyage. From a security standpoint, this carrier would be considered as one of the last types of vessels that a terrorist would use to carry out a hostile mission.

Oceangoing tugs are used for several different types of undertakings. They may be contracted to tow a disabled vessel, a barge, or an oil rig. Weather has a major effect on their schedules, and with very few exceptions, these tugs are not on a set schedule. But since some have larger engines than ships and a very small crew, they may pose a security threat if their operation were taken over by a hostile faction.

Tankers

In this section we begin to discuss in more detail the various classes of oceangoing ships. The first main category is oil tankers. Often when you see an advertisement on television for an oil company, you see mostly the image of a very large tanker navigating across a beautiful blue sea. The type of ship usually pictured is a ULCC (See Fig. 2.5). These mammoth ships are generally more than 350,000 dwt. Most of them exceed 1000 feet long, have a beam or width of more than 150 feet, and require or draw more than 60–80 feet of water. With these dimensions, there are few ports in the world that can receive these large ships. As a result, many of them call at offshore oil terminals, which to the untrained eye appear to be very small oil rigs sticking out of the water (see Fig. 2.6). The pipelines leading to offshore moorings or terminals are submerged in the sea bed and run to tank fields that are usually miles away on the shore. It is common for the tank farms to be positioned on hillsides or even mountaintops, which allow the force of gravity to be used for loading oil onto the tankers. All that is required of the chief mate is to open the valve, wait for the oil to fill the tanker, and close the valve. This simple method of liquid cargo loading helps to prevent spills and other environmental impacts rather than serves as a means of conservation of energy.

FIGURE 2.5 An ultralarge crude carrier, also referred to by its initials *ULCC*. *Photo credit:* Shutterstock.com.

FIGURE 2.6 The single mooring buoy (SMB) is an offshore transfer site where tankers load or unload their product, which is connected to the land-based location by underwater pipes.

VLCCs generally are between 100,000 and 350,000 dwt in size (see Fig. 2.7). These are very large ships by any measure, but since they often draw only 50–60 feet of water, it is possible for them to come into some of the world's larger ports. The typical VLCC is about 1000 feet long but may have a beam of 125–150 feet. Both of these types of ships have a top speed under 15 knots. In recent years, the diesel slow-speed engine has been the choice of most shipbuilders.

FIGURE 2.7 *A very large crude carrier (VLCC). Photo credit:* claffra/Shutterstock.com.

These tankers carry just one type of cargo—crude oil. To prevent the collection of explosive gasses in the tanks, an inert gas system is required by international convention. When the oil is loaded, the inert gas is purged off at the discharge terminal. Fresh inert gas becomes a byproduct of the ship's generators and is pumped into the tanks as the oil is pumped ashore. At all times, the excess tank capacity is filled with inert gas. This is done for two reasons: first, this is to maintain an atmosphere in the tanks during loading and discharge that cannot sustain combustion; and second, the tanker is always carrying the same cargo as it is being discharged—therefore, the tanks are automatically washed with pressured crude oil that is sprayed on the insides. This procedure is referred to as *crude oil washing* and allows for nearly all the oil cargo to be discharged ashore. As an added bonus, this inert gas also prevents most crude oil tankers from being desirable targets for terrorists. Inert gas systems have been installed on crude oil tankers for about 50 years. Their development had everything to do with safety and efficient tanker operations, and little consideration was given to terrorists back in the early 1970s.

Another type of tanker that is generally much smaller than most is the *product carrier.* These ships can range from just a few thousand tons to nearly 70,000–80,000 dwt. Those used in ocean service tend to be more than 50,000 tons and range from 500 to 900 feet long with a beam of less than 110 feet and a draft of less than 40 feet. They often are segregated in such a way as to be able to carry three or four different grades of oil without comingling the cargoes. The pump rooms of these product tankers have several different systems, allowing multiple cargoes to be discharged simultaneously. The smaller size of these ships enables them to sail from a refinery to the destination port desired. Segregated ballast tanks allow for clean salt-water ballast to be taken onboard, while the oil cargo is being discharged ashore. This ballast is not contaminated with the oil and can be discharged later without causing pollution. At the loading port, the clean ballast is pumped out as oil

FIGURE 2.8 A liquefied natural gas tanker underway.

is loaded. Cruising speed may vary from 15 to 19 knots generally. This type of ship could be a target for terrorist activities due to its slow speed and low *freeboard*—the distance from the waterline to the main deck—which may permit easier boarding from a smaller vessel.

Liquefied Natural Gas Tankers

The next type of tanker is called *liquefied natural gas* (LNG) ship (see Fig. 2.8). Natural gas is cooled as it is loaded onboard these specially constructed vessels. The gas is refrigerated the entire time it is onboard while being held in pressurized tanks. Special insulation and large segregated ballast tanks surround these tanks. The LNG ships are rather complex and ideally operate from isolated terminals away from major populated centers. They tend to range from 900 to 1100 feet long with a beam of more than 120 feet. The water depth required for these ships needs to be more than 50 feet. Since the Panama Canal most likely would not allow their transit, most builders have built the ships wider than the 106-foot Canal limitation. Although it may seem that such tankers would be a prize for terrorist organizations, the ship's outer hull as well as the ballast tanks and void spaces surround the pressurized tanks that are normally built out of stainless steel, making it very difficult for penetration.

Chemical Tankers

Chemical tankers carry many different grades of petroleum and liquid chemical cargo (see Fig. 2.9). It is not unusual for one of these ships to have more than 30 different piping systems and tanks, allowing for 30 or more different cargoes to be carried at any given time. In the industry, these ships are often called *floating drugstores.* On one particular ship, it is not unusual to carry cargo ranging from inks used in the food packaging industry to

FIGURE 2.9 A chemical tanker in port. *Photo credit:* Shutterstock.com.

acids used in the beverage industry to chemicals used in the dry-cleaning industry. These ships tend to be much smaller than the other tankers—only 5000–25,000 dwt and 200–400 feet long.

Container Ships

Container ships vary greatly in size and speed. Most container ships are in liner service, referring to their published schedule service. Shippers are able to plan their shipment months in advance, knowing exactly when the cargo needs to be ready for transit and when it will arrive at the port of destination. Most oceangoing container ships stack the containers six to eight high below the main deck and up to six high above the main deck. The corners of these containers have socket fittings sporting special twist locks. These twist locks hold the containers to each other, making a rigid stack. Shore-based gantry cranes lift the containers on and off the ship. These automated and expensive marvels lift containers weighing 35 tons or more. The operator can snatch and drop with great speed and accuracy up to 45 containers per hour (Figs. 2.10 and 2.11).

The newly built liner service ships tend to be faster and larger than those constructed only 10 years ago. The average liner is about 3700 TEUs, but several companies are constructing mammoth ships that are able to load 20,000 TEUs. Ships carrying fewer than 4000 containers can generally transit the Panama Canal. As mentioned previously, those just meeting the Panama Canal's limits are known as *Panamax* container ships. The large container ships are referred to as *post-Panamax*, which means they are too large to transit the Canal.

The container business has grown so large that it is now possible for companies to maintain fleets that trade exclusively in the Atlantic or Pacific Oceans. The Suez Canal was

FIGURE 2.10 This specially designed and built container ship has "open-top" cargo bays and high-speed ship cranes, eliminating the requirement of shoreside cranes.

FIGURE 2.11 A view inside the hatch of the "open-top" cargo bay reveals the guide rails and easy access to the reefer motor of the container.

built without the need for locks like the Panama Canal. As a result, in recent years, major container shipping companies have instituted around-the-world service. The voyage may start in Los Angeles, loop through a few Asian ports, and proceed through the Straits of Malacca before calling in Oman; then transit the Suez Canal, stop in Mediterranean ports located in Italy, Spain, and perhaps France; head up to northern Europe; and cross the

FIGURE 2.12 A RO–RO/LO–LO combo vessel.

Atlantic to some American ports before reversing the entire route. The entire round trip may be accomplished in just 60 days.

Container ships are some of the fastest ships with service speeds ranging from 21 to 25 knots. Schedule reliability is a major selling point for the companies in this business. Since most storms track at less than 15 knots, these ships are able to avoid or outrun many storms. Also with such speeds, the crossing from Rotterdam to New York can be accomplished in less than 5 days. Nearly every container ship built in the past 20 years has been diesel powered.

The Panamax ships are about 900 feet long with a beam of 105 feet and a deep draft of less than 40 feet. The post-Panamax ships are being built to more than 1100 feet long with a beam of about 150 feet. They require ports that have been dredged to about 45 feet. It is not cost effective to have these large container ships calling at a large variety of ports on each side of the ocean. Generally speaking, the larger the ship, the fewer ports of call it will make. Feeder or shuttle ships are smaller versions of these large container ships and are able to call at nearby ports, picking up and delivering containers. This is much like what you undoubtedly have experienced with airlines in the United States, where regional jets bring passengers to the major hubs so they can board a transcontinental flight. Also, some ships are LO/LO (loading containers on and off) and RO/RO (Figs 2.12 and 2.13). Another variation is referred to as *island hoppers* or *self-unloading container ships.* They have one or more cranes onboard which can be used to load and discharge the ship. Though much slower than the large gantry cranes found at container terminals, these island hoppers are able to work ports that just a few years ago they may have bypassed.

FIGURE 2.13 A view of the interior deck of an RO–RO ship and the tying down of trailers and containers mounted on chassis.

Before reading this chapter, you may have thought merchandise found on store shelves arrived via cargo airplanes. In a few rare cases, this happens. But keep in mind that only a few containers can hold as much merchandise as an entire 747. Airfreight is reserved for extremely valuable or time-sensitive shipments. One of the concepts that has driven the expansion of containerized shipping is that the goods are secure and concealed from all but the shipper. From a security perspective, there is a large opportunity for criminal or terrorist entities to ship explosives, persons, or equipment via containers.

Freighters

Before the advent of container ships, goods, merchandise, food, machinery parts, automobiles, and just about every consumer good were transported across the world's oceans on board freighters. Today, few of these "conventional" freighters remain in service. Freighters now are used in specialized trades or call in ports in the Third World. Often these ships are fitted with special equipment to load or unload the cargo where shore-based facilities are lacking. Or, they are fitted onboard with special stowage compartments to protect and transport unusual types of cargo. These freighters tend to be shallow draft vessels requiring less than 25 feet of water to safely navigate. As far as size goes, they range the spectrum. Because of the unique cargo situation, you may sight a 300-foot-long freighter heading across the South Atlantic Ocean bound for the Canary Islands. The population and trade of these islands do not justify a stop by a large container ship (see Fig. 2.14).

FIGURE 2.14 View of a conventional "freighter," which travels the coasts of the Americas and through the Caribbean.

Bulkers

Thousand of tons of raw materials are imported, exported, and transported every day in our country and to every other nation around the world. Gypsum, a white powdery substance, is used to make dry wallboard. Iron ore is used to make steel. Coal is used to generate electricity. Farmers everywhere need fertilizer that comes in powder form. Cement is powder used to make concrete. In small quantities, these cargoes can be hauled over the road in hopper trucks. But the majority of this cargo moves from ships to railcars, by barges, or sometimes directly into pipelines or used at the port of discharge. Unless you live close to a rail line or frequent the banks of a major river, these bulk cargoes are hidden from sight. The ports tend to be noisy, dusty operations in the industrial part of town.

Bulk carriers, or bulkers, are built similar to tank ships. There is normally no requirement for high-speed transits, so the service speed is only around 15 knots. The ships range in size from 50,000 dwt to 200,000 dwt. Some need a 60-foot deep channel to safely navigate. Like tankers, bulk carriers have a segregated ballast tank that is flooded as the cargo is being discharged. At the loading port, these same ballast tanks will be pumped out as cargo is loaded. It is not unusual for a bulk carrier to be 1000 feet long. Some can discharge cargo with fitted equipment. But many require shore-based conveyors, bucket scoops, and suction systems to load and discharge the cargo.

These ships are designed to carry a great deal of cargo. Since it takes days or even weeks to load and unload, tight schedules are not maintained. Weather and adverse sea conditions also affect the schedule. Since commodities often change ownership during an ocean crossing, a change in destination port is probable. Due to the nature of this type of shipping, such vessels are an unlikely target for terrorist actions. The cargo itself is rarely dangerous, and a terrorist wouldn't know when or where the ship would call on next (see Figs. 2.15 and 2.16).

FIGURE 2.15 A bulk carrier unloading its cargo of cement at the port.

FIGURE 2.16 Bulk carriers range in length and can carry dozens of different types of products.

Oceangoing Tugboats

Tugs are used in harbors to assist with the mooring and unmooring of ships and barges. Oceangoing tugs are generally too large and heavy to be used with ship-assist operations. There are two main purposes for really large tugs: salvage and towing. Maritime disasters occur every day. The salvage tug is dispatched to make an attempt to save the ship and cargo from even greater loss. Charters are negotiated with tug operators to tow just about

FIGURE 2.17 Tug pulling a barge loaded with trailers arriving in the bay of San Juan, Puerto Rico.

anything that floats from one port to another, although tugs have also towed submerged objects at great distances. The more common long hauls are oil rigs, ships bound for a shipyard for repair or modification, ships bound for the "breaking yard" at the end of a useful life, floating dry docks being delivered to a new "home," and cargo barges. Salvage tugs head off on a voyage never knowing if the owners will earn any money. Like some attorneys, salvage tugs are generally compensated only after a successful outcome. The rule is "No Cure—No Pay." If the salvage is a success, the tug's owners will share in part of the value of the ship as well as part of the value of the cargo onboard. This is much different than ocean towing, where the charter party or contract will provide financial payments to the tug's owners if certain conditions are successfully met.

From a terrorist point of view, tugboats and their relatively small crew may be an easy target. But determining a schedule may make them less reliable as a suitable platform to stage an attack. Tugs are seldom as fast as ships but may be far more powerful. It is not unusual for some tugs to have 15,000–20,000 hp engines. A ship three times the length, displacement, and/or gross tonnage may have a less powerful engine. The typical oceangoing tugboat is 125–250 feet long; has a raised bow or forecastle, allowing it to head into heavy seas; draws 15–20 feet of water; and may have as few as eight in the entire crew. Whereas most ships have just one propeller, nearly all tugboats are fitted with two or sometimes three. These propellers are driven by medium- or high-speed diesel engines. From a security standpoint, the sheer power to tonnage ratio of these vessels could be a concern (see Fig. 2.17).

Cruise and Passenger Ships

Cruise ships and passenger ships, while sounding similar, are actually quite different from one another. Cruise ships have become very popular in the vacation business. Cruise ships can be defined as destination vacation spots. Though they make ports of call, most of the

FIGURE 2.18 A modern, very large cruise ship in port. *Photo credit:* Shutterstock.com.

passengers have selected this mode of transport for the shipboard experience. It is common for these ships to have nearly as many crewmembers onboard as passengers, and their jobs are to serve and comfort their guests during the voyage. Compare this to a passenger ship, which can be defined as a means to move people from point A to point B. Though many of these ships are comfortable, the crew-to-passenger ratio is usually low, and the guests remain for only a short period of time. Passenger ships are common in Asian, European, and African waters and at one time were the main means for crossing the Atlantic, although, with the advent of jet airline travel, true passenger ships disappeared from the Atlantic Ocean in the 1970s. On a cruise ship, the crew will have a chance to really become familiar with their assigned passengers. On a passenger ship, this isn't always the case. On a passenger ship, the attire may vary greatly among the passengers. Some may be traveling businessmen. Others may be very common folk traveling by ship since they cannot afford to fly. Still others may be college-age people traveling to a destination only served by ship (see Figs. 2.18 and 2.19).

The Race for Greener and Ever-Larger Ships

With the goal being to reduce the cost of per container/tonnage transport, as well as comply with a sea of environmental protection regulations, shipping lines are taking receipt of ever "greener" and larger ships. Almost all commercial ships plying the oceans today use low-grade bunker fuel for their diesel engines—which is a huge polluter! When the M/V Emma Maersk is transporting containers around the globe she is burning nearly 350 tons of bunker fuel a day. The giant diesel engine emits more than 300,000 tons of CO_2 a year, making it the oceangoing equivalent of a medium-sized coal power plant. In a year, this single ship can emit cancer and asthma-causing pollutants

FIGURE 2.19 Some cargo ships also carry "passengers" who want a no-frills experience visiting the ports of call on the ship's established cargo route.

equivalent to that of 50 million cars. The low-grade bunker fuel used by the world's 90,000 cargo ships contains up to 2000 times the amount of sulfur compared to diesel fuel used in automobiles.[1] Pollution from cargo ships using bunker is a worldwide problem. And bunker fuel is not cheap! Consider that even with bunker prices dropping in 2014 and 2015, the cost still represent the largest expense item for vessels—accounting for 30–40% of total operating costs of the ship.[2] To address this very serious pollution issue, in 2012, the U.S. Environmental Protection Agency issued a set of landmark regulations, one of which included creating the North American Emission Control Area, or ECA. The regulation requires that by 2015 all ships traveling within 200 nautical miles of the non-Arctic U.S. and Canadian coasts use fuels with a sulfur content limit of 1000 ppm or below. The regulation also requires an 80% reduction in smog-forming oxides of nitrogen by 2016. The European Community likewise implemented regulations setting similar limits. Of broader impact, the IMO plans to apply a global cap on sulfur emissions as of 2020 but may postpone the date the global cap takes effect until 2025.[3] So, as discussed above, the economic and environmental drivers clearly are present for a shift to alternative fuel sources, and, in kind, reducing operational costs. And, change already is underway.

In April 2015, TOTE Maritime took delivery of the *M/V Isla Bella*, the world's first LNG-powered container ship. Built by General Dynamics NASSCO, she will significantly decrease emissions (reducing NOx emissions by 98%, SOx by 97%, and carbon dioxide by 72%), while increasing fuel efficiency, and is heralded as being the most "green" of its kind and size anywhere in the world.[4] Also in April 2015, the United Arab Shipping Company accepted receipt of the first of six ordered LNG-ready ultralarge container ship (ULCS). The *M/V Barzan* is an 18,800 TEU vessel, presented as the "greenest" ULCS in the world, and complies with the IMO emissions requirements.[5] The *M/V Isla Bella* and the *M/V Barzan* are soon to be joined by 50 other LNG-fueled ships—46 in greater Europe, 3 in Asia and the Pacific, and 1 in the United States. While it is a start in the right direction, that still leaves nearly 100,000 ships plying global trade routes, all powered by bunker oil, one of the dirtiest fuels on the planet. Nevertheless, international regulations and long-term profit will likely lead to change in the next decade from fossil fuels to natural gas as a marine gas.

The goal of reducing costs per container/tonnage transport also is what has led to the designing and purchasing of larger ships, as the efficiencies of scale of larger ships and more containers/tonnage onboard result in lower per unit costs and greater productivity. Container shipping is a $6 trillion industry and containers move 95% of the world's manufactured goods. The trend recently has been to Vessel Sharing Agreements, Vessel Pooling Alliances (such as the 2M of Maersk and MSC), and the ordering of ULCS of 20,000 TEU size.[6] In mid-2015, Maersk ordered a total of 10 ships with a 20,000 TEU capacity, for delivery in 2017 and at a price tag of $155 million per ship, which followed similar capacity orders by CMA CGM, Mitsui OSK Lines, OOCL, and interest by three other mega shipping lines. Imagine, just 47 years ago, the M/V Encounter Bay carried 1530 containers. Since 2013—just 12 years ago—container ships have grown in capacity from 9000 TEUs to just under 20,000 TEUs. This is an overall growth rate of 1200% since 1968.[7]

The Evolution of Polar Class Ships

The gradual, but expanding, usage of the Polar Passages (discussed in chapter 1: Commercial Seaports and Strategic Maritime Passages in Transformation) and requirements of the new Polar Code are leading shipping lines to order an increasing number of Polar class ships. There are increasing developments in cold weather technologies and Polar class ships in order to meet the need and interest of the commercial shipping industry in the Polar Passages. Prior to 2000, tankers and cargo vessels for use in these cold waters tended to be small and medium size. In the early 2000s, the construction of larger commercial vessels for Arctic operations commenced with the line of 70,000 dwt Arc6 shuttle tankers. Currently, new Arc7 LNGC shuttle tankers are under construction at Samsung and Daewoo and these will soon be the largest vessels operating in the Russian Northern Sea Route (also known as the Northeast Passage). These large, reinforced vessels are able to safely operate in ice up to 6 feet thick.[8] Numerous ice class ships now are on the order books and some notable orders and deliveries are those of Nordic Bulk, with their Baltic ice class new builds, and Canada's Fednav (in October 2014, their M/V Nunavik was the Polar Cargo Ship which made the successful solo journey via the Northwest Passage). It is likely that as the Arctic ice continues to recede, and the Passages continue to become more navigable near or year-round, the commercial shipping industry will take advantage of these new routes and use special purpose ships for these trade lanes.

Summary

Commercial shipping is the locomotive for our economy, as well most economies worldwide, and ships have evolved dramatically—specifically in size and technology—over the past 50 years. Ships are designed based on specific usage, type of product or commodity to be transported, trade routes, and canal restrictions. Ships have rapidly grown in capacity as the efficiencies of scale of larger ships and more containers/tonnage onboard results in greater productivity. Environmental protection regulations are leading to "greener" ships and will change the currently used marine gas. Malcom McLean's creation of the shipping container truly revolutionized how goods are moved around the world and served as the catalyst for the development of the container ship, globally the primary type of ship used to transport goods.

End Notes

1. http://www.aiche.org/chenected/2015/07/anchors-away-worlds-first-lng-powered-container-ship; http://www.gizmag.com/shipping-pollution/11526/
2. https://www.bcgperspectives.com/content/articles/transportation_travel_tourism_energy_environment_forecasting_future_marine_fuel/
3. Ibid.
4. http://toteinc.com/tote-launches-worlds-first-lng-powered-containership/
5. http://www.uasc.net/en/news/150429/uasc-names-worlds-most-environmentally-friendly-ultra-large-container-vessel
6. http://www.wsj.com/articles/costly-bet-on-big-cargo-ships-comes-up-short-1433151181
7. http://www.worldshipping.org/about-the-industry/liner-ships/container-ship-design
8. http://ea45bb970b5c70169c61-0cd083ee92972834b7bec0d968bf8995.r81.cf1.rackcdn.com/TOAug-Sept15.pdf

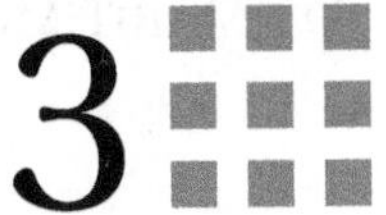

3 Documentation, Financial Transactions, and Business Entities in Commercial Maritime Transportation

OBJECTIVES

After studying this chapter, you will be familiar with

1. The process and steps in the transport of ocean cargo through the supply chain—from the ordering of factory goods to delivery to the importer;
2. The types, content, and usage of documentation utilized in the export and import of ocean cargoes;
3. Documentation requirements for compliance with U.S. Customs and Border Protection (CBP) policies;
4. The definition of key terminology used in commercial ocean maritime transportation;
5. The roles, functions, and interactions of the primary business entities involved in the transport of ocean cargo through the supply chain.

Introduction

The exporting and importing of goods is one of the world's oldest trades, dating back to a period before the invention of money, when people bartered for goods. The trade is open to anyone with the perseverance and willingness to learn the mechanics of the business with its many rules and regulations. Merchandise transiting in and out of a country is documented to show ownership, origin, financial arrangements, and destination, among a host of other requirements. Documentation rules and regulations vary from country to country, but the basics are the same worldwide. In each step of the transport of goods—from the factory to the import destination (see the flowchart in Fig. 3.1)—there is at least one document which records the activity as the goods move through each link in the supply chain. In this chapter, we examine the different types of documents needed to export and import goods—from the factory where it is manufactured through to the end user warehouse at the destination—and review the different business entities involved in commercial maritime transportation.

The word *document* is defined as proof or evidence in support of something. When you document goods for the purpose of exporting or importing them, you are evidencing the amount and type of goods; how they are packaged; their origin; their ownership; their

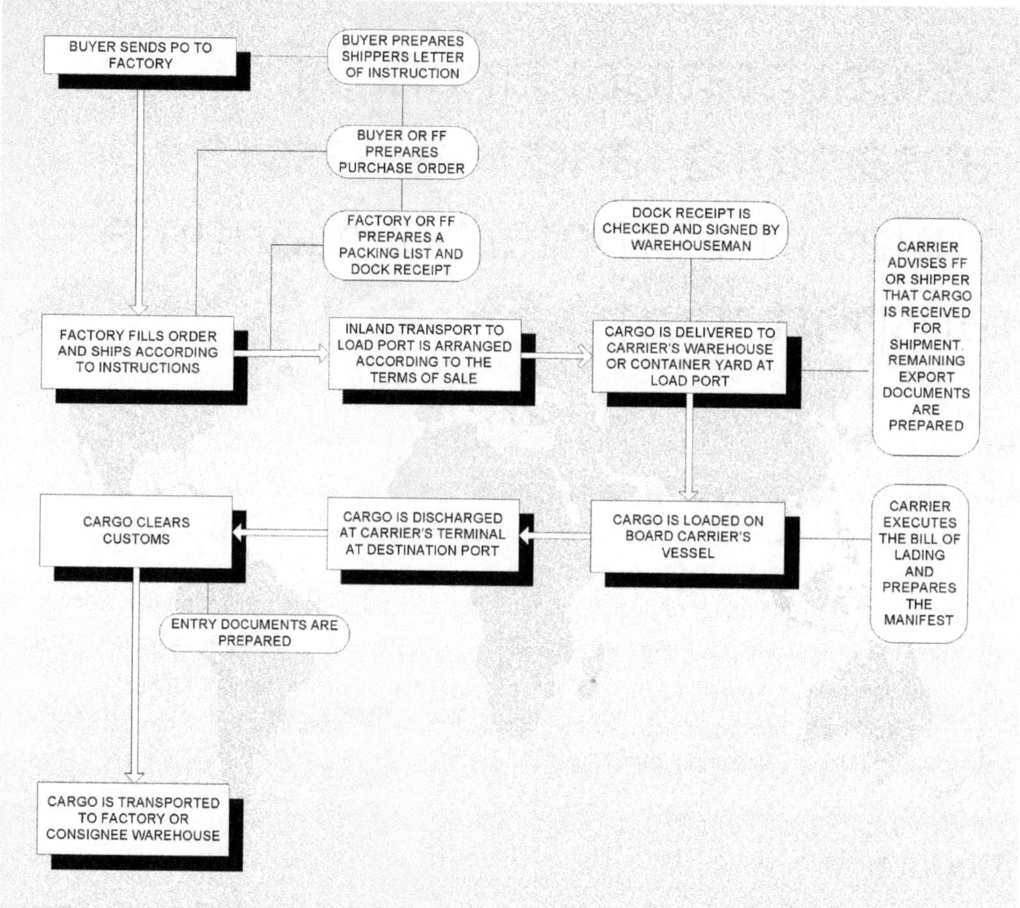

FIGURE 3.1 The general process steps and documentation utilized in the shipment of goods.

destination; and their value for insurance, taxes, and duty purposes. Ocean transportation documents can be prepared by the exporter or importer; however, most sellers and buyers rely on the services provided by an *international freight forwarder* and/or *customs broker,* also known as an *ocean transportation intermediary* (OTI). Improperly prepared documents can severely delay a shipment, ultimately causing a loss of service and money and possibly negating the sale of the merchandise if the terms of the sale are not met.

Purchase of Goods

We start by examining a purchase order (PO), which is the first document needed and a good foundation for all the documentation that follows. A PO is a document issued by the seller to the buyer, evidencing the product, quantity, and agreed price, as well as any pertinent information about the buyer. The PO sets the terms of the sale and delivery of the product.

The PO is often the first commercial document produced and is used to clearly communicate the intention of the buyer to purchase a product. It offers legal protection to a seller in case the buyer either refuses or returns the shipment or refuses to pay for it. The buyer will negotiate the purchase with the seller and set the terms of the sale, such as packaging and labeling instructions, shipping and delivery instructions, cost, quality, and quantity. Once an agreement is reached, the seller will usually request a PO from the buyer. The PO contains a unique serial number; the date the order was placed; a shipping address and billing address; the type, size, quantity, and quality of the merchandise; the terms of the sale; and the agreed price. Once the order is filled, the factory will then produce a packing list. The PO and a copy of the packing list accompanying the merchandise when it is shipped are usually matched to the seller's invoice before it is paid. In today's marketplace, many companies use electronic POs, or they may use the standard paper variety, but all must follow acceptable business-to-business standards and practices. The PO can be used to prepare a master bill of lading (BL) or a shipper's letter of instruction, both of which are explained later in this chapter.

Filling the Order

The next step in the process is the factory's packing of the ordered merchandise and preparation for shipment. The primary document utilized is the export packing list (see Fig. 3.2). The *export packing list* is a detailed itemization of the merchandise being shipped, which also serves as the definitive count, weight, and measurement.

In addition to obvious inventory-control uses by the factory, information on this list also is used to reserve the space needed if the cargo is to be part of a consolidated shipment (shipments of two or more different exporters loaded together in the same container). Likewise, the U.S. CBP use this document to verify outbound and inbound cargo, so it must be accurate and complete to avoid delays, and for the importer to inventory the shipment upon receipt at its destination. An export packing list form can be obtained from a commercial stationery store or a freight forwarder. The packing list is usually attached to the outside of the packaged merchandise.

Container Stuffing

Now that the order has been filled and packed for export, it is ready to be moved to the port for loading. If the terms of the sale require the seller to arrange and pay for the inland transportation, a few different transportation options are open to him. First, it must be determined if the product requires the exclusive use of a container; ie, the order large enough to warrant the cost of using a shipping container exclusively? Sometimes, the shipment may be small but the nature of the merchandise may require it to be loaded in its own container, or this may be a requirement of the buyer or seller. Once it is determined that the merchandise should be loaded into an exclusive-use container, then container size must be determined. All containers are the same width, but they are available in different lengths

Acme Exports
123 West Street, Ste 7
Anywhere, USA 00000
Tel: 555-1000

Packinglist

For account and risk of Messrs.		Commercial Invoice No. Date Letter of Credit No. Date Issuing Bank
Buyer's P.O. or Contract No. Date		Import Permit/License No. Date
Buyer's Department/Store No.		Marks & Numbers
Carrier-Voyage/Flight No.	Shipment on or about	
From (Port of Loading)	To (Port of Discharge)	
Via (Tranship At)	For Transhipment To	

Package No.	Item No.	Description of Goods	Quantity	Weight (Kgs./Lbs.)	Measureme (CBM/Cft.)

FIGURE 3.2 A typical "packing list."

and sometimes different heights. Additionally, there are special function containers, such as refrigerator containers (reefers) and open-top containers. Depending on the weight and volume of the merchandise, it may need a 20-foot, 40-foot, or 45-foot long container.

The next decision the seller must make is whether the product should be loaded at his warehouse/site or at the carrier's warehouse. Where the product is loaded depends on the terms of sale, the ability of the seller to accommodate loading of a container, and the cost to transport the product to the port. In evaluating the options, the seller will call an ocean carrier or an OTI to request a price quotation. If it is determined that there is not enough merchandise to warrant the exclusive use of a container, the seller will make arrangements to have the product delivered loose to the carrier's warehouse, where it will be loaded (consolidated) into a container with other cargo that is bound for the same destination. If the terms of the sale did not include transportation, the buyer or the buyer's agent, a freight forwarder or OTI, will make the transportation arrangements.

Making a Booking

Making a booking—the next step in the process of cargo shipment—is an industry term for reserving space on a vessel voyage from a specific loading point or port to a specific discharge port or point. Before a shipper (exporter, freight forwarder, etc.) makes a booking with an ocean carrier, he will call the carrier and ask for a rate quote. Rates are published in tariffs by the ocean carrier under strict regulations of the Federal Maritime Commission (FMC). A *rate filing* considers the product, the point of receipt (in the case of inland transport), the port of loading, the port of discharge, the point of final destination (and if there will be inland transport), and the size of the container or the loose cargo dimensions. If the seller is satisfied with the rate quotation, he will then make a booking (reserve space). Bookings are made electronically in most cases, and their purpose is to reserve space on the vessel. The following information is needed at the time of the booking:

- Shipper's name and contact information;
- Consignee's name and contact information;
- Freight forwarder (if any);
- Inland point of origin (if the carrier is arranging the transportation);
- Port of loading;
- Port of discharge;
- Final inland destination (if the carrier is arranging the transportation);
- Size of container or dimensions and weight of loose cargo;
- Type of movement—for example:
  - *House-to-House:* The shipper loads at his facility, and the consignee unloads at his facility. The shipper and consignee arrange inland transportation independent of the ocean carrier.
  - *Pier-to-House:* The carrier loads the loose cargo at his facility, and the consignee unloads at his facility. The shipper arranges delivery of the cargo to the carrier's facility for loading, and the consignee arranges transportation of the loaded container to his facility, where the cargo will be unloaded.
  - *House-to-Pier:* The shipper loads at his facility, and the carrier is responsible to deliver only to the pier. The shipper arranges delivery of loaded containers to the carrier's facility, and the carrier unloads the cargo at the pier.
  - *Pier-to-Pier:* The carrier loads at the pier and unloads at the pier.
  - *Door-to-Door:* The shipper loads at his facility, and the consignee unloads at his facility. This type of movement is similar to house-to-house movement, with the difference being that the carrier is responsible for transportation from the shipper's facility to the consignee's facility.

As part of the booking information, if the carrier is performing the inland transportation for the shipper (door-to-door), then the carrier will require instructions detailing where and when to deliver the empty container. The shipper can always use an independent trucker or inland carrier to arrange transportation to the load port (house-to-house); however, he must make sure the company he chooses has an agreement with the ocean carrier to move its containers. This is called an *interchange agreement* (for a trailer or a container).

If the booking is made for a container, then an empty is dispatched for loading per instructions. Either the carrier's trucker or the shipper's trucker will arrive at the terminal (or container yard) with a booking number to pick up the booked container for loading. The terminal issues an empty-out *trailer interchange report* (TIR) or *equipment interchange report* (EIR) that attaches the container number to the booking number. This is known as an *Out Empty TIR/EIR*, and it notes the booking number, container number, container size, name of the inland carrier/trucker, and condition of the container. Many TIRs/EIRs also serve as a means to document damages or other conditions of the container at time of dispatch and transfer of custody.

When the fully loaded container is returned to the terminal, it is driven over a scale at the carrier's facility, where a weight ticket is issued. Then an *In Full TIR/EIR* is produced, showing the container number, size, weight of the container, loaded weight, date and time of arrival at the terminal, booking number, name of the vessel on which it will be loaded, port of loading, and port of discharge; it also notes the condition of the container. If damages are noted, the carrier will compare the remarks made on the Out Empty TIR/EIR to determine if the damage was done while in the possession of the trucker.

Once this paperwork is completed, a copy of the TIR/EIR is provided to the inland carrier for his records, another copy is sent to the equipment control department for inventory updating, and a third copy is sent to the export documentation department where it is matched to the booking. When an In Full TIR/EIR is matched to a booking, the export documentation department will call the shipper or OTI to request the export documentation. After the complete documentation is received, reviewed, and evaluated for accuracy, the shipment can be placed on the loading guide. It is at this point where the carrier's documentation personnel can be most effective in identifying indicators of contraband smuggling and potential terrorist activities. Careful scrutiny of the information contained in the documents may identify suspect shipments.

The *loading guide* (also known as the *load list*), as Fig. 3.3 shows, is a listing of full containers and loose cargo ready to be loaded onboard the vessel. It is divided by the destination of the cargo and size of the equipment. It is used to advise the carrier's operations department and the vessel's master what is scheduled to be loaded onboard. The United States and foreign customs will usually request a copy of the load guide to determine if any shipments appear to be suspicious and may require examination.

The same booking process is required for loose cargo. If a shipment is being delivered loose, when the merchandise arrives at the ocean carrier's facility, it is accompanied with a dock receipt or warehouse receipt. A *dock receipt* or *warehouse receipt* is a document used to transfer accountability from the domestic carrier when merchandise is moved to the port of exit and left with the ocean carrier for export.

A dock receipt or warehouse receipt serves the shipper as proof of delivery of the cargo to a land, rail, ocean, or air carrier. It records the type of merchandise, quantity, weight and measurements, and other vital information. The dock receipt is prepared on the carrier's

		LOADING GUIDE		VESSEL: DUOMO II	Voy. 104		
		POL: MIA, FL			POD: GEO, GUYANA		
	SIZE	CONTAINER NO.	SEAL #	BOOKING #	WEIGHT	HAZARDOUS	
1	40'HC	GSTU432567-0	808	54670	56000	Y	CLASS 3
2	40'HC	SCZU678567-1	908	98765	59000	N	
3							
4							
5							
6							
7							
8							
9							
10							

FIGURE 3.3 A standard "load list."

form usually by the freight forwarder, but the exporter can prepare a dock receipt as well if there is no freight forwarder involved.

When the merchandise is delivered to the carrier's warehouse, the warehouseman will check the receipt against the merchandise and note any visible discrepancies, such as the condition and count of the packages. This receipt can be a vital document if there is damage to or shortages or overages of the merchandise determined at destination. Recording, reporting, and investigating these discrepancies are vital parts of the industry's antiterrorism efforts.

When the merchandise is accepted at the carrier's warehouse, the warehouseman will notify the export department of its arrival, and in turn, the export department will notify the buyer or freight forwarder and get clearance to load the merchandise into a container and then onboard the vessel. As soon as the shipper releases the cargo for loading, he should present the export documents. The shipment will not be loaded without them.

If the shipper chooses to use a freight forwarder, he will prepare a shipper's letter of instruction, like the one shown in Fig. 3.4. The *shipper's letter of instruction* is a "letter" from the shipper instructing the freight forwarder how and where to send the export shipment. This document aids the freight forwarder in preparing the documents required by the carrier to export the cargo and add it to the manifest.

A shipper's letter of instruction is a fundamental document prepared by the shipper and sent to the freight forwarder. It contains all the information required by the freight forwarder to prepare a master BL (see Fig. 3.5), which is required by the ocean carrier in order to manifest the merchandise. It contains, among other things, the following information:

- Shipper's name and address;
- Intermediate and ultimate consignee;
- Inland carrier;
- Booking number;
- Point of origin;
- Country of ultimate destination;

SHIPPER'S LETTER OF INSTRUCTION

SHIPPER (*NAME AND ADDRESS INCLUDING ZIP CODE*)		INLAND CARRIER	SHIP DATE	PRO NUMBER
	ZIP CODE			
EXPORTER EIN NO.	PARTIES TO TRANSACTION			
ULTIMATE CONSIGNEE:				
INTERMEDIATE CONSIGNEE:				
FORWARDING AGENT:		POINT (STATE) OF ORIGIN OR FTZ NO.	COUNTRY OF ULTIMATE DESTINATION:	
SHIPPER'S REF NO.	DATE:	SHIP VIA		

SCHEDULE B DESCRIPTION OF COMMODITIES						VALUE
D/F	MARKS, NOS., AND KIND OF PACKAGES SCHEDULE B NUMBER	QUANTITY - SCHEDULE B UNIT(S)	SHIPPING WEIGHT (Kilos)	SHIPPING WEIGHT (Pounds)	CUBIC METERS	(U.S. dollars, omit cents) Selling price or cost if unsold

LICENSING NUMBER OR SYMBOL	ECCN (When required)	PAYMENT METHOD
DULY AUTHORIZED OFFICER OR EMPLOYEE	Exporter authorizes forwarder named above to act as forwarding agent for export control and customs purposes.	C.O.D. AMOUNT
SPECIAL INSTRUCTIONS:		
SHIPPER REQUESTS INSURANCE:	If shipper has requested insurance as provided for at the left hereof, shipment is insured in amount indicated (recovery is limited to actual loss) in accordance with provisions as specified in Carrier's Tariffs. Insurance is payable to shipper unless payee is designated in writing by shipper.	SHIPPER'S INSTRUCTIONS IN CASE OF INABILITY TO DELIVER CONSIGNMENT AS CONSIGNED:

Shipper or his Authorized Agent hereby authorizes the above named Company, in his name and on his behalf, to prepare any export documents, to sign and accept any documents relating to said shipment and forward this shipment in accordance with the conditions of carriage and the tariffs of the carriers employed. Shipper guarantees payment of all collect changes in the event consignee refuses payment. The Company is to use reasonable care in the selection of carriers, forwarders, agents, and others to whom it may entrust the shipments.

FIGURE 3.4 A typical "shipper's letter of instruction."

Ocean Bill of Lading

Exporter (Name and address including ZIP code)	Document Number	Booking Number
ABC Export Inc. 3212 Calle 5 Colon Free Zone Republic of Panama	X- 123456	B-5678902
	Export References	

Consigned To	Forwarding Agent (Name and address)
John Doe Imports 1234 Central Ave Washington, D.C. 31272	

Notify Party	Point (State) of Origin or FTZ Number
John Doe Imports 1234 Central Ave Washington, D.C. 31272 212-555-1234	Republic of Panama

Pre-Carriage By	Place of Receipt By Pre-Carrier	Domestic Routing/Export Instructions
Exporting Carrier: Maersk Line	Port of Loading/Export: Panama	
Foreign Port of Unloading: Manzanillo Intl - Panama	Place of Delivery By On-Carrier: port of Baltimore	Type of Move

Marks and Numbers	Number of Packages	Description of Commodities in Schedule B Detail	Gross Weight (Kilos)	Measurement
ML2013569	2749	Yuca	3000	XX

There are: pages, including attachments to this Ocean Bill of Lading

These commodities, technology or software were exported from the United States in accordance with the Export Administration Regulations. Diversion contrary to U.S. law prohibited

Carrier has a policy against payment solicitation, or receipt of any rebate, directly or indirectly, which would be unlawful under the United States Shipping Act, 1984 as amended

FREIGHT RATES, CHARGES, WEIGHTS AND/OR MEASUREMENTS

SUBJECT TO CORRECTION	PREPAID	COLLECT
	$1550.0	
GRAND TOTAL		

Received by Carrier for shipment by ocean vessel between port of loading and port of discharge, and for arrangement or procurement of pre-carriage from place of receipt and on-carriage to place of delivery, where stated above, the goods as specified above in apparent good order and condition unless otherwise stated. The goods to be delivered at the above mentioned port of discharge or place of delivery, whichever is applicable

IN WITNESS WHEREOF original Bills of Lading have been signed, not otherwise stated above, one of which being accomplished the others shall be void

DATED AT ________

BY ________

Agent for the Carrier

Mo. Day Year

B/L No.

FIGURE 3.5 A "bill of lading."

- Shipper's references and tax numbers;
- Date the shipment was dispatched;
- Desired method of shipment;
- Description of the merchandise;
- Marks, numbers, and types of packages;
- Weight and cubic measurement of each package;
- Value of the merchandise;
- License numbers, if any;
- Special shipping instructions;
- Container number, weight, and seal number(s) in the case of containerized cargo.

Nearly all the information required on a shipper's export declaration (SED) can be found on the shipper's letter of instruction. Finally, the form should be signed by the exporter or an authorized agent of the exporter.

Documents Used to Export and Import Cargo

When the carrier notifies the exporter or freight forwarder that the cargo has arrived, this person will verify the vessel on which it will be carried. Once the buyer or freight forwarder knows the name of the vessel, the remaining export documents can be prepared. What documents are needed depends on the country of destination, the terms of the sale, and the nature of the merchandise.

Bill of Lading

The one document that must be prepared for all cargo carried on a vessel is the ocean carrier's BL. The BL is a contract between a carrier and another party sometimes referred to as the *freighter,* but more commonly known as the *shipper,* wherein the carrier agrees to carry the goods in or on his vessel/truck/train or allow the shipper the use of all or part of the vessel/truck/train for a specified voyage or time, and the shipper agrees to pay a specified price for the carriage of the goods or the use of the ship/truck/train.

This document is issued by the carrier to the shipper as an acknowledgment that the merchandise is received and is being placed on a vessel for transportation to the agreed destination. It states the terms of carriage and, when fully executed, is a binding contract between the shipper and carrier. The carrier is obliged to deliver the goods in the same count and condition as stated on the BL, and the shipper and/or consignee agree to pay the freight charges, thereby completing the terms of the contract. It is important that the carrier note any count or condition discrepancy when processing the BL and, in the case of a full container load, assuring that a *Shipper's Load, Stow and Count clause* is stated in the body, thus absolving the carrier of any liability for shortages or damages that may have occurred before taking possession.

The executed BL is also used as a receipt for the shipment and gives the holder an endorsed original title to the merchandise, allowing him to take delivery of the goods.

When shipments are made via an ocean carrier, two types of liner bills of lading are commonly used. The first is called a *straight BL,* which means it must be delivered to the consignee who is named on the document. This is a *nonnegotiable instrument,* not to be bought, sold, or traded while in transit. The second type is a *negotiable* or a *"to order" BL.* This second type is consigned to the order of the shipper and can be bought, sold, or traded while the goods are in transit. Where payment is made through a bank, such as a letter of credit (LC), then such shipments must move on a negotiable BL. In any case, the liner BL form is the same for both types.

The BL should contain the following information:

- The name and contact information of the shipper;
- The name and contact information of the consignee (if it is not a "to order" or negotiable BL);
- The name and contact information of the notify party;
- The name of the inland carrier, if inland delivery was performed by a party other than the carrier;
- The inland point of origin, if the carrier is responsible for transporting the merchandise from the factory;
- The name of the ship and its voyage number;
- The port of loading;
- The port of unloading or discharge;
- The point of delivery, if the carrier is responsible for delivering the merchandise to its final inland destination;
- The final port of delivery for transshipment cargo;
- A detailed description of the merchandise, including the number and types of packaging, the cargo weight and measurement, appropriate clauses, eg, antidiversion clause and freight prepaid or collect clause. In the case of a full container load, the container number and seal number should appear in the Marks and Numbers column;
- The export license number, if any;
- The exporter's references, if any;
- The freight forwarder's name, address, and license number;
- The point and country of origin of the goods;
- Special shipping instructions and "also notify" party and contact information.

The entities on the BL are the shipper, the consignee, and the notify party or parties, as there can be more than one:

- The *shipper* is commonly defined as the owner of the merchandise or the person whose name or on whose behalf a contract of carriage of goods has been conducted.
- The *consignee* is the person, company, or representative of the company to which a seller or shipper sends merchandise. This party is also responsible for appointing an import broker who will clear the cargo at its destination.

- The *notify party* could be the same as the consignee or it could be the import broker. The notify party is responsible for advising both the consignee and import broker of the arrival of the merchandise.

After a master BL has been prepared by the exporter or OTI, the carrier's export department issues the ocean carrier's BL. When the ocean carrier processes the BL, it will provide the BL number, freight charges, and the aforementioned information, as well as sign and date it on behalf of the master.

The carrier's BL form provides the terms and conditions of the contract of water carriage printed on the back of the form. It includes standard clauses regarding the shipper's and carrier's responsibilities under this contract.

Exporter's Electronic Export Information

In addition to the BL, when exporting cargo from the United States, an Electronic Export Information (EEI) must be filed. An EEI is an electronic document submitted to the U.S. Department of Commerce to control exports and acts a source document for U.S. export statistics.

Exporters must file an EEI when shipping any one commodity valued over $2500, when shipping merchandise that requires a license, or when shipping to certain foreign countries. The EEI confirmation number must appear on the shipping documents provided to the carrier. If a shipment does not require an EEI to be submitted, a statement to that effect—eg, NOEEI 30.37 (a)—should be made somewhere in the body of the BL. An exporter can file the EEI online by registering at https://aesdirect.census.gov.

A freight forwarder can also file the EEI on behalf of the exporter. EEI is a free service and does not require a software investment.

The data contained in the EEI are used by the Census Bureau to compile export statistics. The EEI information is similar to the information in the BL and the commercial invoice with a few exceptions, such as the commodities Schedule B or Harmonized Code number and a declared value.

Certificate of Origin

The commodity being shipped and its destination will determine whether a certificate of origin (CO) is required. A CO is a signed statement attesting to the origin of the merchandise being exported. It is not required by all countries. A *North American Free Trade Agreement (NAFTA) CO* is needed for transportation of goods traded among the NAFTA countries: Canada, the United States, and Mexico (See Fig. 3.6 for an example).

A CO is used to authenticate the country where the goods were manufactured or produced. Nearly every country in the world considers the origin of imported goods for a variety of reasons, some of which include treaty arrangements with the country of origin, preferential duty rates, and quantity restriction of the import of a particular commodity or, conversely, preferences for manufactured goods from a particular country.

Most countries will accept a general CO form, provided it supplies the required information. This information includes the identity of the seller; the method(s) of transportation;

Canada Border Services Agency   Agence des services frontaliers du Canada

PROTECTED (When Completed)

NORTH AMERICAN FREE TRADE AGREEMENT

CERTIFICATE OF ORIGIN

(Instructions Attached)

Please print or type

1 Exporter's Name and Address: Tax Identification Number: ▶	2 Blanket Period: From DD - MM - YY To DD - MM - YY
3 Producer's Name and Address: Tax Identification Number: ▶	4 Importer's Name and Address: Tax Identification Number: ▶

5 Description of Good(s)	6 HS tariff Classification Number	7 Preference Criterion	8 Producer	9 Net Cost	10 Country of Origin

11 I certify that:

- the information on this document is true and accurate and I assume the responsibility for proving such representations. I understand that I am liable for any false statements or material omissions made on or in connection with this document;
- I agree to maintain, and present upon request, documentation necessary to support this Certificate, and to inform, in writing, all persons to whom the Certificate was given of any changes that would affect the accuracy or validity of this Certificate;
- the goods originated in the territory of one or more of the Parties, and comply with the origin requirements specified for those goods in the North American Free Trade Agreement, and unless specifically exempted in Article 411 or Annex 401, there has been no further production or any other operation outside the territories of the Parties; and
- this Certificate consists of ______ pages, including all attachments.

Authorized Signature:		Company:
Name:		Title:
Date (dd-mm-yy)	Telephone:	Fax:

B232 E (05)
Printed in Canada

Canadä

FIGURE 3.6 A "NAFTA certificate of origin."

the date of exportation; the name and contact information of the receiver (BL consignee); and a description of the goods, including the quantity, weight, and packaging type. This information should match the commercial invoice or import license.

The CO is usually prepared by the exporter or his agent (freight forwarder). COs require an authorized signature of a local governmental organization such as a local chamber of commerce, but some may require only the signature of the supplier or manufacturer.

Every country has its own set of rules, regulations, and forms. Check with the Department of Commerce and Trade for a list of countries that require a CO, a list of commodities, and the proper forms for each.

Commercial Invoice

The commercial invoice plays an important role in exporting and is often the foundation upon which the freight forwarder/OTI relies. A *commercial invoice* is a bill for the merchandise sold; it contains all the pertinent information about the goods, including its generally accepted true value. It is often used by governments to assess customs duties and control imports.

A commercial invoice is similar to any ordinary sales invoice, with the exception that there are specific references to the export–import trade (see Fig. 3.7). The following information is required on a commercial invoice:

- Seller's and buyer's contact information;
- Consignee's contact information (if different from buyer);
- The invoice date;
- A unique invoice number;
- Terms of the sale (*usually in international commerce terms—incoterms*);
- Payment terms;
- Currency;
- Full quantities and description of merchandise (merchandise should be described the same as on the PO);
- Statement certifying that the invoice is correct.

Some countries might require that the commercial invoice be written in the language of the importing country and that the declarations made on the invoice be done in a specific format and with specific text. The exporter should check these requirements with the foreign government's Department of Trade and Commerce in the country of destination.

Typically, a commercial invoice contains a sworn statement from the exporter attesting to the fact that the goods represented in the invoice were manufactured in the exporting country and that the amount shown on the invoice is the true value. Often, duties and taxes are levied based on the value represented on the commercial invoice.

Some countries require the commercial invoice to be certified or legalized. As in the case of the CO, certification of a commercial invoice is usually performed by a local chamber of commerce in the exporting country, and legalization is done by the importing country's consulate or the commercial section of its embassy. Certification and/or legalization

COMMERCIAL INVOICE

Date of Exportation	Export Reference (i.e. Order No. Invoice No., etc.)
Shipper/Exporter (Complete Name and Address)	Consignee (Complete Name and Address)
Country of Export	Importer-If Other than Consignee
Country of Manufacture	
Country of Ultimate Destination	
Air WayBill No.	

Marks/ Nos.	# of Pkgs	Type of Packaging	Full Description	Qty	Unit of Measure	WT	Unit Value	Total Value
	Total # Pkg.					Total Wt.		Total Invoice Value

NO COMMERCIAL VALUE/FOR CUSTOMS DECLARATIONS ONLY $
PROMOTIONAL MATERIAL FOR FREE DISTRIBUTION
WILL BE RETURNED TO THE U.S.A.

THESE COMMODITIES ARE LICENSED FOR THE ULTIMATE DESTINATION SHOWN.
DIVERSION CONTRARY TO UNITED STATES LAW IS PROHIBITED.

I DECLARE ALL THE INFORMATION CONTAINED IN THIS INVOICE TO BE TRUE AND CORRECT.

SIGNATURE OF SHIPPER/EXPORTER (TYPE NAME AND TITLE THEN SIGN)

______________________________ DATE: ______________________

FIGURE 3.7 A standard "commercial invoice."

of the document are usually evidenced by a stamp or official seal. Processing could take up to a week, so it is vital that the certification or legalization is completed in sufficient time as not to delay the exporting of the merchandise.

The following terms are published by the International Chamber of Commerce. The original and official version of *incoterms* is in English and has been endorsed by the United Nations Commission on International Trade Law (UNCITRAL).

Incoterm 2010	Export Customs Declaration	Carriage to Port of Export	Unloading of Truck in Port of Export	Loading on Vessel/ Airplane in Port of Export	Carriage (Sea/Air) to Port of Import	Insurance	Unloading in Port of Import	Loading on Truck in Port of Import	Carriage to Place of Destination	Import Customs Clearance	Import Taxes
EXW	Buyer	Buyer	Buyer	Buyer	Buyer	Buyer	Buyer	Buyer	Buyer	Buyer	Buyer
FCA	Seller	Seller	Buyer	Buyer	Buyer	Buyer	Buyer	Buyer	Buyer	Buyer	Buyer
FAS	Seller	Seller	Seller	Buyer	Buyer	Buyer	Buyer	Buyer	Buyer	Buyer	Buyer
FOB	Seller	Seller	Seller	Seller	Buyer	Buyer	Buyer	Buyer	Buyer	Buyer	Buyer
CPT	Seller	Seller	Seller	Seller	Seller	Buyer	Seller	Buyer/Seller	Seller	Buyer	Buyer
CFR(CNF)	Seller	Seller	Seller	Seller	Seller	Buyer	Buyer/Seller	Buyer	Buyer	Buyer	Buyer
CIF	Seller	Seller	Seller	Seller	Seller	Seller	Buyer/Seller	Buyer	Buyer	Buyer	Buyer
CIP	Seller	Seller	Seller	Seller	Seller	Seller	Seller	Buyer/Seller	Seller	Buyer	Buyer
DAT	Seller	Seller	Seller	Seller	Seller	Seller	Seller	Buyer	Buyer	Buyer	Buyer
DAP	Seller	Seller	Seller	Seller	Seller	Seller	Seller	Seller	Seller	Buyer	Buyer
DDP	Seller	Seller	Seller	Seller	Seller	Seller	Seller	Seller	Seller	Seller	Seller

EXW	Ex Works	Buyer pays all transportation costs and bears all risks to final destination.
FCA	Free carrier	Seller delivers goods to first carrier, where risk passes to buyer. Buyer pays for transportation.
FAS	Free alongside ship	Seller pays transportation costs to load port. Buyer pays all other costs associated with getting goods to their final destination. Risk passes from seller when goods are delivered to load port.
FOB	Free on board	Similar to FAS but the seller pays all costs and assumes all risk until the goods pass the ship's rail at load port. Internationally, the term states the load port, eg, "FOB Rotterdam." In the United States and Canada, "FOB shipping point" or "FOB destination" indicates when risk and cost passes from seller to buyer.
CPT	Carriage and insurance paid to	Seller pays for costs to transport goods (including multimodal) to the named destination. Risk passes from seller when goods are delivered to the custody of the first carrier.
CFR	Cost and freight	Seller pays transportation to load port, loading costs, and freight. Buyer pays insurance and cost to destination. Risk passes from seller to buyer when goods pass the ship's rail at load port.
CIF	Cost, insurance, and freight	The selling price includes the cost of the goods, cost to transport goods to destination, and cost of marine insurance.
CIP	Carriage and insurance paid to	Same as CPT except the seller pays for insurance. Risk passes when goods are delivered to the first carrier.
DAT	Delivered at terminal	Applies to goods regardless of mode. Seller pays for transportation to a named terminal. Buyer arranges customs clearance and costs to transport to the final destination. Risk passes at the terminal.
DAP	Delivered at place	Same as DAT except risk does not pass from seller until delivered at the final destination. Risk passes at the final destination.
DDP	Delivered duty Paid	Seller is responsible for all charges, including duties and taxes, to the final destination. Risk passes at the time of delivery.

Insurance Certificate

It is advisable to insure all shipments against damage and/or loss. If a loss should occur, a carrier's liability is limited by international agreements. An *insurance certificate* is issued to the buyer as proof that the shipment will be protected against any loss during transit for its full value.

Because of damaging weather conditions at sea, rough handling by carriers and port operators, road hazards, and other hazardous conditions that may exist, an exporter is well advised to insure his merchandise during transportation. An exporter can consult an international insurance carrier or a freight forwarder regarding insuring merchandise. Insurance can be purchased by the seller or buyer, depending on the terms of sale, and coverage is usually placed at 110% of the cost, insurance, and freight (CIF) value.

There are two types of insurance an exporter can purchase: an *open policy* or a *specific policy.* An open policy is issued by the insurer to the exporter one time and covers all shipments made by that exporter over a specified period of time and is subject to renewal. A specific policy, also known as a *voyage policy,* is issued to cover a particular shipment during a specific time period and is not renewable. When a shipment is covered by an open policy, proof of insurance coverage is evidenced by the insurance certificate. Blank insurance certificates are supplied by the insurer, are signed, and have the open policy number of the exporter printed on them. They name the insured, the insured value, and all pertinent information regarding the cargo.

Export License

Most countries regulate the export of high-tech products, weapons, including biological weapons, certain chemicals, nuclear material, and other products involving national security, foreign policy, crime control, or terrorist concerns. For those commodities, a shipper may need an export license. An *export license* is a document regulated by a government authorizing the export of certain merchandise and specific quantities to some destinations.

Sometimes an item's licensing requirements depend on end use and the activities of the end user. A country's Department of Commerce or similar agency will govern the listing of commodities that must be licensed and the process required for licensing.

What commodity is being exported, where is it going, who will receive the item, for what purpose will the item be used, and is the product being exported to a country that is subject to embargo are some of the questions that should be asked in determining if an export license is needed.

If it is determined that the merchandise does not require a special license, then the exporter can ship under a general license. It must be determined if shipments traveling under a general license will require a *destination control statement.*

If the shipment requires a validated export license, the exporter must fill out an Application for Export License form. Approval depends on attention to detail when completing this application. When the application is approved, it will be returned to the applicant and will contain an authorization number to be used on all other documents associated with exporting the goods. Complete and accurate records are to be kept for each shipment moving under this license for a period of no less than 5 years.

Consular Invoice

Some countries require a shipment to be validated by their consulate in the country of exportation. If this is a requirement, then the shipper or his agent must prepare a consular invoice. A *consular invoice* describes the type and quantity of goods, gives information about the shipper and consignee, and states the value of the merchandise.

This invoice is used by the importing country's customs officials to verify the quantity, value, and nature of the goods entering the commerce of the country of destination. The format of the form varies, but they all contain essentially the same information as the commercial invoice and packing list. The form is usually in the language of the importing country or a combination of that language and English. Special care should be taken when filling out a consular invoice, as it must be error free. The forms can be purchased from the consulate and, when completed, must be presented with the commercial invoice for legalization. The legalization fee charged can be a percentage of the FOB value. If the consular invoice has not been legalized, the shipment cannot be exported.

Inspection Certificate

Some merchandise requires that it be inspected and certified that it meets the requirements of the buyer and sometimes the country. In that case, an independent surveyor is appointed to carry out the inspection prior to shipment. An *inspection certificate* is a document required by some buyers and countries attesting to the fact that certain specifications of the merchandise have been met prior to shipping.

If an inspection is required, it is generally performed by an independent party or testing organization such as an assayer or surveyor. The findings are prepared in a report, and the report is identified by a number and date. If a shipment is moving under a LC, the inspection certificate may be mentioned as a required document, or proof of the inspection may be shown on the invoice in the form of a label or stamp bearing the certificate number and date of the corresponding report. An inspection report identifies the merchandise by brand name or generic name, has a description of the merchandise, the size of the lot and sample size being tested, percentage of sample inspected or tested, and the testing methods and results.

Phytosanitary Certificate

Some countries require certification that the exported merchandise be pest free to protect their environment. A *phytosanitary certificate* certifies to a foreign country that the plants or plant products described in the certificate were inspected and are free from pests of specific concern to the importing country.

Countries that are signatories to the International Plant Protection Convention (IPPC) have agreed to inspect and treat exported plants and plant products for noxious pests. Once the inspection and/or treatment have been performed to the requirements of the importing country, a certification to such is made on the phytosanitary certificate. This document is then sent along with the other export documents for this shipment. Requirements for exporting vary with the commodity and from country to country.

Packing Materials

IPPC requires wood packing materials (pallets, crates, blocking/bracing materials) be subject to treatment to prevent invasive species from being transported internationally.

The accepted treatment methods are heat treatment or fumigation with methyl bromide. While legal, methyl bromide is a pesticide, and use of this treatment is falling out of favor with many importers and exporters. Packing materials not subject to the treatment requirements are paper/cardboard, plastic, plywood, and particle board. When required the IPPC stamp must be clearly visible on the packing materials. It is recommended that the IPPC stamp also be facing the door of the shipping container to facilitate inspection by regulatory agencies (See Fig. 3.8 for sample).

The Next Step for the Ocean Carrier

Now that all the documents needed for export have been prepared, certified, and presented to the ocean carrier, the shipment can be loaded onboard the vessel. Once the export department has been notified that the merchandise is loaded, it can execute the BL and prepare the cargo manifest.

The *cargo manifest* is an itemized list of BLs by number of all the cargo loaded on a vessel. It describes the kind and quantity of cargo and is usually presented to customs by the vessel's master or his representative.

The manifest is prepared by the carrier based on the information presented by the exporters, shippers, or freight forwarders; and it contains the following information:

- The place or point of origin of the merchandise, port of loading, port of destination, and final destination;
- The name, description, and build of such vessel; its tonnage; her country of origin; the name of each owner according to her register; and the name of her master;
- A detailed description of the cargo as it is described on each BL to include the marks and numbers of each package; in other words, it must be a duplicate list of each BL;

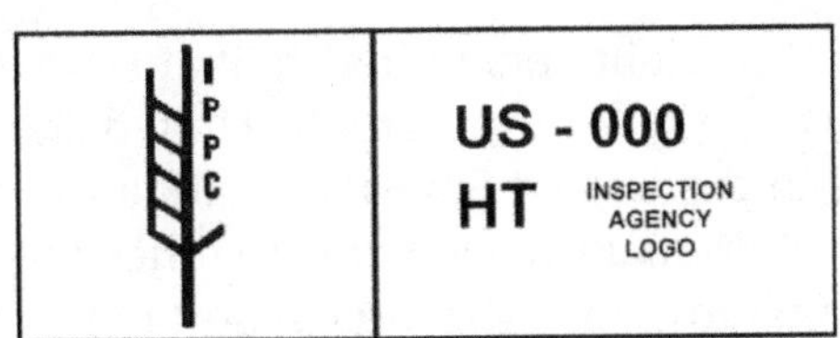

FIGURE 3.8 International Plant Protection Convention stamp.

- The name of the shipper, consignee, and notify parties as they appear on the BL; if there are passengers onboard the vessel, they and their baggage must also be manifested;
- The BLs listed in numerical order according to their discharge port with the discharge ports arranged according to the routing of the vessel;
- Hazardous/dangerous cargo manifested separately and in a list known as the *dangerous cargo manifest.*

A copy of the manifest is transmitted to the carrier's agent at each destination port as notification and to begin cargo clearance arrangements with the authorities at each port. An original set, along with a copy of each BL and any other shipping document, is placed onboard the vessel in a separate pouch addressed to each port agent. Once all the cargo is loaded onboard the vessel and the manifest is complete, the vessel can sail.

24-Hour Advance Manifest Rule and the Importer Security Filing

There are two important notifications and filings that the carrier must make to U.S. CBP prior to the loading of cargo onboard the ship in a foreign port. In 2002, U.S. CBP enacted the "*24-Hour Advance Manifest Rule,*" which requires carriers to transmit to CBP in the port of unlading a copy of the cargo manifest no less than 24 h in advance of the cargo being loaded. Automated NVOCCs and Shipping Lines file their manifests directly via the Automated Manifest System (which is in the process of being fully replaced by ACE, scheduled for late 2016).

The *Importer Security Filing* and Additional Carrier Requirement came into effect in 2009, and in the trade is known as the "10+2 Rule." This rule applies to all cargo arriving via maritime conveyance and requires that the carrier or agent (customs broker, etc.) provide certain cargo information 24 h in advance of the cargo or container being loaded onboard the ship at the port of export. The additional information to be submitted includes

1. Seller (if different from Shipper)
2. Buyer (if different from Consignee)
3. Importer of Record Number
4. Consignee Number (s)
5. Manufacturer (or Supplier)
6. Ship-to-Party (if different from Consignee)
7. Country of Origin
8. Six Digit HTSUS (Harmonized Tariff Schedule of the United States) Number
9. Container Stuffing Location
10. Consolidator (stuffer)

Additionally, for all *FROB* (Freight Remaining on Board—cargo transiting the U.S. ports for discharge at foreign locations), *IE* (Import to the United States and immediate Export), and *TE* (Cargo importing to the United States, transiting the United States for ultimate foreign export), there are additional five elements that need to be submitted through the shipping line, 24 h prior to cargo load at the foreign port of loading:

- Booking Party
- Foreign Port of Unlading
- Place of Delivery
- Ship-to-Party
- Commodity HTSUS (Harmonized Tariff Schedule of US)

Documents Specific to Import Cargo Only

When a vessel arrives at a destination, it immediately begins discharging the cargo that was loaded to that destination. Since most vessels are on a scheduled voyage, it is important that the discharging of cargo goes smoothly and the vessel can continue its voyage. What happens now that the cargo is on the pier? In the following sections, we discuss the documents needed during the import process that we have not previously discussed.

Arrival Notice

The cargo that was discharged onto the pier has just gone through the exact process we described. It was packaged and shipped to the ocean carrier's facility according to the shipper's instructions. It was manifested and had a BL issued by the carrier. All the proper documents required for a smooth delivery to the consignee and/or ultimate buyer were prepared and executed before it left the port of loading. How does the consignee know his cargo has been discharged and he should begin the import process?

Just prior to the vessel's arrival, a notification of arrival form, or *arrival notice*, is issued by the carrier or his agent at the destination port to advise the consignee and import broker of the pending arrival of his cargo. These notices are prepared from the information on the manifest and copies of the BLs that were issued at the load port and sent electronically to the carrier's agent at the destination port. This documentation should be carefully reviewed in an effort to stem the flow of illegal or potentially dangerous cargo into the country before the notice is issued. Unknown shippers and/or consignees, odd or inadequate cargo descriptions, and unusual lapses of time for the movement to take place are all indicators of a suspect shipment.

The arrival notice contains the following information:

- Carrier's name;
- Vessel's name and voyage number;
- Point of origin;
- Ports of loading and discharge;
- Final destination;
- Container number, size, and seal number(s).

In addition, the arrival notice gives a short description of the cargo, including the quantities, weight, and dimensions. It specifies the date of arrival and at what terminal the cargo will be discharged, any pending charges to be collected, and all required documents to be presented before the cargo can clear customs and be released. Cargo can clear customs only if the proper custom entries are prepared and filed.

Most importers use an import broker to clear cargo through customs and arrange delivery. An *import broker* is a licensed entity appointed by a consignee/importer to transact customs business on his behalf.

Before a customs entry can be prepared, however, the importer or import broker must have a commercial invoice, an original and nonnegotiable BL, entry forms, and any other documents required by the destination country, such as a CO, phytosanitary certificate, inspection certificate, consular invoices, etc. These documents, with the exception of the entry forms, were all prepared prior to export, as we discussed previously. Part of the OTI or freight forwarder responsibilities are to forward these documents to the import broker or the importer.

Pro Forma Invoice

In some cases, a commercial invoice is not available at the time of export, and the import broker may have to prepare and present a pro forma invoice. A *pro forma invoice* is an advanced copy of the final invoice. In some countries, the term *sales conformation* is used instead. This invoice is used by the importer to apply to a bank for a LC as proof of the estimated value of the merchandise and the cost of its transportation.

When a commercial invoice is required but is not available at the time a foreign shipment arrives at customs, the importer or the import broker may prepare a pro forma invoice, which generally contains the same information required on a commercial invoice. The pro forma invoice is a device that speeds the movement of goods through customs. With this invoice, the importer must give a bond guaranteeing that he will file the required invoice with the district or port director of customs within 6 months from the date of entry of the shipment. If the invoice does not arrive in that time, the importer will incur a liability under the bond. The entry form can be prepared using the value on the pro forma invoice.

The due duty is usually estimated on the entry form and can be paid to customs directly and immediately, or a bond may be placed. A bond guarantees against a possible failure to pay duties, taxes, or penalties at a later date. It is important to understand that the import broker who files these documents with customs vouches for the truth of the documents, as well as the accuracy of the entry and other documents that are filed. The presentation of any false documents or statements is subject to penalties.

Customs Entries Forms

Customs entries forms are used by the country of destination to determine the type, quantity, and value of the imported merchandise, where it came from, and what its final destination is. When the forms are submitted and approved by customs, the merchandise is "cleared" to enter the country.

The import broker is responsible for all the transactions with customs concerning the entry and admissibility of the merchandise, how it is classed, and its value. He is responsible for making payment, on behalf of his client, of duties, taxes, and any other charges assessed against the merchandise by customs or the ocean carrier. The broker prepares the entry forms required by the customs bureau of the country of destination.

All imported merchandise requires a formal entry, with the exception of those valued under a limit set by the country of destination. In the United States, it is any merchandise valued at less than the US$2500.00. In such case, there are four steps in processing import shipments for clearance:

1. Entry preparation or filing of documents;
2. Inspection and control;
3. Classification and valuation or setting the duty rate;
4. Liquidation of final determination of the duty.

All governments regulate import through the use of documents, physical inspection of shipments, and appraisal of goods. After an arrival notice has been issued, the carrier allows a specific period of time, usually five working days, to present the required entry documents, file the appropriate entry paperwork, and pay all duties and other customs fees.

There are 22 different types of customs entries. The most common are as follows:

- *Consumption Entry (CE):* This is the most common type and is used when goods are intended for resale or are brought directly into the importer's stock.
- *Immediate Transportation (IT):* This type of entry is used when the importer wishes to move the cargo from the port to an inland destination where it will clear customs. In this case, the import broker will arrange to have the goods shipped under bond and without appraisement.
- *Warehouse Entry (WE):* A WE allows the consignee to store certain commodities in a customs-bonded facility for 5 years. Perishables or explosives are not allowed.
- *Warehouse Withdrawal for Consumption Entry (WWCE):* This type of entry works the same as a WE, with the exception that the import broker withdraws portions of the goods as they are needed and pays duty only on the portion removed.
- *Immediate Export Entry (IE):* This type allows goods to be routed to a foreign country via its port of entry. In simple terms, the merchandise moves between two shipping companies within a port of entry for export to another country.
- *Transportation and Export (T&E):* This type of entry involves moving merchandise between two ports of entry within the customs territory of the country of entry for export.
- *Continuous Entry (CE):* In this type of entry, a 1-year bond is made for all entries made in a single year with up to US$50,000 coverage required only under special circumstances.
- *Live Entry:* This type of entry typically requires a visa license from the export country, when mandated by the U.S. CBP, such as for textiles.

Freight Release

Following acceptance of the entry and payment of duties, the shipment may be examined to assure its contents, and then it is released from customs, providing no legal or regulatory violations that have occurred. In addition to preparing the entry and coordinating any inspections required by customs, the broker is responsible for verifying the BL for completeness, making sure all the information is correct, and arranging delivery to its final destination. Before the broker can do this, he must first receive a freight release from the ocean carrier.

A *freight release* is a simple form prepared by the ocean carrier stating that the merchandise has met the terms stated on the BL. This usually means that the freight charges have been paid and the merchandise has cleared customs.

Now that the merchandise has cleared customs and been released by the ocean carrier, the broker can arrange delivery. The inland carrier must be provided with authorization to pick up the cargo and an inland BL showing where it is to be delivered.

Delivery Order

A *delivery order* (DO) is issued by the import broker or the carrier requesting delivery of the arrived cargo. This form provides delivery instructions to the inland carrier once the cargo has been cleared and released, and it is ready to be transported to its final destination.

Duty Drawback

An additional responsibility of an import broker is to prepare and execute duty drawbacks. A *duty drawback* is a document prepared for a refund of all or part of customs duties or domestic taxes paid on imported merchandise that was subsequently either manufactured into a different article or reexported.

A full or partial refund of duties is possible for merchandise moving under a duty drawback. There are several kinds of drawbacks; the most common are as follows:

- Unused merchandise;
- Substitution unused merchandise;
- Rejected merchandise;
- Direct identification manufacturing and substitution manufacturing.

Customs can provide the procedures for filing the drawback claim, which can be completed as late as 3 years after duties were paid.

There are four exceptions in which duties are not refunded:

1. When articles manufactured or produced in the United States with the use of imported merchandise are exported, a refund of 99% of the duties paid on the imported merchandise is refundable;
2. When the imported goods do not agree with the specifications of which they were ordered, or were shipped without the consent of the consignee, the importer may secure a refund of 99% of the duties paid by returning the goods to customs' custody within 90 days after they were released and exporting them under customs supervision;

3. When goods are exported in the same condition as they were imported or destroyed within 3 years from the date of importation, the importer can get 99% of the duty paid refunded to him;
4. When imported goods are not allowed to enter the commerce of the United States and are exported under customs supervision, a refund of the entire amount of duties paid on the rejected goods is allowable.

Finally, there are two financial documents used during importing and exporting of merchandise. They are briefly explained in the following sections.

Bank Draft

A *bank draft* is a draft drawn on one bank against funds previously deposited into its account at another bank that authorizes the sending bank to make payment to the party named in the draft.

A bank draft is a useful tool in helping to secure payment for merchandise when the parties have not done prior business or do not have an established relationship. The draft is in the form of a check and is usually drawn on the head office of the issuing bank. Since a draft is not a guarantee, as is a LC, it must go through the same clearing process as any other check. It is wise not to release the merchandise until the funds have cleared the bank.

Letter of Credit

A LC is a letter of guarantee from a bank that a buyer's payment to a seller will be received on time and for the correct amount.

The bank, acting on behalf of the buyer, who is the holder of the LC, assures that the payment will be made only when the terms of the sale have been fully met as specified in the LC and upon proof of shipment. The buyer makes specific and detailed requirements of the seller in the LC. For payment to be made, the seller must present all the documents that are required in exacting detail.

Business Entities in Commercial Maritime Transportation

The following sections examine the roles, functions, and interactions of the primary business entities involved in the transport of cargo through the supply chain. These entities are freight forwarders, customs brokers, ship's husbands/agents, ship managers and operators, VOCCs and NVOCCs, Protection and Indemnity Insurance (P&I) clubs, the International Maritime Organization (IMO), classification societies, and flag states.

Freight Forwarders

The role of *freight forwarders* is to represent the exporter in arranging the transportation of the merchandise to a foreign destination. Freight forwarders are knowledgeable of the import rules and regulations of foreign countries and the export regulations of the country from which the merchandise will be exported. The proper application of the information will assist the exporter in arranging delivery of the merchandise without costly delays. If requested by the exporter, the freight forwarder will assist in the recommending and arranging of packaging and transportation, providing guidance on marking and labeling of the merchandise, obtaining quotations for all services, booking space with the carrier, advising on import regulations in the destination country, and arranging cargo insurance and export clearance. The freight forwarder also prepares the export documents required by both the inland and ocean carriers, as well as those that may be required by customs or foreign consulates. For all this expertise and valuable service, the freight forwarder charges a fee that is usually included as part of the entire quotation. Most exporters use a licensed and bonded freight forwarder to expedite their overseas shipments. Because freight forwarders have a long established relationship with the inland and ocean carriers and are familiar with each one's particular requirements, this usually allows for the expeditious handling of the merchandise.

It is important to select a freight forwarder based on the needs of the exporter, importer, and merchandise. There are freight forwarders who specialize in handling certain types of cargo—for instance, agricultural products—while others specialize in shipments to specific foreign destinations. Following are some considerations when choosing freight forwarders:

- Are they familiar with the requirements of shipping your product type or to the destination you desire, or both if necessary?
- Do they hold a valid license and bond? Do they carry errors and omissions insurance?
- Do they have offices in the destination port(s) with sufficient staff to handle any unforeseen problems?
- Do they have electronic data interchange capabilities?
- Can they provide references from other clients?
- Are they large enough and have enough locations to handle your business?
- Do you feel comfortable talking with them, and are they a good fit for your business?
- Do they take the time to explain the process to you?

Freight forwarders are licensed by the FMC in the United States and by its counterpart in foreign countries.

Customs Brokers

A *customs broker* is similar in many ways to a freight forwarder, and many customs brokers are also freight forwarders. The main difference between a freight forwarder and a customs broker is that the former arranges the export of merchandise, and the latter arranges the clearance of that merchandise once it arrives at its destination. Customs brokers are not licensed by the FMC or its foreign counterpart as are freight forwarders; instead, they are licensed in the United States by the U.S. Department of Treasury and by a similar government organization in a foreign country.

As described earlier in this chapter, a customs broker must be well versed in international trade regulations to handle the complex business of cargo clearance. There are thousands of regulations and tariffs to consider when importing merchandise into a country. A well-versed broker who is familiar with the workings of customs regulations and its myriad of intricacies can be worth his weight in gold. He must have a thorough knowledge of commodity classifications, duty tariffs and dutiable values, and, most importantly, knowledge of commodities subject to import quotas.

Before the merchandise arrives at its destination, the customs broker will begin preparing the necessary customs entries and arranging the payment of duties based on the documentation forwarded to him by the exporter, or the exporter's agent, the freight forwarder. For this reason, the documents must be complete and error free. The customs broker will examine each document for omissions or errors that may prevent the speedy release of the merchandise from customs' custody.

Once the merchandise is released by customs, a broker may advise on transportation beyond the port or recommend shipping routes and methods.

Customs clearance can be a risky business and, if not handled properly, can cause delays and added expenses. An importer is well advised to seek the assistance of a licensed customs broker to clear his merchandise through customs and represent his interests in the country of destination. The same set of criteria used to select a freight forwarder should be considered when choosing a customs broker.

Ship's Husbands/Agents

A *ship's husband* or *ship's agent* is appointed by the owner and represents the interests of the vessel. The ship's husband has the authority to appoint surveyors to assess damages caused to a vessel during a voyage and to make repairs when necessary. He also attends to the management of the vessel as it relates to equipment, furnishings, and supplies to assure the seaworthiness of the ship. His general duties can be expanded to include arranging for crewing; assuring that the master, mate, and crew are properly licensed and possess valid credentials; and to provide services, either medical or other, to crew members while the vessel is in port. He is responsible for maintaining the proper certificates, surveys, and documents for the ship as a hedge against disputes with insurers, freighters, or charters. In some instances, the ship's husband is granted the authority to enter into charter parties or to generally engage the vessel for a voyage.

Ship Managers/Operators

A *ship manager* is an individual or company, entrusted by a ship owner, to maintain his ship in order to maximize the freight return while maintaining the residual value of the vessel. The components of ship management are mainly commercial management and technical management. The ship manager also offers administrative functions and personnel training. A ship owner may agree to outsource all or some of these components to a ship manager.

Commercial management can consist of keeping the vessel chartered by evaluating the market trends and developments, forecasting market cycles, understanding and evaluating the new building marketplace, voyage estimating, and performing other components that keep the vessel profitable.

Technical management can include manning and crew maintenance, seafarer retention, seafarer identity requirements, maintenance and repairs, classification societies and class survey requirements, maintenance of stores and supplies, insurance for hull and machinery, safety and security requirements, and a host of others.

Vessel Operating Common Carrier and Nonvessel Operating Common Carrier

A *vessel operating common carrier* (VOCC) is a person or entity representing itself to the general public as one that provides transportation by water of cargo by utilizing a vessel operating on the high seas and between foreign ports for all or part of the movement. A *nonvessel operating common carrier* (NVOCC) provides the same type of transportation but usually for smaller quantities of cargo by consolidating several shippers' cargoes to the same destination into containers, and then booking space to that destination on the VOCC vessel for those containers. Both issue BL, maintain a tariff, and are subject to the same rules and regulations governing the export and import of cargo.

P&I Clubs

During the mid-19th century, ship owners found that their traditional hull insurers were unwilling or unable to cover them for certain liabilities. They developed a unique way to address this problem by forming groups of ship owners into associations that would share in one another's claims. Today, these associations have grown to 13 worldwide and have come to be known as *Protection and Indemnity Clubs* or *P&I Clubs* as they are commonly called. It is not the vessel itself that is insured through a P&I Club. That is done through traditional hull insurance companies. What the P&I Clubs cover is the ship owner's liabilities—for example, death or injury to seamen or passengers or any third parties involved in the event. They cover liabilities concerning stowaways, their health, well-being, and humane treatment while onboard the vessel. Liabilities that arise from collisions with other vessels or docks, pollution liabilities, and so on, are all examples of coverage provided.

In addition to insuring the casualty, part of the club's function is to assist a ship owner acting as a legal representative and claims adjuster. A club has access to a large network of specialists to advise and assist with a loss. For losses that occur with vessels owned by large corporations, this function of the club might only be to advise; but for vessels owned by smaller companies that do not have the resources or manpower to handle a major loss, the ship owner may request the club to completely act on his behalf and look after his interests.

It is estimated that the 13 P&I Clubs insure nearly all trading tankers and therefore play a large role in every oil spill. Even though cleanup is usually conducted by a government agency or by the ship owner, the club pays close attention to the process and the expense. The club almost always provides the insurance guarantee known as the *Civil Liability Convention Certificate.* In the United States, where this convention is replaced by the Oil Pollution Act, known as *OPA90,* clubs still provide the actual coverage guarantee. P&I Clubs operate on a nonprofit basis, requiring from their members only enough money to meet the costs and expenses of the members' claims for that year. In this way the members of the associations insure each other. The second major function of the P&I Clubs is to cooperate as a group to represent the interests of their members with maritime organizations, such as the IMO in legislative matters that will impact the maritime trade. It is estimated that nearly 100% of the world's tonnage is insured by membership in a P&I Club.

International Maritime Organization

The IMO is a specialized agency of the United Nations that is responsible for improving maritime safety and preventing pollution for ships. Although international safety regulations have been followed by shipping nations since the middle of the 19th century, it was not until 1948 that the United Nations adopted a convention that formally established the IMO. The purpose of the organization can be summarized in Article 1 of the convention "to provide machinery for cooperation among Governments in the field of governmental regulation and practices relating to technical matters of all kinds affecting shipping engaged in international trade; to encourage and facilitate the general adoption of the highest practicable standards in matters concerning maritime safety, efficiency of navigation and prevention and control of marine pollution from ships." In its charter, the United Nations empowered the IMO to deal with administrative and legal matters related to these purposes.

Classification Societies

Classification societies are nongovernmental organizations or groups of professional ship surveyors, engine surveyors, steel testing surveyors, forging inspectors, and electrical engineers. Classification societies originated in London in the 18th century when marine insurers wanted to develop a system by which a vessel that was presented to them for insurance coverage could be rated. The function of a classification society, typically referred to as a *class,* is to establish and apply technical standards to the design and construction of marine facilities, including ships and offshore structures. Class sets its standards out in the form of rules and regulations that must be met by those vessels or marine structures seeking certification. These vessels and structures are classified according to the soundness of the structure and design for the type of facility it is. A certificate of compliance from class does not imply the fitness of the vessel or structure and in no way is a guarantee of its safety or seaworthiness. It simply implies that the vessel or structure has met the standards required by the rules of that society. The rules developed by a classification society contribute to the structure of the essential parts of a ship's hull, its power generation, its propulsion and steering systems, and any other systems built into the ship that help it maintain the integrity of service it provides. A ship that is built according to a society's rules is assigned a class designation upon successful completion of the various surveys performed by the society. Class survey inspections are carried out on vessels already in service on a regular basis to determine their compliance with the rules of the class society. All flag states require that ships and marine structures that fly their flag meet required standards. A vessel is considered to have met those standards if it carries a valid certificate of compliance issued by an approved classification society. There are more than 50 organizations worldwide that perform the work of a classification society. Of those, 10 organizations form the International Association of Classification Societies (IACS). Between them, they class approximately 94% of commercial tonnage involved in international trade.

Flag States

The term *flag state* is used to refer to a country that maintains a vessel registry. That country is also sometimes referred to as *the administration.* A vessel must agree to abide by the international rules and regulations set forth by the country in which it wishes to be flagged.

Although each vessel that flies a country's flag is ultimately responsible for its own safe operation and the welfare of its crew, the flag state has an overall responsibility for the implementation and enforcement of international maritime regulations. The flag state is also responsible for enforcing the rules of the International Labor Organization (ILO) and the International Oil Pollution Compensation (IOPC) Fund.

It is not unusual for the owner of a vessel to be located in a country other than the country where the vessel is flagged. There are many factors that determine in what country a vessel may be registered or "flagged," some of which are financial considerations, terms of the ship's charter, or employment of certain nationalities of seafarers. When choosing a flag state, an owner should consider one that has ratified, at a minimum, the following core international maritime conventions:

- International Convention for the Safety of Life at Sea (1974) and its amendments;
- International Convention for the Prevention of Pollution from Ships and its amendments;
- International Convention on Load Lines and its amendments;
- International Convention on Standards of Training, Certification, and Watchkeeping for Seafarers and its amendments;
- International Labor Organization Merchant Shipping and its amendments;
- International Convention of Civil Liability for Oil Pollution Damage and its amendments.

In addition to the preceding, an owner should consider the rating and reputation of the registry. How well a flag state performs is rated by the compliance of the vessels flying its flag. The number of vessels flying a state's flag that are detained for violations by Port State Control determines the rating of the flag state. If the flag state is rated poorly, then vessels flying that flag are more likely to be detained for inspection even if that vessel has a good reputation of compliance.

Summary

In closing, we have reviewed the multiple processes and steps in the importation and exportation of ocean cargo, which shed light on the various links in the cargo supply chain. Likewise we have become familiar with the types, content, and usages of shipping documentation, to include those required for compliance with U.S. CBP, and the terminology used in commercial ocean cargo transport. And last, our review of the interactions and roles played by the primary business entities in the maritime transport of cargo provide insight into the truly global nature of the commercial cargo shipping business.

4

International and U.S. Maritime Security Regulations and Programs

OBJECTIVES

After studying this chapter, you will be familiar with

1. The ISPS Code, Parts A and B, and SOLAS Amendments;
2. The World Customs Organization's SAFE Framework of Standards to Secure and Facilitate Global Trade;
3. MTSA: Core tenets of the U.S. "Maritime Transportation Security Act";
4. C-TPAT: CBP's flagship antiterrorism cargo supply chain program;
5. CBP's "Importer Security Filing," "24-Hour Rule," and "Container Security Initiative" (CSI); and
6. Goals of the nuclear detection "Secure Freight Initiative" program.

Introduction

The September 11, 2001, terrorist attacks on the World Trade Center towers and the Pentagon constituted a pivotal event of history that changed the world—and dramatically affected the world of trade and transportation. In response to the increased threat of terrorism—and specifically concerns about threats to ports and commercial ships and their cargoes—the International Maritime Organization (IMO) and the United States implemented new protective measures and requirements that have a significant impact on the processes of purchasing and moving goods throughout the supply chain of international commerce and the conveyances that transport those goods. Every enterprise engaged in international trade is required to comply with specific legislation and implement policies and procedures which significantly increase protection of ports, ships, and cargoes and mitigate potential security threats. The global cargo supply chain offers terrorists many significant targets of opportunity. Of particular concern is the possible use of a supply chain or a maritime transportation conveyance to deliver a weapon of mass destruction (WMD). Cargo containers are especially vulnerable to terrorist and criminal manipulation. While the IMO enacted the International Ship and Port Facility Security Code (ISPS Code), which requires the implementation of security polices, plans, and procedures for ports and ships, the U.S. government enacted the Maritime Transportation Security Act (MTSA) of 2002, which mirrors the ISPS Code, and the Safe Ports Act of 2006, as well as implemented via U.S. Customs and Border Protection (CBP) four initiatives designed to enhance security policies and procedures through the entire cargo supply chain. This chapter focuses on current international and U.S. maritime security laws, voluntary

Maritime Security.

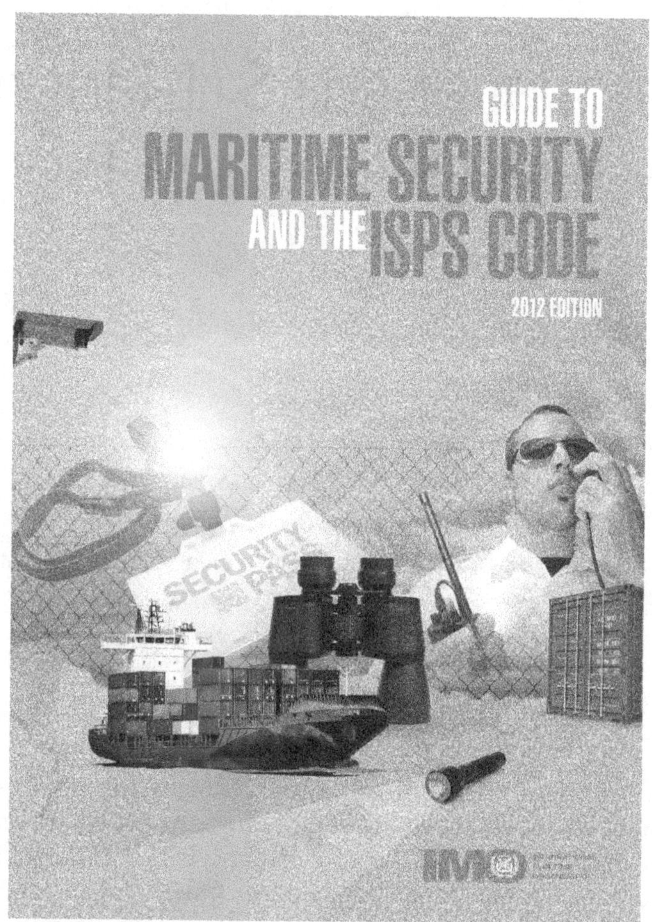

FIGURE 4.1 *The IMO's Guide to Maritime Security and the ISPS Code 2012 Edition.* Copies can be purchased from IMO Authorized Distributors *(http://www.imo.org/en/Publications/Distributors/Pages/default.aspx).* International Maritime Organization, 4 Albert Embankment, London, SE1 7SR, United Kingdom.

initiatives, and pertinent security regulations. First, let's review the ISPS Code, its purpose, scope, requirements, and recommendations for implementation (Fig. 4.1).

The International Ship and Port Facility Security Code[1]

After the September 11 attacks, the international maritime community reexamined its existing laws addressing safety at sea, chiefly the International Convention of Safety of Life at Sea, known as the *SOLAS Convention*, and found it in crucial need of revisions and additions to effectively protect ports and ships around the world from acts of terrorism. After discussions on the security and safety vulnerabilities of the international maritime transport industry, the ISPS Code was created, and together with other amendments to SOLAS 74 was adopted by the Conference of Contracting Governments in December 12, 2002 which took effect on July 1, 2004. The objective of the ISPS Code was to establish an international framework of "standards" to be achieved involving governments, government agencies, local administrations, and the shipping and port industries to detect and assess security threats and standardize the requirements of the maritime industry in taking preventive measures against potential security incidents that could affect ships or port facilities used in international trade. The Code requires ships and port facilities to have properly trained personnel to carry out their security duties, gather and assess information, maintain communication protocols, restrict access, prevent the introduction of unauthorized weapons and contraband, establish the means to raise alarms, ensure pertinent training and periodic drills are conducted, establish threat-based security levels and their relevant security countermeasures and procedures, and provide guidance of the topics for the ship and port security assessments and security plans. It is important to note that the "security threats" addressed are not just "terrorism," but also include stowaways, piracy, drug and contraband smuggling, sabotage, hijacking, unauthorized use, cargo tampering, hostage-taking, vandalism, use of the vessel to carry perpetrators and their equipment, and the use of the vessel as a weapon.

Let's review **Part A** of the Code, which is mandatory for the ships and port facilities covered by the Code, but first learn its objectives and functional requirements, as listed in **Section 1**.

Section 1.1, *Introduction,* states "This part of the International Code for the Security of Ships and of Port Facilities contains mandatory provisions to which reference is made in Chapter XI-2 of the International for the Safety of Life at Sea, 1974, as amended."

Section 1.2 defines the *objectives* of the Code as

- To establish an international framework involving cooperation among contracting governments, government agencies, local administrations, and the shipping and port industries to detect security threats and take preventive measures against security incidents affecting ships and/or port facilities used in international trade;
- To establish and standardize the respective roles and responsibilities of the contracting governments, government agencies, local administrations, and the shipping and port industries, at the national and international level, for ensuring maritime security;
- To ensure the early and efficient collection and exchange of security-related information;
- To provide a methodology for security assessments so as to have in place plans and procedures to react to changing security levels and prepare the security plans; and
- To ensure confidence that adequate and proportionate maritime security measures are in place on a continuous basis.

Section 1.3 states that the Code embodies a number of *functional requirements* to achieve the objectives, including

- Gathering and assessing information with respect to security threats and exchanging such information with appropriate contracting governments;
- Requiring the maintenance of communications protocols for ships and port facilities;
- Preventing unauthorized access to ships, port facilities, and their restricted areas;

- Preventing the introduction of unauthorized weapons, incendiary devices or explosives to ships or port facilities;
- Providing means for raising the alarm in reaction to security threats or security incidents;
- Requiring ship and port facility security plans (PFSPs) be based upon security assessments; and
- Requiring training, drills, and exercises to ensure familiarity with security plans and procedures.

Section 2 identifies key terminology in the Code and states their *definitions*:

- **Convention**—The International Convention for the Safety of Life at Sea (SOLAS), 1974, as amended.
- **Regulation**—A regulation of the Convention.
- **Chapter**—A chapter of the Convention.
- **Contracting Government**—The government of the territory in which the port is located.
- **Recognized Security Organization (RSO)**—A nongovernment company that has proven expertise in relevant aspects of ship and port facility security.
- **Ship Security Plan (SSP)**—A plan developed to ensure the application of measures onboard the ship, designed to protect persons onboard, cargo, cargo transport units, ship's stores, and the ship from risks of a security incident.
- **Port Facility Security Plan (PFSP)**—A plan developed to ensure the application of measures designed to protect the port facility and ships, persons, cargo, cargo transport units, and ship's stores within the port facility from the risks of a security incident.
- **Ship Security Officer (SSO)**—The person onboard the ship, accountable to the master, designated by the company as responsible for the security of the ship, including implementation and maintenance of the SSP, and for liaison with the *company* and *port facility security officers.*
- **Company Security Officer (CSO)**—The person designated by the company for ensuring that a *ship security assessment* is carried out; that a *ship security plan* is developed, submitted for approval, and thereafter implemented and maintained; and for liaison with the port facility and ship security officers.
- **Port Facility Security Officer (PFSO)**—The person designated as responsible for the development, implementation, revision, and maintenance of the *PFSP* and for liaisons with the *ship and company security officers.*
- **Security Level 1**—The level for which minimum appropriate protective security measures will be maintained at all times.
- **Security Level 2**—The level for which appropriate additional protective security measures will be maintained for a period of time as a result of heightened risk of a security incident.
- **Security Level 3**—The level for which further specific protective security measures will be maintained for a limited period of time when a security incident is probable or imminent, although it may not be possible to identify the special target.

Section 3 defines the *application* of the Code, ie, the types of ships and ports to which the Code applies. The Code applies to passenger ships, including high-speed passenger craft, and cargo ships of 500 GTs and above, which are engaged on international voyages, mobile offshore drilling units (MODU), and port facilities serving such ships engaged on international voyages. This section also allows for contracting governments to decide the extent of application for port facilities within their territory which, although used primarily by ships not engaged on international voyages, are required occasionally to serve ships arriving or departing on an international voyage. This section also clarifies that the Code does not apply to warships, naval auxiliaries, or other ships owned or operated by a contracting government and used only on government noncommercial service.

Section 4 sets forth the *responsibilities of contracting governments*, ie, the governments to which the Code applies. This section states that contracting governments will set security levels and provide guidance for protection from security incidents. Higher security levels indicate the greater likelihood of occurrence of a security incident. The section also lists the factors to be considered in setting appropriate levels, including

- The degree that the threat information is credible;
- The degree that the threat information is specific or imminent; and
- The potential consequences of such a security incident.

Section 4 allows contracting governments to delegate to an RSO certain of their security-related duties, noting six exceptions, which are

- Setting of the applicable security level;
- Approving a *port facility security assessment* and subsequent amendments to an approved assessment;
- Determining the port facilities which will be required to designate a *PFSO*;
- Approving a *PFSP* and subsequent amendments to an approved plan;
- Exercising control and compliance measures pursuant to regulation XI-2/9; and
- Establishing the requirements for a *Declaration of Security* (DoS).

Importantly, this section also requires that contracting governments appropriately test the effectiveness of the approved *SSPs* or the *PFSPs* and any amendments made to those plans.

Section 5 sets the requirements for a DoS. The contracting governments determine when the DoS is required by assessing the ship/port interface or ship-to-ship activity risk posed to persons, property, or the environment. A ship can request completion of one when

- The ship is operating at a higher security level than the port facility or an interfacing ship;
- There is an agreement on a DoS between contracting governments covering certain international voyages or specific ships on those voyages;
- There has been a security threat or a security incident involving the ship or the port facility, as applicable;
- The ship is at a port which is not required to have and implement an approved *PFSP*; or
- When the ship is conducting ship-to-ship activities with another ship not required to have and to implement an approved *SSP*.

Requests for completion of this document will be acknowledged by the applicable port facility or ship. The DoS will be completed by the master or the *SSO* on behalf of the ship(s); and if appropriate, the *PFSO* or, if the contracting government determines otherwise, by any other body responsible for shore-side security, on behalf of the port facility. Section 5 also addresses some other issues pertaining to the declarations, ie, security requirements decided by the contracting governments or administrations that could be shared between shore and ship, stating the responsibilities of each, and the minimum period for which the declarations shall be kept by the port facilities and by ships entitled to fly their flag.

Section 6 enumerates the *obligations of the company*. The company shall ensure that the *SSP* contains a clear statement emphasizing the master's authority. The company shall establish in the *SSP* that the master has the overriding authority and responsibility to make decisions with respect to the safety and security of the ship and to request the assistance of the company or any contracting government as may be necessary. The company shall ensure that the *CSO*, the master, and the *SSO* are given the necessary support to fulfill their duties and responsibilities in accordance with SOLAS XI-2 and this part of the Code.

Section 7 describes, under the topic *Ship Security*, how ships are required to act at each of the three security levels, these being set by the governments. A brief definition of Security Levels 1, 2, and 3 was listed in Section 2; however, they are expanded in Part B of the Code. At Security Level 1, the following measures will be executed, through appropriate means, on all ships:

- Ensuring the performance of all ship security duties;
- Controlling access to the ship;
- Controlling the embarkation of persons and their effects;
- Monitoring restricted areas to ensure that only authorized persons have access;
- Monitoring of deck areas and areas surrounding the ship;
- Supervising the handling of cargo and ship's stores; and
- Ensuring that security communication is readily available.

This section also mandates that at Security Level 2, additional protective measures, as specified in the *SSP*, will be implemented for each activity detailed in the preceding list, while incorporating the guidance given in the Code, Part B. It adds that further specific protective measures be activated at Security Level 3 and implemented for each activity detailed in the list. Whenever Security Level 2 or 3 is determined by the administration, the ship shall acknowledge receipt of the instructions on change of the security level. Prior to entering a port or while in a port within the territory of a contracting government that has set Security Level 2 or 3, the ship shall acknowledge receipt of this instruction and confirm to the *PFSO* the initiation of the implementation of the appropriate measures taken. In the case of Security Level 3, the ship shall report any difficulties in implementation of compliance, and the *port facility and SSOs* shall liaise and coordinate the appropriate actions. This section specifies further obligations by the administration, contracting governments, and ship personnel in executing security measures for addressing security incidents.

Section 8 establishes the need for a *ship security assessment,* an essential procedure and integral part of the process of developing and updating the *SSP*. The *CSO* will ensure that the *ship security assessment* is carried out by persons with appropriate skills, and subject to the provisions of Section 9, an *RSO* may carry out this duty. The *ship security assessment* will include an on-scene security survey and, at least, the following elements:

- Identification of existing security measures, procedures, and operations;
- Identification and evaluation of key shipboard operations to be protected and identification of possible threats;
- The likelihood of their occurrence, in order to establish and prioritize security measures; and identification of weaknesses, including human factors.
- The ship security assessment shall be documented, reviewed, accepted, and retained by the company.

Section 9 outlines the topics required, at a minimum, to be addressed in the *SSP*. An administration-approved plan must be carried onboard, making provisions for the three security levels. Additionally, an RSO may review and approve the *SSP* for a specific ship but may *not* be involved in both the preparation of the *ship security assessment* or *SSP* and the approval. The text of the plan will be written in the working language(s) of the ship, and if not in English, French, or Spanish, a translation into one of those languages will be included, and address, at least, the following:

- Measures designed to prevent dangerous items and substances intended for use against persons, ships, or port;
- Identification of the restricted area and measures to prevent unauthorized access to them;
- Measures to prevent unauthorized access to the ship;
- Procedures for responding to security threats or breaches of security, while maintaining critical operation of the ship or ship/port interface;
- Procedures for responding to any security instruction contracting governments may give at Security Level 3;
- Procedures for evacuation in case of security threats or breaches of security;
- Duties of shipboard personnel responsible for security and of other shipboard personnel on security aspects;
- Procedures for auditing the security activities;
- Procedures for training, drills, and exercises associated with the plan;
- Procedures for interfacing with port facility security activities;
- Procedures for the periodic review and updating of the plan;

- Procedures for reporting security incidents;
- Identification of the *SSO* and the *CSO* with 24-hour contact details;
- Procedures to ensure the inspection, testing, calibration, and maintenance of any security equipment provided onboard, and the frequency for those procedures;
- Identification of the locations of ship security alert system (SSAS) activation points; and
- Procedures, instructions, and guidance on the use of the SSAS, including the testing, activation, deactivation, and resetting and to limit false alerts.

The rest of Section 9 details the conduction of internal audits of the security activities, changes to the plan, the allowance of the *SSP* to be in electronic format with proper precautions taken for the protection of it, and actions to ensure the plan's implementation, and further steps to be taken when the ship is suspected of noncompliance.

Section 10 specifies that all *records* pertaining to the *SSP* should be kept onboard for the time period specified by the administration. These records include training drills and exercises; security threats and security incidents; breaches of security; changes in security level; communications relating to the direct security of the ship such as specific threats to the ship or to port facilities the ship is or has been in; internal audits and reviews of security activities; periodic reviews of the *ship security assessment*; periodic reviews of the *SSP*; implementation of any amendments to the plan; and maintenance, calibration, and testing of any security equipment provided onboard, including testing of the ship alert system.

This section also mandates that records be kept in the working language(s) of the ship, but if the language(s) used are not English, French, or Spanish, translation into one of these languages must be included. If records are kept in electronic format, they must be protected from unauthorized use or change of any kind. All records must be protected from unauthorized access.

Section 11 allows that one person may be designated as *CSO* for one or more ships, but the plan must always list the person responsible in the role for its ship. It also lists the duties for this person, which include, but are not limited to, the following:

- Advising the level of threats likely to be encountered…using appropriate sources;
- Ensuring that the *ship security assessments* are conducted;
- Ensuring the development, submission for approval, implementation, and maintenance of the *SSP*;
- Ensuring that if the *SSP* is modified, it satisfies the security requirements of the ship;
- Arranging for internal audits and reviews of security activities;
- Arranging for the initial and subsequent verification of the ship by the administration;
- Ensuring that deficiencies and nonconformities identified in the plan are addressed and dealt with;
- Enhancing security awareness and vigilance of the ship's personnel;
- Ensuring adequate security training for the responsible personnel;
- Ensuring effective and cooperative communication between the *ship* and the *PFSOs*;

- Ensuring consistency between security requirements and safety requirements;
- Ensuring that, if sister ship or fleet security plans are used, each plan reflects the ship-specific information; and
- Ensuring that any alternative arrangement approved for a particular ship or group of ships is implemented and maintained.

Section 12 notes one different requirement for the position of *SSO* and then lists the duties and responsibilities required of this person. Unlike the *CSO*, an *SSO* is designated for each ship. In addition to those specified elsewhere in the Code, the duties and responsibilities of the *SSO* include, but are not limited to

- Making regular security inspections of the ship to ensure security measures are maintained;
- Maintaining and supervising the implementation of the *SSP* and approved amendments;
- Coordinating the security aspects of the handling of cargo and ship's stores with other shipboard personnel and with the relevant *PFSO*;
- Proposing modifications to the *SSP*;
- Reporting to the *CSO* any deficiencies and nonconformities identified during internal audits, reviews, and verifications of compliance and implementing any corrective actions;
- Ensuring that adequate training has been provided to shipboard personnel, as appropriate; reporting all security incidents; enhancing security awareness and vigilance onboard;
- Coordinating implementation of the *SSP* with the *CSO* and the relevant *port security officer*; and
- Ensuring the security equipment is properly operated, tested, calibrated, and maintained.

Section 13, while taking into consideration the guidance provided in the Code, Part B, assigns the responsibilities of *training, drills, and exercises on ship security*. The *CSO* will provide knowledge and training to the appropriate shore-based personnel, the *SSO*, and pertinent shipboard personnel, and to ensure the effective implementation of the Plan, drills will be conducted, and will ensure the effective coordination and implementation of the Plan by participating in exercises at appropriate intervals.

Section 14 addresses an ongoing security concern to the maritime industry, *port facility security*. The ship/port interface area, a logical target for terrorist activity, requires the port facility to meet specific standards of operations. These requirements always keep the goal of addressing threats, while maintaining a minimum of interference with, or delay to, passengers, ship, ship's personnel and visitors, goods, and services of optimum importance. A port facility is required to act upon the security levels set by the territory's contracting government with appropriate measure and procedures. Using the guidance from

Code B, at Security Level 1, the following activities will be carried out through appropriate measures to identify and thwart security threats:

- Ensure the performance of all port facility security duties;
- Control access to the port facility;
- Monitor the port facility, including anchoring and berthing areas and restricted areas to ensure that only authorized persons have access;
- Supervise the handling of cargo and of ship' stores;
- Ensure that security communication is readily available; and
- Provide information for operation at Security Level 2, which requires using additional protective measures, as specified in the *PFSP*, and at Security Level 3, further specific protective measures, listed in the *port security plan*, are to be implemented. All responses will be consistent with direction provided in Part B. Additionally, at Level 3, port facilities are required to implement security instruction given by the territory's contracting government;
- When a *PFSO* is advised that a ship is at a security level higher than that of the port facility, the *PFSO* will report it to the competent authority and then liaise with the *SSO* to coordinate appropriate actions.

Section 15 explains the hows and whys of another procedure, *port facility security assessment*, which is essential to a successful security plan. As with the *ship security assessment*, the *port facility security assessment* is fundamentally a risk analysis of all aspects of a port facility's operation in order to identify any vulnerabilities to security threats and is a necessary and integral part of a fully functional security plan. It will be carried out by the contracting government, which may authorize an RSO to carry out the assessment of a specific port facility located within its territory. However, when that assessment is completed, it will be reviewed and approved for compliance by that same contracting government. Persons conducting the assessments must have appropriate skills and knowledge to perform the job competently, reflecting the guidance given in Part B. Assessments are to be periodically reviewed and updated, reflecting changing threats or changes in the port facilities.

Section 16 outlines the requirements of the *PFSP*. This document will be developed and maintained, based on the *port facility security assessment*, adequate for the ship/port facility, making provisions for the three security levels as defined in this Part of the Code. This *PFSP* will be approved by the contracting government in whose territory the port facility is located. It will be written in the working language of the port facility. The Plan stipulates the inclusions of measures and procedures to minimize terrorist threats, at least, including the following:

- Prevention of entry or unauthorized carrying of weapons or dangerous substances and devices intended for use against persons, ships, or ports into the port facility or onboard a ship;
- Prevention of unauthorized access to the port facility and its restricted areas, and to the ships moored at the facility;

- Prompt and appropriate response to security threats or breaches of security while maintaining critical operations of the port facility or ship/port interface areas;
- Response to any security instructions from the contracting government where the port facility is located when operating at Security Level 3;
- Evacuation in case of threats or breaches of security;
- Instruction given to port facility personnel assigned security responsibilities and all facility personnel on security aspects;
- Interfacing with ship security activities;
- Periodic review and updating as needed of the *PFSP*;
- Reporting of any security incidents;
- Identification of the *PFSO*, including 24-hour contact details;
- Security of the information contained in the Plan;
- Effective security of cargo and the cargo handling equipment at the port facility;
- Periodic auditing of the *PFSP*;
- Response when the SSAS at the port facility has been activated; and
- Facilitating of shore leaves for ship's personnel, as well as visitors to the ship, including representatives of Seafarers' Welfare and Labor Organizations.

Section 16 further states that personnel conducting internal audits of security activities specified in the *PFSP* or evaluating its usage will be independent of the activities being audited unless the size and nature of the port facility makes this impracticable. The *PFSP* must always be protected from unauthorized access or disclosure; it may be combined with or part of the port security plan or any other port emergency plan or plans. The contracting government in whose territory the port facility lies will determine which changes to the Plan will be approved and implemented. While this Plan may be kept in electronic form, it must be protected from unauthorized deletion, destruction, or change. The contracting governments may also allow a *PFSP* to cover more than one port facility if those facilities are similar, and this alternative arrangement with its particulars should be communicated to the organization.

Section 17 explains the duties of a *PFSO* and notes that while every port facility must have a designated person for this position, one person may serve this role at one or more port facilities. The *PFSO* is responsible for the following duties, including any others specified elsewhere in Part A of the Code:

- An initial comprehensive security survey of the port facility, basing it on its security assessment;
- Development and maintenance of the *PFSP*;
- Implementation and exercise of this Plan;
- Regular security inspections of the port facility to ensure the application of appropriate security measures;
- Suggestions to modify the Plan in order to correct deficiencies and keep it relevant to the facility;
- Heighten security awareness and vigilance of port facility personnel;
- Adequate training to be provided for personnel responsible for security of the port facility;

- Reporting to relevant authorities and recording of occurrences which threaten the security of the port facility;
- Coordinate implementation of the Plan with the appropriate company and SSOs, and with security services, as appropriate;
- Standards for personnel responsible for security of the port facility be met;
- Ensuring security equipment is properly operated, tested, calibrated, and maintained; and
- Upon request, assisting *SSOs* in confirming the identity of those seeking to board the ship.

Section 17 concludes with the assurance that the *PFSO* will be given the necessary support to fulfill the duties and responsibilities imposed on that position.

Section 18 assigns accountability for the *training, drills, and exercises on port facility security*. The responsibility for providing the education and ongoing training necessary for the port security personnel lies with the port facility security office and appropriate port facility security personnel responsible for the security of the port facility. All aspects of this section advise taking into account the guidance of Part B of the Code. Security personnel should have understanding of and receive training sufficient to perform their tasks adequately. Drills will be carried out at appropriate intervals to ensure the effective implementation of the PFSP, allowing for the types of operation, personnel changes, the type of ship being served, and other relevant circumstances. It is the PFSO's role to ensure the effective coordination and successful execution of the Plan by participating in exercises at appropriate intervals.

Section 19 specifies that each ship shall have onboard a *verification and certification for ships*. This applies to each ship covered by Part A of the Code. Verifications will be carried out by officers of the administration, who may, however, entrust the verifications to an RSO, and in every case, the administration will fully guarantee the completeness and accuracy of the certificate and ensure arrangements to satisfy this obligation. Each ship is subject to an initial verification before the ship is put into service or before the certificate required is issued for the first time, which is to include a complete corroboration that its security system and any associated security equipment as mentioned in the approved *SSP* are in satisfactory condition and functional for the service for which they are intended. A renewal verification at intervals specified by the administration, but not exceeding 5 years, and at least one intermediate one, ensures that the security system and other security equipment are functional for the purposes. All verifications are to ensure the ship's security system and any associated security equipment are being maintained to function properly and after verification, no changes will be made, nor will be made to them, nor any to the approved *SSP* without the sanction of the administration. After the initial or renewal verification in accordance with the provisions listed above has been completed, an *International Ship Security Certificate* is issued or endorsed by either the administration or by an RSO on behalf of the administration. Another contracting government may, at the request of the administration, cause the ship to be verified, and if satisfied that the provisions comply with this section, shall issue a certificate to the ship. If the language of the certificate's text is not in English, French, or Spanish, the text will include a translation into one of these languages.

Duration and validity of certification is set forth in this chapter also. An International Ship Security Certificate will be issued for a period specified by the administration, but not to exceed 5 years. Whether the renewal verification is completed before or within 3 months before the expiry date or after the expiry date, the new certificates will be valid from the date of completion to a date *not* exceeding 5 years after the expiry date of the existing certificate. A certificate becomes invalid in any of the following cases:

- If the relevant verifications are not completed within the designated periods;
- If the certificate is not endorsed properly;
- When a company assumes the responsibility for the operation of a ship not previously operated by that company; and
- Upon transfer of the ship to the flag of another state.

The Code lays out the procedures to rectify these situations. Interim certificates, granted when all requirements are met to the administration's satisfaction, are valid for a period of 6 months and may not be extended. A current certificate and all relevant paperwork must be on the ship at all times. It is crucial that verification of all security equipment to be fully functional is primary to an effective security plan.

Part B of the Code provides guidance for the processes and procedures necessary to implement the requirements and standards in Part A. The Code states that nothing in Part B should be read or interpreted to be in conflict with any of Part A, and the guidance provided in Part B should always be read, interpreted, and applied in a manner which is consistent with the aims, objectives, and principles established in the Part A.

The *responsibilities of contracting governments* (the governments within whose territory the port facilities are located) listed in Part A are repeated in the Introduction to Part B, and it is reiterated that while these governments can designate RSOs to carry out certain work in port facilities and ship security duties, the governments or their designated authorities are ultimately responsible. The RSO may also advise or provide assistance to companies or port facility on security matters. A competent RSO should demonstrate the following:

- Expertise in relevant aspects of security;
- Appropriate knowledge of ship and port operations, including knowledge of ship design and construction if providing services in respect of ships, and of port design and construction if providing services in respect to port facilities;
- The capability to assess the likely security risks that could occur during ship and port facility operations, including the ship/port interface, and how to minimize such risks;
- The ability to maintain and improve the expertise and trustworthiness of personnel and to maintain appropriate measures to avoid unauthorized disclosure of, or access to, security-sensitive matter;

- The knowledge of the requirements of the Code and relevant national and international legislation and security requirements;
- Familiarity with the current security threats and patterns and of recognition and detection of weapons, dangerous substances, and devices;
- The ability to recognize, on a nondiscriminatory basis, the characteristics and behavioral patterns of persons who are likely to threaten security, as well as the techniques used to circumvent security measures; and
- The knowledge of security and surveillance equipment and systems and their operational limitations.

While delegating specific duties to an RSO, contracting governments cannot transfer the following responsibilities:

- Set applicable security level;
- Determine which port facilities located within the territory of the contracting government are required to designate a *PFSO* and to prepare a *PFSP*;
- Approve a *port facility security assessment* or *PFSP*, or any subsequent amendments to previously approved ones;
- Exercise control and compliance measures; and
- Establish the requirement for a DoS.

Contracting governments also determine and assign Security Levels:

Security Level 1, normal: The level at which ships and port facilities normally operate and when minimum appropriate protective security measures shall be maintained;

Security Level 2, heightened: The level applying for as long as there is a heightened risk of a security incident, for which appropriate additional protective security measures will be maintained for that same period of time;

Security Level 3, exceptional: The level applying for the period of time when there is credible evidence of a probable or imminent risk of a security threat or incident, and requiring further specific protective security measures be maintained for that same time frame, although it may not be possible to identify the specific target.

The *SSP* should indicate the operational and physical security measures the ship itself should take to ensure that it always operates at Security Level 1. Every company operating a ship, covered by the Code, must designate a *CSO* for the company and a *SSO* for each of the ships. The duties, responsibilities, and training requirements of these officers and requirements for participation in drills and exercises are defined in Part A. Moreover, each ship must carry an approved *SSP* and International Ship Security Certificate onboard.

Section 5 reviews a DoS. The main purpose of the DoS is to ensure an agreement is reached between ship and port facility regarding security responsibilities (ie, who is responsible for what). Each side must determine which security measures it will take in accordance with the provision of their respective security plans. Contracting governments and ships will determine when a DoS is required, often based on the information provided by the *port facility risk assessment.* The agreed DoS should be signed and dated by both parties to indicate compliance with Part A, and completed in English, French, or Spanish or a language common to both the port facility and the ship.

Section 6 specifies the company's security obligations. The *SSP* shall contain a statement emphasizing the master's authority. The company will give necessary support to the master, *SSO*, and *CSO* to fulfill their duties efficiently.

Sections 8 and **9** are key sections of **Part B. Section 8** defines who is responsible for conducting the *ship security assessment* and their suggested expertise, the documentation and records to be assembled in advance, and all elements to be addressed and evaluated in the SSA, and its on-scene security survey. Let's review some of the requirements of this important section. First, persons involved in conducting the SSA should have expertise in

- Knowledge of current security threats and patterns;
- Recognition and detection of weapons, dangerous substances, and devices;
- Recognition, on a nondiscriminatory basis, of characteristics and behavioral patterns of persons who are likely to threaten security;
- Techniques used to circumvent security measures;
- Methods used to cause a security incident;
- Effects of explosives on a ship's structures and equipment;
- Ship security;
- Ship/port interface business practices;
- Contingency planning, emergency preparedness, and response;
- Physical security;
- Radio and telecommunications systems, including computer systems and networks;
- Marine engineering;
- Ship and port operations.

Next, what types of documents and records should be assembled and reviewed in preparing to initiate an SSA? They would include

- The general layout (general arrangement or "GA") of the ship;
- The location of areas which should have restricted access, such as navigation bridge, machinery spaces of category A, and other control stations as defined in Chapter II-2, etc.;
- The location and function of each actual or potential access point to the ship;
- Changes in the tide which may have an impact on the vulnerability or security of the ship;
- The cargo spaces and stowage arrangements;
- The locations where the ship's stores and essential maintenance equipment are stored;
- The locations where unaccompanied baggage is stored;
- The emergency and standby equipment available to maintain essential services;

- The number of ship's personnel, any existing security duties, and any existing training requirement practices of the company;
- Existing security and safety equipment for the protection of passengers and ship's personnel;
- Escape and evacuation routes and assembly stations which have to be maintained to ensure the orderly and safe emergency evacuation of the ship;
- Existing agreements with private security companies providing ship/water-side security services; and
- Existing security measures and procedures in effect, including inspection and control procedures, identification systems, surveillance and monitoring equipment, personnel identification documents and communication, alarms, lighting, access control, and other appropriate systems.

Third, what areas should be covered in the SSA? The SSA should address the following elements:

- Physical security;
- Structural integrity;
- Personnel protection systems;
- Procedural policies;
- Radio and telecommunication systems, including computer systems and networks; and
- Other areas that may, if damaged or used for illicit observations, pose a risk to persons, property, or operations onboard the ship or within the port facility.

And, the SSA should evaluate the continuing relevance of existing security measures—and make recommendations—for

- The restricted areas;
- The response procedures to fire or other emergency conditions;
- The level of supervision of the ship's personnel, passengers, visitors, vendors, repair technicians, dock workers, etc.;
- The frequency and effectiveness of security patrols;
- The access control systems, including identification systems;
- The security communications systems and procedures;
- The security doors, barriers, and lighting; and
- The security and surveillance equipment and systems, if any.

The SSA also should consider the persons, activities, services, and operations that it is important to protect. This includes

- The ship's personnel;
- Passengers, visitors, vendors, repair technicians, port facility personnel, etc.;
- The capacity to maintain safe navigation and emergency response;
- The cargo, particularly dangerous goods or hazardous substances;

- The ship's stores;
- The ship security communication equipment and systems, if any; and
- The ship's security surveillance equipment and systems, if any.

What types of threats should the SSA take into consideration? They include

- Damage to, or destruction of, the ship or of a port facility, eg, by explosive devices, arson, sabotage, or vandalism;
- Hijacking or seizure of the ship or of persons onboard;
- Tampering with cargo, essential ship equipment or systems, or ship's stores;
- Unauthorized access or use, including presence of stowaways;
- Smuggling weapons or equipment, including weapons of mass destruction;
- Use of the ship to carry those intending to cause a security incident and/or their equipment;
- Use of the ship itself as a weapon or as a means to cause damage or destruction;
- Attacks from the waterside of the ship while at berth or anchor;
- Attacks while at sea.

How about "vulnerabilities"? The SSA has to take into account

- Conflicts between safety and security measures;
- Conflicts between shipboard duties and security assignments;
- Watchkeeping duties, number of ship's personnel, particularly with implications on crew fatigue, alertness, and performance;
- Any identified security training deficiencies; and
- Any security equipment and systems, including communication systems.

An SSA cannot be prepared without an onsite survey, in the code called the "On-scene Security Survey," which is walking the ship in-person and evaluating existing protective measures, procedures, and operations for

- Ensuring the performance of all ship security duties;
- Monitoring restricted areas to ensure that only authorized persons have access;
- Monitoring of deck areas and areas surrounding the ship;
- Controlling the embarkation of persons and their effects (accompanied and unaccompanied baggage and ship's personnel personal effects);
- Supervising the handling of cargo and the delivery of ship's stores; and
- Ensuring that ship security communication, information, and equipment are readily available.

Section 9 provides extremely thorough guidance in creating the *SSP*, assigning the final responsibility to the *CSO*—who also must submit it for approval. While an RSO may prepare the plan or review the plan, it may *not* do both. As specified in Part A, the creation of and submission for approval of the *SSP* lies again with the *CSO*. The contents of each ship's *SSP* vary depending on the information gleaned by its *SSA*, on which the Plan is based, addressing physical features and threat vulnerabilities peculiar to that ship. It must be written in English, French, or Spanish and may have a translation to the working language of the crew. An approved *SSP* must always be onboard and should

- Detail the organizational structure of security for the ship;
- Detail the ship's relationships with the company, port facilities, other ships, and relevant authorities with security responsibilities;
- Identify the SSO;
- Identify the CSO and 24-hour contact information;
- Detail the communications systems—internal and with other ships and ports;
- Define in detail the duties of shipboard personnel with security functions;
- Define policies, plans, and procedures for training, drills, and exercises;
- Explain how, when, and under what conditions the ship will interface with the port facility, to include coordination of the DoS;
- Designate and identify restricted areas;
- Define policies and procedures for the inspection, testing, and calibration of security equipment;
- Detail the SSAS, its location, usage, and its access;
- Define the security measures and procedures to be implemented when the ship is at Security Level 1, and additional measures and procedures which will be implemented at Security Levels 2 and 3 with respect to
  - Access control to the ship by crew, passengers, visitors, stevedores, etc., via authorized and unauthorized points;
  - Restricted areas on the ship;
  - Handling of cargo;
  - Delivery of ship's stores;
  - Handling unaccompanied baggage;
  - Monitoring the security of the ship.
- Identify procedures for responding to security threats and security instructions from the contracting governments;
- Define procedures for how and when to report security incidents to contracting governments;
- Detail methods for the *CSO* and/or *SSO* to develop procedures to assess continued effectiveness of the *SSP* and amend Plan, as necessary;
- Identify policies and procedures for reviews and audits of the SSP;
- Define procedures and measures when the ship is at a higher Security Level than a destined port; and
- Identify measures when the ship interfaces with a port of a state that is not a contracting government or is not required to comply with the Code, or a ship which is not covered by the Code.

Section 10 states that *security records* should be available to duly authorized officers of the contracting governments and should be kept in any format but must be protected from unauthorized access or disclosure and stored in a safe place. Accurate and complete record keeping is essential to determine ship and crew readiness and to assist security/safety auditors in their postincident investigations.

Sections 11 and 12 describe the duties and responsibilities of the *CSO* and *SSO*. The company designates a CSO. The CSO can be responsible for the company security operations and the conduct of the SSO. However, the assignment of a designated SSO to each ship must be clearly explained in writing and included in the SSP. The duties of the CSO include ensuring the development, implementation, and modification of SSP, arranging for internal audits and reviews and addressing nonconformities. In addition, the CSO must ensure adequate training of crew. The SSO reports to the CSO, and the SSO's duties include

- Undertaking regular security inspections;
- Maintaining and supervising the implementation of the SSP;
- Coordinating the security aspects of cargo handling;
- Proposing modifications to the SSP;
- Enhancing security awareness;
- Ensuring adequate training to shipboard personnel;
- Documenting and reporting all security incidents;
- Coordinating implementation of the security plan with a CSO;
- Ensuring that security equipment is properly operated, tested, calibrated, and maintained; and
- Interface with the PFSOs.

Section 13 addresses all aspects of security-related *training, drills, and exercises*. The quality and consistency of maritime security training for the CSO, SSO, crew with specific security duties, and other support personnel have a significant impact on the ability of a ship and port to effectively prevent and respond to a terrorist threat and other types of threats and incidents. The requirement to conduct drills and exercises, which have the objectives of ensuring that crew are proficient in their security duties and identifying security deficiencies, is defined in this section. Drills must be conducted once every 3 months and also when more than 25% of the crew has been changed at any one time and they have not participated in a drill in the past 3 months. Drills should test the individual threats to the ship—specifically those threats anticipated in the SSA. Exercises are more strategic in nature and may include participation of the CSO, PFSO, and relevant authorities of contracting governments. Exercises should be conducted once per calendar year (with no more than 18 months between exercises) and should test communications, coordination, resource availability, and response. Exercises may be full-scale or live, table-top simulation, or combined with other exercises held, such as search and rescue exercises.

The CSO and appropriate shore-based personnel should receive training in some or all of the following topics:

- Security administration;
- Relevant international conventions, codes, and recommendations;
- Relevant government legislation and regulations;
- Responsibilities and functions of other security organizations;
- Methodology of the ship security assessment;
- Methods of ship security surveys and inspections;
- Ship and port operations and conditions;
- Ship and port facility security measures;
- Emergency preparedness and response and contingency plans;
- Instruction techniques for security training and education;
- Handling of sensitive security-related information and communications;
- Knowledge of current security threats and patterns;
- Recognition and detection of weapons, dangerous substances, and devices;
- Recognition, on a nondiscriminatory basis, of characteristics and behavioral patterns of persons who are likely to threaten security;
- Techniques used to circumvent security measures;
- Security equipment and systems and their operational limitations;
- Methods of conducting audits, inspection, control, and monitoring;
- Methods of physical searches and nonintrusive inspections;
- Security drills and exercises, including with port facility authorities; and
- Assessment of security drills and exercises.

The SSO should receive training in all the preceding subjects (for CSOs) and some or all of the following topics:

- The layout of the ship;
- The SSP and related procedures;
- Crowd management and control techniques;
- Operations of security equipment and systems; and
- Testing, calibration, and at-sea maintenance of security equipment and systems

Crew with specific security duties have training in and sufficient knowledge of

- Current security threats and patterns;
- Recognition and detection of weapons, dangerous substances, and devices;
- Recognition, on a nondiscriminatory basis, of characteristics and behavioral patterns of persons who are likely to threaten security;
- Techniques used to circumvent security measures;
- Crowd management and control techniques;
- Security-related communications;
- Emergency procedures and contingency plans;
- Operations of security equipment and systems;
- Testing, calibration, and at-sea maintenance of security equipment and systems;

- Inspection, control, and monitoring techniques;
- Methods of physical searches of persons, personal effects, baggage, cargo, and ship's stores.

All other shipboard personnel should receive training in and be familiar with the following topics:

- The meaning and the consequential requirements of the different Security Levels;
- Knowledge of the emergency procedures and contingency plans;
- Recognition and detection of weapons, dangerous substances, and devices;
- Recognition, on a nondiscriminatory basis, of characteristics and behavioral patterns of those who are likely to threaten security;
- Techniques used to circumvent security measures.

Section 15 covers the *port facility security assessment* in much more detail than in Part A, as Part B sets forth many considerations for inclusion to make the PFSA as effective as possible. While it may be conducted by an RSO, approval of a complete assessment should be given only by the relevant contracting government. Personnel involved in conducting a *port facility security assessment* should have expertise in or be able to draw expert assistance in areas relating to

- Ship and port operations;
- Knowledge of current security threats and patterns;
- Recognition and detection of weapons, dangerous substances, and devices;
- Recognition, on a nondiscriminatory basis, of characteristics and behavioral patterns of persons who are likely to threaten security;
- Techniques used to circumvent security measures;
- Methods used to cause a security incident;
- Effects of explosives and structures on port facility services;
- Port facility security;
- Port business practices;
- Contingency planning, emergency preparedness, and response;
- Physical security measures, eg, fences, etc.;
- Radio and telecommunications systems, including computer systems and networks; and
- Transport and civil engineering.

A thorough *PFSA* should address the following elements within the port facility:

- Physical security;
- Structural integrity;
- Personnel protection systems;
- Procedural policies;
- Radio and telecommunication systems, including computer systems and networks;

- Relevant transportation infrastructure;
- Utilities;
- Other areas that may, if damaged or used for illicit observation, pose a risk to persons, property, or operations within the port facility;
- Identification and evaluation of assets and infrastructure, prioritized based on importance, and their impact on port operations if damaged or destroyed, as well as the replacement cost. Assets and infrastructures may include
  - Accesses, entrances, approaches, anchorages, and maneuvering and berthing areas;
  - Cargo facilities, terminals, storage areas, and cargo handling equipment;
  - Electrical distribution systems, radio and telecommunications systems, and computer systems and networks;
  - Port vessel traffic management systems and aids to navigation;
  - Power plants, cargo transfer piping, and water supplies;
  - Bridges, railways, and roads;
  - Port service vessels;
  - Security and surveillance equipment and systems;
  - The waters adjacent to the port facility.
- Identification of possible threats to port assets and infrastructure and their likelihood of occurring, to include the following types of security incidents:
  - Damage to, or destruction of, the port facility or of a ship by explosive devices, arson, sabotage, or vandalism;
  - Hijacking or seizure of a ship or persons onboard;
  - Tampering with cargo, essential ship equipment or systems, or ship's stores;
  - Unauthorized access or usage, including the presence of stowaways;
  - Smuggling weapons or equipment, including weapons of mass destruction;
  - Use of a ship to carry those intending to cause a security incident and their equipment;
  - Use of the ship itself as a weapon or as a means to cause damage or destruction;
  - Blockage of port entrances, locks, approaches, etc.;
  - Nuclear, biological, and chemical attack.
- Evaluation of any particular aspect of the port or calling vessels which make the port a more likely target, capability and intent of those likely to mount such attack, and the possible types of attack;
- Identification of vulnerabilities to port assets and infrastructures and definition and evaluation of security countermeasures and procedures to mitigate these vulnerabilities and potential threats.

Section 16 offers a detailed discussion of the preparation of and content in the PFSP. The PFSP defines, standardizes, and establishes all security policies, plans, procedures, and measures in the port. Each port is different—construction, assets, infrastructure, ships, cargoes, vulnerabilities, risks, threats, security configuration, and response capabilities. With this fact in mind, it's logical that each PFSP would, to some degree, also have port-specific security policies, plans, and procedures. The PFSP should address the threats, vulnerabilities, and mitigation strategies developed in the PFSA and elaborate in detail on

- The security organization of the port facility;
- The organization's links with relevant authorities and the necessary communications systems to allow the effective continuous operation of the organization and its links with others, including ships in port;
- The establishment of all restricted areas and their signage;
- The basic Security Level 1 measures, both operational and physical, that will be in place and additional security measures that will allow the port facility to progress without delay to Security Level 2, and when necessary to Security Level 3 with regard to
    - Access to the port facility;
    - Restricted areas within the port;
    - Handling of cargo;
    - Delivery of ship's stores;
    - Handling unaccompanied baggage;
    - Monitoring the security of the port.
- Scheduling regular review or audit of the *PFSP* for any amendment in response to experience or changing circumstances;
- Reporting procedures to the appropriate contracting government contact points;
- The role and structure of the port facility security organization;
- The duties, responsibilities, and training requirements of all port facility personnel with a security role and the performance measures needed to allow their individual effectiveness to be assessed;
- The port facility security organization's links with other national or local authorities with security responsibilities;
- The communication systems provided to allow effective and continuous communication between port facility security personnel, ships in port and, when appropriate, with national or local authorities with security responsibilities;
- The procedures or safeguards necessary to allow such continuous communications to be maintained at all times;
- The procedures and practices to protect security-sensitive information held in paper or electronic format;
- The procedures to assess the continuing effectiveness of security measures, procedures, and equipment, including identification of, and response to, equipment failure or malfunction;
- The procedures to allow the submission, and assessment, of reports relating to possible breaches of security or security concerns;
- The procedures to maintain, and update, records of dangerous goods and hazardous substances and their location within the port facility;

- The means of alerting and obtaining the services of waterside patrols and special search teams, including bomb searches and underwater searches;
- The procedures for interfacing with ships, to include policies and processes for the issuance/coordination of the DoS;
- The procedures when a ship is at a higher Security Level than the port.

All PFSPs must be approved by the relevant contracting government, and this authority will issue the port facility a "*statement of compliance of a port facility,*" which records the port's compliance with Chapter XI-2 and Part A of the ISPS Code. This statement can be valid for up to 5 years.

Section 18 addresses *training, drills, and exercises on port facility security.* Because ships depend on the training of the security personnel at the port facilities they use, Part B of the Code lists a comprehensive array of training topics for all personnel working in the port. As with ships, the port is required to conduct drills and exercises. Drills and exercises are designed to ensure that port facility personnel are proficient in their security duties and identify security deficiencies. Drills must be conducted once every 3 months and focus on the threats anticipated in the PFSA. Exercises are more strategic in nature and may include participation of relevant authorities of contracting governments, CSOs, and SSOs. Exercises should be conducted once per calendar year (with no more than 18 months between exercises) and should test communications, coordination, resource availability, and response. Exercises may be full-scale or live, table-top simulation, or combined with other exercises held, such as search and rescue exercises.

The PFSO should receive training in some or all of the following topics:

- Security administration;
- Relevant international conventions, codes, and recommendations;
- Relevant government legislation and regulations;
- Responsibilities and functions of other security organizations;
- Methodology of the port facility security assessment;
- Methods of ship and port facility security surveys and inspections;
- Ship and port operations and conditions;
- Ship and port facility security measures;
- Emergency preparedness and response and contingency plans;
- Instruction techniques for security training and education;
- Handling sensitive security-related information and communications;
- Knowledge of current security threats and patterns;
- Recognition and detection of weapons, dangerous substances, and devices;
- Recognition, on a nondiscriminatory basis, of characteristics and behavioral patterns of persons who are likely to threaten security;
- Techniques used to circumvent security measures;
- Security equipment and systems and their operational limitations;

- Methods of conducting audits, inspection, control, and monitoring;
- Methods of physical searches and nonintrusive inspections;
- Security drills and exercises, including with ships; and
- Assessment of security drills and exercise.

Port facility personnel with specific security duties have training in and sufficient knowledge of

- Current security threats and patterns;
- Recognition and detection of weapons, dangerous substances, and devices;
- Recognition, on a nondiscriminatory basis, of characteristics and behavioral patterns of persons who are likely to threaten security;
- Techniques used to circumvent security measures;
- Crowd management and control techniques;
- Security-related communications;
- Emergency procedures and contingency plans;
- Operations of security equipment and systems;
- Testing, calibration, and maintenance of security equipment and systems;
- Inspection, control, and monitoring techniques; and
- Methods of physical searches of persons, personal effects, baggage, cargo, and ship's stores.

All other port facility personnel should receive training in and be familiar with the following topics:

- The meaning and the consequential requirements of the different Security Levels;
- Recognition and detection of weapons, dangerous substances, and devices;
- Recognition, on a nondiscriminatory basis, of characteristics and behavioral patterns of those who are likely to threaten security;
- Techniques used to circumvent security measures.

Amendments to Safety of Life at Sea

The IMO recognized that amendments were needed to the International Convention for the Safety of Life at Sea (SOLAS), enacted in 1974, because SOLAS would provide for a fast-track enactment and implementation vehicle for the ISPS Code, as well as provide the Code with needed technical and policy guidance. Key regulations within SOLAS were amended and/or expanded and a new subchapter was created, titled "Special Measures to Enhance Maritime Security." These additions and modifications to existing regulations are far-reaching, reflecting the IMO's grave concern about terrorist acts and its determination to address all aspects of safety onboard ships and in the ship/port areas, as well as ship/port interface areas. The amendments entered into force on July 1, 2004, simultaneous with the ISPS Code. Let's review important tenets of these amendments.

SOLAS Chapter V, Regulation 19, was revised to require that an *automatic identification system* (AIS) be installed on all ships, other than passenger and tanker ships greater than 300 GT, no later than December 31, 2004. Notwithstanding where international agreements provide for the protection of navigational information, the AIS must be in operation at all times. As way of explanation, the AIS functions similarly to the transponder system utilized by air traffic controllers to track aircraft. The AIS allows international law enforcement agencies and defense departments to better track and monitor the movement of maritime traffic and respond to calls for assistance.

SOLAS Chapter XI-1, Regulation 3, was modified to require that the *ship identification number*, also known as the "IMO Number," be permanently marked on the hull or superstructure, clearly visible, and in contrasting color. In the past, pirate and drug smuggling ships displayed temporary numbers applied with nonpermanent paint, confusing law enforcement authorities by impeding identification. This requirement is designed to promote better tracking and accountability of ship traffic around the world.

SOLAS Chapter XI-1, Regulation 5, is a new regulation and requires that the administration (flag state) issue a *continuous synopsis record* for each ship to which SOLAS applies and that this CSR be maintained onboard the ship. The CSR provides an onboard record of the history of the ship and documents

- The name of the ship, identification number, the name of the state under whose flag it operates, date, port, and the state where it is registered;
- The names of the registered owners and their registered addresses; the names of the registered bareboat charterers and their registered addresses, if applicable;
- The name of the company, its registered address and the addresses from where it carries out its safety-management activities;
- The name of all classification societies with which the ship is classed;
- The names of the administrations or the contracting governments or the recognized organizations which issued the ISM Statement of Compliance, Safety Management Certificate, and the International Ship Security Certificate; and
- The date on which the ship ceased to be registered with that state.

The Continuous Synopsis Record must be kept in English, French, and Spanish and stay with the ship, even if the flag, registry, or ownership changes. It must also be available for inspection onboard ship at all times. This document assists in establishing an audit trail of every ship's activities and management. This regulation assists intelligence, defense, and law enforcement services in tracking and evaluating the activities of ship, its owners, and crew.

SOLAS Chapter XI-2 is new and titled "Special Measures to Enhance Maritime Security." This subchapter establishes definitions related to maritime security and incorporates within the SOLAS Convention key policies and requirements of Part A of the ISPS Code. This new chapter covers the following issues:

Regulation 1 lists a brief glossary of common terms used in the Code and maritime security.

Regulation 2 states that the chapter applies to all ships to which the ISPS Code also applies.

Regulation 3 requires that administrations (flag states) set Security Levels and provide Security Level information to ships flying their flag. Likewise, contracting governments are instructed to set Security Levels for and provide Security Level information to port facilities in their jurisdiction.

Regulation 4 states that "all companies and ships shall comply with Part A of the ISPS Code, taking into account the guidance given in Part B of the ISPS Code" and that ships must comply with Security Levels of the ports, set by the contracting governments.

Regulation 5 requires that companies ensure that the master maintains onboard record and documentation which establishes who is responsible for appointing crew, who decides the employment of the ship, and—if applicable—who are the parties under the terms of a charter party agreement.

Regulation 6 decrees that all ships subject to the Code must have a SSAS installed and that, when activated, the SSAS transmit a ship-to-shore security alert to a competent authority of the administration, indicating the name of the company and name/IMO number of the ship. The alarm is silent onboard the ship, and activation buttons are to be located on the bridge and at least one other location on the ship. The SSAS can be compared to a "home panic alarm," which sends a silent signal to a monitoring center, notifying the police to respond. In the case of the SSAS, when an administration receives notification, the administration will immediately notify the state in the vicinity of the ship.

Regulation 7 tasks contracting governments with providing a point-of-contact for ships to seek advice and assistance and to report security concerns. And, when a risk of attack has been identified, the contracting government is required to advise the affected ships and their administrations of the current Security Level, any measures to be put in place, and security measures that coastal states have decided to implement.

Regulation 8 reiterates that the master has overriding authority and that in cases of a conflict between security and safety the master will give priority to the safety of the ship.

Regulation 9 establishes the different control and registry documents that a contracting government may require from a ship entering its port. If the contracting government has clear grounds for believing the ship is in noncompliance with the Code, then it may require or implement additional security measures, relocate the ship to another location, or deny or expel a ship from the port.

Regulation 10 reaffirms that port facilities participating in international commerce will comply with Part A of the Code, taking into consideration the guidance given in Part B. Contracting governments are tasked with ensuring that PSFAs and PFSPs are conducted, reviewed, and approved and security measures identified in the PFSP are, in fact, implemented.

Regulations 11 and 12 offer contracting governments the options to allow ships or ports under their authority to implement alternative or equivalent security arrangements to those defined in Part A of the Code, as long as these alternative or equivalent security measures are at least as effective as those defined in the Code.

Regulation 13 tasks contracting governments with reporting to the IMO, no later than July 1, 2004, all information of their points-of-contact; port facility details; and a list of approved PFSPs, SSAS monitoring/responding entities, RSO information, and information concerning any approved alternative or equivalent security arrangements.

In sum, the ISPS Code and SOLAS Amendments are the first major international regulations to specifically address ship and port security, and the policies and standards of **Part A** and processes and procedures of **Part B** are a significant step forward for the commercial maritime industry and, if fully implemented, will serve to mitigate threats of terrorism and other criminal activities.

Now, let's briefly review the World Customs Organization's (WCO's) initiative to attempt to standardize customs activities in global commerce.

WCO's Framework of Standards to Secure and Facilitate Global Trade[2]

The WCO has taken a position on supply chain security, due to its belief that international trade is an essential driver for economic prosperity. The global trading system is vulnerable to terrorists' exploitation and therefore capable of damaging the global economy. The WCO believes that customs organizations are uniquely qualified and positioned to provide increased security to the global supply chain. Also, due to the international nature of commerce, the WCO believes that its organization should endorse a strategy to assist in securing the movement of global trading. At the June 2005 World Customs Organization Council Sessions in Brussels, WCO Members adopted the SAFE Framework of Standards to Secure and Facilitate Global Trade. This unique international instrument ushered in modern supply chain security standards and heralded the beginning of a new approach to the end-to-end management of goods moving across borders while recognizing the significance of a closer partnership between Customs and business. The 2007 version of the SAFE Framework incorporated, via a separate document, provisions on the conditions and requirements for Customs and Authorized Economic Operators (AEO), and subsequently this was incorporated into SAFE Framework in 2010. Another revision, in 2012, included new parts 5 and 6 to address Coordinated Border Management and Trade Continuity and Resumption and amplification of Annex I. The June 2015 version of the SAFE Framework, which is the most current, includes:

- A new Pillar 3 to foster closer cooperation between Customs and other government agencies;
- Standards for "Pre-loading Advance Cargo Information (ACI)" (air cargo);
- New definition of "container";
- Updating of the relevant text in view of the development of the WCO Risk Management Compendium Volumes 1 and 2;
- Revised "Guidelines for the Procurement and Deployment of Scanning/NII Equipment;
- New "Guidance Material on Threats and Technology Solutions"; and
- WCO Recommendations Concerning Customs Formalities in Connection with the Temporary Admission of Container Security Devices (CSDs).

According to the WCO, the objectives of the 2015 SAFE Framework are as follows:

- Establish standards that provide supply chain security and facilitation at a global level to promote certainty and predictability.
- Enable integrated and harmonized supply chain management for all modes of transport.
- Enhance the role, functions, and capabilities of Customs to meet the challenges and opportunities of the 21st century.
- Strengthen cooperation between Customs administrations to improve their capability to detect high-risk consignments.
- Strengthen cooperation between Customs administrations and other government agencies involved in international trade and security
- Strengthen Customs/Business cooperation.
- Promote the seamless movement of goods through secure international trade supply chains.

The WCO identifies four core elements of the SAFE Framework, which are as follows:

1. Harmonize the advance electronic cargo information requirements on inbound, outbound, and transit shipments.
2. All countries joining commit to employing a consistent risk management approach to address security threats.
3. The Customs of the export nation will, based upon a comparable risk targeting methodology, perform an outbound inspection of high-risk cargo and/or transport conveyances, preferably using nonintrusive detection equipment such as large-scale X-ray machines and radiation detectors.
4. Customs will provide benefits to businesses that meet minimal supply chain security standards and best practices.

Lastly, in this latest version, WCO identifies three pillars of the SAFE Framework, which are based on the four core elements, and include the Customs-to-Customs network arrangements; Customs-to-Business partnerships; and the Customs-to-other government agencies cooperation.

Now, let's look at key U.S. laws and programs designed to enhance maritime security.

U.S. Laws and Programs

Maritime Transportation Security Act[3]

The MTSA of 2002 was signed into Public Law 107-295 on November 25, 2002, came into force on July 31, and it continues to be the primary law governing maritime security in the United States. There are some 11,000 vessels that arrive yearly in U.S. seaports, which in 2012 carried about 20 million Twenty Foot Equivalent Units (TEUs) (about 10 million FEUs - Forty Foot Equivalent Units) of cargo. The overarching goal of MSTA is to prevent Transportation Security Incidents (TSI), which include Loss of Life,

Environmental Damage, Transportation System Disruption, and Economic Disruption to a Particular Area. Recent modifications to the MTSA either were not passed in Congress (such as in 2010) or make no changes to port and ship security criteria defined in the original 2002 law. The development of the MTSA was the result of terrorist attacks in New York and Washington on September 11, 2001 and extreme concern on the part of the U.S. government that terrorists would target ports and ships in additional attacks. MTSA was developed concurrent with work being performed by the IMO to develop the ISPS Code; however, the United States was concerned about the historically long lead time for IMO legislation—similar ground-breaking conventions and codes occasionally had taken decades to be adopted—and the United States desired to implement a law that had greater reach for domestic ports and trade. In a nutshell, the requirements within the MTSA are similar to the ISPS Code, with the exception that it applies to a large group of vessels and ports, and MTSA has "teeth." In practical implementation, MTSA makes many of the security policies, measures, and procedures in Part A and Part B of the Code mandatory and eliminates the wishy-washy application words like "should" and "some or all." Since the implementation of the MTSA, there have been numerous times when the U.S. Coast Guard has shut down U.S. terminals, detained ships, and even expelled ships or denied access to U.S. ports—quite the contrary from many ports and states of the world that rubber-stamped PFSPs and paid only lip service to the ISPS Code and view the terrorist threat to maritime commerce as a "U.S. problem."

The MTSA applies to any owner or operator of any:

- MODU, cargo, or passenger vessel subject to SOLAS;
- Foreign commercial vessels greater than 100 GT and not subject to SOLAS;
- U.S. flag commercial vessels greater than 100 GT (remember the ISPS applied only to cargo ships of 500 GT or more) and almost all uninspected vessels;
- Passenger vessels certified for 12 passengers or more; and
- Tugs and barges (primarily those with dangerous cargoes).

With respect to ports, the MTSA applies to 361 public terminals and ports (within which there are 3200 independent, regulated facilities), and which mostly are domestic cargo and passenger terminals and ports, including all terminals handling dangerous cargoes.

Additionally, the MTSA:

- Requires each terminal or port to have an approved facility security assessment and facility security plan (FSP). The terminal or port-level FSPs are integrated into an Area Maritime Security Transportation Plan and then at the national level into the National Maritime Security Transportation Plan. This is a departure from the ISPS Code, which simply requires that PFSPs be conducted and approved, but doesn't integrate them into a national strategy.

- Directs the Secretary of Transportation to develop and approve "standardized" curriculum for crew and persons working the ports. This is a far cry from the ISPS Code, which offers a number of topics for training but doesn't require standardized or comprehensive training.
- Codifies the USCG Sea Marshall Program (called Maritime Safety and Security Teams).
- Requires that the AIS be installed on all commercial vessels over 65 feet in length (practically, all commercial vessels that are larger than small fishing boats!).
- Creates standards for container seals and locks.
- Directs the secretary to conduct port facility assessments of foreign ports from which vessels travel to the United States or pose a terrorist threat; provides for training and assistance to foreign ports.
- Requires all U.S. flag vessels that conduct international voyages to comply with the ISPS Code.
- Directs the USCG to create and implement a MARSEC Threat Level system (similar to the ISPS Security Levels) and support communication protocols and response plans and procedures.
- Orders the design and implementation of a transportation identification card (also known as the TWIC)—a biometric ID card for all persons with authorized access to a terminal or port. The issue of the ID to a worker is subject to passing a criminal background investigation. There have been many delays and obstacles with this program and as of September 2015 the program has not been fully implemented.
- The United States Coast Guard, U.S. CBP, Transportation Security Administration (TSA), and Maritime Administration (MARAD) work together as a team in implementing and maintaining the requirements of the MTSA.

There are four *key differences* between the MSTA and the ISPS Code:

1. The ISPS Code applies to passenger ships and cargo ships of 500 gross tons or more that engage in international travel and offshore drilling units. MTSA enlarges the net to include any fixed or floating MODU, all passenger vessels that carry more than 150 passengers, and all cargo vessels—to include tankers and towing vessels—or 100 gross tons or greater that engage in international voyages. MTSA also applies to certain vessels carrying dangerous cargos. So, if a foreign-flag vessel is 100 GTs but less than 500 GTs (and would not be regulated under the ISPS Code definition), she must have a USCG-approved Vessel Security Plan if desiring to call in the U.S. seaport.
2. The MTSA *requires* that regulated vessels and facilities agree upon and sign a DoS before embarking or disembarking of passengers or beginning any cargo handling activities, however, the ISPS Code states that vessels and port facilities be prepared to engage in a DoS if asked or if determined to be necessary by the contracting government. Nevertheless, in many foreign ports, the use of the DoS is the norm.

3. Also, the MTSA defines *facility* as "any structure of any kind located in, on, under, or adjacent to any waters subject to the jurisdiction of the US...," so there can be many facilities—all regulated—within a single port. In fact, in the United States, there are some 3200 regulated facilities within the 361 seaports. Conversely, the ISPS does not refer to a single building or unit and lumps all with a "Port facility." So, in a foreign (non-US) port, there could be five, seven, or more independent facilities which are within the single, regulated "Port"—and but there would be only one PFSP.
4. Lastly, the MTSA requires the SSAS or equivalency for small passenger vessels, 100 GTs or larger, with SOLAS documents. As noted above, the ISPS Code does not regulate passenger vessels under 500 GTs.

Customs-Trade Partnership Against Terrorism[4]

The U.S. government realized that the American economy was the true target of the September 11, 2001 terrorists and in November 2001, U.S. CBP Commissioner Robert C. Bonner introduced the Customs-Trade Partnership Against Terrorism (C-TPAT) program, which was adopted on April 16, 2002. C-TPAT was officially launched with the participation of seven major U.S. companies, which served as charter members and helped start the program. As of 2015, over 10,650 importers, air carriers, sea carriers, rail carriers, brokers, NVOCCs, warehouses and manufacturers, trucking companies, and air freight consolidators/OTIs are signatories to C-TPAT. According to CBP, *C-TPAT Partners now import 54.1% of all good entering the United States.* It is important to appreciate that C-TPAT is just one program in CBP's multilayer cargo security strategy, with the other programs discussed in the pages following this section. In the United States, we imported over $2.38 trillion in goods in 2012 and this has continued to grow in the past few years.

C-TPAT is a voluntary, joint government-business initiative that recognizes that the U.S. CBP can provide the highest level of security only through close cooperation with the ultimate owners of the supply chain. In this program, CBP requires that the businesses implement security policies and procedures to mitigate threats to and ensure the integrity of their supply chain and offers "incentives" for those participants whose security programs are validated by CBP. It is important to note that while C-TPAT is a "voluntary" program, most major U.S. importers (Wal-Mart, Home Depot, Target, Dole Fresh Fruit, etc.) are C-TPAT certified and will not contract a vendor or supplier within their supply chain that is eligible to be a C-TPAT member and is not. This commercial decision by those importers has a greater impact than any law that could be written! There have been cases during the past several years in which stowaways were found onboard commercial cargo ships arriving in the United States, and subsequently CBP threatened to suspend the shipping line's C-TPAT certification. In these cases, the presidents of the shipping lines and an army of lawyers immediately became involved in assuring CBP that an investigation would be immediately conducted and aggressive steps taken to prevent future cases.

Let's review the key elements of the C-TPAT program, focusing on sea carrier requirements and the benefits. Companies must apply and be approved to participate in C-TPAT. Participants complete an online electronic application at the C-TPAT security link portal and submit company information, point-of-contact, a supply chain security profile, and an acknowledgment of an agreement to voluntarily participate. Prior to completing the supply chain security profile, the company must conduct a comprehensive *Security Risk Assessment* (self-assessment) of its supply chain security procedures, using the C-TPAT security criteria or guidelines jointly developed by CBP and the trade community for their specific enrollment category. The Assessment must define a mitigation solution or corrective actions/measures to address each of the identified vulnerabilities and risks. The criteria areas in the Assessment include business partner requirements, procedural security, physical security, personnel security, education and training, access controls, manifest procedures, information security, and conveyance security. The company representative completing the profile must address, in narrative format, each of these criteria areas. Upon completion and submission of the application, a CBP supply chain security specialist (SCSS) will review and approve or reject each section of the profile. Any areas "rejected" must be corrected and amplified as necessary. It is worth noting that CBP has prepared a detailed "C-TPAT Supply Chain Security Best Practices Catalog," which shares security policies, procedures, and measures that have been found to be effective, and also the "C-TPAT Security Criteria," which is used to complete the security profile. CBP has up to 90 days to approve or reject an application. If approved, CBP will conduct a validation of the Profile/Assessment within one year of the Certification.

C-TPAT Security Criteria for Sea Carriers

Sea carriers must conduct a comprehensive assessment of their security practices based on the following C-TPAT minimum-security criteria. Where a sea carrier does not control a specific element of the cargo transportation service it has contracted to provide, such as marine terminal operator or a time-chartered vessel with whom it has contracted, the sea carrier must work with these business partners to seek to ensure that pertinent security measures are in place and adhered to. The sea carrier is responsible for exercising prudent oversight for all cargo loaded onboard its vessel, pursuant to applicable law and regulations and the terms of this program.

C-TPAT recognizes the complexity of international supply chains and security practices, and endorses the application and implementation of security measures based on risk. Therefore, the program allows for flexibility and the customization of security plans based on the member's business model. Security measures, as listed throughout this document, must be implemented and maintained as appropriate to the carrier's business model and risk understanding. CBP's C-TPAT validation process will include a review of the carrier's assessment and program.

C-TPAT recognizes that sea carriers are already subject to defined security mandates created under the ISPS Code and the MTSA. It is not the intention of C-TPAT to duplicate these vessel and facility security requirements; rather, C-TPAT seeks to build on the ISPS and MTSA foundation and require additional security measures and practices which enhance the overall security throughout the international supply chain.

Continued

C-TPAT Security Criteria for Sea Carriers—cont'd

ISPS and MTSA compliance are prerequisites for C-TPAT sea carrier membership, and only vessels in compliance with the applicable ISPS code requirements may be utilized by C-TPAT members. Marine terminals operated by C-TPAT members must also comply with ISPS code requirements. The physical access controls and physical security provisions of these criteria are satisfied for ISPS-regulated vessels and port facilities by those vessels' or facilities' compliance with the ISPS Code and Coast Guard regulations.

Business Partner Requirements

Sea carriers must have written and verifiable procedures for the screening of carrier's agents and service providers contracted to provide transportation services for the carrier. Sea carriers must also have screening procedures for new customers, beyond financial soundness issues to include indicators of whether the customer appears to be a legitimate business and/or poses a security risk. Sea carriers will also have procedures to review their customers' requests that could affect the safety of the vessel or the cargo or otherwise raise significant security questions, including unusual customer demands, such as specific stowage placement aboard the vessel (beyond a request for below-deck or on-deck stowage).

Security Procedures

Sea carriers must have written or web-based procedures for screening new customers to whom they issue bills of lading, which identify specific factors or practices, the presence of which would trigger additional scrutiny by the sea carrier, up to and including a detailed physical inspection of the exterior of the suspect customer's container prior to loading onto the vessel. These procedures may also include a referral to CBP or other competent authorities for further review. CBP will work in partnership with the sea carriers to identify specific information regarding what factors, practices, or risks are relevant.

Sea carriers should ensure that contract vessel services providers commit to C-TPAT security recommendations. Periodic reviews of the security commitments of the service providers should be conducted.

Container Security

For all containers in the sea carrier's custody, container integrity must be maintained to protect against the introduction of unauthorized material and/or persons. Sea carriers must have procedures in place to maintain the integrity of the shipping containers while in their custody. A high security seal must be affixed to all loaded containers bound for the United States. All seals used or distributed by the sea carrier must meet or exceed the current PAS ISO 17712 standards for high security seals.

Sea carriers and/or their marine terminal operators must have processes in place to comply with seal verification rules and seal anomaly reporting requirements once promulgated and mandated by the U.S. government.

- Container Inspection

The requirement to inspect all containers prior to stuffing (to include the reliability of the locking mechanisms of the doors) is placed on the importers through the C-TPAT Minimum Security Criteria for Importers dated March 25, 2005. Sea carriers must visually inspect all U.S.-bound empty containers, including the interior of the container, at the foreign port of lading.

- Container Seals

Written procedures must stipulate how seals in the sea carrier's possession are to be controlled. Procedures should also exist for recognizing and reporting compromised seals and/or containers to U.S. CBP or the appropriate foreign authority consistent with the seal anomaly reporting requirements once promulgated and mandated by the U.S. government.

- Container Storage

The sea carrier must store containers in its custody in a secure area to prevent unauthorized access and/or manipulation. Procedures must be in place for reporting detected, unauthorized entry into containers or container storage areas to appropriate local law enforcement officials.

Physical Access Controls

The sea carrier will establish access controls to prevent unauthorized entry to its vessels and cargo facilities, maintain control of employees and visitors, and protect company assets. Access controls must include the positive identification of all employees, visitors, service providers, government officials, and vendors at all restricted access points of entry. Shore employees and service providers should have access only to those areas of the vessel where they have legitimate business. Vessel and facility access controls are governed by the International Ship and Port Security Code and MTSA. The Physical Access Control provisions of these criteria are satisfied for ISPS-regulated vessels and port facilities by those vessels' or facilities' compliance with the ISPS Code and MTSA regulations.

- Boarding and Disembarking of Vessels

Consistent with the vessel's ISPS security plan, all crew, employees, vendors and visitors may be subject to a search when boarding or disembarking vessels. A vessel visitor log must be maintained and a temporary visitor pass must be issued as required by the vessel's security plan. All crew members, employees, vendors, and visitors, including government officials, must display proper identification, as required by the applicable ISPS/MTSA security plan.

- Employees

An employee identification system must be in place for positive identification and access control purposes. Employees should be given access only to those secure areas needed for the performance of their duties. Company management or security personnel must adequately control the issuance and removal of employee, visitor, and vendor identification badges. Procedures for the issuance, removal, and changing of access devices (eg, keys, key cards, etc.) must be documented.

- Visitors/Vendors/Service Providers

Visitors, vendors, government officials, and service providers must present photo identification for documentation purposes upon arrival at carrier's vessels or cargo facilities, and a visitor log must be maintained. Measures described by the approved ISPS/MTSA security plan addressing the escort of visitors and service providers, including, when appropriate, the use of temporary identification will be followed.

- Challenging and Removing Unauthorized Persons

Procedures must be in place to identify, challenge, and address unauthorized/unidentified persons.

Continued

C-TPAT Security Criteria for Sea Carriers—cont'd

Personnel Security

In compliance with applicable laws and regulations for that location, written and verifiable processes must be in place to screen prospective employees and to periodically check current employees.

- Preemployment Verification

Application information such as employment history and references must be verified prior to employment.

- Background Checks/Investigations

Depending on the sensitivity of the position, background checks and investigations will be conducted for prospective employees as appropriate and as required by foreign, federal, state, and local regulations. Once employed, periodic checks and reinvestigations should be performed based on cause and/or the sensitivity of the employee's position.

- Personnel Termination Procedures

Companies must have procedures in place to remove identification, facility, and system access for terminated employees.

- Crewmen Control—Deserter/Absconder Risk

CBP will work with the U.S. Coast Guard and sea carriers to identify specific factors which may indicate when a crewman poses a potential risk of desertion/absconding. When such factors are identified and provided to the carriers, the carrier will provide this information to its vessel masters and to the vessels under charter to the carrier, and such vessels will establish procedures to address the potential risk of desertion/absconding. Added security measures appropriate to the risk present should be employed on arrival into the U.S. port/territories.

- Deserter/Absconder Notifications

Vessel masters must account for all crewmen prior to the vessel's departure from the U.S. port. If the vessel master discovers that a crewman has deserted or absconded, the vessel master must report this finding by the most practical means to CBP immediately upon discovery and prior to the vessel's departure.

Procedural Security

Security measures must be in place to ensure the integrity and security of processes relevant to the transportation, handling, and storage of cargo. Consistent with the carrier's ISPS Code security plan, procedures must be in place to prevent unauthorized personnel from gaining access to the vessel. In those geographic areas where risk assessments warrant checking containers for human concealment in containers, such procedures should be designed to address the particular, identified risk at the load port or the particular port facility. CBP will inform the sea carriers when it is aware of a high risk of human concealment or stowaways at particular ports or geographic regions. Documented procedures must also include predeparture vessel security sweeps for stowaways at the foreign load port and during normal watch activity while en route to the United States as warranted by risk conditions at the foreign load port.

- Passenger and Crew

Sea carriers must ensure compliance with the U.S. Coast Guard Notice of Arrival and Departure requirements so that accurate, timely, and advanced transmission of data associated with international passengers and crew is provided to the U.S. government and CBP.

- Bill of Lading/Manifesting Procedures

Procedures must be in place to ensure that the information in the carrier's cargo manifest accurately reflects the information provided to the carrier by the shipper or its agent and is filed with CBP in a timely manner. Documentation control must include safeguarding computer access and information.

Bill of lading information filed with CBP should show the first foreign port (place) where the sea carrier takes possession of the cargo destined for the United States.

- BAPLIEs

At the request of CBP, sea carriers will provide a requested bayplan/stowageplan occupied and empty locations message (BAPLIE) and/or stowage plan, in a format readily available. Such requests will be made on a voyage-specific basis when CBP requires additional voyage information and will be honored by the sea carrier in a timely manner. CBP recognizes that these are not regulated documents and that the data included may not always match the manifest filing.

- Cargo

Customs and/or other appropriate law enforcement agencies must be notified if illegal or highly suspicious activities are detected, as appropriate.

Security Training and Awareness

A security awareness program should be established and maintained by the carrier to recognize and foster awareness of security vulnerabilities to vessels and maritime cargo. Employees must be made aware of the procedures the sea carrier has in place to report a security concern or incident.

Additionally, specific training should be offered to assist employees in maintaining vessel and cargo integrity, recognizing internal conspiracies, and protecting access controls.

Physical Security

Carriers shall establish written and verifiable procedures to prevent unauthorized personnel from gaining access to its vessels, including concealment in containers, and to prevent tampering with cargo conveyances while they are in the carrier's custody. Such measures are covered by a vessel's and a port facility's ISPS security plan. Physical security provisions of these criteria are satisfied for ISPS-regulated vessels and port facilities by those vessels' or facilities' compliance with the ISPS Code and MTSA regulations. Non-ISPS Code regulated cargo handling and storage facilities and container yards operated by the carrier, in domestic and foreign locations, must have physical barriers and deterrents that guard against unauthorized access. Sea carriers should incorporate the following C-TPAT physical security criteria as applicable.

Continued

C-TPAT Security Criteria for Sea Carriers—cont'd

- Fencing

Perimeter fencing should enclose the areas around cargo handling and storage facilities, container yards, and terminals. All fencing must be regularly inspected for integrity and damage.

- Gates and Gate Houses

Gates through which vehicles and/or personnel enter or exit must be manned and/or monitored and secured when not in use.

- Parking

Private passenger vehicles should be prohibited from parking in or adjacent to cargo handling and storage areas and vessels.

- Building Structure

Buildings must be constructed of materials that resist unlawful entry. The integrity of structures must be maintained by periodic inspection and repair.

- Locking Devices and Key Controls

All external and internal windows, gates, and fences must be secured with locking devices. Management or security personnel must control the issuance of all locks and keys.

- Lighting

Adequate lighting must be provided inside and outside the facility including the following areas: entrances and exits, cargo handling and storage areas, fence lines, and parking areas. While at port, the pier and waterside of the vessel must be adequately illuminated.

- Alarms Systems and Video Surveillance Cameras

At those locations determined appropriate by the carrier's risk assessment, alarm systems and video surveillance cameras should be utilized to monitor premises and prevent unauthorized access to vessels, cargo handling, and storage areas.

Information Technology Security

- Password Protection

Automated systems must use individually assigned accounts that require a periodic change of password. IT security policies, procedures, and standards must be in place and provided to employees in the form of training.

- Accountability

A system must be in place to identify the abuse of IT including improper access, tampering, or the altering of business data. All system violators must be subject to appropriate disciplinary actions for abuse.

Security Assessment, Response, and Improvement

Carriers and CBP have a mutual interest in security assessments and improvements and recognize that specific, implemented security procedures may be found in the future to have weaknesses or be subject to circumvention. When a security shortcoming or security incident is identified, the carrier and CBP officials will meet in an effort to ascertain what led to the breakdown and to formulate mutually agreed remedial measures. If CBP determines that the security incident raises substantial concerns or a security weakness requires substantial remediation, CBP headquarters officials will meet with the carrier's senior management to discuss such concerns and to identify appropriate remedial measures to be taken.

While CBP has the authority to suspend or remove a sea carrier from the C-TPAT program for substantial noncompliance with the security criteria of the program, such authority is exercised only in the most serious circumstances.

The last step in the process is the validation of the participant's security profile, which is needed to ensure the accuracy of the information and verify that the stated security measures are actually in place. C-TPAT participants are given approximately 30 days' advanced written notice along with a request for any supporting documentation that is needed. A validation team consisting of C-TPAT SCSSs and a representative of the C-TPAT participant will conduct the C-TPAT validation visits. Prior to the commencement of the validation, the C-TPAT SCSS team will review the participant's C-TPAT security profile, any supplemental information received from the company, and any CBP headquarters instructions, to determine the intended scope of the validation. A validation visit is a detailed review of the participant's import supply chain security procedures to determine whether sufficient security procedures are in place to meet current C-TPAT guidelines or criteria. The specific sites of the validation visits are be determined based on the C-TPAT SCSS validation risk analysis and coordinated with the C-TPAT participant representative.

A validation may require multiple visits at foreign locations. The visits are usually performed in no more than a day per visit location. Validation visit findings are documented in a validation report and forwarded to the C-TPAT participant. The report findings will identify supply chain security recommendations or best practices. If significant supply chain security weaknesses or recommendations are found, a participant's C-TPAT benefits may be suspended or removed depending on the circumstances. If a company has its C-TPAT benefits suspended, C-TPAT will recommend that the company implements an action plan containing corrective actions to address specific supply chain security weaknesses.

C-TPAT and Foreign Customs Mutual Recognition Agreements

C-TPAT Partners also have the opportunity to be recognized as a *Trusted Trade Partner* by Foreign Customs participating in the Mutual Recognition Agreement program—thereby reducing cargo examinations and inspections at ports of export and importation. According to CBP, Mutual Recognition occurs when two Customs Administrations agree that the security requirements or standards of one program, as well as its validation or audit procedures, are equivalent to those of the other program, leading both Customs Administrations to recognize the validation findings of each other's programs. As of September 2013, CBP has signed seven Mutual Recognition Arrangements with top trading nations, to include New Zealand, Canada, Jordan, Japan, Korea, European Union, and Taiwan. Discussions are ongoing with Customs Administrations of China, Israel, Singapore, Mexico, and Switzerland. Combined, these 12 nations represent 53% of all trade with the United States in 2013.[5]

C-TPAT Benefits

What are the benefits for a company to be a partner in C-TPAT? The most recent analytical survey was conducted by the University of Virginia's Center of Survey Research in 2010, a follow-up of their initial survey in 2007, with 3901 C-TPAT Partners responding with feedback. According to the survey results, the C-TPAT Partners reported that:

- Benefits outweighed or equaled the affiliated costs
- There was an improved work force security and decreased disruptions to the supply chain
- Carriers experienced a decreased wait time for release cargo by CBP
- Decreased time in CBP inspection lines and increased predictability in moving goods
- 87.6% agreed that their ability to assess and manage supply chain risk has been strengthened as a result of joining C-TPAT.[6]

This holistic security approach provides the U.S. government and the company owners with a comprehensive examination of the organization's business processes and operations. The intention is to successfully identify and reduce security vulnerabilities that could allow a terrorist organization to successfully attack and destroy commercial and public assets. C-TPAT is one of the four prongs of CBP's efforts focused on securing the maritime cargo supply chain, with the other two being the 24-hour Advance Manifest Rule and Container Security Initiative (CSI).

24-Hour Advance Manifest Rule, Container Security Initiative, and the Importer Security Filing

Effective December 2, 2002, U.S. CBP enacted a new rule, the "*24-Hour Advance Manifest Rule*," which requires carriers to transmit to CBP in the port of unlading a copy of the cargo manifest no less than 24 hours in advance of the cargo being loaded. In practice, most shipping lines now are closing their cargo booking 48 hours prior to container lading, which allows a time cushion of 24 hours before the required reporting to CBP. Automated NVOCCs and Shipping Lines file their manifests directly via the Automated Manifest System (which is in the process of being fully replaced by ACE in late 2016). This initiative is in support of the CSI program and permits CBP teams in CSI ports adequate opportunity to evaluate and screen all cargo container documentation for indicators of heightened risk—while still at the foreign port of lading.

In January 2002, U.S. CPB launched the "*Container Security Initiative*," whose goal is to prevent global containerized cargo, specifically those destined for the United States, from being exploited or manipulated by terrorists. The initiative is designed to enhance the security of the sea cargo container—a vital link in global trade. U.S. CBP CSI teams work in the host country with host governments to identify and target for prescreening containers that may pose a risk for terrorism. Host governments conduct the inspections while the U.S. CSI team observes. Low-risk and CSI prescreened containers enter the U.S. ports without additional delay, unless more information dictates otherwise.

As of 2013, CSI is operational at 58 ports in North, Central, and South America; the Caribbean; Europe; Africa; the Middle East; and throughout Asia. The four core elements of CSI are

- *Identify high-risk containers.* CBP uses automated targeting tools to identify containers that pose a potential risk for terrorism, based on advanced information and strategic intelligence.
- *Prescreen and evaluate containers before they are shipped.* Containers are screened as early in the supply chain as possible, *generally at the port of departure.*
- *Use technology* to prescreen high-risk containers to ensure that screening can be done rapidly without slowing down the movement of trade. This technology includes large-scale X-ray and gamma ray machines and radiation detection devices.
- *Use smarter, more secure containers,* which will allow CBP officers at U.S. ports of arrival to identify containers that have been tampered with during transit.

There are several benefits provided by the CSI program. The program significantly increases the ability to intercept containers that may pose a risk for terrorism before they reach U.S. shores and increases the security of the global trading system. CSI also facilitates a smooth movement of legitimate trade while simultaneously protecting port infrastructures.

The fourth component of CBP's multilayered cargo supply chain security strategy is the *Importer Security Filing* and Additional Carrier Requirement. This rule came into effect in January, 2009, and in the trade is known as the "10+2 Rule." This rule applies to all cargo arriving via maritime conveyance and requires that the carrier or agent (customs broker, etc.) provide certain cargo information 24 hours in advance of the cargo or container being loaded onboard the ship at the port of export. The additional information to be submitted includes:

1. Seller (if different from shipper)
2. Buyer (if different from consignee)
3. Importer of record number

4. Consignee number(s)
5. Manufacturer (or supplier)
6. Ship-to-party (if different from consignee)
7. Country of origin
8. Six digit HTSUS (Harmonized Tariff Schedule of the United States) number
9. Container stuffing location
10. Consolidator (stuffer)

Additionally, for all FROB (Freight Remaining on Board—cargo transiting U.S. ports for discharge at foreign locations), IE (Import to U.S. and immediate Export), and TE (Cargo importing to U.S., transiting U.S. for ultimate foreign export), there are additional five elements that need to be submitted through the shipping line, 24 hours prior to cargo load at the foreign port of loading as hereunder:

- Booking party
- Foreign port of unlading
- Place of delivery
- Ship-to-party
- Commodity HTSUS

Secure Freight Initiative

An important program underway in limited foreign seaports is the "*Secure Freight Initiative*" (SFI), a joint effort of Department of Homeland Security and the Department of Energy's National Nuclear Security Administration (NNSA). The SFI, announced in December 2006, was mandated by Congress in the SAFE Port Act of 2006. DHS has always been worried about a poor man's missile—a terrorist hiding a nuclear weapon or other WMD in a container destined for the U.S. port. "Our highest priority and greatest sense of urgency has to be aimed at preventing a nuclear weapon or dirty bomb attack against the homeland," said DHS Secretary Michael Chertoff at the time of the enactment.[7]

SFI deploys integrated nuclear detection devices, X-ray or gamma ray imagining machines, and container identifying optical character recognition devices to a small number of foreign seaports. This equipment scans for nuclear and radiological material. The pilot program is testing the feasibility of inspecting 100% of U.S.-bound containers at foreign ports. As of 2015, the SFI program currently is operational in Port Qasim, Pakistan, Puerto Cortes, Honduras, and Southampton, UK. A limited program footprint (small amount of scanning equipment) has also been set up in the port of Salalah, Oman, the port of Singapore, and the Port of Busan, South Korea. The concept is that data collected during the scanning will be transmitted in near real time to CBP personnel in foreign ports and the DHS National Targeting Center. Again, as with the CSI goal, SFI's objective is to provide alert information for investigation and resolution in the foreign ports, and prior to the cargo being loaded on U.S.-bound ships.

Safe Port Act of 2006

The **Security and Accountability for Every Port Act of 2006** (SAFE Port Act) was passed by the U.S. House of Representatives on May 4, 2006. It was signed into law by President Bush on October 13, 2006. The Safe Port Act of 2006 is a logical extension of the Maritime Transportation Act of 2002. The SAFE Port Act created and codified programs and initiatives and amended some of the original provisions of MTSA. The act included provisions that codified CBP's CSI and the C-TPAT; required that all containers entering high-volume U.S. ports be scanned for radiation sources by December 31, 2007 (the SFI and Megaports Initiatives); set an implementation schedule and fee restrictions for the Transportation Worker Identification Credential (TWIC); and established port security interagency operational centers at all high-risk ports.

The Megaports Initiative and the SFI, discussed earlier, address the requirement in the act to scan containers for radiation sources. The Megaports Initiative, a program administered by the Department of Energy's National Nuclear Security Administration, works with foreign governments to install specialized radiation detection equipment in order to deter, detect, and interdict illicit shipments of nuclear and other radioactive materials. The Megaports Initiative has completed deployments of radiation detection equipment at six international seaports and is at various stages of implementation in 12 additional countries around the world.

The TWIC program, also codified in the SAFE Port Act, is a TSA and U.S. Coast Guard initiative. The TWIC program provides a tamper-resistant biometric credential to maritime workers requiring unescorted access to secure areas of port facilities, outer continental shelf facilities, and vessels regulated under the MTSA, and all U.S. Coast Guard credentialed merchant mariners. An estimated 750,000 individuals will require TWICs. Enrollment and issuance will take place over an 18-month period. To obtain a TWIC, an individual must provide biographic and biometric information such as fingerprints, sit for a digital photograph, and successfully pass a security threat assessment conducted by TSA. The TWIC regulations will be split into two phases. Phase 1 relates to the issuance of TWIC cards and began in March 2007. Card issuance will be done on a rolling basis, predicated on the timeline provided in the SAFE Port Act. That schedule dictated that the 10 highest priority U.S. ports, as designated by the Homeland Security Secretary, must begin issuing cards no later than July 1, 2007. The 40 U.S. ports that are next in order of priority must begin issuing cards by January 1, 2008, and all other U.S. ports must begin issuing cards by January 1, 2009. Mariners will have until September 25, 2008, to get TWICs. The DHS, however, may implement the TWIC card issuance process more quickly. TWIC phase 2 relates to card readers and other facility requirements. The final requirements for phase 2 have not been released. A second comment period for the reader requirements will take place, and a card reader pilot program will commence, before ports will have to install readers. DHS may also provide an approved reader technology list for port facilities to use. The SAFE Port Act of 2006 requires regulations for facilities to become effective January 2009.

The U.S. Coast Guard has met the April 1, 2007, deadline mandated by the SAFE Port Act of 2006 to track all large commercial vessels within U.S. waters. "Using the full range of classified and unclassified vessel tracking information available to the Coast Guard, we are meeting all vessel tracking requirements of the act," said Admiral Thad Allen, commandant of the Coast Guard. "Beyond the SAFE Port Act, we need to focus our attention on closing other gaps in maritime security, including long-range tracking of vessels outside U.S. waters and coming to grips with potential threats posed by smaller vessels. While we have done a lot since the terrorist attacks of 9/11,

Continued

Safe Port Act of 2006—cont'd

we need to build a maritime security architecture that does more than just simply react to the last threat or terrorist event".[8] The Coast Guard is working with the IMO, the recreational boating community, small commercial vessel operators, and others to close existing gaps in maritime security. The IMO's long-range identification and tracking system will provide an unclassified system for tracking more than 40,000 ships worldwide by the end of 2008. The United States will be able to obtain tacking information for ships navigating within 1000 nautical miles of the coast under the new system.

The SAFE Port Act also called for establishing interagency operational centers at all high-risk ports in the United States within 3 years. Three ports currently have such centers, which are designed to have a unified command structure that can act on a variety of incidents ranging from possible terrorist attacks to search and rescue and environmental response operations.

The Safe Ports Act of 2006 is a noble effort by U.S. elected officials and federal agencies to more effectively protect our ports by investing in an integrated and international maritime security strategy. It appears that U.S. agencies are successfully meeting their compliance deadlines as part of collective efforts to make our nation safer and more secure. These initiatives along with increased CBP and Coast Guard personnel, resources, and assets—as well as the creation of the Domestic Nuclear Detection Office—have pushed our layered defenses overseas and substantially increased security at America's ports since September 11, 2001.

Summary

The international and U.S. laws and program we have examined have a common theme. Each of them is designed to protect the supply chain of international commerce from terrorism and criminal activity. International economies depend on a safe and secure maritime industry to facilitate global trade. For that reason, there must be an international standardization of port and SSPs, policies, measures, and procedures. The maritime security measures mandated by international and U.S. laws and encouraged by other international organizations require the maritime industry to make a significant investment of time, effort, and financial resources to protect our economies and our civilizations. But, both governments and private industry must embrace and fully implement the laws and programs and their tenets if we are to mitigate threats to the cargo supply chain.

Suggested Additional Regulations for Review by U.S. FSOs

1. 6 CFR Part 25 (Safety Act—support use of technologies to fight terrorism)
2. 6 CFR Part 27 (Chemical Facility Anti-Terrorism)
3. 6 CFR Part 29 (Procedures for Handling Critical Infrastructure Information)
4. 21 CFR Parts 1 and 11 (Bio-Terrorism–FDA)
5. 33 CFR Part 101 (MARSEC Directives)

6. 33 CFR Part 102 (Set-aside)
7. 33 CFR Part 103 (Area Maritime Security Committee)
8. 33 CFR Part 104 (Vessel Security)
9. 33 CFR Part 105 (Facility Security)
10. 33 CFR Part 106 (Outer Continental Shelf Security)
11. 33 CFR Part 126 (Handling of Class 1 (Explosives) materials or Certain Dangerous Cargo)
12. 46 CFR Part 4 (Maritime Casualties and Investigations by the USCG)
13. 49 CFR (Hazardous Materials)
14. 49 CFR Part 1520 (Sensitive Security Information)
15. Maritime Security Directives (MARSEC Directives)
16. Navigational Inspection Circular (NVIC)

End Notes

1. http://www.imo.org/Safety/mainframe.asp?topic_id=583&doc_id=2689
2. http://www.wcoomd.org/en/topics/facilitation/instrument-and-tools/tools/safe_package.aspx
3. http://www.uscg.mil/hq/g-m/mp/pdf/MTSA.pdf
4. http://www.cbp.gov/xp/cgov/import/commercial_enforcement/ctpat/
5. http://www.cbp.gov/sites/default/files/documents/C-TPAT%20Program%20Benefits%20Guide.pdf
6. Ibid.
7. http://www.cbp.gov/xp/cgov/border_security/secure_freight_initiative/
8. http://www.cbp.gov/xp/cgov/border_security/international_activities/csi/

5

Vulnerabilities in the Cargo Supply Chain

OBJECTIVES

After studying this chapter, you will be familiar with

1. The key security vulnerabilities of the links in the supply chain of ocean cargoes;
2. The impact of a serious maritime incident, such as a terrorist attack in a U.S. seaport, on the U.S. economy, or in the cargo supply chain;
3. The security policies and procedures which have proven successful in antinarcotics smuggling programs established by maritime shipping companies and private seaports;
4. Recommended physical security measures, monitoring and detection systems, procedural security standards, and personnel security practices at each phase in the cargo supply chain;
5. The history, impact, and types of cargo theft;
6. Internal conspiracies and techniques used by criminal and terrorist elements to circumvent security;
7. The types, usage, and tactics for defeating container seals.

Introduction

The cargo supply chain which transports the products we eat, wear, drive, and utilize daily is vulnerable to penetration and unauthorized access by criminal and terrorist elements; therefore, aggressive security procedures and countermeasures are necessary in order to mitigate the threats posed by these elements. Cargo thieves, stowaways, pirates, drug smugglers, and terrorists constantly attempt to negate, circumvent, or manipulate security measures designed to protect the cargo in the supply chain. The supply chain is made up of various "links," which may span the globe and pass through several countries. For example, a product supply chain may start at a textile factory in an industrial park in China. Once ready for export, the cargo is loaded into a 40-ft container and transported by truck to a marine terminal in Shanghai, China. There, the cargo container is placed onboard a feeder vessel that sails to the port of Nagoya, Japan. In Japan, the cargo container is discharged from the small vessel and then reloaded to another larger vessel (on a different shipping line), which carries some 9000 other 40-ft containers. This vessel transports container across the Pacific Ocean to the port of Balboa, Panama, is disembarked, and placed on a Panama Canal Railway railcar and transported across the isthmus to Manzanillo International Terminal—Panama, on the Caribbean side of the Panama Canal. At Manzanillo, the container is discharged from the vessel, staged in the port, and then reloaded to another "feeder-size" vessel (again, another shipping line) and transported to the port of

Maritime Security.

Houston, Texas. At the U.S. port, the container is drayed to the rail link, loaded on a flat car, and transported by train to a rail hub in Kansas City. In Kansas City, the container of Chinese-origin cargo is placed on a chassis and trucked to a merchandise distribution center (such as Wal-Mart, Kmart, Target, Home Depot, etc.) in Indiana. At the distribution center, the container is stripped, cargo staged in the center, and then reloaded into contract trailers for ferrying to stores in the region (see Fig. 5.1). As one can see, literally hundreds of persons may participate in the movement of this or any other cargo shipment from point of production to arrival at final destination. In this chapter, we discuss key vulnerabilities in the different links in the cargo supply chain, offer security recommendations, and focus on a few special vulnerabilities in the maritime environment.

Vulnerabilities and Their Potential Impact

The security threats to the different links in the supply chain, their vulnerabilities, and the postincident impact vary greatly and depend on the type of criminal or terrorist activity and intended target, the location in the supply chain, and the ability of the link's security program to deter, detect, or contain the security breach. In subsequent chapters, we discuss in detail the tactics and techniques of cargo thieves, stowaways, drug smugglers, terrorists, and other criminal elements. For now, let's acknowledge that cargo theft, stowaway incidents, drug smuggling, and in some cases piracy are serious problems for the commercial businesses involved in the product supply chain and in the end cost the consumers of the world billions of dollars annually in passed-on losses. However, the targeting of the supply chain by terrorists—because of the potential ramifications—is viewed with great concern by governments, specifically the United States. Each entity that is a link in the cargo supply chain—whether manufacturer, warehouse, carrier, AFC/OTI/NVOCC, broker, or importer—is a potential target of terrorists. Terrorist organizations could use the global trade network to transport or deliver a weapon of mass destruction (WMD, whether chemical, biological, radiological, or nuclear) into the United States or another target country via cargo or a shipping container; just as they have in the past used these same transport methods to move conventional explosives, other terror equipment and devices, and personnel. Terrorists may want to penetrate or negate a company's security controls for the purpose of placing a terrorist device inside U.S.-bound cargo or its container, or the terrorists' cargo may actually be a "terrorist" utilizing the cargo, container, or conveyance as a means of entering the United States undetected. Terrorists may also intend to "taint" the cargo with a biological or chemical agent or poison for the purpose of causing harm to the innocent persons handling the product or the ultimate consumer or to cause widespread panic.

You may remember several years ago there were two high profile cases, one involving the tainting of Chilean grapes and the other being the targeting of Tylenol products. These cases cost the companies tens of millions of dollars and actually changed the way most medicines and many food products are packaged and shipped. Imagine the economic and human cost to our nation if a cargo shipment was tainted with a biological or chemical agent (weapon of mass destruction). The port, shipping line, and the entire cargo

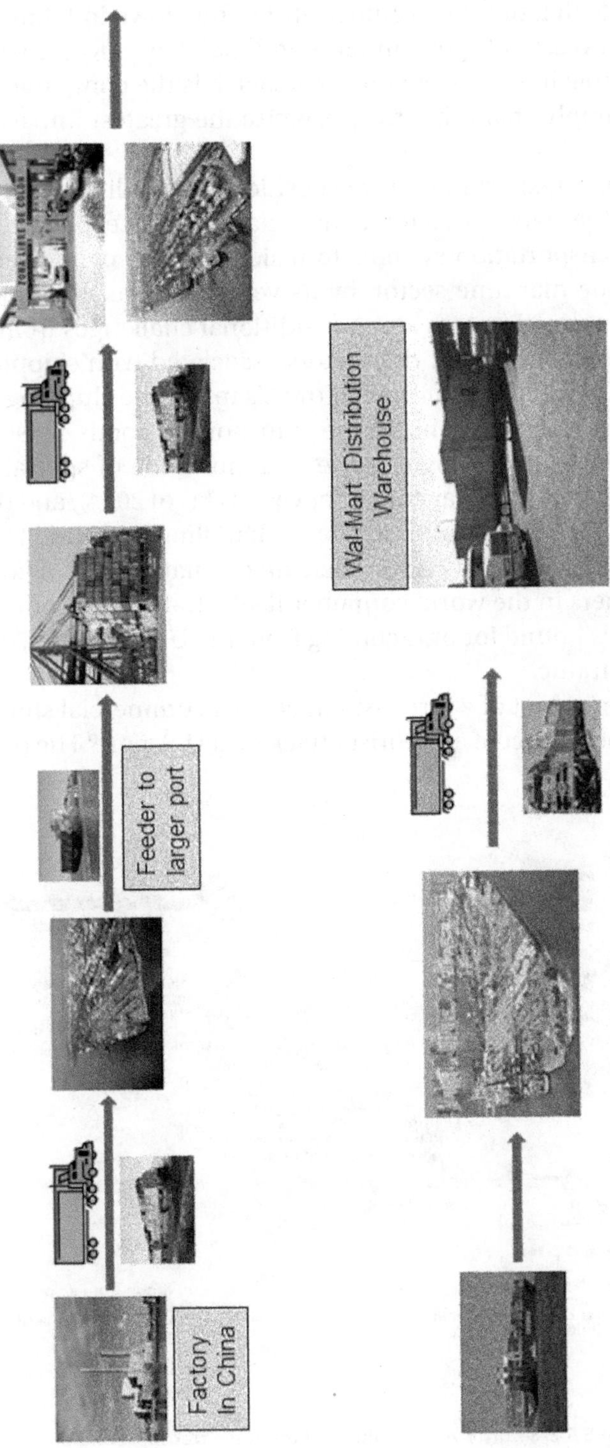

FIGURE 5.1 A typical cargo supply chain incorporates various modes of transport, multiple transhipments, and hundreds of persons interacting with and managing the cargo shipment.

supply chain related to that product would likely be shut down indefinitely, and many persons could lose their lives. While governments and their law enforcement and intelligence agencies play a vital role in mitigating these threats, it is the companies and persons that make up the cargo supply chain that truly exercise the greatest impact in the security of the supply chain.

While all modes of transportation have specific vulnerabilities to criminal operations and terrorist attacks, perhaps no sector is more dangerously exposed than ports and the intermodal freight transportation systems to which they are connected (see Fig. 5.2). In addition to its size, the maritime sector, by its very nature as a complex, international, open transportation network, poses several additional challenges from a security standpoint. One of these is the variety of risk factors associated with shipping. As of 2015, an estimated 95% of the world's nonbulk cargo travels in marine shipping containers. These standardized boxes have revolutionized the transport of goods by sea since their first appearance in the 1950s and have given rise to a multitude of specialized road and rail carriers, a fleet of over 5100 modular container vessels (as of 2014), and the emergence of a global network of over 430 highly automated port handling facilities.[1] How many containers are in circulation today? In 2012, there were an estimated 31.5 million 20-ft equivalent units, or TEU containers in the world container fleet.[2] Today, one container in every nine carrying global trade is bound for or is coming from the United States, comprising 11% of worldwide container traffic.

What has been the impact of a terrorist attack on a commercial ship in recent history, and what would be the impact of a terrorist attack on a U.S. port? The potential direct cost

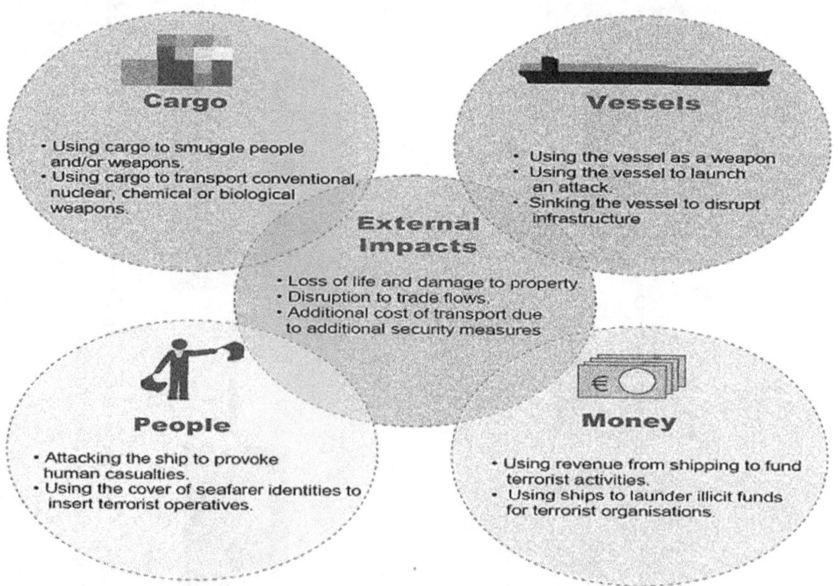

FIGURE 5.2 Security vulnerabilities of maritime transport and ports.

of a terrorist attack on shipping or maritime infrastructure varies tremendously according to the scope of the attack, its target, and its location. As a case in point, consider the costs stemming from the infamous 2002 terrorist attack on the tanker M/V Limburg. Immediately following the attack, underwriters tripled insurance premiums for vessels calling on Yemeni ports. These premiums led some shipping lines to cut Yemen from their schedules and/or switch to ports in neighboring countries despite attempts by the government to put in place a loss guarantee program. Yemeni terminals saw throughput plummet and laid-off as many as 3000 port workers. What do you think would be the impact of a terrorist attack on a major U.S. port? According to a U.S. Department of Transportation Study titled "The Economic Impact of Nuclear Terrorist Attacks on Freight Transport Systems in an Age of Seaport Vulnerability"[3] the economic impact of even a single nuclear terrorist attack on a major U.S. seaport would create disruption of U.S. trade valued at \$100–200 billion, property damage of \$50–500 billion, and 50,000 to 1,000,000 lives could be lost. According to the study, global and long-term effects, including the economic impacts of the pervasive national and international responses to the nuclear attack, though not calculated, are believed to be substantially greater.

Before we discuss the vulnerabilities and recommended security countermeasures for each of the links in the cargo supply chain, let's look at some valuable insight gained from experiences in another war against criminal elements attacking the supply chain—the War on Drugs.

Lessons Learned From the Drug War

There is much value to reviewing the lessons learned from the War on Drugs and how they may apply to securing the supply chain against terrorist activities. For the commercial sector, two primary lessons have relevance in this issue. First, the security procedures, techniques, and measures which proved to have a positive impact in preventing drug smuggling in cargo and containers have application in preventing terrorists from penetrating and manipulating the cargo supply chain. Second, given the extensive relationships between terrorist and narcotics trafficking organizations, it's likely that the terrorists will utilize the same smuggling techniques perfected by the narcos or simply "contract" one of the narcologistics/transportation groups to move their devices or cargos. In either case, the operational "fingerprint" will be similar, and successful countermeasures developed and implemented to address the drug smuggling issue will likewise serve for addressing the terrorism issue.

Let's take a more detailed look at the first point noted here. An estimated 70% of all illegal narcotics enter the United States without detection or seizure, and the War on Drugs generally has been a dismal failure. However, some shipping lines and other companies in the supply chain implemented rigorous and aggressive antinarcotics smuggling programs that scored—and continue to score—many successes. These successful security programs were, and still are, truly the exception and focused on deterrence, detection, denial, and containment, ie, keeping the drugs from entering the cargo, containers, and conveyances (air, sea, trucking) or detecting and seizing them. If we look at the cargo in the supply chain as akin to "criminal evidence that needs to be secured and managed via a chain of custody," attempts to penetrate the supply chain by narcotics traffickers frequently were mitigated. Case studies of successful antismuggling programs reveal that each "link" in the supply chain was viewed as integrated—but yet functionally separate—from a security perspective. And each "link" developed and implemented a security system that, to varying degrees, included the establishment of "layered security rings," defined proactive procedures and policies, professional security management, and security education and training. The result for companies that implemented this security program model was an overall increase in cargo, facility, and conveyance security and a decrease in contraband smuggling and several other types of criminal activities (cargo theft, stowaways, piracy, etc.). From a business perspective, their goal was not to be an arm of law enforcement but simply to avoid being manipulated or penetrated by these criminal elements and let other, less secure, competitors become the targets. This concept is occasionally referred to as the "cockroach fumigation approach to security design and implementation." This approach is based on the premise that when someone sprays his/her apartment for roaches, the insects leave the sprayed apartment to infest the apartments of his/her neighbors and are deterred from returning. Applied to supply chain security, when a business secures its supply chain using these proven, successful security procedures and mitigation strategies, the criminal elements and terrorists generally target other supply chains which have inferior security programs and ineffective security procedures. Therefore, it seems logical that a business can take many of the "best practices" proven successful in antinarcotics smuggling programs and use them in developing an antiterrorism program.

The second point mentioned at the beginning of this section—the working relationship between terrorist and narcotics smuggling organizations—is discussed in more detail in chapter "Targeting and Usage of Commercial Ships and Port by Terrorists and Transnational Criminal Organizations." For now though, let's acknowledge that this relationship exists, that techniques and tactics are shared between these groups, and that the terrorists have been known to contract narcologistics and transportation organizations to ship weapons, explosives, and personnel. With this in mind, you can appreciate the usefulness of looking at how narcotics smuggling organizations function and operate as a means of gaining insight into how terrorist organizations may target the cargo supply chain. So, let's take the information gained from the limited successes in the War on Drugs and combine it with the security best practices and then look at security program design and implementation at the links in the supply chain.

Recommended Security Practices at the Production/Loading Phase

Manufacturer, Factory, and Plant

It's very important to appreciate two key tenets in addressing efforts to significantly enhance the security of the supply chain. One, security measures and procedures must be initiated at the beginning of the supply chain (production/loading phase). Two, as in the case of illegal narcotics, it is a lot easier to prevent a terrorist device from entering the cargo shipment at the production/loading phase than it is to try to find it later on up the supply chain. However, unlike the War on Drugs, in the battle to keep the supply chain safe from terrorists, there is no room for error. Let's be honest, if a load of 500 kilos of cocaine gets through security and makes it to the streets of the United States, that's unfortunate but a daily reality. However, if a terrorist's nuclear bomb gets through and detonates in downtown Washington, then that's quite another event. The potential consequences of failure on this issue are far more devastating. So, we recognize that security efforts must begin in earnest at the production and cargo loading phase. This applies for all products, from textiles to bananas to frozen shrimp to washing machines to ballpoint pens. For the manufacturers, factories, and plants (as well as container yards and warehouses), this means having in place adequate and effective basic *physical security measures*, including

- *Perimeter barrier*: At least 8 feet in height, chain link fence or concrete wall, and topped with baled concertina wire;
- *Gates*: At least 8 feet in height, chain link fence or metal door, and topped with baled concertina wire;
- *Security gate house*: Vehicle and personnel control logs, visitor badges, telephone, radio, post orders, emergency notification rooster, fire extinguisher, flashlight, etc.;
- *Lighting*: Perimeter, exterior of buildings and loading docks, parking areas, container staging areas, and all cargo storage and packing areas;
- *Segregated parking areas*: Privately owned vehicles (POVs) separate from company vehicles, no POVs parked near loading docks or cargo or container staging areas;
- *Building door and window locks/protection*: Deadbolt locks on all exterior doors, wire mesh, or bars on all windows below the second floor.

Manufacturers, factories, and plants need to have in place *procedural security standards and monitoring and detection systems* such as

- *Access control*: Challenging, screening, inspection, and documenting of all vehicles, cargo, and persons at perimeter, gates, and building entrances and exits;
- *Security officers*: Deployed at all entrances/exits and on patrol;
- *Intrusion detection*: Alarms, PIR system, taut wire, buried cable, etc., at the perimeter and at access points to all restricted areas;
- *Closed-circuit television (CCTV) system*: Cameras mounted at perimeter, entrances/exits, container and cargo staging areas, loading dock and restricted areas—monitored/recorded 24/7 in central monitoring office;
- *Contraband detection systems*: K-9 teams and nonintrusive technology;
- *ID cards*: For employees, vendors, visitors;
- *Key*: Issue and control program;
- *Raw materials and finished product*: Controlled, inspected, inventoried, secured, monitored;

- *Container seals*: Inventory controls, issue logs, reconciliation procedures;
- *Security standard operating procedures manual*: Written, comprehensive, implemented, audited.

They should also have in place *personnel security policies and procedures*, including

- Screening all applicants for employment:
  - Completion of detailed employment interview by manager;
  - Criminal history and credit checks;
  - Interviews of references and prior employers;
  - Interview of two neighbors;
  - Lifestyle evaluation (to determine whether applicant is living beyond his or her means);
  - Polygraph (sensitive positions);
  - Employee personnel file, which includes all above records.
- For all vendor and service providers:
  - Completed profile form;
  - Background investigation by professional security company;
  - Personnel file, which includes all above records.

The importer of the cargo being produced at these locations should know who the product suppliers are and maintain the following documentation:

- Written standards for service providers' physical plant security;
- Quality controls on production processes to ensure system integrity;
- Financial assessment process to determine service provider's fiscal soundness and ability to deliver goods and services within contract parameters;
- Internal controls for the selection of service providers;
- Profiles of tier 1 suppliers.

Now let's look at some security tips for securing the cargo at the beginning of the supply chain and "maintaining product integrity" during its transport to the United States:

- Procedures for the handling of incoming and outgoing raw materials and export cargo that protect against the introduction, exchange, or loss of any legal or illegal material should be implemented. The security of all cargo should resemble the "chain of custody of evidence" in a criminal investigation.
- Raw materials unloaded at the factory or plant dock should be checked by a security officer to ensure proper markings, weight, count—as verified against relevant documentation—and screened for contraband (see Fig. 5.3). This activity should be monitored/recorded by CCTV and access to this area restricted.
- Raw materials and packaging materials should be stored separately, properly secured, access restricted, and under monitoring of CCTV (see Fig. 5.4).
- The packing of finished goods into boxes or shipping crates should be under observation of security officers and CCTV to ensure that no contraband or illegal

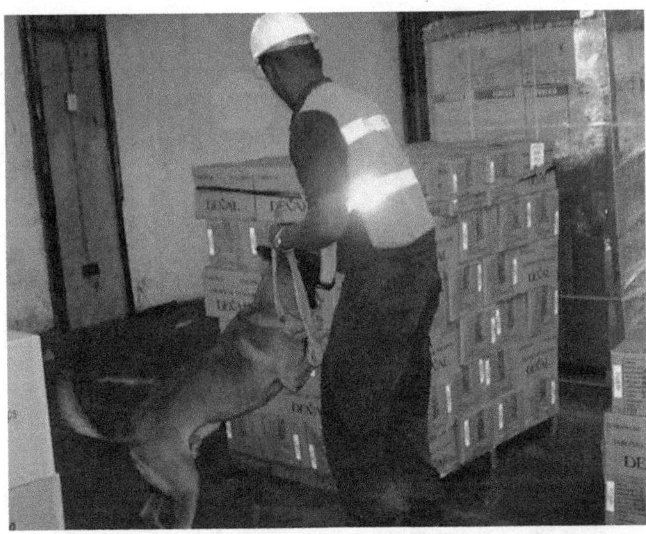

FIGURE 5.3 Raw materials should be screened to ensure that no contraband has been inserted.

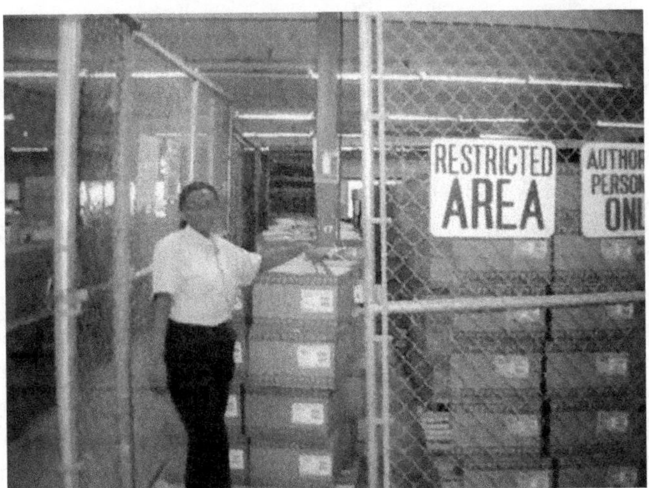

FIGURE 5.4 Raw materials should be secured.

materials are inserted into the boxes or crates (see Fig. 5.5). Security officers should verify the markings, weight, and count against relevant documentation. Any discrepancies noted should be immediately reported to management. The company should have a written procedure for the immediate investigation of suspicious circumstances and, as appropriate, notification of local law enforcement.

Finished, packed goods should be stored in a segregated area and under observation of security officers and CCTV to ensure that no contraband or illegal materials are inserted into the boxes or crates.

FIGURE 5.5 The packing of finished goods should be monitored.

- Prior to the loading of cargo into a container, a physical inspection of the interior and structure of the container should be conducted by specially trained personnel, and if possible a K-9 team or nonintrusive inspection device, to detect any contraband or false compartments. This inspection should be documented on the equipment interchange report (EIR) and other relevant shipping documentation. If the inspected container is not to be immediately loaded with cargo, then a seal should be affixed and the number recorded on appropriate security documentation. This inspection area should be a restricted zone with access only to authorized personnel. A security officer should patrol this area, and a CCTV camera(s) should be mounted so as to record all activity.
- A checker and security officer should be present at the time of cargo loading to ensure that there are no shortages or overages and observe that cargo is properly marked, weighed, counted, and documented. Narcotics and explosives detection K-9 teams, X-ray machines, or other nonintrusive inspections devices should be used to detect contraband. Any discrepancies noted should be immediately reported to management and investigated.
- Following the proper and complete loading of a container, the checker should affix a high security seal to the container (see Fig. 5.6). The seal number should be properly recorded on the EIR, shipping documents, and seal and security documentation.
- Proper seal storage, issue, and control are key issues. Seals should be treated as if they were "high-value" cargo. Upon receipt of an order of seals, they should be physically inventoried (for missing or duplicate numbers—which does occur), a record made, and secured in a locking storage box. They should be inventoried on a bimonthly basis, used in sequential order, and issued to authorized persons via a seal issue log. Seals should be reconciled regularly, utilizing gate logs, shipping documents, and other records.

FIGURE 5.6 A checker applying the high security seal once the container is loaded.

- If the loaded, sealed container is not to be immediately transported to the port or airport, then it should be staged in a segregated area and positioned door-to-door with another container.
- When the loaded container exits the factory or plant gate, the security officer should review all documentation, conduct a physical inspection of the seal, and record all relevant information on a gate log.

Recommended Security Practices at the Export Phase

Carriers and Seaports

The second primary phase in the cargo supply chain is the transport of the loaded container or break-bulk cargo from the production and loading location to the seaport. If the cargo or container arrived at this phase in a "sanitized and secure state" (no contraband, terrorist devices, or unauthorized persons within same), and it can get through this second phase in the same condition, it's probable that it will arrive at the port of entry and to the importer's location free of any contraband, terrorist devices, or unauthorized persons. However, it is at this point where numerous entities now begin to interact with and participate in the cargo shipment. There are truckers who physically transport the container or break-bulk cargo to the foreign seaport (possibly via a container terminal), customs brokers who coordinate documentation needs, port agents who provide myriad services related to the movement, port drivers and equipment operators who move the cargo/container within the terminal, stevedores who load the cargo and containers into/onboard the conveyance, and a host of government officials—and other folks if the cargo has to cross an international border or transit a free zone—who process the export of the cargo and containers. When the cargo arrives at the seaport, it is further documented, possibly inspected to some degree, and finally staged in the seaport awaiting loading. During this entire phase—the transport to the seaport (possibly via a container yard), staging in the port, and the loading of cargo or containers onto the conveyance—there may be various criminal elements (container hijackers, cargo thieves, drug smugglers, stowaways, and terrorists) that are interested in gaining access to the cargo and/or container.

In essence, lots of criminals are looking for a break in the security configuration! So, security at this phase must be vigilant. Generally, the carrier has a special responsibility for this phase of movement in the supply chain, for two reasons. First, in many cases the carrier or its in-country carrier agent directly contracts the truckers and customs brokers and therein has potential legal exposure for claims or losses. Second, U.S. Customs and Border Protection (CBP) places the onus on the carrier concerning "unmanifested cargo and unmanifested persons" brought into the United States. Drug-related fines and penalties levied on carriers by CBP have exceeded $20,000,000 per incident.

Under the C-TPAT program, CBP has moved the responsibility even further up the supply chain and encourages importers to ensure their entire supply chain is properly secured. So what are some of the points that the carriers (and now importers) should be looking at in every cargo shipment?

- The Exporter
  - Who is it?
  - Is it a "known shipper"? Is it new?
  - Has it passed a background investigation?
  - Do the owners or managers have a known history of criminal activity or association?
  - Has the load location been surveyed (does it exist and look "real")?
  - Are they shipping their standard cargo or is it unusual?
  - To the usual consignee or a new party?
  - Were there any strange equipment requests (a reefer container for dry cargo, unknown pickup site, etc.)?
  - Is the value of the cargo less than the shipping costs?
  - Is the type of cargo being shipped illogical (shipping a commodity to a country that does not import that commodity or is a producer of that same commodity, etc.)?
  - Is the reported weight of the cargo at time of booking the same as the actual weight at time of entering the port, and is it consistent with norms for this cargo?
  - Is the shipment being booked "at the last minute"?
  - Is this cargo being transloaded in a manner which is illogical (change of shipping lines and containers or unnecessarily via a free zone)?
  - Is the exporter attempting to maintain anonymity (prepaid freight via third party, etc.)?
  - Is the routing of the cargo shipment illogical (via multiple countries or unnecessary transshipments)?
  - Are the full details provided for completing the manifest?

If any of these questions give the carrier a reason to think "warning," then the cargo shipment should be immediately reported to U.S. Customs and the situation further investigated or the shipment denied. As always, all new or infrequent shippers and suspicious cargo shipments should be reported to U.S. Customs 48 h in advance of lading on a vessel.

- The Trucker
  - Who is it?
  - Is it a legitimate trucking company?
  - Has the company passed a background investigation?
  - Do the owners or managers have a known history of criminal activity or association?
  - Are all drivers screened for criminal history and issued ID badges prior to deployment?
- Transit to Seaport
  - Was the transit direct and no stops made?
  - Are the date, time, seal number, and mileage recorded on the EIR or relevant document when departing the factory/plant/manufacturer?
  - Are the transit times and mileage reviewed upon arrival at the seaport for discrepancies, unusual time delays, or excessive mileage?
  - Any change in drivers during transit?
  - Is the container seal physically inspected upon arrival at the seaport gate and the number verified against relevant documentation?
  - Are all transit documents completed in entirety and signed by the exporter, trucker, and seaport gate security?

Again, if any of these questions give rise for concern, then the circumstances of the shipment should be immediately investigated and, if warranted, reported to the U.S. CBP.

All loaded containers should be staged in segregated and well-lit areas, under constant vigilance (security officers and CCTV), and container and seal numbers checked and recorded on a blind tally when loaded onboard a vessel. If possible, all break-bulk cargo and containers should be inspected (using K-9 teams, gamma-ray systems, X-ray machines, etc.) for contraband and explosives prior to loading onboard. The carrier and port management need to ensure that all shipping documentation is screened and analyzed and that seal controls and usage reconciliation procedures are rigorously enforced.

Although vessel security is addressed in detail in chapter "A Strategic Blueprint for World-Class Seaport Security" let's cover a few key points here. First, the vessel should be fully inspected for contraband and unauthorized persons upon arrival in the seaport. Second, security officers should be deployed at all times to control access of persons and materials, search all items carried on and off the conveyance, inspect all break-bulk cargoes and the exterior of all containers (interior of empty containers), and maintain general defensive security. Third, following the completion of cargo loading into a cargo bay, the cargo bay again should be checked and then the hatch secured and sealed (numbers recorded on a security certificate). Last, at the termination of cargo operations, the vessel should be thoroughly and systematically searched for contraband and unauthorized persons.

Recommended Security Practices at the Importation/ Distribution Phase

Ports of Entry and Importers

The last primary phase in the supply chain is the importation of cargo or a loaded container through a port of entry (seaport) and transport to the importer. Again, at this phase an additional cast of entities interacts with and participates in the cargo shipment. There are the U.S. government officials who "clear" the conveyance and stevedores, checkers, top-pick drivers, terminal hustlers, and others who discharge and transport the containers and cargo within the seaport. Also, carrier importation personnel, customs brokers, consignee staff, and others coordinate documentation and the "release" of the cargo and containers for transport to the destination, and finally truckers transport the cargo and containers from the port of entry to this final location. Some of the areas to observe to ensure effective security in this phase in the supply chain and maintain product integrity during transit are described next.

Seaport Operations: The security program and configuration in the seaport should be comprehensive and designed to address today's very real threats and comply with all requirements set forth in the U.S. Maritime and Transportation Security Act (MTSA) or the IMO's ISPS Code, depending on the jurisdiction. The security program should also include basic requirements for vessel access control and inspections and establish the port–vessel interface processes and procedures. At this phase, it is critically important for the carrier, port, and importer to perform the necessary actions to ensure that the cargo and container still are "sanitized and secure." In part, this can be attained by validating the security of the vessel; inspecting and recording the seals at time of discharge (verifying no seal conflict); screening the cargo and container for contraband, explosives, WMDs, and unauthorized persons (using K-9 teams, X-ray machines, or other detection equipment); staging cargo and containers in segregated and well-lit areas (under constant observation by security officers and CCTV); and ensuring a safe and secure transit of the cargo and container to its final destination (see Fig. 5.7).

The Trucker: The carrier or importer (whoever contracts for the drayage or transport of the cargo) has to ask the following questions (and receive positive answers!). Is it a legitimate trucking company? Has the company passed a background investigation? Do the owners or managers have a known history of criminal activity or association? Are all drivers screened for criminal history and issued ID badges prior to deployment?

Transit to Importer's Location: The importer is ultimately responsible for ensuring that the cargo and container arrive at their destination in the same state as when they were dispatched from the seaport. To meet this goal, the importer needs to confirm that the transit was direct; that the date, time, seal number, and mileage were recorded on the EIR when departing the seaport; the seal number matches upon arrival at destination; and there were no unusual delays in the transit. Again, if any of these questions give rise for concern, then the circumstances of the shipment should be immediately investigated and, if warranted, reported to the CBP, FBI, or local law enforcement.

Documentations and Seals: The carrier, port management, and importer each need to ensure that for their respective area of responsibility all shipping documentation and seal

FIGURE 5.7 A loaded, import container being screened for contraband.

records are fully analyzed and reconciled. It is imperative that any seal discrepancies or unusual observations are immediately investigated and, as warranted, reported promptly to the relevant government authority.

Supply Chain Security Database: A common theme running through our security recommendations involves the collection, analysis, evaluation, and distribution of information. The timely receipt of information indicating a potential breach in the integrity of or threat to the cargo or container (or vessel) may result in the successful mitigation of the threat or incident. The primary function of this database is to enhance information exchange among the links in the supply chain and provide indications and warning of a potential or developing security breach or incident. The importer—because ultimately it is the responsible entity—should develop and maintain this database. At a minimum, the types and fields of information should include detailed data on the following:

- Current or prospective suppliers (manufacturers, factories, plants, and warehouses);
- Current or prospective carriers, brokers, ports, and logistics agents;
- Current or prospective vendors (truckers, container yards, security companies, stevedore companies, etc.);
- Foreign and U.S. law enforcement-provided reports and corporate security intelligence (from all links in the supply chain);
- New techniques and tactics used for circumventing or negating security measures or procedures;
- Alerts of suspicious cargo shipments.

While the database will receive reports generated from the initiative of security managers within companies in the supply chain (tips from employees, etc.), it likewise should serve as a platform for tasking these same personnel to collect follow-up and additional information on suspect companies, persons, shipments, and incidents. This database should generate alerts to trusted entities within the importer's supply chain; warning of emerging or specific threats, suspicious suppliers, and vendors; and new techniques and tactics for circumventing or negating security measures or procedures.

We have discussed the complex supply chain that provides the products we consume and utilize in our daily lives; the vulnerabilities to this supply chain; and the fact that cargo thieves, stowaways, pirates, drug smugglers, and terrorists constantly attempt to negate, circumvent, or manipulate security measures designed to protect the cargo in the supply chain. We have also discussed the recommended security policies, measures, and procedures for each primary link in the cargo supply chain, which, if properly implemented, will serve to mitigate threats posed by these criminal and terrorist elements. Now, let's look at a few of the special issues and threats in the maritime environment.

Special Vulnerabilities in the Maritime Environment

Cargo Theft

Cargo theft has boomed since the advent of the maritime container—an unfortunate by-product of the efficient transport of a single box carrying tons of valuable merchandise—however, new government supply chain security initiatives are offering a ray of hope in both assessing the magnitude of the problem and possibly reducing the level of vulnerability and the numbers of incidents. Historically, before the proliferation of cargo containers, cargo theft on the docks generally was the "setting aside" of a box of merchandise for the longshoremen supervisor. With the containerization of the maritime cargo industry, the setting aside of one box of cargo has turned into the theft of a whole container of cargo. The theft of a container no longer is a single-person operation but is the effort of a number of persons cooperating together and most often has the mark of organized crime groups. How much are the losses? The International Cargo Security Council estimates the annual cargo losses in the United States to be about $10 billion;[4] however, this does not take into consideration the indirect losses to companies, ie, costs related to expediting the replacement goods, disruption of customer service, claims processing, insurance premium increases, and damage to the company reputation. Indirect losses may be five times those of the direct losses. The collection of data on cargo theft, up to now spurious and woefully inadequate, will become more comprehensive and accurate in the next few years, thanks to a 2006 change in the PATRIOT Act. When Congress reauthorized the PATRIOT Act, they required the FBI to compile statistics on cargo theft in a national database. Since 2007, the FBI's Uniform Crime Reports will have a separate category for cargo theft.

According to the U.S. DOT's Volpe Center Report of 1999, titled "Intermodal Cargo Transportation: Industry Best Security Practices,"[5]

[t]he "container revolution," which has increased transportation efficiency and spawned the rapidly growing intermodal freight transportation industry, may have inadvertently encour-

aged increased organized criminal presence in freight transportation. Traditionally (before the 1960s), high-value cargo was moved using break-bulk packaging and shipping techniques. During the "break-bulk" era, high-value cargo was packaged in cases or pallets for shipment and loaded and unloaded on a piece-by-piece or pallet-by-pallet basis. Easy access encouraged the theft of electronics, appliances, clotZzzhes, engine parts, liquor, cosmetics, and cigarettes from terminals (including warehouses, docks, and transfer points) and during loading, unloading, and shipment. When first introduced, containers successfully reduced pilferage. Estimates indicated that during the early years of the container revolution, theft of containerized cargo dropped to less than one-tenth of 1 percent of all cargo shipped in containers. Unfortunately, "after an initial honeymoon period, during which criminals adjusted to the new container system, other patterns of theft developed."

Organized crime recognized the potential for big business. Containers, stacked in terminals, could be stolen as a whole, opened and made subject to pilferage, or serve as a conduit for drug smuggling. "Much larger 'packages' containing higher value cargoes could now be spirited away with comparative ease and the spoils made it worth using more elaborate methods of deception and daring. Whereas, previously ten televisions might go missing because that was all thieves could carry or secrete, now two hundred could be stolen at a go in a container." For example, computer laptops, cellular telephones, perfume, and wearing apparel are among the top items stolen and could be worth from hundreds of thousands of dollars to millions of dollars per container load. A pallet of these devices can command upwards of $250,000. Sixty-four pallets can be loaded into a single 40-ft container, with a net value of $16 million.

Containerized cargo theft is carried out primarily as an organized criminal conspiracy. Substantial evidence supports the hypothesis that most theft of containerized cargo is systematic in method. Often, criminals act with apparent information about cargo manifests, suggesting that collusion is occurring with transportation employees. Cargo terminals are particularly vulnerable to employee penetration at intermodal transfer points, warehouses, rail yards, and docks. In its Ports of the World: A Guide to Cargo Loss Control, the CIGNA Corporation reports that the majority of cargo loss claims "involve cargo taken from transportation facilities by personnel authorized to be there and on vehicles controlled or similarly authorized by management."

This immense network of importers, wholesalers, freight brokers, truckers, and dock workers create problems for law enforcement and transportation operations in pinpointing instances of bribery, extortion, or "purchased" information. Estimates indicate that "well over 80 percent of all theft and pilferage of transportation cargoes is accomplished by, or with the collusion of, persons whose employment entitles them access to the cargo that is stolen."

Criminals use a variety of methods to steal cargo, including:

- *Opening containers stacked at terminal yards or transfer facilities, removing goods, and transporting them from ports or intermodal facilities by personal automobile or delivery trucks.*
- *Falsely claiming that a truck was hijacked leaving a port or warehouse, when the driver is actually complicit in the crime, and receiving a cut of the profits.*

Continued

—cont'd

- *Dismantling containers, removing key merchandise, re-sealing containers and continuing shipment.*
- *Relying on an organized network for spotting, stealing, and fencing merchandise.*
- *Driving off in a loaded tractor trailer via fraudulent paperwork.*
- *Speeding through fences and security checkpoints.*
- *Stealing loaded trucks off the street or from storage yards.*

Once stolen from a terminal, the cargo merchandise is quickly repackaged in a nearby warehouse or facility for transportation to an out-of-state fencing location or out of the country. These goods may re-enter the United States and be sold at a discount, providing an effective way to legitimize illegal profits (referred to as transshipment). The FBI estimates that most stolen cargo remains in the possession of those who stole it for less than twenty-four hours.

Organized criminal groups are becoming transnational, facilitating theft of containerized cargo in one country and trafficking of stolen goods in another. Transnational criminal operations use the entire international shipping cycle, in particular, the maritime and trucking transportation shipping system and the freight-forwarding sector, to support stolen merchandise trafficking. Organized criminals enjoy the same efficiencies and economies of scale as legitimate transnational businesses, but can elude national efforts to restrict their activities.

The most common form of cargo theft is pilferage, which is most often perpetrated by employees. The practice of handlers pilfering cargo has long been an institution in the shipping industry. Manufacturers have been known to over-ship cargo to allow for the "shrinkage" that occurs due to pilferage. In the case of containerized cargo, access is achieved through the following methods:

- *After offloading from the ship while the container is idle awaiting pickup/delivery in the terminal yard.*
- *While the cargo is undergoing consolidation or de-consolidation either at the terminal or an off-site freight forwarder.*
- *Anywhere along a trucking or rail route where the shipment is idle.*

Instances occur in which high-value, high-technology equipment is deliberately "sidetracked" inside a carrier's terminal by employees. When it fails to arrive at the consignee, it is treated as a loss. After a period of time it legally belongs to the carrier; and, after appropriate arrangements are made between the perpetrators and associated liquidators, the shipment is sold at a fraction of its value.

The value of computer hardware and components makes such shipments an attractive target of theft. Exchanges now take place where cocaine shipments bound for the United States are traded for computer chips stolen from cargo shipments. In this scenario, both commodities have the capacity for significant increase in value as they are passed along. Further, as an alternate method to shipping drug profits (that are in the form of cash) out of the United States, those profits are invested in stolen cargo purchased at a fraction of its value (computer hardware, memory chips, etc.) and shipped overseas as legitimate cargo, thus maximizing the capital generation of illicit activity.

One means for pilfering cargo is by removing the contents of one container and placing all or part of the contents into an adjacent container (for example, one that is empty or carrying low value cargo) that will not be monitored. Thieves have devised several ways of gaining access into shipping containers, some of which involve removal and replacement of all or part of the door hardware fasteners so that the seals and locks will not appear to have been disturbed. Once transferred, the perpetrator can arrange for removal and delivery of the stolen goods with minimal risk.

Internal Conspiracies and Techniques Used to Circumvent Security

Criminal organizations and terrorist groups are seasoned experts in developing *internal conspiracies* within maritime transport-related companies and over the years have developed many techniques and tactics for circumventing security policies, measures, and procedures. Internal conspiracies have plagued the maritime cargo business for many years. While internal conspiracies originally focused on the theft of cargo, the advent of drug smuggling—a very high-value business—served as a catalyst for this criminal activity to evolve into a more sophisticated criminal enterprise and one that may involve targeting several links in the supply chain.

Internal conspiracies may involve participation by employees or contractors within any company in the supply chain. Criminal conspirators may include personnel at the factory or plant, warehouse or container yard, truck or seaport, carrier or U.S. port, broker or freight forwarder, or in the importer's company. These persons generally are knowledgeable of the movement of the legitimate cargo; the documentation, international trade, and loopholes in the security configuration; and U.S. CBP or law enforcement procedures and presence in their work area.

As we discussed earlier, terrorists may use techniques used by drug smugglers to transport (smuggle) their explosives or devices into the supply chain of cargo destined for the United States, or they may contract a narcotics smuggling organization to transport their "cargo" for them. In both of these cases, it's likely that employees of one or more companies (links) in the supply chain would participate in this conspiracy (possibly unwitting that this is a terrorist-inspired operation). What are some of the methods used by internal conspirators to move contraband? U.S. CBP describes the following three types of internal conspiracies[6] used in cargo theft, drug smuggling operations, and other contraband operations:

- *The Tap*: This term is used to describe the illegal opening of international cargo or containers for the purpose of "extracting" the contraband prior to routine inspection by U.S. Customs. However, in the case of terrorists, they likely would open *(tap)* the cargo or container at some point prior to loading on the conveyance at the foreign seaport and *insert* explosives, a WMD, or unauthorized person(s) into the cargo or container.

- *The Switch*: This term describes the technique for exchanging a "clean" shipment for one that contains contraband. In the case of terrorists, this activity could occur at any link in the supply chain. It likely would depend on the terrorist's purpose and target.
- *The Pull*: This term describes the taking of an entire shipment, either manifested or unmanifested, prior to customs inspection. In the case of a terrorist operation, this most likely would occur after the cargo or container arrives in the United States and would be for the purpose of "extracting" terrorist materials or personnel which arrived undetected in the U.S. seaport.

A company can take several actions to assist in preventing or detecting internal conspiracies:

- Perform effective preemployment screening for past criminal activity or dishonest behavior.
- Perform preemployment and periodic background investigations, to include a "lifestyle evaluation" of all employees. Fortunately, employees involved in criminal activity have a tendency to want to spend the extra money soon after receiving it! Look for changes in their lifestyle that reflect unexplainable surges in spending (expensive new cars, new home, extravagant jewelry, new girlfriends, increased amount of "partying," etc.).
- Create an internal security team which liaises with law enforcement, collects information related to terrorist and other criminal threats to company operations, and monitors the activities of employees.
- If permissible, conduct polygraphs of employees suspected to be involved in criminal activity.
- Have security officers and supervisors conduct frequent inspections of the facilities and cargo handling areas observing for suspicious activity, signs of unauthorized access, and indications that cargo or containers have been tampered with or seals violated.
- Rotate personnel between positions or shifts, as practical and permissible.
- Observe for altered or forged documentation, unusual changes to cargo documentation and computer databases, violations of access control and password procedures to databases, and unauthorized modifications/updates to shipping documentation files.
- Be vigilant for fake bills of lading, tally logs, EIRs, gate logs, and cargo release documents.

One of the primary purposes of port and vessel security systems is to *deny, deter, detect, and contain* intruders in order to protect personnel and physical assets. However, history has taught us that no security system is perfect. Every security system may be circumvented. Let's look at some of the methods.

- Techniques for circumventing facility access controls include
  - Gaining access to offices that issue passes, decals, and ID cards and stealing items.
  - Entering unlocked cars or breaking into cars with passes and ID cards.
  - Scraping off decals from cars and placing them on other vehicles.

- Tactics for circumventing gates, locks, and fences include
  - Taking advantage of locks left open and removing/replacing them with their own locks. As a result, the criminals/terrorists can now enter the facility at a time convenient to them.
  - Removing gate base and hardware from the ground.
  - Driving vehicles through the fence.
  - Climbing over the fence.
  - Gaining under-the-fence access due to the absence of a bottom rail.
  - Making duplicate keys from inexpensive locks that have visible numbers or are easy to replicate.
  - Utilizing bolt cutters to cut off the locks.
- Methods for circumventing lock/key controls include
  - Creating duplicate keys or stealing keys from an employee or an unsecured key storage location. This can more easily occur when there are poor key control records, improper storage arrangements, or keys not collected from terminated employees.
  - Taking advantage of the lack of rotation of keys or locks.
  - Giving an extra key to a criminal/terrorist for usage. For example, a corrupt or comprised employee may report the loss of a key and the issuance of a replacement. If there are poor key controls, a new one may be replaced without further investigation.
  - Standing near an employee opening a combination lock and that employee doesn't cover the lock with his or her hand or other protection device.
- Techniques for circumventing CCTV security systems include
  - Cutting off the power supply.
  - Damaging the cameras.
  - Testing the CCTV effectiveness during nighttime. If there is no security response to a fake penetration attempt, then it's likely the camera clarity is not effective during the night.
  - Evaluating the coverage of a CCTV camera—checking for "dead zone" and inadequate coverage of the perimeter extremes. Again, if there is no security response to a fake penetration, then the weakness has been identified.
- Tactics used to circumvent security communications include
  - Using a scanner to monitor the activities and actions of port security—unless the channel is encrypted (unlikely).
  - Stealing a radio from the port and during the criminal/terrorist operation communicating false information or instructions in order to confuse and tie up police, security, and emergency response units.
  - Calling in a large volume of phony bomb threats, fires, and suspicious person reports in order to overwhelm the switchboard and distract police and security forces from actual terrorist activities.

- Methods for circumventing security at the port facility gate include
  - Driving through the main entrance and waving a driver's license, acting as if authorized to enter.
  - Obtaining a security badge, ID card, or decal from an authorized person and using it to gain access.
  - Obtaining a copy of a parking pass and ID badge/card, making color copies at a copy store, laminating the items in plastic, and then simply waving them at the security officer at the main entrance. Intruders have made false law enforcement credentials simply by downloading images off the Internet.
  - Convincing the security officer that a criminal/terrorist is authorized and talking his or her way into the facility; for example, claiming to be a contractor meeting a ship or an employee.
  - Hijacking delivery vehicles and replacing the driver with a terrorist/criminal and talking his or her way onto the facility.
  - Posing as a jogger and jogging through the main/side gate and waving to the security officer.
  - Taking a taxi cab and telling the driver the criminal/terrorist has to meet a ship. Allowing the cab driver to tell the security officer he is taking him or her to meet the ship. (The listing of ship arrivals is published in the business pages and on the port/shipping line websites.)
  - Stealing government/military/contractor vehicles and driving them past the security officer without being challenged.
  - During the evening, driving a vehicle up to the gate at a high rate of speed with bright lights turned on.
  - Wearing sunglasses and baseball hats in order to conceal identity from the security officer when showing identification cards to security officers.
  - Either as a friend or as a hostage taker, accompanying an authorized person in his or her automobile and gaining access to the facility without being questioned by security.
- Techniques used to circumvent ship access control procedures include
  - Insisting that the criminal/terrorist was already cleared by the main gate security and that he or she resents being checked again by security/police positioned either near the ship or on the ship.
  - Developing first name relationships with all police and security personnel. This will require at least a few weeks; however, it will increase opportunities for unrestricted access to the ship.
  - Developing close relationships with the ships' captains. They can help the criminal/terrorist circumvent security by "vouching for" him or her to police and security people.
  - Wearing a suit and tie and "looking important." Acting as if the criminal/terrorist is supposed to be near the ship or on the ship.

- Wearing a hard hat and carrying a clipboard. Bringing a two-way radio so that the criminal/terrorist appears to be conducting an inspection. Claiming to be a classification surveyor.
- Obtaining a stevedore uniform and/or port badge (real or forged) and walking up the gangway and flashing an ID.
- Utilizing the "honey trap"—a prostitute—to accompany the criminal/terrorist (pretending to be her driver) and claiming to have a scheduled visit with the captain or officer. This has a high probability of success in most ports of the world.
- Claiming to be a ship chandler with a delivery and hiding weapons or contraband inside the delivery packages.

Container Seals

Seals are utilized as a means of detecting unauthorized access into a container; however, over the years drug smuggling and other criminal elements have repeatedly demonstrated that the perfect seal has yet to be built. First, it is important to clarify that a "seal" is not a "lock." While a seal may have several characteristics of a lock—material used in the manufacture of the device, sturdiness, etc.—it's primary purpose is as a tamper-evident device and not to prevent unauthorized access. Seals are placed on loaded containers as a means of detecting whether the cargo has been pilfered, manipulated, switched (ie, name brands for knock-offs, etc.), or extra items (ie, narcotics, explosives, etc.) inserted or extracted. Seals are also placed on empty containers at time of dispatch to an exporter or loading onboard a ship to detect if unauthorized persons (stowaways, terrorists, etc.) or unauthorized materials (all forms of contraband) gain access.

It is probably a fair assumption that the day after the first seal was affixed to a loaded cargo container, criminal elements targeting containers began investigating ways to defeat these tamper-evident devices. Criminal elements go to great expense and dedication of time to develop strategies for negating the effectiveness of the different types of seals. It is well known in law enforcement circles that in key drug source and transit countries, such as Colombia, Panama, Venezuela, and Mexico, major transnational narcotics trafficking organizations employ persons referred to as *surgeons*. Surgeons are experienced in areas such as jewelry and watch repair, metallic and plastic manufacturing, mechanical engineering, and structural design. The sole function of these craftsmen is to develop ways to compromise seals, while showing no signs of tampering.

There are many types of seals utilized in maritime cargo transportation; however, there is a relatively short list of seals commonly utilized in commercial cargo container shipping. All seals utilized in commercial cargo transport have a unique serial number, and some have a barcode for an additional level of security. The seal number is recorded at time of issue to truckers or exporters, and subsequently as it passes through links in the cargo supply chain. Some exporters purchase and provide their own seals, as a means of control and security.

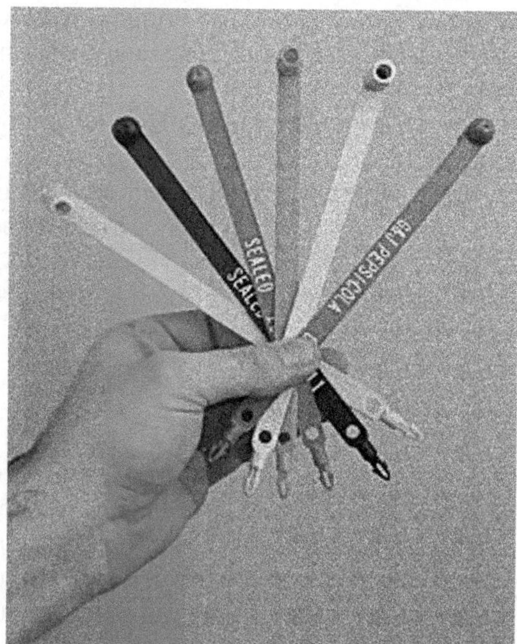

FIGURE 5.8 Plastics seals are used to seal empty containers.

Let's review the primary seals used in commercial cargo transport and techniques practiced by criminal elements to alter or manipulate these security devices. First, though, it is important to appreciate that modifications detected under a microscope or under the bright lights in a law enforcement office are much more difficult to detect at 0200 h on a poorly lit dock and in the driving rain. This is the reality and one under which security officers, dockside checkers, and crewmembers typically conduct these inspections.

Plastics seals, such as those in Fig. 5.8, are used to seal empty containers when staged in ports or terminals and following inspection dockside to be loaded on a ship or when dispatched to a client. These seals are considered "low-level security," tamper-evident devices and extremely easy to defeat and with no signs of detection. A criminal can defeat these devices by simply using an Exacto knife, or single-edge razor blade to cut the plastic strap at the point where it enters into the locking base and then later reattaching it using a couple of drops of super glue.

Metal strap seals, such as the one shown in Fig. 5.9, also are used to seal empty containers when staged in ports or terminals and following inspection, either dockside as the containers are to be loaded on a ship or when dispatched to a client. Occasionally, this seal is used on loaded containers being shipped internationally, but not those destined for the United States. While some believe these seals to be superior to plastic seals, in fact, they are just as easy to defeat without signs of detection. Metal strap seals can be opened by inserting a hair or safety pin or sturdy piece of thin wire into the locking ball base to release the spring that locks in the male strap portion.

FIGURE 5.9 A metal strap seal.

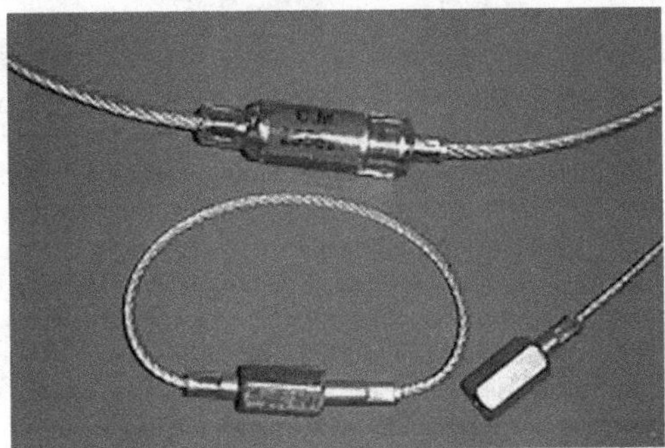

FIGURE 5.10 Typical cable seals.

Cable seals, such as the ones in Fig. 5.10, provide a higher level of protection than plastic and metal strap seals and are viewed by some as having some of the benefits of a lock and a seal. Typically, these seals are used in areas of high levels of pilferage, theft, and container hijacking. However, cable seal can be compromised simply by cutting the cable near the point of insertion into the female bolt, drilling out the portion inside, and then when ready for reattachment, reseating the male portion using a simple bonding compound from a local hardware store.

The high security cable seal identified in the top left photo of Fig. 5.11, by appearances, would seem to be very secure; however, as indicated in the subsequent photos in this figure, the seal can be defeated in well under 10 min by using a common drill and a coat hanger and—with the use of a bit of green plastic fill—leaves no sign of alteration and is reusable.

The seals shown in Figs. 5.12 and 5.13 are commonly called *bolt seals*—because the male stud portion resembles a bolt. The lower portion of the bolt has one or two indentations in which a ring(s) snaps into place when the bolt is inserted into the female portion. This system was first defeated over 15 years ago and memorialized in a video prepared

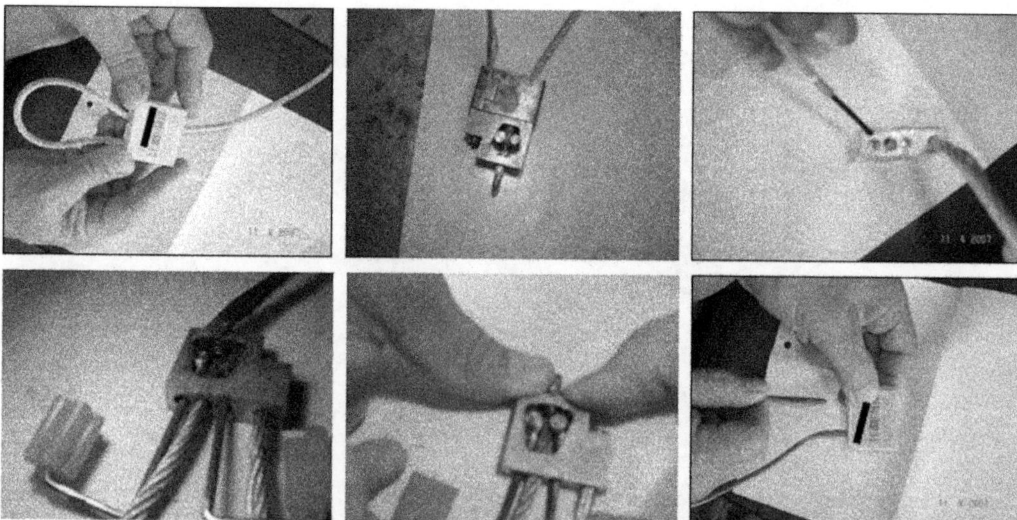

FIGURE 5.11 A technique for defeating a cable seal. The top left photo shows a typical cable seal. The top center photo is the view once the plastic cover is removed (note that cable is fed through housing and between two "barrels," with the spring keeping pressure on the barrel making it "lock" and secure the cable). The top right photo shows two pilot holes which were drilled through the green plastic cover and upper "aluminum" seal housing. This metal is very "soft" and penetrated easily with a common hand drill. The bottom left photo shows the insertion of wire coat hanger pieces into the drill led holes. The bottom center photo shows that when pressure is applied to the coat hanger pieces, the spring is released and the seal cable easily slides out. The bottom right photo shows that once the seal is reassembled, the drilled holes in the plastic cover can be filled to camouflage the penetration and compromise of the seal and the cable seal can be reused again, like a new seal. The time required for this seal compromise is less than 10 minutes.

FIGURE 5.12 A bolt seal.

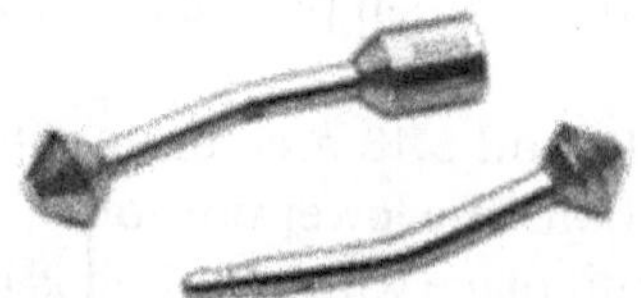

FIGURE 5.13 Another version of a bolt seal.

by a shipping line in Guatemala. In the video, a Guatemalan truck driver showed how, by inserting a thin metal sleeve around the bolt and forcing it down into the locking rings, the locking rings are forced outward and the bolt released. And, with needle-nose pliers, the rings could be extracted, clipped or readjusted, reinserted, and the seal ready for use again. Basically, this concept is similar to using a credit card to open a door-knob-style lock on a door. Another method utilized with some bolt seals is simply using bolt cutters to cut off the male portion of the seal, drill out the remains from the inside of the female portion, adjust the interior rings, and use a new male portion when ready to reseal the container. Many models of the bolt seal do not have the serial number etched on the male bolt portion—just on the female portion—so another bolt would also work. There have been numerous cases of the serial numbers of bolt seals being altered—both those etched into the metal and those etched into the plastic-coated bolt seals. The level of quality of the alteration is determined by the skill of the craftsman; and many cases require the use of a magnifying glass to note the alteration.

Another very commonly used high security seal is the *bottle seal* (see Fig. 5.14). This seal uses a plastic-coated rigid metal cable, in lieu of a sold metal bolt as with the bolt seal. The female portion is hardened metal with a plastic-coated casing. This seal has several of the same flaws as the bolt seal. As in the case of the bolt seal, a criminal can simply cut off the male portion, drill out the remains in the female portion and, when ready, use a new unnumbered male stud. Most models of the bottle seal do not have the serial number etched on the male stud, so any other male stud would work fine. There have been numerous cases of the serial numbers of bottle seals being altered, with the quality of the work varying and based on the skill of the craftsman. Some cases require the use of a magnifying glass or microscope to note the difference. It is very important for the security personnel and checkers screening bottle seals and recording seal numbers to physically—and vigorously—tug on the seals. As noted above, the locking rings on the interior of the female

FIGURE 5.14 A standard bottle seal.

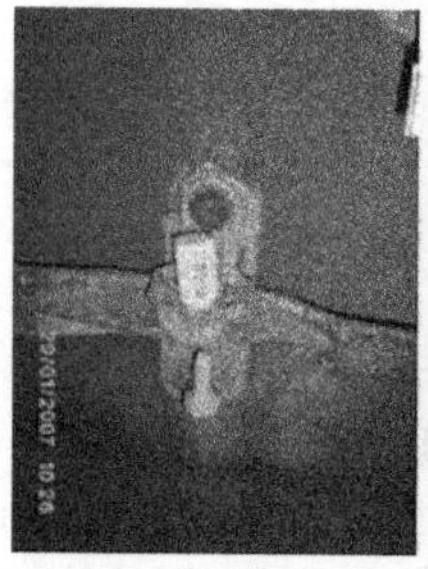

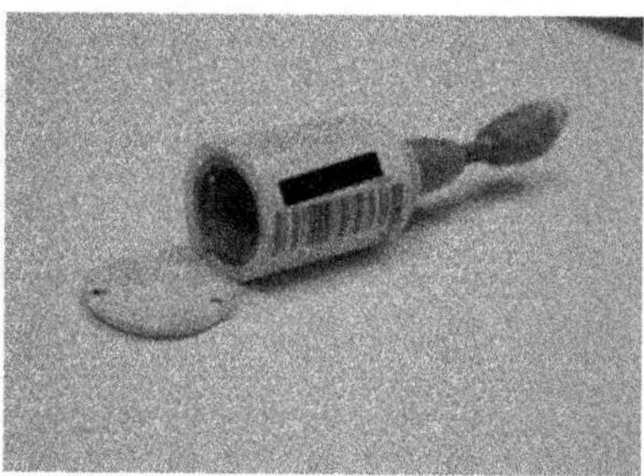

FIGURE 5.15 The compromise of a bottle seal. The photo on the left is the position of the seal when affixed at the exporter warehouse after cargo loading (note the bottle portion is *above* the locking arm latch). The center photo is the position of the seal when the container arrived at the importer in the United States (note the bottle portion is *below* the locking arm latch). The picture on the right reveals that upon close examination the bottom of the bottle portion was likely cut with a jeweler's knife or Exacto blade along the seam, exposing the metal bottom once removed. The bottom was drilled out and the locking rings expanded and manipulated to permit undetected removal/reaffixing of the seal. The plastic bottle-covering was reassembled using super glue. The workmanship was very good and not easily detected—not even at the importer's location.

portion can be manipulated or compromised and reconnected (sometimes using a bit of super glue). During 2014 and 2015, there were numerous incidents of containers arriving in Colombia from Europe (intransit to Central America and the U.S.) that had bottle seals manipulated as noted above. These container seals were "opened," drug inserted, and resealed—all while the containers where staged in ports or onboard the ships, the latter cases with stevedore participation.

Bottle seals also are vulnerable to modification as shown in Fig. 5.15. In this case, the modification was actually performed in the seaport and likely would have been successful had there not been a communication and coordination disconnect between the narcotics smugglers. First, the seal was removed and modified efficiently but reaffixed upside-down from when it was originally affixed at the exporter's location—a telltale flaw since this exporter and importer photograph the container and seals at time of loading and time of arrival at destination and compare the photos/information. Second, while the seal had been modified to permit the stud portion to be removed and reaffixed multiple times, the drugs were not extracted at the Port in Miami or en route to the consignee—a lost opportunity. And, third, as so often happens in the smuggling world, the Panama-based representative for the Colombian narcotics smuggling organization became greedy and short-shipped the majority of the drug load (he stole about 150 pounds of cocaine). The Colombians—and the Mexicans—involved in these operations do not give second chances to people who steal from them. On the evening that the drugs were seized in Miami, the Panama-based representative was assassinated.

In the narcotics smuggling case noted previously in the chapter, the drugs were loaded into the container at a warehouse in the Colon Free Zone, Panama. The original seal-of-record was affixed to the container by the driver at time of pickup. However, a few days earlier—when

FIGURE 5.16 This carton contained part of a 500 lb. shipment of cocaine and had been resealed after the drugs were inserted in place of the legitimate cargo.

the seal-of-record was sent to the exporter—the drug smugglers acquired a seal with almost the same serial number from the company's seal custodian. The second seal was altered to read the same number as the seal now affixed to the drug-laden container. After receiving a tip, U.S. CBP in Port Everglades was waiting for the ship and immediately opened the container upon unloading from the ship. The box shown in Fig. 5.16 had an "altered" seal taped to the top. The narcos' plan had been for participating stevedores to move the container to a low-visibility area in the terminal, cut off the original seal, extract the 500 pounds of cocaine contained in boxes marked with a small piece of red tape in the top corners, and then affix the altered seal before U.S. CBP had the opportunity to inspect the container or it was dispatched to the consignee.

For reasons of enhanced detection of unauthorized access to containers and facilitating quicker and more accurate container information processing (cost savings), it is likely that in the future *electronic seals,* or *e-seals,* will be used to secure an increasing percentage of the loaded cargo containers arriving in the United States and traveling around worldwide. Electronic seals are designed to help companies track shipments and monitor whether a container has been tampered with or if its security has been compromised. Adding sensors and GPS capability can enhance an e-seal's functions and provide the ability to indicate whether conditions inside a container have changed, as well as a container's location while in transit—data which is recorded and transmitted to the entity monitoring the seal status. Approved in mid-April 2007, the ISO 18185 standard addresses technical and application standards for e-seals, which the ISO describes as "nonreusable freight container seals" that "electronically evidence tampering or intrusion through the container doors."[7]

Electronic seals are an emerging class of active radio-frequency identification (RFID) devices that incorporate both a mechanical locking mechanism and an active RFID module to provide wireless alerting and location capabilities not currently possible with traditional bolt seals, which are easily breached. ISO 18185 specifies the requirements for data protection, device authentication, environmental characteristics (resistance to vibration, mechanical shock, rain, dust, and electrostatic discharge, for example), and the communications (air-interface) protocol between read-only active RFID e-seals and associated interrogators. All compliant e-seals must be capable of communicating at 433 MHz and 2.45 GHz.

With all seals currently in use, it is important to appreciate that conducting visual and physical inspections is very important. Seals are much more vulnerable to successful tampering when they can be manipulated prior to application and closing. U.S. CBP advises that seals should never be handled by unauthorized/untrained individuals and C-TPAT Partners can minimize the possibility of seals being tampered with by establishing a seal integrity process. The U.S. CBP "VVTT" seal verification and inspection process call for the following steps to be conducted prior to seals are put in place and closed:

V-View seal and container locking mechanisms.
V-Verify seal number for accuracy.
T-Tug on seal to make sure it is affixed properly.
T-Twist and turn seal to make sure it does not unscrew.[8]

All container seals used in international commerce must meet a "standard" set forth by the International Organization for Standardization (ISO). The ISO is the world's largest developer of international standards. A standard is a document that provides requirements, specifications, guidelines, or characteristics that can be used consistently to ensure that materials, products, processes, and services are fit for their purpose. The most current standard for container seals is ISO 17712:2013, which establishes uniform procedures for the classification, acceptance, and withdrawal of mechanical freight container seals that are acceptable for securing freight containers in international commerce. This regulation became effective on May 15, 2014. In brief, ISO 17712:2013 focus on three areas:

- It defines three types of classes of *seal strength* or barrier capacity: "I" for Indicative; "S" for Security; and "H" for High Security. ***C-TPAT Partners are required to use "H" class seals.***
- The *auditing of manufacturer's security-related business processes*. Annex "A" defines over two dozen required practices, such as facility risk assessments and access controls to production and storage areas. Conformance is validated through an independent certification provider that is accredited to audit compliance with the ISO standards.
- Seals be designed and constructed with *tamper indicative features* that generate telltale evidence of tampering. The 2013 regulation makes changes to the earlier regulation of 2010 and no longer requires independent third party laboratory testing and certification against specific tamper-related criteria. Instead, the 2013 version

permits internally generated and internally managed tests of tamper evidence, as part of a manufacturers' documented ISO 9001 quality program (*must* be ISO 9001 certified). This is more practical for manufactures and also is consistent with other ISO mandates. The testing now is measured against the manufacturers' test protocol and specification versus a defined list—as noted in the 2010 version. Auditable processes must assure explicit attention is given to tamper issues in design and manufacturing.

"Red Flags" of Possible Criminal/Terrorist Surveillance

Efforts to circumvent security measures and procedures frequently leave a "footprint" or indicator of unusual or unauthorized activity that should raise suspicion. According to the U.S. Department of Homeland Security and the U.S. Coast Guard,[9] the following activities are indicators—"red flags"—of possible criminal or terrorist surveillance:

- Unknown persons approaching (in-person or via telephone) employees or their family members inquiring about the facility;
- Unknown or suspicious workmen trying to gain access to the facility to repair, replace, service, or install equipment;
- Suspicious package drop-offs/attempted drop-offs;
- Unknown persons photographing or attempting to gain access to facilities;
- Theft of "standard" operating procedures documents, ID badges, vehicle passes, employee uniforms, or facility vehicles;
- Unusual or prolonged interest by suspicious persons in the security measures or personnel, entry points and access controls, or perimeter barriers such as fences or walls;
- Unusual behavior by unknown person(s), such as starting or quickly looking away from personnel or vehicles entering or leaving designated facilities or parking areas;
- Unauthorized observation of security reaction drills or procedures;
- Increase in anonymous telephone or e-mail threats to facilities in conjunction with suspected surveillance incidents indicating possible surveillance of threat reaction procedures;
- Unknown persons conducting foot surveillance (involving two or three individuals working together);
- Unknown person(s) conducting mobile surveillance, using bicycles, scooters, motorcycles, cars, trucks, sport utility vehicles, or boats;
- Suspicious general aviation aircraft operating in proximity to facilities;
- Prolonged static surveillance using operatives disguised as panhandlers, demonstrators, shoe shiners, food or flower vendors, news agents, or street sweepers not previously seen in the area;
- Unknown persons noted to make discreet use of still cameras, video recorders, or note taking at nontourist-type locations;
- Use of multiple sets of clothing, identifications, or the use of sketching materials (paper, pencils, etc.).

Summary

In this chapter, we have discussed a wide range of vulnerabilities in the different links in the cargo supply chain, special vulnerabilities and issues related to maritime cargo transport, internal conspiracies and how they function, as well as the techniques, tactics, and methods utilized by criminal and terrorist organizations to circumvent security policies, measures, and procedures to gain access to ports and ships. The cargo supply chain is highly vulnerable to penetration and unauthorized access by criminal and terrorist elements; therefore, aggressive security procedures and countermeasures are necessary in order to mitigate the threats posed by these elements.

End Notes

1. http://www.statista.com/statistics/264024/number-of-merchant-ships-worldwide-by-type
2. https://web.archive.org/web/20150718151432/http://www.csiu.co/resources-and-links/world-container-fleet
3. Abt, Clark C., PhD., *The Economic Impact of Nuclear Terrorist Attacks on Freight Transport Systems in an Age of Seaport Vulnerability,* Contract # DTRS57-03-P-80130, April 3003.
4. Tyska, Lou, Guidelines for Cargo Security & Loss Control. 2000. National Cargo Security Council.
5. http://www.volpe.dot.gov/infosrc/strtplns/nstc/cargo/index.html
6. http://www.cbp.gov/xp/cgov/toolbox/publications/trade/
7. http://www.iso.org/iso/iso_catalogue/catalogue_tc/catalogue_detail.htm?csnumber=41125 (this is the ISO website, but you have to buy the doc to read it).
8. http://www.cbp.gov/sites/default/files/documents/Bulletin%20-%20April%202014%20-%20ISO%20 17712%20High%20Security%20Seals.pdf
9. http://esisac.com/publicdocs/Other_Advisories/DHS_ib_03-004_aq_survevil.pdf

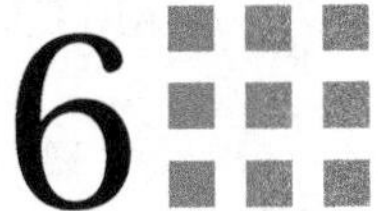

Perils of the Seas: Piracy, Stowaways, and Irregular Migration

OBJECTIVES

After studying this chapter, you will be able to

1. Define piracy and be familiarized with its history;
2. Recognize the current trends and impacts of piracy and armed robbery against ships;
3. Explain the tactics and techniques utilized by pirates;
4. Understand the motivations of stowaways and the business of international human trafficking;
5. Appreciate the techniques and tactics utilized by stowaways to access a vessel;
6. Understand the trends in large-scale irregular migration; and
7. Appreciate the legal requirements placed on commercial shipping related to large-scale irregular migration and the challenges and dangers for Crew tasked with the rescue of migrants.

Piracy and stowaways, the former of which can be traced back to 1200 BC, and the more recent tsunamis of irregular migrants crossing the seas, are costly perils for the commercial maritime industry and present challenges to ships and ports and the Navies that patrol the seas. Irregular migration, specifically into Europe, currently is a humanitarian crisis of epic proportions and costly to the point of straining the coffers and Navies of governments of the region, as well placing seafarers in increased dangers. In this chapter, we will discuss the history, techniques, trends, and ramifications of these three challenges.

Piracy and Armed Robbery Against Ships

What is piracy? Many people hold romantic ideas of pirates, with some forming a mental vision of a swashbuckling Sir Francis Drake assaulting a Spanish galleon in the Caribbean Sea. Unfortunately, this vision is not reflective of the reality of today. The International Maritime Bureau (IMB) defines *piracy* and *armed robbery against ships* as follows: "an act of boarding or attempting to board any ship with the apparent intent to commit theft or any other crime and with the apparent attempt or capability to use force in the furtherance of that act." And, Article 101 of the 1982 United Nations Convention on the Law of the Sea (UNCLOS) defines *Piracy* as follows:

(a) any illegal acts of violence or detention, or any act of depredation, committed for private ends by the Crew or the passengers of a private ship or a private aircraft, and directed
   (i) on the high seas, against another ship or aircraft, or against persons or property on board such ship or aircraft;
   (ii) against a ship, aircraft, persons or property in a place outside the jurisdiction of any State;

(b) any act of voluntary participation in the operation of a ship or of an aircraft with knowledge of facts making it a pirate ship or aircraft;

(c) any act of inciting or of intentionally facilitating an act described in sub-paragraph (a) or (b).

The IMO defines Armed Robbery in Resolution A.1025 (26) "Code of Practice for the Investigation of Crimes of Piracy and Armed Robbery against Ships" as:
"Armed robbery against Ships" means any of the following acts:

a. any illegal act of violence or detention or any act of depredation, or threat thereof, other than an act of piracy, committed for private ends and directed against a ship or against persons or property on board such a ship, within a State's internal waters, archipelagic waters and territorial sea;

b. any act of inciting or of intentionally facilitating an act described above.

There are two important points to make regarding the definitions noted above. First, what defines whether an act is registered as "piracy" or "armed robbery" is related to the jurisdiction where the act occurs, eg, whether "at sea" or in a "State's waters" of legal authority. Second, the definitions are *very* broad. In practice, the legal definition of *piracy and armed robbery of ships* bundles together a variety of acts, ranging from the hijacking/seizing of ships to the kidnapping of Crew to the stealing of cargoes to such minor acts of an unarmed person boarding a ship and absconding with a loaf of bread, screwdriver, or a bucket of rags. One has to review the details of cases before understanding exactly the type of incidents, methods and purpose of attack, and trends.

Historically, the first acts of piracy can be traced back over 3000 years. The earliest act of piracy was pioneered by a group called "The Sea Peoples." These seafaring raiders lived around 1200 BC and sailed to the eastern shores of the Mediterranean, causing political unrest, and attempted to enter Egyptian territory during the late 19th dynasty and during Year 8 of the reign of Ramesses III of the 20th dynasty. Most memorable in more recent history were the two centuries from 1500 to 1700 when buccaneers Sir Francis Drake, Captain Kidd, and Captain Morgan sacked galleons and coastal cities, and Edward "Blackbeard" Teach and Bartholomew "Black Bart" Roberts terrorized the seas and became icons of piracy.

Some 200 years ago, piracy was even a military tactic in the early days of the United States. During the American Revolutionary War, colonial ship owners took part in a concept called *privateering*. This allowed privately owned vessels to attack and seize British vessels and keep a substantial share of the profits. Over $16 million in British maritime assets were seized by these privateers during the Revolutionary War. John Paul Jones, the founder of the American naval tradition, was referred to as a "pirate" by the British Navy. His tactics included flying British flags in order to sneak up on British ships and raiding the British coast, seizing three ships, spiking the guns of a fort, and setting fire to a ship in port and attempting to kidnap a British dignitary. Today, we would likely consider these the tactics of a pirate or terrorist.

Current Piracy and Armed Robbery Incidents and Their Impact

As of early 2016, the majority of piracy and armed robbery against commercial shipping occur in two regions of the world—*Southeast Asia* and the *greater Gulf of Guinea*.[1] Just a few years ago, this wasn't the case. During the early 2000s, the coast of Somalia and the Gulf Aden were rife with Somali pirates and piracy off the east coast of Africa was constantly in the world news and the subject of numerous diplomatic and political initiatives, as the level of piracy there dwarfed statistics in other regions of the world and this is a major shipping lane for tankers, bulk carriers, and container ships. The hijacking of the *M/V Maersk Alabama* and the drama and military operations which followed brought the subject into the living rooms of families in the United States and Europe and served as yet one more example of how small the world is and the local impact of events from the other side of the planet. Over a period of several years, the United Nations, world Navies, and the commercial maritime industry took concrete steps to effectively eradicate this scourge off of the coast of Somalia, Gulf of Aden, and the far western Indian Ocean. An Internationally Recommended Transit Corridor (IRTC) for commercial shipping was established and patrolled by Naval assets of NATO, the European Union, and Combined Maritime Forces (a 30 nation Naval partnership), commercial ships were hardened and made more difficult to be boarded via the implementation of measures and procedures defined in Best Management Practices guidelines (BMP4), and finally, exasperated Shipping Lines broke the age-old restriction and deployed Armed Private Security Companies onboard the ship. This latter point was the true *game changer* in the equation, as the lethal engagements and denial of boarding of pirates by armed security teams soon proved an effective deterrent and pirates generally turned away from any ship when they heard a "warning shot" or noted the armed presence. Since 2012, there has not been a single successful hijacking off the coast of Somalia. Now, let's view the current state of and trends in piracy and armed robbery against ships in the two most active regions (Figs. 6.1 and 6.2).

Southeast Asia

This geographic area includes Indonesia, the South China Sea (SCS), Straits of Malacca and Singapore (SOMS), and Vietnam. Overall, piracy and armed robbery in this region in the first 9 months of 2015 jumped 25% (from 129 to 161) over the same period in the previous year, according to Singapore-based Regional Cooperation Agreement on

FIGURE 6.1 Straits of Malacca and Singapore/South China Sea: actual and attempted incidents of piracy and armed robbery against ships from January to September 2015. *source: International Maritime Bureau (IMB).*

Combating Piracy and Armed Robbery against Ships in Asia (ReCAAP).[2] ReCAAP also notes that the region is at a 10-year high for piracy and armed robbery, with a total of 12 *Very Significant* incidents, while in 2013 there were none.[3] There were several other *sea changes* in piracy and armed robbery in this region during 2015 versus the previous year. For example, actual attacks decreased by 80% in Bangladesh and by 60% in Indonesia and the SCS. However, in the case of the SCS, the waters still were a breeding ground for the majority of the *Very Significant* incidents in 2015, specifically the hijacking of tankers for the purpose of stealing the cargoes of oil. Similarly, Indonesia served as the area for the second most number of *Significant* attacks.[4] Vietnam, which in the first 9 months of 2014 registered only one attack on a ship, saw a surge to 19 incidents in 2015, mostly on ships at anchorages in the southern portion of the country. The vast majority of the attacks were conducted during the night and resulted in the petty theft of unsecured ship supplies (accessible paint, ropes, etc.). Within the region, the primary "hot spot" for piracy and armed robbery in 2015 was the SOMS. Piracy and armed robbery there represent about 59% of the total of incidents in Southeast Asia and experienced a whopping *threefold increase* over the same time period in 2014 (from 26–96 incidents). Three of the attacks were *Very Significant* (hijacking and theft of cargo of oil) and twelve were just one tier down, labeled as *Significant.* The remaining 112 incidents in the SOMS were of *Minor Significance and Petty Theft.*[5]

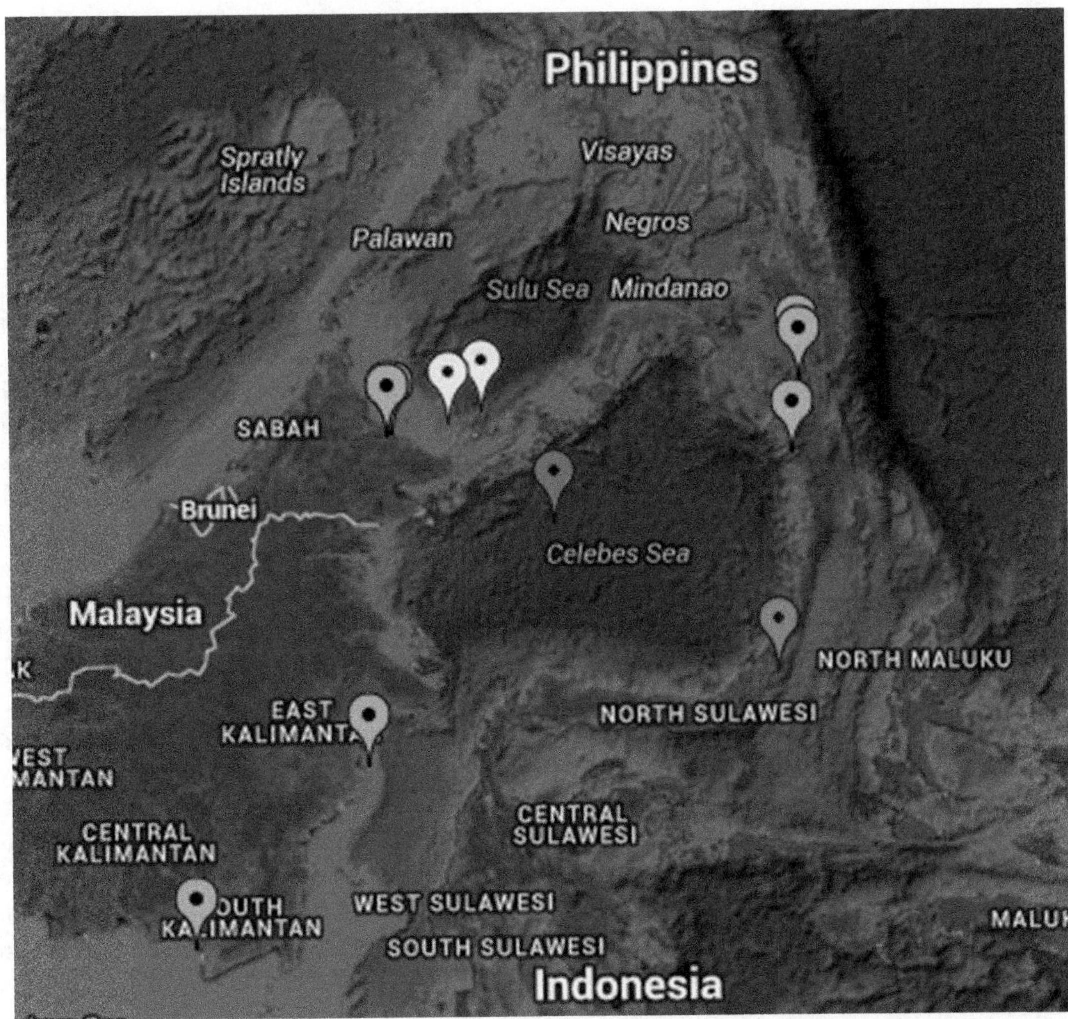

FIGURE 6.2 Indonesia/Philippines: actual and attempted incidents of piracy and armed robbery against ships from January to September 2015. *source: International Maritime Bureau (IMB).*

The majority (90%) of incidents in the SOMS occurred while ships were underway in the eastbound lane of the Traffic Separation Scheme in the Singapore Strait (an area which requires slow speed, making ships susceptible to boarding).[6] Two-thirds of the actual and attempted attacks occurred when ships were underway (87% of these occurred in the SOMS), while the remaining third of the incidents occurred at anchorages and port berths—mostly Vietnam and Indonesia. The majority of targeted vessels were bulk carriers, but the types also included tankers, container ships, tugs, and supply vessels. All of the *Very Significant* incidents involved the targeting of product tankers for the purpose of siphoning the oil and fuels. As the majority of piracy and armed robbery against ships incidents were of *Minor Significance and Petty Theft*, the tactics are reflective of these data.

For example, as documented by ReCAAP, in the majority of the incidents there were one to six perpetrators, 65% of the incidents reported the criminals either were not armed or there was no mention of whether they were armed (28% were armed with knives and machetes and 7% with noted to have guns and knives), and in 78% of the incidents no Crew injuries were reported—however (and importantly), in 16% of the incidents Crew were physically assaulted, seriously injured, and/or temporarily held hostage.[7]

Greater Gulf of Guinea

This geographic area is the span of the waters bordering West Africa, some 5000 nautical miles in length, from Cape Verde in the north to Angola to the south. Piracy and armed robbery against ships in the greater Gulf has been in a slow decline since 2008, when the IMB registered the high point, however, the propensity for violence, temporary hostage-taking, and kidnap for ransom is what makes this region so distressing and dangerous for Mariners. The vast majority of incidents of piracy and armed robbery against ships in the greater Gulf are perpetrated by Nigerian ex-militants and criminal gangs. The former have many years of combat experience and an ample supply of military-grade weapons (Fig. 6.3). The Nigerian criminal gangs are equally as dangerous and armed and they participate in moving an estimated 35–45 tons of Colombian cocaine and many tons of Afghan heroin through West Africa and onward to Europe and Canada, as well the international transshipment of black market arms (Fig. 6.4).

Before discussing incident statistics, one has consider that up to *70% of the actual and attempted piracy and armed robbery incidents are* ***not*** *reported*, largely due to the desire by ship owners to avoid having their insurance rates raised and because governments of the region seek to downplay the problems of insecurity.[8] So, appreciate that the actual numbers likely are much higher. Nevertheless, what the reported numbers do indicate are three key trends, which include: the number of incidents continues to gradually decline; overall violence is rising; and the kidnapping and hostage-taking of Crew steadily are increasing. Let's review some general statistics. According to the IMB, in the greater Gulf of Guinea,

FIGURE 6.3 Pirates operating in Straits of Malacca and Singapore/South China Sea use various types of weapons. (Courtesy of NATO)

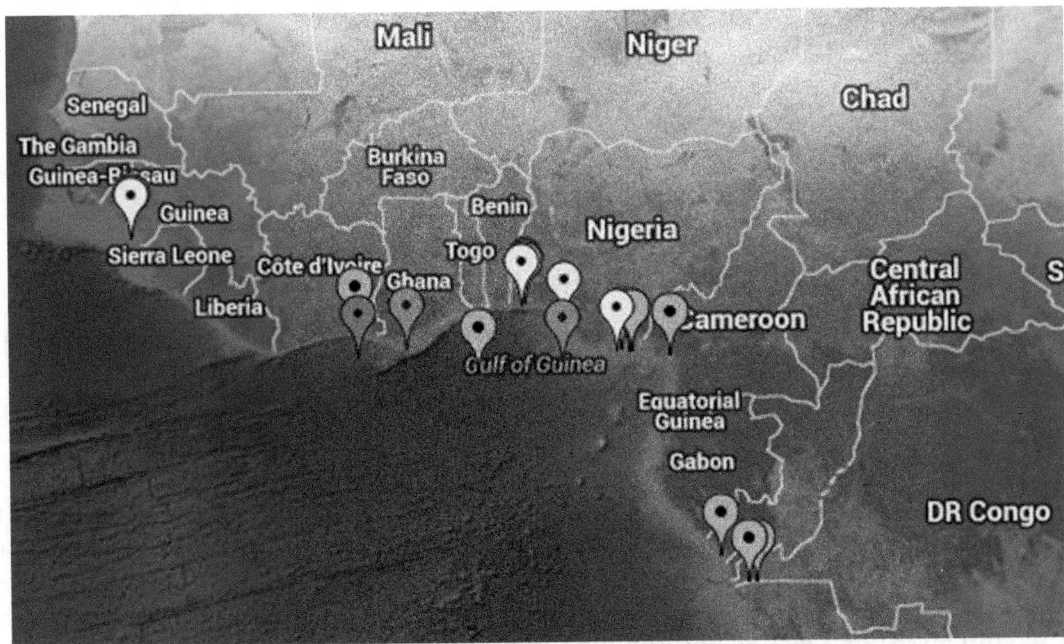

FIGURE 6.4 Greater Gulf of Guinea: actual and attempted incidents of piracy and armed robbery against ships from January to September 2015. *source: International Maritime Bureau (IMB).*

there were 62 pirate and armed robbery attacks against ships in 2012, 51 in 2013, 39 in 2014, and 22 in the first 6 months of 2015. In 2015, the primary types of ships attacked included product tankers, bulk carriers, reefer cargo vessels, general cargo ships, and offshore supply ships. The pirate success rate has been about 40%, only 2 of the 14 ships attacked in 2014 were within 12 nautical miles of the coast, and the two primary motivations for the attacks were to steal oil cargoes and kidnap Crew for ransom, according to the IMB and Dryad Maritime, a UK-based maritime intelligence company.[9]

Attacks have expanded beyond the normal Naval patrol areas and demonstrate the ability of the Nigeria pirates to project their operations both far north and south of Nigerian territorial waters (Fig. 6.5). For example, in 2014, Nigerian pirates hijacked the tanker MT KERALA in Angola anchorage—some 900 nautical miles from the nearest Nigerian waters, and in 2015, heavily armed Nigerian pirates conducted attacks off the coasts of Guinea, Ivory Coast, Ghana, Benin, Togo, Nigeria, Cameroon, and Angola. Some of these attacks were a couple hundred miles off the coast![10] Unfortunately, kidnappings of Mariners in 2015 continue to go at *full steam ahead*. A few cases in 2015 to demonstrate this trend:

- In February, three Crewmembers were taken from a tanker operating off the coast of Nigeria,
- In March, two Crewmembers were kidnapped from an offshore supply boat operating in waters near the Nigeria/Cameroon border,
- In April, three Crewmembers were kidnapped off the MV SURFER 1440 while anchored off the Niger coast,

- In May, a total of nine Crew were kidnapped from a supply boat and barge operating off the coast of Port Harcourt Nigeria, and
- In late October, armed pirates robbed reefer cargo ship MV Solarte, underway near Port Harcourt, Nigeria, and kidnapped four European officers. The Navy subsequently arrested eight pirates, but the Crewmembers were taken ashore by the criminals prior to the arrival of the Navy.[11]

The Impact of Piracy and Armed Robbery Against Ships

The impact of piracy and armed robbery against ships can be seen both at the *macro-* and *microlevels.* At macrolevel, there is a significant economic cost for the countries—regardless of the variances in estimates—and even more so for the world shipping industry. For example, in late 2015, the President of Togo stated at the United Nations that the cost of piracy for the countries of the Gulf of Guinea is estimated to be US$7 billion.[12] This rather high estimate likely is derived from the combination of the loss of revenues from petroleum products and other imported/exported goods, the cost for deployment of Naval forces to patrol the areas, and the heightened costs to citizens when purchasing imported products—due to "passed on" charges assessed for cargo and ship losses and claims and the high cost of "war risks" insurance premiums, all which are paid by commercial shipping lines and eventually filter down to the consumers. (In 2011, the total annual monetary cost of worldwide piracy to the international shipping community was estimated to be between US$4.9 and US$8.3 billion.[13]) Another estimate for the cost of piracy in the Gulf of Guinea, by Oceans Beyond Piracy, noted it was US$983 million in 2014, which likely is closer to a more realistic approximate.[14] Suppressing piracy in Somalia/Western Indian Ocean has been equally costly to the nations of the world which deploy counter-piracy Naval forces there and to the

FIGURE 6.5 Pirates operating in greater Gulf of Guinea generally are from Nigeria, and they are heavily armed and quick to resort to violence.

international shipping industry whose vessels ply the waters of this region. In 2012, the deployed Naval forces cost their respective countries a combined total over US$1 billion; however, the larger burden was borne by the commercial shipping industry—a staggering US$5–6 billion.[15]

At the microlevel, there is a very sobering cost paid by a number of the Mariners onboard the ships that are victimized by pirates. Crewmembers can become traumatized, injured, killed, or kidnapped by pirates or accidentally injured or killed during a military response or rescue. In the latter situation, in the Gulf of Guinea, it is somewhat common for the pirates to exchange gunfire with Naval units and military security teams deployed onboard cargo ships. For example, in July 2013, Nigerian Naval units surrounded the MT NORTE which was in the process of being hijacked, leading to a 30-minute-long gun battle and the death of 12 of the 16 pirates. Similarly, the following month, along the Cameroon border, pirates onboard a hijacked passenger vessel opened fire on a Nigerian Naval boat, which led to a firefight and the killing of six pirates.[16]

All to frequently, Crewmembers have been traumatized, injured, killed, or kidnapped by pirates in attacks. In 2014, some 1035 Crewmembers on ships in the Greater Gulf of Guinea were subjected to the trauma that occurs when violent armed pirates attack a vessel, while 170 of these Crewmembers were held hostage or kidnapped for ransom and 1 was killed. In Southeast Asia, in 2014, some 3654 Crew were onboard ships attacked by pirates, generally unarmed, and 289 were taken hostage, with about 60% of those hostages held less than 1 day. However, in two of those incidents, in the waters of Philippines and the SCS, a total of three Crew paid with their lives. In the first half of 2015, in Southeast Asia, 4 Crew were injured during boarding by pirates and 193 Crew were temporarily taken hostage during the theft and robbery during the pirate operations. During this same time period in the Gulf of Guinea, 1 Crewmember was killed, 2 assaulted and injured, and total of 10 Crew were kidnapped and taken ashore for ransom.[17] As one can see in the above data, Mariners onboard ships in the high threat regions of Southeast Asia and the Gulf of Guinea frequently are subjected to trauma, injury, death, or kidnapping by pirates in attacks. The last several years have seen, specifically in Southeast Asia and Greater Gulf of Guinea, a progressive escalation in level of violence in these attacks.

In South America, the ports of Buenaventura, Colombia and Guayaquil, Ecuador, have been two of the most active ports for piracy, a fact that, while not reflected in reports of international organizations due to underreporting, is well known to captains of commercial cargo vessels that call on ports in this hemisphere. As can be seen in the picture of Buenaventura in Fig. 6.6, ships are anchored along the waterway to the approaches of the port. Buenaventura is infamous for pirate attacks while ships are at anchorage, as well as when ships are traveling at low speed for the 3-hour journey from the sea buoy to the port or inner anchorage. Similarly, the port of Guayaquil continues to this day to be plagued by piracy. The travel time from sea buoy to port is 7 hours, traveling at a slow rate of speed up the narrow Guayas River. Ships also are targeted by pirates when at the various anchorage

Continued

—cont'd

FIGURE 6.6 Pirates operating out of Buenaventura, Colombia, have attacked ships while at anchor, during the transit through the channel to the port, and at berth.

points along the river, but pirates have mastered the tactics of boarding commercial ships while still underway, as noted in the preceding case.

Tactics and Techniques in Piracy

When and where do most pirate attacks occur? In the first 6 months of 2015, worldwide, about 40% of all pirate attacks took place while the ship was at anchorage, 50% while the ship was underway/steaming, and 10% when the vessel was at berth in port, according to the IMB. In Southeast Asia, where the majority of attacks occurred in the SOMS, the majority of ships were attacked while underway. In the greater Gulf of Guinea, according to the Maritime Trade Information Sharing Centre—Gulf of Guinea (MTISCGOG), incidents of piracy and armed robbery at sea and cargo theft are most frequently recorded off the coasts of Benin, Ghana, Nigeria, and Togo. The majority of attacks occur close to shore, in rivers and in ports; however, attacks have been reported over 150 nautical miles from the coast. Chemical and petroleum product tankers at anchor, drifting, or conducting ship-to-ship (STS) operations are particularly vulnerable because of the high demand and ease of selling the cargo. Attacks against vessels underway may occur when proceeding at slow speed and occasionally involve some form of deception to force the vessel to stop.[18]

What are some of the tactics and techniques for boarding? Piracy attacks usually involve boarding the ship from one or more high-speed small boats, using a rope or rope ladder with a grappling hook (for hooking to the deck side rail or deck floor), or a light-weight ladder (single or double pole and with hooks at the top) (Figs 6.7 and 6.8). If the vessel is at anchor and the hawse cover is not in-place and secured, the pirates also may climb up the anchor chain to gain access to the ship. In cases in which the Crew makes

FIGURE 6.7 Lightweight ladders like the one in the photo are used by pirates to board ships.

FIGURE 6.8 A grappling hook with a knotted rope or a rope ladder are frequently used by pirates.

the serious mistake of not retracting the Pilot ladder, this provides a means of access for pirates (as well as terrorists, stowaways, and contraband smugglers). According to Phoenix Group Maritime Security Team supervisors—who have repelled dozens of pirate attacks—if a pirate craft is attacking a vessel while underway, it is generally accomplished by the high-speed small craft approaching from an angled position and sweeping in along the hull, at the aft. Once the craft is alongside, a ladder is raised to the deck or a grappling hook thrown up and hooked. Agile pirates can be on deck in only a few minutes. Pirates will not hesitate to shoot, as a means to escape once detected, or to coerce the vessel into stopping. In reference to the greater Gulf of Guinea, the MTISCGOG report that attacks in an anchorage may involve just two to four individuals, while an attack on a tanker for the purpose of stealing the oil may involve between 10 and 20 well-armed individuals. Similar to other hotspots, the types of vessels used in attacks on ships include high-speed small craft, fishing vessels, and small merchant vessels. While the majority of attacks on ships at anchorages occur at night, many of the attacks further out to sea occur during the day.[19]

What are the targets once onboard? On container ships and freighters, the pirates may plan to steal cargo, electronic and navigation equipment, valuables from unsecured Crew accommodations, and money from the captain's safe. In the case of tankers (chemical, product), especially in Southeast Asia and West Africa, it is most likely that the target is the entire ship. As noted above, in the Gulf of Guinea, the Crew themselves may be the primary target of the attack—for taking ashore and ransom. According to the MTISGOG, the hijacking of a product tanker typically will last a number of days while the vessel is moved frequently across a maritime border to waters of another State. During this time, the vessel may be moved to a number of rendezvous locations to enable ship-to-ship (STS) transfers of cargo. The distance from the coast of the illegal STS position often is determined by the size of the transloading vessel—the larger the vessel, the further out the STS can be conducted (which decreases the chance of detection by Naval forces).

What are the typical arms utilized by pirates? The attackers usually are armed with knives, machetes, or handguns, but it is less common in Southeast Asia for pirates to have automatic rifles. In the Gulf of Guinea, military-grade weapons are the norm, so it is typical to see pirates with AK-47s and rocket-propelled grenades (RPGs). Nigerian pirates are quick to use their firearms to frighten or coerce Crew. In 2015, there were multiple known incidents where pirates fired shots in the direction of the ship for it to stop or near Crew or the Captain to coerce them to comply with a demand.

The Linkages Between Piracy, Organized Crime, and Terror Groups

The linkage between piracy and organized crime has become clearer, while the thin line between whether an attack is piracy or terrorism occasionally becomes difficult to discern. Case studies of piracy incidents during the past decade, specifically in Southeast Asian and African waters, reveal increasing sophistication in tactics and equipment and, moreover, highlight the high level of logistics and international coordination effected by these international criminals. With increasing frequency, entire ships and their cargoes have been stolen, the ships repainted and reflagged, new documentation issued, and the cargoes sold to international buyers. Just the reflagging and issue of new vessel documentation requires conspiratorial participation by government authorities, ship management companies, and other shipping entities—demonstrating a diverse breadth of international contacts, something which only Transnational Criminal Organizations (TCO) possess. While procuring information on cargoes loaded on a specific ship is easy, the sale of an entire shipload of cargo again requires black market access, and if it is unrefined petroleum, then business relations with third-country refineries willing to turn a blind eye and purchase and/or process stolen petroleum products. In these cases, the pirates truly are the de facto operational arm of or partner with a TCO. Additionally, the numerous cases of ships being seized for the sole purpose of holding the Crew hostage—to negotiate a ransom—demonstrate, as in the cases of entire ships stolen, the intricate level of planning, preparation, and international coordination implemented by and capabilities of these pirate organizations. "Piracy for Kidnapping" in Somalia was a good example of this phenomenon. Law Enforcement investigations of Somali kidnappers' communications and following the *money trail* revealed an extensive web of international intelligence and coordination contacts for target selection (cargo manifests, Crew profiles, ship GAs), hostage negotiations, and the facilitating the movement of ransom funds—which connected the Somali pirates to entities in London, Yemen, Dubai, Suez Canal, Odessa—and, in some cases, indicated the involvement of a Russian TCO.

As we discuss later in this chapter, the large-scale transporting of stowaways and trafficking in human cargoes is a business, and one in which pirates have now entered. For example, the European shipping association BIMCO reported an incident on the Ivory Coast in which stowaways apparently obtained access to a vessel's rudder room during an attempted boarding by pirates. The incident happened at an anchorage about 2 miles off San Pedro's breakwater when the ship was waiting for a berth. According to the BIMCO report, at approximately 0200 hours, at least six boats each carrying three to six people approached the vessel. The Crew mustered and managed to repel two separate attempts by the pirates to board. Interestingly, calls for assistance to San Pedro Port Control Authority went unanswered. During the attempted boarding, Crewmembers overheard conversation near the propeller area but were unable to investigate immediately. After berthing, eight stowaways (five Nigerians and three Ghanaians) were found hiding in the rudder room, from which preventive wire netting had been removed. An inspection at the ship's previous call, another West African port, had found the netting secure and no sign of stowaways. This incident clearly suggests that the stowaways had boarded during the "pirate attack." There has been other cases reported in which piracy was used as a diversion for human smuggling operations.

Would it be possible for terrorists to fund their operations by committing acts of piracy? Has there ever been a proven linkage between pirates and terrorists? The answer is Yes. One such example is the Free Aceh Movement (GAM), a separatist group which—according to research conducted at the Singapore-based Institute of Defense and Strategic Studies—utilizes piracy to fund its fight against the Indonesian government. The GAM seeks to create an independent Islamic kingdom in the northern province of Aceh and reportedly conducts piracy operations in the Strait of Malacca to obtain funds to assist in the purchase of arms and equipment. These acts of piracy are criminal and, while probably for the purpose of supporting their separatist movement, are not in themselves acts of terrorism.[20]

The line between acts of piracy and acts of terrorism occasionally blur. As an example, on March 26, 2003, heavily armed pirates off the coast of Sumatra boarded the chemical tanker *Dewi Madrim*. After commandeering the bridge and driving the ship for an hour through the Strait of Malacca, the pirates suddenly fled with the ship's first mate and captain but inexplicably made no request for ransom money, according to *The Economist*.[21] Was this the first such incident of its kind? Not likely, as the IMB estimates that 70% of the maritime attacks are not formally reported. Moreover, since 2013, there have been several other, similar, suspicious incidents in the waters of Southeast Asia.

Another example of a case difficult to categorize concerns the frustrated pirate attack on the cruise ship *SS Seabourn Spirit* in 2005. In this incident, Somali pirates in two boats used automatics rifle fire and RPGs to attack the cruise while steaming 100 miles off the Somali coast, however, the onboard security team implemented the used of the Long Range Acoustic Device (LRAD) system and the Master used evasive measures—leaving the pirates in the wake. What could have been the expectation and goal of the pirates in this incident? The cruise ship does not carry valuable cargo and would be impossible to reflag. Were the pirates hoping the ship would stop and they could ransom the ship and passengers—probably the true valuable cargo? It is most likely that the latter scenario is accurate and that the real goal was a misguided attempt to commandeer the vessel and ransom the passengers. It is worth noting that, as demonstrated by IMB statistics on piracy, the vast majority of piracy cases—and especially those incidents where Crews are shot and the weapons used are military grade—occur in the waters of Southeast Asian and African countries.

Stowaways

Stowaways can be an expensive and disruptive experience for the Crew and the shipping line. It also can be quite deadly for the actual stowaways. In 2014, the IMO noted that the P&I Clubs had reported that from February 20, 2011 to February 20, 2012 there were 774 stowaway incidents, involving 1640 stowaways, for an annual cost to shipping lines and the Clubs of USD$15.3 million.[22] The evolution of stowaways from the single person, unaided, and stowing away on a freighter to today's organized stowaway operation has changed the methods and techniques used by stowaways and, unfortunately, has placed the human cargo in a greater risk of death. *Webster's New World Dictionary* defines *stowaway* as "a person who hides aboard a ship, airplane, etc. to get free passage, evade port officials, etc." Stowaways have been the subject of novels and news articles since at least the early 1800s and, in truth, probably originated not long after the first commercial ships started international trade. What motivates a person to stow away, what is a typical profile, what are the financial and human costs to Shipping Lines and Crew, and how has the desire for a better life evolved into an international business?

The Motivation of the Stowaway

The overwhelming majority of stowaways are looking for economic opportunity and a better life for themselves and their families. Why do they take the risk? They could be trying to escape Port-au-Prince, Haiti, where the trash in the streets is piled higher than many of the buildings and people hack each other to death with machetes over the discarded remains of a lunch. Or stowaways may seek a way out of a ghetto in Rio Haina, Dominican Republic, where the average daily wage—if they can get a job—is less than US$3.

Think these people are desperate? When you observe 30 or more would-be stowaways in the water encircling the ship and none of them move away when the security officers start firing their shotguns into the water, then you get a feel for their level of determination—and desperation. The house in Fig. 6.9 is a typical bamboo structure built by the thousands along the Guayas River, near Guayaquil, Ecuador. This structure has no electricity, running water, toilet facilities, or any other amenities of modern life. Sadly, these folks generally fish and obtain water from the same water below their houses—where their excrement also is disposed of through a hole in the floor. This same quality of life is replicated in many of the countries of Africa. So, stowaways have a real motivation for departing their home and will try repeatedly until successful or they die in an attempt.

While there are many exceptions to the rule (specifically Chinese stowaways), a general profile of a typical stowaway is as follows:

- Male;
- 15–35 years old;
- Economically poor;
- May have some type of national identification but no passport;
- Carries a minimal amount of water, food, and clothing;
- Has point-of-contact information in the country of destination;
- Paid for the opportunity (eg, professional human trafficking organization, security guard at gate, Crewmember on ship, etc.);
- May be trading right of passage for smuggling a modest amount of illegal narcotics;
- Has made multiple prior attempts;
- Generally nonviolent (will immediately try again if caught so there is no need for violence).

Notwithstanding the individual stowaway who, without additional assistance, manages to stow onboard a commercial ship, the majority of stowaway incidents actually are part of an organized human smuggling operation and managed by local or transnational human or narcotics trafficking organizations. To better illustrate this situation, let's review comments from maritime security professionals. According to Phoenix Group Vessel Security Teams, who have captured in excess of 500 stowaways while deployed at seaports and onboard cargo ship operating in Latin America during the past 25 years. In some ports in poor countries—such as Colombia, Venezuela, Ecuador, Peru, Haiti, Honduras, and Dominican Republic—a port security guard or police officer may make his "real" pay collecting bribes and in some instances must pay his supervisor for the opportunity to be positioned closer to the dock. Why? Because the closer he is to the dock, the greater the opportunity for an increased number of bribes and those which are of larger amounts (for cargo theft, drug smuggling, etc.).

This also includes bribes paid by individual stowaways and, more importantly, bribes paid by stowaway organizations. In these ports, it is an open secret who directs the stowaway organizations. This scenario is likely replicated in some ports in West Africa—which are the locations of embarkation for the majority of the world's stowaways.

Stowaway smuggling organizations tend to function like an effective "cargo shipping agent." These organizations have an infrastructure within the port and contacts developed within the port entities, such as port police, stevedores, local security guards deployed onboard the ship, container, and seal checkers, etc. The would-be stowaway pays a flat fee for the right of passage and to cover the logistics and bribes necessary. Frequently, the stowaways—who are literally dirt poor—do not have the money to pay, so they may offer to become *mulas* (drug couriers) for all or part of the payment. The success of the agreement is "guaranteed" in that the stowaway is given, if necessary, repeated opportunities to get to his intended destination. All persons involved in the operation at the port of embarkation—and in many cases in the destination port—share in the fee. The fees for transit to the United States vary from US$2000 per stowaway in a port in Colombia to US$60,000 per stowaway in a port in China. This is big business. Imagine, 1 kg of cocaine at a source

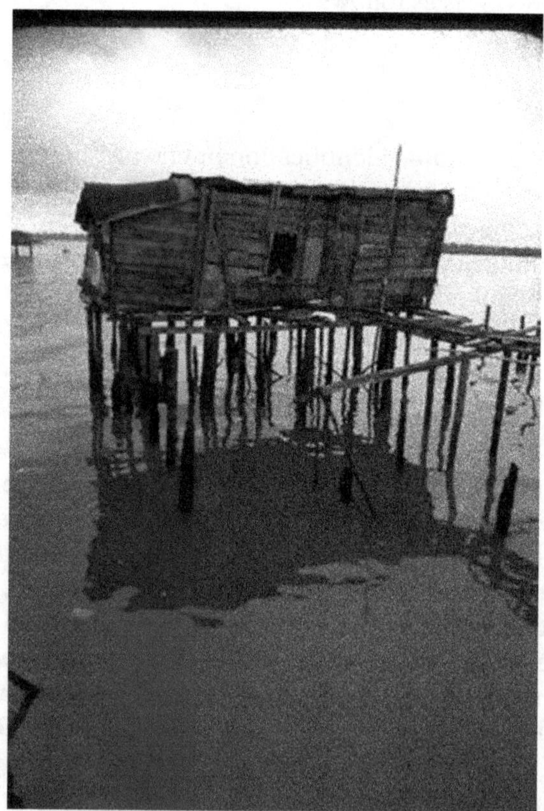

FIGURE 6.9 Living conditions like in this picture provide motivation for some persons to become stowaways.

country port can be purchased for $2000—basically the same price as what a stowaway pays. In fact, stowaway smuggling organizations view their clients as just another commodity. The person who directs the tactical portion of the operation, ie, organizing and placing the stowaways inside the container or supervising the small boat transporting the stowaways to the anchored ship, is called a *coyote* or *snakehead.*

The High Costs and Burdens of Stowaways

Stowaways can be an expensive and disruptive experience for the shipping lines and pose safety and medical hazards to the Crew. According to the P&I Club GARD, in 2013, the average insurance cost of each stowaway case was approximately US$22,000 and in cases where numerous stowaways had to be cared for and repatriated (costs borne by the shipping line victimized), the costs have been known to escalate to US$100,000 or more.[23] The IMO's Convention on Facilitation of International Maritime Traffic (commonly referred to as the "FAL Convention" and updated in the 38th Session in 2014) establishes the legal framework which governs the standards of care and security of stowaways when onboard ships and the procedures for their repatriation.[24] The IMO requires that when stowaways are discovered onboard, the Master immediately must inform the flag state, next port of call, and port authorities of embarkation of the stowaways, make all attempts to establish the identity and nationality of the stowaway (s), and disembark the stowaways at the next Port of Call (if agreeable to the government). Now here is where things being to get real murky and complicated, specifically regarding the latter two requirements. First, how many Crewmembers on the ocean-going cargo and container ships speak the dozens and dozens of languages and tribal dialects of countries of West and Central Africa, as well as Afghanistan, Iraq, and Syria, so they can interview the stowaways? Not too many that I've ever met! Second, this places the Master and Crew in the awkward and possibly dangerous position of being an "interrogator" of stowaways who may turn violent. Third, the convention doesn't mandate that the next Port of Call or any subsequent port accept the stowaway—only that they "should"—and permits local and national level safety and security concerns and laws to override this clause in the Convention. So, it is not unusual for ships with stowaways to become "floating hotels" for several months or longer. The IMO also requires that the ship provide clean, humane, and secure living quarters, food, showers, and any needed medical assistance needed. Lastly, unless a security team is brought onboard, the Crew also is tasked with performing the function of "security" round-the-clock until the stowaway is disembarked. Completing the latter two requirements potentially is dangerous for two reasons. First, the sanitary and medical conditions of the stowaways generally are *very poor* and diseases and other medical illnesses easily can be exposed or transmitted to the Crew. Second, while most stowaways are nonviolent, stowaways from West and Central Africa are extremely desperate and come from a culturally violent region, so the potential for injury or death to Crew is a concern.

A large portion of the "cost" of stowaways for the victimized Shipping Line is due to multitude of expenses involved in the repatriation. For example, when stowaways are repatriated from the United States via airlines, there is a standard for two Security officers per each stowaway to accompany the stowaway all the way back to the country of origin—which may be across the globe. Even processing the stowaways off the ship into a country willing to take them involves the local ship agent having to obtain passports or identity documents for the stowaways from the nearest consulate (possibly in another country if the country of origin doesn't have an embassy or consulate in the discharge country), a visa, health examinations and certificates, numerous other legal and immigration fees and documentation, hotel and food until all is ready (sometimes a month or more), airline tickets for stowaways and security officers, etc. And, this is if any of the following Ports of Call permit the disembarkation of the stowaways! The aforementioned represents a huge financial cost and manpower burden for the Shipping Line and insurance underwriter (P&I Club). A few examples to illustrate these challenges and costs:

- On one occasion, Phoenix Group was contracted to deploy an eight-man security team onboard a ship berthed in a port in Florida with 23 Jamaican stowaways in a cargo bay. The security teams provided custody of the large group of stowaways down in the cargo bay, through various port calls, until the ship returned to the waters of Jamaica—some 2 weeks later. The ship actually diverted from its new trade route to stop off the coast of Jamaica, where the stowaways were transferred to a Navy patrol boat and taken ashore. The shipping line was stuck paying the bill for all of these expenses.
- On another occasion, a cargo ship arrived in a port in Louisiana with 15 Haitian stowaways in a container. As no airlines nearby had direct flight to Haiti, or was even willing to take the large group onboard a commercial flight, Phoenix Group contracted a private jet to transport the stowaways and security escort personnel to the airport in Port-au-Prince, Haiti. Since the dysfunctional government in Haiti typically would not receive back stowaways, we disembarked the stowaways on the runway and immediately departed for the United States.
- In 2014, Ebola was ravaging Liberia, Guinea, and Sierra Leone. During this time period, a cargo ship called in the port of Dakar, Senegal (which was free of Ebola), and two stowaways (mingling in with stevedores) boarded undetected. The stowaways were not discovered until arrival in the following port in Africa. At that port, officials refused to permit the disembarking of the stowaways due to the fear of them having the deadly virus and their lack of identity documents. What followed was a 6-month-long headache and costly experience for the ship and the Shipping Lines as no port would permit the stowaways off the ship due to the hysteria related to Ebola. Finally, the ship returned to West Africa and the stowaways could be disembarked.

Techniques and Tactics Used by Stowaways

Stowaways utilize many techniques and tactics to gain access to the vessel, including via authorized or unauthorized vessel access points, in containers, or in cargo. As shown in Fig. 6.10, the typical load on/load off (LO–LO) container ship (as well as roll-on/roll-off

[RO–RO], tanker, and general cargo vessels) provides many points of access—authorized and unauthorized—for stowaways. The most common points of access for stowaways are as follows:

- The gangway serves as the authorized access point for stevedores, Crew, government officials, and visitors. However, it is very common for stowaways, generally with the assistance of stevedores, to pose as legitimate stevedores (in uniform and with fake or real stevedore IDs), day laborers, etc., and try to enter the vessel.
- Not fully retracted Jacob's or Pilot ladders, as shown in Fig. 6.11, present an opportunity for stowaways arriving by small launches or for swimmers. Some swimmers use the infamous "stowaway pole," shown in Fig. 6.12. This bamboo pole has a metal hook (could be a piece of rebar) attached to the top for hooking on to the deck rail and handholds fashioned from pieces of rubber tied at intervals along the pole. The bamboo has natural air pockets, so it will float in the water, which serves two purposes: (1) this makes it somewhat easier to swim with and (2) it provides its own projection capability. When alongside the ship, the stowaway forces the pole underwater and then releases it. When the pole shoots up, the swimmer guides it so the hook latches onto the deck rail. Agile stowaways, like the young men in Fig. 6.12, can climb the pole and be on deck in about 1 minute. For ships at berth, the waterside of the vessel—whether via a ladder or not—is a favorite point of entry for most stowaways not boarding within the cargo or a container. As in the case of pirates and drug couriers, stowaways boarding from small craft generally use a grappling hook attached to a rope (or rope ladder), a lightweight ladder, or a knotted rope tossed down to the waterline by a participating stevedore, Crewmember, or security officer. Also, stowaways use supply and bunker vessels—which frequently tie up on the waterside of the ship—as a platform to access the target ship's waterside.
- Mooring lines and the anchor chain present additional means of entry into the vessel by stowaways. During the nighttime, unmonitored mooring lines, especially if the vessel is at low tide and heavy with cargo (which lowers the vessel in relation to the dock), permit stowaways to climb hand-over-hand from the dock to the vessel. The anchor

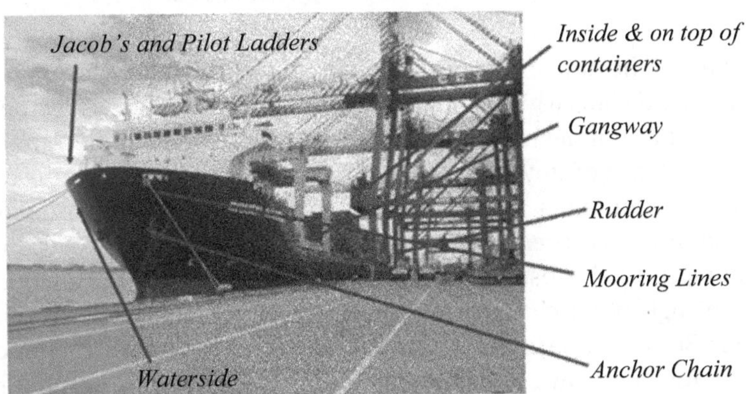

FIGURE 6.10 Access points where stowaways attempt to board the ship.

FIGURE 6.11 A partially retracted Pilot or Jacob's ladder presents an opportunity for stowaways arriving by small launches or swimming alongside.

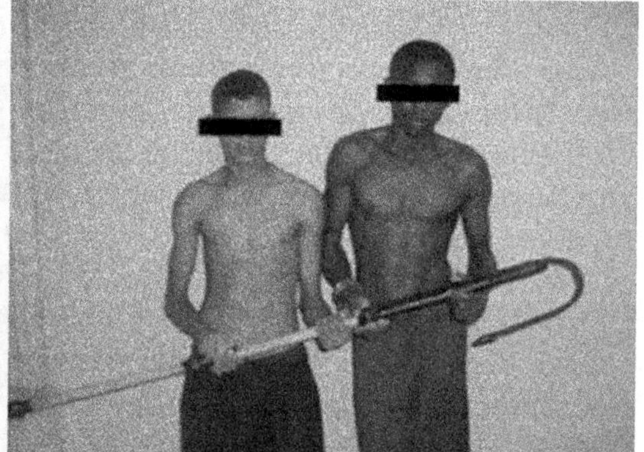

FIGURE 6.12 The infamous "stowaway pole."

chain, especially if the hawse cover is not secured, is the primary access point for stowaways to board ships while at anchorage. As an example, typically there are some 30–40 ships waiting at inner and outer anchorage at each end of the Panama Canal. Of the couple of dozen of stowaways that Phoenix Vessel Security Teams (which were deployed onboard container vessels at Canal anchorages) have captured or denied access, the majority have tried to gain access via the anchor chain. On some ships, such as the one in Fig. 6.13, the distance from the water to the top of the anchor chain is very short, and the angle of the chain from the ship to the water denies easy observation from on deck. Both of these factors make the access via the ship's anchor chain an inviting target for stowaways, as well as other criminal elements. Another method used by human smuggling groups is the "love boat." In high volume ports and waterways

FIGURE 6.13 Access via the anchor chain is a favorite method of stowaways boarding at anchorage.

that have active anchorages, it is not uncommon for water taxis and launches filled with prostitutes to visit commercial cargo ships while waiting at anchorage. Frequently, these love boats also carry stowaways and drug couriers.

- There has been much written, in alerts from Protection and Indemnity (P&I) Clubs, Customs and Border Protection (CBP) bulletins, and news reports, about stowaways (and drug smugglers) accessing the rudder compartment and traveling inside this compartment to the port of destination. As mentioned in chapter "Drug Smuggling via Maritime Cargo, Containers, and Vessels," drug smugglers use this method to move illegal narcotics to their destinations. This is a very risky technique for stowaways because the constant loud noise, regular spray of ocean water (which damages any unprotected food), and the jolting movements of the ship can easily create dangerous situations. There have been numerous cases of stowaways having their food damaged by salt water spray and being found exhausted and near death. Worse yet are those who have fallen down into the propeller. This tactic has been especially popular via tankers and break-bulk vessels from ports in Africa, Venezuela, and Colombia. For example, in May 2015, while at berth in Dakar, Senegal, the Crew of a vessel was conducting the predeparture inspection and detected three stowaways hidden into the rudder trunk space. The stowaways had entered the trunk by forcing open the security grating.

If stowaways successfully enter the vessel, where do they hide? There are an almost infinite number of locations. However, this author's 25 years of experience in searching for and capturing stowaways on commercial ships and barges have revealed that some of the commonly used locations include the following:

- Inside ventilation shafts and crawlspaces within the cargo bays/hatches;
- Behind or inside coiled mooring lines and other equipment in unsecured storage lockers (see Fig. 6.14);

FIGURE 6.14 Stowaways have been discovered underneath stacked and coiled mooring lines.

FIGURE 6.15 Empty containers, either unsealed or with a low-level security seal, are easily accessed by stowaways.

- Between and on top of containers in the hatches, including wedging between containers that are stacked four or five high (a risky method);
- Inside unsecured empty containers or loaded ragtops (push back the tarp cover) (see Fig. 6.15);
- On the main (poop) deck, between and on top of containers, hiding in unsecured equipment rooms and inside the ship crane compartments (see Fig. 6.16);
- Inside lifeboats and the smoke stack access hatch (see Fig. 6.17);
- In the engine room, steering room, engineering, and spare parts lockers (including submerged in oily water under the raised floor in the engine room and breathing through a straw or narrow plastic tube);

FIGURE 6.16 Ship's gear (cranes) can be accessed via hatches at two levels.

FIGURE 6.17 Persons conducting the vessel search must physically board the lifeboats to inspect all storage areas.

- Inside cargo bays, hiding with bulk cargo. This is especially dangerous because some cargoes emit toxic fumes. In May 2015, a stowaway from the Ivory Coast was found dead inside the cargo bay of a ship arriving in Philadelphia. The bay was holding a load of cocoa beans. It was suspected that the stowaway died from breathing –for two long weeks– the insecticide or other chemical sprayed on the beans.
- In unsecured Crew accommodations, hospital room, and passenger/pilot rooms;
- In linen lockers, food storage areas, and other common areas.

The other primary means that stowaways utilize are hiding inside break-bulk and palletized cargo and via containers and related equipment:

- Stowaways hide inside pallets of cargo—boxes of fruit, vegetables, etc.—generally with the assistance of persons at the packing station. With this technique, a void is created by extracting several boxes from the finalized pallet, as shown in Fig. 6.18. The stowaway sits in a ball position, while only box ends are used to build a façade. To the untrained eye, it looks like a normal pallet of bananas. Due to the small space, the stowaway can carry only a limited amount of water and food, as shown in Fig. 6.19, for the voyage, which in this case was 6 days. However, a stowaway is more likely a seasoned *drug courier* when you find him well dressed and clean and his supplies include multiple knives, passport, stevedore identification card, radio with port authority frequencies, two cell phones with SIM cards for various countries, and cash, as shown in Figs. 6.20–6.22.
- Empty containers/trailers and open-top (ragtop) containers frequently are targeted by stowaways. Empty containers and trailers offer the stowaways adequate space for supplies, movement, and additional air to breathe if the container becomes boxed in, and because empty containers hold no cargo, they are typically left unsealed in the port (easy access) and earn a low level of interest. Ragtop containers are designed to hold some types of bulk cargoes and large pieces, such as heavy generators, engines, etc., that need to be moved by crane which are not well suited for a conventional container. However, the canvas top easily can be pulled back or the tie rope cut, stowaways inserted, and the rope retied. Also, because these containers generally are stowed on deck (and not in the closed cargo bays) and have a very porous canvas top, there is regular access to fresh air (See Fig. 6.23).

FIGURE 6.18 A stowaway is discovered hiding in the center of a pallet of boxes of bananas.

FIGURE 6.19 Foodstuff, water, and weapon carried by a captured stowaway.

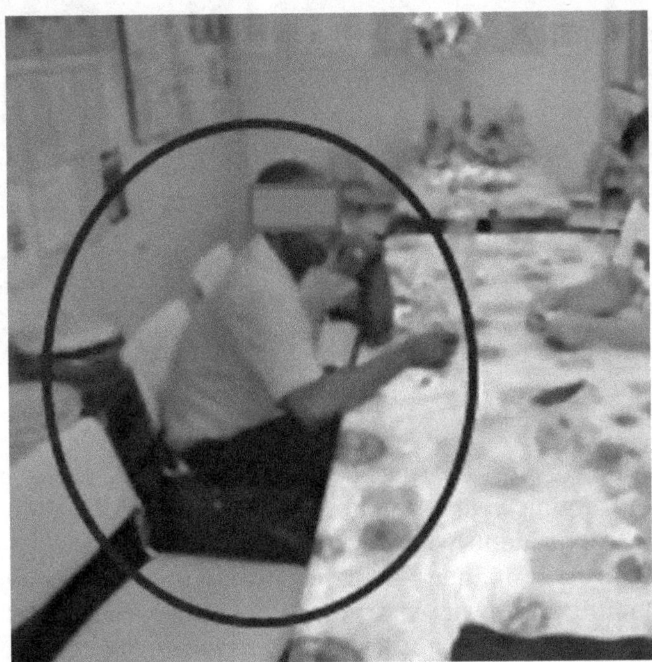

FIGURE 6.20 Note that this "stowaway" is well dressed, clean, and dry.

- Human smuggling organizations utilize loaded containers and *supposedly* loaded containers to transport stowaways. In the Dominican Republic and Haiti, hundreds depart each year either as stowaways in containers or onboard cargo ships or in boats crossing the Mona Passage to Puerto Rico in the hope of reaching the shores of the United States. Dominican authorities estimate that as many as 100 of these persons die some months of the year trying to accomplish this goal—mostly in boats

FIGURE 6.21 The presence of a passport, multiple knives, two cell phones, SIM cards for multiple countries, and a port authority radio suggests that this stowaway actually is a drug courier.

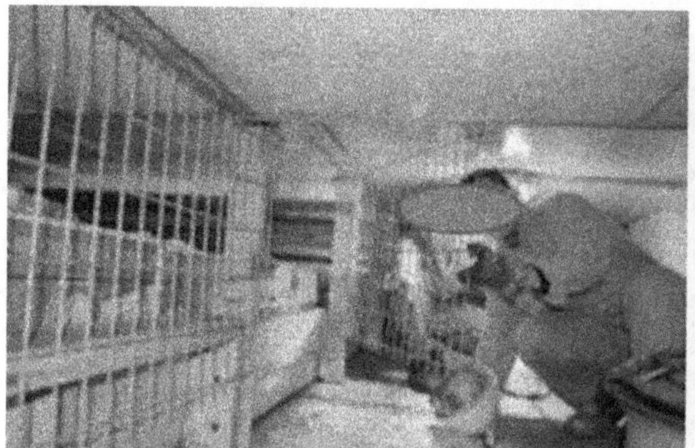

FIGURE 6.22 Note that the metal cage bars separating the cargo area from access to another cargo bay area were cut, most likely by participating stevedores. This is an indication that the "stowaway" was in truth a "drug courier."

that sink attempting to cross the treacherous Mona Passage. However, it is also all too common for Dominican and Haitian stowaways to perish inside cargo bays and containers. Two incidents which occurred in June and July 2006 illustrate the smuggling method via containers—and the perils of utilizing this technique. In the first case, six Dominican stowaways accessed a container being loaded at a garment-sewing factory near the Haitian border. (The Dominican Republic and Haiti, like China, Honduras, and Indonesia, have many *maquillas*, which cut and sew fabrics and textiles utilizing inexpensive labor, and these containers are favorite targets of stowaways.) Unfortunately, a delay in port cargo operations and poor ventilation in the container resulted in the suffocation of five of the stowaways. In the July 2006 case, four stowaways again accessed a loaded textile container, and again with fatal results. The container was already loaded onboard the MV Tokai in the port of Puerta Plata when security officers patrolling the vessel heard screams coming from the container. Two stowaways were found dead, and the other two were very weak. Generally, human

FIGURE 6.23 "Ragtop" containers, which do not have a fixed metal roof, are designed to hold some types of bulk cargoes and large pieces of equipment; however, their canvas top is easily manipulated.

smuggling in 807 cargo containers (the 807 designation refers to the value-added duty provisions under Section 807 of the Tariff Schedules of the United States, which offer significant tax incentives for having fabrics manufactured/cut/sewed at the *maquillas* in the Caribbean and Central America) is performed by loading the stowaways to the front of the container, with a wall of cargo to the rear—providing adequate concealment for visual inspections. Another technique utilized is to build a false wall one-half or two-thirds into the container, with the stowaways and their provisions loaded in the empty space and cargo fully loaded to the rear.

Chinese *snakeheads* have raised human smuggling via containers to an art form, learning from their earlier mistakes. Organized human smuggling is a $10 billion a year business worldwide. Following are a few examples. In April 2005, a total of 29 Chinese stowaways were captured while trying to exit the port of Los Angeles. The stowaways had arrived in two containers from mainland China and showed no wear for the 2-week trans-Pacific journey. The containers had an adequate amount of food, water, blankets, sleeping bags, small fans which ran on car batteries and circulated fresh air from holes cut in the floor, and precut "pop-out" holes in the roof for quick and undetected exit via ladders, as shown in Fig. 6.24. A fake exporter and importer were created and used by the snakeheads, and the container weight corresponded to the weight noted at the time of booking and on the bill of lading. In a similar case a few months earlier in January 2005, a total of 32 Chinese stowaways were captured

Continued

—cont'd

FIGURE 6.24 This container was packed with Chinese stowaways and had an adequate amount of food, water, blankets, sleeping bags, small fans, and precut "pop-out" holes in the roof for quick exit via ladders.

FIGURE 6.25 22 Chinese stowaways were found in very good condition in a container arriving in the port of Shanghai.

in two containers arriving in the port of Los Angeles from China and Hong Kong. The preparation of the containers and fake booking details were consistent with those in the later April case. These two cases mirror an incident in the port of Seattle, in April 2006, when 22 Chinese stowaways were found in very good condition in a container unloaded from the MV Rotterdam (see Fig. 6.25), having arrived from the port of Shanghai, China. Noteworthy, the port of Shanghai is a U.S. Customs CSI port, and the snakeheads were able to slip through scrutiny by U.S. CBP documentation analysis and container inspection measures. (Luckily, they were only stowaways and not terrorists with a nuclear bomb!) Over the past several years, the Chinese snakeheads have refined their logistical and operational skills and learned from earlier errors. In 1999, 3 of the 18 Chinese stowaways found inside a container onboard a ship arriving in Seattle died. The following month, 12 Chinese stowaways were found semiconscious in a container in the port of Hong Kong as it was about to be loaded on a ship destined for Long Beach, California. And, in June 2000, 58 of 60 Chinese stowaways who traveled in a container from China to England died during the drayage to the container's final destination. In just 1 year, the snakeheads learned how to make their operations more efficient and safely transport the "commodity" to the destination port.

- Stowaways also are found hiding on the undersides of trailers, mafis, and chassis equipment. Mafis, such as those shown in Figs. 6.26 and 6.27, are very low to the ground, and it is difficult to observe the undersides. Also, the structural design creates hidden pockets in corners where stowaways and drug couriers can easily hide themselves. Typically, stowaways suspend themselves under mafis, trailers, and chassis utilizing ropes and harnesses to maintain their bodies as close as possible to the underside and decrease the opportunity for observation by security.

Irregular Migration

Irregular migration, specifically into Europe, currently is a humanitarian crisis of epic proportions and is placing huge burdens on commercial shipping and Navies operating in the Mediterranean, as well as potentially exposing ships and Crews to physical violence and disease. The combination of the ruins left in the wake of the ill-fated Arab Spring, the spread of the Islamic State, and wars in Syria, Yemen, Iraq, Afghanistan, and West and Central Africa have resulted in the largest mass migration since World War II. Over 250,000 desperate irregular migrants made the trip via sea from North Africa/Turkey to Southern Europe in 2014; however, the pace of migration in 2015 has accelerated *incredibly*, as seen in Table 6.1.[25] Note that in *just* October 2015, the number of migrants reaching Europe via the sea was almost the same as for the *entire year of 2014*! According to the UNHRC, some 3500 migrants reportedly perished in 2014 attempting to make the voyage, although this number likely is an underestimate. For instance, in September 2014, an estimated 500 migrants drowned off the coast of Malta after they departed from Egypt and a confrontation erupted with the human smugglers. In April 2015, in the worst maritime disaster to date, a total of 800 migrants, 100 of them children, drowned when their boat capsized after departing Libya for Italy.[26] In October 2015, a boat packed with some 280 migrants capsized in the Mediterranean amid near-gale-force winds and all perished.[27] Rescue operations and

FIGURE 6.26 The *mafi* is used to transport containers and heavy equipment.

FIGURE 6.27 The design of the underside creates areas which are difficult to inspect.

death statistics from the central Mediterranean route (departing from Libya and Egypt for Greece, Italy, Malta and Spain) recorded an 83% increase in refugees and migrants crossing the Mediterranean from January to June 2015—137,000, versus 75,000 in the same period last year. Statistics also note that the eastern Mediterranean route (from Turkey into Greece) has now surpassed the central Mediterranean route as the main route for maritime transit. According to the UNHRC, one-third of the men, women, and children who arrived by sea in Italy or Greece were from Syria, with the two other countries of origin being Afghanistan and Eritrea—making them qualified for refugee status or other forms of protection.[28] Almost assured "refugee status" and the accompanying financial and legal benefits likely will ensure an ever-increasing number of mixed migrants (refugees and

Table 6.1 Comparison of Monthly Mediterranean Sea Arrivals (Information source: UNHRC)

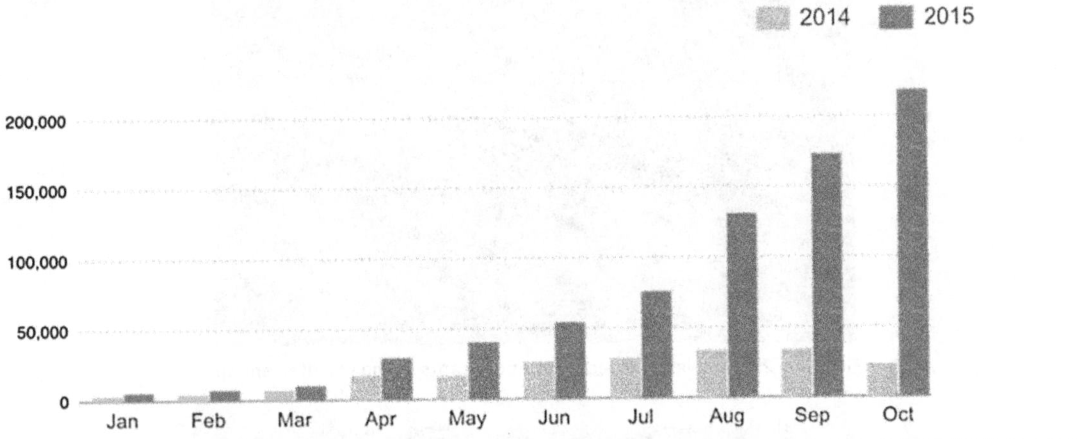

irregular migrants) making the maritime transit to Europe, as the underlying problems driving the migration are as yet unresolved.

It is worth noting that the western Mediterranean likely will become another route to Southern Europe, however, these migrants will be from West Africa (mostly Nigeria, Mali, Ivory Coast, and Cameroon). As of late 2015, an estimated 100,000 migrants from West Africa, mostly young males, now are living in Morocco and more than 500,000 are in Libya.[29] Those living in Morocco are hoping to make the 9-mile journey across the Gibraltar Strait to Spain. These migrants are fleeing poverty, lack of jobs and opportunity, and an expanding war by Islamist (Boko Haram and the Islamic State). It is unclear when the situation in Morocco may boil over and lead to a third major front (western Mediterranean route) developing.

From January 2014 to May 2015, well over 1000 commercial cargo and container ships have been tasked with conducting migrant rescue operations in the Mediterranean, assisting in the rescue of more than 50,000 people.[30] These rescue operations are not small in scope. For example, in April 2014, the M/V EVELYN MAERSK responded to a request from one of the Maritime Rescue Coordinating Centres (MRCC) in the Mediterranean and rescued 352 migrants from a sinking boat. Similarly, in August 2014, the M/V NYK ORION responded to distress call the MRCC in Malta and subsequently rescued 257 migrants. The migrants travel in very overcrowded rubberized boats and rafts, fishing boats, and small coastal freighters which are operated by human smugglers (See Figs. 6.28 and 6.29). The vast majority of the migrants pay human smugglers for transport across the Mediterranean. According to interviewed Italian Naval Officers who served onboard patrol ships conducting Migrant Search and Rescue operations in the Mediterranean, the human smugglers are keenly aware that European Navies maintain a heavy presence off the coast of North Africa and are legally bound to provide assistance once notified that a vessel is in distress in international waters and must rescue all migrants and take them to Italy for immigration processing. The Italian Naval Officers related that the Smugglers have satellite telephone with the telephone

FIGURE 6.28 An overcrowded boat of migrants in the Mediterranean.

FIGURE 6.29 Rubberized boats and rafts like the one in the picture are used to reach just beyond Libian territorial waters and await rescue by a Naval vessel or a dispatched commercial ship.

numbers of the MRCC in the Mediterranean and the Naval Search and Rescue operations centers "preprogrammed on speed dial" in their phones. They are cognizant that as long as they are outside the territorial waters of Libya, Egypt, and Morocco, they simply have to make the telephone call and Naval and commercial ships are duty-bound to provide rescue and care until arrival in Europe or, in the case of commercial ships, transfer to a Naval vessel.[31]

Obligations of the Master of a Commercial Ship—Legal Framework

International law decrees that the Master of a commercial ship, once notified via any means of a ship in distress, has a *legal obligation* to render assistance to those in distress at sea without regard to their nationality, status, or the circumstances in which they are found. This requirement is defined in the following two international conventions:

- The *1982 United Nations Convention on the Law of the Sea* (UNCLOS Convention) states that "Every State shall require the master of a ship flying its flag, in so far as he can do so without serious danger to the ship, the crew or the passengers: (a) to render assistance to any person found at sea in danger of being lost; (b) to proceed with all possible speed to the rescue of persons in distress, if informed of their need of assistance, in so far as such action may reasonably be expected of him." (Art. 98 (1))

- The *1974 International Convention for the Safety of Life at Sea* (SOLAS Convention) states that the "master of a ship at sea which is in a position to be able to provide assistance, on receiving information **from any source** that persons are in distress at sea, is bound to proceed with all speed to their assistance, if possible informing them or the search and rescue service that the ship is doing so...." (Chapter V, Regulation 33(1)).[32]

Note the phrase above "on receiving information **from any source** that persons are in distress at sea." The majority of migrant rescue operations are not because the Deck Watch observed a sinking migrant boat nearby. To the contrary, in most cases, the commercial ship is instructed by a Naval ship or one of the MRCC in the Mediterranean to conduct a rescue of a ship is in distress at a location given. The commercial ship Master may also be notified by another commercial vessel or any other means.

As the majority of migrants currently crossing the Mediterranean likely will receive "refugee status," the below International law also must be considered by Masters:

- The *1951 Convention relating to the Status of Refugees* defines a "Refugee" as a person who "owing to a well-founded fear of being persecuted for reasons of race, religion, nationality, membership of a particular social group, or political opinion, is outside the country of his [or her] nationality, and is unable to or, owing to such fear, is unwilling to avail himself [or herself] of the protection of that country" (Article 1A(2)) and prohibits that refugees or asylum-seekers be expelled or returned in any way to the "frontiers of territories where his [or her] life or freedom would be threatened on account of his [her] race, religion, nationality, membership of a particular social group or political opinion" (Article 33 (1)). The term "territories" refers principally to the country from which the individual has fled but also includes any other territory where he/she faces such a threat. The term "asylum-seeker" is defined as *an individual who is seeking international protection and whose claim has not yet been finally decided on by the country in which he or she has submitted it.* Not every asylum-seeker will ultimately be recognized as a refugee, but *every refugee initially is an asylum-seeker.* So, this Convention must also be considered by ship Masters.[33]

Potential Dangers for Ship and Crew

The conducting of these large-scale migrant rescue operations by commercial ships places the ship and Crew in potentially dangerous situations and are fraught with opportunities for things to go wrong. A few points for consideration:

- Migrants generally have traveled many thousands of miles, crossed various countries, and lived in unhealthy conditions prior to being rescued by a commercial ship. Many are in poor health and may have been exposed to viruses and diseases along the way, thereby placing the rescuing Crew at increased risk of contracting diseases or other illness.

- Migrants willing to risk their lives crossing the Mediterranean in unseaworthy boats and rafts certainly are extremely desperate and there have been numerous incidents where migrants had fought and killed each other or attacked the human smugglers. What is to keep 500 desperate migrants from attacking the small number of Crew onboard a typical commercial ship or of commandeering the ship to go to a desired final destination in Europe (such as England or northern Europe)?
- Numerous press reports note that the Islamic State may (or is) inserting terrorists into the throngs of migrants crossing into Europe and the November 2015 attacks in Paris, of which at least one terrorist entered as a Syrian refugee, gives credence to this concern. Could these terrorists, once rescued by a cargo or container ship, commandeer the ship for use as a platform in a terrorist attack on a Naval ship or European seaport or turn a well-intentioned, life-saving act into a deadly hostage situation?
- Commercial ships are designed and equipped to transport cargo and containers and not as large-scale rescue platforms or function as "hospital ships" and Crew are not trained medical professional. Can a ship or Crew be held negligent and liable if the rescue doesn't save all migrants, medical care given by nonmedically trained Crew doesn't save the life of a migrant, or if the ship exhausts its medical provisions and does have enough to care for all migrants?
- What if a ship rescues a large group of migrants but the nearest country won't accept them? One such case occurred when a cargo ship rescued migrants from a sinking rubber raft off the coast of Tripoli. The migrants were rescued within the territorial waters of Libya, however, when the ship retuned the migrants to Libya, officials there refused to accept them because they were not "Libyans." When the Captain protested, he was threatened with being charged as a "Human Smuggler." The ship was required to travel into the Mediterranean and rendezvous with a European Naval vessel to transfer the migrants.

As one can see from the above points, while there is a legal obligation for commercial shipping to assist in the large-scale migrant rescue operations, they are not conducted without a high level of risk and complications. Now let's reviews some recommended advise for ship Masters.

Recommendations for Ship Masters

The United Nation's IMO and UNHRC have published Guidelines for steps to be taken once a Master is notified to conduct a migrant rescue operation, and the International chamber of Shipping and a few P&I Clubs have issued Instructional Booklets and Circulars advising of the actions to be taken prior to sailing into a high-risk area for migrant smuggling, as well the conducting of rescue operations and the care of rescued migrants. The UK P&I Club and the UNHRC note, with respect to reporting requirements, that when requested to provide assistance to the rescue of persons in distress at sea and diverting to the location, the Master of the ship should, if possible: identify the ship's equipment and life-saving appliances that may be appropriate for the rescue operation; determine if any special arrangements, additional equipment, or assistance may be required for the rescue operation; implement any plans and procedures to safeguard the safety and security of the Crew and the ship; and inform the ship's owner/operator and agent at the next intended port of call of the rescue operation.[34]

Once migrants are onboard, the Master must advise the MRCC of the details of the rescued persons, including total number; name, gender, and age; apparent health and medical condition (including any special medical needs); actions completed or intended to be taken by the Master; the Master's preferred arrangement and location for disembarking or transferring the rescued persons, mindful that rescued persons should not be disembarked or transferred to a place where their life or safety would be at risk; any help needed by the assisting ship (ie, due to limitations and characteristics of the ship's equipment, available manpower, stocks of supplies, etc.); and any special factors (eg, safety of navigation, prevailing weather conditions, time-sensitive cargo). Masters who have embarked persons in distress at sea should treat them with humanity, within the capabilities of the ship. If rescued persons appear to indicate that they are asylum-seekers or refugees or that they fear persecution or ill treatment if disembarked at a particular place, the Master should contact/advise the MRCC and UNHRC and inform the rescued persons concerned that the Master has no authority to hear, consider, or determine asylum requests. Additionally, the Master/Crew should not ask to or conduct disembarkation in the country of origin or from which the individual has fled and should not share personal information regarding the asylum-seekers with the authorities of that country, or with others who might convey this information to those authorities. UNHCR should be contacted if there are difficulties reaching agreement regarding arrangements for the treatment or disembarkation of rescued people who may be asylum-seekers or refugees. Asylum-seekers and refugees have a right to contact UNHCR. This would usually take place as soon as possible after embarkation.[35]

The International Chamber of Shipping's *Large Scale Rescue Operations at Sea—Guidance on Ensuring the Safety and Security of Seafarers and Rescued Persons, Second Edition 2015* is an excellent product and source for Masters and Crew and addresses, among many topics:

- *Preparations:* Plans and Procedures, Training, Life Saving Equipment, Food and Provisions, First Aid and Supplies, and Shelter for Migrants
- *Conducting Large-Scale Rescue Operations:* Coordination, Responding to the Distress Call, Recording Events, Assessing the Situation, Monitoring the Situation, Rescue Planning, Considerations for the Rescue, and Embarkation of Rescued Persons
- *Management of Rescued Persons:* Security of the Crew and Ship, Accommodations of the Rescued and Management of the Migrants, Medical Care, Infectious Diseases and Viruses, and Sanitation and Hygiene
- *Disembarkation of Rescued Persons:* Disembarkation in Port, Disembarkation at Sea, Personal Effects, Post Disembarkation Actions, and Crew Welfare Considerations and Action

The booklet also includes step-by-step instructions for the conducting of the rescue operations and sample forms and documents for the registration and safety of the rescued migrants.[36]

Summary

In this chapter, we discussed the definition and history of piracy, recent trends in piracy and armed robbery against ships, the tactics and techniques utilized by pirates, and the linkage to organized crime and terrorism. Similarly, we reviewed the motivations of stowaways and the business of international human trafficking, as well as the techniques and tactics utilized by stowaways to access the vessel. Lastly, we reviewed the legal obligations, potential dangers, and current state of irregular migration via sea into Europe, as well as guidance for commercial shipping when conducting large-scale migrate rescue operations. Clearly, the problems and perils of piracy, stowaways, and irregular migration will continue to challenge commercial ships, and their Crew, and ports for the foreseeable future.

End Notes

1. http://www.recaap.org/Portals/0/docs/Reports/2015/ReCAAP%20ISC%20Half%20Yearly%202015%20Report.pdf http://www.hellenicshippingnews.com/wp-content/uploads/2015/01/2014-Annual-IMB-Piracy-Report-ABRIDGED.pdf. (It is important to appreciate that the different Piracy and Armed Robbery Reporting Centres define sub-regions differently from a geographic perspective and also receive and collect data from different sources, all of which results in some variances in the statistical data fields and subsequent analyses.)
2. http://www.recaap.org/Portals/0/docs/Reports/2015/ReCAAP%20ISC%203rd%20Qtrly%20Report%202015%20%28Open%29.pdf. Of note, Dryad Maritime reports a 38% increase in piracy and armed robbery in the first three quarters of 2015 versus the same time period in 2014.
3. "*Very Significant*" is defined an incident involving a large number of perpetrators usually nine or more, armed with guns and knives, Crew is exposed to physical violence and held hostage/kidnapped, and the ship was either hijacked or the cargo on board was stolen, for example siphoning of cargo oil.
4. "*Significant*" is defined an incident involving a moderate number of perpetrators (usually 4-6), armed with knives and machetes, Crew likely is threatened or temporarily held hostage while cash and ship's property is stolen.
5. "*Minor Significance and Petty Theft*" is defined an incident involving from 1 to 6 perpetrators, generally unarmed but may have a knife, bat, or stick, Crew is not injured but may be verbally challenged, and nothing is stolen or just minor ship's stores or spare parts. In the vast majority these cases, the attacker (s) disembark as soon as Crew sees them and/or sounds the alarm.
6. http://www.recaap.org/Portals/0/docs/Reports/2015/ReCAAP%20ISC%203rd%20Qtrly%20Report%202015%20%28Open%29.pdf
7. Ibid.
8. http://www.dryadmaritime.com/combating-piracy-gulf-guinea/; http://oceansbeyondpiracy.org/sites/default/files/attachments/SoP2014ExecutiveSummary.pdf
9. http://www.dryadmaritime.com/maritime-crime-figures-2014-analysis/; http://oceansbeyondpiracy.org/sites/default/files/attachments/SoP2014ExecutiveSummary.pdf; http://shipandbunker.com/news/apac/652620-obp-state-of-maritime-piracy-report-se-asian-piracy-is-especially-dangerous-continuing-at-unacceptable-levels
10. http://www.mtisc-gog.org/recent-incidents/
11. http://www.thetidenewsonline.com/2015/10/26/navy-nabs-eight-suspected-oil-thieves-moves-to-rescue-foreign-abductees/; http://www.mtisc-gog.org/recent-incidents/

12. http://maritime-executive.com/article/four-mariners-kidnapped-in-nigeria
13. http://www.igpandi.org/downloadables/piracy/news/Marsh%20Piracy%20implications.pdf
14. http://oceansbeyondpiracy.org/sites/default/files/attachments/SoP2014ExecutiveSummary.pdf
15. http://oceansbeyondpiracy.org/publications/economic-cost-somali-piracy-2012
16. http://www.dryadmaritime.com/combating-piracy-gulf-guinea/
17. http://oceansbeyondpiracy.org/sites/default/files/attachments/SoP2014ExecutiveSummary.pdf; http://www.hellenicshippingnews.com/wp-content/uploads/2015/01/2014-Annual-IMB-Piracy-Report-ABRIDGED.pdf.; ICC-IMB, Piracy and Armed Robbery Against Ships Report – 01 January – 30 June 2015
18. Ibid.; http://www.mtisc-gog.org/
19. http://www.mtisc-gog.org/
20. Raymond, Catherine Zara, The Malacca Straits and the Threat of Maritime Terrorism, August 24, 2005 issue of Power and Interest News Report.
21. http://www.economist.com/business/displaystory.cfm?story_id=2102424
22. http://www.imo.org/en/MediaCentre/MeetingSummaries/FAL/Pages/FAL-38th-session-.aspx
23. http://gcaptain.com/stowaways-complicated-messy-expensive-and-possibly-dangerous/#.Vjj2lSundoM
24. http://www.uscg.mil/hq/cg5/cg523/ANNEX%20to%20the%20FAL%20convention%204th%20period%202.pdf
25. http://www.nytimes.com/...rkey-greece-mediterranean-kos-bodrum-migrants-refugees.html?action=click&contentCollection=Europe&module=RelatedCoverage®ion=Marginalia&pgtype=article; http://www.unhcr.org/5592b9b36.html; http://www.vox.com/2015/11/3/9663492/migrant-crisis-chart-mediterranean; http://www.reuters.com/article/2015/09/09/us-europe-migrants-idUSKCN0R71EX20150909;
26. http://www.theguardian.com/world/2015/apr/20/italy-pm-matteo-renzi-migrant-shipwreck-crisis-srebrenica-massacre
27. http://www.vox.com/2015/11/3/9663492/migrant-crisis-chart-mediterranean
28. http://www.unhcr.org/5592b9b36.html
29. http://www.wsj.com/articles/african-migrants-hit-a-wall-in-morocco-on-way-to-europe-1446508748
30. http://www.ics-shipping.org/docs/default-source/resources/safety-security-and-operations/large-scale-rescue-at-sea.pdf?sfvrsn=10
31. Interview at NATO with Italian Naval Officers, April 2014.
32. http://www.unhcr.org/450037d34.html
33. Ibid.
34. http://www.ics-shipping.org/docs/default-source/resources/safety-security-and-operations/large-scale-rescue-at-sea.pdf?sfvrsn=28; http://www.unhcr.org/450037d34.html'; http://www.ukpandi.com/fileadmin/uploads/uk-pi/Latest_Publications/Circulars/2015/UNHCR-Rescue_at_Sea-Guide-ENG-screen.pdf
35. Ibid.
36. http://www.ics-shipping.org/docs/default-source/resources/safety-security-and-operations/large-scale-rescue-at-sea.pdf?sfvrsn=28

7

Drug Smuggling via Maritime Cargo, Containers, and Vessels

M.A. McNicholas*, G.R. Draughon¶

*MANAGING DIRECTOR, PHOENIX GROUP; ¶UNITED STATES CUSTOMS AND BORDER PROTECTION (RETIRED)

OBJECTIVES

After studying this chapter, you will be familiar with

1. The origins, cultivation, and production of the three primary illegal drugs—cocaine, heroin, and marijuana—smuggled to the United States and Europe via commercial maritime transport;
2. The key maritime drug smuggling routes and trends and what factors influence change;
3. The various methods and techniques used to smuggle illegal drugs via cargo, containers, and vessels;
4. The role of "front companies" and free trade zones to facilitate drug smuggling by international criminal organizations.
5. "The proliferation of and evolution in the *Narco Submarine*"

The majority of illegal drugs smuggled from their points of cultivation and/or production to transnational markets of consumption are transported via maritime cargo, containers, and vessels, and this criminal activity presents a significant challenge to the targeted seaports and commercial vessels. The surges in the production of heroin in Afghanistan and Mexico and cocaine in Colombia between 2013 and 2015 have significantly increased the amount of illegal drugs available for shipment worldwide, specifically heroin and cocaine destined for the United States and Europe. The methods and techniques used to smuggle drugs via maritime cargo and conveyances are extensive, difficult to detect, and ingenious in design and variation. In this chapter, we review illegal drug origins and production, maritime smuggling routes and trends, and maritime smuggling methods and techniques. First, let's look at the origins and production of the primary drugs smuggled via international maritime transport.

Illegal Drug Origins and Production

The primary types of illegal drugs smuggled to the United States and Europe via international commercial maritime transport are cocaine, heroin, and marijuana. The United Nations Office on Drugs and Crime (UNODC) estimated in its 2015 Annual Report that a total of 246 million people—slightly over 5% of those aged 15–64 years worldwide—used

Maritime Security.

an illicit drug in 2013.[1] The cultivation of coca—for production of cocaine—and opium—the base product of heroin—has increased dramatically in 2013 and 2014.

In Colombia, in 2014, the area under coca cultivation rose 44% to 69,000 hectares, which yielded a whopping 53% increase in cocaine production from just the previous year—from 290 to 442 tons. Much of this expansion has occurred in the south of Colombia, in areas under the control of the Narco-terrorist group, the FARC. Conversely, coca cultivation in Peru has dropped 30% since 2012, which, when assessing total worldwide production, moderates the impact of this increased cultivation in Colombia.[2] Colombia now is the primary country of origin and production of cocaine. In Colombia, the continued participation of local terrorist organizations in the security of cultivation fields, laboratories, transport, and custody of the finished product complicates interdiction and law enforcement efforts. While Colombia's coca cultivation in 2014 reversed a multiyear decline in production, cocaine usage in United States continues to decrease and has stabilized in Europe. To add a twist to the "coca cultivation to cocaine production ratio," according to the UNODC in Peru, recent advancements in the coca leaf refinement method now require less leaves in the processing stage. Previously, 370 kg of dry coca leaf were required to produce 1 kg of cocaine HCL. With the newly discovered method, only 240–260 kg are needed to obtain 1 kg of cocaine.[3] Once this knowledge is implemented in Colombia, the amount of cocaine available for export will be even greater. The primary consumption markets for cocaine are the United States, Europe (with their some 4 million users), Russia, China, and several countries in South America.[4]

Cocaine is categorized as a stimulant and is extracted from the leaves of the coca plant (*Erythroxylum coca*), which is indigenous to the Andean highlands of South America. Native Indians of this region historically (and still do) chewed or brewed coca leaves into a tea to relieve fatigue and for use in religious and cultural ceremonies. The processing of cocaine starts with the stripping of the leaves from the coca plant. The leaves are dried in the sun, pulverized (by the use of a weed eater, etc.), and then an alkali (lime or cement) is mixed in to break down the leaves and release the coca alkaloids. Gasoline or kerosene is then added, and the mix either is physically stomped by people walking on it or stirred to macerate the leaves and extract the coca alkaloids, which dissolve into the gasoline or kerosene. After it is strained, the initial substance is mixed with sulfuric acid, again strained and then dried, resulting in the formation of cocaine base. The cocaine base is then mixed with sulfuric acid and potassium permanganate and dried. The final phase is the mixing of the refined coca base with acetone and hydrochloric acid, the straining of the mix to remove the hydrochloric acid, drying, and netting of the final product—cocaine hydrochloride (HCl). Cocaine HCl is a white crystalline powder or off-white chunky material.

It is important to note that there is a variation of the standard white cocaine, one that was developed to deter detection by law enforcement and narcotics detection K-9 teams. This cocaine is black in color (*coca negra* in Spanish), was first discovered in 1998, and resembles organic fertilizer or black dirt. In the preparation process, charcoal, cobalt, iron dust, and/or ferric chloride are mixed with the white cocaine HCl to change the color, odor, and appearance. The use of this variation continues today. In September 2015, police in Colombia seized 1 ton of the black cocaine—cocaine mixed with black ink toner—for shipment to Mexico. Another ton of black cocaine was shipped days earlier and passed through undetected.

Cocaine HCl generally is snorted or dissolved in water and injected. "Crack," the chunk or "rock" form of cocaine, is a ready-to-use freebase. On the illicit market, it is sold in small, inexpensive dosage units that are smoked. Smoking crack delivers large quantities of cocaine to the lungs, producing effects comparable to intravenous injection.

Opium poppy is the source for the production of heroin. The vast majority of the heroin consumed in the United States comes from poppies grown in Colombia and Mexico, with only a very small fraction coming from Afghanistan. The sourcing of heroin from Afghanistan for U.S. markets may grow due to the recent establishment of the presence of Mexican transnational criminal organizations (TCOs) in the Middle East and Turkey—major transit gateway for Afghan heroin. Mexico's geographic proximity to the United States serves as a benefit to major Mexican TCOs, like the Sinaloa Cartel, who control the product supply chain—from the opium fields in Mexico to major distribution center in Chicago and Los Angeles.[5] However, the ballooning use of heroin in the United States is driving major changes on the supply side of the equation. Over the past decade, heroin use has increased steadily across the United States and more than doubled among young adult ages 18–25.[6] In major U.S. cities, heroin addiction has risen to epidemic levels and the rate of heroin-related overdose deaths has quadrupled in the past 10 years.[7] Tragically, deaths from heroin overdose rose an alarming 175% just from 2013 to 2014. So, as the demand for heroin in the United States has increased substantially, major narcotics trafficking organizations have in turn responded to the market demand by increasing the supply. Between 2013 and 2014, opium production in Colombia and Mexico has skyrocketed—with the largest expansion in Mexico. Analyses of opium crop surveys reveal that in 2014, Colombia cultivation increased by 30% from 2013, but surged 50% in Mexico in just this 1 year.[8] Less than 10 years ago, Mexico was the source for only 20% of the heroin consumed in the United States. In 2015, this now has jumped to a full 50%, with the remaining 50% mostly from Colombia.[9] The Sinaloa Cartel, the largest drug smuggling organization in the world, with operations in 50 countries, has *23,000 square miles of opium and cannabis growing* in the Mexican State of Guerrero. This cultivation area is the size of the country of Costa Rica! Previously, a majority of this illicit cultivation was marijuana; however, in the past couple years the planting quickly has shifted and the current majority of plants are poppies.[10]

Afghanistan supplies the vast majority of the heroin consumed in Canada, Europe, Russia, Ukraine, Africa, and augments consumption in Asia. Interestingly, the United States' northern neighbor, Canada, reports that at least 90% of the heroin seized originated in Afghanistan.[11] This difference between the origins of the heroin consumed in the United States and that in Canada likely is a testimony to the strength of the grip that Mexican TCOs exert in the drug distribution markets in the United States and Latin America, and of the prominence of Albanian, Turkish, and Pakistani criminal organizations in Afghan heroin smuggling in Canada–where there are diaspora communities of each of these three ethnic groups. In 2014, opium cultivation in Afghanistan ascended to historic level—in fact the highest since the 1930s when recording was established—to 224,000 hectares, and now accounts for over *77% of global heroin production and 85% of the opiates trafficked.*[12] Why the huge expansion? While heroin usage has remained steady in Western Europe and Canada, the number of heroin addicts has grown in Eastern and Southeastern Europe, Russia, Ukraine, Africa, Southeast Asia, and China.[13] The heroin markets in Russia and Ukraine now are larger than the combined markets of all Western Europe.[14] Asia remains the largest market for opiates, and the new increase in heroin users in China and Southeast Asia likely is being supplied by the heroin from Afghanistan, supplementing opium production in Myanmar. Heroin use is rising in Africa, probably a consequence of the major role played by Nigerian and Pakistani criminal organizations in directing the smuggling of Afghan heroin via East and West African seaports using the "Southern Route" to Northern European seaports. Historically, when an area become a transit point for drugs, there is a spillover into the local communities, as there is new wealth and frequently locals partially are paid in product—which is sold locally. The likely factors facilitating the surge in opium cultivation in Afghanistan are the expansion of control of the Taliban in Afghanistan (who fund their terror operations via proceeds from heroin and opium sales) and the incorporation of newly available technologies for accessing water from deep wells—which is providing the ability to irrigate arid land and the growing of crops in areas where previously nothing grew. The consequences of this large increase in cultivation already are being seen on the streets—in the form of cheaper heroin, increased purity, spike in overdose deaths, and expansion to new markets.[15]

Heroin is produced from extracts of the poppy plant. When the plant reaches maturity, the petals fall off the flower, leaving a capsule. Raw opium gum is harvested from this capsule. The surface of the capsule is cut, or "scored," with a knife containing three or four small blades, and the opium gum oozes out through these cuts. The gum is scraped off the capsule and then "rescored," usually three to five times. Once the gum is collected, it is dried for several days and then wrapped in a banana leaf or plastic. Refining raw opium into heroin is a tedious, potentially dangerous, multistep process. At a refinery or lab, the opium gum is converted into morphine, an intermediate product. This conversion is achieved primarily by chemical processes and requires several basic elements and tools. Boiling water and lime are used to dissolve opium gum, and burlap sacks are used to filter and strain liquids. When dried, the morphine resulting from this initial process is pressed into bricks. The conversion of morphine bricks into heroin requires acetic anhydride, sodium carbonate, activated charcoal, chloroform, ethyl alcohol, ether, and acetone. The two most commonly produced heroin varieties are *No. 3 heroin,* or smoking heroin, and *No. 4 heroin,* which is for injecting.

Marijuana is the most widely used and broadly cultivated of the three illicit drugs. There are over 180 million users of cannabis in the world and just in the U.S. consumers spend over $40 billion a year on purchasing marijuana.[16] According to the UNODC 2015 Annual Report, marijuana usage continues to increase in the United States, Europe,

New Zealand, and Australia. Several countries in Europe and several states in the United States have decriminalized marijuana use or fully legalized its possession in small, personal usage quantities, which likely is resulting in further expansion of the market.[17] Cannabis is grown *all over the world.* Cannabis (marijuana) cultivation is a multibillion dollar cash crop industry in several U.S. states, Mexico, Colombia, Canada, Afghanistan, Morocco, and Jamaica. Due to the large physical volume and footprint of a typical export load, shipments generally are smuggled via maritime containers or overland via trailers. Cannabis plants generally are cultivated on sizable tracts of land (an acre or more), to include nationals parks and areas under environment protection, and sometimes camouflaged by mixing within crops of corn, sugarcane, tall-growing plants, or trees. The term *marijuana* refers to the leaves and flowering tops of the cannabis plant that are dried to produce a tobacco-like substance. The level of tetrahydrocannabinol (THC) in the plant determines its potency and value. THC is one of the cannabinoids in the cannabis plant. Marijuana usually is smoked in the form of loosely rolled cigarettes. Hashish consists of the THC-rich resinous material of the cannabis plant, which is collected, dried, and then compressed into a variety of forms, such as balls, cakes, or cookie-like sheets. Hash oil is produced by extracting the cannabinoids from plant material, with a solvent. Generally, hash oil is a thick brown liquid, similar in appearance to molasses or melted brown sugar.

Maritime Smuggling Routes and Trends

The majority of illicit drugs destined for consumer markets in the United States, Europe, Asia, and Oceana are smuggled via maritime conveyances, with the lion's share being transported unwittingly by commercial cargo/container vessels engaged in legitimate business and plying normal trade lanes, as reflected in maps of the major drug trafficking routes in the UNODC's World Drug Report 2015.[18] Maritime smuggling routes therefore shift and modify when, for commercial reasons, shipping trade lanes or seaport operations change. Additional factors impacting on smuggling routes are the expansion into new or increasing consumer markets and as a reaction to law enforcement interdiction actions. As discussed earlier in this chapter, the surge in opium production in Afghanistan has increased the availability of cheap heroin in the European Community, Russia, and the former Eastern European countries, and the continuing escalation in heroin consumption in the United States, which now has reached epidemic levels, is driving increased opium cultivation and heroin smuggling from Colombia and Mexico. Recent changes in the supply and demand of drugs, as well as interdiction concerns, have led major transnational drug trafficking organizations to modify their smuggling routes and modes of transport.

Most illicit drugs are shipped via maritime transport. Analyses by the United Nations of drug seizures globally during 2014 revealed that over *60% of all drugs seized were during maritime transport.*[19] Nevertheless, it is most probable that this number (60%) actually is an "underestimate" and the true percentage is much higher. In fact, Ana Lilia Perez, author of *Mares de Cocaina* (*Seas of Cocaine*), states in her book that, based on her research,

70–80% of the cocaine consumed worldwide is at some point transported via maritime conveyance. As further support for this thesis, in August 2015, the U.S. Coast Guard Commandant announced that during 2014, antismuggling operations netted 59 tons of narcotics off the Pacific and Caribbean coasts of Mexico and Central America, *more than the previous 3 years combined.*[20] From 2000 to 2013, with the dominance of Mexico TCOs directing the cocaine, marijuana, and heroin shipments from South America to the United States, a significant percentage of drugs were flown to Central America or directly to Mexico, or traveled overland and crossed the United States–Mexico land border. However, with the deployment of U.S.-funded ground-based radar systems in Colombia, Panama, Honduras and key locations in the Caribbean—as well as the installation of X-ray and other nonintrusive inspection systems at several land border checkpoints in Central America—air and overland transport has been severely hindered. During 2014 and 2015, drug flights to Honduras and Guatemala, previously major air transit zones, were almost nonexistent and overland transport through Central America has lost its favor due to numerous seizures by law enforcement.[21] Echoing this sea change, the El Salvadorian antinarcotics police spokesman in early 2015 stated that 89% of the drugs from South America reaching the United States and Canada do so via maritime routes.[22] Based on drug seizures and law enforcement reporting during the past couple years, it appears that drug smugglers operating in the Americas are expanding their utilization of maritime transport; via the use of containers in the normal shipping trade lanes, coastal freighters, Narco Submarines, and *pangas* (open-top long canoes with large motors).

The smuggling of cocaine to the United States and Europe from Colombia follows the depiction seen in Fig. 7.1; however, for maritime shipments there is a preference for the use of transshipment ports in Central America and Ecuador, and, to a lesser, but increasing degree, via West Africa. The U.S. government estimated in the 2015 International Narcotics Control Strategy Report that 83% of the cocaine smuggled into the United States first transited Central America (which includes Panama). In 2014, cocaine seizures in Panama were 35 and 26 tons in Costa Rica, leading the region.[23] However, these seizure amounts *do not* include drugs seized off of the Panamanian and Costa Rican coasts (another 4+ tons for Panama). Costa Rica has evolved from being primarily a transit country to a country of both transit and temporary storage. The depth of penetration by TCOs in Costa Rica is substantial and can be evidenced clearly in the degree of money laundering. According to the Director of Costa Rica's National Intelligence Service (DIS), US$4.2 billion is laundered in Costa Rica every year by foreign TCOs.[24] The Sinaloa Cartel, the Zetas, Colombia's Clan Usuga, the Russian Mafia, and TCOs from Eastern Europe all have members deployed in Costa Rica to coordinate and manage transnational criminal activities (drugs and weapons shipments, money laundering). Ecuador plays a role similar to that of Costa Rica and has numerous TCOs operating in the country, specifically those from Mexico, Colombia, Ukraine, Albania, Bulgaria, Romania, China, Japan, and Colombian Narco-terrorist FARC. Ecuador, like Costa Rica, does not cultivate or process cocaine or heroin in sizable quantities and functions primarily as a transit gateway for an estimated 110+ tons of cocaine destined for Europe, Australia, Russia, Asia, and the United States. In 2014, 43.7 tons of cocaine

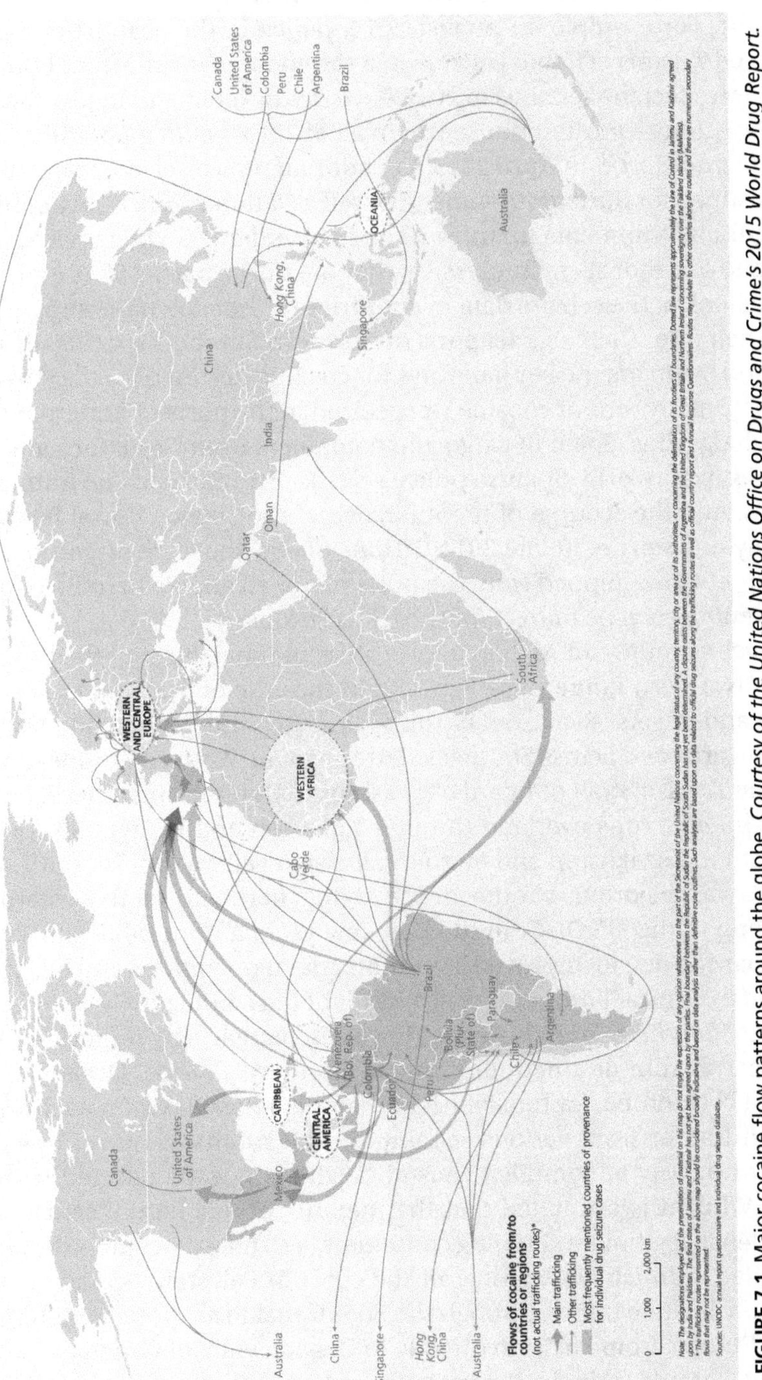

FIGURE 7.1 Major cocaine flow patterns around the globe. *Courtesy of the United Nations Office on Drugs and Crime's 2015 World Drug Report.*

was seized in Ecuador, of which the vast majority was in process of being shipped via maritime transport. For example, in August 2014, police in the seaport of Guayaquil, Ecuador, discovered 7.8 tons of liquid cocaine in a shipment of disinfectant bound for Valencia, Spain.[25] Of note, cocaine seizures in 2015 have skyrocketed and in just the first half of the year stand at 42 tons—the amount seized in all of 2014—*with all of this cocaine departing via maritime transport.*[26] In April 2015, Ecuadorian police seized 2 tons of cocaine in the seaport—destined for Rotterdam—and arrested a National Police LT. Colonel who was in-charge of multiple shipments to Antwerp and Rotterdam.[27] While the seizure numbers in Costa Rica and Ecuador seem impressive, they are only a partial view of the whole picture as one has to look at the seizure data in countries further down the supply chain to better appreciate their role. The mega seaports of Northern Europe—specifically Rotterdam and Antwerp—and Spain are the key gateways for cocaine destined for the Western Europe. In 2014 and 2015, many tons of cocaine were seized in the ports of Rotterdam, Antwerp, and Valencia and Algeciras, Spain in cargo and containers from Costa Rica and Ecuador. During just *1 week* in May 2014, Spanish police seized 4.5 tons of cocaine from the Costa Rican port of Moin. And the scourge of the influence of the Sinaloa Cartel has spread to Peru, where in only one seizure in late 2014, 10 tons of cocaine were discovered hidden inside sacks of coal set to be shipped from the ports of Callao and Paita to Belgium and Spain.[28] Of note, the entire cocaine market for the UK is 20 tons.

The smuggling routes for Afghan heroin are expanding beyond the traditional "Balkan Route" and "Northern Route" (see Fig. 7.2). In the case of the *Balkan Route*, heroin exits Afghanistan and traverses Pakistan or the Islamic Republic of Iran and then on to Turkey, Greece or Bulgaria, and across Southeast Europe to the Western European market or from Turkey via the Turkish Strait onboard cargo ships to Ukraine and other Black Sea seaports. The *Northern Route* runs overland through Tajikistan and Kyrgyzstan (or Uzbekistan or Turkmenistan) to Kazakhstan and on to the Russian Federation. Up until about 2010, the *Balkan Route* was the primary route for the Afghan heroin to get to Western Europe; however, according to the UNODC, in the past few years a noticeable shift to the *Southern Route* has occurred due to improved law enforcement operations and border checks along the route and in Central Europe, as well a result of the conflict in Syria.[29]

The newer "*Southern Route*" is emerging as an increasingly important maritime gateway for Afghan heroin destined for Canada, Northern Europe, Oceania, and consumption in Africa.[30] Hundreds of tons of Afghan heroin enter Pakistan each year and depart west through Iran or from various seaports in the south—via unwitting container and cargo ships or by way of complicit coastal freighters (locally referred to as ocean-going "Dhows").[31] While it is estimated that the majority of this heroin sent via the *Southern Route* is hidden in legitimate shipping containers, a sizable percentage transported to East Africa is loaded onto Dhows waiting off the coast of Pakistan. Primary subroutes of the *Southern Route* include transit through the Suez Canal to seaports in Italy and other ports in Southern Europe, from Pakistan directly to Canada (90% of Canada's heroin arrives via Pakistan) and Oceania (principally, Australia and New Zealand), or from Pakistan, transiting the Indian Ocean to the East Coast of Africa (Kenya and Tanzania) and South Africa.

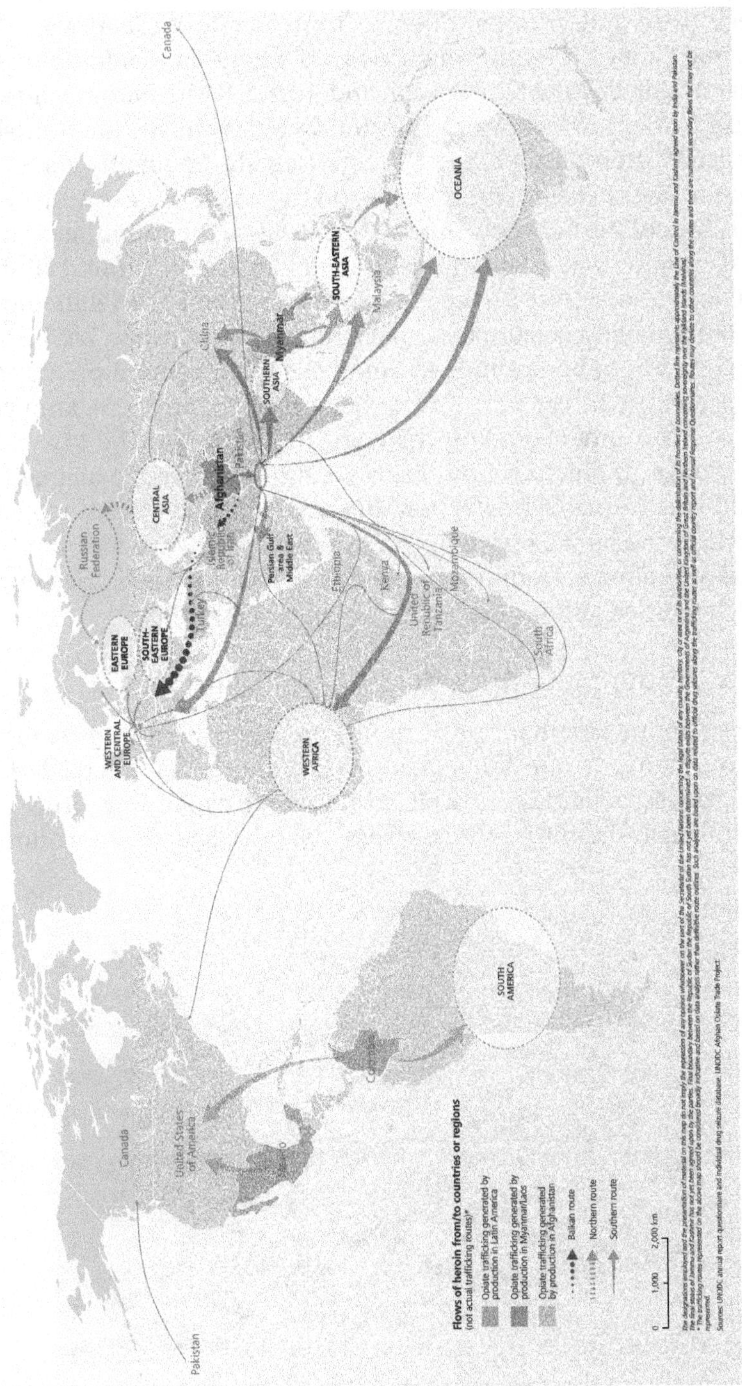

FIGURE 7.2 Major heroin flow patterns around the globe. *Courtesy of the United Nations Office on Drugs and Crime's 2015 World Drug Report.*

Heroin arriving at ports in or off the coast of East Africa and South Africa, generally makes its way via legitimate and criminal-directed transport to West Africa (Nigeria, Ghana, Mali, Senegal, and Guinea-Bissau), which also are emerging as additional transit centers for Colombian cocaine destined for Europe and Russia.[32] The heroin loads, while feeding developing local markets in East Africa transit port cities, mostly are transshipped to seaports in Northern Western Europe, the UK, and Canada-frequently via South Africa and West African countries. Recent large seizures off the coast of East Africa underscore the growing importance of the *Southern Route*. During 2014, the Combined Maritime Forces, a multinational antipiracy naval task force formed to protect commercial shipping off the coast of Somalia, seized almost 3.4 tons of heroin on a total of 18 different vessels in the Indian Ocean.[33] The largest seizure took place in April 2014, when an Australian warship found more than a ton of heroin hidden among sacks of cement on a dhow in international waters (see Fig. 7.3). The *MV Al Noor* had set off from the Makran coast in southwest Pakistan and was intercepted off the coast of Mombasa. The MV Al Noor was one to two dhows setting off together from Pakistan and transporting a large load of heroin, with the second vessel escaping detection. In such smuggling cases, typically the heroin is unloaded from dhows and cargo ships off the shores of Kenya and Tanzania and taken ashore on small speedboats. Heroin seizures off the coast of East Africa in 2014 were four times the total combined amount seized between 1990 and 2009.[34]

What Factors Influence Change to Smuggling Routes?

It is important to appreciate that transit routes and trends for drugs smuggled via commercial maritime transport are influenced by changes in commercial shipping routes and seaport business activities, as well as new and expanding drug markets. Why? First, the commercial shipping routes across the two oceans—and into the Western

FIGURE 7.3 Ocean-going "Dhows" like these are used to transport heroin from Pakistan to Africa and Southern Europe. *Courtesy of Byelikova Oksana*/Shutterstock.com.

Hemisphere—resemble two great pendulums, swinging east from Asia to the U.S. west coast and Central America and west from Europe to the U.S. east coast and the Caribbean Basin. The large cargo and container ships ply these ocean routes and call on the mega transshipment ports, such as, Los Angeles/Long Beach, United States; Kingston, Jamaica; Manzanillo, Mexico; Balboa and Manzanillo International Terminal, Panama; Cartagena, Colombia; and Freeport, the Bahamas; Antwerp, Belgium; Rotterdam, the Netherlands; and Shanghai, Shenzhen, Hong Kong, and Ningbo, China. At these mega transshipment ports, feeder vessels of various sizes shuttle the cargo and containers in north-south route configurations to their destination ports. These routes, both of the transocean and feeder vessels, are determined by global trade factors and other economic forces. So, transnational drug smuggling organizations that operate via commercial maritime cargo mold their smuggling operations and routes around the legitimate commercial cargo routes, for reasons of functionality and in an effort to "blend in." Let me offer a couple examples to demonstrate this concept.

A number of years ago, a commercial cargo vessel carrying boxes of bananas arrived in the port of Ilychevsk (Odessa), Ukraine, from the port of Santa Marta, Colombia. During the unloading of the cargo, one of the stevedores noticed something unusual about several boxes and advised the captain. A detailed inspection of the cargo hold turned up 245 suspect boxes carrying a combined total of 1500 packets of marijuana, each packet weighing 2 kg. Each box was found to be "marked" with a piece of tape and loaded with a small quantity of bananas (as camouflage) and several black plastic bags, which contained the compressed marijuana. Why the port adjacent to the city of Odessa? What was the catalyst? A subsequent investigation revealed the following information:

- This smuggling operation was the third—with the first two getting through—so this was not a fluke.
- The shipping line which transported the cargo had some 6 months prior to the smuggling operation *initiated calling in this Ukrainian port* from the port of Santa Marta, Colombia.
- Participants who organized these smuggling operations were Colombia's Atlantic Coast Cartel (a narcotics trafficking organization which operates in the port of Santa Marta), the right-wing paramilitary commander, and the Russian Mafia.
- These smuggling operations were to barter drugs for weapons.
- Approximately 4 months prior to the drug seizure, four representatives of the Atlantic Coast Cartel—who had previously coordinated narcotics smuggling operations with paramilitary commander—relocated to Odessa.

So when the shipping line opened up this route and linked these two ports, one penetrated by Colombia narcotics traffickers and the other by the Russian Mafia, an opportunity presented itself for paramilitary forces in need of arms and with access to large quantities of drugs. *The shipping line's route for legitimate cargo directly influenced the planning, operations, and seaports utilized by the narcotics smuggling organization.* A similar situation may present itself when a new major seaport is built or existing clientele change. The construction of a new seaport, especially a transshipment port, where there was not a port before may change the dynamics because now there may be cargo and containers coming from many points in the world, some of which may be drug production or transit locations. Or, a port may sign a contract with a shipping line that has a history of drug seizures or significant penetration by narco organizations or whose vessels call on ports in drug production/transit countries. Either of these two scenarios affects the drug smuggling threat for the seaport, as well as for the seaports up and down the cargo supply chain. So, there may be a port that previously never had a major drug seizure in cargoes or onboard vessels; however, one day U.S. Customs and Border Protection (CBP) start to make seizures of large quantities of drugs in this port. Why? An investigation may reveal that the cargoes are from a new "load" port located in a drug production or transit country. Or, possibly the shipping line recently began calling in this U.S. port (route change), and this shipping line had a "history" of drug smuggling issues. Or, the investigation might reveal that a previously "drug issue-free" shipping line, for purely business reasons, began to "slot charter" cargo or container space on its ships (a common practice) to a shipping line with a somewhat more problematic history. The previously "issue-free" port and shipping line would be victims of increased vulnerability and targeting because of legitimate "commercial changes." Narcotics smuggling organizations constantly analyze changes in vessel routing, seaport commercial activities, and commercial shipping agreements for opportunities to exploit vulnerabilities and ship their product via the most efficient and secure method.

Drug Smuggling Methods and Techniques

The techniques and methods used by drug smugglers continue to evolve, traverse the globe, and are limited only by the imagination and determination of the narcotics smuggling organizations. While some involved in counter-narcotics law enforcement may profess the adage "there's nothing new under the sun" with regard to drug smuggling methods, this belief is not fully accurate because the drug smugglers constantly are modifying or tweaking old techniques and methods to increase the likelihood of the drug load going undetected and are open to experimenting with new technology (such as submarines). Additionally, it is interesting to note that a new or revised smuggling or concealment method discovered in, for example, Colombia, will most assuredly be discovered a few months later in bordering countries or in ports up the supply chain and literally circle the globe over a period of time. Of note, most major drug trafficking organizations appear to favor the "shotgun approach" regarding tactics and techniques. For example, Colombia's "Clan Usuga" (also known as Los Urabeños—of paramilitary roots), arguably the most success Colombian TCO, is known to utilize a diverse array of smuggling techniques. They range from transporting up to 8 tons of cocaine inside Narco Submarines launched from the Caribbean and Pacific coasts and destined for the United States and Mexico, to stuffing 7 tons of cocaine into fruit boxes loaded in containers for Europe, to sending a multiton liquid cocaine shipments hidden in large generator, to using scuba divers to attach "torpedoes" filled with multihundred kilo loads of cocaine to the undersides of cargo ships. This multiprong ("shotgun") strategy makes good business sense as diversifying the smuggling techniques and tactics likely reduces the financial impact when a load is seized (as there are many other loads in parallel supply chain pipelines); enhances operational security by permitting more strict compartmentalizing of tactical level information and planning; and, increases the overall percentage of successful operation. Tremendous ingenuity, imagination, money, and effort are dedicated to constantly "looking for a better method or *truco* (trick)." It is common knowledge in drug enforcement circles that major drug trafficking organizations in locations such as Colombia and Mexico have teams of "surgeons" on-staff. These "surgeons" are engineers, chemists, scientists, and logistic experts who focus exclusively on developing new and improved smuggling methods, techniques, and tactics to circumvent or mitigate security measures and procedures and discover security "holes," all to increase the probability of success. In the following sections, we review some of the primary smuggling methods and techniques used in cargo, containers, and vessels.

Drug Smuggling via Cargo

Drug smugglers conceal their consignments inside the cargo, in lieu of the cargo, fabricated with the merchandise, mixed with the cargo, and within the structure of the packing/pallet. It is common for illegal drugs to be hidden inside cargo, such as inside concrete blocks, fence posts, batteries, ceramic products, vehicles, pineapples, bananas, squash, or hundreds of other products. For example, in 2014–2015, in Spain and Rotterdam, many tons of cocaine were discovered in shipments of hollowed-out bananas and pineapples from Costa Rica and Ecuador. The more complicated concealment methods generally involve the secreting of the drugs inside the cargo at a factory or warehouse. A technique frequently utilized is the hiding of drugs inside a mechanical device, engine, or other machinery, such as a wheel rotor or hydraulic pump or within the floor of vehicles, all which are fully assembled and difficult and time-consuming to inspect (see Figs. 7.4–7.12).

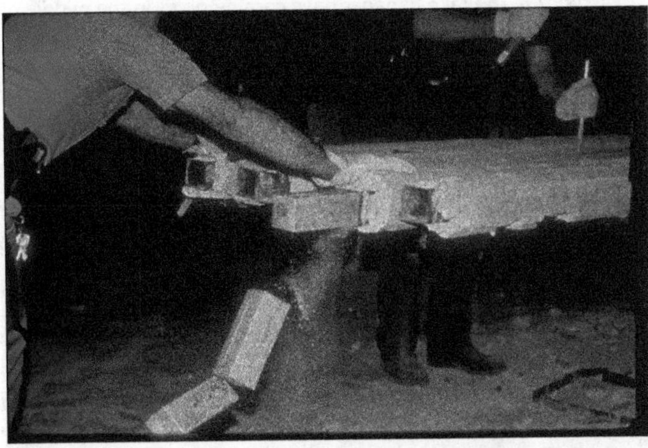

FIGURE 7.4 Cocaine hidden inside concrete fence posts.

FIGURE 7.5 Can you tell which bananas are real and which are fake?

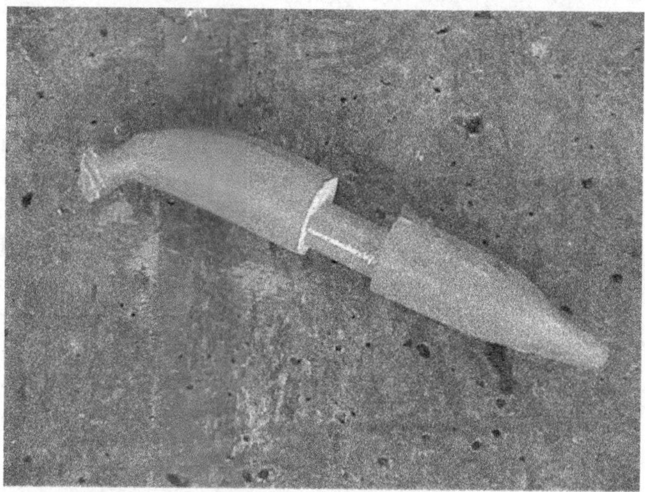

FIGURE 7.6 The fake bananas have cocaine plugs in the middle.

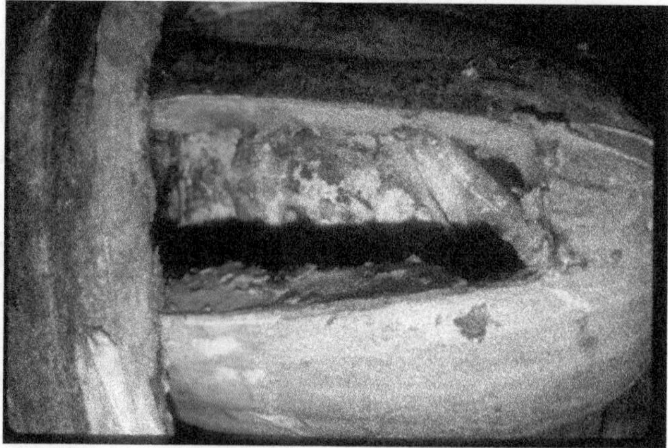

FIGURE 7.7 This pumpkin squash is hollowed-out and kilos of cocaine inserted.

FIGURE 7.8 The container was loaded with "stuffed" pumpkins.

FIGURE 7.9 Drugs were found hidden within the hollow area of a shipment of mechanical drums.

FIGURE 7.10 The interior of hydraulic pistons contained cocaine.

FIGURE 7.11 Removal of the piston cover revealed that the drug package ruptured and dusted the inner side of the cover.

FIGURE 7.12 A K-9 team alerted on several of the vehicles being loaded onboard a ship.

It is likewise common for drug smugglers to create real, operational businesses, factories, etc., both at the point of drug packing/transit and in the destination countries – to facilitate the successful shipment of their cargo. In such cases, no drugs are shipped until the companies have established themselves as "legitimate"; ie, they have made several shipments of legitimate cargo and no longer are priority targets by Customs and law enforcement agencies. Similarly, "paper companies" (those which exist only on paper) are also a common technique, as they provide a level of anonymity and may not have any physical assets to track or investigate.

Another technique utilized by drug smugglers is to pack the drugs inside hermetically sealed cans or cartons, in lieu of the listed legitimate cargo. For example, in the case

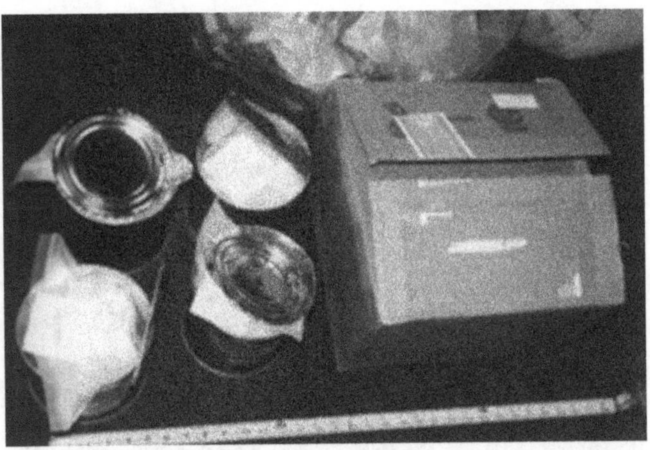

FIGURE 7.13 Drugs packed inside hermetically sealed cans.

depicted in Fig. 7.13, a total of 50,000 pounds of compressed marijuana was loaded into cans which supposedly held juice. The drug-filled cans were packed in boxes which filled an entire 40-foot shipping container. Post-seizure investigation revealed that the cargo had been loaded in a container in the port of Buenaventura, Colombia, and shipped to Panama. In Panama, the container was drayed to a container freight station (CFS) in the seaport and the cargo transloaded to a new container of a different shipping line. A new Bill of Lading was prepared, showing Panama as the point of loading (all quite legal, but an indicator of potential contraband smuggling). This container was scheduled to be shipped to Istanbul, Turkey, where it was to be again transloaded (again, a new Bill of Lading created) and routed to a business in College Park, Maryland, the actual final destination. This container was one of three in a multicontainer shipment, with the other two also carrying large loads of cocaine and marijuana.

A smuggling method developed to elude detection is the mixing of cocaine or heroin with a liquid substance to create liquid cocaine/heroin, a tactic for camouflaging the drugs. The nondrug liquid substance can vary from gasoline/industrial oils to fruit juice to vegetable/coconut oil to water to cleaning liquid substances. Once the cargo shipment reaches its destination, the smugglers mix in acetone or ether and allow the drug to separate from the legitimate liquid. In Fig. 7.14, cocaine was mixed with cocoa butter oil and placed back inside the plastic bottles, which were part of a larger shipment. A similar case occurred in August 2014, in Ecuador, when 7.8 tons of cocaine was mixed with disinfectant for shipment to Spain.[35] In Fig. 7.15, cocaine was mixed with clear oil in 55 gallon drums; the total weight of the cocaine in this shipment from Ecuador to the United States was 870 kg. This method of mixing oil and cocaine also was seen in mid-2014 in the seizure of almost 3 tons of liquid cocaine (mixed with the diesel oil) in an electronic transformer in the port of Cartagena, Colombia, which was being shipped to Guatemala.[36]

Another form of camouflage used by drug smugglers is the impregnating of cocaine or heroin into fabrics (cotton, wool, etc.). In this method, somewhat heavy or bulky

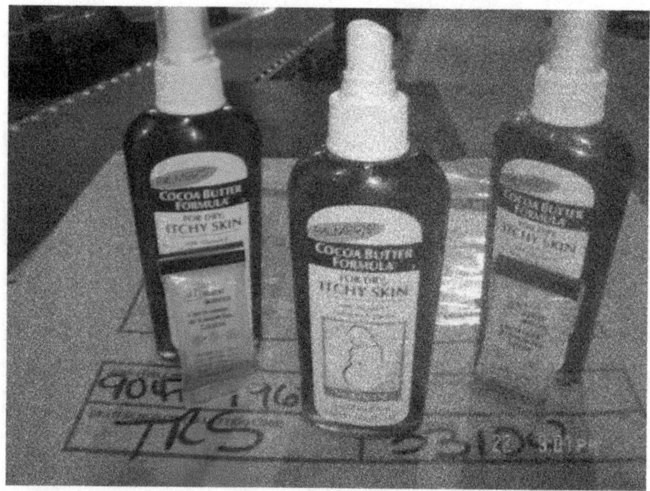

FIGURE 7.14 A shipment of bottles of cocoa butter oil with liquid cocaine mixed with the oil.

FIGURE 7.15 A total of 870 kg of cocaine was mixed with oil in a shipment from Ecuador to the United States.

clothings—such as jeans, shirts, winter pants, jackets, etc.—are soaked in liquid cocaine or heroin and then allowed to dry. The drug particles adhere to the fabric, making it appear coarse and stiff. The same extraction process noted earlier is also utilized to separate the cocaine and heroin from the clothing. In September 2015, an innovative twist on this method was discovered in Argentina in which cocaine was soaked and impregnated into rice and the dried rice packaged for commercial sale. The additional benefit of this method is that the drug doesn't have to be extracted, as the rice can serve as the "cutting agent" for preparation for sale on the street. The rice was being shipped to Guinea-Bissau in West Africa for forwarding to Europe.[37]

FIGURE 7.16 Cocaine was mixed with the plastic used to form a large shipment of battery terminal cleaners.

An especially creative smuggling method involves the mixing of cocaine or heroin in the fabrication of merchandise that is plastic-based. Items such as PVC tube, toilets, sinks, furniture, tools, household goods, and ornaments have been formed or molded using a mixture of plastic and cocaine or heroin. In the case of battery terminal cleaners, shown in Fig. 7.16, a review of the shipping documentation showed the point of loading as Colombia, South America; however, the actual individual package of each item listed "made in Taiwan." When the plastic portion of one of the battery terminal cleaners was rubbed against concrete, it smelled of burned cocaine. There were tens of thousands of these items in the shipment. In a similar case, the plastic ornaments in Figs. 7.17 and 7.18 were formed of a cocaine-plastic mix. The separation process is identical to the one described previously, where acetone is used to separate the plastic from the drug.

One of the most common techniques used by drug smugglers—especially when there is an internal conspiracy involving dock workers or truck drivers—is the placing of drug-filled boxes and bags near the rear door of the container, for quickly identification and extract. This tactic frequently is referred to as the "rear rip" or "rear rip-off." This technique is very popular in ports that have X-ray systems to check import containers prior to dispatch from the port, as in these instances terminal labor extracts the drugs prior to local Customs having the opportunity to inspect the container. In cases where drug smugglers are utilizing an unwitting, legitimate exporter, and consignee, generally the drug shipment is inserted

FIGURE 7.17 These ornaments were found to be a mix of cocaine and plastic.

FIGURE 7.18 Close-up view of one of the ornaments.

within the container during the time between when the container departs its initial load point and it's laden onboard the vessel. In such cases, as shown in Figs. 7.19–7.22, the drugs may be tossed on top of the cargo and at the rear door or the drug-laden boxes may be visibly marked (piece of tape or hand marking on the boxes) and positioned for immediate identification and retrieval. A common tactic in this smuggling method is for equipment operators (top-loader, RTG, forklift, etc.) in the destination port to arrange containers or cargo in a "box configuration" with the target container/cargo pallet in the center of the circle—to limit visibility by port security while participating stevedores or terminal workers extract the drug shipment. How quickly can this be accomplished? In 2014, Dutch Customs in Rotterdam videotaped stevedores open a container, extract three bags with 70 kg of cocaine, and reseal the container—*all in less than 3 min.* In 2013–2014, the "rip-off" method was the most popular in the ports of Antwerp and Rotterdam in Northern Europe. In other related scenarios, a truck driver delivering a drug-filled import container to the Consignee

FIGURE 7.19 A "rear rip-off"—drugs are loaded just inside the door for quick extraction in the U.S. port.

FIGURE 7.20 Because of the positioning just inside the door, note the ease with which the bags of kilos of cocaine can be extracted.

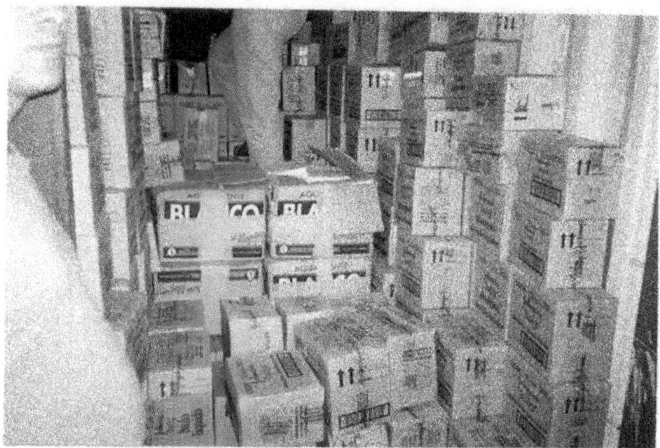

FIGURE 7.21 Contraband-filled boxes (different markings) were mixed with the legitimate cargo.

FIGURE 7.22 The boxes with a piece of tape on the side were loaded only with cocaine.

from the destination port may detour from his route or stop on the side of the road, where accomplices will be waiting to quickly off-load the drugs—made more practical and time efficient when the drugs are loaded just inside the door.

The technique of secreting drugs inside crating and packing materials, as well as within the structure of pallets, has been used frequently (see Figs. 7.23 and 7.24). However, the drug smugglers in the case identified in Figs. 7.25 and 7.26 made up for this restriction by increasing the number of cargo-loaded pallets they were shipping from Ecuador to the United States. Incomplete information for the Consignee raised suspicion, and a K-9 alert on the pallets led to a more detailed inspection. A total of 210 kg of cocaine was discovered within the pallets. Similarly, drugs are hidden within the cardboard structure of boxes, either by inserting very flat packages within hollowed-out portions, the glued cardboard pieces, or affixing as a second layer covering the inside sections of the box. In September

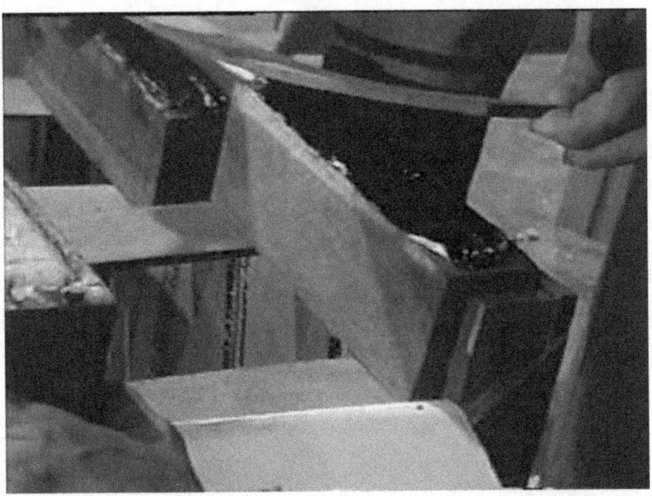

FIGURE 7.23 K-9s alerted on a container load of pallets.

FIGURE 7.24 Close inspection of the pallets revealed the wood had been hollowed out and packed with cocaine packages.

2015, U.S. CBP in the port of Philadelphia discovered 165 kg of cocaine formed in long, thin packages (a pound each) laminated to the inside of the fruit case box flaps of boxes of Costa Rican pumpkins and squash.[38]

In smuggling operations where the Exporter and/or Consignee is complicit, or the plan is to hijack or redirect the container once exiting the destination port, it is common to find very large loads and the drugs mixed with the cargo or throughout the entire container. Typically, the kilo packages will be inside the boxes of legitimate cargo, hidden among the cargo on pallets, or between or on top of the boxes or crates

FIGURE 7.25 Drilling of the wood corner blocks produced white residue on the drill bit—cocaine.

FIGURE 7.26 Breaking open the corner blocks revealed the contraband.

(see Figs. 7.27–7.29). A few more examples include the following: in April 2014, antinarcotics police in the port of Cartagena, Colombia discovered 7 tons of cocaine in containers loaded with boxes of pineapple pulp. The drugs were located in between the boxes of legitimate cargo, and destined for Rotterdam. The previous month, in the nearby port of Santa Marta, two other containers loaded with 2 tons of cocaine in each one—with the same smuggling method—were seized prior to loading onboard ships, one for the United States and one for Europe.[39] In 2014, multiple containers were prepared to depart or were shipped from Costa Rica with tons of cocaine (and in one case, 16,000 LSD pills) mixed between or inside the boxes of yucca (also referred to as "cassava"), tubers, ornamental

FIGURE 7.27 This shipment of ceramic tile had one pallet with a large wood box which could not be seen until the adjacent pallets were moved.

FIGURE 7.28 Removal of the tiles on top revealed large bags filled with kilos of cocaine.

flowers, and pineapples to Spain, Rotterdam, and Antwerp. Costa Rica has become so "hot" a transit point that some Narcos have even begun shipping to loads from Costa Rica to Panama, to then jump to Europe and the United States.[40]

Drug Smuggling via Containers

The ingenuity, effort, and persistence invested in the designing and implementing of drug smuggling techniques via cargo are equaled or surpassed by the techniques utilized in the smuggling of drugs via containers and associated equipment. Secret compartments, fabricated inner structures, and the disassembly and reassembly of container structures are common techniques and tactics. Some of the primary methods are described next.

FIGURE 7.29 Kilos of compressed marijuana packed in boxes of bananas.

The hollowing out of insulation in the walls, floor, and roof of refrigeration (reefer) containers is a method for smuggling large quantities, up to 500 kg or more, of drugs. As shown in Figs. 7.30 and 7.31, the roof is peeled back to permit the removal of the insulation and insertion of the kilos. As observed in Fig. 7.32, a similar practice is implemented when drugs are hidden in the walls and floor. The refrigeration unit of the container is located at the front wall, behind a removable wall. There is adequate space around the refrigeration unit and in the air channels to hide many kilos of drugs, as shown in Figs. 7.33–7.36. However, the smuggler must ensure that there is adequate airflow in the channels; otherwise, the reefer temperature gauge will show a malfunction—and require a technical inspection and probable detection of the smuggling attempt. But, if they target an *empty reefer container* (intransit or repositioning which is not running) or have corrupted the reefer technicians (who are tasked with checking the temperatures and malfunctions), then this goes a long way toward eliminating the potential "Red Flag."

The top and bottom rails of the container, as well as the portions of the doors and their support beams, are hollow and serve as locations where drugs can be inserted (see Fig. 7.37). The rails can hold hundreds of kilos of drugs. Prepared with care and by professional container repairmen, this method of smuggling is very difficult to visually detect. Most

FIGURE 7.30 The insulation of the roof of this refrigerator container was gutted and replaced with packages of cocaine.

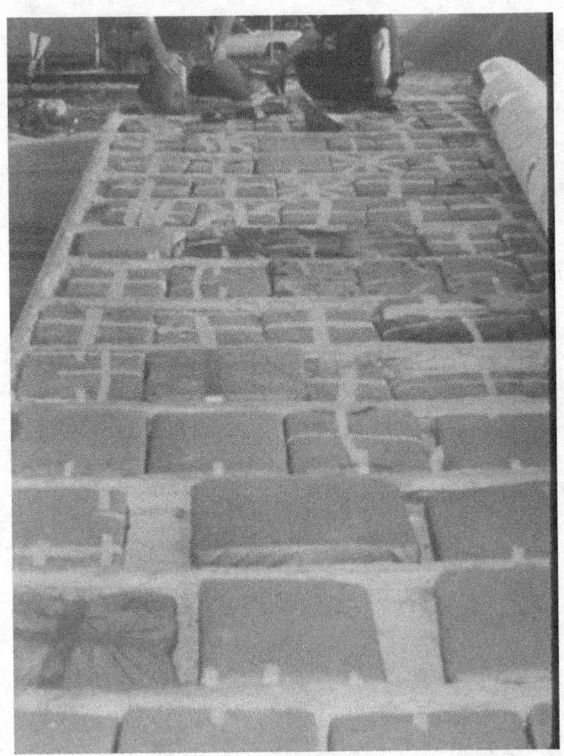

FIGURE 7.31 Removing the insulation allows for the insertion of hundreds of kilos of cocaine and heroin.

FIGURE 7.32 The floor insulation of this refrigerator container was removed and replaced with drugs.

FIGURE 7.33 The front wall of this refrigerator container had been removed and 125 kg inserted in the side airflow ducts of the refrigeration unit.

FIGURE 7.34 The upper airflow chambers of the reefer unit can hold a couple dozen kilos.

FIGURE 7.35 If airflow is blocked, an alarm is triggered and registered in the control panel data base.

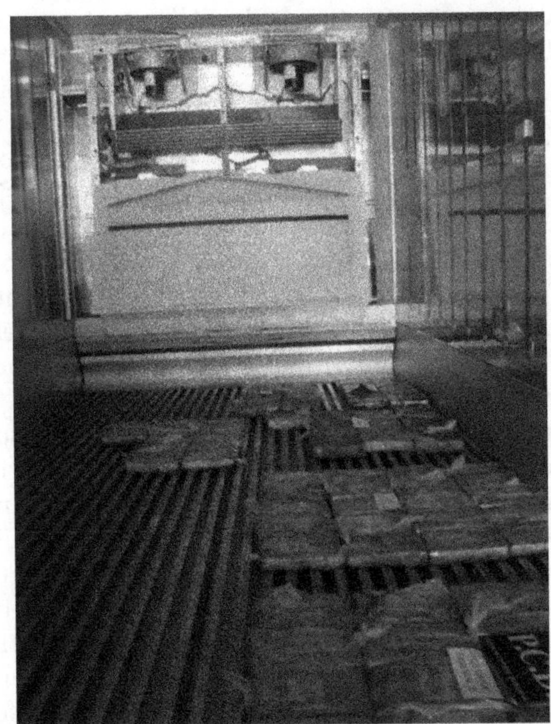

FIGURE 7.36 View of reefer unit fully opened and discovered kilos of cocaine on the floor.

FIGURE 7.37 The top rail of the container is hollow and can hold many kilos.

detections of this method are the result of scanning by nonintrusive inspection equipment or K-9 detection. Obviously, as in the cases of removal of the reefer insulation, a fair amount of labor and skill are required to utilize these smuggling tactics.

The fabrication of false walls inside the container—especially the front wall—is a clever method that requires great attention to detail if the smuggler is to be successful (see Fig. 7.38). The fake wall cannot be too deep, or it will be easily detected and can appear to be a new modification. A well-designed wall is one which uses just 12 inches or less of space—enough for stacking 500 kg of heroin or cocaine—and appears to be the same age and construction as the rest of the container. Nonnormal appearing corner blocks, poorly matched paint colors, a different inside/outside rib count, off-position or missing rivets, missing ventilation ribs, or welding "burn" marks are some of the telltale signs of a false wall or secret compartment. The smugglers must also take care with weight distribution, especially when drugs inserted in the front wall. If there is an imbalance and the container is lifted by cable slings of a vessel crane or hoist, the container will tilt and immediately raise suspicion.

The construction of false compartments in the doors, under the chassis, and the insertion of drugs into air handler tanks, as shown in Figs. 7.39–7.42, are methods which require limited sophistication but time to set up. Somewhat more time-consuming is the technique of creating a false compartment in a reefer fuel tank. Some reefer trailers are equipped with large fuel tanks (similar in appearance to a 55-gallon drum) to accommodate longer voyages. Smugglers have been known to swap out these fuel tanks at an exporter's location or while enroute to the port. The drug smugglers will mount a fuel tank which has been prepared in the following manner: the fuel tank is cut in half, drugs are placed on the bottom portion, a plate is welded across the bottom half, the two halves are then welded together; paint and then dirt or grease are applied, and the tank is filled up (filling only the segregated upper portion). Detection is difficult unless the tank is "sounded" (a procedure which requires

FIGURE 7.38 Discovery and opening of a false front wall in this dry container reveal a load of contraband.

FIGURE 7.39 Container doors have compartments which can be used to hide drugs.

FIGURE 7.40 The false bottom of the underside of this container, straining under the weight of a heavy load of cocaine, broke away when this container was lifted from its chassis.

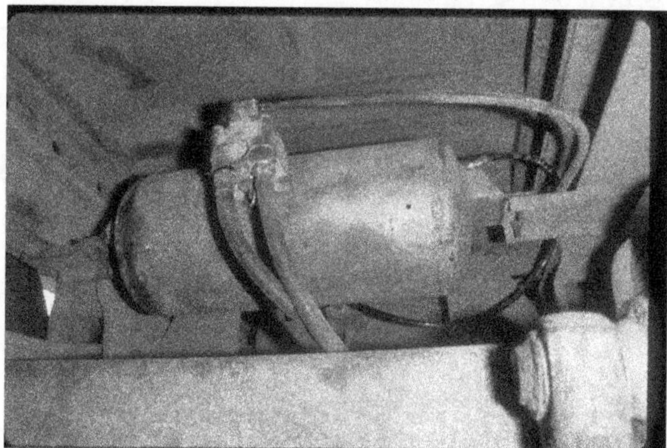

FIGURE 7.41 This air handler tank has new paint and a new hose. Indicators of manipulation?

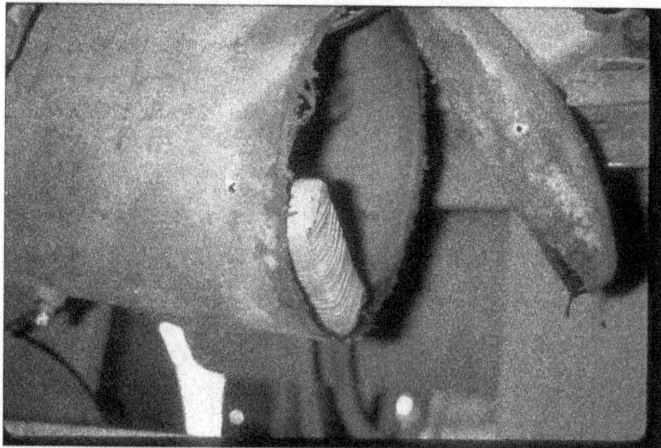

FIGURE 7.42 Once opened, the tank revealed several kilos of cocaine.

tapping on the top and bottom portion to note a different tone) or a probe is inserted into the tank to check the depth. Other low-technology techniques and methods to smuggle drugs include the placement of drugs in a "hammock" or rope harness under the chassis or Mafi (shown in Fig. 7.43), hiding kilos inside the trailer inspection plate (shown in Fig. 7.44), and the secreting of drug packages inside the fifth wheel cover (shown in Fig. 7.45).

A common smuggling tactic used over the past 20+ years is the hiding of drugs in the tires of cargo trailers or chassis that are being repositioned from one port to another; eg, from Santo Tomas, Guatemala, to Jacksonville, Florida (see Figs. 7.46 and 7.47). Heroin, cocaine, and marijuana have all been discovered inside tires. Depending on whether a tire tube is used, drug packages either will be "molded" around the rim or attached to the inside of the actual tire. The chassis platforms themselves are also used to transport drug shipments (see Fig. 7.48). Portions of the platform can be removed or modified to accommodate the insertion or placement of dozens or hundreds of kilos of contraband.

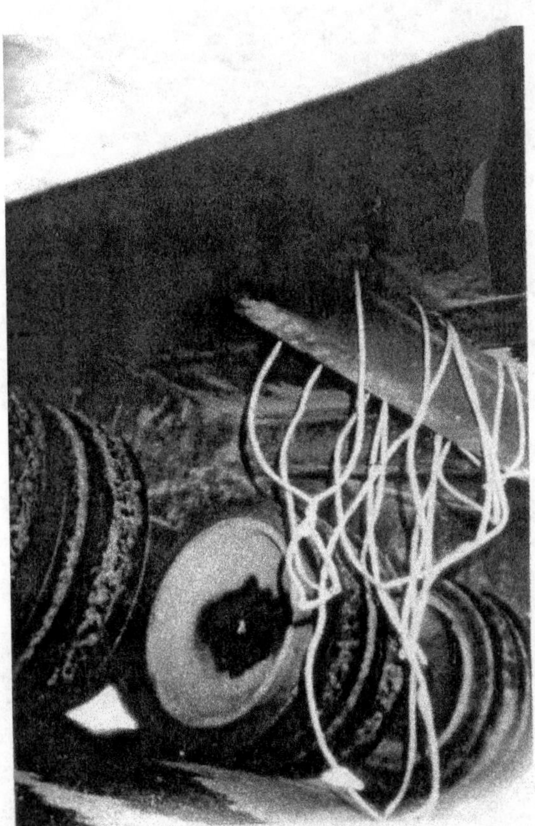

FIGURE 7.43 A dozen kilos of contraband were secured via ropes to the underside of this Mafi.

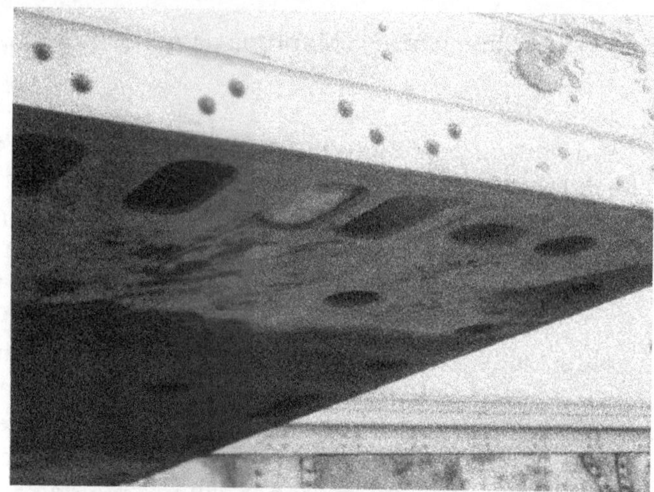

FIGURE 7.44 Kilos hidden in the void above the container's inspection plate.

FIGURE 7.45 The container's/trailer's "fifth wheel" cover offers the smuggler a location to hide a dozen or more kilos.

FIGURE 7.46 Marijuana bricks line the interior of the tire between the tube and the tire walls.

FIGURE 7.47 Hiding of drugs in trailer and chassis tires is a common practice.

FIGURE 7.48 The chassis floor flatbed is easily modified to permit the smuggling of dozens of kilos.

Drug Smugglers use a number of *sleight-of-hand* tactics to mask their targeting of specific containers, so the containers with contraband raise less interest on the part of security and authorities. Let's review a couple popular tactics. In 2014 and 2015, there were over a dozen known incidents—and probably several dozen more that went undetected—in the Colombian port of Turbo of containers that were violated and drugs inserted even though they never went ashore. In several incidents, the containers were temporarily removed from the ship's main deck (poop deck) so the cargo bay hatches could be opened for loading cargo/containers below the main deck. These containers were moved to barges alongside the ship, while the cargo bay was being unloaded or loaded, during which time drug smugglers broken the seals, inserted the drugs (up to 500kg), and resealed the containers. In some of the cases, empty reefer containers were targeted and the front wall was opened and drugs inserted into the reefer ventilations passages. In other cases, during the night time, drug smugglers secretly boarded the ships and opened containers on deck (some even at the *second level high above the deck*) and placed drug loads inside the containers. These containers (both loaded and empties) were "intransit" from the United States to Central America or from Europe to Central America and the United States.

Continued

—cont'd

Because these containers officially "never left the ship," they would receive little attention versus those embarked in Colombia. In Costa Rica, there were numerous such incidents where cocaine was discovered stacked on the floor or hidden in the front wall of reefers—even though these containers never left the ship![41] In one incident, a container laden on the ship in Philadephia was found to have had bolts of the locking arms drilled out and replaced in Colombia and 350 kg of cocaine loaded inside (the container was stacked on the second level on deck and was not moved while in Colombia). This is a very clever tactics for targeting low risk containers and using them to move drugs to major transshipment locations or directly to the destination markets in the United States or Europe. Phoenix Group Post-Seizure Investigations in Colombia of several of the incidents indicated Stevedore and Vessel Security participation—or turning of the head—due to death threats from Narcos; threats which can't be taken lightly. In just a 6-month time period in 2014, at least seven security officers working on cargo ships in the port of Turbo were assassinated following drug seizures from vessels they worked on.

A somewhat similar scenario is active in Panama. On a daily basis, thousands of containers are unloaded from ships transiting the Panama Canal, due to restrictions, and transported via the Panama Canal Railway or truckers to the other side of Panama to be reembarked on the same ship. Also, as the five primary seaports of Panama serve as major transshipment hubs in the Western Hemisphere, hundreds of thousands of containers are unloaded from one ship in their trade service and loaded on a ship in another trade lane. During 2013–2015, there have been numerous incidents, especially in the ports of Balboa and Cristobal, when these transshipment/repositioned containers have been targeted by drug smugglers. A smaller number of these containers have been penetrated at the rail load points. Police in Panama repeatedly have seized cocaine loads ranging from 300 to 900 kg to be loaded into these containers, frequently arresting port workers and security personnel.[42] On multiple occasions, altered high security seals have been found with the drug loads, for applying at point of extraction in the destination seaport. In one incident in February 2015, police arrested five workers in the port of Balboa and seized 250 kg of cocaine when the port workers were caught in the act of transloading the cocaine from one container to another. However, what is highly interesting is that the drugs and seven altered high security container seals had been loaded onboard the vessel *at sea*, stashed in a container from the United States (obviously by Crew), and in the port was to be loaded in another container destined for the United States.[43] Obviously, these cases indicate a high level of communications and coordination between the port of origin, Crew on the ship (in the latter incident), the port workers in Panama, and the Narco-controlled stevedores in the destination ports. It is important to appreciate that the primary Colombian TCO, Clan Usuga, and the Colombian Narco-terrorist organization, the FARC—as well as Mexican Cartels—oversee the drug smuggling through these seaports.

Drug Smuggling via Vessels

Drug smuggling via the commercial vessel, her crew, or drug couriers presents special challenges to the vessel master, crew, and shipping line. While the quantities may be smaller than drug loads found in containers and cargo, there is an increased risk that when drugs are seized onboard the vessel by law enforcement agencies, the vessel may be delayed, detained, or a fine assessed by government authorities. Additionally, drug couriers—who are transporting very valuable cargo—may become desperate or violent if confronted by Crewmembers. Moreover, Crew frequently are targeted for recruiting or threatened to participate in the smuggling operations.

There are hundreds of locations to hide drugs inside commercial container, bulk, and break-bulk ships. The insides of the cargo bays, ventilation shafts, crawl spaces, rope and storage lockers, engine room, accommodations, supply closets, life boats, etc., provide an almost infinite number of places to hide a box or duffle bags containing kilos of drugs. In September 2015, in Costa Rica, while conducting the postarrival search of a ship arriving from Colombia and destined for Europe, Phoenix Group security officers discovered 200 kg of cocaine in a cable passage in a deck of the ship (see Figs. 7.49 and 7.50). Similarly, on another ship destined for the United States, several kilos of cocaine were discovered on

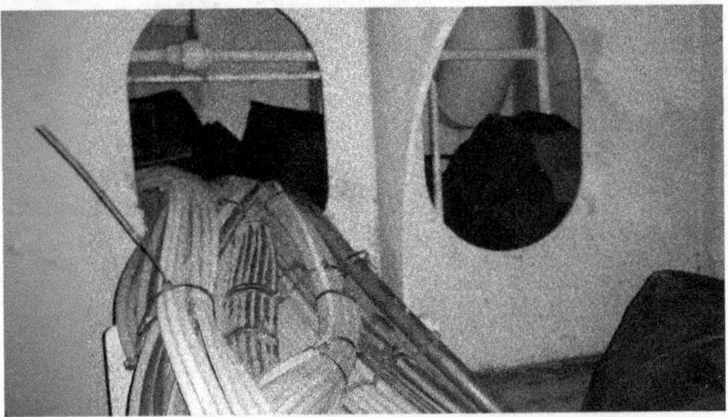

FIGURE 7.49 Crew and/or Stevedores hid these bags in a cable passage area, difficult to access and only by Crew, which were discovered by Phoenix Group security officers during the postarrival vessel inspection.

FIGURE 7.50 The bags held 200 kg of cocaine. Ship had arrived from Colombia.

a ledge in a cargo hold (see Fig. 7.51). Equipment and supply storage lockers are readily accessible by stevedores and good hiding locations for smaller, 20–100 kg loads (see Fig. 7.52). In 2014, there were at least six incidents in Santa Marta, Colombia, where smugglers hid drugs inside the anchor room and chain locker of ships destined for seaports in

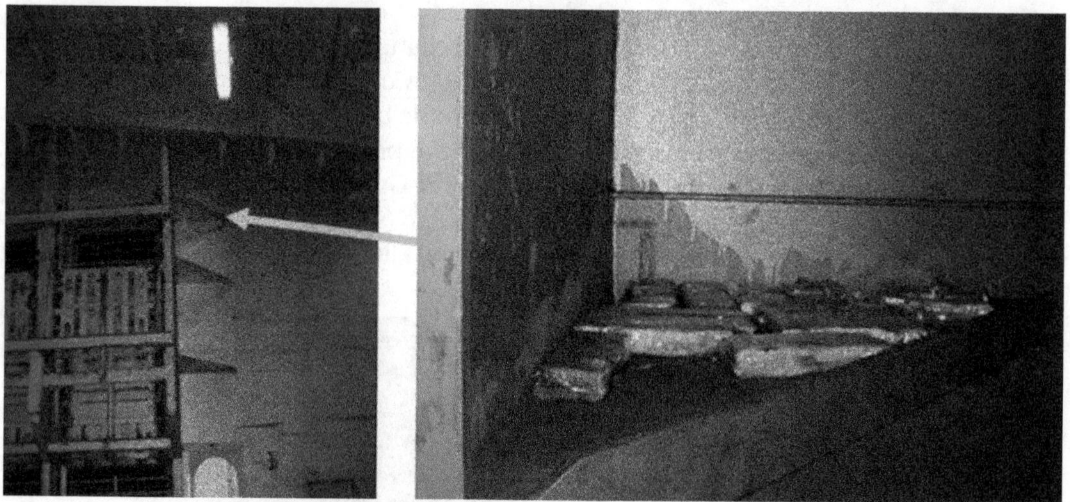

FIGURE 7.51 The ledges in the Cargo Bays are good locations to hid 6–12 kg.

FIGURE 7.52 These 5 gallon cans of grease held more than just grease! A total of 76 kg were hidden in the cans in a main deck storage locker on this ship destined for Europe.

Northern Europe (see Fig. 7.53).[44] Reefer ships, which load fruit and vegetable pallets and loose boxes in lower decks of cargo bays have raised flooring for cold air circulation. These removable floor gratings frequently are used as concealment areas for drug load of up to several hundred kilos in size (see Figs. 7.54 and 7.55). *The key to effective vessel security is denying access to all contraband and unauthorized persons!*

Fig. 7.56 shows a depiction of the access path for drug couriers and drugs entering the vessel rudder compartment. The hatch above the rudder compartment is always maintained closed and secured from the inside, so there is no opportunity to enter the interior of the vessel from this space. When a ship is loaded with cargo the access hole to the rudder compartment is submerged below the water line. In one of the first major incidents, in the early 1990s, six Colombian drug couriers—armed with pistols and transporting 900 kg of cocaine—were captured in the port of Tampa, Florida. The usage of this method waned for more than a decade and then in 2014 rebounded in force. In 2014 and 2015, this tactic was used repeatedly by smugglers in Colombia and Peru as a "*stash*" location for cocaine

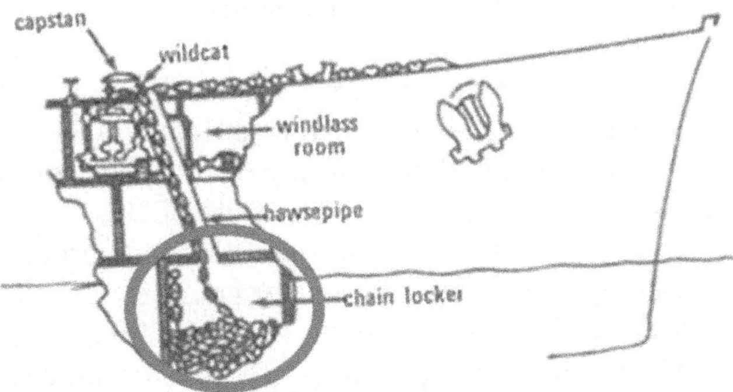

FIGURE 7.53 In Santa Marta, Colombia, in 2014, there were more than five incidents of drugs being found in the chain locker or anchor rooms. Typically, the duffle bags or suitcases are lowered into the space via ropes, which are then discreetly tied to the ladder.

FIGURE 7.54 View of kilos of cocaine hidden below the grating of the floor in the cargo bay of a Reefer Ship.

FIGURE 7.55 The amount of kilos hidden in these smuggling operations typically range from 50 to 200 kg. In 2014 and 2015, this method was very popular in fruit ports in South America.

shipments (100–400 kg) to be retrieved by divers in destination ports in Scotland, Spain, the Netherlands, Mexico, and the United States.[45] In mid-2014, the U.K. National Crime Agency arrested a Dutch SCUBA team in Scotland that traveled across Northern Europe retrieving loads from the rudder compartments of ships. The SCUBA team was set to retrieve the drugs in a ship arriving from Santa Marta, Colombia. In February 2015, a Colombian Navy SCUBA team in Cartagena discovered two drug couriers and 102 kg of cocaine in the rudder compartment of a tanker about to depart for Baton Rouge, Louisiana. In September 2015, the Peruvian Navy likewise encountered a load of cocaine (211 kg) in the rudder compartment of an LNG tanker, this ship destined for the port of Manzanillo, Mexico.

In the smuggling operation noted in Figs. 7.57 and 7.58, four *drug couriers* boarded the vessel while in a Colombian port—with two vests totaling 46 kg of cocaine—initially hid in an unsecured container and then moved to a storage locker. The drug couriers were captured by Phoenix Group Panama security officers during a postarrival inspection of the vessel in port. Fig. 7.59 shows how a drug courier with 22 kg of cocaine had hidden inside a banana pallet but was captured during cargo discharge operations. In most of these cases, the drug courier is inserted at the packing station (where the pallet is "built") or intransit to the ship, and the inner boxes are gutted and others positioned around the person and his "cargo." There are two variations of *drug couriers,* both of which use many avenues to access the vessel and are a potential physical threat to Crewmembers. The first type of drug courier is the *stowaway,* who, in lieu of paying corrupt port officials or the local mafia (snakehead) boss for the opportunity to stow away onboard a ship, agrees to "transport" a small amount of drugs (usually 2–5 kg) to its destination—a type of barter arrangement. This drug courier is on a "one-way, one-time" trip, is not a professional smuggler, and usually remains unarmed. The second type is the *professional drug courier,* who makes trips on a frequent basis, works for an

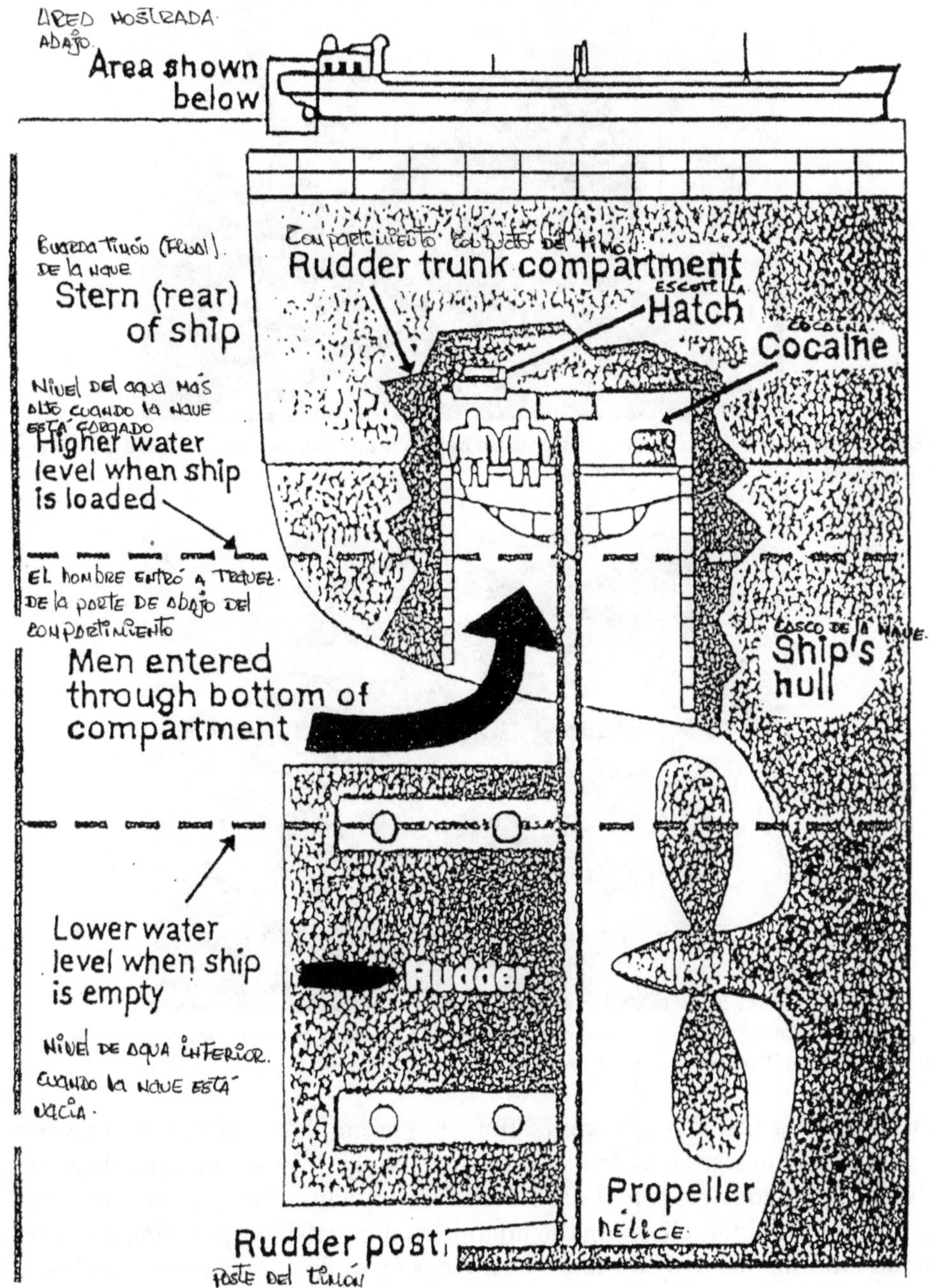

FIGURE 7.56 Diagram depicting how drug couriers access the rudder room and travel to the port of destination.

FIGURE 7.57 Part of the provisions and two vests carried by four drug couriers who boarded a container ship when she was in the port of Buenaventura, Colombia.

FIGURE 7.58 A total of 46 kg of cocaine were in the pockets of the two vests when they were discovered and captured in Panama by Phoenix Group security officers.

international drug trafficking organization, has a good knowledge of vessel security measures and the design and structure of the vessel, and may be armed (with a knife, pistol, etc.). Drug couriers may board the vessel by climbing the mooring lines, pilot ladder, or Jacob's ladder; climbing the anchor chain; walking up the gangway posing as a stevedore; hiding inside a container or the cargo, under the chassis, inside the cab of Ottawa, or secreted inside a pallet of boxes (bananas, pineapples, etc.). Drug couriers who gain access to the ship's decks hide in unsecured containers, open cargo bays, ventilation shafts, crane access areas, unlocked storage lockers, in between/on top of/under containers and other unmonitored or unsecured locations.

FIGURE 7.59 A drug courier with 22 kg of cocaine was hiding in the center of this banana pallet.

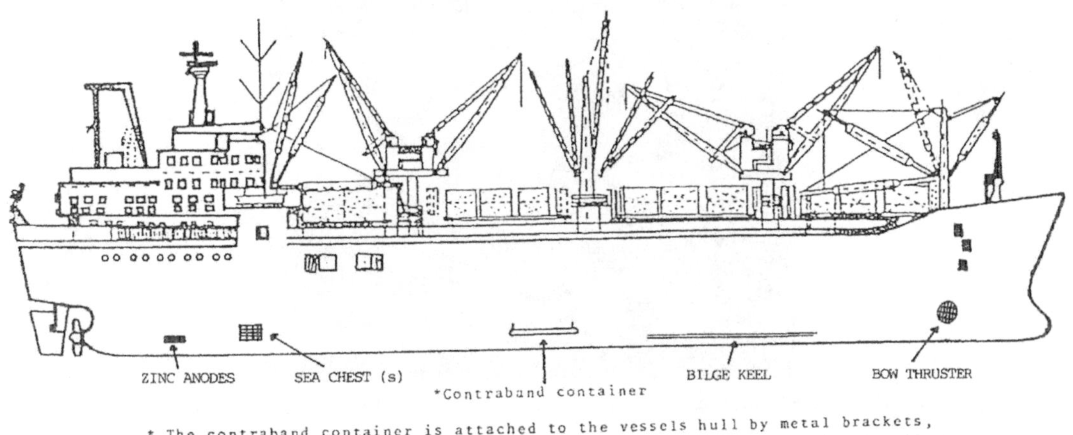

FIGURE 7.60 Locations on the exterior of the hull where drug-laden torpedoes or bags are attached.

The design, development, and usage of drug-filled "hull attachments" and "torpedoes" originated in Colombia in the late 1980s, and the technique has spread across the globe (see Figs. 7.60–7.66). Each of the torpedoes in the figures is from a different incident, yet, as one can see there is a significant similarity in the construction. All torpedoes were mounted in Colombia and most likely by representatives of Clan Usuga. This

FIGURE 7.61 This drug-filled torpedo was discovered during an inspection of the hull by scuba divers in Costa Rica.

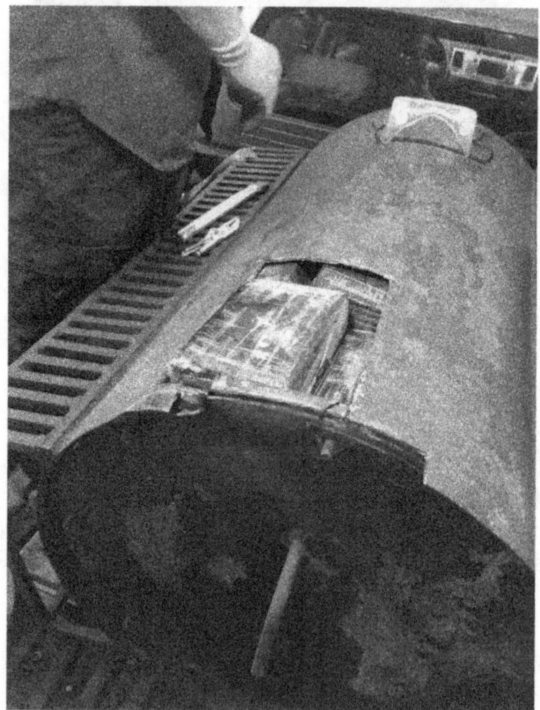

FIGURE 7.62 Once opened, the torpedo was found to hold 300 kg of cocaine.

smuggling method requires the use of SCUBA divers to attach and detach the device and occurs while the vessel is in port or at anchor. The drugs within the torpedoes—ranging in quantity from 200 to 500 kg—are destined for the United States and Europe. In 2014, there was a large uptick in the use of this method and this wave continued in 2015. While some torpedoes are used in "door-to-door" delivery (origin to destination), torpedoes also are used as a "platform" to transit drugs to a transshipment site, where either the torpedo is reattached to another ship or it is detached and the drugs are repacked in a container for

FIGURE 7.63 All of the torpedoes in the photographs were mounted to the ship when in a Colombia seaport. They all have a very similar construction design and hull affixing system.

FIGURE 7.64 This torpedo was longer in length than the others in the photographs and held 500 kg of cocaine. All torpedoes noted in the photos were discovered in 2014–2015.

transport to the final destination. This latter usage is a frequent scenario for torpedoes arriving in Panama and Costa Rica from Colombian ports on the Caribbean and Pacific coasts.[46] There have been a variety of attachments systems used, to include, cable hooks, chains, magnets, and U-bolts to hold the "torpedo" in-place, some temporary and others permanent. The sea chest and bow thrusters are the favorite attachment sites. Also, drug-filled duffle bags have been discovered inside sea chests, latched to the grill-like cover of the bow thruster. Heroin and cocaine are the typical drugs smuggled via this method.

Crew conspiracy and participation in the smuggling of drugs are significant problems in commercial shipping. Low-level Crewmembers (nonofficers) are paid a meager salary—as

FIGURE 7.65 View of a Bow Thruster of a cargo ship.

FIGURE 7.66 These hook cables were used to secure the torpedo to the Bow Thruster grating.

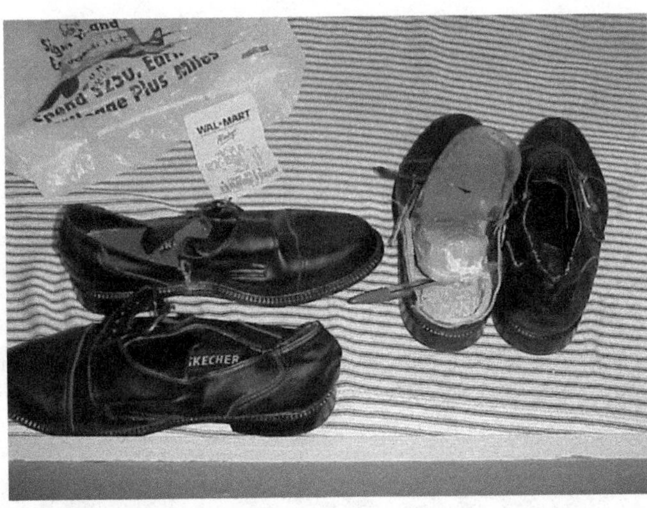

FIGURE 7.67 The heels of these Crewmember's shoes were modified to each hold a pound of pure cocaine.

low as $300 per month—so the opportunity to make up to $2000 or more per kilo smuggled is very enticing. Imagine, a Crewmember participating in a single smuggling operation of only 30 kg of cocaine would earn some $50,000—equal to his salary for 14 years. Crewmembers have carried drugs on and off the vessel taped to their bodies, within their luggage or personal effects, in backpacks, and inside ship property. Narco-influenced Crewmembers assist in bringing drugs onboard and hiding them in containers and areas of the ship. According to U.S. Customs and Border Protection field reports, Crewmembers have been arrested wearing "girdles" and vests with hidden pockets where drugs were secreted. In the case of the smuggling operation observed in Fig. 7.67, the Crewmember who wore the shoes onboard had been recruited in an Ecuadorian bar by a prostitute who introduced him to cocaine usage and subsequently presented him to the smuggler. (The *honey trap* is the primary method for recruiting Crewmembers.) Foolishly, the Crewmember decided to try some of the cocaine he was smuggling—which was highly pure. He died immediately and was found in his cabin.

It is not uncommon for narcotics trafficking organizations to form "front" companies and purchase ships solely for the purpose of smuggling illegal narcotics and other contraband. Some of the largest drug seizures in history were made in cargo and/or ships dedicated to this illegal trade. In March 2007, the U.S. Coast Guard stopped the coastal freighter GATUN off the Pacific coast of Panama and made one of their largest maritime drug seizures. As shown in Figs. 7.68–7.70, the 20 tons of cocaine discovered inside two containers practically covered the deck when unloaded from the otherwise empty containers. The seizure was the result of a 2-month investigation in Panama, started when two logistics representatives of the Mexican-based Sinaloa cartel made two key errors which were unusual business practices and in turn raised a red flag to law enforcement. It is worth reviewing this case because it shows the projection south of the largest Mexican cartel and provides examples of indicators of suspicious activity.

Continued

FIGURE 7.68 The U.S. Coast Guard Cutter SHERMAN hailing the coastal freighter GATUN after it departed Panama.

FIGURE 7.69 U.S. Coast Guard boarding team officers extracting large bags of cocaine from a container on deck.

FIGURE 7.70 The 20 tons of cocaine seized almost cover the deck of the freighter.

In January 2007, Mondragon and Jose Nunez, of the Sinaloa cartel, arrived in Panama and set up a front company named Marine Management & Chartering, which purchased the coastal freighter GATUN. For the next 2 months, the GATUN made a few runs from Guyana, through the Panama Canal, and then up the coast to the Mexican port of Topolobampo, in the state of Sinaloa, Mexico. The few trips from Guyana to Mexico likely were to establish a pattern of legitimate maritime commerce, which is correct practice in this illegal trade. However, what followed next were three critical errors:

- First, the Mexicans made arrangements for the GATUN to stop in a port in Colon, Panama, and pick up two containers—empty containers. Why would any legitimate business go through the trouble of having two empty containers exported out of the Colon Free Zone and be transported to the port for loading onboard for Mexico? This effort costs money, and no cargo was booked—as would be the norm—to offset costs. That it didn't make sense was the first indicator of suspicious activity and one which drew the attention of the Panamanian police and DEA.
- Second, this would be the **first time** the GATUN called in a port in Panama, and the only cargo to be loaded was two empty containers. Unusual? Yes! It costs money to call in a port, and these empty containers were the only cargo loaded. While ships regularly load empty containers, they always also load break-bulk cargo or loaded containers. Again, this was another indicator of suspicious activity.
- On March 17, 2007, the GATUN exited the Canal and made a turn south and dropped anchor. High-speed launches were tracked departing the northwest coast of Colombia to rendezvous with the GATUN, and the drugs were loaded onboard and into the two empty containers—but not resealed! The U.S. Coast Guard cutter Sherman stopped the GATUN off the Panamanian coast, and a boarding team went on deck. Their observation was that 2 of the 12 containers on deck were not properly sealed. The third error! The USCG opened the containers and had an unobstructed view of 20 tons of cocaine.

Another maritime smuggling method which has been embraced by major Colombian narcotics smuggling organizations is the use of the "Narco Submarine."[47] There are four types of vessels under this label: low-profile vessels (LPV), self-propelled semisubmersibles (SPSS), fully submersible submarines (like those of Naval Forces), and towed torpedoes (towed by cable attached to a boat, usually a fishing boat). Frequently, LPVs are referred to as an SPSS; however, the distinct difference is that the SPSS has a "snorkel like apparatus" which can be used to provide surface air while the vessel very briefly submerges when spotted by law enforcement/military. The first Narco Submarine was detected in 1993 and built from wood and fiberglass. These initial subs were very rudimentary and could not submerge, were slow, and resembled more a fast boat with a top affixed. From these trial-and-error learning efforts, Colombian Narco-terrorists (FARC) and TCOs honed their skills and by the mid-2000s were producing LPVs and SSPS that masked their heat signature, could evade sonar and radar, and used lead siding/top to help mask their infrared signature—making detection very difficult. Current LPVs/SPSS are equipped with radar systems and advanced GPS systems for navigation. The first SPSS captured was in 2006 by the U.S. Coast Guard when detected off the coast

FIGURE 7.71 "Bigfoot" was captured in the Pacific Ocean off the coast of Costa Rica. This Narco Submarine is on display at the Truman Annex, Naval Air Station Key West, in Florida.

of Costa Rica and carrying 3000 kg of cocaine – and was subsequently known as "Bigfoot" (see Fig. 7.71). In the 3 years following this first capture, the Joint Interagency Task Force—South (JIATF-South), a combined US law enforcement and Military Task Force, detected 60 Narco Subs and by late 2014 this grew to a total of 214 sightings in the Pacific Ocean and Caribbean Sea.[48] Unfortunately, because of budget restraints and a lack of available assets, *only 21% of the sightings were investigated by the U.S. law enforcement and Military forces.*[49] While the most commonly detected subs are the LPVs and SPSS, fully submersible submarines have been captured (see Figs. 7.72 and 7.73). In July 2010, Colombian and Ecuadorian authorities discovered a Narco Submarine a few miles south of the Colombian border. The 74-foot-long fiberglass/Kevlar-coated submarine had a diesel-electric drive and twin screws, and could dive to 65 feet below the surface. The following year, the Colombian Military captured a 30-m-long fully submersible submarine in Cauca, a Pacific coast province controlled by the FARC and *less than 200 miles from the site of the Ecuador discovery.* Made of fiberglass, the sub carried a four-man crew and had air conditioning, toilets, kitchen, a 16-foot periscope. This fully submersible submarine would be virtually undetectable when deployed and had a capacity to hold 8 tons of drugs. The sub could dive to 30 feet, travel at 12–15 knots, and had a range of 8000 miles (roundtrip from Colombia to California) (see Fig. 7.74).[50]

As of early 2016, a total of three ready-for-deployment, fully submersible submarines have been captured. But, is this the tip of the iceberg? Is there already a *fleet* of fully submersible submarines currently operating in the Pacific Ocean and Caribbean Sea that are beyond detection by U.S. air observation or radar? It's a case of the "*we just don't know.*" DEA estimates that about 30% of drugs transported via maritime methods now are through the use of SPSS/LPVs.[51] In July 2015, the U.S. Coast Guard made a record seizure off the coast of El Salvador of an LPV with 8 tons of cocaine, evidence that the Narcos continue to transport huge loads via submarines for destinations in the United States.[52] As recently as late September 2015, the Colombian military captured a submarine in its final phase of construction in swamp area along the southern Pacific coast of Colombia—an area controlled by the FARC.

FIGURE 7.72 Low-Profile Vessel (LPV), frequently it is incorrectly referred to as an SPSS, however, the distinct difference is that the SPSS has a "snorkel like apparatus."

FIGURE 7.73 A Self-Propelled semisubmersible (SPSS).

Based on seizure cases ("what we know"), the SPSS and LPVs are preferred because they cost much less to build versus a fully submersible submarine—($500,000 versus $2,000,000)—and require less skill sets to build and to operate at sea.[53] Today, we assume that Narco submarines are deployed only for transport of drugs to Mexico and the United States. However, in late August 2014, the President of Guyana announced the capture of the first SPSS in Guyana. The fiberglass SPSS was 65-feet long and 12-feet wide and Guyanese Customs Anti-Narcotics

FIGURE 7.74 Captured by the Colombian military in 2011, this was truly a fully submersible submarine and would be virtually undetectable.

Police believe the submarine was to be used to transport tons of cocaine to West Africa and other countries.[54] If accurate, this would be a significant increase in the area of operation of the Narco submarines. So what is the next iteration in the evolution of Narco Submarines? Maybe a seizure in the coastal jungles of Western Colombia provides insight. In December 2014, the Colombian Navy discovered an unmanned torpedo-like craft under construction, which when deployed would be operated by remote control and GPS navigation aids (think "waterborne drone"). The 5-foot-long vessel was capable of carrying about a third of a ton of cocaine—and, importantly, requires *no humans* onboard, who may provide information if captured and need to breathe air from the surface.[55] It seems logical that in time the length of these vessels will grow to comparable sizes of the LPVs/SPSS and, with their advantages, may even become their replacement.

Summary

The ever-increasing production of and demand for illegal drugs—specifically heroin, cocaine, and marijuana—ensures that commercial vessels, their cargoes, and seaports will remain a target for drug smugglers. Moreover, the ship crews and port security forces will continue to be challenged by the innovative and varied smuggling methods and techniques. The use of semisubmersibles and submersibles, as well as evolutions in these platforms by TCOs, presents a formidable challenge for world law enforcement agencies and militaries.

End Notes

1. https://www.unodc.org/colombia/en/press/2015/junio/informe-mundial-sobre-las-drogas.html; https://www.unodc.org/documents/crop-monitoring/Colombia/censo_INGLES_2014_WEB.pdf
2. https://www.unodc.org/documents/crop-monitoring/Peru/Peru_Informe_monitoreo_coca_2014_web.pdf; http://www.latimes.com/world/mexico-americas/la-fg-colombia-drugs-20150719-story.html
3. http://www.cocaineroute.eu/flows/reported-changes-coca-pastehydrochloride-refinement-methods/
4. http://www.theguardian.com/world/2015/jul/02/colombia-coca-cultivation-rise-stop-herbicide

5. http://www.businessinsider.com/mexican-drug-cartels-and-heroin-in-the-us-2015-8
6. http://www.cdc.gov/vitalsigns/heroin/
7. Ibid.
8. http://www.nytimes.com/2015/08/30/world/americas/mexican-opium-production-rises-to-meet-heroin-demand-in-us.html?_r=1
9. http://latino.foxnews.com/latino/news/2015/02/03/mexican-farmers-expand-opium-production-to-feed-growing-us-heroin-boom/
10. http://elpais.com/elpais/2015/07/13/inenglish/1436790509_614345.html
11. https://www.unodc.org/documents/wdr2014/World_Drug_Report_2014_web.pdf
12. http://www.unodc.org/wdr2015/; http://www.businessinsider.com/afp-record-afghan-opium-output-prompts-cheaper-us-heroin-supply-un-2015-6
13. Ibid.
14. https://www.europol.europa.eu/content/eu-serious-and-organised-crime-threat-assessment-socta
15. Ibid.
16. http://fortune.com/2015/02/18/marijuana-markets-biggest-world/
17. Ibid.
18. http://www.unodc.org/wdr2015/
19. http://www.unodc.org/wdr2015/
20. http://www.breitbart.com/texas/2015/08/13/drug-smugglers-shifting-us-bound-routes-back-to-open-waters
21. http://www.insightcrime.org/news-briefs/no-more-drug-flights-through-honduras-military
22. http://www.insightcrime.org/news-briefs/drug-traffickers-upping-use-of-el-salvador-maritime-routes
23. http://www.state.gov/j/inl/rls/nrcrpt/2015/
24. http://www.insightcrime.org/news-briefs/4-2-bn-laundered-in-costa-rica-every-year-official
25. http://www.globalpost.com/dispatch/news/regions/americas/140220/ecuador-cocaine-submarine-route-drug-war; http://www.ndtv.com/world-news/ecuador-seizes-7-8-tons-of-liquid-drugs-bound-for-spain-652808
26. http://www.andes.info.ec/en/news/ecuador-almost-duplicates-drug-seizure-between-2014-and-2015-adding-400-tons-eight-years.html
27. http://www.eluniverso.com/noticias/2015/04/08/nota/4746591/11-detenidos-casi-dos-toneladas-droga-decomisada-deja-operativo
28. http://larepublica.pe/26-08-2014/incautan-3-toneladas-de-clorhidrato-de-cocaina-en-trujillo
29. http://www.dawn.com/news/731994/over-200-tonnes-of-heroin-is-smuggled-via-pakistan-a-year; http://www.unodc.org/wdr2015/; http://www.economist.com/news/middle-east-and-africa/21639560-east-african-states-are-being-undermined-heroin-smuggling-smack-track
30. Ibid.
31. http://www.dawn.com/news/731994/over-200-tonnes-of-heroin-is-smuggled-via-pakistan-a-year
32. http://ecpr.eu/filestore/paperproposal/9e9dd3da-27fa-42cb-96c6-0bc8b5639c99.pdf
33. http://www.unodc.org/documents/data-and-analysis/Studies/Afghan_opiate_trafficking_southern_route_web.pdf; http://ecpr.eu/filestore/paperproposal/9e9dd3da-27fa-42cb-96c6-0bc8b5639c99.pdf
34. Ibid.
35. http://www.skynews.com.au/news/world/sthamerica/2014/08/24/ecuador-seizes-7-8-tonne-drug-haul.html

36. http://latino.foxnews.com/latino/news/2014/04/15/police-in-colombia-seize-3-tons-cocaine/

37. http://www.reuters.com/article/2015/09/24/us-argentina-drugs-idUSKCN0RO03R20150924

38. http://www.americanshipper.com/Main/ASD/CBP_seizes_over_363_pounds_of_cocaine_at_Port_of_P_61593.aspx

39. http://colombiareports.com/seven-tons-cocaine-seized-cartagena/; http://www.insightcrime.org/news-briefs/colombia-seizes-historic-7-tn-cocaine-load-destined-for-europe; http://news.xinhuanet.com/english/world/2014-03/30/c_133223893.htm

40. http://www.ticotimes.net/2014/12/01/dutch-seize-huge-cocaine-shipment-hidden-in-cassava-roots-from-costa-rica; http://www.nacion.com/sucesos/narcotrafico/Banda-enviaba-coca-cajas-Holanda_0_1415858448.html; http://www.nacion.com/mundo/centroamerica/Policia-decomisa-contenedor-Costa-Rica_0_1444055752.html; http://www.telegraph.co.uk/news/worldnews/europe/spain/10813882/Spain-police-seize-tons-of-cocaine-among-pineapples.html

41. http://new.diarioextra.com/Noticia/detalle/231456/pegan-primera-carga-de-coca; http://www.diarioextra.com/Noticia/detalle/233106/pescan-122-kg-de-coca-en-tres-contenedores

42. http://panamaon.com/noticias/portada/1161933-mas-de-790-paquetes-de-cocaina-en-4-operativos.html; http://www.telemetro.com/nacionales/Decomisan-cocaina-contenedor-Puerto-Balboa_0_779622723.html; http://www.panamaamerica.com.pa/nacion/decomisan-droga-en-puerto-de-balboa-y-chame; https://panamapeligro.wordpress.com/2015/03/15/panama-es-la-reina-de-las-drogas/

43. Ibid.

44. http://worldmaritimenews.com/archives/135277/liberian-flagged-bulker-busted-for-cocaine-smuggling/

45. http://www.dailymail.co.uk/news/article-2830890/Court-hears-16m-Colombian-drugs-slipped-ashore-Scotland-007-plot.html; http://navaltoday.com/2014/08/11/colombian-navy-impounds-246-kilograms-of-cocaine/; http://navaltoday.com/2015/09/10/peruvian-officials-find-cocaine-aboard-lng-vessel/; http://navaltoday.com/2015/02/24/colombian-navy-finds-102-kg-of-cocaine-aboard-tanker/

46. http://navaltoday.com/2014/07/17/colombian-navy-seizes-196-kilograms-of-cocaine/; Interviews of Sources in Panama Customs, Honduran Military Intelligence, and Costa Rican Police in 2015.

47. The U.S. Army's Foreign Military Studies Office, in 2014, produced a highly detailed and excellent research study on the topic of SPSS, entitled, *Narco-Submarines: Specially Fabricated Vessels Used for Drug Smuggling Purposes*. The study documents their history and evolution utilizing open source reporting, case studies, and extensive use of pictures.

48. http://fmso.leavenworth.army.mil/Collaboration/Interagency/Narco-Submarines.pdf

49. Ibid.

50. http://www.csmonitor.com/World/Americas/2012/1205/Colombia-s-narco-sub-museum-gives-a-peek-into-drug-trafficking-tactics

51. http://www.maritime-executive.com/article/NarcoSubmarines-Innovative-technology-by-Drug-Cartels-2014-08-03

52. http://www.businessinsider.com.au/narco-submarine-with-8-tons-of-cocaine-2015-7

53. http://fmso.leavenworth.army.mil/Collaboration/Interagency/Narco-Submarines.pdf

54. http://www.caribnewsdesk.com/news/8468-dea-to-assist-guyana-in-probing-discovery-of-cocaine-smuggling-sub-pres-ramotar

55. http://www.latimes.com/world/mexico-americas/la-fg-colombia-drugs-20150719-story.html

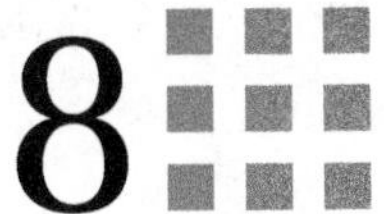

Targeting and Usage of Commercial Ships and Port by Terrorists and Transnational Criminal Organizations

OBJECTIVES

After studying this chapter, you will be

1. Familiar with attacks over the past decade of ships and seaports by terrorist groups and recent game-changing incidents by ISIS and other Jihadists operating in North Africa;
2. Aware of the tactics and technique of terror groups in using commercial shipping and cruise lines to transport terrorists and their materials around the world;
3. Understand the nexus between terrorist groups and transnational criminal organizations (TCOs); and,
4. Explain the evolution and operations of the primary TCOs, how they use commercial shipping and ships to facilitate their criminal contraband activities, and the negative impacts of their enterprises.

Terrorist groups have, for a couple of decades now, targeted ships and ports for attack, as well as used ocean-going commercial cargo vessels and coastal freighters, as conveyances to transport terrorists, weapons, and materials around the world, while Transnational Criminal Organizations (TCO) have used maritime assets to facilitate their criminal operations. The expansion of the Islamic State, and its growing list of "affiliate" terrorist group stretching from West Africa to Southwest Asia, and the use of military weapons systems in maritime terror attacks, likely is an ominous sign for world shipping. A "business alliance" between terrorists and a vast network of profit-oriented TCOs, which include regional gangs and international drug-trafficking organizations, and support from sympathetic nation-states, facilitate the activities of both of these actors. These criminal and threatening activities of terror groups and TCOs targeting the maritime sector present a formidable challenge to the security programs of unsuspecting seaports and ships. First, let's review terrorist targeting of the commercial maritime industry and then discuss how conveyances are used by terror groups to further their causes.

Terrorist Targeting of Ships and Ports

The targeting and attacking of ships and ports by terrorist organizations has been considerably alarming over the past decade, with *game-changing incidents occurring from 2013–2015.*

Maritime Security.

Small vessels continue to be a primary platform for launching or conducting attack, but military-grade weapons also are being used from ashore to conduct attacks on ships. A lingering concern is that terrorists may wish to gain control of maritime conveyances for the purpose of using them as a delivery system for weapons of mass destruction or to create mass causalities. Such crises could occur with the targeting of key infrastructure within the United States and Europe, such as major cities, water supply, agriculture areas, power grids, and the Internet switching sites. Alternatively, terrorists could take control of a large tanker or cargo vessel for the purpose of ramming it into the liquid natural gas or liquefied petroleum gas storage tanks or pipes located on the docks of several major seaports or use a maritime conveyance to deliver and detonate a dirty bomb to create mass panic and evacuation. Many seaports are located adjacent to major cities, so loss of life may well be significant. Let's review some of the key incidents of terrorists targeting ships and ports during the past 13 years.

- On October 6, 2002, the *MT Limburg* was anchored off the coast of Yemen awaiting a pilot when a small vessel came alongside and detonated its load of explosives. The explosion left the tanker of 397,000 barrels of crude oil damaged and a massive fire underway. One crew member was killed in the blast, and the others were rescued. The terrorist attack was claimed by al-Qaeda. It is suspected that terrorists utilized a remote-controlled motorboat loaded with explosives to blow a hole in the side of the tanker.[1]
- In June 2003, Philippine-based terrorist group Abu Sayyaf kidnapped a resort maintenance engineer. Upon his release, the man, a certified scuba diving instructor, reported that Abu Sayyaf had specifically targeted him because of his scuba skills. This report mirrors a similar report from Kuala Lumpur, where a dive shop owner reported that several local Muslim youth had inquired about scuba classes but were interested only in learning how to dive deep and not about issues of decompression or lifesaving techniques. These two reports suggest a potential interest in terrorists to strike ships via motorized underwater sleds, hull-attached mines, or human torpedoes. This concern is supported by a statement made by captured al-Qaeda operative Omar al-Faruq, in Indonesia on June 5, 2002, confessing to planning scuba attacks against U.S. warships.[2]
- In 2004, at the Port of Ashdod, Israel, 10 persons were killed and more than 15 injured, when two suicide bombs detonated. A subsequent inspection in the port identified an empty container with five grenades, weapons, clothing, and a mattress. Gate logs revealed that the container had entered the port 4 hours prior to the suicide attack.[3]
- In 2005, explosives destined for use in attacking American and Israeli cruise ships calling in Istanbul exploded in the apartment in Turkey of an al-Qaeda terrorist, who was the bomb maker. The terrorist confessed to police that he was planning to load the explosives into multiple small fast boats for crashing into the cruise ships (eg, the same tactic used in the attack on the *MT Limburg*).[4]
- In November 2005, terrorists deployed an explosives-laden unmanned launch at the Port of Buenaventura, Colombia, and guided into berths 10 and 11. While the launch was alongside the berth, Navy personnel attempted to board. Explosives detonated, killing two Navy officers and injuring seven other persons. Subsequent arrests by police in reference

to the attack also netted information on the construction in progress of a 5-m long homemade torpedo made by terrorists and designed to carry a large amount of explosives.

- During late July 2010, the al-Qaeda-affiliated Brigades of Abdullah Azzam launched a suicide attack on the *MT M Star*, a Japanese oil tanker, while the tanker was underway in the Persian Gulf. The explosion left a large dent above the water line, on the starboard side, but no serious injuries or ecological incident.[5]
- In April 2012, the German newspaper *Die Zeit* reported that an encrypted data file (hidden within a porno picture) in the possession of a captured al-Qaeda operative, once decrypted, revealed plans for an aggressive terror campaign in Europe. The document also included plans to hijack cruise ships, put the passengers in orange jumpsuits (*a la* Guantanamo), and threaten to behead them unless demands were met—the release of certain prisoners around the world.[6]
- In October 2012, Cypriot security forces seized a large explosive device in the port of Limassol, which was to be used to kill Israeli passengers on a cruise ship in port. Hezbollah was thought to be behind the intended attack (Fig. 8.1).[7]
- In August 2013, terrorists of the Furqan Brigades, an al-Qaeda-affiliated group based in the Sinai Peninsula, fired RPGs (rocket-propelled grenade) at two commercial ships passing through the Suez Canal, causing very minor damage. The second attack, on the container ship *MV Cosco Asia*, was filmed by the terrorists and the video uploaded on the Internet.[8]
- In late 2014, al-Qaeda's English-language magazine *Resurgence* called for attacks on key maritime hubs, to include the Suez Canal, Straits of Malacca and Singapore, Istanbul Strait, and the Strait of Hormuz. The article states, "Simultaneous attacks on western shipping or western oil tankers in more than one chokepoint would bring international shipping to a halt and create a crisis in the energy market."[9]

FIGURE 8.1 The Suez Canal. *Photo courtesy of* Shutterstock.com.

- In July 2015, the Egyptian military arrested 13 terrorists of the Muslim Brotherhood terrorist organization, who were suspected of planting a number of bombs discovered along the Suez Canal, specifically in electrical facilities. The stated intent of the intercepted attack was to disrupt Canal operations and create economic problems for the new government. All bombs were successfully removed without damage (Fig. 8.2).[10]
- In early 2015, the Islamic State (also referred to ISIS and ISIL), moved into the Sinai Peninsula of Egypt, having already taken over large swaths of land and cities in northern Libya in 2014. This Sinai-based Jihadist group has introduced the use of high-tech military weapons to attack maritime assets. In a true wake-up call for the commercial maritime sector—and the Suez Canal—in July 2015, ISIS terrorists positioned on the shore used a Russian-made *Kornet anti-tank-guided missile* system to attack an Egyptian Coast Guard ship patrolling *2 miles off the Sanai coast.* A number of photos taken by the terrorists were posted on the Internet with their statement of claim. Just prior to this attack, ISIS used the same missile system to attack an Egyptian military building. This *Kornet* missile is known to be in use by Palestinian terrorists in Gaza Strip, but also large quantities of the missiles were captured by ISIS in Iraq when they overran Iraqi Army positions.[11]

FIGURE 8.2 The Egyptian ship was attacked by ISIS terrorists using a Russian-made Kornet anti-tank-guided missile system, which has an effective range of 4 kms. *Photo courtesy of NATO.*

Usage of Ships and Containers by Terrorists to Transport Personnel and Materials

There is a plethora of case studies, incidents, and open-source reporting substantiating the widespread usage of commercial maritime conveyances—large ocean-going vessels, cruise ships, and coastal freighters—by terrorist groups to transport personnel and material from one country to another. In some cases, neither the ship nor her crew were complicit; however, in many cases—possibly the majority—the owner or the crew had knowledge of and/or directed or participated in the activity. In the former cases, terrorists that board unsuspecting commercial ships while in port or at anchorage utilize the same tactics employed by drug couriers and stowaways; i.e., climbing the anchor chain, mooring lines, or waterside; hiding in containers to be laden; or posing as and blending in with stevedores. In cases where either the ship owner and/or crew are knowledgeable of or directly participate in these transport operations, this complicity negates the need for individuals to surreptitiously board the ship, and in instances when the vessel is at berth, terrorists access the vessel under the guise of being new crew, visitors, or passengers or bribed port security do not challenge their entering into the port or the ship. Frequently, terrorists board "witting ships" while positioned off the coast. In such operations, terrorists are ferried—via inflatable boats, canoes, fishing boats, and yachts—to waiting freighters. Well-publicized cases in Europe, include the August 2002 incident involving the cargo vessel *M/V Sara*—whose captain radioed an emergency SOS to Italian marine authorities claiming that 15 men brought aboard in Casablanca, Morocco, were threatening him and his crew. According to press reports, the captain stated that he had been "forced" to take the men aboard by the ship's owners, the company—Nova—was suspected of being an al-Qaeda "front" company and, according to U.S. and Italian intelligence sources, had a long history of smuggling illegal immigrants. The Italian authorities discovered that the 15 passengers were all Pakistanis linked to al-Qaeda cells in Europe and were in possession of money, fraudulent documents, and detailed maps of Italian cities. This vessel and the *M/V Twillinger* and the *M/V Tara*—were owned by Nova and had been involved in the transport of terrorist personnel, weapons, and documentation for several years.[12] More recently, ISIS has begun using maritime conveyances—terrorists hiding among irregular migrants—to gain access to Europe and as a means of moving personnel within Southeast Asia. Now, let's look as some specific examples which demonstrate this historical situation and the current trends (Fig. 8.3).

- In late November 2000, a commercial cargo vessel laden with bananas arrived in the port of Ilyichevsk, in Odessa, Ukraine, from Santa Marta, Colombia. During the discharge of the boxes of bananas, 245 boxes packed with compressed marijuana—totaling 6000 pounds—were discovered. The marijuana was seized by authorities, and the resulting investigation established that there had been several similar shipments previously, including via other shipping lines. Also revealed was that the drugs were being exchanged for weapons and these operations had

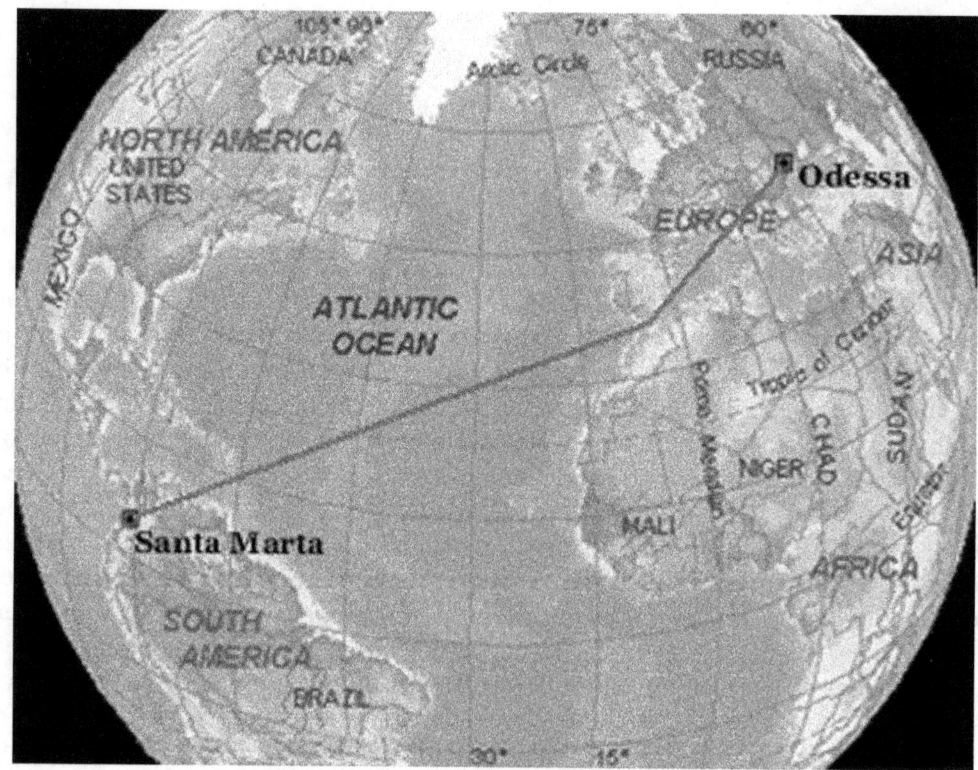

FIGURE 8.3 The drugs-for-guns swap from Colombia to Odessa.

been a coordinated effort of elements of Russian-organized crime, the Colombian "Atlantic Coast Cartel," and the paramilitary United Self-Defense Forces of Colombia (AUC) command in northeast Colombia. Additionally it was revealed that 5 months prior to the seizure, four narcotics smugglers aligned with AUC commander Hernan Giraldo had relocated to Odessa, Ukraine, to coordinate the smuggling operations.[13]

- In October 2001, an Egyptian terrorist was discovered in an empty container in the southern Italian port of Gioia Tauro. The container was to be loaded onboard a commercial container ship destined for Canada and the United States. The container was outfitted with a bed, toilet, and food, as along with a laptop computer, cellular and satellite telephones, and forged airport ID badges and aircraft mechanic certificates for New York's John F Kennedy, Los Angeles International, and Chicago's O'Hare airports.[14]
- Also in 2001, the U.S. Coast Guard racked up two drug seizures which yielded a total of 21 tons of cocaine. The drugs were discovered in fishing vessels crewed by Russians and destined for Mexico. Colombian authorities reported that these cocaine shipments were owned by the terrorist group FARC, elements of

Russian-organized crime were performing the transportation function, and the drugs were to pay for arms from Mexico. Investigations related to multiple drug seizures in Mexico and onboard coastal freighters in the Pacific Ocean identified the presence of a strategic alliance between the FARC, a Russian TCO, and the Mexican drug-trafficking organization "Arellano Felix Organization" (AFO). Moreover, according to press reports, Mexican law enforcement reported the discovery of documentation in raids on AFO locations detailing an ongoing business relationship between the FARC and this drug-trafficking organization.[15]

- In November 2001, the coastal freighter M/V *Otterloo* departed from the Nicaraguan port of El Rama after having loaded 14 containers onboard. The containers held a total of 3000 AK-47s and 2.5 million rounds of ammunition. Supposedly destined for the Panamanian National Police, Panama-based Israeli arms broker Simon Yelinek diverted the ship to Turbo, Colombia and its arms shipment into the waiting arms of the paramilitary United Self-Defense Forces of Colombia command (AUC).[16]
- In May 2002, the news media cited a U.S. Coast Guard report that 25 Islamic extremists had recently stowed away onboard commercial cargo vessels in two Latin American port anchorages and successfully disembarked at major U.S. seaports on the east and west coasts.[17]
- In 2003, according to press reports, al-Qaeda senior leader Khalid Shaikh Mohammed (KSM) attempted to invest in a Pakistani clothing factory for the purpose of shipping undefined weapons within their loaded containers which were destined for New York.[18] Cases like this one and other similar investigations are useful because they offers a view of the global nature of shipping and sheds light on how legitimate commerce can easily shroud probable contraband operations.
- According to a 2006 report by London-based Protection and Indemnity Club, in the previous 2 years there had been several instances of "pirate attacks" occurring off Somalia, in the Malacca Strait, and other waters off Indonesia, where terrorists were left onboard the "attacked" vessel for use of the vessel as a conveyance to travel undetected from one country to another.[19]
- In November 2008, 10 Pakistanis of the terror organization Lashkar-e-Tayyiba (LT), used automatic weapons and grenades to attack multiple resort hotels, a theater, restaurant, and two hospitals in Mumbai (India), killing 164 persons and injuring over 300 more persons. Nine of the terrorists were killed during the multiple battles. Subsequent investigation revealed that the terrorists traveled from Sir Creek (east of Karachi) on the *Al Husaini*, a Pakistani coastal merchant ship, to the territorial waters and then hijacked the Indian trawler, *Kuber*, to transport the terrorist to the coast waters of Mumbai—where they were shuttled ashore on rubber dinghies. Fast-forward 7 years. On the morning of New Year's Eve, 2015, Indian Coast Guard forces intercepted an unusually large Pakistani fishing trawler 364 km off the coast of Porbandar in Gujarat—an area not typical for fishing. More importantly, the Coast

FIGURE 8.4 A cruise ship in a Turkish seaport—Turkey is a favorite maritime debarkation point for recruits for ISIS in Syria and Iraq. *Photo courtesy of* Shutterstock.com.

Guard was acting on specific information from communications from the ship that was intercepted by the Indian National Technical Research Organization (the Indian version of NSA and GCHQ) and indicated that the ship was carrying terrorists and explosives. When the ship was ordered to stop, the crew started a fire onboard, the ship exploded, and there were no survivors (Fig. 8.4).[20]

- In late 2014, INTERPOL Counter-Terrorism Director Pierre St. Hilaire sounded the alarm that numerous reports from mid to late 2014 indicated that Jihadist Fighters were traveling onboard cruise ships and disembarking in ports in Turkey (and not reboarding) to continue forward to Syria and Iraq to join ISIS.[21]
- In early 2015, the British "Quilliam Foundation" (a UK- based counter-extremism think tank with a staff of former members of extremist organizations), published a number of ISIS documents, which describes their plans to send terrorists posing as migrants across the Mediterranean on migrant ships departing from Libyan ports. Other documents mention attack on maritime ships, including cruise ships. From ISIS-controlled cities on the Libyan coast, Malta, Sicily, and Greece mainland are only 300 miles away and Lampedusa is just a 100-mile hop.[22]
- News reports in June 2015 state that *at least 30 ISIS terrorists had been captured in Italy* by law enforcement after arriving from Libya on boats with other migrants.[23]

- In late September 2015, Indonesia's Counter-terrorism chief warned that ISIS is using existing human smuggling networks to transport foreign terrorists via ships from Malaysia to terror-training camps in Indonesia. Indonesia forces have already foiled plots by ISIS-supported local terrorists to attack police station and churches in the region.[24]
- In early November 2015, German press reported that Senior al-Qaeda terror leader Ben Nasr Mehdi, a Tunisian also affiliated with ISIS in Tunisia and who previously served 7 years in an Italian prison for plotting terror attacks in 2007, had been captured in October trying to reenter Italy by hiding within a group of 200 migrants arriving from Libya. Nasr had provided a false name but his true identify was revealed via fingerprint check. The news report states that Italian authorities intentionally did not release the incident for fear of creating panic and criticism of Europe's lax border controls and asylum policy.[25]

The Caribbean Rim of Central and South America has been, and continues to be, highly active as a transit route for terrorists arriving from countries that serve as terror breeding grounds. Over the past 10 years, the migration of Hezbollah, Hamas, and al-Qaeda terrorists to South America generally has followed a route from the Middle East, Near East, and North/East Africa to Venezuela, Guyana, and Ecuador. While some of these terrorists travel to diasporas in the Tri-border Region, Iquique, Chile or port towns in Ecuador, a large percentage travel west from Venezuela and Guyana—or north from Ecuador—onboard general cargo and coastal freighters to Riohacha, Colombia (closest port to Maicao) or to Panama. At these South American and Panamanian locations, the terrorists are staged in the homes, businesses, and secret residences of cooperating Muslim businessmen. Interestingly, many of these terrorists carry valid Venezuelan passports or UN Refugee identification. Once in the Muslim communities of the Caribbean Rim, the terrorists take on a "Western" appearance (jeans, polo shirts, short hair, clean shaven, etc.) and receive instruction in the English and Spanish languages. From Panama, the terrorists either travel onboard coastal freighters to seaports in Honduras, Mexico, or Cuba or overland in commercial trucks or buses to Mexico.[26] For example, according to Panama press reports, on September 18, 2010, Panamanian law enforcement raided a beach house along the upper coast of Colon, seizing 500 kilos of cocaine and capturing several persons subsequently identified by Customs officials as probable FARC and Jihadists[27] and interview of confidential source in Panamanian law enforcement, September 2010. The route from the west coast of South America begins at the coastal locations of Iquique, Chile or Guayaquil, Ecuador to Tumaco and Buenaventura, Colombia–via cargo coastal freighters. From the west coast of Colombia, the terrorists board coastal freighters destined for Panama's Pacific coast or nearby islands.[28] As an example, in March 2012, Yaee Dawit Tadese (distant relative of the late Osama bin Laden) was arrested in Quito, Ecuador, along with 66 recently arrived person from Asia, East and North Africa (specifically Somalia), and the Middle East. Tadese, who was immediately deported to the United States on terrorism charges, was the mastermind of a vast human smuggling network transporting immigrants—some of them terrorists—from Somalia and the Middle East to Ecuador and Venezuela and then north Figs. 8.5 and 8.6.

Continued

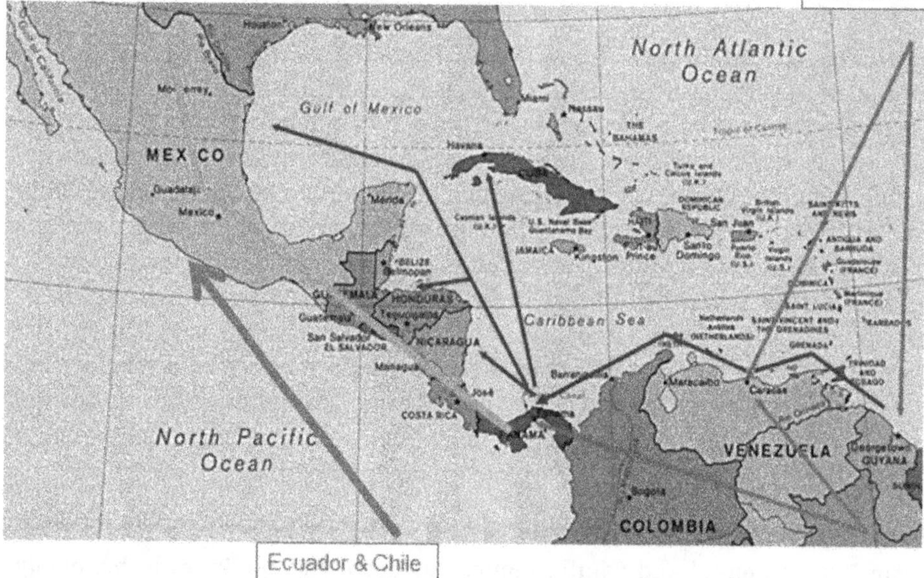

FIGURE 8.5 Migration routes of Hezbollah and al-Qaeda terrorists to South America and north to Central America/Mexico and destined for the United States.

FIGURE 8.6 A typical coastal freighter. This type of ship is used to transport contraband and humans, as well as legitimate cargo, in the Caribbean and coasts of Latin America.

The Nexus Between Terror Groups and TCOs

The existence of a "business alliance" between terrorists and a vast network of profit-oriented TCOs, which include regional gangs and international drug-trafficking organizations, greatly enhances the operational control, complexity, and likely success of these activities, and in the Western Hemisphere is the primary driver directing the transport of terrorists and materials via commercial maritime transport. A fundamental tenet in this discussion is an appreciation that TCOs are "for-profit" enterprises that view terrorists and their materials simply as "commodities to be delivered for a paying client." The Central American-based gangs M-18 and MS-13, like the Mexican *Los Zetas*, now operate from the United States to Brazil—with MS-13 having already established a foothold in Spain, Italy, and several countries in northern Europe—and are highly organized and extremely violent TCOs. Throughout Central America there exists a strategic and tactical alliance between M-18, MS-13, Muslim businessmen involved in money laundering, and transnational DTOs, specifically Mexico's Gulf Cartel and the Sinaloa Cartel. The roles played by M-18 and MS-13 in this triangular alliance include: international "couriers" (*mules*), "personal security escorts," and "enforcers"—in support of the operations directed by Muslim money launders and Mexican DTOs (drug-trafficking organizations) and their subordinate entities. Gang members escort terrorists and illegal drugs from Panama to Honduras, via land and maritime routes, and then—in the case of the Islamic terrorists—north to Mexico and to the U.S. border, as a "for-profit" service. (Fig. 8.7).

One such operation was interrupted in April 2010 by the U.S. Coast Guard. According to press reports in Panama, the U.S. Coast Guard intercepted a coastal freighter off the

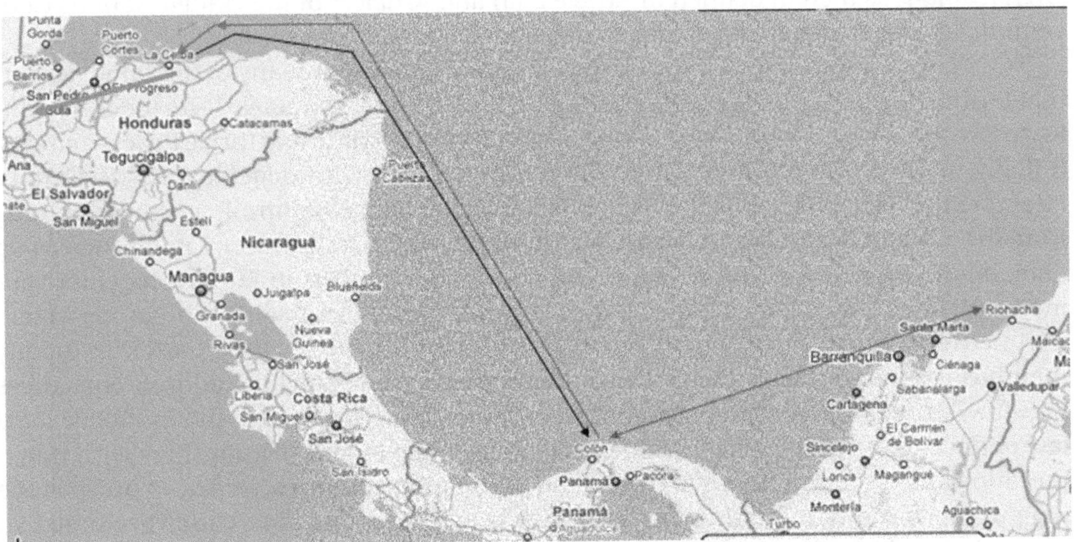

FIGURE 8.7 The south-to-north and north-to-south routes used to transport humans and drugs to north and money and weapons to south.

Caribbean coast of Panama and detained five MS-13 members found onboard. The gang members were brought to port, transferred to the U.S. Embassy personnel, and flown out of Panama. Panamanian law enforcement identified the coastal freighter as one in the fleet noted above.[29]

Transnational Criminal Organizations and the Commercial Maritime Sector

TCOs are corrosive to security, governance, and regional stability, and their seaborne criminal activities pose a daunting challenge to the integrity and security of legitimate maritime commerce and to the world's Naval forces charged with its protection. TCOs exploit the vast expanse of the oceans to advance their criminal enterprises, which include the maritime smuggling and trafficking of illegal drugs, weapons, humans, and counterfeit merchandise and piracy and armed robbery at sea. There are more than 3600 TCOs active just in the European Union.[30] In 2009, they generated an estimated USD$870 billion in annual revenue, which is equivalent to 7% of the world's total exports or the GDP of Mexico or South Korea, and worldwide the UNODC estimates that TCOs generated well over US$2 trillion (3.6% of the global GDP).[31] This section of the chapter briefly discusses the evolution and caustic effects of TCOs and their primary criminal activities in the maritime environment.

For the purposes of this chapter, the term "Transnational Criminal Organizations" is used synonymously with the term "Transnational Organized Crime Groups," with the former being more preferred in the United States and the latter used in EU documents and United Nation Conventions. Additionally, we define the term *Transnational Criminal Organizations* as therein defined in Article 2 (a) and Article 3 of the United Nations Convention Against Transnational Organized Crime (UNTOC).[32]

TCOs have evolved significantly during the past 30 years, for many of the same reasons that legitimate international corporations alter their business strategies—to increase profits, improve operational efficiency and security, and expand into and thrive in new markets. Initially, major drug-trafficking cartels of the 1980s, such as the Medellin and Cali Cartels, attempted to establish vertically integrated supply chains—controlling the drug trade from the production level to wholesale distribution in the U.S. However, rapidly increasing demand throughout the United States and developing markets in Europe, together with increased law enforcement actions and the complexities of managing multimodal transport networks across the globe, served as catalysts for these early drug Cartels to modify their business strategies. These new business strategies also sought to address challenges presented by culture and language differences, the ability to corrupt and influence local law enforcement and other authorities, and knowledge of and relationships with transportation links at various levels in transit and destination countries. Hence, to prosper, the organizations evolved. In this evolution, Cartels in drug production countries forged ad hoc and formal relationships with regional and local criminal organizations in transit and destination countries—to facilitate and ensure the secure and efficient logistics support, transportation, and wholesale distribution. These alliances have facilitated the formerly "regional" crime groups to "go global." Today, for example, of the TCOs operating in Belgium and Portugal, many also are operational in more than 35 other countries.[33] Similarly, Nigerian TCOs involved in drug smuggling are known to maintain personnel in the countries where the drugs are produced, the various transit countries, and the final destination countries; eg, the entire product supply chain.[34] The Sinaloa Cartel, which functions more like a federation of the heads of major organizations, has its tentacles (members) in 50 countries and in every continent of the world, according to Insight. The stranglehold of the Sinaloa Cartel off the Pacific coast of Mexico and Central America is so tight that they charge a "*derecho de pisar*" (right to access)—a fee paid by other drug traffickers to Sinaloa for freedom to use the route for smuggling.[35]

What has emerged today resembles a spiderweb, with alliances and business arrangements between TCOs at all levels of the international supply chain and across the globe. As example, arrests resulting from several multi-ton cocaine seizures in the seaport of Guayaquil, Ecuador in 2013–2014, revealed extensive business alliances and cooperation/coordination between the Mexican Sinaloa Cartel and Colombia's ex-paramilitary group "Los Urabeños" (also known as "Clan *Úsuga*") operating in Colombia and Ecuadorian seaports and Albanian, Bulgarian, Portuguese, Ukrainian, Dutch, and Russian organized crime groups at seaports in Belgium, the Netherlands, and Spain.[36] As evidenced by numerous press reports and post-seizure investigations over the past several years, representatives from the "partner" or contracted groups maintain a presence in the origin, transit, and destination countries to liaise and coordinate information, logistics, and payments. Likewise, there are the Nigerian mafia groups and Chinese triads, each of whom maintains a presence in Ecuadorian seaport cities for the coordination of cocaine shipments to West Africa and Asia.[37] Last, for years, numerous press reports have noted that Colombian TCOs have maintained "collection offices" in Spain, Italy, Belgium, and the Netherlands to facilitate the receiving of funds from the various partner groups for subsequent laundering or transport back to Latin America. Importantly, quality of service, competitive pricing, efficiency, and future business opportunities are the key factors which determine whether an alliance is created and/or continues – and profit *always* trumps ideology, tribal/cultural/national allegiance, and religion. There is no discrimination or hand-wringing regarding whether or not to transport a particular consignment. *Business is business* and a shipment of cocaine, counterfeit cigarettes, weapons, explosives, women and children destined for prostitution, or a transiting terrorist truly are just a "package" for delivery to a destination by a paying customer.

Increasingly, TCOs are "multiproduct/service" enterprises, employing a network form of structure, and newer TCOs are more heterogeneous with regards to the nationalities of their members. Of the estimated 3600 TCOs active in Europe, more than 30% are poly-crime enterprises, such as being engaged in drug smuggling operations and trafficking in human beings, and over 40% have a network type of structure—making them flexible and quick to react to market opportunities and building cooperative alliances and subcontractual relationships.[38] The top earning TCOs offer a view of the two primary types of business structures utilized and the incredibly lucrative earnings being amassed. The most financially successful TCO is the Yamaguchi Gumi (also known the "Yakuza"), with annual revenues estimated at US$80 billion and origins dating back hundreds of years, they earn their billions through drug trafficking, gambling, and extortion.[39] Their organizational structure is highly centralized and member ethnic makeup is exclusively homogeneous—possibly due to their hundreds of years in existence and idiosyncrasies of Japanese culture. Conversely, the Solntsevskaya Bratva (the most prominent of the Russian Mafia groups), earns an estimated US$8.5 billion via drug and human trafficking, but is highly decentralized and its 9000 members are divided among 10 semiautonomous "brigades."[40] The majority of TCOs are heterogeneous with regards to the nationalities of their members. In the EU, some 70% of the TCOs are identified as multinational, with two or more nationalities making up their composition.[41] Non-EU nationalities include persons from Latin America, former Soviet Union countries, Afghanistan, Pakistan, East-Asian countries, and the Maghreb.[42] This evolution is not limited to only the EU. In the Americas, even the ultra-nationalistic MS-13, the TCO previously made up exclusively of persons of El Salvadorian heritage; have opened membership to other Latins and even non-Latins.[43] Prolific global migration and the TCOs conducting business in countries not of their national or ethnic origin appear to be significant factors in this development.

Violence and corruption perpetrated by TCOs in the conducting of their business result in the loss of lives, degrade good governance, and, in some areas, challenge regional stability. Drug production, shipment, transit, and destination areas frequently appear to resemble active combat zones, with higher than normal levels of violent crime and murders, and bodies littering the streets. Frequently, violence erupts between TCOs for control of drug smuggling "routes" or corridor, or when one gang attempts to intercept and steal a drug shipment from another gang. In 2013, there were several incidents of running gun battles in the port of Antwerp, a major drug destination seaport, between rival Albanian and Bulgarian crime groups specifically for the aforementioned reasons.[44] Currently, Honduras is the murder capital of the world, and most of these murders are related to drug trafficking and fighting between rival TCOs. In Mexico, during 2013, 40–60% of all homicides were identified as "organized crime homicides."[45]

TCOs can also present challenges to effective governance and regional stability. Opium profits in Afghanistan fuel Taliban weapons purchases and their ability to finance services for communities under their control—undercutting the power and authority of the national government and efforts at regional stability. Effective governance is depleted when the criminal activities of TCOs reduce the monies entering the treasuries of sovereign states. For example, in United Kingdom, 25% of all cigarettes purchased are counterfeit or smuggled into the country—which represents a US$3.3 billion loss in taxes collected by the government, according to a 2011 report by the British HM Revenue and Customs.[46] TCOs also make billions of dollars—and risk tens of thousands of innocent deaths and as well rob tax income from governments—in counterfeit vaccines and lifesaving medicine. For example, it is estimated that more that 50% of the antimalaria and antibiotics in Southeast Asia and Africa are counterfeit and do not contain the active ingredients in the real dosages. The World Health Organization estimates that one million people die each year from malaria, which could be significantly decreased if fake antimalarial pills were removed from the supply chain. The vast majority of these counterfeit medicines are produced in illegal laboratories in China and, based on worldwide seizures, some 66% of *ALL* counterfeit merchandise and products are manufactured in China[47] And how much profit do TCOs make from counterfeit goods from East Asia, mostly from China, to the United States and the European Union? The estimate is that for the year 2010, TCOs generated US$24.4 billion in profits.[48]

The United Nations Convention Against Transnational Organized Crime (UNTOC) is the primary international convention and legal instrument addressing the problem of TCOs and their activities. The UNTOC sets forth a series of measures to combat TCO activities through global cooperation in matters relating to the confiscation of property, extradition, mutual legal assistance, and technical assistance and training. The Convention also requires parties to implement domestic measures to achieve criminalization of the various aspects of organized crime.[49] The UNTOC contains two important Annexes; first, the "Protocol to Prevent, Suppress, and Punish Trafficking in Persons, Especially Women and Children," and second, the "Protocol against the Smuggling of Migrants by Land, Air, and Sea.". Two other key legal instruments related to TCOs are the "Protocol against the Illicit Manufacturing and Trafficking in Firearms" and the "United Nations Convention against Illicit Traffic in Narcotic Drugs and Psychotropic Substances." The United Nations Office on Drugs and Crime (UNODC) is the UN guardian for these Conventions and associated Protocols.[50]

Primary TCO Criminal Activities in the Commercial Maritime Environment

While the single most profitable venture for TCOs across the globe continues to be drug trafficking, trafficking in counterfeits, human and migrant smuggling, and arms smuggling likewise are very lucrative, and *the majorities of these criminal activities are perpetrated via the commercial maritime transport.*[51] Global **profits** for TCOs from their crimes – i.e., combining proceeds from drug trafficking; counterfeiting; human trafficking; trafficking in oil, wildlife, timber, fish, art and cultural property, gold, human organs, and small and light weapons – in 2009 were estimated to be US$882 billion, of which some 70% was subsequently laundered. Of this huge figure, 50% of these proceeds come from drug trafficking.[52] The profit from drug trafficking is grossly disproportional to other criminal and legitimate business activities. An analysis of the profit-cost ratio for the global cocaine trade reveals that of the estimated US$85 billion in worldwide sales, only a little over 1% were incurred in "costs"—permitting TCOs to reap a hefty US$84 billion in wholesale and retail profits.[53] Modern communications systems and devices, and the Internet, have greatly impacted on how TCOs do business and communicate.[54] Most TCOs have vigorously embraced the use of the Internet– (using e-commerce, the Dark Net, secure chat rooms, encrypted web mail, mobile communications, and Legal Business Structures to conduct business, coordinate operations, enhance operational security, extend their global reach—all which translate into greater efficiency and profit.[55]

While we have discussed in detail the drug-trafficking operations of TCOs, in many global criminal operations TCOs leverage the infrastructure, resources, and assets of one criminal network chain/activity to enhance the success of other criminal ventures. Let's briefly look at an example to better understand this strategy. In September 2015, the U.S. authorities charged three Colombians partnering with a Chinese TCO based in Guangzhou to launder more than $5 billion in drug profits from the United States, parts of Africa, Europe, and several countries in Latin America. In this criminal enterprise, the Colombians wire transferred the drug money to Hong Kong-based banks owned by Chinese casinos and importers/exporters. The funds were then used to purchase counterfeit goods that were shipped and sold internationally in exchange for money not linked to drug trafficking.[56] Note that the vast majority of drugs smuggled from Latin America to those destination markets and the counterfeit merchandise shipped from China (the port of Guangzhou is a major departure point for containers loaded with fake cigarettes, medicines, auto parts, etc.) would be via commercial maritime transport. Colombian TCOs and Chinese TCOs—referred to as "*Red Dragons*" in Latin American, also coordinate human smuggling and trafficking in human beings from China to Colombia, Ecuador, and Peru. These *Red Dragon* TCOs charge US$60,000 per Chinese national smuggled from mainland China to Latin America. For those migrants "fully paid in advance," the Colombians facilitate the movement of the Chinese migrants via coastal freighters to Guatemala and Mexico, where they are escorted into the United States or Canada. Other Chinese smuggled into Mexico, Guatemala, and South America—with promises of jobs and a new life—are forced into indentured labor, slavery, and the sex trade, as a means of paying for the transport.[57] Very similar alliances exist in other regions of the world, with other TCOs cooperating for "*profit reasons.*"

Summary

In this chapter, we discussed the historical and current trends in terrorists targeting ships and seaport for attack, and how ships and containers are used by terror groups to transport terrorists, weapons, and materials around the world. Importantly, we highlighted the growing threat of ISIS to maritime assets and the jihadist attacks in the Suez Canal. We also reviewed how TCOs cooperate with each other and terrorist groups and use commercial shipping to smuggle drugs, counterfeit merchandise, and humans around the world – and the negative consequences of these crimes, to include increased violence, broken lives, and the corrosion of security and governance for the nations impacted.

End Notes

1. http://articles.latimes.com/2002/oct/11/world/fg-tanker11; http://www.globalsecurity.org/security/profiles/limburg_oil_tanker_attacked.htm
2. http://www.ecop.info/documents/mricfeb04.pdf
3. http://archive.adl.org/israel/israel_attacks.html

4. http://www.cruiselawnews.com/2012/04/articles/terrorism-1/al-qaeda-planned-to-seize-cruise-ships-execute-passengers/
5. http://www.telegraph.co.uk/news/worldnews/middleeast/unitedarabemirates/7930642/Al-Qaeda-attack-on-supertanker.html
6. http://www.cruiselawnews.com/2012/04/articles/terrorism-1/al-qaeda-planned-to-seize-cruise-ships-execute-passengers/
7. http://www.cruiselawnews.com/2012/10/articles/terrorism-1/terror-plot-against-israeli-cruise-pasengers-thwarted-in-cyprus/
8. http://www.esisc.org/upload/publications/briefings/egypt-expansion-of-the-suez-canal-and-increased-operational-capabilities-of-is-terrorists-raise-concerns-over-the-security-of-the-strategic-waterway/Suez%20Canal.pdf
9. http://shippingwatch.com/secure/carriers/article7128599.ece
10. http://english.aawsat.com/2015/07/article55344287/egypt-arrests-13-brotherhood-members-over-alleged-suez-canal-terror-plot-sources
11. http://www.esisc.org/upload/publications/briefings/egypt-expansion-of-the-suez-canal-and-increased-operational-capabilities-of-is-terrorists-raise-concerns-over-the-security-of-the-strategic-waterway/Suez%20Canal.pdf; http://www.breitbart.com/national-security/2015/07/17/world-view-isis-linked-terrorists-sink-egyptian-navy-ship-amid-suez-canal-expansion/; http://www.janes.com/article/53070/sinai-militants-attack-egyptian-patrol-boat
12. http://www.washingtonpost.com/ac2/wp-dyn/A56442-2002Dec30?language=printer
13. Phoenix Group Report of Investigation, Santa Marta, Colombia, December 2000.
14. http://www.cbc.ca/canada/story/2001/10/25/stowaway_farid011025.html
15. http://www.latinamericanstudies.org/drugs/mexicans-russians.html
16. La Prensa, Republic of Panama, February 19, 2003
17. http://www.foxnews.com/story/0,2933,52628,00.html
18. http://www.freerepublic.com/focus/f-news/968461/posts
19. Interview of confidential source in London P & I Club, December 2006
20. http://www.cnn.com/2013/09/18/world/asia/mumbai-terror-attacks/; http://www.dailymail.co.uk/indiahome/indianews/article-2894894/Mumbai-like-terror-attack-averted-coast-guards-intercept-Pakistani-vessel-Gujarat-coast.html
21. http://www.maritime-executive.com/article/Jihadists-Using-Cruise-Ships-to-Sneak-Into-War-Zones-2014-11-07
22. http://www.gatestoneinstitute.org/5301/islamic-state-libya;
23. http://www.foxnews.com/politics/2015/06/14/sources-isis-terrorists-using-chaotic-libya-west/
24. http://thediplomat.com/2015/09/indonesia-warns-of-islamic-state-threat/
25. http://www.breitbart.com/london/2015/11/09/al-qaeda-terror-boss-discovered-on-migrant-boat-authorities-tried-to-hide-news/
26. Kimery, A., *Unholy Trinity*. Homeland Security Today, p. 24-36., August 2009.
27. http://mensual.prensa.com/mensual/contenido/2010/09/18/uhora/local_2010091810310567.asp and interview of confidential source in Panamanian law enforcement, September 2010.
28. Interview of Colombian Military advisor, October 2010.
29. http://mensual.prensa.com/mensual/contenido/2009/04/12/hoy/panorama/1750394.asp and interview of confidential source in Panamanian law enforcement, April 2009.
30. European Police Office. (2013). EU Serious and Organized Crime Assessment 2013. EUROPOL SOCTA 2013, p 33.

31. INTERPOL (2014). Against Organized Crime. *INTERPOL Trafficking and Counterfeiting Casebook 2014*, p 14.; ONODC (2011) *Estimating illicit financial flows Resulting from drug trafficking and Other Transnational Organized Crimes*, p 9.

32. UNTOC, *Article 2 (a)* states: "Organized Criminal Group" shall mean a structured group of three or more persons, existing for a period of time and acting in concert with the aim of committing one or more serious crimes or offenses established in accordance with this Convention, in order to obtain, directly or indirectly, a financial or other material benefit. *Article 3* states that an offense is "transnational" in nature if: it is committed in more than one State; it is committed in one State but a substantial part of its preparation, planning, direction, or control takes place in another State; it is committed in one State but involves an organized crime group that engages in criminal activities in more than one State; or, it is committed in one State but has substantial effects in another State.

33. European Police Office. (2013). EU Serious and Organized Crime Assessment 2013. *EUROPOL SOCTA 2013*, p 34.

34. International Scientific and Professional Advisory Council of the United Nations Crime Prevention and Criminal Justice Program. (2011). International Organized Crime: The African Experience *ISPAC, 2011*, pp 34–39. The Center for Investigative Journalism in the Americas, 2014, August. Drug Trafficking: Has Ecuador Lost the Pacific? Retrieved from http://thecija.org/blog/2014/08/24/part-one-drug-trafficking-has-ecuador-lost-the-pacific.

35. http://www.insightcrime.org/mexico-organized-crime-news/sinaloa-cartel-profile?highlight=WyJzaW5hbG9hIiwic2luYWxvYSdzIiwiJ3NpbmFsb2EiLCJjYXJ0ZWwiLCJjYXJ0ZWwncyIsImNhcnRlbCciLCInY2FydGVsIiwiJ2NhcnRlbCciLCJzaW5hbG9hIGNhcnRlbCJd; http://www.insightcrime.org/news-analysis/maritime-drug-trafficking

36. El Universo, 2014, April. Decomisan 400 kilos de cocaina en Ecuador, *El Universo*, Retrieved from http://www. eluniverso.com/noticias/2014/08/01/nota/3304351/policia-decomisa-cocaina-durante-operativo-jujan-guayaquil. INTERPOL, 2014, August. Albanian Fugitve targeted by INTERPOL arrested in Ecuador, *INTERPOL*, Retrieved from http://www.interpol.int/News-and-media/News/2014/N2014-149. The Center for Investigative Journalism in the Americas, 2014, August. Drug Trafficking: Has Ecuador Lost the Pacific? Retrieved from http://thecija.org/blog/2014/08/24/part-one-drug-trafficking-has-ecuador-lost-the-pacific.

37. Ibid.

38. European Police Office. (2013). EU Serious and Organized Crime Assessment 2013. *EUROPOL SOCTA 2013*, p 33.

39. Matthews, C. (2014, September 14). Fortune 5: The biggest Organized Crime Groups in the World. *Fortune Magazine*, Retrieved from http://fortune.com/2014/09/14/biggest-organized-crime-groups-in-the-world.

40. Ibid.

41. European Police Office. (2013). EU Serious and Organized Crime Assessment 2013. *EUROPOL SOCTA 2013*, p 34.

42. Ibid.

43. Wills, S. (2013). Retrieved from http://abcnews.go.com/ABC_Univision/ABC_Univision/mara-salvatrucha-gang-mexican-cartel-united-states-problem/story?id=18920021.

44. Interview of Belgium Customs Officers, June 2014.

45. Heinle, K., et al. (2014). *Justice in Mexico Project.* University of San Diego. pp. 22–24.

46. INTERPOL (2014). *Against Organized Crime: INTERPOL Trafficking and Counterfeiting Casebook 2014*, p 13.

47. INTERPOL (2014). *Against Organized Crime: INTERPOL Trafficking and Counterfeiting Casebook 2014*, p 54. United Natons Office on Drugs and Crime (2013). *Transnational Organized Crime in East Asia and the Pacific, A Threat Assessment*, p 123.

48. UNODC (2013). *Transnational Organized Crime in East Asia and the Pacific, A Threat Assessment*, p 121.
49. United Nations General Assembly (2001). *United Nations Convention Against Organized Crime.*
50. United Nations Office on Drugs and Crime (2013). Combating Transnational Organized Crime Committed at Sea, Issue Paper, p 1.
51. INTERPOL (2014). *Against Organized Crime: INTERPOL Trafficking and Counterfeiting Casebook 2014*, p 14.
52. United Nations Office on Drugs and Crime (2011). *Estimating illicit financial flows resulting from drug trafficking and other Transnational Organized Crime*, pp 35–36.
53. United Nations Office on Drugs and Crime (2011). *Estimating illicit financial flows resulting from drug trafficking and other Transnational Organized Crime*, pp 9–10.
54. European Police Office. (2013). *EU Serious and Organized Crime Assessment 2013.* EUROPOL SOCTA 2013, p 34.
55. Ibid.
56. http://www.businessinsider.com/us-charges-3-people-in-multibillion-dollar-drug-money-laundering-scheme-2015-9; http://www.insightcrime.org/news-analysis/colombians-charged-china-drug-money-laundering-scheme
57. http://www.insightcrime.org/news-analysis/rising-dragon-the-chinese-mafia-threat-in-latin-america

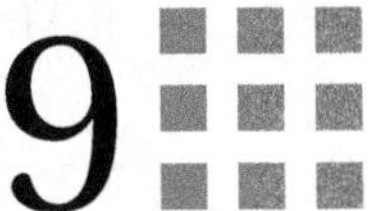

9 Cyber and Information Threats to Seaports and Ships

R. Sen

UNITED STATES DEPARTMENT OF DEFENSE AND NATIONAL INTELLIGENCE COMMUNITY

OBJECTIVES

After studying this chapter, you will be familiar with

1. The current and emerging cyberthreats and their impact;
2. The specific cyberthreats to the commercial maritime sector;
3. Why seaports and ships are especially vulnerable to cyberattacks;
4. Who are the actual and potential actors targeting ships and seaports;
5. The key components to a cybersecurity plan for businesses and organizations which builds Resiliency.

Introduction

It seems that every time one looks at the news these days a new major cyberattack has occurred. From the data breach of government employees of the Office of Personnel Management by a foreign intelligence agency to major financial and health care providers having their customer and patient databases plundered. Equally concerning, hackers have recently started to show their ability to attack everything from airliners to cars and seemingly everything in between. Costs of cyberattacks on industry vary widely, based on data and methodology, but range from $300 billion a year on the low side to over $1 trillion a year on the more realistic side. This number is projected to double—to $2 trillion a year—by 2019.[1] However, these costs do not take into account the long-term losses in terms of trust, brand damage, and damage to national security of various countries. Equally alarming, the picture emerging actually is more worrisome when one *really* analyzes the data and incidents. For example, few news outlets report on an increasing trend in cybersecurity, one which has the potential to impact 90% of world trade. This trend is the growing wave of attacks on maritime assets and organizations.[2]

Most computer-based technical, mechanical, operations, and communications systems used in ports and onboard ships and gas/oil platforms increasingly are automated. And most ships and platforms utilize a vast array of sensors, such as weather sensors, RFID, onboard radio, Wi-Fi, and satellite-based Internet systems. Numerous evaluation tests and

Maritime Security.

several criminal cases from 2013 to 2015 have demonstrated that all of the aforementioned port and ship equipment and system, to include the main ship navigation systems—the Automatic Identification System (AIS), the Electronic Chart Display and Information System (ECDIS), and GPS—are susceptible to penetration or manipulation, including those that interfaced via satellite.[3] These vulnerabilities create openings for hacktivists, terrorists, and criminal elements, who may want to cause an environmental disaster, to use a ship as an attack platform, steal cargo, hijack a ship, or release private information to embarrass organizations. Criminal organizations have hacked the computers and networks of shipping lines and their agents, port authorities, and terminal operators to obtain information on ship-sailing schedules, ports of call, the specific cargoes and containers onboard, load/manifest data, trucker information, cargo release information in destination ports, and which security measures are in place. Frequently, this is done to facilitate cargo theft/container hijackings and drug-smuggling operations in ports, but there are indications that criminal gangs, especially those in Asia, have used information from hacked systems to target ships for attack and piracy at sea. All the data and indicators point to this trend worsening as maritime assets become evermore automated and reliant on their onboard information technology (IT) systems. Nevertheless, even though the cyberthreat continues to spiral upward in sophistication, there are real steps, processes, and protocols that can be implemented to greatly reduce and ameliorate the threat. In this chapter, we will review the current and emerging cyberthreats to maritime systems and organizations, as well as look at why maritime systems are such an attractive target. Finally, we will look at the new reality in cybersecurity—which recognizes that your organization will, at some point, most probably become compromised—and how one can build resiliency to these attacks.

Before discussing ways to mitigate the current and emerging cyberthreats to maritime security, it's first important to have some understanding of the current cyberthreats in general and maritime threats in specific. It is not necessary to understand exactly how, at a technical level, many of the attackers perform their attacks, but to understand the risk they represent. It is also not necessary to have a technical understanding of information security to design and implement high-level security policies and procedures, thus we will not delve into a highly technical discussion. Finally, we will not perform an exhaustive examination of every type of threat possible in the Cyber Realm. Entire rows of books are dedicated to each of these topics! Rather, we will try to give you a sense of the breadth, depth, and severity of the threat. At the end of this chapter, you will note a listing of suggested additional readings and resources for those persons desiring to delve deeper into the topics of computer security and cybersecurity standards of leading organizations. It is important to appreciate that to seriously address the cybersecurity threats in your organization, and make it resilient to cyberattack, you and your organization must commit resources to this issue, bring in experts and outside third-party testers, and align the security goals with the major organizational goals. With this in mind, let's first look at the growing threat of cyberattack and some of the current trends in the industry.

A Growing Threat

Cyberattacks have not only been increasing in number but they have been increasing in severity, complexity, and sophistication. Cyberattacks have started to become the *go-to* method for intelligence gathering by many nation states, as well as unethical corporations who attack vulnerable IT systems or individuals for the purpose of illegally acquiring intellectual property (IP), business intelligence, and other information to provide a competitive or economic advantage. The total costs from types of attacks are very difficult to quantify, varying from hundreds of thousands of dollars to many billions. In some cases, damage caused just from simple data breaches have caused companies to shut down, delay launches of service, and/or resulted in damaging law suits. In the case of the U.S. F-35 Fighter Jet, Chinese attackers were able to retrieve significant documentation, plans, software, and other IP, allowing them to replicate the F-35 for their fifth generation aircraft.[4] The F-35 program cost U.S. taxpayers more than *$400billion* and is only one of a number of multibillion dollar weapon programs whose IP has been stolen in the last few years. Most importantly, the pace of these data breaches, from 2004 to June 2015, has continued to increase in number, scope, and severity (as shown in Fig. 9.1).

While cyberattacks have become a major issue in the loss of data, they also have become popular methods for state actors, criminal networks, activists, and other malcontents to cause harm to organizations' ability to maintain business continuity. These attacks have moved from simple defacing of websites and Distributed Denial of Service (DDOS)[5] attacks to very sophisticated attacks against systems, sensors, and infrastructure. For example in late 2014, hackers attacked the control system of a German steel mill causing the improper shut down of a blast furnace. The result was a "massive," though unspecified, damage to

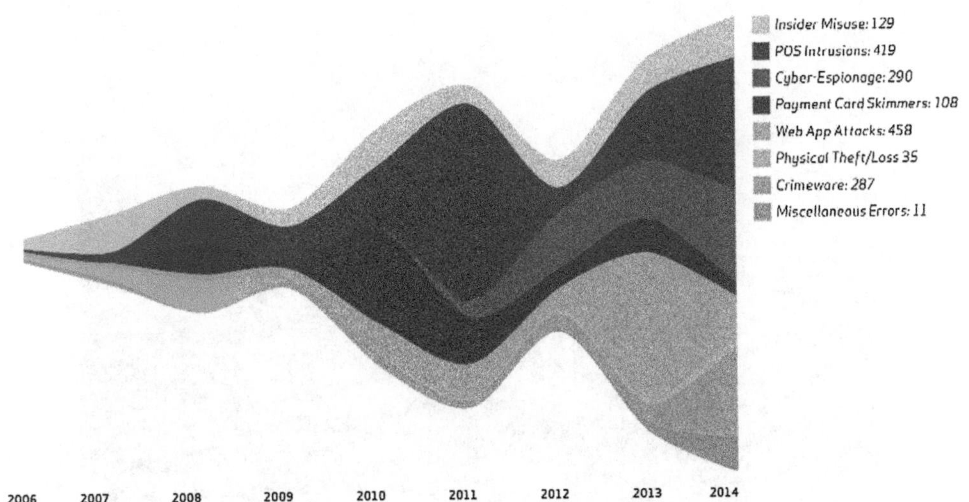

FIGURE 9.1 Trends in source of data breeches from 2006 to 2014 showing increasing diversity of attacks as well as depth.

the furnace and steel works.[6] Such attacks deeply trouble security experts because they demonstrate that not only can attacks steal data but they can do actual, and serious, physical harm to systems and critical infrastructure.

Cyberthreats to Maritime Security

One problem with maritime cybersecurity comes from the low-level attention the maritime industry has paid to the problem, in large, because until recently it has not been a major issue. That has changed though in the last five years, as commercial maritime and affiliated industries increasingly have come under attack. Moreover, an increasing trend by organized crime, and even some smaller criminal networks, is to gain unauthorized access to shipping and port computer systems for the purpose of obtaining information to facilitate cargo theft, piracy, and contraband (drugs, humans, counterfeit products, etc.) smuggling operations. Perhaps one of the most well-known and fascinating examples of such cyberattack activity happened in the European port of Antwerp (Belgium) in 2013, and made possible the successful smuggling and dispatch from the port of numerous containers of many tons of Colombian cocaine and heroin over more than 2 years (See Fig. 9.2).[7] This smuggling operation came to light when law enforcement investigated complaints by shipping lines that loaded containers were missing cargo when arriving at the importers' sites and other various containers had simply disappeared from the ports. Subsequent investigation revealed that a Dutch transnational criminal organization, operating in several seaports in Northern Europe, initially had contracted two hackers to send spear phishing messages to several port workers, who were tricked into downloading malware. The malware collected the user names and passwords of port employees working in operation,

FIGURE 9.2 Container entrance and exit gate at the Port of Antwerp.

permitting the criminals to gain access to vessel arrival and manifest information, the Terminal Container Yard Management system, and the Gate Dispatch system. Once the terminal operator detected the system breach, a firewall was installed to block the intrusions. However, as evidence of the criminal organization's perseverance and willingness to take risks for the huge rewards reaped, criminal, with hackers in tow, surreptitiously accessed the Terminal offices and computers, and installed key-logging software/hardware and secret Wi-Fi devices in the computers and electrical outlets. This software and hardware permitted the criminals full access to the terminal's operations, yard management, and dispatch systems and the ability to view, manipulate, and change data and records. With this capability and information, hackers changed the cargo release data to note the truckers employed by the criminal organization, facilitate the dispatch of the containers before the legitimate truckers arrived, and then cover-up the entire transaction—displaying that the containers had not left the port terminal. At the conclusion of the investigation, police in Belgium and the Netherlands raided 20 homes and businesses, arresting 15 criminals and hackers, and seizing 2 tons of cocaine and heroin and over $1 million in cash.[8] While the Antwerp port case is a notable example, it is very likely that many other cases have happened but simply were not detected. In part, this is because much of the technology and infrastructure used to operate and manage ports, ships, and trucking is very vulnerable to cyberattack.

The maritime sector relies heavily on the use of wireless technologies, such as satellite networks to enable digital communications, tracking of ships, and navigation. Wireless networks are notably hard to secure but many satellite networks, often decades old, are incredibly insecure, using no or very simple encryption and allowing anyone with technical know-how to intercept communications between the satellite and its intended audience. Hackers could use that information to track ships, or the cargo on it, for pirate attack or actually manipulate the data between the ship and satellites to misdirect them on to a new course.[9] In January 2014, a UK cybersecurity firm found flaws in one ECDIS system that would allow an attacker the ability to access and modify ship electronic-navigation charts—which is the primary system used for charting a course.[10] In late 2013, University of Texas researcher gave a live demonstration onboard a superyacht, taking over the navigation system and changing its course using a $2000 easy-to-assemble devise—which *spoofed* the navigation system using a fake GPS signal.[11] Hackers have also shown that they can manipulate security flaws in the ship AIS, which is onboard virtually every commercial cargo/container ship over 100 gross tons—over 1 million ships in the world—and was first mandated with the implementation of the International Ship and Port Facility Security (ISPS) Code. The AIS transceiver is a key data communications system that is used to report a ship's location, type of cargo, and the positions of nearby vessels. However, it also is used in ship-to-ship communications, course plotting, and collision avoidance. Likewise, the data broadcast continuously by the AIS is used by port authorities and the world's navies and coast guards to maintain near real-time awareness of the locations of ships worldwide and for use in identifying threats and respond to emergency calls for assistance. At a major shipping conference in 2013, researchers showed how using inexpensive radio

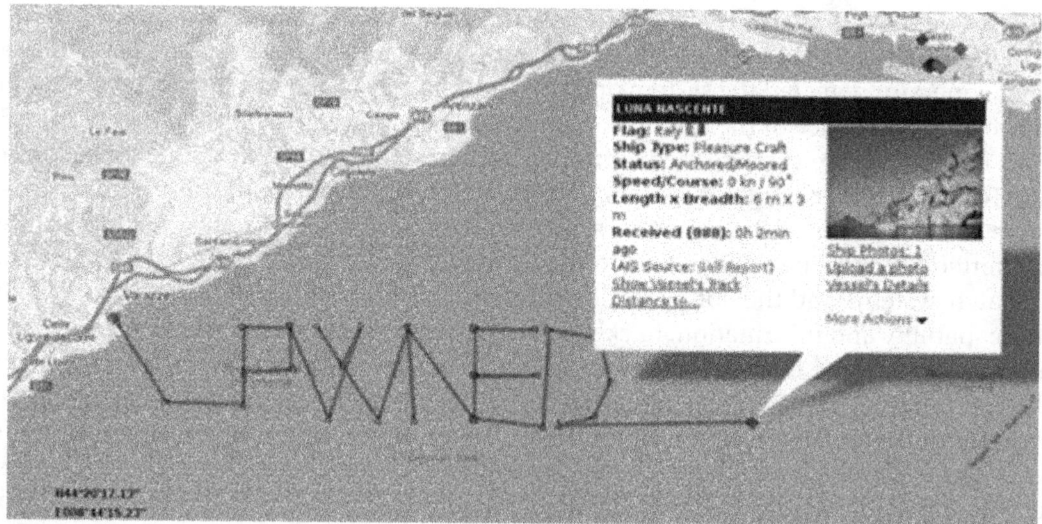

FIGURE 9.3 Hackers demonstrate their ability to push false data Automatic Identification System spelling out the word "PWNED." *Illustration courtesy of* http://www.technologyreview.com/news/520421/ship-tracking-hack-makes-tankers-vanish-from-view.

equipment they were able to hack and spoof the AIS system, making the ship disappear on the map, portray the ship sailing on dry land (projecting at a false location), show false alerts—"man-in-the-water" and "collision warning," and sail a track which spelled out a word—"PWNED" (See Fig. 9.3).[12] As one can imagine, this vulnerability offers tremendous opportunities for criminals, pirates, and terrorists to obtain sensitive information and also project false information. While these threats are real, and serious, there are other cases that point to a concerning trend of hackers causing physical damage to maritime assets.

Over the last few years, a number of offshore oil drilling platforms have been taken off-line by malicious software downloaded or accidently placed onto computers by employees. In one incident in 2013, a group of hackers remotely attacked a floating oil rig off the coast of Africa and gained control of its stabilization systems and programmed the platform to tilt dangerously to one side. The platform had to be shut down for 19 days while IT security professionals removed numerous viruses and malware from its computer systems and permit the rig to again become seaworthy.[13] Various reports also suggest that numerous oil companies have had their oil rigs attacked by sovereign states, perhaps China. In these cases, the attackers seem to have attempted to access and take control of oil platform's supervisory control and data acquisition (SCADA) systems. In most cases, the oil companies who ran and owned the platforms had no idea that the attacks had happened until they were contacted by the U.S. Federal Bureau of Investigation. In 2012, the Saudi Arabian Oil Company reported that 30,000 computers' hard drives were destroyed by malicious software in multiple major attacks.[14] While one can only speculate why these attacks have happened, hackers have already shown that they can take oil and power facilities off-line, as well as control everything on an oil rig to, for example, create a massive oil spill and environmental disaster.[15] Such a capability might be leveraged by a criminal network for extortion or by a hostile State to create economic damage to a country. As such, the current trends in maritime cybersecurity have moved from enabling more mundane crime, such as shipment of illicit goods, to cyberespionage and sabotage and the trafficking of billions of dollars in illegal drugs.

Why the Maritime Sector Is Particularly Vulnerable

As mentioned earlier, the maritime sector is highly vulnerable to cyberthreats, in large part, because it has not had to deal with the same level of cyberthreats that other sectors have seen and therefore funding and attention has been slow in shifting to focus on the issue. For example, a 2013 Brookings Institution study of six major ports found all six vulnerable to cyberattack, but only one port had conducted a threat assessment, and none had developed contingency plans to address a major cyberattack.[16] Moreover, while federal funding to enhance port security in 2013 totaled over $2.6 billion, less than 1% of this money was directed for cybersecurity projects.[17] Shipping lines and agents are likewise highly susceptible to attack. In 2013, maritime cybersecurity company "CyberKeel" probed the online defenses of the world's 20 largest container shipping lines and found that 16 had serious security gaps.[18] And, as noted above, the oil and gas sector are feeling the pain more than any other private sector industry. An April 2015 study by Symantec Corporation revealed that computer-system hackers had attacked 43% of all global mining, oil and gas companies at least one time in 2014.[19] The Norwegian gas and oil sector experienced more than 50 cyberattack incidents just in 2014.[20] The commercial maritime shipping industry was not left untouched. The Classification Society leader DNV (GL-Maritime division) reported in March 2015 that shipping industry had already seen cyberattacks of AIS, ECDIS, and GPS data—the three key navigation and communication systems on vessels.[21] With these points in mind, let's review a number of other factors which make the maritime sector so vulnerable.

Over Reliance on Outdated Technology

One major problem that the maritime industry suffers from, as do other industrial verticals, is the over reliance on outdated technology and security practices. For example, many people, even some in the IT-security field, believe that firewalls and antivirus software are sufficient to protect most IT systems. Unfortunately, this is not the case! Attackers have moved to using tools and technologies that allow them to easily create viruses, Trojans, and other assorted malware often with the push of a button. This allows them to quickly and easily alter their code or make viruses that they will only use once—making it nearly impossible for the typical antivirus vendors' software to keep up. Indeed, a report from FireEye shows that 82% of all malware it detects stay active for a mere hour, and 70% of all threats only surface once, as malware authors rapidly change their software to skirt detection from traditional antivirus solutions (See Fig. 9.4).[22] What this means is that hackers and bad actors can

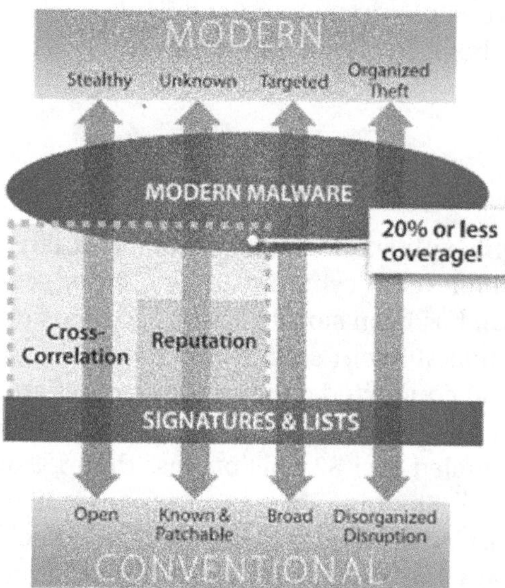

FIGURE 9.4 *Conventional Defenses are effective against only 20% or less of Modern Malware Illustration courtesy of* http://www.nle.com/literature/FireEye_modern_malware_exposed.pdf.

often easily exploit the weak and outdated security used by most maritime organizations to protect their systems. The industry as a whole needs to look at other industries, as well as emerging best practices that focus on a much more holistic approach to cybersecurity. While it may be intellectually difficult to accept, the maritime industry should assume that intrusions and data breaches will happen and thus focus on how to ameliorate and respond to threats via rapid detection, reporting, and coordinated response. While we will get into this more in the Chapter Section entitled "Securing Maritime Assets," the only way to meet the future of emerging cybersecurity threats is to invest in training and planning, as well as technologies that are designed to help support a robust continuity of operations plan.[23]

General Ignorance of IT Security

Another reason the maritime industry is such a ripe target for cyberattacks is its general lack of knowledge of IT security and disinterest in the subject; although that is changing. As we have already discussed in the previous section, maritime cyberthreats are increasing in complexity and severity yet most maritime companies have done little to nothing in response. Furthermore, and equally perplexing, vendors who manufacture, install, or service maritime automation and communication equipment are also generally slow and somewhat disinterested in securing their products and systems from attack.

High Value—Low Risk

The maritime industry's total economic value in the United States in 2009 was worth $436.6 billion.[24] Worldwide, maritime assets moved trillions of dollars in goods and commodities. As such, it makes an attractive target to criminal networks, as well as those interested in causing major economic damage. Hackers and other malicious actors also are very attracted to the maritime industry not only because of the high value it represents but also because of the low chance of punitive action. As the targets are unlikely to have sophisticated cybersecurity or even know-how to respond to attacks, the downside is minimal.

Lack of Standards

The maritime industry currently lacks serious standards, unlike other industries, in hardening against cyberattack. While many problems exist with maritime IT security, usually one of the easiest ways to address these problems is to develop comprehensive standards and frameworks that can be used as foundation for making more secure systems. Specifically, some very good standards and frameworks exist, for example, the U.S. National Institute for Standards and Technologies (NIST) Cyber Security Framework, and can be used as a starting point in lieu of spending a long time creating initial maritime-specific cybersecurity standards.[25]

Complexity

Ships are often floating office spaces and multicargo logistics centers with sophisticated navigation, communication, instrumentation, and IT systems—to include for staff or passengers, who also bring their own devices (See Fig. 9.5). With the trend toward increased automation and use of technology comes increased complexity, making it much harder for maritime crews and service people to know exactly how everything works, what security threats to computers exist, and how to mitigate those problems. A report in 2015 looked at a random set of maritime company sites and found that 37% of them had Microsoft servers that were vulnerable to an attack simply because the available Microsoft patch was not downloaded and installed.[26] This simply means that, for whatever reason, these organizations or crews left their systems vulnerable to attack even though there was a simple mechanism for protecting them. If organizations are too stressed, busy, or unable to keep up with even the simplest of security practices, how are they expected to understand and manage the more esoteric threats of SCADA networks and satellite commutations systems? Furthermore, as these systems get more complex, it becomes harder to understand what's connected to what, how different technologies may affect another system; and likewise, appreciate the natural human tendency of workers when faced with complex IT systems to cut corners and not follow best practices. As such, the increasing complexity of maritime IT systems is heightening their vulnerability to cyberattack.

Easy Targets

Many organizations in the commercial world have had to harden their infrastructure, in part, due to constant, malicious attacks by hackers. Frequently, their operations at some point manage data—from IP to customer data to digital money to trade secrets—and this

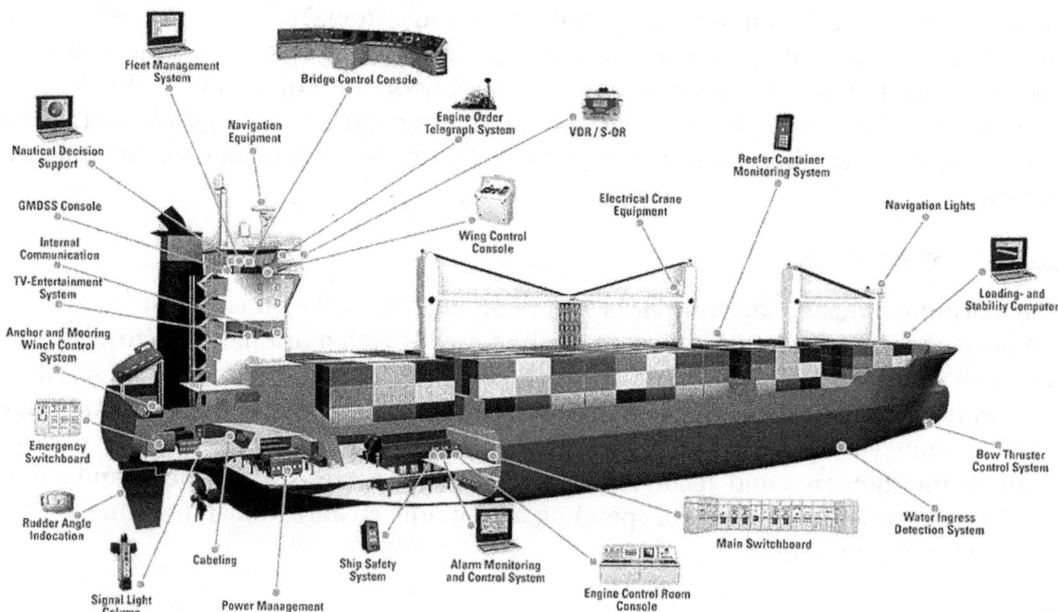

FIGURE 9.5 A view of the complex automation and digital communication systems on most modern commercial ships. Almost all of these systems are highly vulnerable to hostile hackers (http://www.pa-en.com/media/course_img/80eb6f4e2d0194b7ddaa5a37ec56f6bc.gif).

attracts the attention of transnational criminal organizations and State intelligence services. So these organizations and companies, for evolutionary reasons and survival, have had to keep up with the growing cybersecurity and information-security threats. Maritime companies and their assets have not been seen as interesting to criminal actors using cyberattacks, until more recently, when they realized the opportunities to extort them, steal cargo, and leverage maritime shipping for moving their illicit products. For a longer period of time, state actors have paid attention to ports, tankers, oil platforms, and ships, as their focus has been on identifying and exploiting vulnerabilities and the potential consequences of physical and economic disruption to an opposition's maritime sector.

Hacking Is Easy

Hacking used to be the domain of highly skilled and intelligent individuals who would spend considerable time developing skills, knowledge, and expertise to exploit complex systems. Overtime, malicious hackers realized they could make money not only from hacking systems but by developing specialized tools to assist in exploiting systems and selling those tools to others. The result of this, over the last 15 years or so, is the development of point and click tools that allow computer illiterate attackers to generate viruses, Trojans, and various attacks on the target of their choosing. The popularity of these software tools has created multimillion dollar black markets for the tool creators who compete to offer the best attacks and services for an increasingly large audience of cybercriminals. This readily available software and increasing larger pool of adequately skilled hackers, intersecting with marine equipment and systems manufacturers who have been slow to take the security threats seriously, are creating a perfect storm for exploitation by criminal organizations, terrorists, hacktivists, and hostile intelligence actors. So, while maritime organizations continue to automate and load their ships, ports, and various other assets with higher-technology and Internet-connected systems, in truth, they are continuing to add easily attacked vectors that often require very little effort to compromise. Criminal hackers have moved away from being very sophisticated technology savants to technicians who simply operate tools they purchase, which are adequate in attacking the vulnerability of the target's current technology.

Understanding Who are the Bad Guys

State Actors

Numerous sovereign States have military, intelligence, and related organizations that support their State's interests through cyberespionage, cybersabotage, and cyberwarfare.[27] While almost every major country, and some minor states, use electronic means to infiltrate friends and foes alike to collect intelligence, some states like China, Iran, and Russia have been at the forefront of using their cyber capabilities to attack and do damage to maritime systems. State actors typically are driven by political and strategic goals in their actions, in contrast to criminal networks, which are driven by financial rewards.

Criminals Networks

Criminal networks and gangs have turned to the internet *in a big way* to support their illicit activities and were some of the first to realize how they could exploit IT systems and networks for financial gain. As evidenced earlier in the cited incidents, criminals use everything from extortion to data theft, and everything in between, to make money and they are the primary threat to commercial organizations. Today, cybercriminals do not even really need to understand in detail how to program or use the Internet, as there is a subniche of cybercriminals who sell point and click hacking tools on various cyber-black markets. The result of this development has been an explosion of people participating in cybercrime, a rapid increase in the sophistication and quality of cybercrime tools, and criminals looking for easier niches to exploit due to the ferocious competition (See Fig. 9.6).

Private Companies

An increasing trend in information security is the tendency of unethical people in companies, or, more specifically, unethical companies, to use hacking or cyberattacks to gain competitive advantage against their competitors. This may include obvious attempts to collect proprietary information, such as customer lists and intellectual property, and a company contracting a criminal gang to perform DDOS attacks against their competition to damage their reputation, financial base, or delay service or product launches. Indeed,

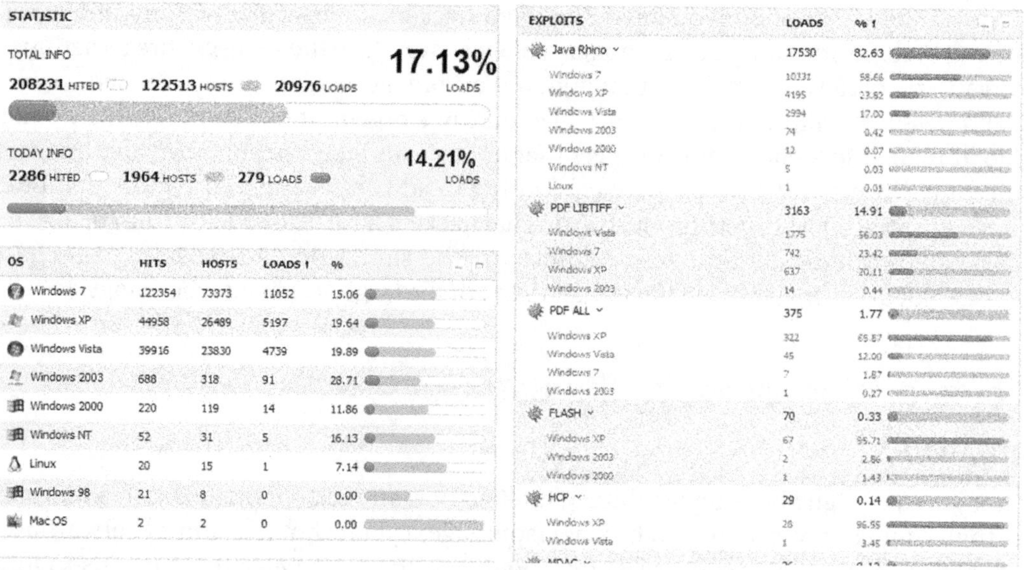

STATISTIC

TOTAL INFO

208231 HITED 122513 HOSTS 20976 LOADS

17.13% LOADS

TODAY INFO

2286 HITED 1964 HOSTS 279 LOADS

14.21% LOADS

OS	HITS	HOSTS	LOADS	%
Windows 7	122354	73373	11052	15.06
Windows XP	44958	26489	5197	19.64
Windows Vista	39916	23830	4739	19.89
Windows 2003	688	318	91	28.71
Windows 2000	220	119	14	11.86
Windows NT	52	31	5	16.13
Linux	20	15	1	7.14
Windows 98	21	8	0	0.00
Mac OS	2	2	0	0.00

EXPLOITS	LOADS	%
Java Rhino	17530	82.63
Windows 7	10331	58.66
Windows XP	4195	23.82
Windows Vista	2994	17.00
Windows 2003	74	0.42
Windows 2000	12	0.07
Windows NT	5	0.03
Linux	1	0.01
PDF LIBTIFF	3163	14.91
Windows Vista	1775	56.03
Windows 7	742	23.42
Windows XP	637	20.11
Windows 2003	14	0.44
PDF ALL	375	1.77
Windows XP	322	65.87
Windows Vista	45	12.00
Windows 7	7	1.87
Windows 2003	1	0.27
FLASH	70	0.33
Windows XP	67	95.71
Windows 2003	2	2.86
Windows 2000	1	1.43
HCP	29	0.14
Windows XP	28	96.55
Windows Vista	1	3.45

FIGURE 9.6 Example screens from a point and click cyberattack tool kit. The user simply picks what operating systems they want to attack, what outcome they want, and the tool provides them with a number of options, including how they want to deliver the attack, for example via email (http://www.group-ib.ru/index.php/7-novosti/1362-group-ib-pomogla-presech-deyatelnost-izvestnogo-khakera-s-psevdonimom-paunch%22).

corporate espionage performed by other corporations or state governments represents most cyberespionage attacks.

Hacktivist

Hacktivists are activists who use the same hacker techniques but to promote political causes and movements. While they do not always break the law, they can be a major threat and headache to the targeted organization's continuity of operation and brand, as seen by one of the more infamous hacktivists groups; *"Anonymous"*. Hacktivists tend to be drawn to targets that will also gain them media attention.

Terrorists

While terrorists have not performed much in the way of cyberattacks, they extensively use the Internet, and occasionally hacking, to communicate, plan, manage, and execute terrorist attacks. Somali pirates and terror groups like al-Qaeda, al-Shabaab, and others have all used the Internet and weaknesses in online maritime tracking tools to help select targets for pirate and terror attacks. Terrorists, unlike most criminal networks, are not motivated just by money but want to push their political and ideological agendas via violence. Heretofore, terrorists haven't concentrated on conducting cyberattacks; however, this could change soon as it becomes easier to target critical infrastructure and their convergence with transnational criminal organizations continues to blossom. Hacking would give terrorist groups an additional weapon in their arsenals and another means of causing massive natural disasters and disruption to entire energy grids and economic and commerce sectors.

Employees and Former Employees

"Insiders" represent the greatest cyberthreat to almost any and all organizations. Indeed, one of the first oil platforms to be compromised by a hacker was hacked by an employee whose contract was not renewed. One of the reasons for these incidents occurring is that few companies have good policies to manage employee access to sensitive systems, to track it, and revoke it when they leave employment.

Lone Actors

This is a broad description for individuals who perform actions solely according to their own agenda and may include disturbed individuals, disgruntled employees, as well as simply curious persons who have no malicious intent but attack systems solely to see what will happen.

Dealing with the Threats

For most of this chapter, we have focused on why you need to worry about cyberthreats, what sort of attacks have happened and what is possible from a technology standpoint, and who conduct attacks and what are their motives. In many ways, it seems like the threat of cyberattacks is impossible to stop without having advanced technology and a horde of information security employees. The reality is that methods to mitigate cyberthreats, including new and emerging ones, are similar to the ways one counters any other security threat—which is through a well thought-out and continuous process that is rigorously defined, executed, and measured. At a very high level, a cybersecurity plan will have major components which include: identifying the organization's priorities, defining the standards, assessing the risks, remediation planning for vulnerabilities, penetration testing, and monitoring (See Fig. 9.7). It is important to appreciate that a good cybersecurity plan is always being updated and changing in response to the organization's changes and new and emerging threats and technology. With this point in mind, in order to have an effective cybersecurity plan, your cybersecurity planning processes must be constantly in evolution and part of the risk management culture of your organization. Now let's discuss general and specific actions you can take to start developing an organization resilient to loss and disruption from the increasingly ever present threat of cyberattack.

Identifying Your Organization's Priorities

This may seem like an obvious idea. Defining what's really important to your organization and what you want to protect. Why not just protect *everything all the time* and equally? The

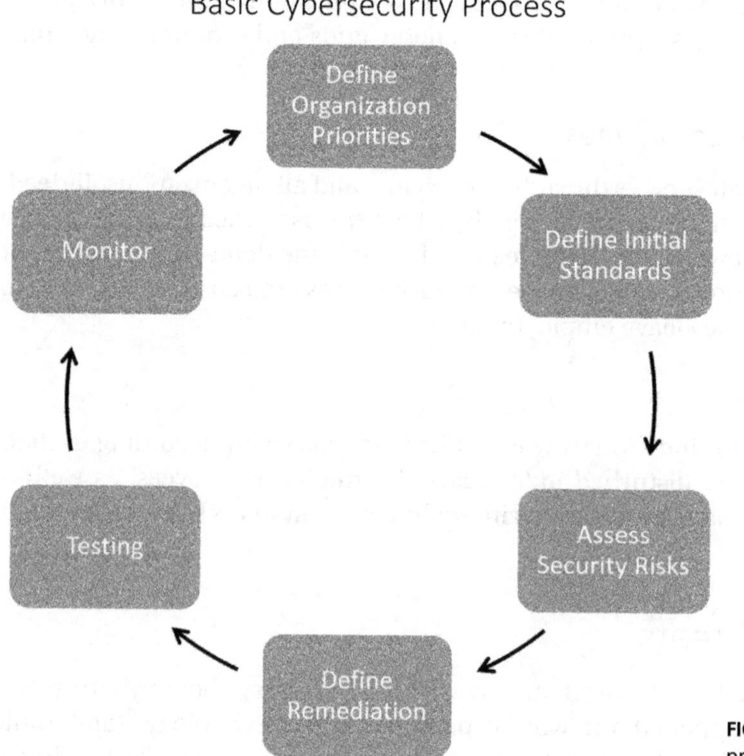

FIGURE 9.7 High-level view of the process.

reality is that security is an *expense* and there are costs represented in money, time, staff, and other resources. Furthermore "total" security can rapidly become a never ending, all-consuming quest that is impossible. Rather, the best way to look at security is that it is in a constant state of "action," shifting and changing as the threat evolves. The first step in implementing security policies, processes, procedures, plans, and systems is to first identify the things, tangible and intangible, that are most important to your organization and its continuity of operation. These may include your customers, your people, the ships, the cargo, the seaport terminals, your business reputation/credibility, or a combination of several of these things. Once you have determined the top priorities, you can start to quantify the value of each one and how much of your organization's budget you want to allocate to securing these valued resources.

Defining Standards

There are a number of excellent *frameworks* for use in developing security standards, for example, the NIST Security Framework.[28] Understand though, that no general security framework will perfectly address the needs of your organization and your specific business. What is suggested is to use a recognized framework, like NIST's framework, as a model straw man and bring together the internal stakeholders and your security team to customize and develop a process and framework that meets your specific needs—without deviating significantly the best practices model framework that was selected originally.

Another important step in defining your initial standards for your security analysis and assessment is to take into consideration the laws and regulation which the company must comply with or have indirect impact on the operations. For example, in the United States, marine facilities may be subject to 33 CFR 101.105, Health Insurance Portability and Accountability Act (HIPAA), Sarbanes–Oxley, and others rules for protecting and securing your data. Ensuring that your cybersecurity plan is built to fully comply with these regulatory standards is a critical task. However, one should evaluate and consider compliance with *voluntary* standards, as well as keep abreast of emerging regulations and best practices. One simple reason for this is that as cybersecurity becomes more of a pressing concern to the maritime sector—or there is a significant incident involving cybersecurity—it is likely that P & I Clubs, the IMO, Registries, and, for the United States, the U.S. Coast Guard—will codify those *voluntary* standards into actual regulations and rules.[29]

Assessing Your Risk

Assessing your *real* risk is very hard. Risk assessment of cyberattacks is one place where both mature and immature organizations fail to even move from initial investigation to determining their exposure. In part, this is because it seems that anything that runs on electricity or has a network connection is at risk. At this point, many organizations simple give up or pick some arbitrary subset of their IT infrastructure, let's say their web servers and only assess the security risks from that facet—while ignoring the rest of their organization. So while they might harden their web servers and forward-facing IT infrastructure, the rest of their organization likely is open and vulnerable to attackers—who most often take a broad look for ways to attack you. And, because of the aforementioned, their attack will be successful. While most organizations have limited resources to devote to security, and protecting everything equally well is more or less impossible, one wants to stay focused on protecting your identified most important assets and remove your largest risks. So to maximize your resource investment in security and make sure you correctly prioritize, it is important to have a solid risk assessment framework.

There are a large number of excellent threat-modeling frameworks available for consideration. Some of these include Microsoft's DREAD framework, the U.S. NSA's MORDA, MITRE's TARA, and Carnegie Mellon's OCTAVE.[30] There are many more frameworks, but regardless of which one you select, occasionally you should use a different one just to gain new perspectives on your threat-modeling. All risk assessment frameworks have similar approaches that focus on defining what you need to protect, what are the possible attack vectors, what are possible threats, how much damage a specific threat could cause, and finally what is the probability of a specific threat occurring.

ID	TTP Name	Source Reference
1	Subverting Environment Variable Values	CAPEC-13
2	Target Programs with Elevated Privileges	CAPEC-69
3	Cryptanalysis	CAPEC-97
4	XQuery Injection	CAPEC-84
5	SQL Injection through SOAP Parameter Tampering	CAPEC-110
6	Using Escaped Slashes in Alternate Encoding	CAPEC-78
7	Subvert Code-signing Facilities	CAPEC-68
8	Cross Site Tracing	CAPEC-107
9	HTTP Request Smuggling	CAPEC-33
10	HTTP Request Splitting	CAPEC-105

FIGURE 9.8 Example of a list of threats generated during a risk assessment.

In MITRE's framework, report writers and stakeholders define a set of tactics, techniques, and procedures (TTPs) that an attacker might use to attack the organization. MITRE has a common attack pattern enumeration and classification (CAPEC) database which it uses to keep track of common TTP's and links to counter measures (CMs) and information on the attacks.[31] Report creators can then link to them in their report by their CAPEC reference (See Fig. 9.8). In many cases, this can and should be followed up with penetration testing. This is where testers actually attack systems using automated tools and techniques, in a controlled manner so as to do no harm, but to expose potential threats and verify risks. While penetration testing is not necessary in all cases to assess security risks, it is critical for generating independent risk assessments for completeness. Third party penetration tests are also often required by many industrial standards and certifications.

Once those working on the risk assessment project have selected the common threats, these threats then are ranked by severity or concern. In the MITRE framework, the risk assessment team develops a tailored risk scoring model (See Fig. 9.9). Most frameworks do something similar but some frameworks already have defined TTP risk-scoring models. The next step is to develop a *Threat Matrix*, based on their specific risk scoring and relative to a specific asset (See Fig. 9.10). When completed, typically, report developers' next define the CMs, before addressing remediation planning.

Remediation Planning

Once you have performed your initial risk assessment, it is important to start considering high-level to low-level remediation plans. These plans may include specific technical tasks such as patching servers, adding firewalls, etc., but may also include human processes and procedures, such as the communication plan when there is an incident, how to report breeches to the public, and the like. Indeed the most critical aspect, and most often ignored, part of remediation planning in cybersecurity is *human responses to events.*

Factors for assessing TTP Risk						Factor Value [1...5]	Factor Weight
Factor Range	1	2	3	4	5		
How localized are the effects posed by this TTP?	no noticeable effects	effects limited to targeted asset	targeted asset and supporting network	noticable effects to external enclave/domain	effects experienced globally	1	0.2
How long would it take to recover from this TTP once the attack was detected?	no recovery needed	< 1 hour	< 24 hours	< 72 hours	> 72 hours	1	0.1
What is the estimated cost to restore or replace affected cyber asset?	no restoration required	< $10K	< $20K	< $50K	> $50K	1	0.1
How serious an impact is loss of data confidentiality resulting from successful application of this TTP?	no adverse effects	limited adverse effects	serious adverse effects	severe adverse impact	catastrophic impact	1	0.2
How serious an impact is loss of data integrity resulting from successful application of this TTP?	no adverse effetcs	limited adverse effects	serious adverse effects	severe adverse impact	catastrophic impact	1	0.2
How serious an impact is loss of system availability resulting from successful application of this TTP?	no adverse effects	limited adverse effects	serious adverse effects	severe adverse impact	catastrophic impact	1	0.2
Is there evidence of this TTP's use in a security incident database?	Incident database not consulted	evidence of TTP use possible	confirmed evidence of TTP use in database	frequent use of TTP reported	widespread use of TTP reported	0	0
What level of skill or specific knowledge is required by the adversary to apply this TTP?	no specific skills required	generic technical skills	some knowledge of targeted system	detail knowledge of targeted system	knowledge of both mission and targeted system	0	0
Would resources be required or consumed in order to apply this TTP?	no resources required	minimal resources required	some resources required	significant resources required	resources required and consumed	0	0
How detectable is this TTP when it is applied?	not detectable	detection possible with specialized monitoring	detection likely with specialized monitoring	detection likely with routine monitoring	TTP obvious without monitoring	0	0
Would residual evidence left behind by this TTP lead to attribution?	no residual evidence	some residual evidence, attribution unlikely	attribution possible from characteristics of the TTP	same or similar TTPs previously attributed	signature attack TTP used by adversary	0	0

FIGURE 9.9 Tailored tactics, techniques, and procedures risk-scoring model. *Courtesy of* https://www.mitre.org/sites/default/files/pdf/11_4982.pdf.

Organizations often completely focus on technical process and technical remediation and blindly ignore key points—such as training, education, and plans to respond to the inevitable; a successful cyberattack. In most cases, your remediation plans will follow along closely to the findings in the risk assessment. In general, one will follow these steps:

1. Select which TTPs to mitigate
2. Identify plausible CMs
3. Assess CM merit—in MITRE's TARA; this results in a CM Matrix (See Fig. 9.11)
4. Identify an optimal CM solution
5. Prepare recommendations

It is recommended that when evaluating the merits of a CM, also identify the estimated costs of employing the CM, so stakeholders can more intelligently make decisions on what CMs to deploy—versus the costs associated with an incident.[32] Finally, while the report writers will make recommendations on the best solution or mitigations to the threats assessed, it is up to the business stakeholders to make the final decision on where to place their resources. This often results in trade-offs between risk, security, and cost. This is normal and to be expected but it is important to continuously, or cyclically, perform security analyses on your infrastructure since not only will threats change but also the effectiveness and cost of CMs. Once the initial mitigation plan is formed, the focus shifts to implementing the remediation plan and testing it.

TTP ID	TTP Name	Source Reference	Risk Score	LAN Switch			VOIP Gateway		
				External	Insider	Trusted Insider	External	Insider	Trusted Insider
25	Malicious Software Download	CAPEC-185	4.3			4.3			4.3
22	Simple Script Injection	CAPEC-63	4.2	4.2	4.2	4.2		4.2	4.2
12	Manipulating Writeable Configuration Files	CAPEC-75	4.1			4.1			4.1
24	Man in the Middle Attack	CAPEC-94	3.8		3.8	3.8		3.8	3.8
15	Filter Failure through Buffer Overflow	CAPEC-24	3.6	3.6	3.6	3.6	3.6	3.6	3.6
13	Overflow Buffers	CAPEC-100	3.6	3.6	3.6	3.6	3.6	3.6	3.6
2	Target Programs with Elevated Privileges	CAPEC-69	3.5	3.5	3.5		3.5	3.5	
1	Subverting Environment Variable Values	CAPEC-13	3.5		3.5	3.5		3.5	3.5
11	Brute Force	CAPEC-112	3.3	3.3	3.3		3.3	3.3	
23	Cross Site Request Forgery (aka Session Riding)	CAPEC-62	3.3		3.3	3.3			
3	Cryptanalysis	CAPEC-97	3.2	3.2			3.2	3.2	3.2
6	Using Escaped Slashes in Alternate Encoding	CAPEC-78	3.2					3.2	3.2
20	Lifting Data Embedded in Client Distributions	CAPEC-37	3.0				3.0	3.0	
9	HTTP Request Smuggling/Splitting	CAPEC-33/105	2.8	2.8	2.8				
17	Accessing/Intercepting/Modifying HTTP Cookies	CAPEC-31	2.8	2.8	2.8				
16	Exploiting Trust in Client (aka Make the Client Invisible)	CAPEC-22	2.7	2.7	2.7		2.7	2.7	
8	Cross Site Tracing	CAPEC-107	2.5	2.5	2.5	2.5			
	Aggregate Scores			32	40	33	23	38	34
					105			**94**	

FIGURE 9.10 *Threat Matrix* based on their specific risk scoring and relativeness to a specific asset

System name: **System XYZ**			Assurance Level: **Medium**					
Countermeasure (CM)			Mitigation Effectiveness (by Attack Vector ID)					
ID	Countermeasure Name	Cost Index	T000105	T000008	T000016	T000049	T000001	T000021
			2.1	1.9	1.8	1.7	1.6	1.4
C000023	Change default SNMP community string values	1		P				
C000062	Disable client side scripting	3	P		P			
C000194	Disable hyperlinks in email	1	M		M			
C000015	Verify BIOS implemented security controls after BIOS image update	2					P	
C000018	Use checksums to verify the integrity of downloaded BIOS image updates	2					P	
C000024	Restrict SNMP community string value reuse	2		P				
C000081	Use strong mutual authentication	3						P
C000083	Use cryptography that is sufficient strong	3						P
C000136	Utilize processor-based protection capabilities	1				M		
C000238	Enforce sofware quality standards and guidelines that improve software quality	2				M		
C000090	Validate input fields use of NULL, escape, backslash, meta, and control characters	3	M		M			
C000002	Verify BIOS image write protection	2					M	
C000101	Verify buffer sizes	2				M		
C000247	Ensure trustworthiness of key personnel	3						M
	Totals	30	3	2	3	3	3	3

FIGURE 9.11 Impact of Countermeasures versus cost and mitigation effectiveness

Penetration Testing

Testing is one of the most important components of any cybersecurity plan since it provides objective evaluation of not only risks but also the effectiveness of your CMs. Unfortunately, most organizations only do penetration testing infrequently and then often do not further test their CMs. If they do testing, it's often only using automated tools instead of humans and subject matter experts. To truly understand the effectiveness of your CMs to mitigate security issues, it is critical you test not only your technical systems under real world conditions and using real thinking testers, but also test your organization's responses to simulated attacks, breaches, and security failures. These sorts of tests should be tightly aligned and integrated into your overall organization disaster recovery or business continuity plans, since certain cyberattacks, as we have discussed, threaten loss of life and overall organization viability. It also is advisable that the cybersecurity testing plan for regular simulated attacks and war games that test your organization's actual response to situations like a data breach, denial of service attack, or critical system failure due to a cyberattack.

Monitoring

Monitoring is the final phase of the cybersecurity process. At a high level, monitoring means more than just technical monitoring of systems, such as networks and computers. It also includes monitoring all areas of security, as well as the organization's compliance with all regulations and laws which address cyber topics. While much of monitoring can be automated, humans still are necessary to review automated system alerts, abnormalities in logs or sensor data, etc., and make reasoned decisions about risk. This often will require further training and practice via tests and war games to assure monitoring processes and reactions to attacks at effective and efficient rates. Monitoring is one of the most important cornerstones in points in building an organization which is resilient to cyberattacks.

Implementation

Once the cybersecurity plan is fully developed and defined, the next step is implementation, which will be guided by your business goals, budget, and mitigation strategy. For organizations without mature IT security departments, it's crucial to bring in experienced advisors who can coach and guide the implementation and management of the plan, as well as train the staff to maintain CMs and continually improve upon your cybersecurity plan.

Continuity Planning

Cybersecurity should always be seen as a component of your general continuity plan and overall security planning. While cyberattacks can cause real damage to systems and create major disruptions in business continuity, few organizations actually integrate their cybersecurity plan into their business continuity plans. Many savvy cyberattackers are aware of this, and there are numerous instances where attackers compromised a business or organization due to the lack of clear business continuity plans. In these cases, unfortunately, the organization lost valuable time while trying to determine what immediate steps to take, who had authority to make cyber-related decisions—such as shutting down IT systems, and when to communicate with law enforcement and notify customers. Indeed a lack of a clear continuity planning can and should be considered a major risk; one that attackers will exploit.

Summary

In this chapter we have covered, at a very high level, the nature of the cyberthreats, an overview of specific maritime cyberthreats and incidents, why the maritime industry is especially susceptible to cyberattack, and the actors who may pose a cyberthreat to the commercial maritime sector. We have also presented a framework by which maritime organizations can reduce their vulnerabilities to cyber targeting and attacks, and create resiliency, through the development of a cybersecurity plan. This chapter covers just the very tip of the iceberg of cybersecurity. To gain a greater depth of understanding on cybersecurity, one should review the reading and resources in the provided list. Hopefully, this chapter will have conveyed the important point that one does not need an expert to get started planning for mitigating the inevitable cybersecurity event. Indeed, almost all of the steps discussed in this chapter can be performed, at a high level, by a nontechnical layperson.

Suggested Background Reading and Resources

Introduction to Computer Security—Excellent Video Series from MIT that introduces computer security and concepts to laymen https://www.youtube.com/watch?v=zBFB34YGK1U

NIST Cyber Security Framework—http://www.nist.gov/cyberframework/upload/cybersecurity-framework-021214-final.pdf

ISO/IEC 27001:2013: Information technology—Security techniques—Information security management systems—Requirements http://www.iso.org/iso/home/store/catalogue_tc/catalogue_detail.htm?csnumber=54534
ISO/IEC 27002:2013: Information technology—Security techniques—Code of practice for information security controls—http://www.iso.org/iso/home/store/catalogue_tc/catalogue_detail.htm?csnumber=54533
Site Security Handbook RFC 2196: High-level overview of how to develop policies and procedures for cybersecurity—https://tools.ietf.org/html/rfc2196
ICS CERT https://ics-cert.us-cert.gov/Training-Available-Through-ICS-CERT
U.S. COAST Guard https://www.uscg.mil/seniorleadership/DOCS/cyber.pdf

End Notes

1. http://www.juniperresearch.com/document-library/white-papers/cybercrime-the-internet-of-threats.
2. https://business.un.org/en/entities/13.
3. http://www.reuters.com/assets/print?aid=USBREA3M20820140423; http://www.net-security.org/secworld.php?id=15781; http://www.csmonitor.com/World/Security-Watch/Cyber-Conflict-Monitor.
4. http://breakingdefense.com/2013/06/top-official-admits-f-35-stealth-fighter-secrets-stolen.
5. https://en.wikipedia.org/wiki/Denial-of-service_attack.
6. https://ics.sans.org/media/ICS-CPPE-case-Study-2-German-Steelworks_Facility.pdf.
7. http://www.telegraph.co.uk/news/worldnews/europe/belgium/10383504/.
8. http://tmgonlinemedia.nl/consent/consent/?return=http%3A%2F%2Fwww.telegraaf.nl%2Fdigitaal%2F21656421%2F__Hackers_helpen_drugsbende__.html&;clienttime=1438559293469&version=0&detect=true ; https://nakedsecurity.sophos.com/2013/10/17/organised-drug-gangs-increasingly-hooking-up-with-hackers-warns-europol; http://motherboard.vice.com/blog/how-traffickers-hack-shipping-containers-to-move-drugs; http://www.telegraph.co.uk/news/worldnews/europe/belgium/10383504/.
9. http://news.utexas.edu/2013/07/30/spoofing-a-superyacht-at-sea.
10. http://www.reuters.com/assets/print?aid=USBREA3M20820140423.
11. http://www.technologyreview.com/news/517686/spoofers-use-fake-gps-signals-to-knock-a-yacht-off-course.
12. http://www.technologyreview.com/news/520421/ship-tracking-hack-makes-tankers-vanish-from-view; http://www.net-security.org/secworld.php?id=15781.
13. http://www.reuters.com/assets/print?aid=USBREA3M20820140423.
14. http://www.bloomberg.com/news/articles/2015-06-10/hackers-favorite-target-big-oil.
15. Ibid.
16. http://www.reuters.com/assets/print?aid=USBREA3M20820140423.
17. Ibid.
18. Ibid.
19. http://www.bloomberg.com/news/articles/2015-06-10/hackers-favorite-target-big-oil.
20. http://www.tankeroperator.com/allnews.aspx.
21. Ibid.

22. "Ghost-Hunting With Anti-Virus" http://www.fireeye.com/blog/corporate/2014/05/ghost-hunting-with-anti-virus.html.
23. https://blog.kaspersky.com/maritime-cyber-security/.
24. http://www.technologyreview.com/news/520421/ship-tracking-hack-makes-tankers-vanish-from-view.
25. http://www.nist.gov/cyberframework/upload/cybersecurity-framework-021214-final.pdf.
26. http://www.networkworld.com/article/2917856/microsoft-subnet/maritime-cybersecurity-firm-37-of-microsoft-servers-not-patched-vulnerable-to-hacking.html.
27. Contributor and Cybersecurity Expert Robi Sen see's Cyberwarfare slightly different than many security experts. He believes that Cyberwarfare must have a component of physical. destruction or harm and that what most people call Cyberwarfare, electronic intrusion, sabotage, data theft, and are better classified as Cyberintelligence and Cyberespionage when performed by State Actors.
28. http://www.nist.gov/cyberframework/upload/cybersecurity-framework-021214.pdf.
29. A good reference that discusses emerging cyber risks and its relationship to maritime security is the US Coast Guard's "Maritime Cyber Security Public Meeting", https://www.youtube.com/embed/rzOVc1ZOuvY?rel=0.
30. https://msdn.microsoft.com/en-us/library/ff648644.aspx, NSA MORDA https://www.academia.edu/2817116/Mission_oriented_risk_and_design_analysis_of_critical_information_systems, MITRE TARA http://www.dtic.mil/dtic/tr/fulltext/u2/a576473.pdf CMU OCTAVE http://resources.sei.cmu.edu/library/asset-view.cfm?assetID=8419.
31. https://capec.mitre.org.
32. By cost we do not simply mean financial cost to implement a patch. Cost might be measured in man hours, down time, loss of operation efficiency, and the like.

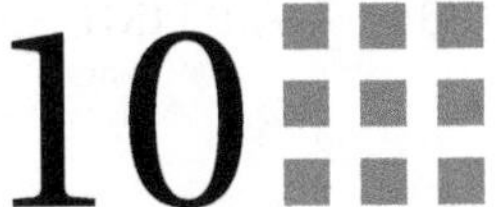

A Strategic Blueprint for World-Class Seaport Security

OBJECTIVES

After studying this chapter, you will be familiar with the following:

1. the Defense-in-Depth concept in port security;
2. the External Security Ring components and their functions;
3. the Perimeter Security Ring components and their functions;
4. the Inner Security Ring components and their functions;
5. the Site and Asset-Specific Security Ring components and their functions;
6. the Vessel Security Ring components and their functions;
7. procedures of security personnel employment and training;
8. the role of the Security Director.

With few exceptions, the seaports of the world increasingly are under threat of penetration, manipulation, and usage by drug smugglers, stowaways, cargo thieves, pirates, and terrorists. Targets of these criminal elements include terminals, vessels, cargo, containers, equipment, and personnel. In addition to concerns during 2014 and 2015 related to the rising number of incidents of violent piracy off the west coast of Africa and the tsunami of irregular migrants and refugees crossing the Mediterranean into Southern Europe, ports in these post-September 11, 2001 times must also face the looming specter of terrorist attacks involving weapons of mass destruction (WMDs) or of a vessel being used by terrorists as a conveyance or an instrument of destruction. To effectively deter or deny these threats, ports must develop a security strategy that identifies the potential security threats, defines critical assets and information, integrates security resources and capabilities, and ensures the successful design, implementation, and management of a world-class seaport security program.

The most comprehensive and effective seaport security program is one based on the military concept called *Defense-in-Depth.* Applied to a seaport, this concept involves the design and establishment of a series of layered security "rings" around and in the port, as well as encircling critical assets within the port (such as cranes, vessels, etc.). The number of security rings established and the specific components (security systems and measures) of each ring will vary and depend on the port's layout and operations, its assets, and the level, type, and duration of the threats. While the rings themselves are permanent or long-standing, the individual components within the rings may be long-term or temporary, as in the case of measures implemented to address a crisis situation or a short-term threat. These security rings should be layered and integrated, but capable of functioning independently. Security ring components include physical security measures, security procedures, specialized assets, and personnel resources. It is important to appreciate that no one component can efficiently or effectively accomplish the overall task without the support of the others. As an example, while a security officer may be deployed at an entrance gate to control access, if there is no written or defined access control procedure or an identification badge system in use, he cannot effectively perform this function. While many of the component systems and measures deployed in a security ring configuration may be permanent, others may be very short-term, such as those enacted during an increase in the port security level (Maritime Security or MARSEC), in response to a terror alert or other emergency situation, or the visit of a prominent dignitary. The temporary implementation or activation of special security components or procedures due to heightened threats should be preplanned, and part of an overall security level status system and detailed in the *port facility security plan* (PFSP). While the security program should be based on the results of the analysis of the *port facility security assessment* and incorporate measures and procedures defined in the ISPS Code and MTSA, every port should have a baseline security design, ie, a blueprint. This chapter discusses one such strategic blueprint. The policies, procedures, and systems defined in this chapter may be considered *Best Practices*, as the locations where they have been implemented resulted in statistically significant improvement in security outcomes and decreases in security breaches and incidents.

A brief outline of a blueprint of a world-class seaport security program—one which is designed for a multithreat environment and utilizes layered security rings—includes the concepts described below.

External Security Ring

Intelligence Operations

The continual tasking, collection, analysis, dissemination, and evaluation of strategic and tactical intelligence and information from confidential informants (persons associated with or inside criminal and terrorist organizations) and sources of information in the communities and regions surrounding and inside the port (such as truck drivers, warehouse laborers, documentation clerks, cargo surveyors, open press, news reporters, etc.) to provide advance indications and warnings of evolving and future criminal activities or threats targeting the port are key tenets of the port security strategy. In many cases, the success of the port security program depends on the ability to receive advanced knowledge of planned criminal/terrorist activities and to direct or manipulate events so that these situations are neutralized or contained outside the port or at one of the security rings.

Government and Law Enforcement Liaison

The establishment of active and ongoing relations with and support from national government agencies, such as the police, customs, military, and intelligence services, is a necessity. Also desirable are working-level contacts with international and nonhost country law enforcement and intelligence agencies, such as Interpol and foreign customs services. These entities can provide vital information concerning activities by transnational criminal and terrorist organizations that may target the seaport or a vessel or its cargo.

Perimeter Security Ring

Physical Security Barrier and Illumination

The entire land boundary of the port is identified and protected by a wall or fence no less than 8 feet in height and topped with three strands of barbed wire or baled concertina wire. The wire topping should be secured to arms that are angled outward at 45 degrees. If the perimeter barrier is fencing, then it should be constructed either of "climb-resistant" stretched steel or 9-gauge chain-link wire mesh, with 2-inch openings, and secured at the bottom with metal tubing or a concrete footing, to deter under-the-fence ingress (see Fig. 10.1).

In most ports, the berths project outward over the water, creating an open area under the berth where swimmers, small boats, and scuba divers could access and contraband could be staged. If above and below water obstructions (bars, heavy wire mesh, etc.) are not installed, then CCTV and or laser or microwave motion detection systems should be installed to detect and view potential threats.

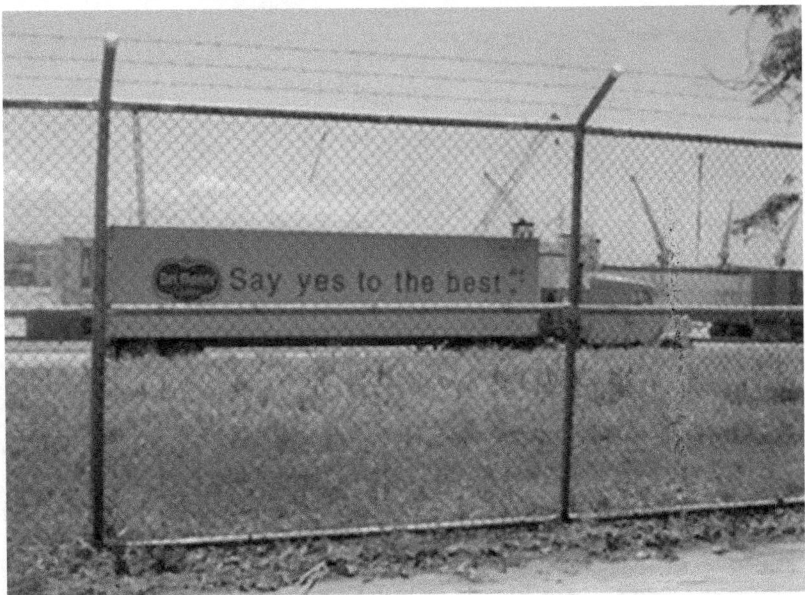

FIGURE 10.1 Perimeter barrier.

The level of illumination along the perimeter barrier should be no less than 2-feet candles at ground level (similar to the level in a well-lit parking lot), projecting 10 feet inside the barrier and 20 feet outside the barrier. This same lighting standard should be met or exceeded in cargo- and container-staging areas, along the berths, and on the exterior of buildings and warehouses. Good lighting arguably is the most effective and least expensive measure of deterrence against cargo pilferage, container theft, drug smuggling, and other similar violations.

Waterside Security Measures

A security launch with armed security officer(s) should patrol along the berth and in nearby waters to deter or prevent approach and access on the waterside of the port by stowaways, smugglers, pirates, terrorists, etc. (see Fig. 10.2). Increasingly, narcotics trafficking organizations are using scuba divers to attach drug-laden torpedoes and boxes to the hulls and bow thrusters of vessels. If this threat is suspected, the port security program should include the use of either underwater security patrols (scuba), an antidiver system, or the installation of underwater CCTV (in ports with somewhat clear water). Likewise, drug smuggling and professional stowaway organizations utilize small boats or launches to transport their stowaways, drug couriers, and contraband to the waterside of the vessels for lading. Moreover, as demonstrated by the attack on the USS Cole in Yemen, terrorists utilize small launches and port services vessels to attack large vessels while in port. The 24-hour security launch patrol increases the probability that threats from the waterside are detected, deterred, or prevented.

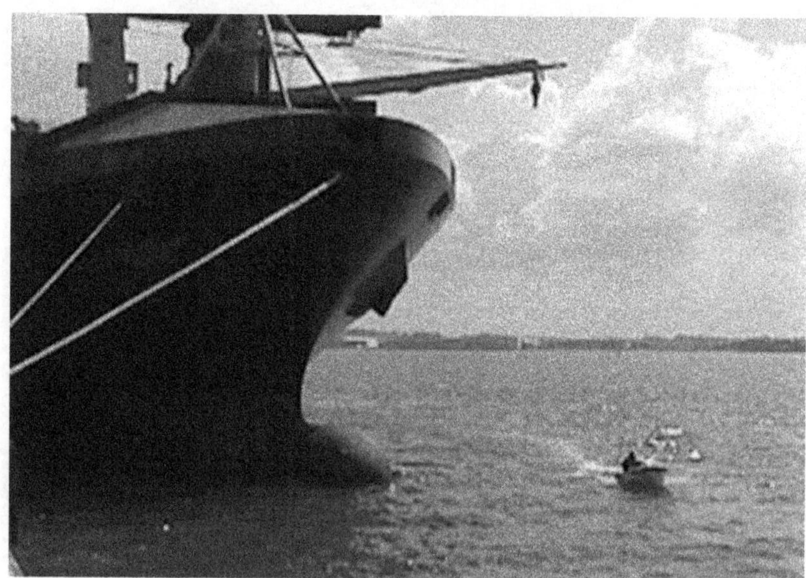

FIGURE 10.2 Waterside security patrol launch.

Perimeter Intrusion Detection

Generally, it is a common practice to deploy security officers at stationary and roving posts along the perimeter. These posts may include security officers positioned in elevated towers along the perimeter (see Fig. 10.3), walking along the perimeter barrier, and patrolling via mobile means. In some port facilities, for increased efficiency and multicapable response, a K-9 patrol team may be utilized to patrol the perimeter. Research by the U.S. law enforcement has determined that the deployment of K-9 patrol teams is a force-multiplier; and one K-9 team is as effective as deploying three individual police officers. Perimeter intrusion detection can also be accomplished by, or significantly enhanced through, the use of technological security systems; among them CCTV cameras, buried or taunt cable, microwave curtains, dual-technology passive infrared (PIR) motion detectors, and laser beams—all of which may be integrated into a manned central monitoring station. With respect to CCTV, the cameras should be color, HD, and automatically switch to low-visibility settings during night hours. Furthermore, there should be a mix of high-profile cameras and hidden cameras, with some cameras (especially those at access control points) having microphone for recording conversations (record bribes being offered, criminal activities discussed, etc.).

FIGURE 10.3 Security tower.

Entrance and Exit Gates

The number of port entrances and exits should be limited to a minimum and their purposes specifically defined. There should be separate gates for pedestrians and vehicles. Likewise, there should be separate gates for the entrance and exit of trucks transporting containers or cargo and those vehicles driven by employees, vendors, clients, and visitors. Physically, the gates should be constructed so as to meet the same minimum standards as the chain-link perimeter barrier. These gates should lock with heavy-duty padlocks, and the keys should be controlled by security personnel. A security gatehouse should be located at each primary access point. The gate house should have the basic items required to accomplish the tasks, such as a fire extinguisher, first aid kit, flashlight, rain gear, vehicle and visitor gate logs, 24-hour chronological security logbook, personnel authorization roster, telephone, emergency telephone notification list, security post orders, and a copy of the relevant contingency plan.

Access Control Policy and Procedures

All access points (gates) should be strictly controlled, and there should be a comprehensive policy and specific written procedures which define the authorized access of persons (employees, visitors, contractors, truck drivers, ship chandlers, etc.), vehicles (employee and visitor cars, trucks, etc.), and items (cargo, containers, trailers, ship's goods, spare parts, etc.) into and out of the port. "Restricted Area," "Authorized Personnel Only," "Identification Checkpoint," the current "MARSEC/Security Level," and "Entry Constitutes Consent to Search of Person & Vehicle for Contraband and Weapons" signs should be posted and highly visible at all access points. Generally, the following recommended procedures and processes should be in effect.

- *Privately Owned Vehicles (POV) Access Gates into non-Restricted Area port property*—many ports have offices and parking for shipping lines, truckers, shipping agents/customs brokers, government agencies, vendors, and their own Admin, which are located within the terminal operators area of control or property but not within the official Restricted Area. Additionally, a wide array of persons—employees, contractors, couriers, visitors, etc.—will need access to these offices and buildings. For the port, it is advisable to exercise a basic level of screening—especially during the evening hours—as these areas border the actual Restricted Area of the Terminal. As such, during nondaytime business hours and on weekends, security officers stop and question persons entering to check IDs and assess whether the persons exhibit suspicious behavior and visually briefly check the interior of the car and trunk (see Fig. 10.4).
- *Pedestrian Gates into Restricted Areas*—Security officers posted at pedestrian gates with access into Restricted Areas should stop and challenge all persons, inspect their identification badges, and search any boxes, briefcases, or other items for contraband. Use of a metal detector or pat-down procedure to check for weapons is strongly recommended (see Fig. 10.5). Employees should present their ID badges to the security

FIGURE 10.4 Vehicle inspection at port POV entrance/exit gate.

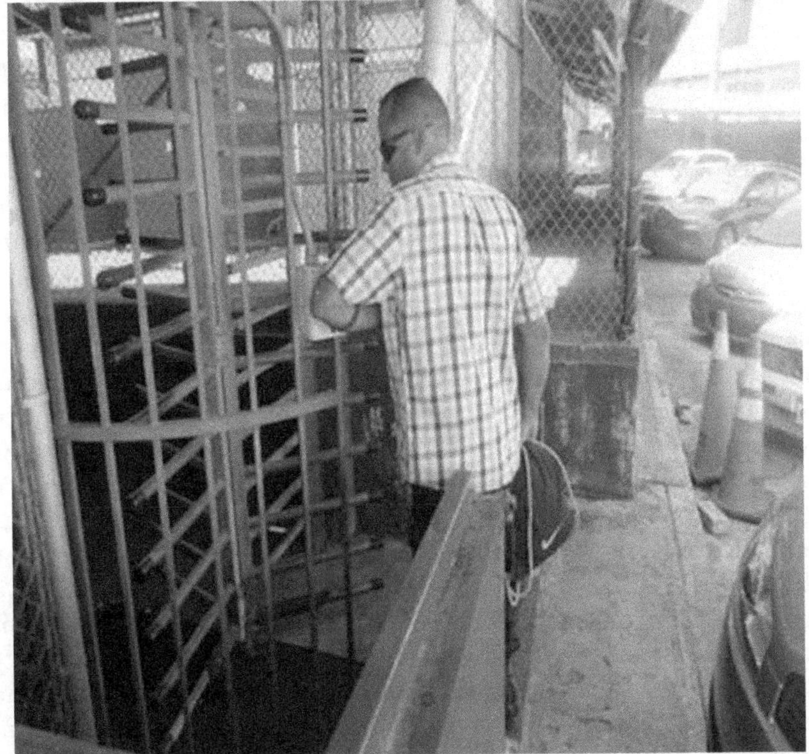

FIGURE 10.5 Employee pedestrian entrance gate.

officer for visual checks and then at the turnstile card reader for access (if badge is valid and the employee is authorized to be in the zone, the turnstile light shows "green" and releases the lock for a single revolution). Adjacent to the turnstile, for viewing by the security officer, should be a screen which presents the photo, name, and department of the employee who is about to enter the turnstile. This presence of the screen permits the security officer to validate that the photo registered in the computer-controlled ID badge system, and displayed on the screen is the same person who presented the ID badge. It is recommended that the turnstile reader also have some type of biometric access control reader (fingerprint, vascular, retina scan, etc.) that provides a second-level validation through interface with the access control database. All visitors (clients, vendors, contractors, etc.) initially should be processed and visitor badge issued at the Terminal's *Visitor Office.* The Visitor Office should be located prior to the access points into the Terminal Restricted Area. Visitors should be "precleared" via an email or memo received in advance from the sponsoring employee or authorized entity, personal and visit data recorded, and identification checked and recorded into the visitor control system. Likewise, the visitor's should be recorded and a one-day use, self-destructive visitor badge issued. At the access gate, the Security Officer will stop and screen the visitor, check the badge, inspect hand-carried items for contraband, and permit the "Escort" to accompany the visitor into the Terminal.

- *Vehicle Gates*—only duly authorized port vehicles—and not POVs—should be permitted in the Terminal. Only the driver should be in the vehicle when passing through this point. Any passengers should exit the vehicle and be processed through the personnel turnstile located adjacent to the vehicle gate. These vehicles should display a port-issued decal which identifies the vehicle as being authorized. The exception to this rule being authorized ship chandlers and delivery vehicles. Ship chandlers and delivery persons are processed as "Visitors" and vehicles and cargo searched by K-9 *prior* to entrance into the Terminal. The driver should show his ID badge to the security officer and the officer should conduct a visual inspection of the interior for contraband. These same processes and procedures are applied when vehicles exit the Terminal.
- *Container/Cargo/Truck Gates*—All trucks, transporting cargo, or containers (empty or loaded) first are processed as the "Pre-Gate," which is located before the access gate into the Terminal. At the "Pre-Gate," all cargo shipping and transaction documentation are presented and processed, Customs fees and clearances completed, pre-Equipment Interchange Report initialed, and other information entered in the Terminal Yard Management. The "Pre-Gate" permits the process and procedures at the actual Gate to be smooth and quicker and detects/resolves any documentation conflicts in advance. When the truck pulls up to the Gate, the driver stops at the Driver's License Verification point and the security officer views the windshield to ensure there is a current port access decal (which validates that the tractor is registered in the port access control system and is properly insured). As this point, the driver step out of the cab and onto an elevated stoop and holds his license up to a reader for validation as being legitimate and that he is recorded in the Terminal access control database as being an authorized and

cleared driver (see Figs. 10.6 and 10.7). If ok, the "red" traffic light turns "green" and the driver's picture and data are visual on the Security Checkpoint screen for viewing by the security officer, as it the "green" (for ok) traffic light. While this process is underway, the checker initiates his inspection of the exterior of the container and a "Seal Inspector" physically checks on the seal and records the number. Container and seal information are validated against the preprepared Equipment Inspection Report (EIR) and information entered into the Yard Management System (which assigns the container staging location in the Yard). Another activity performed at this point is the security officer who conducts an inspection of the interior of the cab for contraband and additional persons (only the driver should be in the cab) (see Figs. 10.8 and 10.9). This entire process should be captured and recorded, in close detail, by CCTV.

Port Identification Badge System

Each person authorized to work within the port should be issued an identification badge. In the U.S. ports, personnel are issued the *transportation worker identification credential* (TWIC). At non-U.S. ports, if possible, the ID badge should mirror the technical specifications of the TWIC and incorporate the use of digital fingerprints or other biometric measures (eg, retina scan). The ID badge program should be managed by a computer-based system which functions with biometric confirmation or proximity/magnetic strip badges, assigns zones of access, permits or denies a person's access into a specific zone, and records this activity into a database. The front of the employee ID badge should have a color photo, the employee's name, a government identity document or passport number,

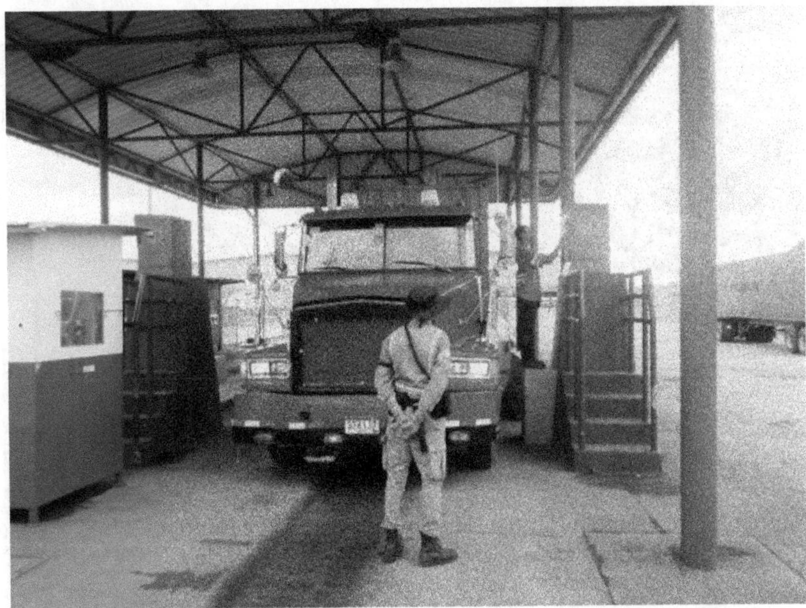

FIGURE 10.6 Driver's license, vehicle insurance, and port authorization validated at the cargo entrance gate.

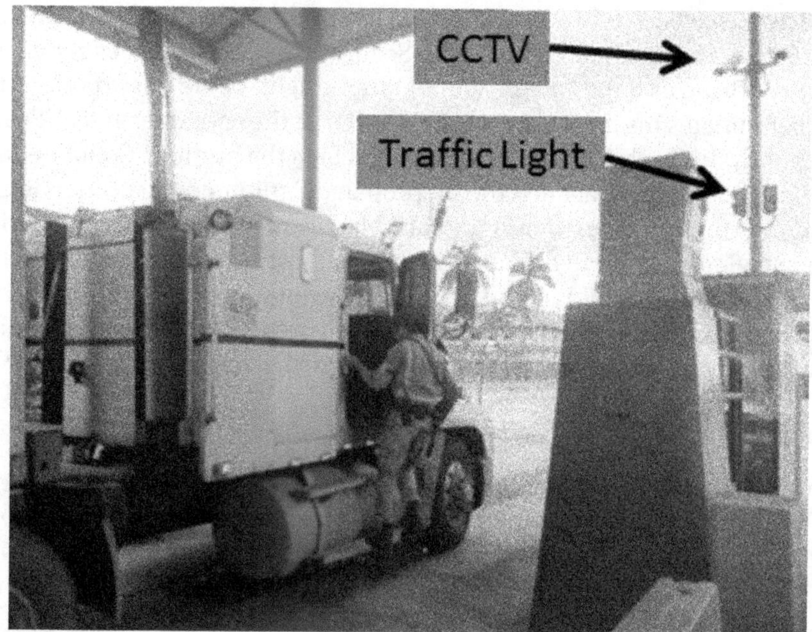

FIGURE 10.7 Once the driver and vehicle are validated as "authorized," the traffic light changes from red to green. The entire process is captured and monitored live by security via CCTV.

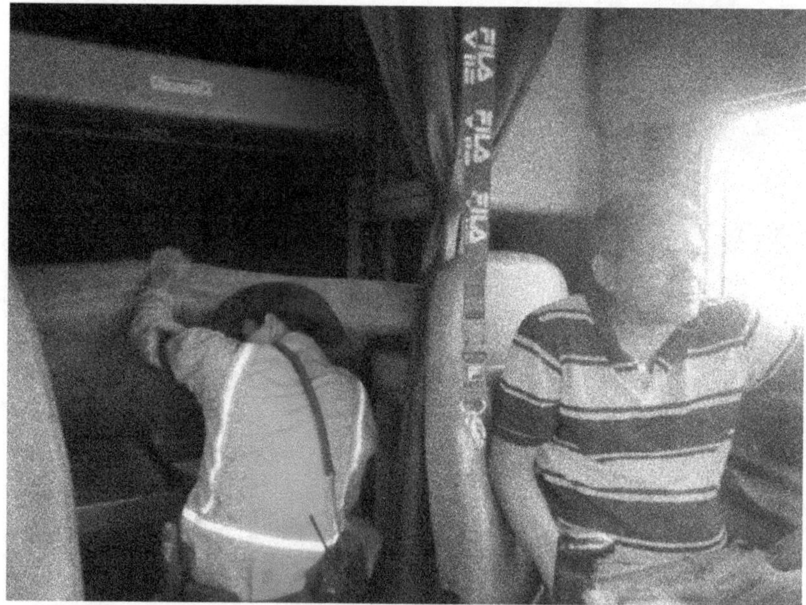

FIGURE 10.8 The sleeping area of the cab is a clever area for hiding illegal drugs.

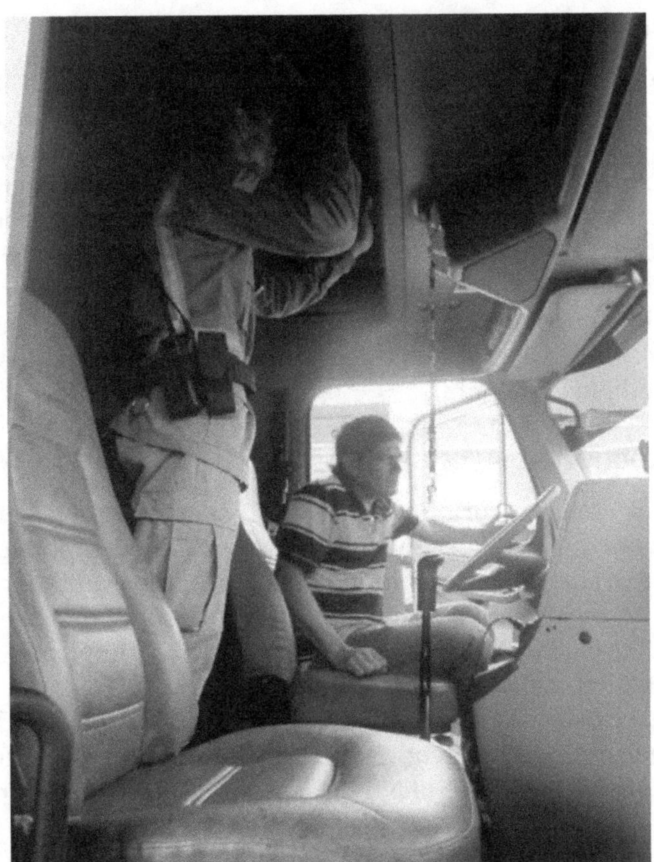

FIGURE 10.9 It is not uncommon for driver to carry weapons.

the employee's position, and an expiration date. If the ID badge system is not computer-based and interfacing with the Access Control System, the back of the ID badge should note the employee's date of birth, height, weight, color of hair and eyes, complexion, and the signature of the port director. Each employee's badge should be programmed to allow access to specific zones, this being based on his or her job or position requirements. Employees who have forgotten or lost their badges should be issued a temporary badge for the day or while a new badge is being prepared. Visitor badges generally are for one-day use; disposable; and should note the name of the visitor, a government identity document or passport number, area or zones visiting, and the date issued. Nonemployees who temporarily or frequently work in the port—such as contractors, clients, and government representatives—should be issued a badge similar to the employee ID badge (but a different color). A permanent record of the issue of all nonemployee badges (with the captured data) should be maintained for at least 2 years after expiration. It is important that the badge is retrieved and deactivated when a port worker is no longer authorized access (fired, resigned, etc.).

Narcotics Control at Access Points

Attempts to smuggle drugs through the access points and into the port may be conducted via hand-carried items, inside vehicles, and in containers or trailers and their cargo. While hand-carried items, such as briefcases, boxes, etc., can be effectively inspected by a hand search by the security officer, it is not as practical (timewise) or effective to do so in the case of a loaded cargo container, empty trailer, or vehicle. For these reasons, highly trained and certified narcotics detection K-9 teams should be positioned at the access points and utilized to inspect the containers, cargo, and vehicles for narcotics (see Fig. 10.10). Alternatively, if financially possible, *nonintrusive inspection* (NII) devices (such as X-ray, VACIS, etc.) should be positioned at the vehicle and container entrance points to screen for narcotics (as well as other contraband).

Explosives Detection at Access Points

During times of heightened security level (MARSEC) due to risks of terrorist attacks, bombing, or violent labor conflicts, extra security measures should be implemented to screen for explosive devices and weapons entering the port. In the event that there is a specific threat or reliable information of a planned attack, the security procedures should be further enhanced. Conversely, these measures should also be implemented on a random, sporadic basis as a form of deterrence—absence of a threat.

The four primary means of searching and screening for explosive devices and weapons are (1) a visual and hand search; (2) the use of a vapor analyzer to detect chemical odors from explosives; (3) the use of NII devices, which vary in size from those used to

FIGURE 10.10 Narcotics and explosive detection K-9 teams are effective for searching cargo containers.

screen letters or parcels to those that inspect vehicles and shipping containers; and (4) an explosives detection K-9 team. These four measures may be used independently or in combination, this generally being determined by the level and type of threat and the items to be searched. Special attention should be given to suspicious mail and delivery packages and unattended vehicles positioned at access points or near key assets or buildings.

Weapons of Mass Destruction Detection at Access Points

Ports must develop, test, and continually update contingency plans for the rapid deployment of systems and measures for the detection of chemical, biological, radiological, and nuclear weapons (typically referred to as *weapons of mass destruction,* or WMDs). In many cases, the port will rely on the national government to provide such technical capabilities and equipment; however, it is critically important that the port security director develop the policies, plans, and procedures which will ensure a successful integration of these measures without significantly impacting the port's business or endangering the safety of its personnel. These contingency plans and procedures should be fully coordinated with the relevant government agencies and tested on a periodic basis. The contingency plans must be clearly documented in the port facility security plan and, if developed, the port's disaster preparedness and recovery plan, which ensures business continuity, and the safety and security of the personnel in the event of an incident.

Inner Security Ring

Mobile Security Patrols

The interior areas of the port, such as the container stacking zones, cargo staging areas, facility and maintenance buildings, equipment storage areas, and berths should be patrolled continuously by security officers in vehicles. These units should patrol in separate, overlapping zones. These security personnel should monitor general yard activities, restrict the movement of truck drivers away from their vehicles, observe the transloading of cargo containers, and view stevedores and laborers working on the docks.

Foot Security Patrols

The conducting of periodic inspections and keeping of tallies of containers and seals throughout the yard by the security officers are effective deterrents to cargo pilferage, drug smuggling, and container manipulation, as well as a means of establishing a specific time period of an incident. The foot security officers should be constantly vigilant that the personnel are wearing valid ID badges and are in their authorized zones, doors and windows of any structures and buildings are secured during nonoperational hours, and drivers are not operating equipment at high rates of speed or in a dangerous manner.

Security Operations Command Center

Security systems and monitoring specialists should be deployed 24 hours per day in the *security operations command center* (SOCC) for the purpose of observing and operating the central monitoring system, which manages and controls all perimeter intrusion detection measures; CCTV deployed in the patio, on the berths, and outside or inside buildings; building intrusion and panic alarms; access control systems; fire alarm systems; etc. CCTV cameras should cover all areas of the port and be of sufficient quality to clearly viewing and recording the employee number printed on the backs of workers' shirts. All security systems should be fully integrated and should support each other in the event of an incident.

Shift Security Superintendent

One person should be designated as the overall Shift Security Superintendent, and he/she should direct, lead, and manage the terminal security supervisor; vessel security team (VST) supervisor, SOCC specialists, and the K-9 operations supervisor; and oversee their respective subordinates. The Shift Security Superintendent should be out "kicking the tires," ie, inspecting the individual terminal security officers, vessel security team (VST) officers, K-9 Handlers; interacting with other port managers and clients; responding to and taking charge of serious security situations and incidents; and generally knowing at all times what is happening in the port. The aforementioned supervisors (terminal, vessel, K-9, and SOCC) report to the Superintendent, and while on duty he/she reports to and is the "eyes and ears" for the port Security Director. Generally, because of the 24-hour responsibilities of the port facility security officer, other Security Supervisors will function as the Port Facility Security Officer (PFSO) while on duty.

Site and Asset-Specific Security Rings

Administrative and Operations Office Buildings

Dedicated resources should be deployed and procedures established so as to ensure the security of the buildings and its contents and the safety of its occupants. The number of entrances and exits should be restricted to a minimum, with doors being secured with deadbolt locks when not in use. A security officer should be posted at each unlocked exterior-access door (see Fig. 10.11). Keys should be kept to a minimum and issued on a restricted basis by a designated key custodian. A computer-based key management system should be utilized. First floor–level windows (and those below) should be protected by bars or wire mesh. Lighting on the exterior of the building should be at the same level as that along the perimeter. At the main entrance, a security officer should screen all persons; check IDs and visitor badges; and search all handbags, briefcases, boxes, etc., for weapons and contraband. A segregated reception area should be located inside the entrance. All visitors should be escorted into the interior offices by the sponsoring port representative. The interior of the building should be divided into functional zones in order to establish access zones for employees and other authorized personnel. Access into each zone should be

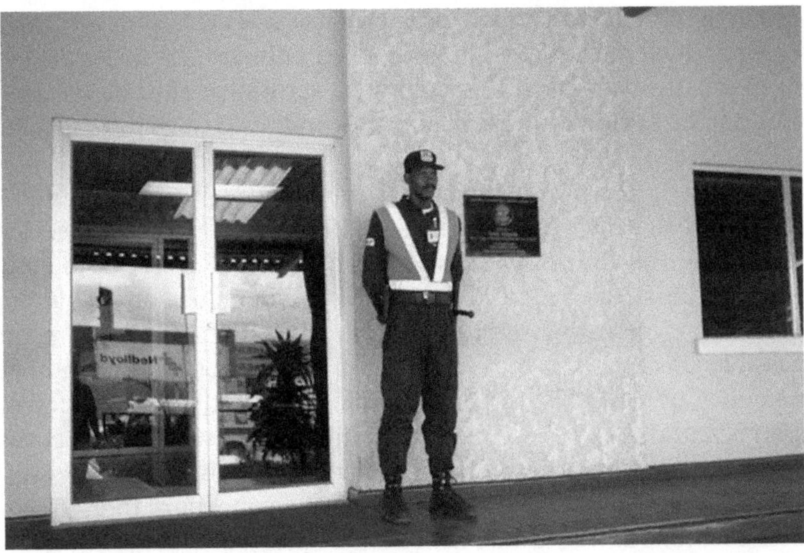

FIGURE 10.11 Security officer posted at entrance of port administration building.

regulated via the ID badge system. The main entrance, secondary access points, and the reception should be under constant surveillance by CCTV cameras, which are monitored and recorded by specialists in the SOCC. Other sensitive areas, such as cashier windows, computer and telephone rooms, etc., should be under observation and security monitoring by intrusion alarms and CCTV cameras.

Bonded and High-Risk Warehouses

Security measures and procedures similar to those noted above for "Administrative and Operations Office Buildings" should be implemented to ensure the security and integrity of the cargo, building, and personnel.

Critical Assets and Essential Equipment

For cranes, electric plants, telephone buildings, etc., security measures and procedures similar to those noted above for "Administrative and Operations Office Buildings" should be implemented, as appropriate, ensuring the effective security and integrity of the assets and equipment.

Vessel Security Ring

Basic Concept

Like other critical assets within the port, vessels must have their own security ring, which is a part of—but necessarily independent from the terminal security apparatus. The keys to effective vessel security and deterring or preventing incidents of stowaways, piracy, drug smuggling, pilferage, and terrorism are to (1) exercise strict access control at the gangway, including a search of all persons and items carried onboard; (2) know who is onboard at all times; (3) maintain the waterside secured; (4) scrutinize all trailers, containers, hustlers, etc., entering or exiting the vessel; and (5) conduct Post-Arrival and Pre-Departure inspections.

All vessels calling on the port should be assigned a VST. The VST should be deployed from the time of arrival until time of departure. Upon each arriving vessel's clearance by government officials, the VST should immediately board the vessel and conduct a quick Post-Arrival inspection of the deck and exterior of the superstructure. This inspection is to detect the presence of stowaways, terrorists, or narcotics; unlocked doors into the superstructure; possible HAZMAT emergencies; etc. All discoveries of undocumented persons, suspected narcotics, or HAZMAT situations should be immediately reported to the captain and VST supervisor and the situation secured until their arrival. Other security discrepancies, such as unlocked doors, should be noted in the gangway logbook and reported to the chief officer for corrective actions. Following this inspection, the VST officers should deploy to their positions and continue with their duties.

Vessel Security Team Deployment for Load On/Load Off (LO/LO) Commercial Cargo/Container Vessels and Tankers

The VST should consist of no fewer than three security officers and one VST team leader:

1. One security officer posted at the gangway to control and document the entrance and exit of persons (stevedores, crew, visitors, vessel agents, government officials, etc.) and search all parcels, bags, water coolers, etc., carried on and off the vessel (see Fig. 10.12). Persons wearing jackets or sweaters must remove them for inspection. The security officer should use a Garrett Metal Detector to check persons for weapons and—via lightly rubbing the Detector against the person's body—"pat-down" persons wearing bulky clothing or who appear suspicious.
2. One security officer patrolling the deck to monitor activities of the stevedores and ongoing cargo operations.
3. One security officer patrolling the waterside, scanning the waters for "swimmer" stowaways, scuba divers, drug smuggler launches, etc. (see Fig. 10.13).
4. One VST team leader constantly patrolling the vessel decks and inspecting and supervising the operations of the security officers and taking charge of security situations. All empty containers not inspected by port checkers, terminal security officers, or K-9 teams should be inspected and sealed dockside at the hook by the VST team leader.
5. K-9 Team—The interior/exterior of all empty containers/trailers and the exterior of all loaded containers/trailers and other equipment (flat racks, mafis, etc.) are to be inspected by K-9 teams (narcotics and, if possible, explosives detection) and following this inspection, the K-9 handler affixes the seal to empty containers and records on a K-9 inspection log. The K-9 team should also inspect stevedores and their items, crew luggage and bags, ship's stores, etc., prior to entrance into the vessel (see Fig. 10.14).

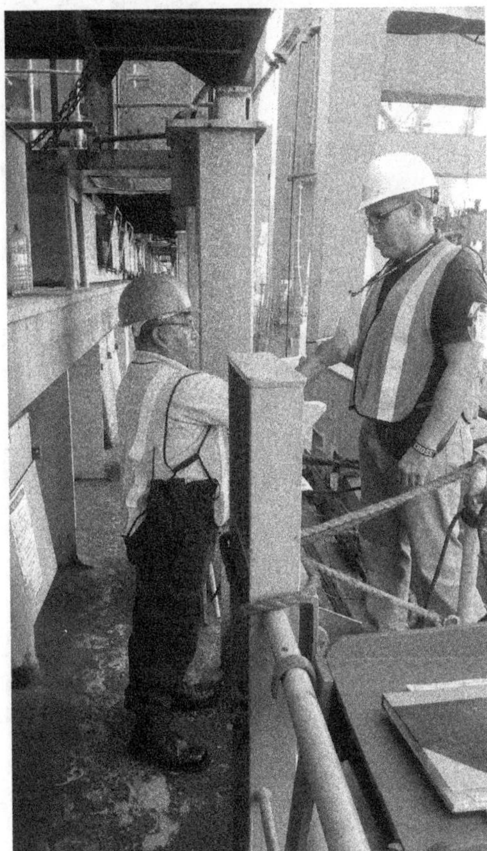

FIGURE 10.12 Security officer at the gangway to verify ID and search all hand-carried items.

Vessel Security Team Deployment for Roll On/Roll Off (RO/RO) Vessels

The VST should consist of no fewer than five security officers and one VST team leader:

1. One security officer posted at the top of the ramp to control and document the entrance and exit of persons (stevedores, crew, visitors, vessel agents, government officials, etc.) and search all parcels, bags, water coolers, etc., carried on and off the vessel. The security officer should use a Garrett Metal Detector to check persons for weapons and—via lightly rubbing the Detector against the person's body—"pat-down" persons wearing bulky clothing or who appear suspicious. This officer should also constantly scan the dockside for unusual activity.
2. Two security officers posted on the ramp to inspect the undersides of trailers, inside vehicles and Ottawas (also referred to as "Mula" or "Hustler," this tractor transports trailers and chassis on and off the ship), and inspect/record the seals of empty and loaded containers on separate tally logs (see Fig. 10.15).
3. One security officer patrolling the internal deck where trailers loading/unloading operations are underway.

FIGURE 10.13 Security officer patrolling the waterside.

FIGURE 10.14 K-9 team inspecting cargo and chassis before entering the vessel.

FIGURE 10.15 Ramp security officer checking the interior of an Ottawa entering the vessel.

4. One security officer patrolling the weather/upper deck waterside, scanning the waters for "swimmer" stowaways, scuba divers, drug smuggler launches, etc.
5. One VST team leader constantly patrolling the vessel decks, and inspecting and supervising the operations of the security officers and taking charge of security situations.
6. K-9 Team—The interior/exterior of all empty containers/trailers and the exterior of all loaded container/trailers and other equipment (flat racks, mafis, etc.) should be inspected by K-9 teams (narcotics and, if possible, explosives detection) and following this inspection, the K-9 handler affixes the seal to empty containers and records on a K-9 inspection log. The K-9 team should also inspect stevedores and their items, crew luggage and bags, ship's stores, etc., prior to entrance into the vessel (see Fig. 10.16).

Key Vessel Security Procedures

Following are the key procedures proven to yield positive results in maintaining effective vessel security.

1. Post a sign at the gangway which advises "Authorized Personnel Only—Present ID to Gangway Security—All bags, packages, etc. will be searched for weapons and contraband."
2. All stevedores and visitors relinquish their port ID badge or national ID card to gangway security officer while onboard.
3. Use a visitors log, stevedore list, shorepass log, and security logbook to document the entrance and exit of persons and all security incidents and activities.
4. Maintain all superstructure doors and cargo and deck hatches secured when not under guard.

FIGURE 10.16 K-9 check of stevedore gang prior to boarding vessel.

5. Keep secure all deck maintenance and storage lockers and crane access hatches when not in use.
6. Maintain rat guards on mooring lines.
7. Secure hawse cover (anchor chain cover) while in port and at anchorage.
8. Restrict stevedores to immediate work areas.
9. Fully retract and secure Jacobs ladder and Pilot ladder.
10. Lock cargo bay access hatches when not in use.
11. Use waterside/dockside illumination during night.
12. Use plastic/paper seals on access points of minimum usage (see Fig. 10.17).
13. Place sawdust or flour on deck around anchor chain and mooring line holes and in key crawl spaces (entry noted by hand- and footprints).
14. Do not allow POVs parked on dock next to the vessel.
15. Have all ship's stores and ship-chandler products searched by narcotics/explosives detection K-9 team dockside.
16. Inspect all empty containers for narcotics and stowaways and seal them prior to lading onboard the vessel. The container and seal numbers for all containers/trailers loaded onboard should be recorded on a tally sheet.

Pre-Departure Search for Contraband and Unauthorized Persons

Upon completion of cargo operations, the VST team leader will coordinate and lead the officers (with the exception of the officer posted at the gangway/ramp) in a systematic and comprehensive search of the vessel for stowaways and narcotics (see Fig. 10.18). The gangway security officer should restrict access to the vessel during this inspection.

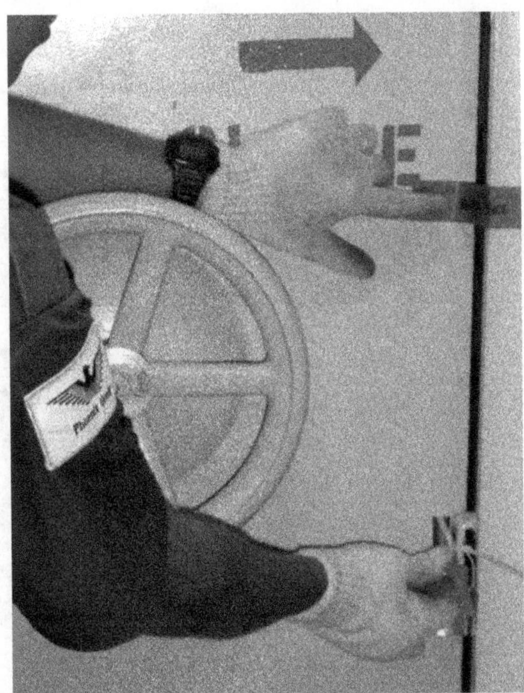

FIGURE 10.17 Tamper-evident, serialized security tape is applied to key doors and hatches of minimal usage.

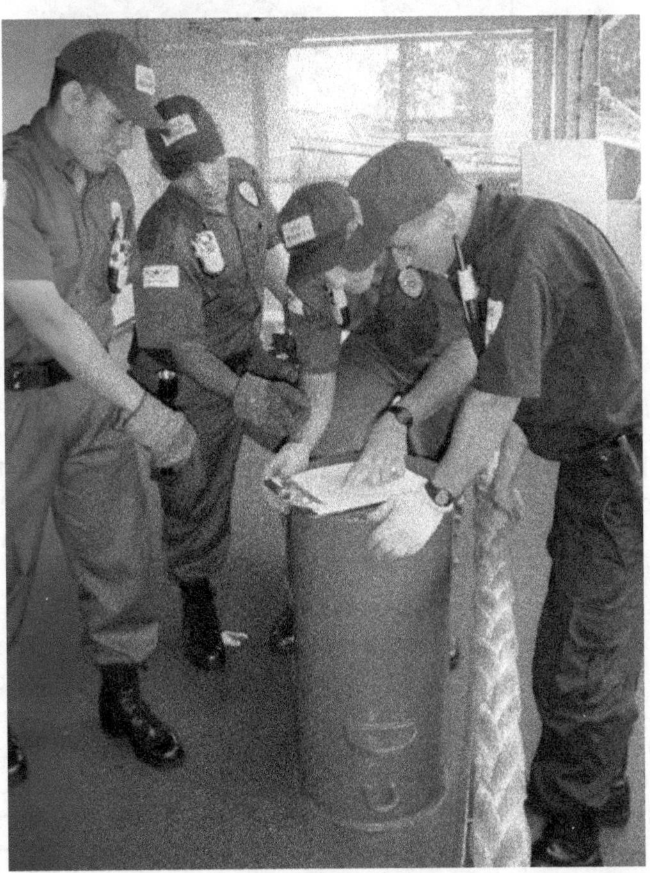

FIGURE 10.18 VST team leader issuing tasks and instruction to security officers participating in the vessel pre-departure inspection.

FIGURE 10.19 Security officer descending into a cargo bay.

In the case of LO/LO vessels, the search will start by the security officers descending to the lowest level of the most forward cargo bay at the bow (usually Bay #1) and checking between and under all containers (ensuring all are sealed), around ribs and support beams along the hull, inside ventilation shafts and air ducts, into crawl spaces, and in all equipment and tool storage locations (see Figs. 10.19 and 10.20). This detailed search will continue upward until arriving at the poop deck (main deck) and then be repeated in each sequential cargo bay.

After each cargo bay is searched and secured, the team will sweep the poop deck, from bow to stern, inspecting under the hawse cover, coiled lines, storage bins, and equipment lockers; underneath and between containers (checking all seals); inside access areas to and compartments of ship's gear (cranes); inside fire house compartments; under air exhaust covers; and inside trash and oil rag cans (see Figs. 10.21–10.24).

Next, the security officers inspect the exterior of the superstructure, checking that all doors are still secured, searching inside lifeboats, first aid lockers, accesses to the smokestack, and retracted ladders. The security officers continue this methodical search

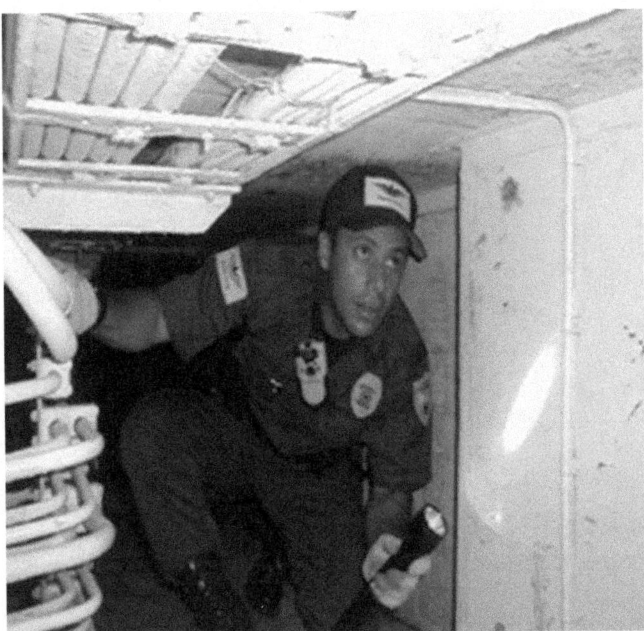

FIGURE 10.20 A physical inspection of all crawl spaces is necessary.

FIGURE 10.21 Security officers checking the main (poop) deck.

upward until they reach the bridge. After checking the exterior of the bridge, a security officer ascends to the top of the bridge and checks the area of navigation and communications aides. Upon completion of the search, the team descends to the poop deck, enters the superstructure, and descends to the steering/rudder room, off the engine room (see Figs. 10.25–10.31).

FIGURE 10.22 A security officer carefully inspecting all spaces on deck.

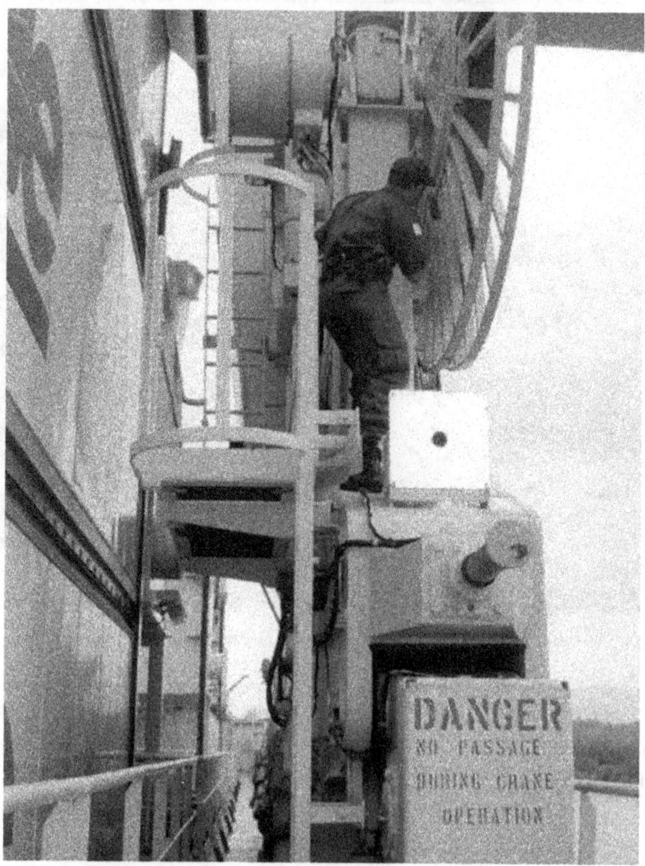

FIGURE 10.23 Checking the exterior of the ship's gear.

FIGURE 10.24 A bin of container locking pins is checked for contraband.

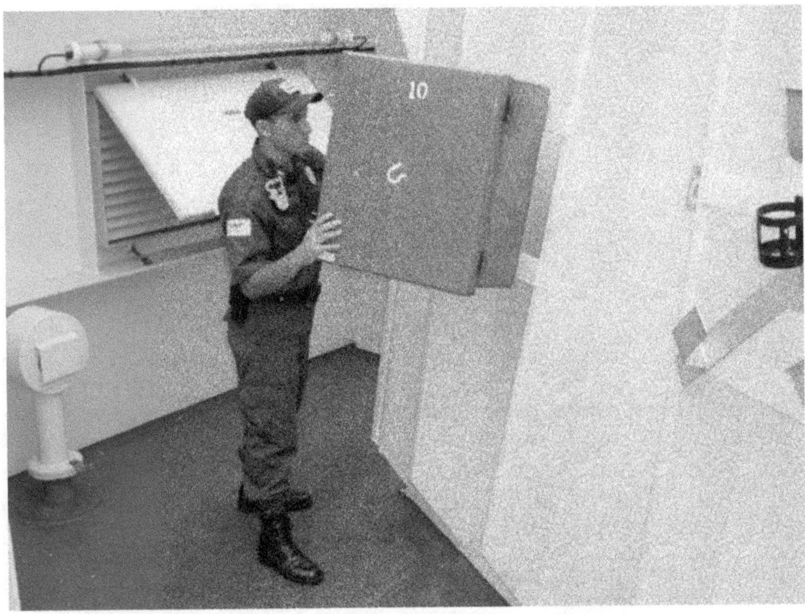

FIGURE 10.25 All fire hose cabinets and first aid boxes are opened.

FIGURE 10.26 Inspecting the stern mooring line guides.

FIGURE 10.27 Oily rag cans and trash disposal bins are opened and inspected.

FIGURE 10.28 Security officer entering the access door to the smokestack.

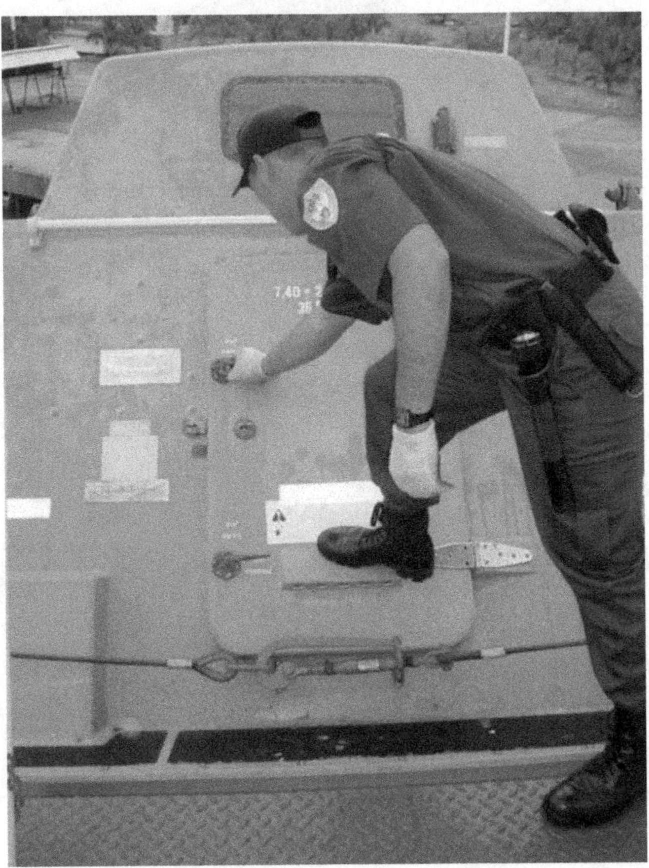

FIGURE 10.29 The enclosed, newer-style lifeboats must be opened and the interior physically inspected.

FIGURE 10.30 Security officer conducting a check of the exterior of the bridge.

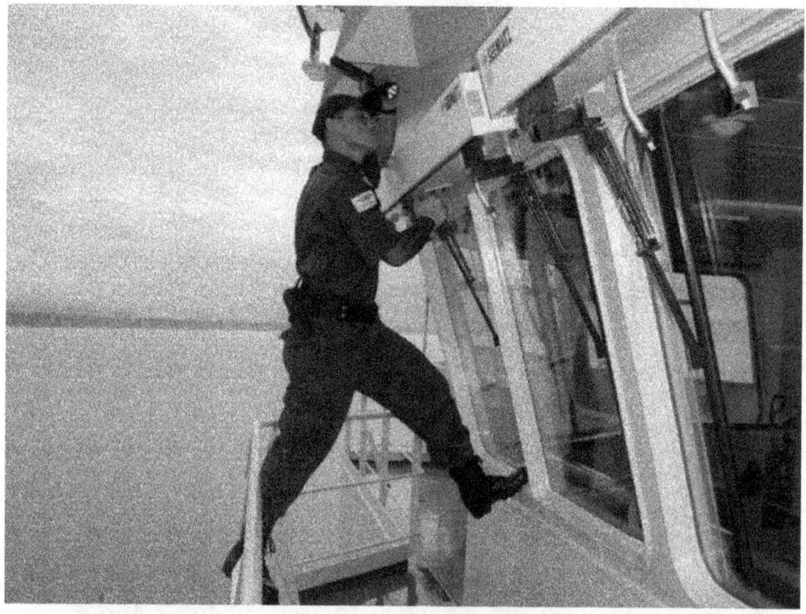

FIGURE 10.31 All areas of the exterior of the superstructure must be inspected.

Once the team is inside the steering/rudder room, the security officers begin by checking under walkways and around pipes. Next, the team moves to the engine room, inspecting the undersides of elevated floors and in any accumulated oil deposits (look for "drinking straws" sticking out of the oil, which submersed stowaways use for breathing), as well as between and under all machinery and pipes. Slowly moving upward, the security officers check inside the mechanic's room, engineer office/room, spare parts room, and control room. Food stuff storage lockers and supply closets are opened and inspected. Continuing upward, the team inspects inside linen closets, dining areas, storage closets, and above pipes in common area walkways. Crew, pilot, and passenger accommodations (especially "unoccupied" rooms) are searched (check removable wall partitions in bathrooms, behind the toilet, and dead space under bunks). Upon reaching the bridge, the security officers quickly review the common areas before completing the vessel search. Upon termination of the vessel search, the VST team leader will complete a "vessel search certificate" and provide signed copies to the captain, vessel agent, and the shift security superintendent (see Figs. 10.32–10.42).

Security Personnel Employment and Training

While not a component of a specific security ring, proper preemployment screening, training, and equipping of security personnel will directly impact on attaining the desired results of security personnel deployed in the various rings and the success of the overall port security program.

FIGURE 10.32 Security officer inspecting the underside of the raised floor in the engine room.

FIGURE 10.33 The web of large pipes and machinery provide numerous locations for hiding contraband and unauthorized persons.

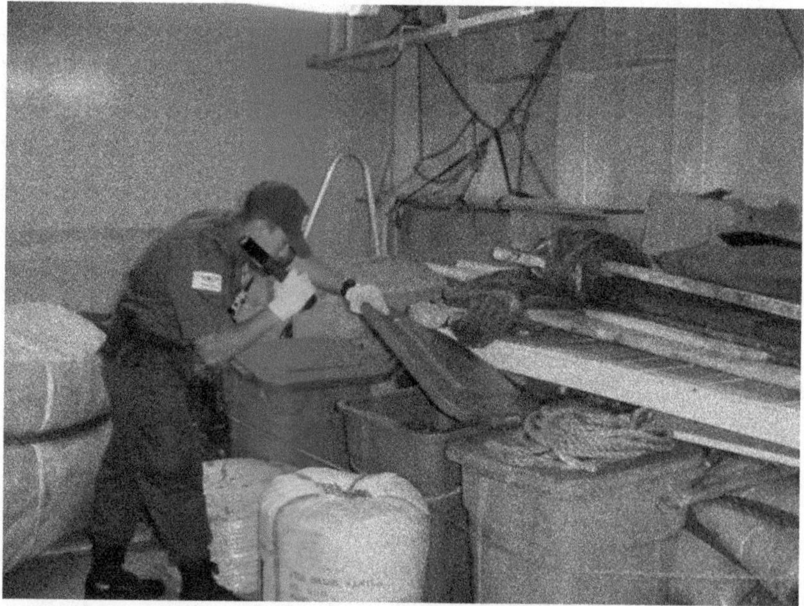

FIGURE 10.34 A security officer methodically inspecting the various storage and supply rooms and lockers.

FIGURE 10.35 Checking the boxes and bins in the mechanic's room.

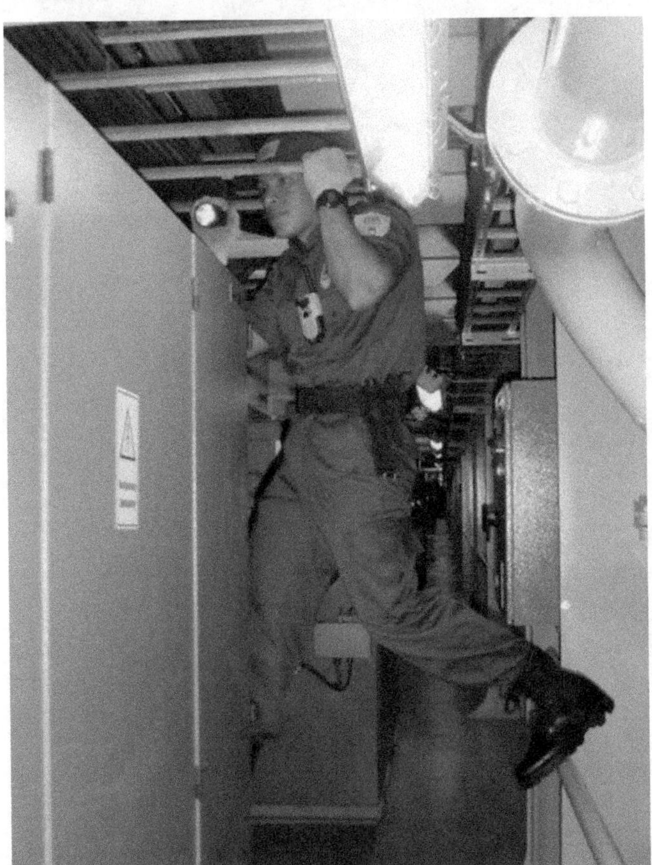
FIGURE 10.36 The tops of electric panels provides ample space to hide contraband.

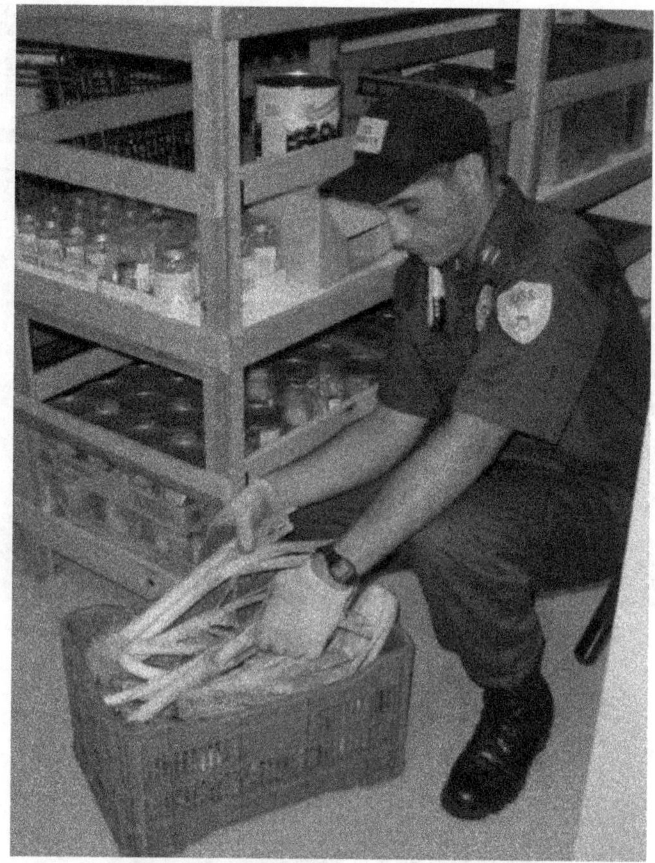

FIGURE 10.37 Food locker undergoing inspection.

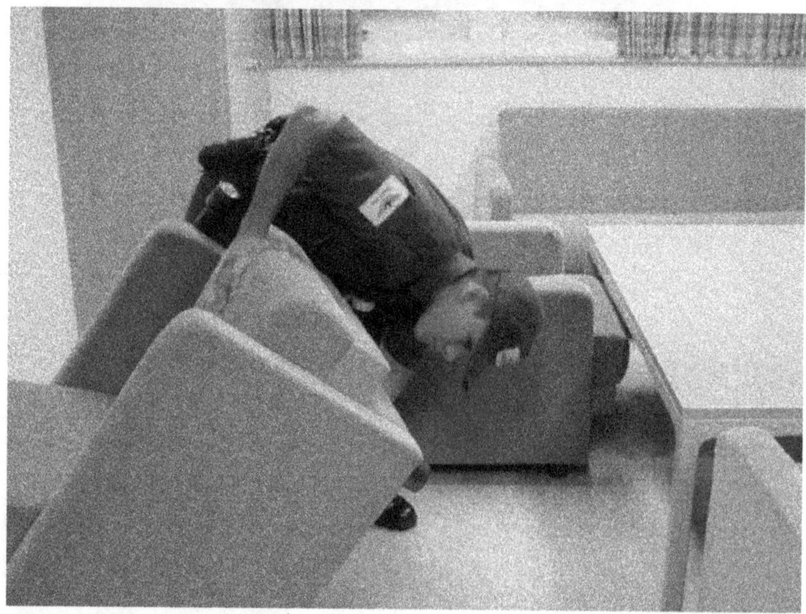

FIGURE 10.38 Ship offices and recreation rooms are not excluded from the pre-departure search.

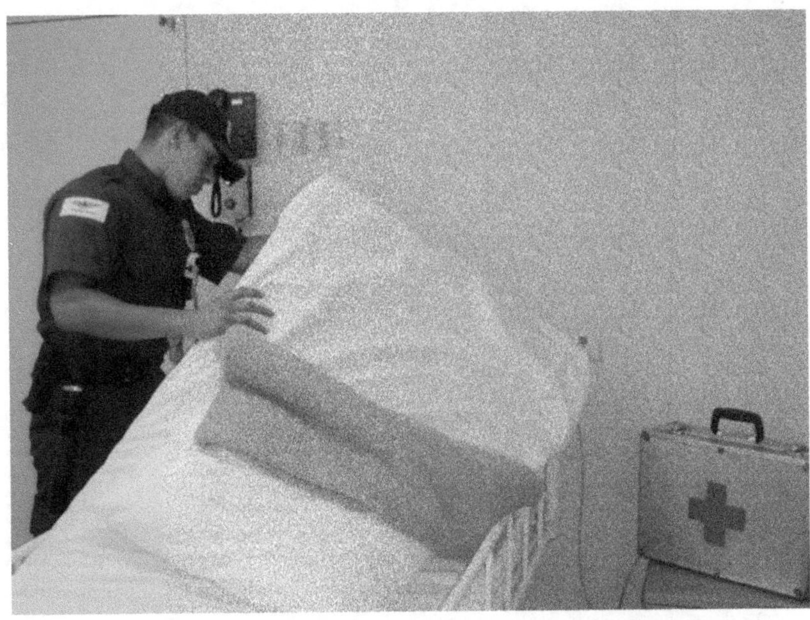

FIGURE 10.39 A security officer checking the ship's hospital.

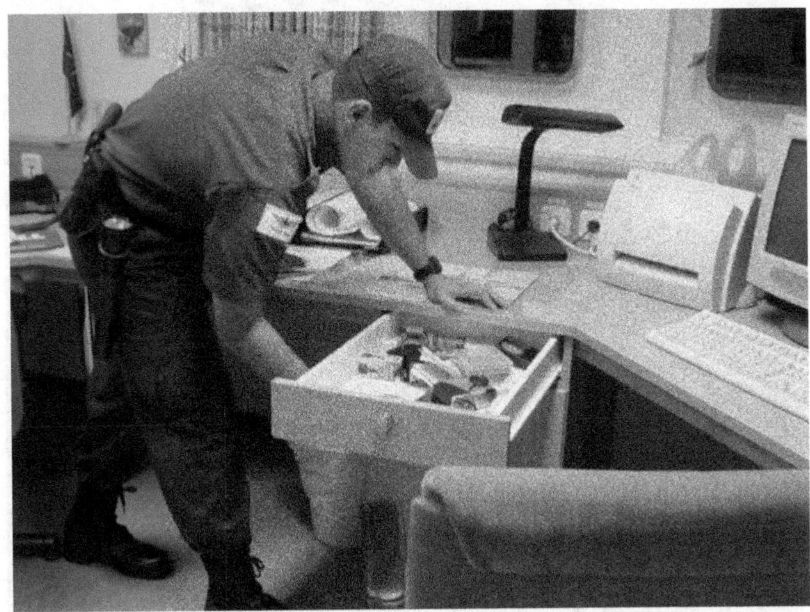

FIGURE 10.40 Inspecting the chief officer's work area.

FIGURE 10.41 Use of the K-9 increases the speed and accuracy of the ship inspection.

FIGURE 10.42 Hiding of illegal drugs in the reefer compartments of containers is common.

Preemployment Screening

The screening of candidates for employment with the security department should follow these steps:

1. The candidate completes a detailed employment application and provides a "good health" certificate, "no police record" certificate, and copies of all education and training documents.
2. The candidate is interviewed by a security supervisor.
3. The human resources (HR) department verifies prior employment and references.
4. An internal security investigator conducts in-person interviews of the candidate's neighbors and checks national police records (convictions, arrest, and ongoing investigations).
5. The candidate undergoes a drug-use test.
6. The candidate receives a final interview by a shift security superintendent.
7. Candidates for sensitive positions (K-9 handler, investigator, supervisor, etc.) undergo a polygraph. If pass, they are scheduled for training.
8. Candidate undergoes the relevant training course (Security Officer, K-9 Handler, Admin, etc.) Upon successful completion, the candidate signs an employment contract. New employee is assigned to his/her Group.
9. HR establishes a permanent personnel file, which includes the signed contract, completed application and photo, and all screening and investigation documentation.

Basic Security Training

All new security personnel, regardless of their permanent assigned position, first should be fully trained in the basics of seaport security (see Figs. 10.43–10.47). A comprehensive security officer course for new security personnel would be approximately 200 hours in duration and include at least the following topics:

1. Security Definitions in a Port Environment
2. Discipline, the Chain-of-Command, and Ethics

FIGURE 10.43 Security officer training is critical to the success of the port security program and must be comprehensive. A quasi-military atmosphere and discipline breeds pride, loyalty, and a work ethic.

FIGURE 10.44 A high level of physical activity eliminates the uncommitted and undedicated.

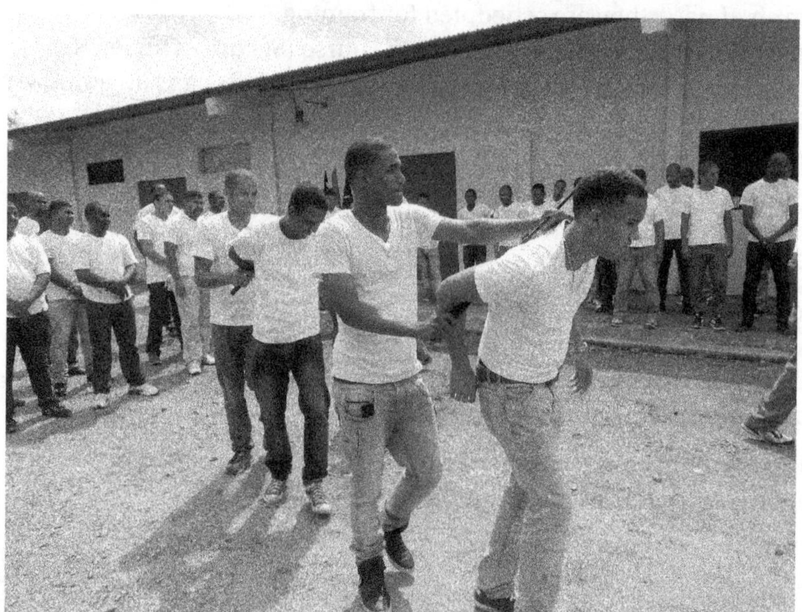

FIGURE 10.45 Students receiving self-defense and detention skills using the ASP Baton.

3. Legal Considerations
4. Uniform and Equipment Presentation
5. Personal Defense Tactics and Apprehension Techniques
6. Use of the ASP or PR-24 Baton
7. Use of CS/CN Gas
8. Access Control and Searching of Vehicles and Persons
9. Security of Installations, Offices, and Warehouses
10. Vehicle and Foot Patrols and Static Posts

FIGURE 10.46 "Hands-on" classes make the training real, relevant, and increase skill retention.

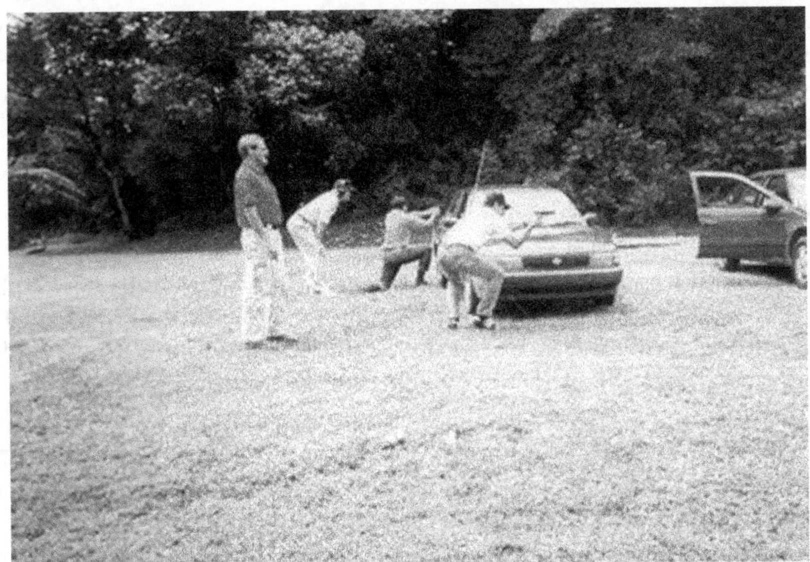

FIGURE 10.47 Firearm and tactics training of the port's "Executive Protection Team."

11. Report Writing
12. Security Forms and Documentation
13. General and Administrative Orders
14. Post Orders and Special Orders
15. Vessel Security Operations and VST Post Orders

16. Detection and Search of Persons and Vehicles
17. Role of Internal Security and Intelligence Operations
18. Role of the Shift Security Superintendent, Shift Supervisor, K-9 Units, and Other Special Services
19. Leadership, Motivation, and Conflict Resolution
20. First Aid and Fire Fighting
21. Use of Radio and Communication Etiquette
22. The Business and Functioning of a Commercial Seaport
23. Usage and Qualification with Issued Pistol and Shotgun
24. HAZMAT Recognition and Emergency Response
25. Bomb Threats and Search Procedures
26. Familiarization with the Port Facility Security Plan
27. ISPS Code Modules for "Port Personnel with Security Duties"
28. C-TPAT and Supply Chain Security Modules
29. Executive Protection Detail (Selected Candidates)

Security Officer Equipment

All security officers and the shift security supervisor should wear a police or military-style uniform, hat, and black military boots. Each should be issued a safety vest and helmet and wear a black nylon military equipment belt which holds a three-dimensional cell Maglite flashlight, two flex cuffs, ASP or PR-24 Baton, radio, CS/CN gas, issued pistol, and extra ammunition. VST officers should not carry a firearm, unless the port or vessel is at a heightened security level and this measure is noted in the PFSP.

Port Security Director

All world-class seaport security programs require the assignment of a highly experienced, full-time Port Security Director and the support of a capable administrative staff. The Security Director is charged with the development, implementation, leadership, and management of the overall port security program. In addition to managing all security operations and resources, the Security Director defines and establishes all security policies, plans, and procedures, including the development and updating of the port facility security plan and supplemental plans, such as disaster preparedness and recovery plan. The Port Security Director directs the Shift Security Superintendents as well, and directly manages the intelligence program. The Security Director should have a military and/or law enforcement background, extensive leadership and management skills, a solid understanding of the commercial maritime business and how a seaport functions, the ability to lead a large and multifaceted security organization, and broad knowledge of and experience in assessing and successfully confronting the various security threats faced by a commercial seaport.

Port Facility Security Plan

There is a military adage which states, "Proper Planning Prevents Poor Performance." This is likewise true for port security. The absence of comprehensive, realistic, and tested written security policies, plans, and procedures will ensure the failure of the port security program. It is critical that the port facility assessment is comprehensive and used to guide the development of a well-designed and practical PFSP.

Summary

In order to meet the increasing and ever-changing security challenges and threats to seaports of the world, port management must design and implement a security strategy that is based on the concepts of "Defense-in-Depth" and "layered, interlocking security rings." This well-planned strategy, when combined with the leadership of a highly professional Port Security Director, deployment of a well-trained security force, and preparation of a comprehensive PFSP, will ensure the success of the security program in deterring, preventing, or denying current and anticipated security challenges and meriting recognition as a world-class seaport security program.

11 Threat Mitigation Strategies

OBJECTIVES

After studying this chapter, you will be familiar with

1. Behaviors and activities of criminals, terrorists, and others likely to pose a security threat;
2. Strategies, procedures, and measures to detect, deter, delay, deny, and contain pirate attacks;
3. Requirements for configuring and equipping an effective Citadel;
4. Recommended actions to survive as a hostage of pirates or terrorists;
5. Container inspection techniques;
6. Security equipment, systems, and devices utilized to detect contraband and unauthorized persons in a container.

Mitigation may be defined, for our purposes, as the avoidance or favorable resolution of a threat or incident through actions either of detection, deterrence, delay, denial, or containment. The mitigation of security threats posed by criminals, terrorists, pirates, and stowaways to ports and commercial shipping is the foremost goal—and challenge—in maritime security. Throughout this book, we have discussed vulnerabilities and threats to ports and ships, as well as to links in the cargo supply chain. Earlier in the book, we reviewed a detailed blueprint for a model port and vessel security program, which in itself defines policies, procedures, and security measures that serve to form a framework of mitigation strategies and concepts. This chapter focuses on additional actions and security equipment, systems, and devices available to aid in mitigation security threats.

Prior to our discussion of mitigation strategies, you can be best served by a brief review of the behaviors and activities you may observe which may indicate targeting by criminal or terrorist entities. Many of us have been conditioned to think of a certain type of person when we hear the word *criminal* or *terrorist.* Unfortunately, that means we look at a person's appearance, language, and culture when evaluating suspicious actions. However, you cannot identify a person who may threaten security by how a person is dressed, what a person eats, where a person is from, or their accent. As an example, consider American terrorists Jose Padilla (the would-be "Dirty Bomber") and John Walker Lindh (the "American Taliban"). Neither of them fit the profile of an Islamic terrorist prior to engaging in terrorist activities on behalf of al-Qaeda. Conversely, observing a person's behavior or activity may well reveal indicators of potential criminal or terrorist targeting. Let's review some of these potential indicators:

- *Surveillance:* Terrorists invest considerable time in selecting and planning attacks against their targets. Successful targeting requires long periods of surveillance and intelligence gathering. The terrorists' preparation for the September 11, 2001 attacks—5 years of planning, skill acquirement, and practice—is an example of the dedication and patience of terrorists. In order to build "target folders," terrorists take photos, make drawings, or shoot videos for use in planning an attack. For this reason, persons observed photographing, videotaping, or sketching diagrams of a port or facility should be challenged and questioned. Also, unusual requests for maps, blueprints, and related documents should be investigated. From the waterside, terrorists have launched boats near commercial and military ships to take photos. If these activities are not challenged, terrorists or criminals will have more confidence in their ability to successfully launch an operation against the port and/or ship.

- *Dry Runs:* Terrorists, drug smugglers, and other criminals have been known to conduct dry runs as part of their planning. As an example, while conducting a vessel predeparture search in the port of Buenaventura, Colombia, Phoenix Group Maritime Security Team officers deployed onboard a container ship discovered a hidden kilo-size package which had the outward appearance of being a narcotics shipment; however, upon opening it, they found the contents were cocoa beans. This act was an example of a dry run by narcotics smugglers to test the effectiveness of the search team. In some cases, the dry run may actually be a probing effort and intended to provide an indication of the vulnerabilities of the security systems protecting the ports and ships and the security response capabilities and procedures. For example, there have been cases of truck drivers (part of a container hijacking organization) arriving at the port claiming to have urgent verbal instructions or a hand-written drayage order to transport a container from the port to an off-port warehouse. However, the real purpose was to probe the reaction of security and gate personnel and see how far the drivers could get without proper documentation.
- *Suspicious Questions:* Terrorists and other criminals may openly ask port employees or vendors for information pertaining to security operations and activities. For example, "How can I deliver some gifts to a friend onboard a ship without going through the hassle at the visitor gate?" "How many security guards work at the port?" "I think I know that security guard at the main gate. What is his name and where does he live?" While the questions may be innocent and genuine, they also may be an attempt to solicit information concerning the security vulnerabilities, procedures, and personnel. Some criminals/terrorists might try to obtain information about the port by approaching port or vessel employees and their family members. Be suspicious of people who ask a lot of questions regarding port and vessel activity.
- *Questionable Workmen* or *Vendors:* Some criminals/terrorists might disguise themselves as workmen or repair personnel in order to gain access to the facilities and sensitive areas of the port. Fake vendors (or real ones with a second agenda) may arrive at the port attempting to gain entrance to the port under the pretext of marketing products and services to the port or port clients. The real purpose of the vendors' activities may be to gather intelligence for use in planning attacks or criminal operations at the port.

Again, behaviors and activities are the keys to recognition. Watch for the following:

- Unknown persons approaching (in person or via telephone) employees or their family members inquiring about the facility.
- Unknown or suspicious workmen trying to gain access to the facility to repair, replace, service, or install equipment.
- Suspicious package drop-offs/attempted drop-offs.
- Unknown persons photographing or attempting to gain access to facilities to photograph port areas.
- Theft of "standard" operating procedures, ID badges, vehicle passes, employee uniforms, or facility vehicles.
- Unusual or prolonged interest by suspicious persons in the port security measures or employees, entry points and access controls, or perimeter barriers.
- Unusual behavior by unknown persons, such as studiously watching personnel or vehicles entering or leaving designated facilities or parking areas.
- Unauthorized observation of security drills or exercises.
- Increase in anonymous telephone or e-mail threats to facilities or employees.
- Unknown persons conducting foot surveillance (involving two or three individuals working together).
- Unknown persons conducting mobile surveillance, using bicycles, scooters, motorcycles, cars, trucks, or boats.
- Suspicious general aviation aircraft operating in proximity to facilities.
- Prolonged static surveillance using operatives disguised as panhandlers, demonstrators, shoe shiners, food or flower vendors, news agents, or street sweepers not previously seen in the area.
- Unknown persons noted to make discreet use of still cameras, video recorders, or note taking at nontourist type locations.
- Use of multiple sets of clothing or identification by an unknown person.

Mitigating Pirate Attacks

The scourge of piracy in Southeast Asia and the greater Gulf of Guinea, a security threat to ships and Crews which we addressed earlier in this book, can be mitigated, in large part, using proven strategies, plans, procedures, and measures. While there are valuable experiences, partnerships, and proven antipiracy ship security procedures and measures developed as a result of the hard-fought success in mitigating piracy in Somalia, they cannot be "cut-and-pasted" to strategies for mitigating piracy in the greater Gulf of Guinea and Southeast Asia. In this section of the chapter, we will briefly contrast the different and unique situations of the three piracy-prone regions and offer a more detailed discussion of mitigations strategies, to include measures and procedures, for commercial ships operating in the high-risk areas of the greater Gulf of Guinea and Southeast Asia. The reader will recognize that the suggested security configuration for the ship is a layered approach, one utilizing a defense-in-depth methodology, which creates a strategy for the detection, deterrence, delay, and denial of a pirate attack.

The political, legal, and military situation of Somalia at the height of the scourge of piracy was vastly different from that of the two current hotspot regions. Somalia was a *failed state* and the administration, known as the Transitional Federal Government (as of August 2012 the Federal Government of Somalia), barely controlled Mogadishu, much less the tribal centers of piracy to the south. At that time, there was no viable Navy or Coast Guard to patrol waters and the rule of law didn't exist. While this vacuum of legal, military, and political powers permitted piracy to flourish, it also allowed the world governments to step in and deploy Naval Forces in territorial waters and a defacto license for the positioning of armed security teams onboard commercial ships in their waters—two of the three pillars of the broad strategy which successfully eradicated piracy off the coast of Somalia. These three pillars were (and still are):

- The deployment of Naval ships in three major armadas—the European Union's "Operation Atalanta," NATO's "Operation Ocean Shield," and the U.S.-led "Combined Maritime Forces" (a 30-nation Naval partnership) to patrol the Gulf of Aden and the western Indian Ocean and escort commercial ships through the Internationally Recommended Transit Corridor (IRTC).
- The implementation of Best Management Practices guidelines (BMP4 being the most recent) by the majority of commercial shipping lines operating in the high-risk area provided shipmasters with a checklist of security measures and procedures for hardening the ship and making it less likely of being attacked and boarded by pirates. These guidelines were developed jointly by several international shipping organizations (ICS, BIMCO, INTERTANKO, IMB, etc.) and with input from some Navies participating in the patrol operations. According to Adjoa Anyimadu, of Chatham House, interviews of shipping lines sailing this route revealed that ships which implemented the security measures and procedures defined in BMP4 were *four times less likely to be hijacked.*[1]
- The deployment of Armed Private Security Companies onboard the commercial ships was a huge departure from a maritime norm of the past 100 years (no military-style firearms onboard commercial ships) and a real *game changer* in warding off the pirates. As evidence of the impact of this measure, not a single ship with an armed security team onboard has been successfully hijacked off the coast of Somalia.

The fundamental objective of Somali pirates was hijacking a ship for the purpose of ransoming the Crew and the ship. So, while Somali pirates were heavily armed with automatic weapons and RPG grenades, the propensity for deadly violence was not directed at on a personal or wanton level. The Crew Lastly, ships attacked by Somali pirates were underway (steaming or drifting) and their approach tactics were a reflection of attacking ships while underway. Now let's contrast the government situation and other factors with the two other primary zones of piracy.

The political, legal, and military situations in the greater Gulf of Guinea and Southeast Asia, as well as pirate behaviors and goals, are quite different from those of Somalia. First, the coastal countries of West Africa—from Senegal in the north to Angola to the south—and those of Southeast Asia (Singapore, Malaysia, Vietnam, Thailand, Philippines, etc.) all have functioning governments, a legal system, and a military—a stark departure from Somalia. Second, while there are a couple multinational Naval patrol operations, made up of Navies of the region and securing the waters of Southeast Asia, Navies of West African nations mostly patrol their own sovereign waters. Third, for the most part, privately contracted armed security guards are not permitted to operate within the territorial waters of Gulf of Guinea countries. Ships armed security personnel onboard while steaming or at anchorage/drifting in the territorial waters of Nigeria, Benin, or Togo may contract the militaries or police to post personnel onboard the ship. There have been several incidents in Nigerian waters of ships being detained or Crew arrested for having local or non-Nigerian private security personnel (armed and unarmed) onboard the ship. For example, in 2012, the M/V Myre Seadiver, a vessel owned by a Russian security firm, and its Crew were arrested by the Nigerian Navy and accused of illegally entering Nigerian waters carrying weapons. The ship's owner stated that the vessel had secured proper permits and licenses from the Nigerian authorities, but this claim was rejected by the Navy and the Crew was charged with illegally possessing and importing arms and ammunition. Conversely, there are a number of private security companies providing armed and unarmed security services to ship transiting the Straits of Malacca and Singapore, as well as in the South China Sea and parts of Indonesia. Whether or not a shipping line or ship utilizes these services appears more related to "cost issues" than regulations. Most of the tankers that are attacked and fuel stolen tend to be Product Tankers that are medium to small in size and not ULCCs or VLCCs, so their operating budgets are much less than the large ships.

The *end game* (goals) for pirates operating in the greater Gulf of Guinea and Southeast Asia generally is quite different than in Somalia, and this is likewise reflected in their tactics and behavior. The goal of pirates in the Gulf is the theft of cargo, with a secondary goal of kidnapping for ransom foreign Crew. In Southeast Asia it varies from petty theft to stealing ship equipment, to robbery of the fuel cargo. So, in the Gulf the value of the lives of Crew is less important and pirates are more likely to harm or kill Crew (or onboard security—including military personnel), while in Southeast Asia, the majority of times when the pirates are discovered they immediately disembark and escape, without resorting to violence. Pirates in the Greater Gulf of Guinea—of Nigerian origin—are very quick to use deadly and mistreat hostages.

Ship Antipiracy Planning Strategies and Recommended Actions

The tried and proven baseline "antipiracy security strategy," developed by preeminent, global Shipping Associations and Naval Forces deployed off the coast of Somalia, is the "Best Management Practices for Protection against Somali Based Piracy" (currently in Version 4).[2] The vast majority of this well-developed, detailed strategy document (95 pages in length) is applicable in other piracy high-risk areas (including GOG and SWA), especially

Continued

Ship Antipiracy Planning Strategies and Recommended Actions—cont'd

the pretransit ship and voyage-specific risk assessment, ship master's planning, deterrence/delaying measures, and actions to take when boarding in imminent. Many of the points in the Risk Assessment emanate from the ISPS Code. A complement to BMP4, which addresses the threat of piracy worldwide, is the IMO's Maritime Safety Committee Circular MSC.1/Circ.1334, entitled, "Piracy and Armed Robbery Against Ships—Guidance to Shipowners and Ship Operators, Shipmasters and Crews on Preventing and Suppressing Acts of Piracy and Armed Robbery Against Ships."[3] This current guidance lists 94 detailed points (30 pages) for preparing, avoiding, deterring, and responding to acts of piracy and armed robbery worldwide.

As the goals, violent behavior, tactics, and targeting of pirates in the greater Gulf of Guinea are somewhat different than pirates in other regions, the Maritime Trade Information Sharing Centre—Gulf of Guinea (MTISC-GOG) issued a set of Guidelines which seek to bridge the gap between the advice currently found in BMP4 and the prevailing situation in the Gulf of Guinea region.[4] In this document, the MTISC-GOG offers some location-specific advice to Masters for planning and actions to take if attack is imminent, to include:

"Given the modus operandi of the pirates operating in the Gulf of Guinea region, the Master should plan according to the following:

- Rendezvous—Where possible, avoid waiting and slow steaming. Consider offering several alternative rendezvous points and advise rendezvous points at the last minute. If waiting, keep well off the coast (up to 200 nm). Do not give away waiting positions. Do not drift and keep engines ready for immediate maneuvers.
- Anchoring—Where practicable, a prolonged stay at anchorage is to be avoided.
- Minimize use of VHF and use e-mail or secure satellite telephone instead. Where possible only answer known or legitimate callers on the VHF, bearing in mind that imposters are likely and may even appear in uniform.
- The greatest risks of piracy are at night and these need to be factored into all planning. Where possible, operations should start and end during daylight hours.

MITSC-GOG suggested Ship Security Protective Measures—the ship protection measures described in Section 8 of BMP4 (except 8.15) also apply in the Gulf of Guinea. Also consider:

- Vessel hardening is likely to be quite effective in this region and a moving ship also makes an effective deterrent since, unlike Somalia-based pirates, ladders are not often used to board ships.
- During STS operations or when adrift, equipment such as fenders, anchor chains, and hawse pipes can potentially provide a vulnerable point of access for attackers, and entry should be physically blocked.
- Pirates detect and target vessels by sight and by the use of Automatic Identification System (AIS). Therefore limit the use of lighting at night and reduce the power or turn off AIS. Unfortunately, this has a major drawback in that it may reduce the likelihood of an intervention by 'friendly forces' if attacked. Consequently, AIS must be switched on immediately if the ship is boarded.

- The use of Citadels is an owner's/master's choice but it should be borne in mind that their successful use in the Indian Ocean was predicated upon their being a strong chance of a Naval Intervention. The principles of their construction and use, however, remain the same as outlined in BMP4. Given the levels of violence perpetrated by pirates, and if control of the engines can be maintained from the Citadel, many think that this option is the safest and also one that prevents the ship from maneuvering in order to prevent cargo theft.
- Owners should consider the placement of hidden position transmitting devices as one of the first actions of pirates is to disable all visible communication and tracking devices and aerials.

MITSC-GOG suggests the following list of actions should be considered *if an attack is imminent*:

- If underway, speed should be increased as much as possible to open the distance between the ship and the attackers. Try to steer a straight course to maintain maximum speed. Consider evasive actions if the circumstances dictate.
- Initiate the ship's preprepared emergency procedures.
- Activate the emergency communication plan.
- Sound the emergency alarm and make an announcement in accordance with the Ship's Emergency Plan.
- Report the attack as soon as possible to MTISC-GOG by phone and follow up with call to the company security officer if the situation permits.
- Activate the ship security alert system (SSAS) which will alert your CSO and flag state. Make a 'Mayday' call on VHF Channel 16.
- Send a distress message via the Digital Selective Calling (DSC) system and Inmarsat-C, as applicable.
- Ensure that the AIS is switched ON.
- All Crew, except those required on the bridge or in the engine room, should move to the Safe Muster Point or Citadel, if constructed.
- If possible, alter course away from the approaching craft. When sea conditions allow, consider altering course to increase an approaching craft's exposure to wind/waves.
- Activate water spray and other self-defensive measures.
- Confirm external doors and, where possible, internal public rooms and cabins are fully secured. If possible pull up external ladders and fenders.
- Place the ship's whistle/foghorn/alarm on auto to demonstrate to any potential attacker that the ship is aware of the attack and is reacting to it.

MITSC-GOG states that violent shipboard robberies can take place as a result of a previously unsuccessful attack on another vessel. Therefore, if pirates take control:

- Great care needs to be taken if your ship is boarded, as life is little valued by pirates. Compliance/submission to attackers is essential once a vessel has been taken.
- Generally minimizing cash carried will make vessels less attractive in the longer run.

Kidnap and ransom in the Gulf of Guinea are a growing trend. Experience shows attackers will board a vessel and loot the ship's stores and steal personal belongings. Once this has been

Continued

Ship Antipiracy Planning Strategies and Recommended Actions—cont'd

done they may kidnap key individuals, eg, the Master and Chief Engineer. Kidnap can serve two key purposes for the attackers:

- Help the attackers escape—the presence of hostages may reduce the likelihood of security forces to engage in a firefight; and
- For ransom—to maximize their profits from the attack or hijack."

Ship Antipiracy Security Measures for High-Risk Areas

When defining the security measures and systems to be incorporated into the antipiracy security configuration, it is important to select and deploy them in a layered format, utilizing the defense-in-depth methodology. The goal of the configuration is to detect, deter, delay, and, if required, deny the pirate attack—at the greatest distance possible from the ship as possible. While several security measures are discussed in detail in BMP4 and other guidance from Shipping Line Associations, below is a broad range of equipment and systems, organized in a layered approach (security rings) for use/engagement at the different distances. It is important to remember that in some areas—such as the Straits of Malacca and Singapore—ships, particularly those at anchorages, typically are very close together and the outer ring may only be 300–500 m away from the ship (Figs. 11.1 and 11.2).

Outer Security Ring (700–1000 m)

At this distance, shipboard watches are in a threat *monitoring and detection* mode. The use of ship radar, long-range CCTV (with laser Illuminator), and *Deck Watches—must be 24× 7 while traveling in high-threat areas* (minimum of one private security officer or crewmember on the starboard side and one on portside, with binoculars and night vision

FIGURE 11.1 Long-Range CCTV for a maritime environment.

attachment for use in darkness)—should be constantly scanning and monitoring the waters for suspicious boats and ones which appear to be approaching the ship. If a potential pirate boat(s) is noted, the focus of the CCTV/illuminator (zooming in on suspect boat) should be on the suspect boat(s) for continuous monitoring (Figs. 11.3 and 11.4).

Threat Evaluation and Initial Deterrence Ring (400–500 m)

At this distance, suspect boats are evaluated and initial efforts are made to *dissuade and deter* their further closing-in on the ship. Nonlethal and nonprovocative measures and

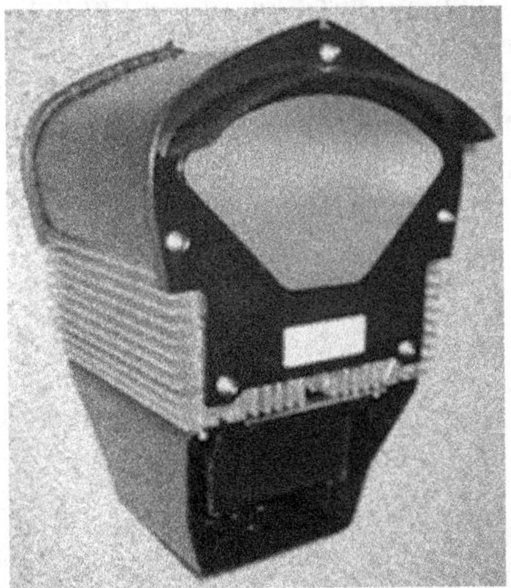

FIGURE 11.2 Illuminators, like in the picture, use focused, high-power Infra-Red to send a narrow beam of light out to 1000 m. Function jointly with CCTV.

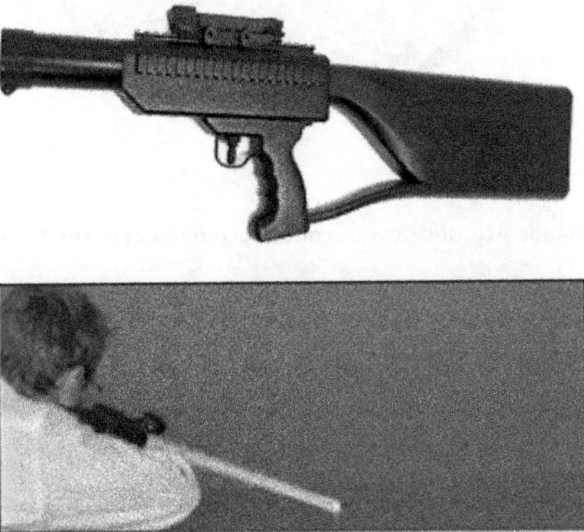

FIGURE 11.3 The Medusa is a completely self-contained high-power green laser device which provides long-range (multiple kilometers) nonlethal deterrence, disorienting the target.

equipment, such as the Medusa long-range laser (works day and night) and the LRAD (long-range acoustic device) will let the suspect boat(s) know they have been spotted, are under observation, and both the nonharmful, but disorienting and temporarily incapacitating, laser and LRAD also serve as a deterrent device to further approach.

Threat Deterrence and Engagement Ring (200–300 m)

If the suspect boat(s) has continued in persevering in closing-in on the ship, more *aggressive deterrence measures* should be implemented. These may include one of more of the following: if armed security personnel are deployed, they should fire two to three warning shots (tracer rounds) in the general direction of—but not at!—the boat(s) and/or a series of warning flares should be fired using the flare shotgun (see Fig. 11.5). The Medusa long-range laser should focus directly on the person driving the boat(s). The Master should conduct evasive actions if underway or prepare for the implementation of emergency measures (sound alarm, turn-on lights, etc.).

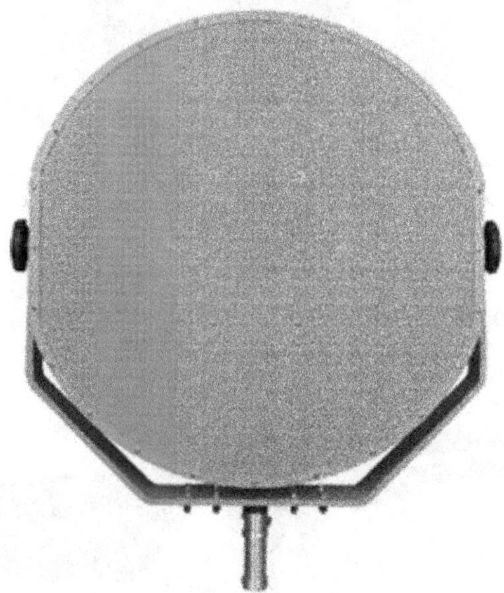

FIGURE 11.4 This Long-Range Acoustic Device sends a focused high pitched noise to a directed location.

FIGURE 11.5 High-speed shotgun-style flare projector.

Threat Trip-Wire Ring (75–100 m)

If the pirates have continued to advance, ignoring the multiple warnings, they have demonstrated a clear intention of wanting to conduct an attack on the ship. Likewise, they—may have already used their firearms or other weapon systems (RPG, etc.) in an attempt to have the ship stop or surrender to boarding. The Master should initiate emergency measures and if armed security personnel are deployed, they should fire multiple rounds into the boat(s) to disable the engine(s) and neutralize any pirates firing weapons at the ship (see Fig. 11.6). Crew and/or security personnel should *implement delaying* measures, to include: use the flare shotgun to shoot incendiary, concussion, and CN Gas flares into the boats; deploy boat nets to clog propellers (see Fig. 11.7); and engage pirates with the remotely controlled water cannons (see Fig. 11.8). Crew should prepare to deploy boarding denial measures.

Boarding Denial Ring (0–50 m)

The Master should implement the emergency notification steps and order Crew Muster to retreat to the Citadel. If armed security personnel are deployed, they should shoot to kill. Crew or security should initiate the installed boarding denial measures, which may include any of the following: swirling concertina wire (see Fig. 11.9); hanging anti-boarding concertina wire barrier (see Fig. 11.10); swirling high pressure water hoses (see Fig. 11.11); and water curtain (see Fig. 11.12). Likewise, if safe to do so, "stun" or CN gas grenades should be dropped into the boats as they come alongside. Typically, prior to entering the high-threat area, the ship will have installed double or triple concertina wire and fencing on the starboard and port sides and around the bridge deck (see Figs. 11.13 and 11.14), electrically charged wire affixed to arms mounted on the poop deck (see Fig. 11.15), or mounted the proven-effective guardian antigrappling hook system in the poop deck rail (see Figs. 11.16 and 11.17).

FIGURE 11.6 Armed private security team. *Courtesy of NATO.*

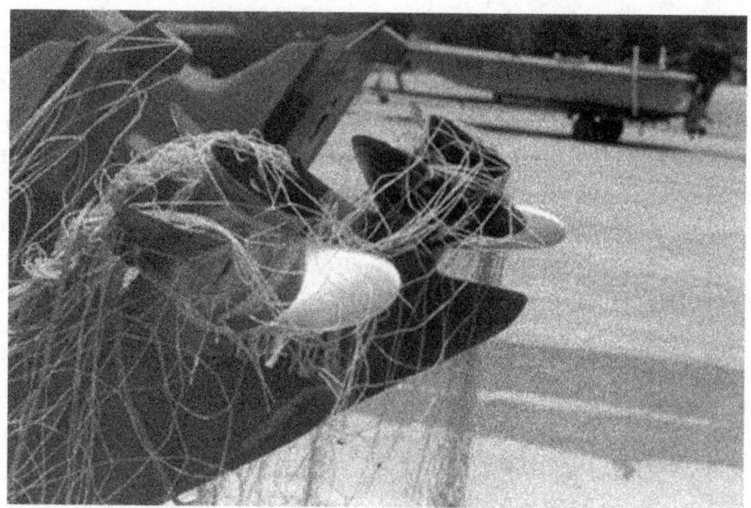

FIGURE 11.7 Boat netting clogs engine propeller. *Courtesy of NATO.*

FIGURE 11.8 Remote-controlled water Cannon. *Courtesy of NATO*

FIGURE 11.9 Whirling razor wire. *Courtesy of NATO.*

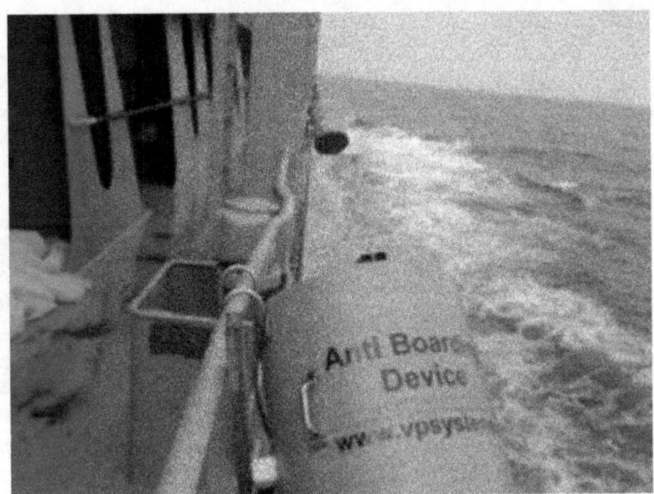

FIGURE 11.10 Deployable hanging antiboarding concertina wire barrier. *Courtesy of NATO.*

FIGURE 11.11 Whirling high pressure water hoses. *Courtesy of NATO.*

FIGURE 11.12 Water curtain. *Courtesy of NATO.*

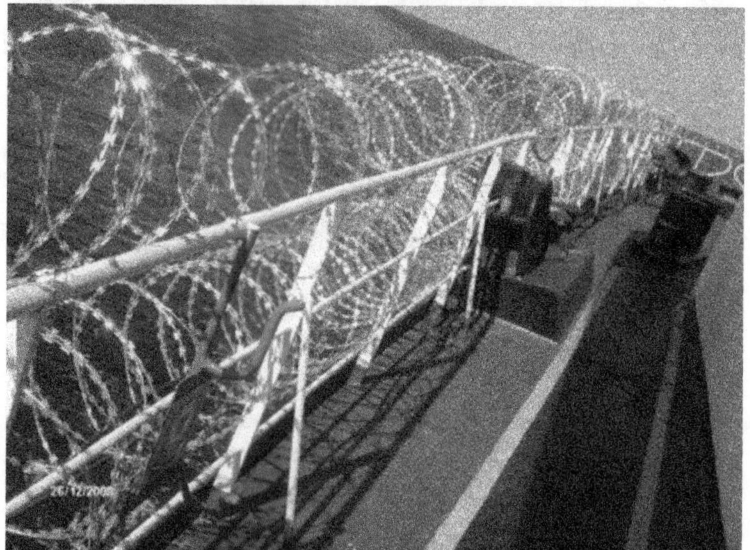

FIGURE 11.13 Concertina Wire on port and starboard sides. *Courtesy of NATO.*

FIGURE 11.14 Fencing on the bridge. *Courtesy of NATO.*

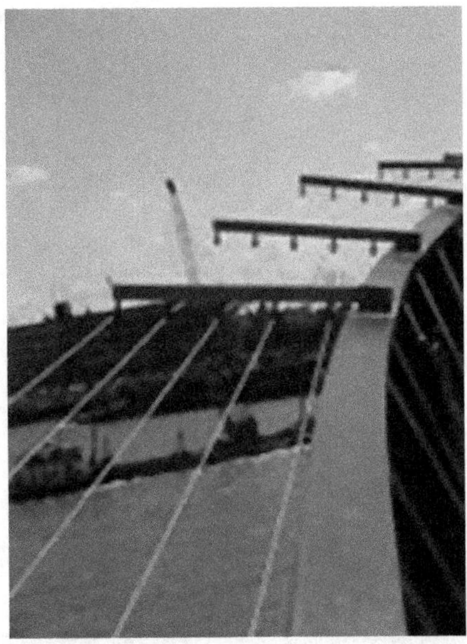

FIGURE 11.15 The "Secure-Ship" high-voltage fence is designed to prevent unauthorized boarding. *Courtesy of NATO.*

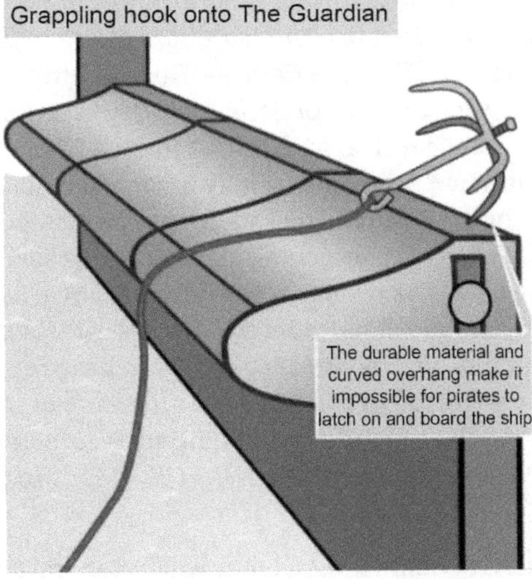

FIGURE 11.16 The Guardian is lightweight, portable, easy to mount and remove, and British Royal Marines who attempted to board couldn't clear the beveled ledge.

FIGURE 11.17 The Guardian was proven successful against Somali pirates.

Citadel

The Citadel is akin to a "panic room" or "safe room" in a house. It is a secure location where Crew can withdrawal to and wait for the calvary (in this case, the Navy) to arrive or the pirates to disembark. A Citadel is defined in BMP4 as *A designated pre-planned area purpose built into the ship where, in the event of imminent boarding by pirates, all crew will seek protection. A Citadel is designed and constructed to resist a determined pirate trying to gain entry for a fixed period of time.* According to the Maritime Security Centre—Horn of Africa, between January 2010 and the first half of 2011, there were 26 cases of Somali pirates boarding ships but unable to take control because the ship Crew were all able to retreat to their Citadel. However, there were also five incidents where Citadels had been successfully breached by pirates—due, in part, to poor construction and location of the Citadel. The Citadel can be located in any room in the superstructure which is fitted with water-tight doors and can be upgraded or reinforced. The Citadel must be prepared in advance of the voyage into a high-risk area, as per the results of the Risk Assessment. *If the Master gives the order to retreat to the Citadel, the ship propulsion needs to be turned off and ship "blacked-out" (power turned off)—a delaying action to the pirates taking control of the ship and intending to sail to a safe haven for them or cargo transit location.*

Before discussing the needed upgrades and equipment to be preplaced there, it is worth noting some important observations from EU NAVFOR's Maritime Security Centre—Horn of Africa, to include:

- "Once the pirates manage to board a vessel they will in general try to make their way directly to the Bridge—usually accommodation doors are locked and the external stairways offer an easier route. Any delaying tactics by blocking access is useful since it will give the vessels crew more time to secure the Citadel and its approaches.
- Pirates cannot operate a vessel without the crew.
- Once access to the Bridge has been gained, the pirates will then systematically search through each cabin and locked compartment gaining access by utilizing small arms fire or any other equipment that they may find on board such as crowbars, fire axes etc.

- Attempts have been made to smoke out the crew from a Citadel, by setting fire to the Bridge and/or accommodation.
- Pirates have been known to force hinges, to use mechanical tools such as disk cutters (if found on board), to breach compartments. They have also attempted to pull off doors.
- Vessels which have locked all doors in the accommodation, and which have effectively secured the inner stairwell doors leading to each deck on board, have in the past generally been successful in delaying the pirates to such an extent that the pirates have been frustrated and departed, or that the delaying tactic has enabled the Naval/Military forces to be given sufficient time to respond and intervene.
- Pirates have been known in the past to use ruse and trickery in an attempt to coerce the crew into voluntarily exiting the Citadel. *It is imperative that all Crew are inside the Citadel, as pirates have threatened to kill captured Crew to force the opening of the Citadel and hostage-taking of the entire Crew.*
- Ensure that all access to the Citadel and the approaches are secure against a sustained physical attack. This includes doors, locks, hatches, portholes/windows and ventilation grilles. Pirates have been known to attempt to gain access to Citadels by forcing locks, by removal of hinges, and by pulling off a door utilizing ships tools. Hinges to any door should be internal, and the door itself should provide a smooth external surface in order to prevent the pirates from taking the opportunity to attach any tools to pull the door off. This may have the added advantage of offering a camouflaged entrance.
- In light of the pirates having been known in the past to try and smoke out the crew, ventilation of the compartment should be considered. In this respect the ventilation should be from a stand-alone power supply and should provide adequate ventilation for the ships entire crew particularly if Citadel procedures involve the vessel 'blacking out.' The inlet for this ventilation should, where possible, be concealed."[5]

As doors, bulkhead walls, and windows of commercial ships are not designed to or capable of stopping 7.62 mm rounds (those used by the AK-47s favored by pirates), one must consider upgrading the structure with ballistic resistant materials—which meet a recognized international ballistic standard. For the Citadel door, one can install a ballistic resistant door, made from steel or a mix of composite and steel, and with a dedicated door frame. For protection via the walls and any windows, ballistic resistant laminated glass or ballistic resistant composite (an aggregate, ceramic, or fiberglass) panels or partitions—think Legos, which connect together and on the inside of the room (room within a room, with option of its own composite door). Composite panels are more lightweight than comparably strong steel, easier to manage, and quicker to assemble, but may be a more expensive alternative. Hopefully, future ship designs will include a dedicated, properly constructed Citadel on all ships.

Inside the Citadel, the following items should be prepositioned and regularly tested and replenished as necessary: independent communications (satellite phone and charger, satellite-based e-mail, preferably with concealed external antenna), list of telephone numbers for notification purposes, a monitor and control stick to observe and manipulate all CCTV cameras (with stand-alone power supply); navigational aids (the routing of a GPS or slave radar feed to the Citadel); medical trauma kit, any required medicines used by Crew; flashlights and extra batteries; fire extinguishers; portable toilets; portable AM/FM radio (and batteries); and sufficient food and water for 3–5 days (time depends on the high-risk area and anticipated military rescue).

Hostage Survival and Rescue

The increase in incidents of hostage-taking by pirates during the past decade requires that crews on commercial ships be familiarized with techniques for surviving a kidnapping by pirates (or terrorists) and properly reacting to a possible rescue operation. Likewise, information contained in a well-prepared ship security plan will provide vital data for operational planners of the rescue team. While there is much written concerning hostage resolution strategies, there are several common basic concepts. One of these—establishing a rapport with the pirates—is demonstrated in a story related by Professor Ed Piper of John's Hopkins University.[6]

Professor Piper was conducting a maritime security seminar in Nigeria when one of the students, a local captain who had previously been taken hostage by pirates in Nigeria's Western Delta State, recounted his experience. The captain stated that after the pirates boarded the petroleum tanker and took him hostage, the pirates instructed him to contact the oil company (the owner of the ship) and ask for a million dollars in ransom. The oil company manager told the captain that he would get back to him. After 2 days of living with the pirates, the captain still had not received a response from his employer and decided to negotiate with the pirates. The captain told Professor Piper's class that he had made the following plea to the pirates:

I am a poor Nigerian and you are a poor Nigerian.

I have a family and you have a family.

I don't have any money and you don't have any money.

The oil company has all the money and they do not care about you or me.

I just want to see my family again and so do you.

Why not just let me and the crew go free?

This negotiation strategy worked! The pirates released the captain and the ship. Most of the best researched information for hostage survival techniques has been extracted from publications of the U.S. military and from the U.S. Department of State. A review of DOD Directive 1300.7 and U.S. Marine Corps Publication MCRP 3-02E 2001, "Individual's Guide for Understanding and Surviving Terrorism,"[7] offers valuable insight into hostage survival techniques, which are equally applicable to our current discussion. Let's review some of the key points in this latter reference:

- Realize that your best chance of escape may be during the first few moments of the incident. (In several cases of commercial ships attacked by pirates at sea, crew members onboard avoided capture by jumping overboard.)
- Observe and gather as much information as possible concerning the number of hostage-takers, their weapons, appearance, tattoos, accents, names, and locations.

- If you are blindfolded, do not attempt to remove your blindfold. It may anger your hostage-takers and result in your death.
- Do not directly challenge or threaten your captors.
- Realize that you will go through a number of phases during your captivity. These phases are anger, denial, regression, and acceptance.
- Establish a rapport with the hostage-takers, but be leery of the Stockholm Syndrome (developing a sympathetic understanding and appreciation for the hostage-takers).
- Focus on survival. Practice good hygiene and, if possible, do exercises to maintain a level of physical fitness. This will help stress reduction during this challenging time.
- Psychologically prepare for the day of rescue and release.
- In the event rescue forces arrive at your location, keep your head down facing the deck and listen for the instructions of the rescue force.
- Realize that you will most likely suffer from posttraumatic stress disorders after this incident. For this reason, you should obtain the services of professional counselor.

A hostage situation aboard a ship provides hostage-takers with a significant advantage over the military and law enforcement hostage rescue teams; however, a well-prepared ship security plan and proper reaction by crew members can play an important role in the successful mitigation of the incident. Accurate intelligence is essential for the rescue force to successfully plan for the liberation of crew and passengers onboard a tanker, cruise ship, or any other type of commercial vessel. The following information, most of which is available in a well-prepared ship security plan, is essential for developing a successful rescue plan:

- Locations of the passageways
- Locations of hatches
- Locations of stairways
- Construction of hull/bulkheads (steel, aluminum, or other material)
- How hatches and portholes open and may be secured
- Access routes to different areas and alternate routes
- Thickness of windows and portholes
- Type of glass utilized
- Height of deck above waterline (freeboard height)
- Type and location of lighting
- Ropes, bumpers, or ladders on the side of the ship
- Boarding ramps in place

All of this information will be gathered, analyzed, and assembled into a set of intelligence reports used to create a hostage rescue plan of the ship. To appreciate the importance of proper reaction on the part of the crew during a rescue operation, let's review a typical rescue scenario, which is discussed in Leroy Thompson's book titled *Hostage Rescue Manual*.[8]

According to Leroy Thompson, once the hostage rescue team has designed and rehearsed its rescue plan, the execution phase will be implemented. Insertion of a rescue team will usually be via fast rope from a helicopter or ascending from an inflatable fast boat. Fast rope insertion directly over the deck of the ship is the most practical insertion method. However, if there are armed hostage-takers onboard the ship, they likely will fire on the arriving rescue forces. For that reason, according to Thompson, it is essential that the rescue forces have a means of providing cover fire during the rescue action. The standard protocol is for a helicopter to approach from the rear, flying at wave top, and sneak in behind the fantail for fast insertion. On the other hand, if the vessel containing the hostages is small, rescue forces can board the ship via a Zodiac or other small boat. Rescue forces utilizing small boats usually insert from the rear. U.S. Navy SEAL Team 6 and the British SAS Special Boat Service are considered experts in this area. Combat swimmers and hostage rescue divers can also be used to gather intelligence or act as part of the rescue force. Some of these personnel might be equipped with assault ladders or telescopic ladders with padded hooks that allow them to be quickly placed on a railing or deck lip.

Thompson states that the rescue force will probably utilize inspection mirrors or tactical video cameras to clear stairwells and passageways aboard ship. It may be necessary to have one or two men crouching or crawling, while others cover them from behind the bulkheads. As the passageways are cleared, it is imperative that the hatches are secured along the route. The hostage rescue team members will usually identify themselves as they enter an area containing hostages. The hostage crew and passengers likely will hear the commands "Hit the deck!" and "Don't move!" It is important that the hostages literally hit the deck and not make any sudden moves.

Hostages must not attempt to take pictures of the rescue team members. It is quite possible that the hostages will be ordered by the hostage rescue force to place their hands on their head and crawl on knees to the hostage rescue force member. Hostages will likely be very briefly questioned by hostage rescue force members concerning the number and appearance of hostage-takers, their spoken language or accents, current locations, weapons, any deployed explosives or booby traps, and position/condition of remaining hostages. Hostages will be searched and their identity verified and may be handcuffed and moved to another area until the situation is secured. The reason for these actions is obvious. Hostage-takers often try to disguise themselves as hostages in order to escape.

If the hostage-takers have placed explosives in the ship, the clearing procedures will take considerably longer. In these cases, it is quite possible that a military *explosive ordinance disposal team* and *explosive detection K-9 teams* will be deployed to the ship. Depending on the scenario, securing the entire ship could take an entire day or longer. After the ship is secured, crew and any passengers taken hostage will be screened and treated by medical professionals and debriefed by government officials. The reaction of hostages and their observations play an important role in the successful mitigation of a hostage-taking incident.

Cargo Container Inspection Techniques

In chapter "Drug Smuggling via Maritime Cargo, Containers, and Vessels," we explored methods used to smuggle drugs in containers and trailers. Now let's review techniques to inspect containers and trailers for contraband and manipulation. Empty containers are inspected in container yards, port terminals, and at the cargo loading location (ie, exporter plant or factory, consolidator warehouse, container freight station, etc.). For the most part, this inspection is conducted by personnel and/or K-9 teams. Personnel conducting the inspection of the empty container or trailer should have the minimum proper tools, which include

- Hammer
- Screwdrivers and pliers
- Portable handheld drill
- Laser measurement meter
- Small inspection mirror
- Flashlights (mini and large)
- Metal probes (short and 5-foot length)
- Fiber-optic scope
- Buster (density reader)

There are seven primary inspection areas of a shipping container, which are noted in Fig. 11.18. When you are initiating the inspection of the empty container, first open the door, step inside, and use your sense of smell. The smell of fresh silicon, soldering, burned metal or material, paint, or other unusual odors may be an indicator of container structure modifications. The presence of human feces or dead animals creates a horrible odor and occasionally is used by contraband smugglers to deter inspectors from

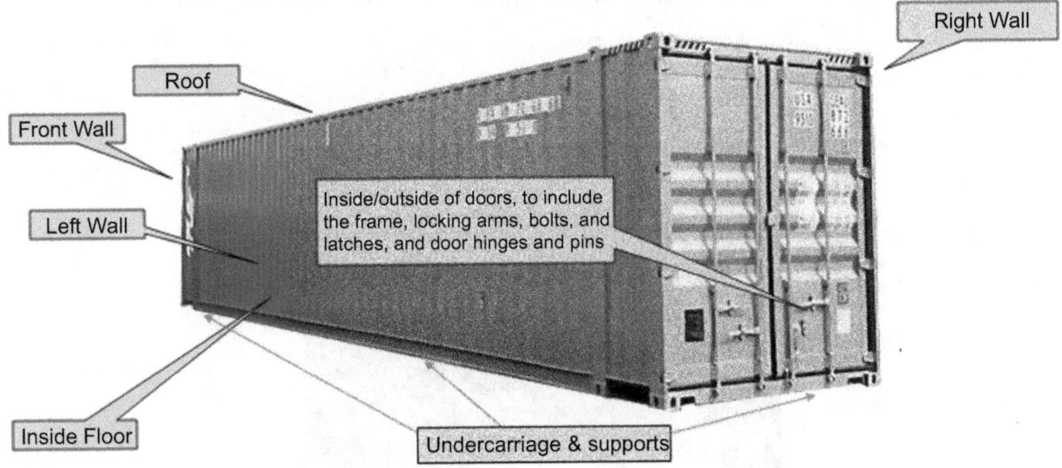

FIGURE 11.18 The seven primary inspection areas of a container.

conducting an inspection. Now let's review basic inspection techniques of the seven primary areas:

- *Front Wall (Interior):* Stand to the rear of the opened right door and view the length of the container on the outside and then the inside. Do the internal and external lengths appear the same? Use the laser meter to check the internal distance against the known container's specification (see Fig. 11.19). Walk to the outside of the container and count the numbers of "ribs" on the right or left external wall. Repeat this process on the inside of the container. Is the count the same? If the count is not the same, there may be a false front wall. View the interior ventilation panels on the front right and left interior walls. Are they missing or partially covered, as in Fig. 11.20? Use the hammer to tap the front wall listening for unusual sounds and the lifting blocks to ensure they are real and not camouflaging a false wall, as shown in Figs. 11.21–11.23. Signs of fresh paint, new silicon, or burn marks may signal a false wall or compartment. Suspicious areas should be further investigated using the buster and/or drill. The interior

FIGURE 11.19 A laser meter can be used to measure the interior length to the front wall.

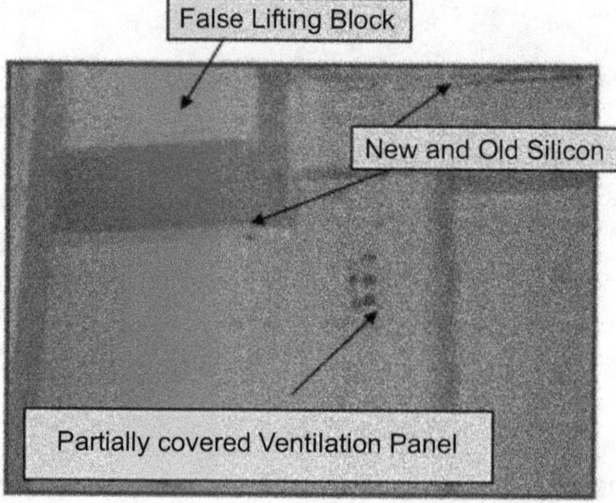

FIGURE 11.20 Indicators of the presence of a false front wall.

front wall of reefers (refrigerator containers) should be checked using a flashlight, inspection mirror, and fiber-optic scope and the reefer system turned on to ensure that the air is circulating unobstructed.

- *Left and Right Walls (Interior):* Use the hammer to tap the walls, high and low, listening for unusual sounds (hollow or solid in areas where it should be the opposite). Observe the panels' rivets for inconsistencies, new replacements, or the presence of screws, as noted in Figs. 11.24 and 11.25. Note new modifications or spot patches on the walls. Areas above arms' reach should be checked, as smugglers will position the contraband at the top of the walls, as shown in Fig. 11.26. Reefer container walls are filled with insulation to maintain the cold air inside the container, so observe for areas where the insulation may have been gutted and contraband or weapons inserted.

FIGURE 11.21 Fake lifting block.

FIGURE 11.22 Real lifting block located behind false wall.

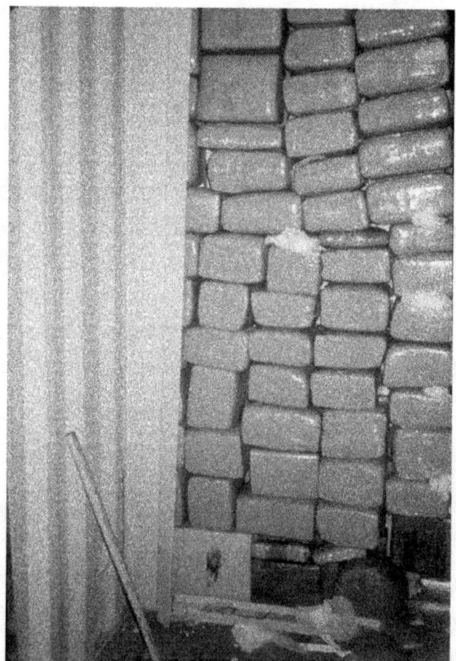

FIGURE 11.23 Removal of the false wall revealed a large load of drugs.

FIGURE 11.24 Note the inconsistency in the rivets.

- *Floor (Interior):* Inspection of the floor begins by viewing the floor from the outside of the container and observing if the floor appears to be raised or altered in any area, such as in Fig. 11.27. Inside, note the floor alignment, uneven floor and wall joints, and new caulking or other bonding materials. A mix of old and new floor materials, loose panels, burn marks from new soldering, new paint over welds, and attempts to make modifications appear dated may be signs of false compartments, as shown in Figs. 11.28–11.30.

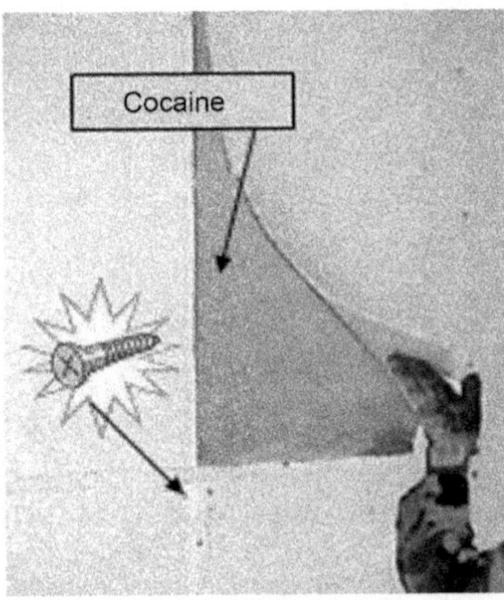

FIGURE 11.25 A screw was detected where typically only rivets are used.

FIGURE 11.26 Drug smugglers affixed the kilos above arms' reach on the assumption that port security would not make the extra effort.

- *Ceiling (Interior):* While many ceilings may appear scarred and scratched, they should have a professionally finished appearance. Bulges, new screws, seams in the ceiling, and rivets and screws which appear new or have been removed merit further inspection. Look for crimp marks, new rivets, caulking, new paint, variations in thickness, mismatched or misaligned ceiling panels, and inconsistent ceiling height above door areas. Don't forget to look at the container floor for evidence of aluminum remnants or other debris left by criminals or terrorists during the ceiling alteration process.
- *Roof (Exterior):* Inspect rooftop rivet lines to ensure uniformity and a professionally finished appearance. While walking the length of the rooftop, look for shoe or boot tracks and feel for the firmness of the roof. Legitimate roofs will have a degree of

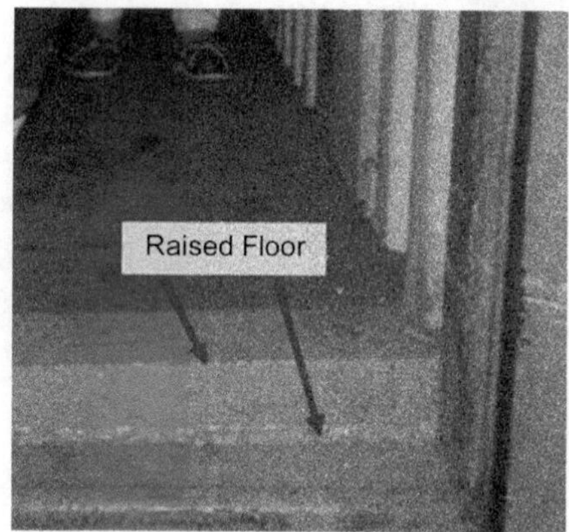

FIGURE 11.27 Note the raised floor.

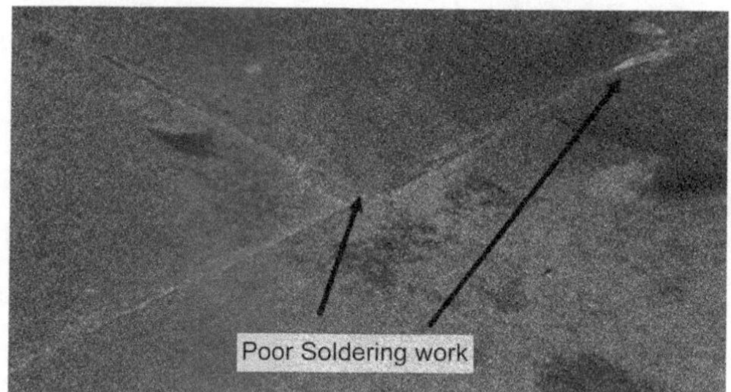

FIGURE 11.28 Marks from soldering raise suspicion.

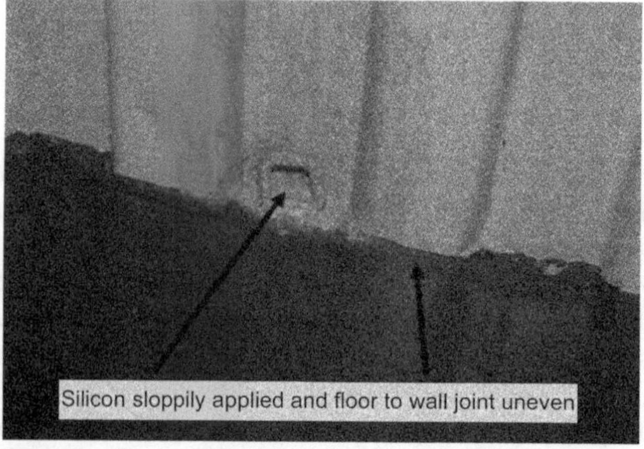

FIGURE 11.29 Check the intersections of the floor to the walls.

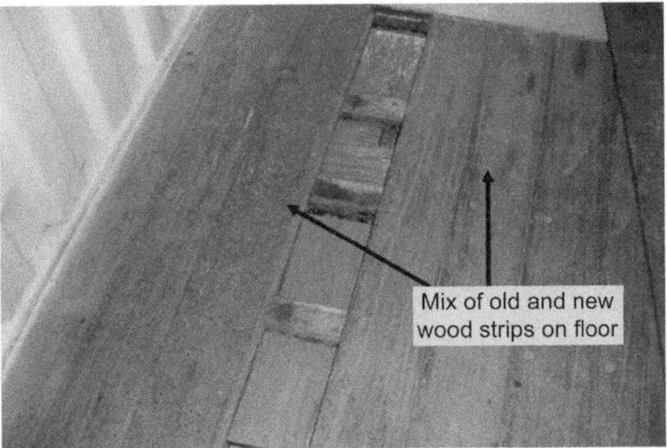

FIGURE 11.30 Different floor panels warrant more intensive observation.

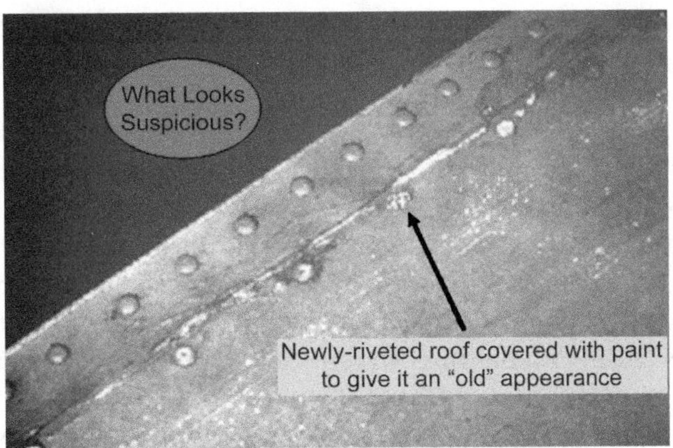

FIGURE 11.31 Indicators of modifications to this roof?

flexibility, while solid areas may indicate a concealed shipment of contraband. Note mismatched and uneven roof panels, unusual crimp marks, and the use of excessive caulking or bonding materials (see Fig. 11.31).

- *Left, Right, and Front Walls (Exterior):* Observe all the panels and front/side posts for unusual patches, repairs, new paint, and modifications. Check the container numbers and markings for alterations. Corner posts, top side rails, bottom side rails, and the upper and lower beams should be scrutinized for new welding, soldering, new painting, and signs of alterations. Reefer containers present a special challenge because a sizable quantity of contraband can be secreted behind the motor and within the airflow canals. As shown in Fig. 11.32, generally there are up to three inspectional panels/plates that can be removed for observation inside via the use of a flashlight, inspection mirror, and/or fiber-optic scope. Suspicious observations may require the removal of the motor, to

FIGURE 11.32 Inspection panels on a reefer container.

check under, to the sides, and behind the motor—which can hold many kilos of illegal drugs and other contraband.

- *Container Doors and Locking Mechanisms:* The right door hardware has long been considered one of the strongest points of oceangoing containers and designed to be the key locking point in container security. However, criminal elements have proven this to be nothing but a myth and a deadly weakness, in spite of its overall strength. Smugglers also have discovered a way to relatively quickly defeat the locking bar handle. Several years ago, when this method first appeared, the perpetrators would use a plain steel chisel and hammer to remove the rivets from the door handle. Now, these rivets are quickly removed by use of an electric drill, and then the rivets replaced with prethreaded hardware—appearing to be a genuine rivets but with nut and bolt (male and female) characteristics or made to hold temporarily with glue—which do not require tools to remove. The container handle can then be dropped out of the handle hub and the door easily opened without disturbing the high security seal (see Figs. 11.33–11.36). Careful observation must be made to the locking bars, handles, hinges, and bolts/rivets for signs of removal, alteration, or modifications. Also, check to ensure that the door hinges have been lock-welded to prevent the undetected removal of the doors from the container (again with the seals still intact). Container doors are made of steel and are structurally sound but have some hollow areas. A standard door is typically heavy; however, altered and contraband-loaded doors will be noticeably heavier. Use the hammer to test the door areas for inconsistent sounds and observe for repainting, spot welds, and the use of grease to camouflage modifications and the odor of illegal drugs. Contraband can be secreted in door panels and the frame, as shown in Fig. 11.37.
- *Undercarriage and Frame:* The undercarriage provides ample opportunities for criminals and terrorists to hide contraband and weapons of various types. As you can

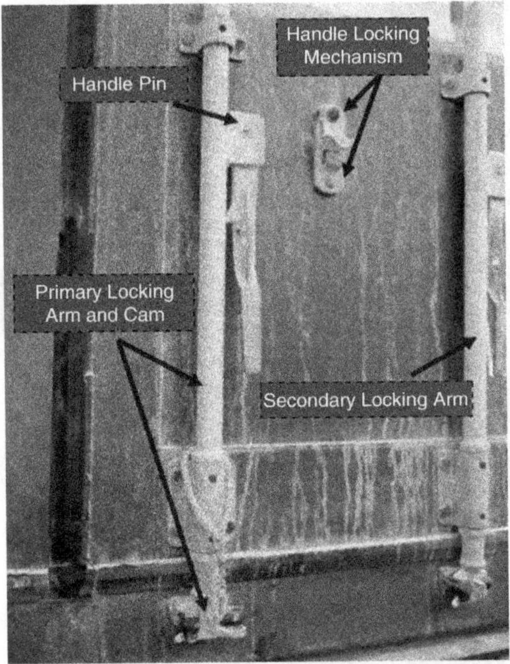

FIGURE 11.33 Points of inspection of the door locking system.

FIGURE 11.34 Areas to check on the locking handle apparatus.

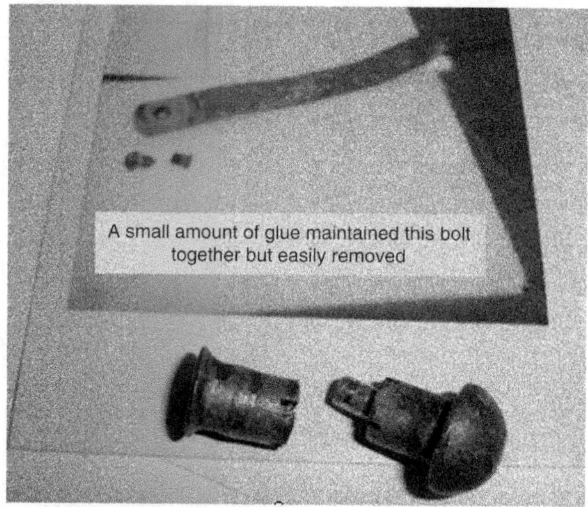

FIGURE 11.35 Bolts held in place with glue.

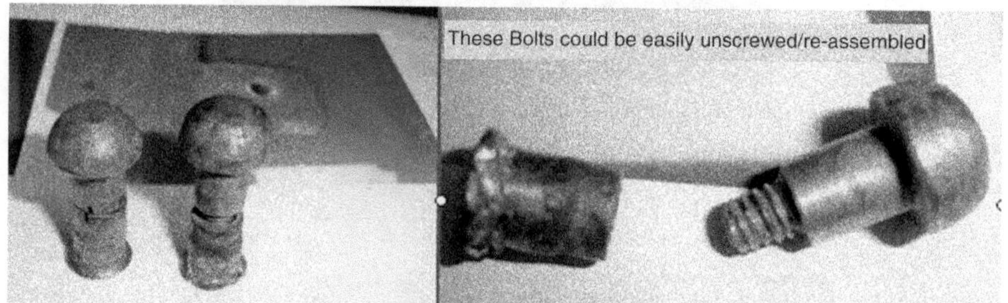

FIGURE 11.36 Smugglers machine-threaded these bolts so they could be removed and reassembled.

FIGURE 11.37 Altered door panels.

FIGURE 11.38 Note unusual modifications, patches, or panels.

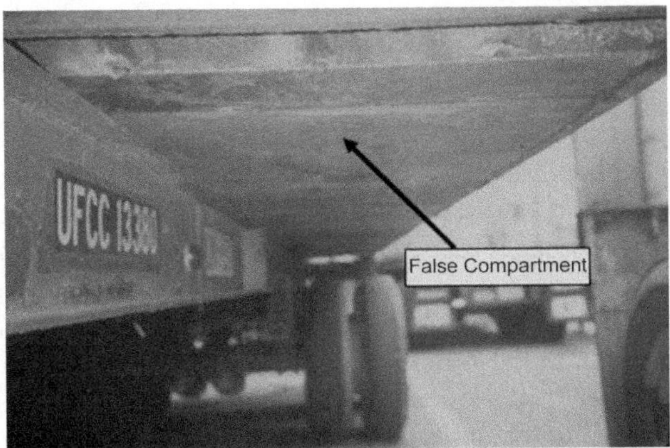

FIGURE 11.39 An inconsistent undercarriage structure should raise suspicion and be closely inspected.

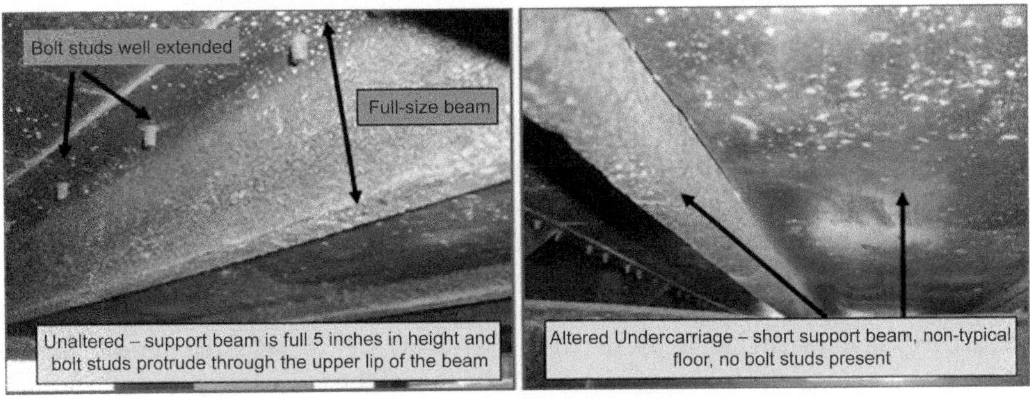

FIGURE 11.40 A comparison of a normal and altered undercarriage.

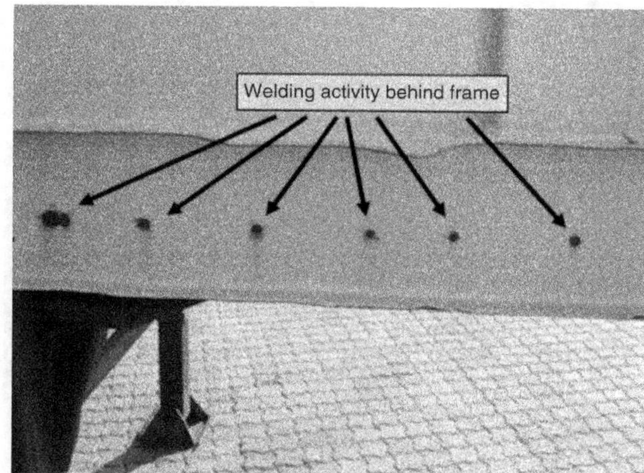

FIGURE 11.41 Unusual burn marks on the exterior walls or upper/lower beams warrant further inspection.

see in Fig. 11.38, containers being moved to the ground, a terminal bomb cart or chassis should be observed during the movement for underside modifications, alterations, new paint, and areas which are clean when the rest of the underside is dirty or greasy. Look for the absence of floor support beams, as shown in Fig. 11.39, or the lack of bolt studs protruding (or barely so) through the floor. Why? Bolts are used to secure the floor onto the beams and will generally protrude an inch or more through the upper side of the beams. The visual absence of floor support beams and bolt studs suggests a modification to the floor (see Fig. 11.40). Support beams should be 5 in. in height, so a short beam requires further inspection. Note the presence of spotted horizontal rust spots or paint touch-ups, as in Fig. 11.41, which may well indicate welding activity occurred to the underside of the lower support rail.

- *Trailers and Chassis:* A trailer, in its most simplistic definition, is a container with a chassis (wheeled frame) permanently attached. Both the trailer wheel base and the chassis, like the container undercarriage, offer many smuggling opportunities to the criminal and terrorist. Some of the favorite areas include the bumpers, air brake tanks, tires, and the fifth wheel. Let's take a closer look. All chassis and trailers have a front and rear bumper structure, similar to the ones on vehicles or trucks.

However, these bumpers are bigger, stronger, and contain voids. Bumpers vary in shape, widths, and height. As you can see in Fig. 11.42, the long center portion of the bumper is hollow and can be used to secrete contraband. Both ends of the bumper have a "lip," either of which can be cut off, contraband inserted, and then the lip rewelded to the bumper (see Fig. 11.43). Fresh paint or recently welded areas on the outside and rear of the bumper are indicators which require closer inspection. A 5-foot long stiff wire cable can be used, as shown in Fig. 11.44, to check the hollow area for secreted items. A hammer can be used to check the integrity of the steel beams of the chassis/trailer and sound the air brake tanks for signs of solid objects inside, as shown in Figs. 11.45 and 11.46. Different colored or new hoses, baffles, and weld marks are indicators of possible alteration. Tires

FIGURE 11.42 Closely check the bumpers of the chassis.

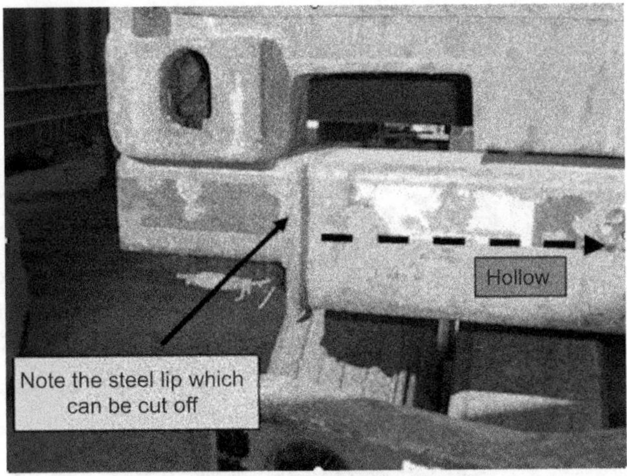

FIGURE 11.43 Inspection point for bumpers.

are used to transport contraband, cash, and other items. When you are inspecting tires, look for signs of abrasions and nicks on wheel hub nuts. If tattle caps are used as a method of detecting tire manipulation, as shown in Fig. 11.47, ensure the serial number is the same number as noted on control documents; however, you need to be cognizant that criminals have mastered the technique of removing tires without taking off the lug nuts or violating the tattle caps. Tap tires with a hammer and listen for the typical echoing sound. If you hear a blunt dead sound, there may be packages or objects inside the tire. If a buster is available, use it to check the density. Lastly, remove some air via the valve stem and smell it for unusual odors. The trailer or chassis attachment platform and pin that attaches to the tractor or Ottawa is called the *fifth wheel*. The fifth wheel housing has a void (hollow) area above both sides of the plate from which the pin protrudes. A flashlight and wire probe or fiber-optic scope is used to ensure that no objects are in the void.

FIGURE 11.44 A metal rod or wire probe can be used to inspect the interior of the bumper.

Use Hammer to check beams and undersides

FIGURE 11.45 A security officer using a hammer to "sound" the undercarriage.

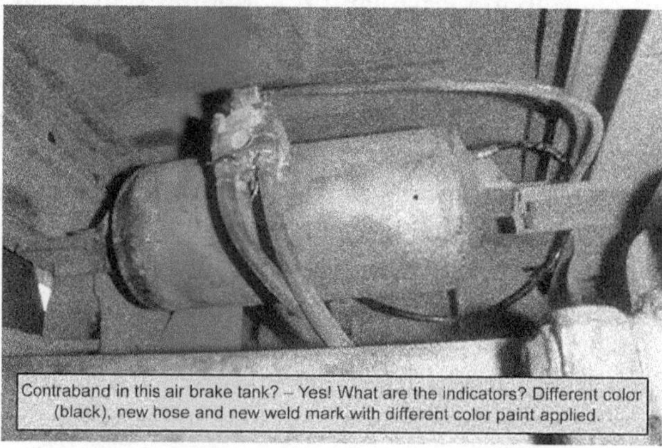

Contraband in this air brake tank? – Yes! What are the indicators? Different color (black), new hose and new weld mark with different color paint applied.

FIGURE 11.46 What is suspicious with this air brake tank?

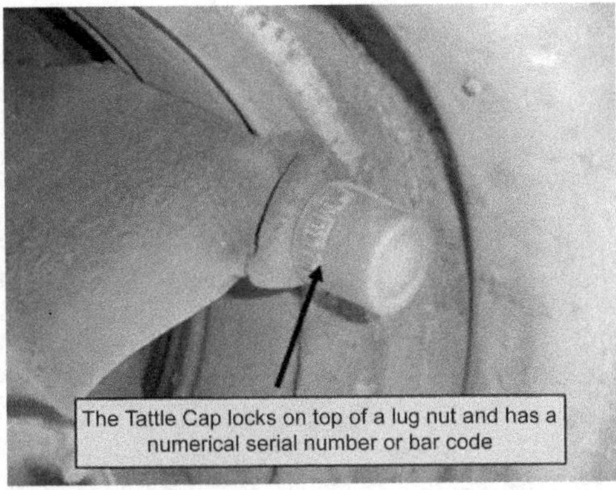

The Tattle Cap locks on top of a lug nut and has a
numerical serial number or bar code

FIGURE 11.47 The tattle cap is easily defeated.

Security Equipment, Systems, and Devices Used to Detect Contraband and Unauthorized Persons in a Container

Technology permits the inspection of containers, for the purpose of detecting various types of contraband and unauthorized persons, in a fraction of the time necessary to conduct such checks manually. Let's review the primary security equipment, systems, and devices in use today.

- *CD-2 Human Occupancy Detector:* This cost-effective handheld unit is battery operated and is attached to a small probe that is inserted between the rubber seal of the doors and the container frame, as shown in Fig. 11.48. The unit measures the carbon dioxide in the container and provides a digital reading on the meter. The location where the probe is inserted must be constantly varied, as criminals and stowaways have attempted to circumvent the effectiveness of the device by covering up the probe with a box or cup, thereby limiting the sampling. Nevertheless, this device is very effective in detecting human smuggling in containers.
- *Radioactive Isotope Identification Device (RIID):* This handheld point-and-shoot device detects the presence of radioactive emissions in field operations where ease of use and simplicity are critically important (as shown in Figs. 11.49 and 11.50). The RIID is a gamma-ray spectrometer that performs three functions in one handheld device. The instrument allows the user to survey (locate radioactive source), measure dose (determine the exposure hazard level), and analyze (identify) nuclides, such as highly enriched uranium (HEU) and plutonium (Pu), for Risk Assessment.
- *Radiation Portal Monitor (RPM):* The Radiation Portal Monitor (RPM) uses advanced passive scanning technology to detect gamma and neutron radiation sources in closed, moving vehicles; containers; and railcars (see Fig. 11.51). The RPM can scan an entire container, trailer, or railcar in seconds, enabling security personnel to screen all traffic passing through a facility or checkpoint with minimal impact on traffic. The two

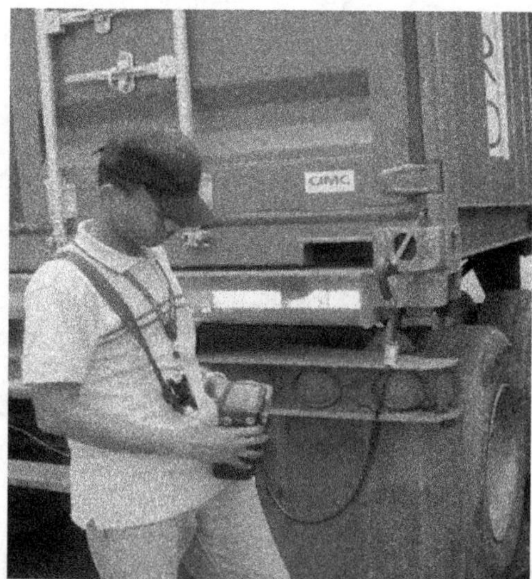

FIGURE 11.48 CD-2 human Occupancy detector.

FIGURE 11.49 Radioactive Isotope identification device.

primary targets are special nuclear material, used in the creation of atomic weapons, and radioactive dispersal devices, which use large commercial radioactive sources coupled with a high explosive to provide a nonnuclear blast but leave significant radioactive contamination.

- *Mobile VACIS Inspection System:* The Mobile VACIS unit consists of a truck-mounted, nonintrusive gamma-ray imaging system that produces radiographic images used in the evaluation of the contents of trucks, containers, cargo, and passenger vehicles to determine the possible presence of many types of contraband (see Fig. 11.52). The gamma-ray imaging system is integrated onto an International Navistar chassis. The onsite typical setup time for a Mobile VACIS system is 10 min. The scanning of a 40-foot

FIGURE 11.50 The radioactive isotope identification device detects the presence of radioactive emissions.

FIGURE 11.51 Radiation portal monitor.

(12.2 m) container can be accomplished in 6 s. Scanning can be performed in a forward or reverse direction on either a stationary or moving object, and a series of containers can be scanned in a single pass using the Quick Save software feature. The gamma image and a video image of the target vehicle are stored in the onboard computer to allow further review and analysis. The Mobile VACIS system utilizes gamma rays as opposed to X-rays, allowing for an overall lower cost, smaller operating space, higher

FIGURE 11.52 Mobile VACIS inspection system.

system reliability/availability, and safer operation. Object penetration is approximately 6.25 in. (15.9 cm) of steel.

- *Relocatable VACIS Inspection System:* The Relocatable VACIS unit utilizes a low-level gamma-ray radiation source to penetrate vehicles and cargo. Absorption of this low-level radiation is progressively measured by a sensitive array of detectors located on the opposing side of the object. The truck, or target, remains stationary during inspection, and the source and detector arrays move synchronously along a set of parallel tracks to cover the target's full length. Absorption data are then fed to a computer, where a digital image is formed and optimized for display on a high-resolution video monitor. The radiographic image is analyzed by the operator, and appropriate steps can be taken if apparent contraband and/or threat objects are present. Further image analysis is available to the operator through the integrated image processing software tools supplied with the system. Image storage, transfer, and recall capabilities are included. The unit typically scans at speeds of about 1 foot (30 cm) a second, allowing for full inspection of a 40-foot (12.2 m) container in less than 1 min. The system is easily relocated, with disassembly and reassembly taking less than a day each.
- *X-ray Imaging System:*This is a compact, high-penetration, high-energy inspection portal that combines small footprint with high throughput. The system comprises a low-dose compact 7.5-MeV X-ray accelerator working in conjunction with a high-efficiency detector array to produce high-resolution, high-contrast images of the target. The inherently low radiation dose produced by the source results in fewer shielding requirements than conventional X-ray units and small radiation restricted area. The system is designed to scan at speeds between 8 and 13 km/h (5–8 mph) and throughput

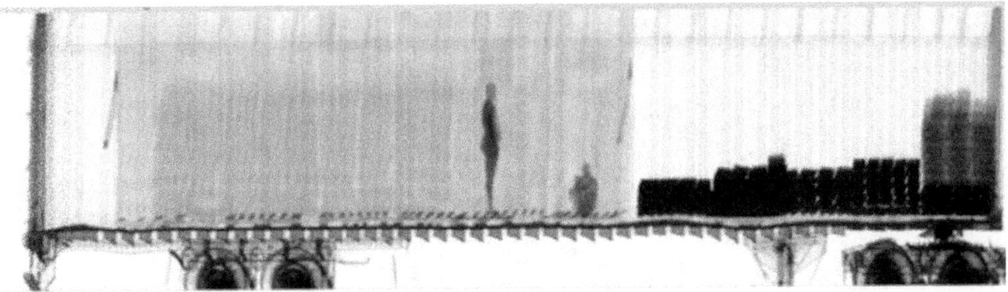

FIGURE 11.53 The X-ray revealed two unauthorized persons (stowaways) inside the container.

rates of up to 150 12-m (40-foot) containers per hour. The system supports imaging of twin 6-m (20-foot) containers in free-flow operation. The system's multiple safety interlocks and low radiation dose—just 2.6 μSv (257 μrem) per scan to cargo at a scan speed of 13 km/h (8 mph)—assure safe, effective operation. The system is designed to scan only the cargo but can also detect humans, such as the stowaways in Fig. 11.53.

Summary

While piracy has become more violent and containers are increasingly utilized by criminals and terrorists, procedures and actions of detection, deterrence, delay, denial, and containment will serve to mitigate the security threats to an acceptable level. Furthermore, technical security equipment, systems, and devices are available to reduce the manpower and time required to conduct inspection and detection functions and increase the effectiveness of the overall mitigation strategy.

End Notes

1. https://www.chathamhouse.org/sites/files/chathamhouse/public/Research/Africa/0713pp_maritimesecurity_0.pdf
2. http://www.mschoa.org/docs/public-documents/bmp4-low-res_sept_5_2011.pdf?sfvrsn=0.
3. http://www.imo.org/en/OurWork/Security/PiracyArmedRobbery/Guidance/Documents/MSC.1-Circ.1334.pdf.
4. http://www.mtisc-gog.org/msg/security-planning/; http://www.mtisc-gog.org/msg/ship-protection-measures/
5. http://www.mschoa.org/docs/secure-documents/industry-citadels-paper-final-3.pdf?sfvrsn=2.
6. Piper, Edward. e-mail message to author, February 17, 2005.
7. http://www.dtic.mil/whs/directives/corres/pdf/130007p.pdf and http://www.usmc.mil/directiv.nsf/6c683984fdle09cc85256c75006e6395/7949e094d6905dd5852572b9006305e9/$FILE/MCRP%20302E%20The%20Individual's%20Guide%20Understanding%20and%20Surviving%20Terrorism.pdf
8. Thompson, Leroy. 2005. Hostage Rescue Manual: Tactics of the Counter-terrorist Professionals, Greenhill Books.

Security Management and Leadership in Seaports

M.A. McNicholas*, E. Piper[¶,§]

*MANAGING DIRECTOR, PHOENIX GROUP; ¶GEORGETOWN UNIVERSITY LAW CENTER; §JOHNS HOPKINS UNIVERSITY

OBJECTIVES

After studying this chapter, you will be familiar with

1. The port security director—leader, manager, and knowledgeable asset to the commercial aspects of the port;
2. The strategic management process, ISO certifications, security metrics management, and the importance of defining job descriptions;
3. Ways to plan and conduct training;
4. The role of intelligence, risk management, and threat assessments;
5. Contingency planning, crisis leadership, and exercises.

According to business management professors Stephen P. Robbins and David A. Decenzo, "management refers to the process of getting things done, effectively and efficiently through other people."[1] Port security management, therefore, is the process of effectively and efficiently protecting things and people in the port, including ships at berth, with the support of senior management, the government, and other people. In this chapter, we review the primary elements of *port security management and leadership*.

The Port Security Director

The *port security director* is to the port security program what a captain is to a ship. The port security director "steers"—by managing and leading—the security program, possibly from its inception, and must possess certain leadership traits and attributes, have the necessary skills and knowledge (specifically of commercial port operations), and take the actions required to accomplish the port security mission. In the preceding chapter, we briefly mentioned the role and functions of the port security director. As with most senior management positions, the port security director needs to be both a manager and leader. Let's look at the latter, leadership, first.

Maritime Security.

One definition of *leadership* is "the process of influencing people by providing purpose, direction, and motivation while operating to accomplish the mission and improving the organization."[2] Much of the business literature and theoretical research on leadership and management, at their roots, is predicated on the experience-based writings of the U.S. military. Military leadership principles and techniques of current business literature likewise have application in port security management. For example, the port security director must effectively communicate the mission and vision of the security program to supervisory personnel and security officers, provide subordinates with clear and focused direction, set tasks that can be measured, and motivate subordinates—through providing positive reinforcement, ensuring discipline, setting the example, and looking out for their welfare—to accomplish the mission of the port security program. These also are keys tenets of military leadership. How do they apply in civilian port security programs?

Let's review a few real-life examples of the application of these leadership principles by the former port security director of Manzanillo International Terminal—Panama.

The first security company Christmas party was a special event for the security officers and supervisors, as the majority of them had never before eaten the main entrée—turkey—or taken their wives to a company Christmas party. When the serving line began to form, the security director instructed the supervisory personnel not to enter the food line until each of their subordinate security officers and families had first received their meal. The security director was the last to eat. While this instruction to the supervisors was contrary to local custom (eg, bosses are catered to first), it was recognized by the security officers as an act of respect and caring for them and served to educate supervisors in the need to think of their personnel before themselves.

Many of the security officers lived in very poor and dangerous housing—including in the attics of decrepit houses—and their family members had to take turns chasing away the rats and watching for poisonous snakes. The security director and staff coordinated a program with the local government which facilitated and fast-tracked the renting or purchasing of low-income housing for these affected security officers. This was a life-changing event for those security officers.

Monthly award ceremonies (held in front of shift formations) were held to recognize the outstanding performance of security officers and K-9 handlers. While the personnel demonstrating exceptional performance were recognized with plaques and cash bonuses, all employees that reached 6 months on the job receive a key chain and pen with the company logo. The value and importance of the awards to the Officer of the Month or K-9 Handler of the Month were evidenced when one entered their homes and observed the certificate or plaque proudly displayed on the wall at the entrance door.

The director had the practice of making checks of security posts at 0200 hours in the morning. During these checks, the director asked each security officer how he liked the company and their supervisors, whether there were any family issues or problems, if he had any recommendations for the security program or company, and generally checked on the welfare of the security officers (that rain gear was available if necessary, coffee, etc.). On more than one occasion, security officers found to be drowsy during these visits either were seen jogging behind the director's vehicle while he made the rounds of the port (a mile or so) or were heard yelling out the count as the security officer performed 50 push-ups. These disciplinary actions were not viewed as demeaning (their fellow security officers cheered and laughed at the spectacles), and the point was made, as evidenced by the low rate of repeat offenders.

What leadership principles do the preceding scenarios describe? Setting the example, ensuring the welfare of subordinate personnel, providing positive reinforcement and recognition of efforts, and ensuring corrective results through immediate disciplinary actions.

The port security director must also be an effective manager, which includes demonstrating technical, organizational, and interpersonal skills. According to Bernard L. Erven, there are five functions of management: planning, organizing, staffing, directing, and controlling. These functions are defined as follows:[3]

- *Planning* is the ongoing process of developing the business' mission and objectives and determining how they will be accomplished.
- *Organizing* is establishing the internal organizational structure of the organization. The focus is on division, coordination, and control of tasks and the flow of information within the organization. It is in this function that managers distribute authority to job holders.
- *Staffing* is filling and keeping filled with qualified people all positions in the business. Recruiting, hiring, training, evaluating, and compensating are the specific activities included in the function.
- *Directing* is influencing people's behavior through motivation, communication, group dynamics, leadership, and discipline. The purpose of directing is to channel the behavior of all personnel to accomplish the organization's mission and objectives while simultaneously helping them accomplish their own career objectives.
- *Controlling* is a four-step process of establishing performance standards based on the firm's objectives, measuring and reporting actual performance, comparing the two, and taking corrective or preventive action as necessary.

In order for the port security director to be successful in his management role, the director must master the implementation and execution of the five preceding functions.

A reference for maritime security (MARSEC) management on a ship or port is the highly stimulating *It's Your Ship: Management Techniques from the Best Damn Ship in the Navy*, by D. Michael Abrashoff. In this book, Captain Michael Abrashoff, USN (Ret.) discusses his tour as commanding officer of the Arleigh Burke-class Aegis guided-missile destroyer *USS Benfold* and the sometimes unusual (for a Navy commanding officer) management techniques he followed to lead his ship. A summary of some of the key management points and their application to port security management follows:[4]

- "See the ship from the eyes of the crew." The crew can provide a valuable perspective of the ship's security issues, problems, and solutions. Look at every security process on the ship and ask the crew if there is a better way. Write down their comments in a journal and then take action on improving the process or operation. This tip also applies to *nonmilitary port security*.

- "Don't just take command—communicate purpose." Traditionally, security officers have a high turnover rate. Do you really know your security officers? Do you know about their backgrounds? Their families? Their aspirations? Do they understand the importance of their jobs as applied to the overall operation of the port? If not, why?
- "Leaders listen without prejudice." Captain Abrashoff met with each person individually and asked three simple questions: What do you like most about the *USS Benfold*? What do you like least? What would you change if you could? Most of these sailors had never even been in a commanding officer's cabin before, let alone asked for their feedback! According to Captain Abrashoff, once they saw that the invitation was sincere, they gave him suggestions for change that made life easier for the whole crew and also increased the ship's combat-readiness ratings. *This technique directly applies to port security management.*
- "Practice discipline without formalism." In many units a lot of time and effort is spent on supporting the guy at the top. The captain relates that anyone on his ship will tell you that he is a low-maintenance commanding officer and that it's not about him—it's about his crew. Those initial interviews set the tone; in his chain of command, high performance is the boss. This means that people don't tell him what he wants to hear; they tell the captain the truth about what's going on in the ship. It also means that they don't wait for an official inspection or run every action up and down the chain of command before they do things—they just do them. Every port is supposed to have a security plan and a set of procedures for all security incidents and emergencies. Are they practical and relevant? Are they effective? Do your security supervisors and security officers know the details of the port security plan and its policies, plans, and procedures? Do they know their role and functions? Do you trust them to do the right thing in an emergency situation? Only you the port security director know the answers to these questions!
- "The best Captains hand out responsibility—not orders." According to Captain Abrashoff, he not only has to train new folks but also has to prepare higher-level people to step into leadership roles. The captain states that if all you do is give orders, then all you'll get are order-takers. What the ship needs is real decision-makers—not people who just sleepwalk through the manual. That means that you have to allow space for learning. As a port security director, do you simply tell security personnel what to do, or do you train them how to do it? There should be two to three people trained for every *key* position. In this way, in case of an emergency, there is always someone qualified to step in and fill a leadership position. The U.S. Army has always advocated this philosophy in the training and development of its commissioned and noncommissioned officer corps, and it has proven to be critically important in combat.
- "Successful crews perform with devotion." According to the captain, at a conference for commanding officers that he attended, more than half of the officers there argued that paying attention to quality of life (QOL) interferes with mission accomplishment. That notion is ridiculous. It doesn't make sense to treat these young folks as expendable, according to Captain Abrashoff. As a port security director, do you take steps to ensure that your supervisors and security officers are equipped with basic

necessities—especially late at night and during inclement weather? Are they being fed properly? Are they physically fit and properly rested? Are they being paid an adequate salary? Do they have medical benefits for themselves and family? Life insurance? Are they able to be contacted by their families in case of an emergency?

In addition to technical expertise and knowledge in MARSEC, it is imperative that the port security director and his staff have a solid understanding of the commercial "business" of the seaport, how it operates, and the functions of port personnel. The port security director and his staff should have spent adequate time with and understand the roles and functions of personnel in the following areas:

- *Administration:* Sales and marketing, accounting, human relations, labor relations, legal, and senior executive staff.
- *Gate and Yard Operations:* Equipment control (dispatching and receiving of containers, tractors, cargo, etc.), yard planning section, equipment operators (top-pick, forklifts, Ottawas, cranes, etc.).
- *Vessel Operations:* Cargo stowage planning, cargo lading, stevedoring.
- *Maintenance and Support:* Container repair, reefer mechanics section, facility maintenance, and computer system and communications sections.

Do the port security director and his staff need to know how to make a sales call, operate the yard management computer system, or operate a gantry crane? No, but they should understand the importance of sales and marketing to the financial health of the port; know the characteristics, capabilities, and any security vulnerabilities of the gate and yard management computer systems; understand the documentation and physical "process chain" for import and export cargo and containers; have observed the operation of all port equipment; and physically toured the interior and all decks of the various types of ships arriving in the port. Neither the port security director nor his staff can be effective if they do not understand and have a working knowledge of the commercial aspects of the seaport.

The Systems Approach, ISO Certifications, Strategic Planning, and Metric Management

The *systems approach* is a "conceptual framework to help organize the subject matter of management and views an organization as a set of interrelated and interdependent parts arranged in a manner that produces a unified whole," according to Professor David A. Decenzo.[5] A port requires an open-systems approach toward security management. The port consists of individual parts constantly responding to changes in the maritime environment and depending on interaction with the environment and stakeholders. As you can see in Fig. 12.1, the diagram of the port of Rotterdam illustrates the systems approach and the *P-D-C-A model* (P-Planning, D-Doing, C-Check, and A-Act) advocated by the International Organization for Standardization (ISO). Ports are the hubs of international commerce and for that reason must be managed efficiently and effectively. This is particularly

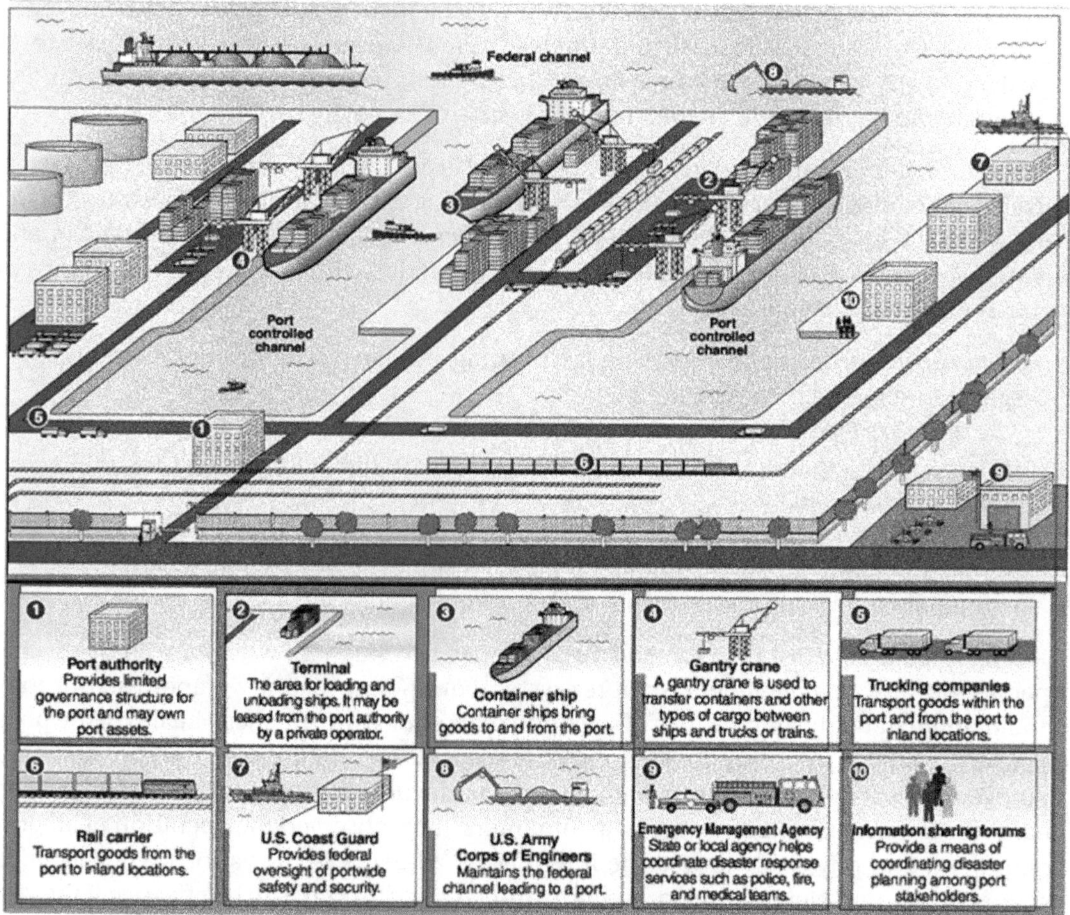

FIGURE 12.1 Stakeholders and assets in a seaport.

true of port security processes and operations. While laws and regulations mandate certain security standards, *total quality management* (TQM) and other quality standards, such as ISO certification criteria, require specific improvements in processes to enhance the productivity and in some cases profitability of port operations. Security is a critical part of each of these elements. For that reason, let's briefly look at developments in Europe regarding MARSEC and *ISO standards.*

The ISO developed two security standards: ISO/IEC 27001 and ISO 28000. ISO/IEC 27001 details IT security management requirements, while ISO 28000 covers security management and the global supply chains. There are various applications and addendums for the 2800 series, which include

- ISO/PAS 20858:2007 (*Ship and marine technology*)—published in 2007, this standard establishes a framework to assist marine port facilities in specifying the competence of personnel to conduct a marine port facility security assessment and to develop a security plan as required by the ISPS Code International Standard, conducting the marine port facility security assessment, and drafting/implementing a port facility security plan (PFSP).

- ISO/PAS 28001 *(Best practices for custody in supply chain security)*—This standard was designed to assist the trade and maritime industries in meeting the best practices outlined in the World Customs Organization Framework.
- ISO/PAS 28004 (*Security management systems for the supply chain*)—This standard provides general guidelines on principles, systems, and supporting techniques to guide users of ISO 28000. This standard references ISO 19011:2002 (*Guidelines for quality and/or environmental management systems auditing*) and the ISO/IEC 17021 (Conformity assessment—Requirements for bodies providing audit and certification of management systems).

ISO/PAS 28000 is the product of the work of ISO technical committees. Another related standard, ISO/TC 8 (*Ships and marine technology*), was drafted in collaboration with other technical committee chairs. Fourteen countries participated in its development, together with several international organizations and regional bodies. They included the International Maritime Organization, the International Association of Ports and Harbours, the International Chamber of Shipping, the World Customs Organization, the Baltic and International Maritime Council, the International Association of Classification Societies, the International Innovative Trade Network, the World Shipping Council, the Strategic Council on Security Technology, and the U.S.-Israel Science and Technology Foundation. Receiving these ISO certifications or "quality labels" for security will be costly. According to a study by Det Norske Veritas (DNV), certifications would affect a total of 4.75 million companies in the European Union states.[6] The initial cost would be 48 billion euros and a further 36 billion euros per year for these companies. Included in this ISO security certification are creation and documentation of security management, provision and further training of personnel, guarantee for physical security (buildings, lighting, and communications), comprehensive access controls (transit, loading, freight sectors, and identification procedures), ensuring procedural security steps (prearrival and predeparture controls of freight, personnel, storage, and documentation), and development and securing of information systems. ISO certification is a detailed and time-consuming investment. Every process and operation of your supply chain security must be analyzed, documented, and approved.

In order to be effective, a security organization must incorporate *strategic planning*. What are some of the questions that come to mind when considering a strategic plan? Think in broad terms. What is the purpose of your security organization? Why does it exist? What are its objectives and goals? How will you know when you reach them? If you don't think this exercise is important, think about what happened with security expenditures across the United States after the September 11 terrorist attacks. Millions of dollars were spent on security technology and various devices and instruments under the auspices of the Department of Homeland Security. What were the results? What was accomplished? In too many cases, these questions cannot be answered! This gives credence to the belief that governments and corporations often throw money at security problems with no real and measurable security strategy. As Department of Homeland Security Secretary Michael Chertoff said, "What should drive our intelligence, policies, operations, and preparedness plans and the way we are organized is the strategic matrix of threat, vulnerability, and consequence. And so, we'll be looking at everything through that prism and adjusting structure, operations, and policies to execute this strategy."

Can you answer the question, "What is the mission of your port security department?" In other words, what are you all about as a security department? Do you understand the mission of senior managers of the port and the senior management of the shipping lines that call on your port? In what ways does your security department's mission statement support and complement their mission statements? This is the first part of the security management process. The next question is, what is your vision for your security department? Where do you see your security department in the next 5 years? What does it look like? Sound like? Feel like? The answer to these questions will drive your hiring, recruiting, training, and budget for the next several years.

Without a mission and vision statement, your security department will always be in reaction mode. You'll find yourself reacting to security threats with whatever resources are available at any given time. Obviously, this is neither an effective nor efficient way to manage a security organization. It will also be difficult to gain new financial resources for your security department when you are unable to explain what you were able to accomplish with the security resources that were already provided to your department.

This leads us to the next topic, *strategic metric management*. There is a critical need to establish *measurable objectives* for your port security department. A few measurable topics to consider include

- If the problem is theft and pilferage, how has your security department reduced the frequency of incidents? What is the decrease in terms a percentage?
- If the problem is stowaways gaining access to ships at your port or terminal, how have your security countermeasures reduced the number of incidents?
- If your port conducted a tabletop exercise or field training exercise, how has your performance as a security department improved?
- If closed-circuit television or security officers have been placed in certain areas, what have been the results of this investment? Are incidents increasing or decreasing? Did you set any goals or objectives for your department in this area?
- Have you surveyed port and ship personnel regarding their perceptions of your security department? How have they rated your performance? Since last year, have comments indicated an improvement or are they deteriorating?
- Have you surveyed the members of your security department? What is their level of satisfaction regarding management and operations? What is the rate of turnover? Is it getting better?
- Are security officers receiving training, promotions, and pay increases?
- What are the rates of criminal incidents at the port and ships while berthed at the port? Did you set any goals for decreasing this rate during the last year?

What is the point of these questions? As a port security director, you must be able to quantify the performance of your port security department. Law enforcement agencies do it every year and justify budgetary expenditures based on this performance. What we have been discussing is called *security metrics management.* According to Dr. Gerald L. Kovacich and Edward P. Haalibozek in their book, *Security Metrics*, a security metrics management program has three parts: data collection (surveys, reports), data analysis, and graphic depiction that tells the story.[7]

While we cannot endorse a product, IRIMS's PPM 2000 is an excellent security metrics data gathering, analytical, and presentation tool to help any port security director and staff measure and evaluate the effectiveness of their department.[8] It is a reality that the port security director must be able to "sell" security solutions to senior management, and the best way to do this is with a visual representation of the security department's performance. IRIMS's PPM 2000 and other incident-reporting management tools provide the port security director with powerful graphs, pie charts, and spreadsheets for presenting professional security reports and briefings to the senior managers and stakeholders of the port.

A Multiorganizational Approach Toward Port Security

In chapter "A Strategic Blueprint for World-Class Seaport Security," we defined a model port security program. Now let's look specifically at a *publicly managed U.S. seaport* and some of the considerations which may require a multiorganizational approach, including the development of a *port security committee (PSC)*. In some U.S. ports, a port police department has been established to work with surrounding law enforcement agencies. For example, the ports of Los Angeles and Long Beach take an integrated, multiagency approach to port security. A partial list of agencies exercising jurisdiction in the port complex include

- Los Angeles Port Police
- United States Coast Guard
- U.S. Customs and Border Protection (CBP)
- Immigration and Customs Enforcement (ICE)
- Los Angeles Police Department
- Los Angeles County Sheriff's Department
- California Highway Patrol
- Los Angeles Fire Department
- Long Beach Police Department

As one of the few police forces in the nation dedicated exclusively to 24-hour port activities, the Los Angeles Port Police are responsible for patrol and surveillance of the Port of Los Angeles and neighboring Harbor Area communities. The LA Port Police are sworn California peace officers and enforce federal, state, and local public safety statutes as well as environmental and maritime safety regulations. Highly regarded among specialized law enforcement agencies, the LA Port Police have as their primary goal maintaining the free flow of commerce and producing a safe, secure environment that promotes uninterrupted port operations. Key components of this port police department are as follows:

- *Port Police Patrol:* Los Angeles Port Police patrol officers are responsible for enforcing all the laws and ordinances within the jurisdiction of the Port of Los Angeles, including its commercial operations; docks and marinas; recreational, residential, and neighboring areas. Patrol officers may also be involved or interface with other programs, such as participation in bicycle patrol, K-9, dive operations, sea marshal operations, detectives, or involvement in narcotics, cargo theft, or antiterrorism task forces.
- *Port Police K-9 Unit:* Canine officers are a vital component of the Port Police. The narcotics detection canines are certified by the California Narcotics Canine Association and are trained to sniff and locate narcotics in any of the thousands of cargo and passenger ships that move through the port each year. The explosive detection canines are specifically trained to sniff out explosive materials and are primarily assigned to patrol cruise ships and the World Cruise Center Terminal.
- *Port Police Dive Team:* Formed in 1989, the Los Angeles Port Police Dive Team serves as an underwater unit that polices the entire port area from the docks to the breakwater. The dive team often assists the U.S. Coast Guard (USCG) to investigate spills, accidents, and suspicious incidents.
- *Cargo Theft Interdiction Program (CTIP):* Formerly known as Cargo CAT (Cargo Criminal Apprehension Team), CTIP is a coordinated multiagency effort responsible for the prevention and investigation of incidents of cargo theft in Southern California. The CTIP partnership includes several major law enforcement agencies at the local, state, and federal levels: Los Angeles Port Police, Los Angeles Police Department, California Highway Patrol, Vernon Police Department, California Department of Insurance, and U.S. Department of Homeland Security CBP.
- *High Intensity Drug Trafficking Area (HIDTA):* The HIDTA is a coordinated antidrug task force that targets drug trafficking in the Ports of Los Angeles and Long Beach. Directed by the Drug Enforcement Agency (DEA), HIDTA is composed of several local, state, and federal law enforcement agencies. This task force replaced the Marine Anti-Smuggling Team (MAST), originally formed in 1994.

Port police officers are assigned to the City of Los Angeles Harbor Department and undergo basic police academy training, followed by field training with a field training officer. They may be assigned to patrol by vehicle or boat. Boat patrols include the enforcement of laws regulating vessel traffic; pollution investigations; handling of navigational hazards; inspections of docks, wharves, marinas, and all port-controlled waterways. Port police officers receive general law enforcement and regulatory assignments designed to promote a safe port. Officers may also independently initiate actions designed to respond to long-term or continuing criminal or safety problems as well as respond to individual criminal activity. Officer duties require considerable public and community contact and cooperation.

In the United States, port security directors are not limited to the services of only local law enforcement in the war against terrorism and criminal activities. The USCG in NVIC 9-02 recommended the creation of a Port Security Committee (PSC). Representatives for each aspect of the safety, security, and commercial interests of the port are encouraged to participate. PSC membership may include

- USCG COTP (chair), air stations, small boat stations, and Maritime Safety and Security Teams
- Federal Bureau of Investigation (FBI)
- Federal Emergency Management Agency (FEMA)
- U.S. Customs and Border Protection (CBP)
- Immigration and Customs Enforcement (ICE)
- Transportation Security Administration (TSA)
- Department of Defense (DoD)
- U.S. Transportation Command (TRANSCOM)
- Military Sealift Command (MSC)
- Military Traffic Management Command (MTMC)
- Environmental Protection Agency (EPA)
- U.S. Department of Agriculture (USDA)
- Animal and Plant Health Inspection Service (APHIS)
- Occupational Safety and Health Agency (OSHA)
- Maritime Administration (MARAD)
- Research and Special Programs Administration (RSPA)
- Federal Railway Administration (FRA)/Federal Highway Administration (FHWA)
- Federal Transit Administration (FTA)
- Army Corps of Engineers (ACOE)
- Local, county, and state police and government officials
- National Guard
- Port Authority Police
- Terminal/Facility Security Force
- Marine Police
- Fish and Wildlife marine units
- Fire departments
- State Department of Natural or Environmental Resources marine units
- State and local health agencies
- State and local occupational safety agencies
- State Transportation Agencies
- Regional Development Agencies/Metropolitan Planning Organizations
- Civil Defense
- Vessel owners/operator security representative
- Facility owner/operators
- Terminal owner/operators
- Labor unions and companies

- Trade organizations
- Recreational boating organizations (yacht clubs, rowing clubs)
- Pilot associations
- Railroad companies
- Trucking companies
- Shipyards
- Tow boat operators
- Marine exchanges
- Industry organizations
- Commercial fishing industry
- Representatives of other facilities within the port having waterside access (eg, refineries, chemical plants, power plants)

PSCs are established to address issues directly involving Maritime Homeland Security (MHLS); however, other committees also operate in the port. Just as legal jurisdictions in the ports are overlapping, some committee responsibilities may overlap. For example, MHLS encompasses national security objectives pertaining to the MTS, including the need to support military operations conducted through the ports by the DoD. These issues have been directly addressed by the Port Readiness Committees (PRCs) and the National Port Readiness Network (NPRN). However, coordination between the PSCs and PRCs is important. Some committees such as the Harbor Safety Committees (HSCs) have subcommittees or ad hoc committees in place already working on port security issues. A Captain of the Port (COTP) may decide to expand HSCs to form port security subcommittees, establish the PSC as a subcommittee of another existing committee, or establish existing PRCs under new PSCs. In the United States, the PSC is led by the relevant COTP. Regardless of the organization, the COTP is responsible for coordinating the MHLS activities of their appropriate committee or subcommittee.

A recommended general organizational structure may be applied to most PSCs. While particular elements of PSC structures may differ from port to port, PSCs may be organized into a tiered organization consisting of a managing board or steering committee, general committee, and ad hoc or standing committees. A general committee of the PSC should be open to participation by all interested port stakeholders. A managing board should be made up of representatives of agencies that the COTP determines have the authority necessary to enact or enforce the scalable activities and procedures decided to be appropriate at each MARSEC level. Managing board members could also include representatives of agencies that have resources that could be utilized in a port security-related function or mission. Ad hoc or standing committees may be made up of people from the general committee. They can work on issues raised by the general committee or by the managing board. The managing board oversees the day-to-day scheduling and operations of the PSC and coordinates the agenda.

Much of the work that the PSC will undertake will involve sensitive security information (SSI). The Department of Transportation has established a new category of information titled SSI. It is not classified material, but it will have some restrictions on its handling and distribution. The Coast Guard's initial procedures for SSI are published in reference (h). The COTP is responsible for developing procedures to protect both SSI and classified information that is developed and used by the PSC. The managing board may consider and evaluate SSI and classified information on behalf of the general committee.

When possible, managing board members should be persons with valid security clearances. Only individuals with appropriate security clearances may have access to classified information. Initially, the full committee (managing board, general, and subcommittees) may meet on a quarterly basis. As chair, the COTP is responsible for notifying all members of meeting logistics. More frequent meetings of the managing board and subcommittees may be held during initial plan development or to respond to special circumstances, significant changes in port operations such as a new dangerous cargo, or to changes in threat levels.

The Importance of Comprehensive Job Descriptions

In the preceding chapter, we discussed in detail the screening, selection, and training of security officers, as well as employees and other persons with access to the port. It is important that the port security director incorporate these personnel policies and procedures into the PFSP/PSP. However, before this employment process can be initiated, the port security director must define a job description for each position.

Why is the job description so important? The answer to this question has a few components. First, the job description will be utilized for recruiting and matching the skill sets of prospective employees with the applicable security job opportunity. Second, it will be used for employee performance evaluations (pay raises, promotional opportunities, etc.). Third, this information will be utilized to design professional development training. And, last, if designed correctly, the job description will directly connect to the strategic security plan for the port facility. The basic functions performed by security officers at different locations are similar. The functions involve the following:

- Protecting people and assets;
- Preventing crimes, fires, and accidents;
- Controlling access;
- Observing and reporting;
- Taking actions to negate or mitigate security breaches and threats.

Most job descriptions are composed of three elements: functions, responsibility and authority, and relationships. The best job descriptions include the following:

- Objective of the position
- Dimension of the position
- Nature and scope of the position
- Position in the organization

- Mission and environment
- Specific functions of the position
- Subordinates' functions
- Primary challenge of the position
- Authority vested in the position
- Relationships
- Requisites
- Primary responsibilities

Sample Job Description for Port Security Captain of Uniformed Security and Port Police

Job Description: Captain

Objective of Position:

To ensure the port protection program of the security department is effective, functional, properly managed, and in compliance with MTSA, C-TPAT, and ISPS Code.

Dimension of the Position:

Directly supervises 5 sergeants and indirectly supervises 28 port security officers.

Nature and Scope of the Position:

Position in the organization: Reports to the port security director. Directly supervises five sergeants.

Mission and environment: Protection of port and tenants' employees and property, 24 hours a day, 365 days a year in a structured regimen with emergency response capabilities.

Specific Functions of the Position:

1. Selects, trains, schedules, and supervises sergeants and indirectly supervises all security personnel.
2. Reviews all security officer-generated or related control documents, forms, logs, and reports.
3. Coordinates corrective and/or maintenance follow-up activities identified by security officers and port supervisors.
4. Analyzes physical protection strategies, assignments, and posts to ensure the work is cost-effective and necessary and recommends appropriate modifications and revisions when appropriate.
5. Develops training programs for security officers to ensure staff is both knowledgeable and productive.
6. Guides, assists, monitors, and councils sergeants to ensure they're motivated, creative, and effective leaders of their subordinates.
7. Subordinates' functions: Sergeants ensure that the necessary security controls are in place and function in each facility through scheduled inspection activity.

Primary challenge of the position: The primary challenge is ensuring that sufficient planning and training have adequately prepared the security staff to effectively respond to and deal with the unusual/emergency/crisis events at any hour in any facility, including, but not limited to, a major conflagration, bombing, earthquake, cyclone, or other natural disaster.

Authority: Captain has the authority to deny access to the facility, deny removal of property, and conversely, if the circumstances warrant, permit acceptable exceptions to the procedure, if in his judgment the action is appropriate. The captain, in conjunction with local law enforcement, Coast Guard, and other public safety organizations, has the authority to help coordinate the evacuation of the facility. Authorized to make arrests and call for public protective assistance.

Relationships: Must be able to effectively deal with law enforcement, employees, vendors, job applicants, business visitors, and all public safety personnel.

Requisites: Knowledge of

1. MTSA, ISPS, C-TPAT, and applicable MARSEC regulations
2. Alarm hardware and operations
3. Port and ship operations
4. Patrol procedures
5. Physical security devices and hardware
6. Security training techniques leadership skills

Experience: A minimum of 3 years' experience as a sergeant in port security or a minimum of 5 years' military or civilian law enforcement supervisory experience whose duties included security and safety training, evaluating performance, scheduling subordinates, handling disciplinary problems, conducting facility surveys or inspections, and preparing written recommendations.

Education: Minimum of 2 years of college with at least 30 credits in security administration and management.

Principal Responsibilities:

1. Ensure that facilities and facility occupants are adequately protected against harm or loss 24 hours a day, 365 days a year.
2. Ensure that the entire port security program is effectively and efficiently supervised by sergeants.
3. Ensure that the sergeants are adequately trained and exercise good leadership skills in dealing with their subordinates.
4. Ensure that a sergeant is officially trained in and knowledgeable of appropriate response strategies to any emergency that presents a serious threat to life or property at the port.
5. Ensure that port security practices are in compliance with MTSA, ISPS, C-TPAT, and supply chain security requirements.

Planning and Conducting Security-Related Training

What is *training*? According to Charles A. Sennewald, in his book titled *Effective Security Management*, training is an educational, informative, skill development process that brings improvement to the anticipated performance through changing comprehensive behavior.[9] The main objective of training is to improve the performance of both the individual and the organization. Training focuses on the acquisition of knowledge, skills, and abilities needed to perform more effectively toward the current job.

What does the port security director need to consider when designing the training curriculum? First, the director needs to review the security department's job descriptions for the various positions, evaluating the knowledge, skills, and abilities needed to successfully perform the job. Second, the director needs to accompany the members of the security department and visually observe them in the performance of their duties. This is to validate that the job descriptions are fully accurate. A record should be made—via photographs or video—of the security officers performing different functions. The photographs and videos would be used for training analysis and, later, training presentation materials. Remember that security officers are like anyone else; they love to see their pictures or their appearance on customized training videos in their own workplace. Third, the director needs to review any local, state, federal, or international security training requirements. Every state in the United States, as well as every country, has a different regulation for security training. In some jurisdictions, there are no security training standards. However, in the commercial maritime community, there are training requirements specified in the MTSA and the ISPS Code Part B. We reviewed these basic requirements and curriculum in chapter "Documentation, Financial Transactions, and Business Entities in Commercial Maritime Transportation." Now let's review considerations the director must contemplate when conducting training.

In order to be effective, training must be designed to match the learning style of the individual learner. Adults learn differently than children. The study of adult learning is called *andragogy* and is based on the assumption that adults want to learn. The styles of learning, according to a University of Illinois resource presentation,[10] are described in the following sections.

Visual/Verbal Learners

Visual/verbal learners learn best when information is presented visually and in a written form. In a classroom setting, they prefer instructors who use visual aids (ie, black board, PowerPoint presentation, etc.) to list the essential points of a lecture in order to provide them with an outline to follow during the lecture. They benefit from information obtained from textbooks and class notes. These learners like to study by themselves in quiet environments. They visualize information in their mind's eyes in order to remember something. The online environment is especially appropriate for visual/verbal learners because most of the information for a course is presented in written form.

Visual/Nonverbal Learners

Visual/nonverbal learners excel when information is presented visually and in a picture or design format. In a classroom setting, they benefit from instructors who supplement their lectures with materials such as film, video, maps, and diagrams. They relate well to information obtained from the images and charts in textbooks. They tend to prefer to work alone in quiet environments and visualize an image of something in their mind when trying to remember it. These learners may also be artistic and enjoy visual art and design. The online environment is well suited for these learners because graphical representations of information can help them remember concepts and ideas. Graphical information can be presented using charts, tables, graphs, and images.

Auditory/Verbal Learners

Auditory/verbal learners learn best when information is presented orally. In a classroom setting, they benefit from listening to a lecture and participating in group discussions. They also benefit from obtaining information from audio tapes. When trying to remember something, these learners will repeat the point out loud and can mentally "hear" the way the information was explained to them. They learn best when interacting with others in a listening/speaking activity. Online learning environments can complement the style of these learners. Although most information is presented visually (either written or graphically), group participation and collaborative activities are accomplished well online. In addition, streaming audio and computer conferencing can be incorporated into an online course to best meet the learning style of these students.

Tactile/Kinesthetic Learners

"Hands-on" activity is best suited for tactile/kinesthetic learners. In the classroom, they prefer to learn new materials in a lab setting where they can touch and manipulate materials. These learners learn best in physically active learning situations. They benefit from instructors who use in-class demonstrations, hands-on learning experiences, and fieldwork outside the classroom. Online environments can provide learning opportunities for tactile/kinesthetic learners. Simulations with three-dimensional graphics can replicate physical demonstrations. Lab sessions can be conducted either at predetermined locations or at home and then discussed online. Also, outside fieldwork can be incorporated into the coursework, with ample online discussion both preceding and following the experience.

Designing Training for Different Types of Learners

The challenge is to incorporate "something for everyone" when designing the training. Let's review some of the considerations offered in Malcolm S. Knowles's book titled *Modern Practice of Adult Education: Andragogy Versus Pedagogy*. They include [11]

- *Lectures* develop knowledge.
- *Reading and research* develop knowledge, develop values, and involve learners actively.

- *Group discussions* develop understanding, develop skills, develop attitudes, develop values, involve learners actively, and obtain feedback.
- *Programmed instruction* develops knowledge.
- *Films and visuals* develop knowledge and develop skills.
- *Case studies* develop understanding, develop skills, develop understanding, develop values, and involve learners actively.
- *Games and simulations* develop understanding, develop skills, develop attitudes, and develop values.
- *Role playing* develops understanding, develops skills, develops attitudes, and develops values.
- *Brainstorming* develops knowledge, develops understanding, and involves learners quickly.
- *Demonstration-practice* develops understanding, develops skills, and involves learners actively.

Additional training design tips and considerations from Russell L. Bintliff's book, *The Complete Manual of Corporate and Industrial Security,*" include:

Plan your training. Good training is well planned.
Determine the standards. How do you successfully perform a gangway watch?
Determine the needs. How does a port security officer check a manifest?
List the objectives. What are the things a security officer should know how to do when responding to a bomb threat?
What are the best techniques? What is the best way to search for a bomb on a ship?
What should be emphasized: skills, knowledge, or information?
What technique is best: performance-oriented lecture, video, or reading assignment?
What are the best resources to provide desired outcomes?
What are our needs: trainers, guest instructors, time? Money?
How will we implement the training program?
How will we present the training standards?
How will we present the objectives?
Will we use a variety of training techniques in our lesson plan?
Will we utilize our training resources effectively?
How will we evaluate the effectiveness of our training?
Will we evaluate outcomes?
Will we look at short-term and long-term performance?
Will we evaluate methods and techniques used? Lecture versus hands-on versus video?
Which method was least effective?
Are there other alternatives?
Do you allow enough time?
Is this a good location for training?
Do you have the right trainer?
Do you have the right training aides?

One of the most important training tools you will need is a good *lesson plan.* Elementary schools and military organizations demand lesson plans. One of the military's highly successful training programs is called the Battalion Training Management System (BTMS), which is based on a recognized training model called Instructional System Design (ISD). In this model, the lesson plan is divided into three primary categories: tasks, condition, and standard. *Tasks* specify exactly what the security officer should do to demonstrate mastery. The *condition* clearly describes and explains under what conditions the task must be performed. The *standard* of acceptable performance describes how well the task must be performed. The following are steps for writing training objectives:

- Begin with an action which is observable and measurable.
- Completely describe the performance.
- Are the objectives clearly relevant to the job or task?
- Be accurate and precise.
- Avoid overlapping other actions.
- State the conditions under which the task must be performed. The condition portions of the training objectives must specify exactly what the personnel will be given and provided to assist them in performing the task; specify restrictions or limitations imposed; identify the tools, equipment, and clothing to be used; list the references and job aides to be used; and describe special physical or environmental conditions.
- State the training standard or acceptable performance. To be usable, the training standard statement must be realistic and attainable, relevant to the job or task, specify clearly the minimum acceptable level of achievement, and be measurable.

As an example, let's review a simple lesson plan for training personnel as the gangway security officer.

Task:

As a gangway security officer covering this post stationed at any port, successfully challenge an unidentified person (during MARSEC level 2/Security level 2) attempting to pass you to gain entrance to the ship. Notify ship and port security about the situation.

Condition:

Given a handheld radio, cell phone, crew roster and security log, clipboard, and pen, assume the role of a shore-based gangway security officer assigned to a commercial ship at a port. It is assumed you are familiar with MTSA and ISPS Code. You will be in a classroom or non-classroom training area. An instructor or fellow student will assume the role of the unauthorized person. An instructor will use another handheld radio and simulate the role of the SSO/master and port security.

Standards:

Gangway security officer must have operable handheld radio, cell phone, and ship roster.

Gangway security officer must challenge all persons attempting to gain access to ship.

Gangway security officer must demand ID from all persons attempting to access ship.
Gangway security officer must verify all persons are duly authorized to board vessel.
Gangway security officer must deny access to unauthorized personnel.
Gangway security officer must provide ship security officer/master and port security with accurate description of the unauthorized person, including

- Race, sex, height, weight, age, color of hair
- Clothing worn
- Distinguishing marks
- Items being carried
- Name on ID—if presented
- Location and direction last seen

Duration of Scenario: 5–10 minutes.

Have class provide feedback on standards compliance after each training performance. Document performance of each student.

Training Resources:

- Two operable handheld radios and two cell phones.
- Clipboard with simulated crew and vendors list.
- Observation/evaluation form for instructor.

Five-Step Instructional Process

1. Preparing:
   a. Preparing the trainer
      i. Know the course content, objectives, materials, and design.
      ii. Review available data about trainees: background, interests, prerequisites.
      iii. Plan ahead, get rest, organize thoughts, and mentally review the day.
   b. Preparing the environment
      i. Check the classroom setup: supplies, materials, training aids.
      ii. Check environmental factors: lighting, heating, space, seating, and safety factors.
   c. Preparing the learners
      i. Put the learners at ease—display a positive attitude.
      ii. Focus learners' interest and attention by showing the value to them in learning the material and relating new learning to past experience and needs.
      iii. Preview course objectives, content, time frames and procedures, and expectations.
2. Delivery:
   a. Effectively use methods, techniques, and training aides to develop content that is appropriate for the subject, course objectives, time constraints, and learners.
   b. Deliver ideas in a logical sequence moving at a pace appropriate to the learners.
   c. Encourage learners' participation and questions, reviewing, and summarizing content.

3. Practicing:
   a. Allow learners to practice under the direct guidance of the trainer; ask effective questions by checking for learners' understanding of new content.
   b. Encourage and support learners, treating mistakes as part of learning process and retrain as needed.
   c. Summarize learning based on course objectives.
4. Testing
   a. Have learners perform a test that is related to course objectives and has standards for minimal performance.
   b. Review test results, providing feedback to learners on their progress.
5. Evaluating
   a. Evaluate the learners regarding their progress toward mastery of content and meeting course objectives, based on learner feedback and trainer objectives.
   b. Evaluate the effectiveness of the training based on learner feedback and trainer observations: content, materials, design, environment, and instruction.
   c. Trainer evaluates his own performance.
   d. Take appropriate action based on the evaluation steps above, such as retraining learners, advising of course design problems, and improving own performance, etc.

Intelligence and Its Role in Maritime Security

What is *intelligence*? There are many definitions of intelligence, and the definition correct for its usage is, in part, determined by the environment and application in which the term is utilized. One definition is, information and/or knowledge about an adversary obtained through observation, investigation, analysis, or understanding. A second definition is, in government and military operations, evaluated information concerning the strength, activities, and probable courses of action of international actors that are usually, though not always, enemies or opponents.[12] Applied in the corporate and business world, the definition of intelligence continues to evolve. Intelligence is an important component of national power and a fundamental element in decision-making regarding national security, defense, and foreign policies.

Intelligence may be strategic (national level, involving broad policy or long-term issues, "big picture") or tactical (focused, operations-oriented, issue- or event-specific, short-term, "street-level"). An example of strategic intelligence would be the collection and analysis of information to develop trends in the proliferation of the use of homicide bombers worldwide. Conversely, an example of tactical-level intelligence would be the collection and analysis of information on a specific targeted narcotics smuggling group which is interested in smuggling heroin in containers from the port of Maraicabo, Venezuela. The means for the collection of information either is "technical" or "nontechnical." Technical means include signals intelligence (SIGINT), measurement and signatures intelligence (MASINT), and imagery intelligence (IMINT). Nontechnical means include human intelligence (HUMINT) and open source intelligence (OSINT).

There are a few "classification systems" used to restrict access and dissemination of intelligence information. The national security classifications—including "Confidential," "Secret," and "Top Secret"—and law enforcement classifications—such as "DEA Sensitive," "Law Enforcement Only," "For Official Use Only"—are used to protect who provided the information (sources), how the raw information was collected (methods), and to whom intelligence reports are disseminated (person duly authorized and with the need to know). The MTSA and 49 U.S.C. 114(s) and 49 CFR 1520.7(k) created a new classification system, SSI. SSI-designated information includes

- Any vessel, maritime facility, or port area security plan required or directed under federal law;
- Maritime security directives issued by the USCG under 33 CFR Part 101.405;
- Navigation Vessel Inspection Circulars (NVICs) issued by the USCG related to MARSEC.

The Intelligence Cycle (Based on the Central Intelligence Agency Model)

1. Planning and Direction

In this step, the entire effort is planned and managed, from identifying the need for data to delivering an intelligence product to a consumer (eg, port security director). It is the beginning and the end of the cycle—the beginning because it involves drawing up specific collection requirements and the end because finished intelligence, which supports policy decisions, generates new requirements. Once the collection requirements are defined, field and operations staffs are tasked with the collection of information through their sources and utilizing available methods.

2. Collection

This step involves the gathering of the raw information needed to produce a finished intelligence report and provide answers to the tasking and collection requirements. Information is gathered from many sources, including "open sources," such as radio reports, newspapers, periodicals, and books; and secret sources of information, such as covert and undercover agents and technical means.

3. Processing

Processing is the converting and organizing of information collected—including translating, decryption, and data reduction if necessary—into a form which is understandable and usable for analysis.

4. All Source Analysis and Production

In this step, all collected information is integrated, evaluated, and analyzed—taking into consideration the source's/information's reliability, validity, access, and relevance—and distilled by analysts into a concise report which addresses the tasking, assesses an issue, and makes judgments regarding implications for the consumer.

5. Dissemination

The last step, which logically feeds into the first, is the dissemination of the final report to the consumers, whose needs initiated the intelligence collection requirement. Additional questions, interest, or a request for clarification by the consumer may result in further collection requirements and tasking, which starts anew the intelligence cycle.

It is impossible to overstate the importance of receiving information that provides an advanced warning of developing or imminent security threats to the seaport or its personnel or assets and the ships and cargoes. In many cases, the success of the port security program depends on the port security director's ability to receive advanced knowledge of planned criminal/terrorist activities and direct or manipulate events so that these situations are mitigated or contained outside the port. It is of the utmost importance that the port security director develops and manages a robust and highly active intelligence program. For the port security director of a private or public seaport, there are three primary sources of information:

- *Government-managed intelligence information (SSI):* This source is generally limited to "unclassified" and "sanitized" analytical reports (such as those generated by Navy and Coast Guard Intelligence Agencies, State Department, etc.) and law enforcement field and analytical reports (CBP, DEA, local and state police, etc.).
- *Open source information:* Newspapers, journals, trade magazines, and private intelligence organizations offer a wealth of information and analysis, both strategic and tactical.
- *In-house intelligence operations:* Developed and directed by senior staff of the port security director, this section of the port security department is charged with the continual tasking, collection, processing, analysis, and dissemination of strategic and tactical intelligence and information from confidential informants (persons associated with or inside criminal and terrorist organizations) and sources of information in the communities and regions surrounding and inside the port (such as truck drivers, warehouse laborers, documentation clerks, cargo surveyors, church groups, labor organizations, news reporters, etc.).

Intelligence information and reports generated from the three preceding sources provide vital support to the port security program in four primary areas:

- Indications and warning of a planned or imminent security threat;
- Background and current information regarding profiles, techniques, and countermeasures of terrorists, criminal organizations, and other entities which may pose a security threat;

- Information concerning compromise of security personnel, port employees, vendors, and port clients by terrorist or criminal organizations, or entities whose efforts may negatively impact on the operation of the port (external labor unions, environmental groups, etc.);
- Information concerning attempts by competitor ports or related entities to collect confidential business data, client and employee information, operational statistics and data, security-related information, and other similar information.

Just how important is the establishment of a successful in-house intelligence operations capability? To shed a little light on the answer, let's review a real-world case conducted by the Phoenix Group's Intelligence Section:

INTELLIGENCE REPORT #PNXXXXXX

***** FLASH *****

SECRET—NOCONTRACT—LIMDIS—ORCON

XX April 20XX, Republic of Panama

ATTN: Port Security Director, Port of XXXX

Managing Director, Phoenix Group

According to a generally reliable source with excellent access, a group of Colombians connected to the terrorist group XXXX are in Colon and are planning to kidnap two unidentified high-level American executives at the seaport. The American hostages will be moved by high-speed boat to Colombia for transfer to XXXX Commandos on standby there and the hostages will be ransomed for $2,000,000 each. According to the source, for an undefined time period the Colombian group has been conducting surveillance of the executives and tracking their daily commute to and from the port. The group knows that the targets do not carry weapons and have no personal security detail. The Colombians are being supported by Colon-based narcotics traffickers and as of this date they have acquired Ingram submachine guns, fragmentation grenades, flashlights, signaling lights, and fuel for an outboard motor. Additionally, today the Colombians requested a stolen 4 × 4 truck from their Colon support group, supposedly for delivery late this evening.

Analytical Comment: The time and date of the planned kidnapping(s) is unknown, however, based on the information above which indicates the terrorists are in their final stage of preparation it seems reasonable to assume that they are planning to execute the operation this weekend or next week. Additionally, our analysis indicates that the probable location of the attack will likely be at XXXX location on XXXX road, due to the absence of cell phone coverage and natural bottleneck created by terrain and road conditions.

After Action Report—

Subsequent to the issue of this report by Phoenix Group Intelligence, protective security detail teams were deployed for the American executives and the National Police were advised. Additionally, Phoenix Intelligence deployed a counter-surveillance team which identified one of the terrorist surveillance vehicles and two suspects. The planned attack was canceled when the terrorists noted the obvious security presence with the executives. The information contained in the report was confirmed by the Panamanian National Police. The "Source" for this report was employed as a XXXX (on the payroll of the Phoenix Intelligence) who had many narcotics trafficking contacts and was contracted by the leader of a narcotics smuggling group to function as the XXXXX for the terrorist group leader while in Panama. The Source was able to overhear conversations and observed the receipt of the weapons. This Source previously provided information concerning a planned attempt to rob the port payroll; information which was validated by the National Police.

Intelligence information and analyses regarding potential security threats or actual incidents are used by the USCG to establish or change MARSEC levels at U.S. ports. Similarly, in foreign countries, the designated authority (usually the National Port Authority, Coast Guard, or Navy) will—as required by the ISPS Code—utilize intelligence information to set the security level in national ports. Local and federal law enforcement can help provide intelligence products to port security personnel dealing with these unique security threats.

The intelligence gathering and analysis are part of a process known as a "threat assessment." A threat assessment identifies adverse events that can affect an entity and may be present at the global, national, or local level. The threat assessment considers the intent of the terrorist agent, capability of the terrorist agents to implement the action, the vulnerability of the target and its impact if damaged or destroyed, and the likelihood of the incident occurring. This information is utilized to establish the appropriate MARSEC level for port facilities and ships.

The USCG has two facilities it calls "maritime intelligence fusion centers" (one in the Atlantic Command and one in the Pacific Command) that provide around-the-clock watch over maritime traffic and developments. These centers monitor areas of interest, track events, follow vessels of interest, provide analysis, and evaluate trends. The two fusion centers provide information to operational units but also work in concert with the USCG Intelligence Coordination Center (ICC) at the National Maritime Intelligence Center in Suitland, Maryland. The ICC is responsible for producing and disseminating intelligence with a USCG perspective to support U.S. policy makers and operations.

Risk Management and Port Security

What are your security priorities at the port? What are the threats you will most likely be facing? How do you reduce the likelihood of these events? These questions, as well as other similar issues, need to be addressed by the port security director to guide the strategic design of the port security program and the deployment of security assets and are answered by conducting an analysis of the risks. Risk management is, in its simplest definition, "an analysis of the security risks and the identification of measures to counter those threats."[13] The USCG, in Enclosure 5 to Navigation and Vessel Inspection Circular

No. 11-02, provides a well-designed risk management methodology and analytical tool. Let's review the concepts of the USCG's multistep risk analysis tool.

Step 1: Potential Threats

To begin an assessment, a facility or company needs to consider attack scenario(s) that consist of potential threats to the facility, under specific circumstances. It is important that the scenario or scenarios are within the realm of possibility and, at a minimum, address known capabilities and intents as given by a threat assessment. They should also be consistent with scenarios used to develop the port security plan (PSP/PFSP). For example, a bomb threat at a major petrochemical facility is one credible scenario. Table 12.1 provides a notional list of scenarios that may be combined with specific critical targets to develop the scenarios to be evaluated in the facility security assessment (FSA/PFSA). The number of scenarios is left to the judgment of the facility or company. An initial evaluation should at least consider those scenarios provided in Table 12.1. Care should be taken to avoid unnecessarily evaluating an excessive number of scenarios that result in low consequences. Minor variations of the same scenario also do not need to be evaluated separately unless there are measurable differences in consequences.

Step 2: Consequence Assessment

For this step a *facility security officer* or company official should determine the appropriate consequence level (3, 2, or 1) determined from Table 12.2. The appropriate consequence level should be based on the "Description" of the facility (ie, one that transfers, stores, or otherwise contains *certain dangerous cargoes* would have a three consequence level).

Table 12.1 Potential Security Threat Scenarios

Typical Types of Scenarios		Application Example
Intrude and/or take control of the target and...	Damage/destroy the target with explosives	Intruder plants explosives.
	Damage/destroy the target through malicious operations/acts	Intruder takes control of a facility intentionally opens valves to release oil or HAZMAT that may then be ignited.
	Create a hazardous or pollution incident without destroying the target	Intruder opens valves/vents to release oil or toxic materials or releases toxic material brought along.
	Take hostages/kills people	Goal of the intruder is to kill people.
Externally attack the facility by...	Launching or shooting weapons from a distance	Shooting at a target using a rifle, missile, etc. to damage or destroy bulk storage tanks, dangerous cargo, etc.
Use the facility as a means of transferring...	Materials, contraband, and/or cash into/out of the country	Facility is used as a conduit for *transportation security incidents*.
	People into/out of the country	

Table 12.2 Consequence Level

Consequence Level	Description
3	*Facilities* that transfer, store, or otherwise handle *certain dangerous cargoes*
2	*Facilities* that 1. are subject to 33 CFR Parts 126 and 154 (other than *certain dangerous cargoes*); 2. receive vessel(s) that are certificated to carry more than 150 passengers (other than those required to comply with 33 CFR 128); *or* 3. receive vessels on international voyages including vessels solely navigating the Great Lakes
1	*Facilities*, other than those above

Table 12.3 Vulnerability Assessment

Availability	The facility's presence and predictability as it relates to the ability to plan an attack.
Accessibility	Accessibility of the facility to the attack scenario. This relates to physical and geographic barriers that deter the threat without organic security.
Organic Security	The ability of security personnel to deter the attack. It includes security plans, communication capabilities, guard force, intrusion detection systems, and timeliness of outside law enforcement to prevent the attack.
Facility Hardness	The ability of the facility to withstand the specific attack based on the complexity of facility design and material construction characteristics.

Step 3: Vulnerability Assessment

Each scenario should be evaluated in terms of the facility's vulnerability to an attack. Four elements of vulnerability could be considered in the vulnerability score: availability, accessibility, organic security, and facility hardness, as defined in the element description in Table 12.3.

The facility security officer or company official should discuss each vulnerability element for a given scenario. The initial evaluation of vulnerability should be viewed with only existing strategies and protective measures, designed to lessen vulnerabilities, which are already in place. After the initial evaluation has been performed, a comparison evaluation can be made with new strategies and protective measures considered. Assessing the vulnerability with only the existing strategies and protective measures will provide a better understanding of the overall risk associated with the scenario and how new strategies and protective measures will mitigate the risk. With the understanding that the facility has the greatest control over the accessibility and organic security elements, this tool takes into consideration only these elements (not addressing availability or facility hardness) in assessing each scenario. The vulnerability score and criteria with benchmark examples are provided in Table 12.3. Each scenario should be evaluated to get an accessibility and organic security score. Then sum

Table 12.4 Vulnerability and Consequence Matrix

		Total Vulnerability Score (Table 3)		
		2	3–4	5–6
Consequence Level (Table 2)	3	Consider	Mitigate	Mitigate
	2	Document	Consider	Mitigate
	1	Document	Document	Consider

Table 12.5 Mitigation Determination Worksheet

Step 1	Step 2	Step 3			Step 4
Scenario/Description	Consequence Level (Table 2)	Vulnerability Score (Table 3)			Mitigate, Consider, or Document (Table 4)
		Accessibility +	Organic =	Total Security Score	
	Once a facility is categorized, the consequence level remains the same.				

these elements to get the total vulnerability score (Step 3 in Table 12.5). This score should be used as the vulnerability score when evaluating each scenario in the next step.

Step 4: Mitigation

The facility or company should next determine which scenarios should have mitigation strategies (protective measures) implemented. This is accomplished by determining where the scenario falls in Table 12.4, based on the consequence level and vulnerability assessment score. Table 12.4 is intended as a broad, relative tool to assist in the development of the facility security plan. "Results" are not intended to be the sole basis to trigger or waive the need for specific measures but are one tool in identifying potential vulnerabilities and evaluating prospective methods to address them. The following terms are used in Table 12.4 as mitigation categories:

- *Mitigate* means that mitigation strategies, such as security protective measures and/or procedures, should be developed to reduce risk for that scenario. An appendix to the facility security plan should contain the scenario(s) evaluated, the results of the evaluation, and the mitigation measures chosen.
- *Consider* means that mitigation strategies should be developed on a case-by-case basis. The facility security plan should contain the scenario(s) evaluated, the results of the evaluation, and the reasons mitigation measures were or were not chosen.

Table 12.6 Mitigation Implementation Worksheet

1	2	3	4	5		
Mitigation Strategy (Protective Measure)	**Scenario(s) that are affected by Mitigation Strategy (from Step 1 in Table 5)**	**Consequence Level (Table 2)**	**New Vulnerability Score (Table 3)**			**New Mitigation Results (Table 4)**
			Accessibility +	**Organic =**	**Total Security Score**	
1.	1.					
	2.					
	…					
2.	…					

- *Document* means that the scenario may not need a mitigation measure and therefore needs only to be documented. However, measures having little cost may still merit consideration. The security plan should contain the scenario evaluated and the results of the evaluation. This will be beneficial in further revisions of the security plan, in order to know if the underlying assumptions have changed since the last security assessment.

Step 5: Implementation Methods

To determine which scenarios require mitigation methods, the facility security officer or company official may find it beneficial to use Table 12.5. The facility or company can record the scenarios considered, the consequence level (Table 12.2), the score for each element of vulnerability (Table 12.3), the total vulnerability score, and the mitigation category (Table 12.4). The objective is to reduce the overall risk associated with the identified scenario. Note that generally it is easier to reduce vulnerabilities than to reduce consequences or threats. To assist the facility security officer or company official evaluate specific mitigation strategies (protective measures), it may be beneficial to use Table 12.6.

The following steps correspond to each column in Table 12.6:

1. For those scenarios that scored as *consider* or *mitigate*, the facility or company should brainstorm mitigation strategies (protective measures) and record them in the first column of Table 12.6.
2. Using the scenario(s) from Table 12.5, list all the scenario(s) that would be affected by the selected mitigation strategy.
3. The consequence level remains the same as was determined in Table 12.2 for each scenario.
4. Reevaluate the accessibility and organic security scores (Table 12.3) to see if the new mitigation strategy reduces the total vulnerability score for each scenario.
5. With the consequence level and new total vulnerability score, use Table 12.4 to determine the new mitigation categories.

A strategy may be deemed as effective if its implementation lowers the mitigation category (eg, from *mitigate* to *consider* in Table 12.4). A strategy may be deemed as effective if the strategy will lower the overall vulnerability score when implemented by itself or with one or more other strategies. For example, for a facility with a consequence level of 2, if a mitigation strategy lowers the vulnerability score from 5–6 to 3–4, the mitigation category changes from *mitigate* to *consider,* and the mitigation strategy is effective. For a facility with a consequence level of 3, the mitigation category would remain the same (*mitigate*) for a similar reduction in vulnerability score from 5–6 to 3–4. It should be noted that if a mitigation strategy, when considered individually, does not reduce the vulnerability, then multiple strategies may be considered in combination. Considering mitigation strategies as a whole may reduce the vulnerability to an acceptable level. As an example of a possible vulnerability mitigation measure, a facility or company may contract for additional security personnel to prevent unauthorized access during times of elevated threat levels. This measure would improve physical security and may reduce the total vulnerability score from a 3–4 to a 2. However, this option is specific for this scenario and also carries a certain cost. A strategy may be deemed feasible if it can be implemented with little operational impact or funding relative to the prospective reduction in vulnerability. A strategy may be deemed partially feasible if its implementation requires significant changes or funding relative to the prospective reduction in vulnerability. A strategy may be deemed not feasible if its implementation is extremely problematic or is cost prohibitive. Feasibility of a mitigation strategy may vary based on the *MARSEC Level.* Therefore, some strategies may not be warranted at *MARSEC Level 1*, but may be at *MARSEC Levels 2* or *3*. For example, using divers to inspect the underwater pier structures and vessel may not be necessary at *MARSEC Level 1* but may be appropriate if there is a specific threat and/or an increase in *MARSEC Level.* Mitigation strategies should ensure that the overall level of risk to the facility remain constant relative to the increase in threat.

Tables 12.7 and 12.8 provide an abbreviated example of how Tables 12.5 and 12.6 would be filled out for a bulk oil facility that is subject to 33 CFR 154 and receives vessels on international voyages. This example assumes that the facility has a fair deterrence capability with respect to organic security but does not have a fenced perimeter to restrict access to the facility.

Contingency Planning: A Critical Part of Port Security Management

After you have defined the risk and considered your prevention and response strategy, it's time to step back and reexamine how you are actually going to respond to a crisis situation. Will you be orderly and efficient, or will it be pure chaos? Let's take a closer look at contingency planning. A contingency plan, drawn up in advance, ensures a positive and rapid response to a changing situation. It often results from scenario planning and may form part of an organization's disaster management strategy. It is an action to be

Table 12.7 Sample Mitigation Determination Worksheet

Step 1	Step 2	Step 3			Step 4
Scenario/Description	Consequence Level (Table 2)	Vulnerability Score (Table 3)			Mitigate, Consider, or Document (Table 4)
		Accessibility +	Organic =	Total Security Score	
1. Gain unauthorized entry into the facility.	2	3	2	5	Mitigate
2. Externally attack the facility with a firearm.		3	2	5	Mitigate
3. Use the facility as a means of transferring people from a ship to a vehicle to illegally enter the U.S.		3	2	5	Mitigate
...		...	...	...	...

Table 12.8 Sample Mitigation Implementation Worksheet

1	2	3	4			5
Mitigation Strategy (Protective Measure)	Scenario(s) that are affected by Mitigation Strategy (from Step 1 in Table 5)	Consequence Level (Table 2)	New Vulnerability Score (Table 3)			New Mitigation Results (Table 4)
			Accessibility +	Organic =	Total Security Score	
1. Perimeter Fence that Restricts Access to the facility (meeting ASIS standards)	1. Intrude to the facility.	2	2	2	4	Consider
	2. Use the facility as a means of transferring people from a ship to a vehicle to illegally enter the U.S.		2	2	4	Consider
	...		...	...	...	...
2...	...		...	...	...	...

implemented only upon the occurrence of anticipated future events other than those in the accepted forward plan. Contingency plans are sometimes called "crisis management plans." The Chinese symbols for crisis represent "danger" and "opportunity." Professor Ed Piper, who teaches contingency planning at Johns Hopkins University, points out that in other words, there is an opportunity to face danger in an organized and predictable fashion in order to save lives.[14] Bob Roemer, an adjunct professor in crisis management at Northwestern University's Medill School of Journalism, in his latest book, *When the Balloon Goes Up*, mentions that an appropriate crisis response strategy could be as follows:[15]

1. Protect people, assets, and the environment.
2. Correct the problem.
3. Connect with key stakeholders.

In Roemer's opinion, the primary focus is to organize people to respond effectively.

How does contingency planning apply to MARSEC? In terms of threat, vulnerability, and consequence, there are few more valuable and vulnerable targets than the U.S. maritime transportation system. Let's elaborate on this concept and the terms:

- *Threat:* While the 9-11 Commission notes the continuing threat against our aviation system, it also states that "opportunities to do harm are as great, or greater, in maritime or surface transportation."[16] From smuggling to piracy, to suicide attacks, to the threat of weapons of mass destruction, the threats are many and varied.
- *Vulnerability:* The U.S. maritime transportation system annually accommodates 6.5 million cruise ship passengers, 51,000 port calls by over 7500 foreign ships, at more than 360 commercial ports spread out over 95,000 miles of coastline. The vastness of this system and its widespread and diverse critical infrastructure leave the nation vulnerable to terrorist acts within our ports, waterways, and coastal zones, as well as exploitation of maritime commerce as a means of transporting terrorists and their weapons.
- *Consequence:* Contributing nearly $750 billion to the U.S. gross domestic product annually and handling 95% of all overseas trade each year, the value of the U.S. maritime domain and the consequence of any significant attack cannot be overstated. Independent analysis and the experiences of 9-11 and the West Coast dock workers strike demonstrate an economic impact of a forced closure of U.S. ports for a period of only 8 days to have been in excess of $58 billion to the U.S. economy, according to Rear Admiral Larry Hereth, USCG, in testimony before the U.S. Senate on May 17, 2005.[17]

Getting the Maritime Community Excited About Contingency Planning: A Brief Look at an Introduction to a Contingency Planning Training Session

According to John's Hopkins Professor Ed Piper,[18] who has trained numerous company security officers, ship security officers, and port security officers on contingency planning as part of the ISPS Code and MTSA compliance, the seasoned ship captains and retired police officers filling these positions benefit from "icebreakers" to spur interest in the topic. So let's review a few of the "icebreaker" exercises utilized by Professor Piper to spike the students' interest:

- *Icebreaker #1:* Divide the class into two sections: natural disasters/acts of God and artificial disasters. Students in each group brainstorm and place their examples on a piece of poster paper. When they complete the assignment, the poster paper is placed on a wall with a piece of tape.

Example of Poster Papers

Artificial Disasters	Acts of God and Nature
1. Arsons	**1.** SARS
2. Pirate attacks	**2.** Typhoon
3. Robberies	**3.** Hurricane
4. Assaults on crew	**4.** Earthquake
5. Oil spills	**5.** Tsunami

The list can continue for pages.

Most PFSPs have a contingency plan section that addresses response measures for the following situations:

1. Fire
2. Explosion
3. Chemical spill
4. Oil spill
5. Mass casualties
6. Cyclone, earthquake, tsunami, or other natural disaster
7. Bomb threat
8. Hostage negotiation/extortion
9. Armed robbery
10. Stowaways/refugees
11. Power failure
12. Communication failure
13. Demonstration/strike
14. Any other threat

We then ask the students: Do you have a contingency plan to deal with each one of these challenges? Usually, the answer is "No." This helps to make the initial case for contingency planning.

- *Icebreaker #2*: Have students list the initials of every agency they might interface with during a crisis situation. The students stay in teams and place initials on a piece of poster paper. When completed, they tape it on the front wall of the training room. Usually, it looks like this:

  USCG
  EPA
  FEMA
  DHS
  FBI

INS
BATF
DOD
LOCAL POLICE
FIRE DEPARTMENT

We then ask the students: Do you have current phone numbers and points of contact for each one? Usually, the answer is "No." This helps to make the second case for contingency planning.

- *Icebreaker #3:* Have students write down the financial losses the port would experience if a crisis situation shut it down for an hour? 8 hours? 1 day? 1 week? 1 month? The students stay in teams and place financial numbers on a piece of poster paper. When the assignment is completed, they tape it on the front wall of the training room. Usually, the numbers quickly jump from thousands to millions. When the port leaders state that they cannot afford to develop a contingency plan and practice for contingencies, these financial numbers make the business case for investing in planning, training, and preparation.

The objective in contingency planning is speedy recovery and return to normal operations as quickly as possible. This also includes financial recovery. Just think of the financial losses to the financial sector, hotel industry, and travel industry after 9-11. This is the first reference to be reviewed when designing contingency plans for ports, facilities, and ships. Everyone remembers the losses in lives and dollars associated with the September 11, 2001, attacks.

The Rand Corporation, in a study on maritime terrorism,[19] expanded the traditional scope of consequences of a maritime terrorist attack to include the following:

1. Fatalities
2. Loss of salary
3. Loss of investments
4. Loss of public services
5. Destruction of ships, facilities, transportation infrastructure; loss of data, life, and injury
6. Disruption in business cycle
7. Lag in delivery, loss of revenue business interruption
8. Increased transport costs
9. Long-term transportation inefficiencies
10. Augmented security measures
11. Increased insurance rates
12. Loss of revenue for government
13. Changes in investment strategies
14. Reduced tolerance for risky investments

15. Loss of future revenue streams
16. Decreased foreign confidence and investment
17. Shift in stock market
18. Decrease in tourism and loss in revenue
19. Unknown political consequences/loss of faith in government

When you examine these losses or consequences in detail, you realize that the root cause can be attributed not only to terrorism but also to all hazards. The FEMA recommends an all-hazards approach in its emergency preparedness policy. FEMA defines an all-hazards approach based on the concept that a preparedness plan features the same principles and actions, regardless of the specific emergency. This means that the plan establishes a single, comprehensive framework for the management of emergency events and applies standardized procedures and protocols. In the public sector, an all-hazards approach enables various parties to communicate and act as quickly and efficiently as possible because they are operating under the same protocols. With this in mind, port security directors can turn to the task of creating a plan that addresses preparedness, response, and recovery operations. A comprehensive approach to emergency preparedness begins to bring a plan into focus.

Looking for Well-Respected Sources and Standards on Contingency Planning

The National Fire Prevention Association (NFPA) is a good source for the port security director in helping to define the standards and best practices of contingency planning. NFPA has been involved in the planning for the response to and mitigation of weapons of mass destruction incidents since the first World Trade Center bombing in 1993. After the Oklahoma City bombing, and reinforced by the events of September 11, first responders have looked to NFPA for information on planning, response, first responder protection, and building and life safety codes and standards. "Many of the areas in which NFPA has been involved with historically have become more important to the country since September 11," says NFPA President James M. Shannon. "Things like firefighter safety, and making sure that first responders have adequate training and clothing and equipment to deal with any emergency, whether it be a HAZMAT emergency or a radiological attack or even traditional sorts of emergencies that they respond day in and day out, things like fires. But I think that there's been a lot more awareness across the country among the first responder community about the need to be prepared for these extraordinary events."[20] NFPA prepared the latest "NFPA 1600, Standards on Disaster/Emergency Management and Business Community Programs" in 2013. This document was developed in conjunction with the FEMA, the National Emergency Management Association, and the International Association of Emergency Planners, and it offers a framework for contingency planning.

Crisis Leadership: Improving Emergency Management and Contingency Planning at Port Facilities

A critical part of contingency planning for ports involves the processes by which the security director plans for and establishes *situational awareness* and *on-the-scene decision-making* in times of emergencies and crises and leads the response to a favorable resolution of the incident or situation. The USCG and DHS, as well as many large organizations, utilize the Incident Command System (ICS) and the National Incident Management System (NIMS) in the crisis and contingency planning, which is the foundation for the National Preparedness System.[21] However, while the ICS and NIMS offer very good planning frameworks and guidelines that should be reviewed and considered by port security directors/manager, they are best suited for large organizations, with a depth and range of resources.

The vast majority of terminals and ports, and their security departments, in the United States are not the size of the New York/New Jersey Port Authority or of Los Angeles/Long Beach and do not have the resources these port can bring to incident planning and response. To the contrary, the majority has a security manager or director, one to less than five persons making up the security support staff, and 4–16 security officers and supervisors who perform the security functions. Their resources are limited, especially in these challenging economic times, and they are among the first targeted in "cost-cutting" reviews by upper management. Moreover, the types of emergencies and crises they will confront likely will have a very short spin-up time, in part because they do not have access to the national and state-level intelligence support to provide advance warning and indications of threats. The recent series of active shooter incidents in the United States and utilization of improvised explosive devices by domestic terrorists at the Boston Marathon dramatically illustrate the need for effective leadership, training and teamwork within security and public safety departments charged with protecting our entire infrastructure, including our port facilities. It is highly probable that the port security team will be the first responders to immediately encounter all hazards including active shooter, HAZMAT disasters, and nuclear, biological, and chemical attacks. For this reason, port facilities need to adopt and adhere to the motto of the USCG, *Semper Peratus*—Always Prepared!

The internal and external environment of the maritime industry continues to change rapidly. Dramatic improvements in communications, technology, processes, and operations mandate that port security managers and supporting organizations constantly reevaluate their current practices and procedures for preventing, responding to and recovering from all-hazard incidents. The effectiveness and efficiency of our mitigation, prevention, and response capabilities are highly dependent on the quality of leadership of the port facility security team. The performances of the team and team leader are a direct reflection of the quality of the training provided to and completed by the organization. In this area of crisis leadership, one has to look beyond the requirements of the USCG, DHS, and International Maritime Organization and seek out other private and government sources and contingency planning and crisis leadership models.

Which organization has the most experience in protecting critical assets and can serve as a repository of lessons learned and best practices? It should come as no surprise that the entity with the most experience in dealing with these scenarios is the U.S. military. Realizing that both law enforcement and security have their roots in the U.S. military, it should come to no surprise that United States military's efforts to review and improve its performance and capabilities to prevent and respond to terrorist attacks around the world has been researched, published, and disseminated to decision-makers in specific military and government leadership positions. Moreover, findings from this research have direct application for port security directors and managers, as well as firefighters and emergency medical technicians. Some of these models and findings include "In Extremis Leadership," the "OODA Loop," and "Team of Teams."

The most *important ingredient to successfully resolve crisis situations is leadership, not management.* As Adm. Grace Hopper, United States Navy (retired), stated during a briefing at the Pentagon during the fall of 1983: "You manage things, you lead people." Advocating a similar philosophy, the United States Military Academy at West Point has made it a practice to only teach evidence-based theories. Under the direction of Brig. Gen. Tom Kolditz, United States Army, this "leadership best practices" model is known as **In Extremis Leadership.**[22] General Kolditz conducted a detailed study focused on how to lead during life-and-death situations with special perspectives from the viewpoints of the followers. Examples included FBI SWAT team leaders, US and Iraqi military officers, and personnel stationed in Iraq and Afghanistan. The research identified several characteristics that helped leaders during these tense times and examined the moderating effect of four human qualities identified in the qualitative study (*self-esteem, self-sacrifice, mental flexibility, and altruism*) on situational awareness and self-efficacy, as they relate to survival criteria in life-threatening situations. "If you look at the research done, the qualities leaders were born with, such as, intelligence and attractiveness, account for 30% of leadership. The rest is through experience and well-designed and delivered leadership training," says General Kolditz, who spent the last 12 years of his career running the leadership program he developed at the U.S. Military Academy at West Point. The application for this research has been expanded beyond the U.S. Army and has value for the number of law enforcement officers, firefighters, emergency medical technicians, military personnel, humanitarian aid workers, and port security personnel working under conditions of physical risk—combined exceeding *5 million people in the United States and 40 million worldwide.* In fact, port security directors/PFSOs/FSOs have the real potential for having to lead in a life-and-death situation and would benefit from the tenets of **In Extremis Leadership**.

One of the most reliable and proven decision-making tools utilized for the survival of the individual and/or the entire organization is the **OODA Loop**, created by Col. James Boyd, United States Air Force (retired). While this concept was initially rejected by the United States Air Force, ironically, the United States Marine Corps immediately adopted the concept and integrated it into its strategy and tactics. What does OODA Loop stand for? The first "O" stands for Observe. The second "O" stands for Orient. The "D" stands for Decide. The "A"stands for Act. First, you need to know what's going on around you

(Observe). Secondly, you assess the situation based on your training and experience (Orient). In a way it is practicing situational awareness. This is where well-developed skill sets or muscle memory comes into play in terms of your reaction speed. This leads us to deciding a course of action and acting without hesitation (Decide). A perfect example would be the case of a security officer confronting an armed intruder. In order to be victorious, the officer must go through the ODDA Loop faster than the armed intruder and take action (Act) or else he will be killed or seriously wounded! Professor Ed Piper relates that he personally utilized the OODA Loop for emergency response planning/training for daycare facility workers on a college campus. The challenge faced by the staff was the overly restrictive command and control model that inhibited the on-the-scene incident team leader from taking corrective action. Acting team leaders with the responsibility for the lives of 70 small children had developed a total dependency on the campus security personnel to tell them what to do. In the event of an active shooter or fire, this habit of freezing in place until one is told what to do by some manager located offsite is life threatening. In order to prevent this paralysis by analysis from occurring, a basic orientation course on the ODDA Loop and a practical application exercise for the team leaders was conducted and this led to an immediate improvement in their ability to practice situational awareness.

The next military model for more effective decision-making and faster response of personnel to rapidly changing environments is the title of Gen. Stanley McChrystal's (U.S. Army retired) recently published New York Times best-selling book, *Team of Teams.* The book detailed the decision-making and leadership concepts developed from an excellent study which focused on the ever-changing nature of Al-Qaeda and the need for the U.S. Army in Iraq to change its organizational design and entire approach in order to outmaneuver these terrorists. General McChrystal concluded that what was needed was a set of small teams—as part of a seamless network—which were able to constantly adapt to the ever-changing environment. These teams within teams were made up of individuals who could perform with general guidance, decentralized leadership and could take the initiative and get the mission accomplished. This philosophy does require a dramatic change in the culture of the organization, this being to push information down to those at the scene of the incident and allow them to resolve the situation without micromanagement. An almost identical challenge is being faced by the first responders today as they attempt to respond to and recover from all-hazards incident; and Ports are no exception. In his book, General Chrystal stated: "Technology has been both a cause of our challenge and a tool for our success." But there was a culture change in the organization that allowed the task force to use it properly. In applying the *Team of Teams* concept to the U.S. Army in Iraq, Gen. McChrystal increased the communications capability of the various organizations working on Iraq, in addition to the U.S. Army, so they could talk to each other on daily basis, each morning face-to-face. He also reorganized the command center to resemble the bullpen of Mayor Bloomberg of New York City. These corrective measures were part of a successful effort to streamline communications in order to evolve teams to be more effective within the U.S. Army and all the organizations that work within Iraq. Now compare these dramatic improvements with the current ability of first responders from various departments to have the capability to even talk to each other (be interoperable with each other) despite the strong recommendations of the United States 9-11 Commission. Port facility security officers/security personnel must have the capability to communicate with other first responders' organizations and with all other entities within the port. General Chrystal goes on to state: "The role of the leader of a Team of Teams is more similar to that of a gardener than the traditional self-confident, omnipotent commander. Leaders who resist the urge to monitor and instruct and leave decisions to those further down the line command get equally good decisions and a more efficient organization."

Researchers Blair and Martindale analyzed active shooter events in the United States 2000 through 2010. Their research, which examined 84 active shooter events, provides fire, EMS, and police administrators with empirical evidence and implications for training and equipment. The researchers also found that many of these events involve the disciplines of police, fire, and EMS responding together but failing to act in a cross-disciplinary manner. Frequently, fire and EMS operate in a "standby" mode and thus do not treat the victims in a timely manner. The current policy, prevalent in most jurisdictions, of EMS personnel not entering the scene until the incident scene or area is declared safe by law enforcement allows victims who have been shot or wounded to continue to bleed and hemorrhage to death. The research also concludes that the active shooter incident scene involves many variables and tasks to include: neutralizing of the shooter(s), securing improvised explosive devices (IEDs), breaching secured areas, and medical interventions such as triage, stabilization, treatment, and transportation of victims. It is painfully obvious there are similarities between the U.S. Army in Iraq and the first responders in the United States.

Dwight D. Eisenhower said, "In preparing for battle I have always found that plans are useless, but planning is indispensable." The intensified speed of critical events mandates the need to reengineer the way we respond to emergency situations. Can the complex and time-consuming "ICS NIMS" model actually be utilized by a small Port during active shooter situations which usually are over in 8–12 minutes? By the time the police arrive, the location is already a mass casualty crime scene. Professor Ed Piper, who also is the Policing Director of a major U.S. University, recently related, "I have personally been involved in several crisis situations in which there was no time to implement ICS/NIMS system." On certain shifts, at different ports, first responder capabilities might be extremely limited thus making it a totally impractical model for emergency management for those particular situations.

In addition, one must consider the increased dangers when security directors and/or senior leadership are unable to deviate from the emergency/crisis management plans or do not take any action until all the facts are in; both instances of inertia may well lead to disastrous consequences. Mistakes are inevitable and the specifics of emergencies rarely confirm to the assumptions made in planning. However, part of the drive to succeed is the desire to confirm the legitimacy of the plan by seeing it succeed. In social psychology terms, the difference between what is happening on the ground and was anticipated in the plan causes cognitive dissonance—two conflicting views on the unfolding events.[23]

Emergency leaders often adopt emerging facts to fit expectations rather than the other way around. The job of the leader is to recognize when circumstances and events don't fit the planned mold and respond appropriately.

The crisis leader at a port facility must have the capability to deviate from a preestablished emergency management plan once he realizes that the scenario he is facing is different from the one that they trained and planned for in the past. In a way, this need for flexibility and adaptation is very similar to that of a quarterback calling an audible during a football game. The play that they had rehearsed and practiced and recorded in the playbook turns out not to be the appropriate response for dealing with this particular situation. It is for this very reason that decision-making tools are absolutely essential to avoid cognitive dissonance and to make the right decisions at the right place at the right time. However, if one does not utilize their crisis management/emergency plan during their decision-making what is the alternative? Is there a practical tool that enables an individual to rapidly assess the situation and take the proper action during a life-threatening event? It is my belief that the *Team of Teams* principles must be applied toward the communication and leadership practices of first responders and port security to quickly and successfully adopt their strategies to the immediate change in environment. Additionally, there is great value in incorporating the tenets of "In Extremis Leadership" and the "OODA Loop" models into the situational awareness and decision-making processes of the port security leadership and the security officers and supervisors.

Testing Training and Planning Through Exercises and Drills

The MTSA and the ISPS Code require that exercises and drills be conducted to test the port security program's response to various types of security incidents and emergencies. We discussed the requirements for exercises and drills and the minimum specific topics in chapter "International and U.S. Maritime Security Regulation and Programs." Now let's discuss the benefits and formats for this testing. Full-scale training exercises involve first responders, port and ship security, and surrounding law enforcement (local, county, city, state, federal, and military) organizations and test their interaction during a well-designed scenario. Are these exercises necessary, and do they have value in identifying conflicts and weaknesses? A 2004 U.S. GAO report described a detailed evaluation of U.S. port security training exercises.[24] The following observations were reported:

- 59% of the exercises raised communication issues, including problems with interoperable radio communications among first responders, failure to adequately share information across agency lines, and difficulties in accessing classified information when needed.
- 54% of the exercises raised concerns with the adequacy or coordination of resources, including inadequate facilities or equipment, differing response procedures or levels of acceptable risk exposure, and the need for additional training in joint agency response.
- 41% of the exercises raised concerns related to command and control, most notably a lack of knowledge or training in the incident command structure.

- 28% of the exercises raised concerns with participants' knowledge about who has jurisdiction or decision-making authority. For example, agency personnel were sometimes unclear about who had the proper authority to raise security levels, board vessels, or detain passengers.

So, it is clear from the analyses by GAO of the exercises that these tests are necessary and do have benefit in identifying critical conflicts and weaknesses.

Port Security Training Exercise Program[25]

Port Security Training Exercise Program (PortSTEP) has been developed to help meet the mandates of the Maritime Transportation Security Act (MTSA). PortSTEP is the result of a partnership between the TSA and the USCG and is designed to provide both maritime and surface intermodal transportation communities nationwide with a series of training exercises to strengthen the nation's ability to prevent, respond to, and recover from a transportation security incident (TSI) in the maritime intermodal environment of the port. The mission of PortSTEP is to

- Develop and implement a port security intermodal transportation security exercise program for use by the national port community;
- Align the program with the nation's infrastructure protection policies and programs;
- Execute through the Area Maritime Security committees;
- Engage all modes of the transportation community to continuously improve readiness;
- Deliver an innovative and comprehensive system of tools and services to strengthen the port security posture;
- Consider the economic impacts of a TSI on affected industries and the movement of people and commerce.

TSA is the lead agency for surface transportation, and USCG is the lead agency for maritime transportation. PortSTEP-participating vendors include Applied Science Associates, Inc. (exercise hardware), Booz Allen Hamilton (exercise services), Community Research Associates, Inc. (training exercises), and UNITECH (training exercises). PortSTEP leverages existing exercise efforts and aligns with current guidance (NVIC, NIMS, HSEEP, etc.) in order to minimize the burden on participants, incorporating concepts such as the following: "Open Team" structure allows participation by government agencies and industry involved in intermodal transportation; "Open Exercise Delivery Strategy" allows integration and coordination with existing exercise programs, resulting in cost savings for participants; and "Comprehensive Outreach Strategy" ensures that the intermodal port community is involved and included in the program.

PortSTEP intends to blend transportation security issues into port exercises where various maritime elements and transportation modes intersect. Most of the issues identified in port security exercises have been operational rather than legal in nature. These issues appeared in most after-action reports the USCG reviewed and in all four of the exercises they observed. While such issues are indications that improvements are needed, it should be pointed out that the primary purpose of the exercises is to identify matters that need attention and that surfacing problems is therefore a desirable outcome, not an undesirable one.

The majority of port security directors, like most managers in the private sector, have a limited amount of time and money for exercises. The good news is that a "tabletop exercise" can allow you to test your security/contingency plan in a safe and controlled environment and within a 2–4-hour time frame. Tabletops are mentioned in the ISPS Code and the MTSA as a cost-effective means for training senior management and security personnel. What is a tabletop exercise? According to the Department of Homeland Security, "a tabletop exercise is a facilitated, scenario-based group discussion."[26] The scenario for the tabletop is chosen on hazards or security threats/incidents likely to occur in the port. Why conduct tabletop exercises? Tabletops do the following:

- Clarify roles and responsibilities: PFSO, CSO, SSO, COP, etc.
- Evaluate port and ship contingency plans.
- Develop effective teamwork before an actual crisis.
- Help to assess resources and capabilities.
- Identify needs and solutions.

According to John's Hopkins Professor Ed Piper,[27] one of the best methods to get started on a tabletop is to follow these steps:

1. Conduct an orientation meeting with proposed participants (CSO, SSO, PFSO, COTP; local and regional police, fire, and emergency medical services; and state and federal law enforcement/military).
2. Conduct a hazard analysis and security threat assessment. (What is the most like problem/crisis to occur at port?)
3. Choose a scenario.
4. Determine whether other agencies need to be invited.
5. Establish objectives.
6. Designate a facilitator.
7. Develop a scenario.
8. Establish a time line and meeting schedule.

The following outline is based, in part, on notes from California Emergency Management, FEMA, and DHS, and will walk you through the developmental process. Experience has shown that it usually takes 1–2 months to develop a good tabletop exercise. Tabletop exercise development steps are as follows:

1. Vulnerability analysis—problem statement
2. Purpose (mission)—intent, what you plan to accomplish
3. Scope—exercise activities, agencies involved, hazard type, geographic impact area
4. Goals and objectives—criteria for good objectives (SMART):
   Simple (concise)

Measurable
Achievable (can this be done during the exercise?)
Realistic (and challenging)
Task oriented (oriented to functions)

5. Narrative—should describe the following:
   Triggering emergency/disaster event
   Describes the environment at the time the exercise begins
   Provides necessary background information
   Prepares participants for the exercise
   Discovery, report: how do you find out?
   Advance notice
   Time, location, extent, or level of damage
6. Evaluation:
   Objectives-based
   Train evaluation teams
   Develop evaluation forms
7. After-action report—compiled using the evaluation reports
8. Improvement plan (IP)—should reduce vulnerabilities

The USCG and surrounding military and law enforcement organizations are usually very interested in participating in tabletop exercises. The port security director, or his designee, should plan on extending invitations 60 days prior to the exercise and request that these government entities also send their alternate emergency management representatives in the event the primary representative is not available when there is a real crisis. The port security director can begin the tabletop development process by gathering the incident command team and brainstorming the most likely threats/scenarios that are faced at the port. Videos and photos should be taken and incorporated into PowerPoint presentations to dramatize the exercise. Evacuation plans, security plans, and crime and unclassified intelligence reports should be assembled and inserted into the tabletop exercise playbooks you will be creating and distributing to all attendees. In some cases, the tabletop exercises will complement larger live-scale exercises for ports conducted by the USCG.

Summary

This chapter on port security management is only a basic primer on the topic. Additionally, you should realize that strong emphasis was placed on the perspective of port security management at U.S. ports, but likewise appreciate that ports in less-developed countries may have minimal available government resources and port security capabilities may be more primitive. Importantly, the chapter focuses on the key areas of leadership and management skills and capabilities; strategic management processes and principles; planning and conducting of training; the role of intelligence, risk management and threat assessments; contingency planning and the ICS; and the development of exercises to test the port security program.

End Notes

1. Robbins, Stephen P. and Decenzo, David. 2004. *Fundamentals of Management,* 4th ed., Prentice Hall.
2. This definition is included in the U.S. Army Field Manual 6–22 (Army Leadership).
3. http://ohioline.osu.edu/~mgtexcel/Function.html#N_1.
4. Abrashoff, Michael, Captain. 2002. *It's Your Ship: Management Techniques from the Best Damn Ship in the Navy,* Warner Books, Inc.
5. Robbins, Stephen P. and Decenzo, David. 2004. *Fundamentals of Management,* 4th ed., Prentice Hall.
6. http://www.bdi.eu/en/Dokumente/Verkehrspolitik/Positionspaper_Security.PDF.
7. Kovacich, Gerald L. and Halibozek, Edward P. 2005. *Security Metrics Management,* Butterworth-Heinemann.
8. See http://www.ppm2000.com/software_IRIMS.htm for details on this tool.
9. Sennewald, Charles A. 2003. *Effective Security Management,* Fourth Edition, Butterworth-Heinemann.
10. http://www.ion.uillinois.edu/resources/tutorials/id/learningStyles.asp.
11. Knowles, Malcolm S. 1970. *Modern Practice of Adult Education: Andragogy versus Pedagogy,* Association Press.
12. U.S. Department of Defense definitions. http://www.answers.com/topic/intelligence-information-gathering
13. Hutchins, Greg. 2006. *Your Future in Risk Management,* American Society for Quality.
14. Piper, Edward. e-mail message to author, April 12, 2004.
15. Roemer, Bob. 2007. *When the Balloon Goes Up,* Trafford Publishing.
16. http://www.9-11commission.gov/report/911Report.pdf.
17. Hereth, Larry, Rear Admiral USCG, May 7, 2005, in testimony before the Committee on Commerce, Science and Transportation, United States Senate.
18. Piper, Edward. e-mail message to author, February 17, 2005.
19. Greenberg, Michael D., Peter Chalk, Henry H. Willis, Ivan Khilko, and David S. Ortiz. 2006. *Maritime Terrorism, Risk and Liability,* Rand Center for Terrorism and Risk Management Study.
20. The National Fire Prevention Association. 2013. NFPA 1600: Standard on Disaster/Emergency Management and Business Continuity Programs, http://www.nfpa.org/
21. https://www.fema.gov/national-incident-management-system
22. http://www.apa.org/news/press/releases/2010/02/battlefield.aspx.
23. Ashkenazi, Isaac, et al., *The Success Paradox: Avoiding the Traps.* Crisis Response Vol. 5 Issue1.https://www.crisis-response.com/archive/?volume=5&issue=20
24. http://www.gao.gov/new.items/d05170.pdf.
25. Port Security Training Exercise Program (PortSTEP), http://www.tsa.gov/what_we_do/layers/portstep/editorial_with_table_0061.shtm
26. http://www.crcpd.org/Homeland_Security/HSEEPv1.pdf.
27. Piper, Edward. e-mail message to author, June 26, 2005.

13

A Networked Response to Maritime Threats: Interagency Coordination

B. Wilson, S.D. Genovese

DEPARTMENT OF HOMELAND SECURITY/UNITED STATES COAST GUARD

OBJECTIVES

After studying this chapter, you will be familiar with

1. The whole-of-government approach in response to maritime security incidents;
2. Challenges presented in defining terminologies used in policies pertaining to coordinated responses to maritime security incidents;
3. National-level Maritime Threat Response Frameworks used by other countries;
4. Key elements and considerations in the formulation of a National-level Maritime Threat Response Framework; and,
5. The U.S. process, as viewed in response to the hijacking of the M/V MAERSK ALABAMA.

Topics addressed in other chapters—transportation, security regulations, vulnerabilities, and legal authorities—represent fundamental elements of the homeland security spectrum. This chapter examines another key portion of the security spectrum by focusing on national-level processes that align civil and military agencies in response to maritime threats.

Whole-of-government processes are a relatively new development in homeland/national security. Maritime security challenges have grown in frequency and complexity, thereby increasing the number of government agencies tasked with, or responsible for, identifying threats and responding. Despite this evolution, governments have generally not sought to consolidate authorities within a single agency. Instead, governments in the past decade have created frameworks that integrate agencies with separate chains of command, authorities, capabilities, and capacities. These frameworks are redefining how governments share information, collaborate, and respond to maritime threats. Issues that could be addressed by a whole-of-government process include the interdiction and prosecution of a potential terrorism threat, a maritime drug trafficker, boarding a foreign-flagged fishing vessel suspected of illicit activity in the exclusive economic zone, or inspecting a container on a vessel possibly contaminated with radiation.

There is no single model for effective national-level maritime response coordination, as each process reflects varying national-level priorities, involved agencies, and organizational structure. Some frameworks solely address maritime security threats, others include environmental or pollution responses. Some constructs are based on response coordination through "unity of effort," others are predicated on the notion of "command and control." Because these interagency frameworks impact how governments respond to maritime threats and homeland security challenges, it is instructive to examine their common themes and best practices.

Terminology Challenge?

The definition of collaboration, coordination, interagency, or whole-of-government is not universally recognized.[1] A study conducted in Europe on "whole-of-government" concluded, "One would search in vain for a uniform definition of such integrated approaches."[2] And in the United States, the term "interagency collaboration" is used more than 20 times in statutes, yet not one includes a definition.[3] A former U.S. Ambassador characterized the interagency as a "mysterious beast."[4]

The Project on National Security Reform defines "interagency space" as the operating area, "below the President and above the Cabinet level departments."[5]

A U.S. Joint Staff document on homeland defense (HD) asserts "interagency coordination" includes "coordinated and integrated activities."[6] And a National Security Enterprise study described the interagency process as seeking "to stitch the seams between (for example, the military, diplomacy, and treasury) institutions and capabilities."[7]

There is no consensus over "unity of effort" either. Within the United States:

- The *Department of Defense* defines this term as "Coordination and cooperation toward common objectives, even if the participants are not necessarily part of the same command or organization—the product of successful unified action";[8] and
- The *Department of State* defines this term as "a cooperative concept, which refers to coordination and communication among U.S. government organizations toward the same common goals for success; in order to achieve unity of effort, it is not necessary for all organizations to be controlled under the same command structure, but is necessary for each agency's efforts to be in harmony with the short- and long-term goals of the mission."[9]

Cooperation, along with collaboration, and coordination represent core elements of a "unity of effort" process, though they are complementary, different concepts. The Government Accountability Office (GAO) defined "collaboration" as "any joint activity by two or more organizations that is intended to produce more public value than could be produced when the organizations act alone."[10] Another GAO study cogently noted, "distinguishing between collaboration and coordination on paper; however, it is complicated in practice."[11]

The interagency (or interministerial) concept is best approached either as a community or in the context of an activity, such as coordination. Interagency coordination frameworks are currently used as a necessary tool for maritime responses by bringing together different agencies within a government to share information, identify courses of action, and collectively respond in the most effective and efficient means available.

National-Level Maritime Threat Response Frameworks

Civil and military agencies now share response responsibilities to threats posed by maritime drug smuggling, migrant trafficking, maritime oil and fuel smuggling, piracy, terrorism, and the proliferation of weapons of mass destruction. Whole-of-government frameworks have been adopted, in part, to replace ad hoc processes and best position those responding to threats with timely information, integration of resources, and a complete situational picture. A study by the Government Accountability Office on piracy, which identified the number of U.S. agencies involved in the response, highlights the coordination imperative (Fig. 13.1).[12]

Interest in whole-of-government maritime response frameworks spans the globe. In Pakistan, for example, Chief of Naval Staff Admiral Muhammad Asif Sandila remarked that multiple agencies in different ministries are concerned with maritime security.[13] "...Information blockage, duplication of efforts and the resultant uncoordinated response

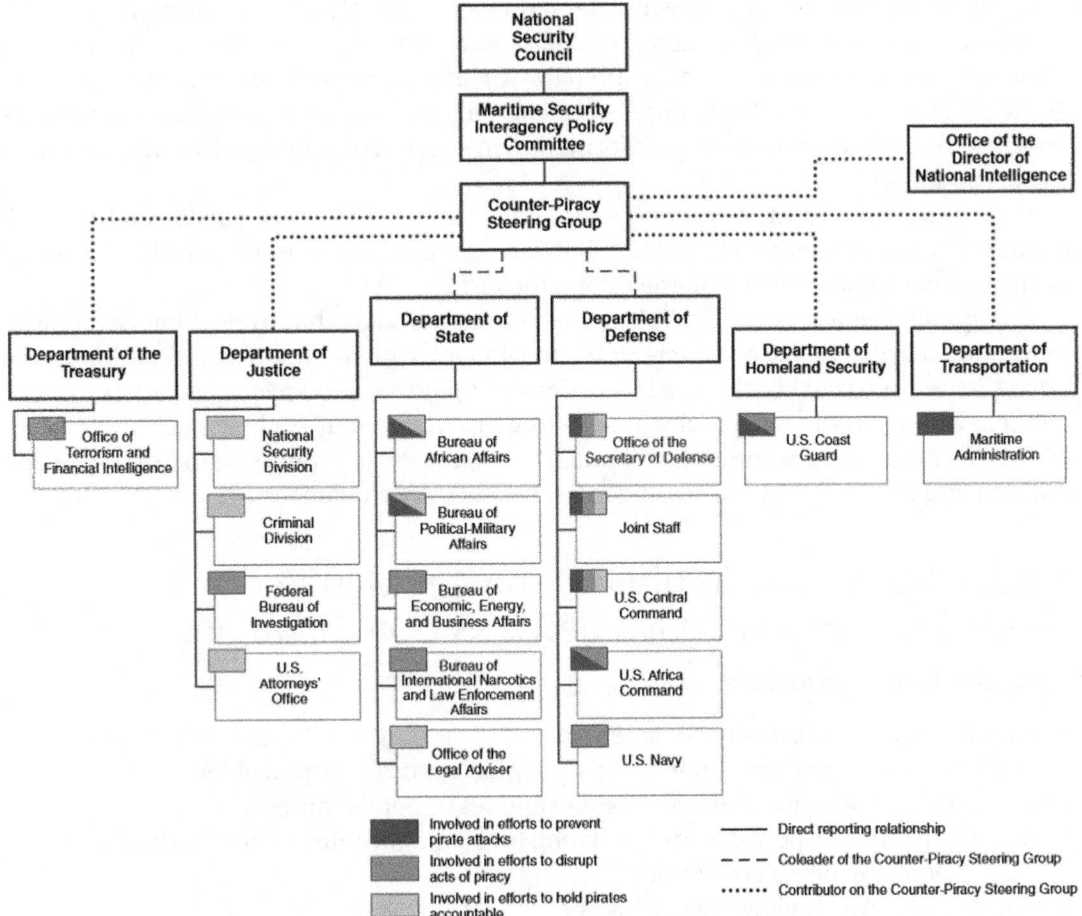

FIGURE 13.1 U.S. Agencies involved in the response to piracy off the Horn of Africa.

to challenges in the maritime arena," led Admiral Sandila to pursue an "inter-ministerial and interagency body, which will bring more synergy in our efforts and become an assured guarantor of our port and coastal security."[14]

Canada's Maritime Event Response Protocol (MERP) formally brings together multiple government agencies to address and respond to maritime events and threats. MERP provides a united and cohesive national-level government response capability while acknowledging that there is no single Canadian federal department solely responsible for maritime security. MERP's multiagency approach to marine security reflects the Government of Canada's approach to emergency management: whole-of-government, collaborative to address all hazards.

The United Kingdom's National Maritime Information Centre (NMIC) is a "cross-government body" that "works in close cooperation with Her Majesty's Government departments" and is accountable to the Home Office. NMIC is tasked with actively monitoring maritime activity around the UK and areas of national interest; enabling a better understanding of maritime safety and security and provide a "single voice" for maritime issues.[15]

New Zealand's Integrated Targeting and Operations Centre (ITOC) incorporates the National Maritime Coordination Centre (NMCC), and personnel from customs and public safety to local police. Their impressive capabilities include the ability to coordinate response assets and the decisional information in support of safety and security throughout the country.[16]

Cape Verde's Maritime Security Operations Center (COSMAR), established in 2010, enables a "more efficient collaboration between national agencies responsible for monitoring and controlling illicit activities along the territory."[17]

Philippine Defense Secretary Voltaire Gazmin remarked "that to deal effectively with maritime security challenges [there must be...] greater inter-agency coordination ...Our armed forces needs to synchronize its actions in operations in specialized areas to complement the efforts of our agencies. Addressing maritime security challenges necessitates our armed forces to collaborate with civilian agencies whose expertise and procedures are relevant and useful in fully addressing maritime security challenges."[18]

National-Level Whole-of-Government Maritime Threat/Event Response Frameworks Considerations

These considerations include:

- How is the process formally documented?
- Does the process require funding, and if so, what agency is responsible?
- Do agencies retain all authorities/responsibilities under the process?
- Is there an office responsible for facilitating (or leading) coordination activities, and if so, to whom are they accountable?
- Is office (or process) viewed as inclusive?
- What decisions/actions can this process/entity take?
- Are triggers to activate process or action documented?

- Are there information acquisition considerations?
- Is there a process to resolve disagreements?
- Is there a capability for those involved in the process to directly forward information to a head of state office?
- Who documents and disseminates decisions?
- Are private sector individuals and organizations (those outside of the government) involved in the process?
- Are lessons learned and best practices documented?
- Is there common terminology?
- Are there "kneeboard" or "quick response cards" to document standard information that is required?

The U.S. Process

Coordination frameworks provide benefits to those in operational and policy positions. An examination of a coordinated response highlights the whole-of-government imperative. At 1300 local time on Tuesday, April 7, 2009, the bridge watch of the 508 foot U.S. flagged container ship MAERSK ALABAMA detected three small skiff-type boats holding in a position approximately 5 miles off MAERSK ALABAMA's quarter. It is likely Captain Richard Phillips, MAERSK ALABAMA'S master, knew immediately why the skiffs were there and their intentions. After all, since 2007, approximately 640 ships had reported pirate attacks in the region he was transiting and that Somali pirates had taken more than 3150 hostages and received millions in ransom payments.

MAERSK ALABAMA, with a ship's company of 20 U.S. citizens, owned and operated by the Maersk Line, was en route to Mombasa Kenya with a shipment of food aid and other cargo. The ship was on the high seas, over 200 miles from the Somali coast and many miles from any naval or coast guard asset. As one skiff increased speed in an attempt to close MAERSK ALABAMA, it began to buck violently in the sea chop and eventually turned away. An omen of things to come.

At approximately 0600 the next morning, a report was received at the United Kingdom's Maritime Trade Organization, in Dubai, that a small boat with armed men was approaching MAERSK ALABAMA and that shots had been fired. Despite the efforts of the ship's company, men, armed with AK-47 rifles and other small arms, managed to board the ship. The ship's company retreated to the steering gear room and a cargo control room. MAERSK ALABAMA'S chief engineer executed an emergency shutdown of the engine room machinery thereby denying the intruders the ability to navigate the ship and cutting off all internal lighting, power, and ventilation. Captain Phillips remained outside of the safe room and, despite his efforts and those of the Chief Engineer, was taken hostage by the group of Somalis.

The first indication for the U.S. federal agencies that there was a potential problem on board MAERSK ALABAMA was the receipt of a signal from the Ship's Security Alert System (SSAS) alarm when the pirates boarded the ship. In less than 5 minutes the U.S. Coast Guard's Pacific Area Command Center contacted the Chief Security Officer for Maersk Lines who was able to confirm the signal was not a false alarm and indicated an ongoing attack.

Shortly after the pirates boarded MAERSK ALABAMA and the SSAS signal was received, the first national-level coordination activity took place in accordance with the U.S. Maritime Operational Threat Response (MOTR) Plan. The MOTR Plan provides guidance and a structure for the U.S. federal interagency coordination response process, including the response to maritime threats conducted by the U.S. military, law enforcement, investigative, diplomatic, and other federal agencies. MOTR was completed in 2005 and presidentially approved in 2006.

On the first day of the attack and capture of MAERSK ALABAMA three interagency coordination events were held. Throughout the time Captain Phillips was held hostage, secure video teleconferences connected agency/watch centers, hostage rescue experts, maritime legal, policy, and other subject matter experts on three continents to discuss and resolve many difficult, complex, and sensitive issues. The series of negotiations and maneuvering by both sides ended on April 12 when one of the pirates pointed an AK-47 at the back of Captain Phillips. The senior officer on scene, Commanding Officer of USS BAINBRIDGE (DDG 96), determined the situation had changed significantly and that Captain Phillips was in imminent danger. The sharp shooters aboard BAINBRIDGE shot and killed the person holding the AK-47 as well as the two other Somali pirates who were positioned near the opened hatch of the lifeboat.

The aligned response to the attack by Somali pirates on MAERSK ALABAMA represented one of the more high-profile instances of coordinated maritime threat response. The whole-of-government coordination framework ensured interagency concurrence on desired national outcomes and alignment of response action.

Conclusion

A prescient article in 1979 asked, "What are the consequences of a number of agencies becoming involved in the same policy area? When the number of agencies is great, there are several detrimental consequences to policy formation. As the number increases, there are greater difficulties in collecting and utilizing information. Communication among the agencies involved becomes more complex and clients are besieged with a bewildering variety of agency requests and requirements."[19] Those considerations exist today; the answers are largely being addressed through whole-of-government frameworks.

When an incident or maritime threat is identified, the questions of who is in charge, how is information going to be disseminated, and what is the desired course of action and outcome(s) for a nation need to be expeditiously resolved by maritime/military, response, and policy officials. Though substantively different, elements in effective whole-of-government frameworks across the globe include:

1. Head of State support and direction;
2. Flexible, agile, and inclusive process that can address emerging threats;
3. Timely, accurate and useful information dissemination;
4. Decisions/information are documented and distributed;
5. Multiple agency/subject matter support and ownership;

6. Used frequently and there is training for those new to the process;
7. Agreed upon dispute resolution provisions; and
8. Operational, implementing guidance

Formal interagency processes have proved tremendously beneficial to operations, diplomacy, and legal accountability. As threats evolve, it will be necessary for coordination processes to similarly evolve to best position timely, decisive responses to maritime challenges. The next phase of whole-of-government collaboration likely includes bilateral and multilateral, or even geographically focused collaborative arrangements.

Summary

In this chapter, we examined the U.S.' Whole-of-Government approach in response to maritime security incidents, as well as discussed those of selected other countries. Challenges posed by differing interpretations of terminologies used in policies pertaining to coordinated responses to maritime security incidents, as well as considerations when developing a, National-level Maritime Threat Response framework likewise were reviewed. A review of the U.S. MOTR plan in action, via the U.S. response to the hijacking of the M/V MAERSK ALABAMA, afforded a window for viewing the U.S. process and how the whole-of-government coordination framework ensured interagency concurrence on the desired national outcomes and an alignment of a response action.

End Notes

1. Christian Bueger, What is Maritime Security, Marine Policy 53 (2015) 159–164. "Since there are little prospects of defining maritime security once and for all, frameworks by which one can identify commonalities and disagreements are needed...Maritime security can first be understood in a matrix of its relation to other concepts, such as marine safety, seapower, blue economy, and resilience. Second, the securitization framework allows to study how maritime threats are made and which divergent political claims these entail in order to uncover political interests and divergent ideologies. Third, security practice theory enables the study of what actors actually do when they claim to enhance maritime security. Together these frameworks allow for the mapping of maritime security."
2. Andrea Baumann, Center for Security Studies (CSS); Whole of Government: Integration and Demarcation, No. 129, March 2013, available at: http://goo.gl/VAmdjQ.
3. Frederick M. Kaiser, Interagency Collaborative Arrangements and Activities: Types, Rationales, Considerations, Congressional Research Service, May 31, 2011, available at: https://www.fas.org/sgp/crs/misc/R41803.pdf.
4. Neumann Speaks on Interagency Process, Simons Center, March 17, 2015, available at: http://goo.gl/u8OceY.
5. Project on National Security Reform (PNSR), Forging a New Shield, November 2008. PNSR was led by James R. Locher III.
6. Joint Publication 3–27, Homeland Defense, July 29, 2013, available at: http://www.dtic.mil/doctrine/new_pubs/jp3_27.pdf. "Unity of effort among all HD participants is fundamental and essential. HD operations are conducted in a complex operational environment that contains thousands of different jurisdictions (federal, state, tribal, and local), many agencies and organizations, and several allies and multinational partners."

7. Roger Z. George and Harvey Rishikof, editors, The National Security Enterprise, Georgetown University Press, 2011. Jon J. Rosenwasser and Michael Warner authored the chapter "History of the Interagency Process for Foreign Relations in the United States: Murphy's Law? "
8. Joint Staff Publication 1–02, Department of Defense Dictionary of Military and Associated Terms, November 8, 2010, as amended through June 15, 2015, available at: http://www.dtic.mil/doctrine/new_pubs/jp1_02.pdf. *See also*, David Grambo, Barrett Smith and Richard W. Kokko, Insights to Effective Interorganizational Coordination, InterAgency Journal, Volume 5, Issue 3, Fall 2014.
9. Ibid., and *see also*, 3D Planning Guide: Diplomacy, Development, Defense, September 2011. "Unity of effort is based on four principles: 1. Common understanding of the situation. 2. Common vision or goals for the mission. 3. Coordination of efforts to ensure continued coherency. 4. Common measures of progress and ability to change course if necessary."
10. Practices That Help Enhance and Sustain Collaboration, Government Accountability Office, October 2005, GAO-06-15, available at: http://www.gao.gov/assets/250/248219.pdf. See also, Kaiser, Interagency Collaborative Arrangements and Activities: Types, Rationales, Considerations, Congressional Research Service, May 31, 2011.
11. Kaiser, Interagency Collaborative Arrangements and Activities: Types, Rationales, Considerations, Congressional Research Service. "It is useful to distinguish coordination from collaboration of multiple organizations. Interagency coordination might be defined as a specific form of collaboration that applies to particular cases and operations. By contrast to collaboration when multiple agencies may perceive mutual benefit in working together, coordination often is more of a top-down exercise. It takes place when a leader with authority over multiple organizations directs them to collaborate to achieve a specified joint purpose."
12. Government Accountability Office; Maritime Security: Actions Needed to Assess and Update Plan and Enhance Collaboration among Partners Involved in Countering Piracy off the Horn of Africa; GAO-10-856, September 2010.
13. Indian nuclear subs cause of concern: Pakistan, The Nation, February 26, 2012, available at: http://nation.com.pk/national/26-Feb-2012/indian-nuclear-subs-cause-of-concern-pakistan
14. Ibid.
15. United Kingdom's National Maritime Information Center (NMIC) Information Guide (2011); available at: http://www.recaap.org/Portals/0/docs/NMIC-information-booklet.pdf.
16. *See*: Briefing for the Incoming Minister of Customs, December 2011, available at: http://www.customs.govt.nz/news/resources/corporate/Documents/bim.pdf.
17. Gustavo Placido Dos Santos, Cape Verde and drug trafficking: A major challenge to rule of law – analysis, Eurasiareview, available at: http://www.eurasiareview.com/05112014-cape-verde-drug-trafficking-major-challenge-rule-law-analysis/.
18. Available at: https://www.iiss.org/en/events/shangri%20la%20dialogue/archive/shangri-la-dialogue-2011-4eac/fifth-plenary-session-30f2/voltaire-gazmin-c351.
19. Betsy C. Cox, Gary Shmerling, Interagency Conflict: A Model for Analysis, 9 GA. J. Int'L & Comp. L 241 (1979), available at: http://digitalcommons.law.uga.edu/gjicl/vol9/iss2/9. The article also noted,"... incentives are necessary to motivate agencies to cooperate in their interactions with other agencies which have overlapping authority or jurisdiction over the same policy task."

Legal Authorities for Maritime Law Enforcement, Safety, and Environmental Protection

R.L. Castaneda*, C. Condit*, B. Wilson†

*UNITED STATES COAST GUARD; †DEPARTMENT OF HOMELAND SECURITY/UNITED STATES COAST GUARD

OBJECTIVES

After studying this chapter, you will be familiar with

1. The United Nations Convention on the Law of the Sea (LOSC);
2. The 1988 United Nations Convention Against Illicit Trafficking in Narcotic Drugs and Psychotropic Substances;
3. The Maritime Drug Law Enforcement Act (MDLEA) and Drug Trafficking Vessel Interdiction Act (DTVIA);
4. The International Convention for the Prevention of Pollution from Ships and its application worldwide;
5. The Fisheries and Environmental Laws of the United States;
6. The U.S. Immigration and Nationality Act (INA); and
7. The Authority, Role, and Operations of the U.S. Coast Guard (USCG) in responding to and enforcing the above International Conventions and the U.S. laws.

Maritime law enforcement is applied across the globe in pursuit of transnational criminal organizations (TCOs), drug traffickers, illegal fishing, and other illicit activity. Whether the response involves an at-sea boarding or a port State control examination, authority is derived from multiple international treaties and domestic laws that advance state interests. This chapter focuses primarily on the U.S. authorities, analyzes maritime law enforcement operations and pollution enforcement along with the relevant authorities for conducting operations in the maritime domain.

United Nations Convention on the Law of the Sea

The United Nations LOSC, referred to as the "Constitution for the oceans"[1] provides a set of authorities for the oceans and protection of their resources. The development of the Convention, which entered into force on November 16, 1994, is the result of more than 12 years of negotiations by more than 150 countries with varying legal and political systems and differing levels of economic and social development. The LOS Convention is widely regarded as the authoritative maritime safety and security instrument of our time, ratified by 166 States (as of September 2015), providing rules for the uses of the oceans and the framework for further development of the law of the sea.[2] The Convention contains more than 320 articles and 9 annexes relating to navigation, environmental control, the Exclusive Economic Zone (EEZ), delimitation, marine scientific research, economic and commercial activities, the transfer of technology, and the settlement of disputes relating to ocean matters.[3] The United States participated in the development of the Convention,[4] recognizes its navigation and overflight provisions as a codification of customary international law, signed the revision of Part XI, but it has not ratified the Convention.

One LOSC article that is utilized often in maritime drug enforcement operations is a right of visit (ROV) boarding. Article 110 states:

1. Except where acts of interference derive from powers conferred by treaty, a warship which encounters on the high seas a foreign ship, other than a ship entitled to complete immunity in accordance with articles 95 and 96, is not justified in boarding it unless there is reasonable ground for suspecting that
   a. the ship is engaged in piracy;
   b. the ship is engaged in the slave trade;
   c. the ship is engaged in unauthorized broadcasting and the flag State of the warship has jurisdiction under article 109;
   d. the ship is without nationality; or
   e. though flying a foreign-flag or refusing to show its flag, the ship is, in reality, of the same nationality as the warship.
2. In the cases provided for in paragraph 1, the warship may proceed to verify the ship's right to fly its flag. To this end, it may send a boat under the command of an officer to the suspected ship. If suspicion remains after the documents have been checked, it may proceed to a further examination onboard the ship, which must be carried out with all possible consideration.
3. If the suspicions prove to be unfounded, and provided that the ship boarded has not committed any act justifying them, it shall be compensated for any loss or damage that may have been sustained.
4. These provisions apply *mutatis mutandis* to military aircraft.
5. These provisions also apply to any other duly authorized ships or aircraft clearly marked and identifiable as being on government service.

A substantial number of law enforcement boardings are based on the ROV. An ROV boarding may be conducted to verify vessel registry, and it cannot be used as a means to conduct a search for evidence of illegal activity. ROV is permitted under customary international law, as codified in LOSC.

Complementing the LOSC, other multinational documents, notably the 1988 Vienna Convention, also support maritime enforcement action and are addressed further.

The 1988 United Nations Convention Against Illicit Trafficking in Narcotic Drugs and Psychotropic Substances (the 1988 Vienna Convention)

The 1988 United Nations Convention Against Illicit Trafficking in Narcotic Drugs and Psychotropic Substances (the 1988 Vienna Convention) entered in to force on November 11, 1990, currently has 189 parties, and is the global framework for which international maritime drug enforcement operations are conducted.[5] The Convention requires States Parties to designate competent authorities to request authority to stop, board, and search, as well as waive jurisdiction of, foreign-flagged vessels during real-time operations. Article 17 provides a framework for States Parties to take appropriate law enforcement action to suppress maritime drug trafficking anywhere on earth, provided, of course, that the enforcing Party has either enacted domestic implementing legislation or adopted the Convention language as positive law. Article 17 reads in part:

1. A Party which has reasonable grounds to suspect that a vessel flying its flag or not displaying a flag or marks of registry is engaged in illicit traffic may request the assistance of other Parties in suppressing its use for that purpose.
2. A Party which has reasonable grounds to suspect that a vessel exercising freedom of navigation in accordance with international law and flying the flag or displaying marks of registry of another Party is engaged in illicit traffic may so notify the flag State, request confirmation of registry and, if confirmed, request authorization from the flag State to take appropriate measures in regard to that vessel.
3. … [A] flag State may authorize the requesting State to … (a) board the vessel; (b) search the vessel; (c) if evidence of involvement in illicit traffic is found, take the appropriate action with respect to the vessel, persons, and cargo on board.

While the 1988 Vienna Convention does not dictate the internal policies and procedures to be set by each respective country in utilizing the authority of the Convention, it does encourage Parties to establish bilateral and multilateral agreements to carry out, or to enhance the effectiveness of, the provisions of Article 17. In response, numerous countries engaged in diplomatic conversation and developed bilateral and multilateral agreements that span wide swaths of the maritime domain. Colombia, Ecuador, Panama, and Costa Rica as well as the United States have been particularly proactive in engaging with international partners to combat illicit maritime activity.

U.S. Coast Guard—Law Enforcement 14 U.S.C. § 89(a)

As the nation's only armed force with domestic law enforcement authority, the USCG has jurisdiction and law enforcement powers pursuant to 14 U.S.C. § 89. The USCG is involved daily in enforcing federal law in the areas of drug interdiction, immigration, marine environmental protection, marine safety, fisheries, maritime security, and general federal law applicable at sea.[6] This statute states in part:

1. The Coast Guard may make inquiries, examinations, inspections, searches, seizures, and arrests upon the high seas and waters over which the United States has jurisdiction, for the prevention, detection, and suppression of violations of laws of the United States. For such purposes, commissioned, warrant, and petty officers may at any time go on board of any vessel subject to the jurisdiction, or to the operation of any law, of the United States, address inquiries to those on board, examine the ship's documents and papers, and examine, inspect, and search the vessel and use all necessary force to compel compliance. When from such inquiries, examination, inspection, or search it appears that a breach of the laws of the United States rendering a person liable to arrest is being, or has been committed, by any person, such person shall be arrested or, if escaping to shore, shall be immediately pursued and arrested on shore, or other lawful and appropriate action shall be taken; or, if it shall appear that a breach of the laws of the United States has been committed so as to render such vessel, or the merchandise, or any part thereof, on board of, or brought into the United States by, such vessel, liable to forfeiture, or so as to render such vessel liable to a fine or penalty and if necessary to secure such fine or penalty, such vessel or such merchandise, or both, shall be seized.

This authority extends beyond the territorial seas of the United States, and can be exercised on the high seas as well as, with coastal state permission, the territorial seas of foreign nations.

Maritime Drug Law Enforcement Act (MDLEA) 46 U.S.C. §§ 70501-7-507

Numerous laws exist for prohibiting the possession, sale, and distribution of controlled substances. For example, 21 U.S.C. § 841 et. Seq. proscribes the manufacture, distribute, or dispense, or possess with intent to manufacture, distribute, or dispense, a controlled substance; 21 U.S.C. § 952 prohibits the importation of controlled substances. 21 U.S.C. § 959 prohibits the manufacture or distribution of controlled substances with intent or with knowledge that controlled substance will be imported into the United States or U.S. territorial seas.

The principal statute for counterdrug enforcement in the maritime domain is the Maritime Drug Law Enforcement Act, (MDLEA), 46 U.S.C. §§ 70501-70507. The MDLEA states in part:

> Congress finds and declares that (1) trafficking in controlled substances aboard vessels is a serious international problem, is universally condemned, and presents a specific threat to the security and societal well-being of the United States and (2) operating or embarking in a submersible vessel (FSV) or semisubmersible vessel (SPSS) without nationality and on an international voyage is a serious international problem, facilities crime, including drug trafficking, and terrorism, and presents a specific threat to the safety of maritime navigation and the security of the United States. 46 U.S.C. section 70501

Under the MDLEA, it is unlawful for any person onboard a vessel of the United States or onboard a vessel subject to the jurisdiction of the United States, or who is a citizen of the United States or a resident alien of the United States onboard any vessel to knowingly or intentionally manufacture or distribute a controlled substance. A vessel of the United States means either a United States-registered vessel or a vessel owned by a U.S. citizen. A vessel subject to the jurisdiction of the United States means

1. a vessel that is without nationality, which is subject to the jurisdiction of any nation;
2. a vessel assimilated to without nationality under the 1958 High Seas Convention;
3. a foreign-flag vessel if the flag state has waived jurisdiction;
4. a vessel in the territorial seas of the United States;
5. a vessel in the territorial seas of a coastal state if the coastal state has waived jurisdiction; or
6. a vessel in the contiguous zone of the United States if the vessel is arriving, departing, or "hovering."

Congress enacted the statute with provisions designed to eliminate defenses based upon a lack of jurisdiction under the U.S. domestic or international law. That is, an individual defendant does not have the standing to assert that a U.S. court, or other court, does not have the jurisdiction to be tried for violating the MDLEA; this issue exists as one to be decided as a question of law by the presiding trial judge at the beginning of an MDLEA prosecution. The government has the burden of proving jurisdiction. If the vessel is without nationality, the government can introduce questions asked during the initial approach of the vessel (Right of Approach questions),[7] and the answers provided by the master, person in charge, and/or crew, evidence that the vessel lacked indicia of nationality, and evidence or lack thereof discovered during a boarding.

The Drug Trafficking Vessel Interdiction Act of 2008 (DTVIA) 18 U.S.C. § 2285

The DTVIA makes it unlawful for any person to knowingly operate, or attempt or conspire to operate, by any means, or embark in any submersible vessel, also known as FSV,[8] or semisubmersible vessel, also known as SPSS,[9] that is without nationality and that is navigating or has navigated into, through, or from waters beyond the outer limit of the territorial sea of a single country or a lateral limit of that country's territorial sea with an adjacent country, with the intent to evade detection.[10]

"The use of submersibles by traffickers is on the rise and presents a transnational security threat."[11] "From 2001 through 2010, approximately 175 documented drug transits from South America to global destinations occurred on SPSS-type platforms. While transporting illicit cargo in the maritime domain is not new, the stealthy SPSS—a long-range vessel that is extremely difficult to identify and track—raised significant national security concerns. "If (SPSS vessels) can smuggle drugs, what else can they smuggle?" asked Drug Enforcement Administration spokesman Rusty Payne. In 2008, Congressman Daniel E. Lungren of

California asserted that the SPSS is one of the most significant threats we face in maritime law enforcement today, "but noted that without a law proscribing the operation of these platforms, narcotraffickers often avoid criminal consequences. The United States closed the legal gap in 2008 with the passage of the DTVIA."[12]

This federal statute criminalizes the operation of FSV or SPSS that are without nationality and are navigating or have navigated outside of a nation's territorial sea with the intent to evade detection. Essentially, the conveyance was outlawed regardless of its contents. At present, dozens of defendants have been convicted under the DTVIA, and there have been no successful appeals of the provisions of the DVTIA. Four Eleventh Circuit opinions issued in the first half of 2011 denied challenges that claimed the DTVIA exceeds congressional authority, that its application violates due process, that its text is too vague, and that the statute improperly shifts the burden of proof to the defendant.

Elements of the DTVIA include

1. operating or embarking any FSV or SPSS;
2. the SPSS/FSV is stateless or properly assimilated to without nationality;
3. the SPSS/FSV was located seaward of any state's territorial sea or transited form one state's territorial sea to another state's territorial sea; and
4. the SPSS/FSV was attempting to evade detection.[13]

It is an affirmative defense to a prosecution for the violation of the DTVIA, which the defendant has the burden to prove by a preponderance of the evidence, that the SPSS or FSV was, at the time of the offense:

1. a vessel of the United States or lawfully registered in a foreign nation as claimed by the master or individual in charge of the vessel when requested to make a claim by an officer of the United States authorized to enforce applicable provisions of the U.S. law;
2. classed by and designed in accordance with the rules of a classification society;
3. lawfully operated in government-regulated or licensed activity, including commerce, research, or exploration; or
4. equipped with and using an operable automatic identification system, vessel monitoring system, or long-range identification and tracking system.

At the time of this printing, both the United States and Colombia do not classify and register SPSS or FSVs. The DTVIA has explicit extraterritorial federal jurisdiction and allows for both civil and criminal penalties with as much as 15 years of imprisonment, if convicted.[14]

"Although the cost of constructing a FSV is high—around $2 million—those costs are mitigated by the fact that such vessels can transport several tons of cocaine in one voyage. Thus, as a result of the tremendously higher street value of cocaine in areas outside of Peru, Colombia, and Bolivia, a TCO could [d]eploy five vessels at a combined total layout of $100 million, successfully deliver one, and you double your investment."[15]

"Stopping vessels before they get underway is certainly preferable, but because the construction and deployment of SPSS platforms occur in rough, rural, and isolated terrain, doing so is not always possible. This is, in part, due to the fact that smugglers are —constantly adapting their techniques to counter U.S. law enforcement activities." Consequently, "identifying and tracking illicit vessels on millions of nautical miles of ocean space poses multiple operational challenges, because traffickers have created intricate methods involving multiple at-sea transfers between commercial and fishing vessels, complex logistics chains along circuitous routes, and extensive use of decoy vessels to confuse interdiction forces."[16]

Joint Interagency Operations

Law enforcement boardings are not conducted in a vacuum. The Department of Defense (DOD) is the lead federal government agency for the *detection and monitoring* of aerial and maritime transit of illegal drugs into the United States. The USCG is the lead federal agency for *maritime drug interdiction* under the National Drug Control Strategy and shares responsibility for air interdiction with the U.S. Customs Service.[17] The shared mission of the DOD and the USCG effectively reduces the supply of drugs from source countries by denying smugglers the use of air and maritime routes in the source and transit zones, an area of more than 6 million square miles, including the Caribbean, Gulf of Mexico, and Eastern Pacific. In meeting the challenge of patrolling this vast area, identifying and tracking smuggling vessels, and interdicting them, the DOD and the USCG closely coordinate with other federal agencies and partner nations in the region to disrupt and deter illicit maritime activity.

MARPOL 73/78

MARPOL 73/78 is the commonly used acronym for the International Convention for the Prevention of Pollution from Ships, 1973 as modified by the Protocol of 1978, which, as the title indicates, is the primary international convention on the prevention of pollution from ships into the world's maritime environment. MARPOL 73/78 came into being more than 50 years after the sinking of the Titanic and more than 20 years after the initial international recognition for the need to protect the sea from oil pollution.

As oil became a major commodity, the transport of oil by sea prompted ever-increasing interest in international shipping via tank ships or "tankers." In 1954, the International Convention for the Prevention of Pollution by Oil (OILPOL) was the first international treaty focused on prohibiting tankers from discharging oil (including oily mixtures of more than 100 parts per million) within specified zones.

However, as the world was switching from coal to oil as a primary fuel source, the need to export, import, and transport oil increased dramatically. As a result of this new demand, vessel manufacturers started making tankers bigger with little concern for engineering standards or safety. The concept of a "super" tanker quickly became a reality and as the capacity to carry massive quantities of oil grew, so did the capacity for accidents to turn into environmental disasters. Among the many significant spills from supertankers during this time period, two attracted attention on an international scale as the catalysts for an international convention that addressed the discharges of pollutants.

A Brief History

The first major oil spill came from the Tank Vessel Torrey Canyon in 1967. (Fig. 14.1) Although the Torrey Canyon was originally built to only carry 60,000 tons of crude oil, it was enlarged to a 120,000-ton capacity in order to increase the export capability. Torrey Canyon was at full capacity when it hit a rocky reef off the coast of Cornwall, England. The resulting spill created an oil slick over 270 square miles, contaminating more than 180 miles of coast along England and France. More than 15,000 sea birds and enormous numbers of aquatic animals were killed before the spill was finally contained. Even today, reminders of the disaster linger in a quarry in Guernsey where the black sludge was pumped as it washed up on local beaches.

At the time of the grounding, the registered owner of the Torrey Canyon was Barracuda Tanker Corporation, but the ship was under a twenty-year time charter to the Union Oil Company of California and registered in Liberia. To complicate the matter further, the crude oil had been shipped by British Petroleum Trading Ltd., under a voyage charter from Union, with freight payable at destination in Wales.[18] The confusion and finger-pointing among the various entities, combined with the ambiguity of international law, and the lack of a comprehensive legal regime, made the recovery of damages tedious and the assignment of liability nearly impossible.

Following the Torrey Canyon disaster, the International Convention on Civil Liability for Oil Pollution Damage (CLC) of 1969 was adopted to ensure adequate compensation for persons who suffer damage as a result of maritime casualties involving tankers. The rewriting of the International Convention on the Safety of Life at Sea (SOLAS) was completed in 1974 to address many of the safety concerns expressed after the Torrey Canyon disaster. The other major international effort came through in the MARPOL Protocol of 1973, which created an obligation to limit the release of harmful substances into the

FIGURE 14.1 The remains of the Tanker TORREY CANYON as she breaks apart on Seven Stones reef off the coast of Cornwall, England.

sea. Although it was adopted, MARPOL 73 had not yet entered force when a series of 14 tanker accidents occurred in a span of 10 weeks, including one off the coast of the United States.

In 1976, the Liberian-flagged tanker, Argo Merchant, grounded off Nantucket carrying 7.3 million gallons of fuel oil, nearly twice the amount of the Torrey Canyon. (Fig. 14.2) Horrible weather conditions prevented removal of the oil before the hull began to break in half, spilling the oil to the sea. This led to the MARPOL Protocol of 1978 which combined with the 1973 Protocol to further prevent and control marine pollution from ships, and particularly oil tankers. This is why the treaty is referred to as "MARPOL 73/78."

The Fundamentals of MARPOL

MARPOL 73/78 entered into force on October 2, 1983 and has been amended numerous times since. The most recent amendment was in 1997 with the addition of Annex VI to regulate the air emissions from vessels.

MARPOL 73/78 consists of the Protocols (1973, 1978, and 1997) and the Annexes. The Protocol essentially cover the obligations of the Parties, definitions, reporting requirements, and arbitration. However, the substance of MARPOL 73/78 lies mainly with the Annexes, which specifically address the operational or accidental release of six different categories of pollutants: I = oil, II = noxious liquid substances in bulk, III = harmful substances in package form, IV = sewage, V = garbage, and VI = air emissions.

FIGURE 14.2 Remnants of Tanker ARGO MERCHANT near Nantucket, Massachusetts.

Application of MARPOL 73/78 depends on a vessel's gross tonnage and certifications. Thus, the application of each Annex differs and should be consulted depending on the pollutant. As with most international instruments, each Annex also includes exceptions, Appendices, and Unified Interpretations, which further clarify, or in some cases, complicate, the landscape. Finally, each Annex in MARPOL 73/78 also includes special areas where there are even more strict limitations on operational discharges.

Annex I is currently the most wide-cited Annex for prevention and enforcement actions in port States and especially in the United States. Annex I entered into force on October 2, 1983, and addresses the prevention of pollution by oil from shipboard operations as well as accidental discharges. It applies to all "seagoing" vessels. Annex I receives the most attention because it is widely argued that the single largest source of man-made oil pollution in the oceans is oily waste spilled from ships. Oil illegally dumped from commercial ships accounts for 46% of all the oil entering the world's oceans from human sources.[19] Annex I thus centers on the equipment requirements for the proper processing and discharge of oily waste. Important to enforcement efforts, Annex I requires any discharge and/or transfer of oily waste to be recorded in an Oil Record Book. Annex I also sets out the equipment requirements for the machinery spaces on all ships as well as specifics geared toward tankers.

Annex II also applies only to seagoing ships and details the discharge criteria for noxious liquid substances carried in bulk. This includes over 250 substances, which are listed in an appendix to the Convention. For these substances, the discharge of residues is allowed only to reception facilities until certain concentrations and conditions (which vary with the category of substances) are complied with. In any case, no discharge of residues containing noxious substances is permitted within 12 nautical miles (nm) of the nearest land.

Annex III controls harmful substances carried by sea in packaged form, and includes general requirements for the issuing of detailed standards for packing, marking, labeling, documentation, stowage, quantity limitations, exceptions, and notifications. For the purpose of this Annex, "harmful substances" are those substances which are identified as marine pollutants in the International Maritime Dangerous Goods Code (IMDG Code) or which meet the criteria in the Appendix of Annex III.

Annex IV concerns the pollution by sewage from ships and places controls on the discharge of sewage into the sea. Discharge is generally prohibited unless the ship has an approved sewage treatment plant or when the ship is discharging comminuted (reduced to particles) and disinfected sewage using an approved system more than 3 nm from the nearest land. Sewage not comminuted or disinfected must be discharged at a distance of more than 12 nm from the nearest land. Please note that the United States has not ratified Annex IV because the Federal Water Pollution Control Act (Clean Water Act) addresses the discharge of sewage through the use of Marine Sanitation Devices.

Annex V prevents the discharge of garbage from ships except when certain controls are in place. The dumping of plastic is always prohibited. However, food wastes and certain cargo residues may be discharged when more than 12 nm from land if properly reduced to less than one inch. Like Annexes I and II, garbage record books are required and often inspected by port States. Unlike Annexes I and II, Annex V applies everywhere in the marine environment.

Finally, Annex VI, the newest kid on the block, institutes limits on air emissions including sulfur oxide and nitrogen oxide. To be compliant, ships entering Emission Control Areas (ECA) are only allowed to use low sulfur fuel oil. For reference, the North American ECA spans the entire length of the North American coastline out to approximately 200 nm. While there are certain permits to promote technology that can "scrub" exhaust, few vessels have requested such permits from their flag state. Further, there are mandatory technical and operational energy efficiency measures aimed at reducing greenhouse gas emissions from ships and a world cap aimed at reducing the total emissions to below 3.5% by 2020. While Annex VI has been on the books since 2008 with the limits slowly phased in, many port States are just now beginning to inspect for noncompliance and establish implementing regulations.

National-Level Authorities to Protect the Maritime Environment, Punish Those Who Exploit It, and Prevent Illicit Activity

MARPOL 73/78 is enforced unevenly across the globe. One of the difficulties in enforcing the treaty arises from the very transient nature of maritime shipping. Where the ship is registered, known as the flag State, used to play a bigger part in the enforcement of regulations. However, in an era of "Flags of Convenience," where ship registration can be easily bought, and flag States are often unwilling or unable to exercise responsibility, the emphasis on regulation and enforcement for pollution and safety laws lies mainly with the port State. The port State is the country that the ship visits in furtherance of its trade. This is distinguished from a coastal State which does have some authority to enforce laws when a vessel enters territorial waters. Simply put, port States can exercise jurisdiction, including criminal jurisdiction, over foreign-flag vessels that voluntarily conduct business in their port. MARPOL 73/78 allows a port State to develop domestic laws to protect their waters, and in accordance with customary international law and the International Maritime Organization, port States conduct inspections on foreign-flag ships to ensure compliance with these laws. If clear grounds exist to indicate the vessel is not in compliance with the domestic or international laws, the port State can expand the examination and take enforcement actions. Further promoting compliance, a port State can detain the ship if it finds significant noncompliance or can refer potential violations to the flag State. Even with a referral option, a 2000 Government Accountability Office (GAO) report documented the poor response rate from flag States, making the port State compliance and enforcement regime all the more necessary.

While MARPOL 73/78 is the international convention that requires parties to implement domestic legislation, the extent of national-level authorities and the enforcement mechanisms in place vary widely among countries, and thus port State actions also vary. Below is a snippet of four nations with domestic laws in place. As you will see, the United States is the only country not a party (but is an observer) to a regional memorandum of understanding (MOU) concerning vessel inspections. The regional MOUs provide the parties with the ability to establish consistency, reduce "port shopping," and limit the strain on resources by sharing information and coordinating the exercise of their port State control authorities. These regional MOUs, however, do not extend to criminal enforcement.

United Kingdom

The domestic laws of the United Kingdom (UK) include the Merchant Shipping Act 1995 and the associated regulations.[20] Under the MSA, an illegal discharge of oil includes a fine of up to £250,000 on summary conviction or an unlimited fine on indictment; failure to maintain the Oil Record Book includes a fine of up to £5000 on summary conviction; and falsified or misleading entries in the Oil Record Book to a fine of up to £5000 or 6 months imprisonment or both or an unlimited fine or 2 years imprisonment or both on indictment.[21] If the matter of an illegal discharge is investigated based on a "view toward prosecution," the suspect will be questioned in accordance with the Police and Criminal Evidence Act (PACE) 1984.

However, the UK has focused on a "pragmatic approach" toward enforcement and went to the European Commission in order to promote a fair and consistent approach throughout the EU, so that the UK ports were not unfairly disadvantaged.[22] Further guidance then came from a European Parliament and Council Directive 2009/123/EC, amended a previous directive to criminalize the accidental discharge of ship-source pollutants for serious negligence, thereby strengthening the European Union's enforcement mechanisms. In support of the Directive, the Commission Vice President emphasized the need for criminal penalties.

> *We must get tough on illegal discharges and gross negligence must be fought at all cost: the threat of criminal penalties hanging over polluted heads will help to protect our coasts. We cannot tolerate deliberate pollution or gross negligence by a minority of operators who tarnish the image of the shipping industry.*[23]

Based on the most recent Organization for Economic Cooperation and Development (OECD) report, between 1997 and 2002, the UK prosecuted 12 cases with fines ranging from 5000 to 35,000.[24]

The UK is also a signatory to the Paris MOU. The Paris MOU is one of the earliest agreements signed in 1982 among port States and was initially agreed upon to inspect labor conditions onboard. Following the sinking of another vessel, the Amoco Cadiz, the Paris MOU parties decided to include safety and pollution within the gamut of the inspection. The Paris MOU currently has 27 maritime administration parties.

As briefly discussed earlier, the purpose of the MOU is to promote consistency in port State inspections and to maximize resources. By each party agreeing to conduct a certain number of vessel inspections, the temptation of vessel to "port shop" and seek the least stringent inspection States is reduced. This also tampers a port States' concern that by conducting inspections, a vessel is apt to take business elsewhere. Through the MOU, the entire region works to prevent substandard or noncompliant vessels from seeking certain ports to avoid inspection. Means for ensuring compliance include the issuance of a deficiency for violations of MARPOL, the detention of the vessel for significant violations, or the total banning of the vessel from a particular region for repeated noncompliance.

Each regional MOU contains a hierarchy of flag States based on their compliance. The "White List" is countries whose flagged vessels have a consistently low detention rate for noncompliance and are considered to be low risk. The Gray List is countries whose flagged vessels are average performers. Depending on where a flag falls on the "Grey List," that nation could be incentivized to improve in order to get on the "White List" or could be in danger of being demoted to the "Black List." The "Black List" includes flag States with the highest detention rates and are considered to be high and even very high risk. A ship with a consistently dismal performance could be banned from the Paris MOU region.

As indicated further, the success of the regional MOUs in deterring substandard vessels and promoting compliance is theoretically observable in the number of deficiencies recorded. However, qualifying the success of any party in an MOU based solely on deficiencies is an approximation and extracted from larger data samples with no ability to characterize the types of deficiencies that resulted in a detention.

Table 14.1 illustrates the number of inspections, deficiencies, and detentions the UK issued under the Paris MOU. However, extrapolation of the data is necessary to determine how many of the deficiencies were due to violations of MARPOL 73/78.

Table 14.2 is an extrapolation of the data to determine the number of deficiencies the UK issued for violations of MARPOL. From the data given earlier, Annex I and Annex V provided the basis for the highest number of deficiencies in the UK.

In sum, the UK accomplishes deterrence and enforcement through the Paris MOU as well as a domestic regime that provide criminal penalties for operational and accidental discharges.

Australia

Australia's domestic law is called the *Protection of the Sea (Prevention from Pollution from Ships) Act of 1983,* which is administered by the Australian Maritime Safety Authority.

Table 14.1 UK Port State Inspections, Deficiencies, and Detentions Compared to Paris MOU Total[25]

Port State	United Kingdom		MOU Total
Inspections	1456	7.9%	18,430
Deficiencies	941	9.2%	10,214
Detentions	63	10.3%	612

Table 14.2 UK Port State Estimated MARPOL Deficiencies Compared to Paris MOU Total[26]

MARPOL	MOU Total	UK (%)	UK Total
Annex I	874	9.2	95
Annex II	27	9.2	2.9
Annex III	4	9.2	0.43
Annex IV	344	9.2	37.4
Annex V	596	9.2	96.1
Annex VI	458	9.2	49.5

Table 14.3 Table of Australia's implementation of the MARPOL Annexes by State/Territory

State/Territory	Annex I	Annex II	Annex III	Annex IV	Annex V
QLD: Transport Operations Act 1995	Yes	Yes	Yes	Yes	Yes
NSW: Marine Pollution Act 2012	Yes	Yes	Yes	Yes	Yes
VIC: Pollution of Waters by Oil and Noxious Substances Act 1986	Yes	No	No	No	Yes
TAS: Pollution of Waters by Oil and Noxious Substances Act 1987	Yes	Yes	Yes	Yes	Yes
SA: Protection of Marine Waters Act 1987	Yes	Yes	Yes	No	Yes
WA: Pollution of Waters by Oil and Noxious substances Act 1987	Yes	Yes	No	No	No
NT: Marine Pollution Act 1999	Yes	Yes	Yes	Yes	Yes

QLD, Queensland; *NSW*, New South Wales; *VIC*, Victoria; *TAS*, Tasmania; *SA*, South Australia; *WA*, Western Australia; *NT*, Northern Territory.

Jurisdiction under this Act extends from 3 nm out to the Australia EEZ (200 nm) and also applies within the 3 nm limits where the State or Northern Territory does not have complementary legislation. The complementary legislation by States or Northern Territories is listed below (Table 14.3).

Section 28 of the *Protection of the Sea Act of 1983* concerns the prosecution of offenses against Act and details the maximum penalty as well as the requisite "state of mind" standard for proceeding against the corporation. Between 1997 and 2009, through the Protection of the Sea Act or complementary States legislation, Australia has 83 criminal prosecutions for oil and chemical pollution from ships with fines ranging from $1000 to $1.6 million in addition to clean-up costs and community service payments.[27] Under the *Protection of the Sea Act and the Navigation Act of 2012,* Australia's regulatory scheme breaks down into "Marine Orders." Marine Order 91 concerns the prevention of oil pollution and incorporates Annex I by reference.[28]

Australia is a party to the Tokyo MOU along with Canada, Chile, Russia, China, New Zealand, Japan, and others.[29] Australia is also a party to the Indian Ocean MOU.[30] As

Table 14.4 Australia Port State Inspections, Deficiencies, and Detentions Compared to Tokyo and Indian Ocean MOUs with estimated percentage related to MARPOL.[31]

	Australia			Tokyo MOU	Indian Ocean
Port State	**Total**	**Tokyo (%)**	**Indian Ocean (%)**	**Total**	**MOU Total**
Inspections	3742	12.3	61.8	30,405	6059
Deficiencies	2357	12.4	67.9	19,029	3469
Detentions	269	22.4	71	1203	379

previously discussed, the regional agreements are similar to the Paris MOU and contain a hierarchy of flag countries based on their compliance. The data on associated inspections and deficiencies are provided below.

Table 14.4 illustrates that Australia had approximately 12.4% of the total deficiencies under the Tokyo MOU, and 22.4% of the detentions, including an estimated 16 detention related to MARPOL deficiencies. This represents a more even distribution of port State activity within the Tokyo MOU compared to Australia's port States accounting for over 67% of the deficiencies and 71% of the detentions under the Indian Ocean MOU. While Australia is likely consistent in conducting inspections within its ports, the discrepancy between the activeness of the other parties to the respective MOUs makes a difference.

Table 14.5 again shows the higher percentage of MARPOL deficiencies issued by Australia under the Indian Ocean MOU compared to the Tokyo MOU. With respect to the specific deficiencies in Australia, both Annex I and V are notable under the Tokyo MOU region, while Annex IV is distinct within the Indian Ocean MOU region.

Like the UK, Australian implementing legislation provides for criminal penalties in certain cases while the MOU obligations make up a large part of the compliance regime.

Japan

Japan adopted the Act on the Prevention of Marine Pollution and Maritime Disaster (Marine Pollution Prevention Act) in 1970 and amended it in 1983 with the ratification of MARPOL.[33] According to Article 1 of the Marine Pollution Prevention Act, the purpose is to "secure appropriate enforcement of international convention on the prevention of marine pollution and maritime disaster."[34] The Japanese Coast Guard, established through the Japan Coast Guard Act includes "prevention of marine pollution" as one of the missions and authorizes administrative and judicial enforcement jurisdiction.[35] Article 17 specifically allows Japanese Coast Guard officers to demand production of official papers, inspect vessels, and question the crew. Enforcement of violations, however, is addressed by means of the bond system, and further enforcement options are rarely pursued.

Japan is also a party to the Tokyo MOU and primarily enforces through port State actions rather than the bond system.

Table 14.6 shows Japan's share of the port State activities under the Tokyo MOU with percentages slightly above those of Australia and MARPOL-related detentions only slight lower.

Table 14.5 Australia Port State Estimated MARPOL Deficiencies Compared to Tokyo and Indian Ocean MOUs[32]

	Tokyo			Indian		
MARPOL	**Total MARPOL Deficiencies**	**Australia (%)**	**Australia Total**	**Total MARPOL Deficiencies**	**Australia (%)**	**Australia Total**
Annex I	1679	12.4	208.2	283	6 7.9	192.2
Annex II	13	12.4	1.6	0	67.9	0
Annex III	33	12.4	4.1	10	67.9	6.8
Annex IV	1199	12.4	148.7	293	67.9	198.9
Annex V	1587	12.4	196.8	204	67.9	138.5
Annex VI	758	12.4	94	110	67.9	74.7

Table 14.6 Japan Port State Inspections, Deficiencies, and Detentions Compared to Tokyo MOU Total

Port State		Japan	MOU Total
Inspections	5337	17.6%	30,405
Deficiencies	3538	18.6%	19,029
Detentions	208	17.3%	1203

Table 14.7 demonstrates Japan's reiteration of Annex I and Annex V as the primary MARPOL Annexes with deficiencies, most likely due to the record-keeping requirements or faulty equipment.

Despite being an early leader in environmental regulation, Japan's enforcement of MARPOL violations beyond the basic port State obligations is lacking. While the illegal dumping of oil accounts for nearly 80% of the marine pollution incidents detected by the Japan Coast Guard, there is little information of enforcement actions taken. However, the 2002 Environmental Performance Review for Japan does indicate an increase in reception facilities, which, in turn, has promoted a decline in illegal Annex I discharges.[36]

United States

The Torrey Canyon disaster "shocked" the American people and put the Coast Guard into the hot seat as the responsible agency for "provid[ing] adequate safeguards for protecting the American public against a Torrey Canyon–type disaster."[37] Since Torrey Canyon, and the multitude of smaller shipping disasters closer to the United States, the emphasis on prevention and compliance has resulted in a robust port State control program totally apart from the regional MOUs discussed earlier.

While the United States is not a party of any MOU, the Coast Guard does observe many of the MOUs and considers recent exams conducted in other countries when determining whether a vessel will be inspected upon entry to a U.S. port. It is important to note the Coast Guard can also conduct an inspection outside of the targeting matrix when there

Table 14.7 Japan Port State Estimated MARPOL Deficiencies Compared to Tokyo MOU Total

MARPOL	Total MARPOL Deficiencies	Japan (%)	Japan Total
Annex I	1679	18.6	312.3
Annex II	13	18.6	2.4
Annex III	33	18.6	6.1
Annex IV	1199	18.6	223
Annex V	1587	18.6	295.2
Annex VI	758	18.6	141

are indications of noncompliance with the law or the vessel present as substandard with respect to safety or the environment. The Coast Guard's port State control program has been effective in improving compliance while the United States is recognized for the most proactive criminal enforcement efforts since the early 1990s.[38]

The United States implements MARPOL 73/78 through the Act to Prevent Pollution from Ships (APPS) and the associated Code of Federal Regulations. The Coast Guard employs the same compliance actions as those under the MOUs, including the issuance of deficiencies, the detention of substandard vessels, and the banning of vessels if detained more than three times in a 12-month period. The Coast Guard also has programs for recognizing vessels with superior safety and environmental records and promotes a voluntary disclosure program, which allows a vessel to report a violation and take on the subsequent investigation.

Over the past 20 years, the United States has increased enforcement of violations of MARPOL 73/78 more than anywhere else in the world. APPS includes a provision that allows a U.S. court to award up to half of a criminal penalty to a crew member, often referred to as a "whistleblower," who provides information that leads to a conviction. Whistleblowers often, but not always, provide information that indicates a vessel is not in compliance with domestic and international law. With these clear grounds, the Coast Guard can expand the exam in order to determine whether there is a violation of law. These expanded exams can result in the administrative, civil, or criminal enforcement actions. The United States has received criticism both for the practice of using whistleblowers as an investigatory tool and for aggressively prosecuting MARPOL violators.

In cases referred for criminal prosecution by the Coast Guard, the Department of Justice often seeks vicarious liability against the vessel owners and operators, and goes beyond monetary penalties to argue for prison time for those who illegally discharge oily water or garbage in violation of Annexes I and V. Because of this aggressive enforcement posture, the Coast Guard has been called into the domestic courts to justify the ability to prosecute foreign-flagged vessels, their owners and operators, for violations that occur outside of the United States' waters. Most criminal cases brought in the United States are based on the entry of a vessel into a U.S. port with an inaccurate Oil Record Book. Criminal penalties can range from $200,000 to $12 million depending on the number of port calls, the number of vessels committing violations, and the egregiousness of the violations. Convictions and settlements often include a probation period ranging from 3 to 5 years and requires the company to establish an Environmental Compliance Plan. The Environmental Compliance plan ensures a system is put in place to prevent future violations and forcibly change the culture on the vessel and within the company.

The United States has led the efforts to enforce against companies in order to promote a cultural change and encourage those with direct control to reduce intentional pollution. However, because shipping is often a race to the bottom, businesses seek the cheapest way to transport goods with little concern for sound environmental practices. A 2003 OECD report on MARPOL and enforcement acknowledges that even though the cost of compliance with MARPOL is only 2% of daily operational costs and in the United States, the penalties awarded have been significant, compliance has not significantly increased because the risk of being caught combined with the cost of a successful prosecution still does not outweigh the cost savings of noncompliance.[39] The lack of economic incentive to comply with MARPOL combined with uneven international enforcement as vessels travel from port to port are two of the reasons compliance remains a difficult objective to meet under the existing regimes.

Living Marine Resources Enforcement

A number of federal agencies are involved in living marine resources enforcement. The USCG is the lead agency for at-sea enforcement of living marine resource laws, and shares the responsibility for overall enforcement with the U.S. National Marine Fisheries Service (NMFS) of the U.S. National Oceanographic and Atmospheric Administration (NOAA) under the Department of Commerce, the U.S. Fish and Wildlife Service (FWS) of the Department of Interior, and state enforcement agencies. NOAA is the primary agency responsible for monitoring the status of fish stocks, setting catch limits, and the U.S. fishery management process within the U.S. EEZ.[40] The USCG ensures compliance with domestic regulations and select international fisheries conventions and through conducting patrols and law enforcement boardings.

In addition to international conventions, the USCG is a party to numerous fishing bilateral agreements including agreements with Canada, Mexico, the People's Republic of China, Russian, and Taiwan. In 2007, during the reauthorization of the Magnuson–Stevens Fisheries Conservation and Management Act (Magnuson–Stevens), Congress found that, "[i]nternational cooperation is necessary to address illegal, unreported, and unregulated fishing and other fishing practices which may harm the sustainability of living marine resources and disadvantage the U.S. fishing industry."[41] Bilateral agreements are reached in conjunction with the Department of State, with the input of the Department of Commerce, and are authorized by Congress under the Magnuson–Stevens Act.[42] Communications through diplomatic channels can take a significant amount of time to process—typically weeks, not days, for clearance of correspondence and proper in-country routing. Bilateral agreements allow for a prenegotiated, streamlined process for communication and for requesting any necessary authorization to stop, board, and search a vessel, or to confirm the flag state registration of a vessel. They also create a quick process for notifying a flag state of the results of a boarding, law enforcement action taken, or to request a waiver of jurisdiction if the United States seeks to enforce domestic law as a result of a law enforcement boarding.

Further, the USCG also has shiprider agreements with several countries including Senegal, Sierra Leone, the Gambia, Palau, Micronesia, Marshall Islands, Nauru, Kiribati, Tuvalu, Tonga, Samoa, and the Cook Islands (New Zealand). These agreements are designed to deter illicit maritime activity beyond the jurisdiction of the United States. A foreign shiprider embarked on a USCG vessel allows for the USCG vessel to enter into another nation's territorial seas or to board a vessel flagged by that country. The shiprider has the authority to provide authorization to stop, board, and search a vessel and to seize contraband or illegal catch.

The Magnuson–Stevens Fisheries Conservation and Management Act (Magnuson–Stevens), 16 U.S.C. §§ 1801-1883

The Magnuson–Stevens Fisheries Conservation and Management Act (MSA), initially passed in 1976 and amended in 2006, is the primary law governing marine fisheries management in the U.S. federal waters.[43] In 1976, the MSA extended U.S. jurisdiction of fisheries management beyond 12 nm, which was previously viewed as "international waters" and fished by foreign fishing fleets, to 200 nm. It also established eight regional fishery management councils that are responsible for fisheries conservation and management in their respective geographic areas.[44] The fisheries councils are compromised of both voting and nonvoting members from the commercial and recreational fishing industries, and from environmental, academic, and government interests, and they are required to "reflect the expertise and interest of the several constituent States in the ocean area" over which the council has authority.[45] The main duties of the councils are to develop and amend fishery management plans,[46] convene committee and advisory panels, prioritize research objectives, establish annual catch limits, and to create and execute fishery rebuilding plans.[47] The MSA provides for both civil and criminal penalties.[48] The Act permits the civil forfeiture of fishing gear, vessel, or illegal catch without prior court approval for the sale of seized fish for at least fair market value.[49] The NOAA and the USCG are the primary federal agencies to enforce the MSA.

The Lacey Act of 1900, 16 U.S.C. §§ 3371-3378

The Lacey Act was the first U.S. federal regulation passed that protected wildlife. The Lacey Act makes it unlawful to import, export, sell, acquire, or purchase fish, wildlife,[50] or plants[51] that are taken, possessed, transported, or sold in violation of any U.S. or Indian tribal law, treaty, regulation, or any foreign law.[52] In 2008, the Act was amended to include additional prohibited plants and plant products including products made from illegally logged woods. The U.S. FWS is the lead federal agency for enforcing the Lacey Act, though other agencies, such as the Departments of Interior and Commerce, also have enforcement authority. The Act provides for both civil and criminal penalties. This Act may not include the regulation of activities that are governed by other living marine resources, such as the Magnuson Fishery Conservation and Management Act, and activity involving the harvest of highly migratory species.

1991 UN Moratorium on High Seas Drift Net Fishing (UN General Assembly Resolution 46/215)

In 1991, the United Nations assembly recognized the impact of large-scale pelagic drift net[53] fishing on living marine resources, including enclosed and semienclosed seas, and adopted UN General Assembly Resolution 46/215. The Resolution recommends that all members of the international community take the following actions:

1. reduce fishing effort in existing large-scale pelagic high seas drift net fisheries by reducing the number of vessels involved, the length of the nets, and the area of operation, so as to achieve a 50% reduction in fishing effort;
2. continue to ensure that the areas of operation of large-scale pelagic high seas drift net fishing are not expanded and are further reduced;
3. ensure that a global moratorium on all large-scale pelagic drift net fishing is fully implemented on the high seas of the world's oceans and seas, including enclosed seas and semienclosed seas.

The Agreement for the Implementation of the Provisions of the United Nations Convention on the Law of the Sea of 10 December 1982 Relating to the Conservation and Management of Straddling Fish Stocks and Highly Migratory Fish Stocks (United Nations Fish Stock Agreement or UNFSA)

In response to the international observation that the management of high seas fisheries were inadequate in many areas, resources were over utilized, problems existed with unregulated fishing, overcapitalization, excessive fleet size, vessel reflagging to escape controls, insufficiently selective gear, unreliable databases, and lack of sufficient cooperation between the international community, the United Nations adopted the United Nations Fish Stock Agreement (UNFSA). Parties to the UNFSA agree to support flag States, port States, and coastal States in the enforcement of conservation and management measures adopted "to ensure the long-term conservation and sustainable use of straddling fish stocks and highly migratory fish stocks."[54] Pursuant to the UNFSA, to ensure compliance with conservation and management measures, the United State may conduct a boarding of any UNFSA party vessel on the high seas that is located within a region managed by a fisheries agreement for straddling stocks or highly migratory species that the United States is a party to, regardless of whether the flag State of the vessel which the United States seeks to board is a member of the regional fisheries body enacted by the agreement.

Regional Fisheries Management Organizations (RFMOs), established by international agreements or treaties, such as UNFSA, are responsible for managing the fish stocks of a particular region.[55] Members share a practical or financial interest in the management or conservation. They also have a duty to conserve all species associated or affected by their fisheries.

The Marine Mammal Protection Act of 1972—16 U.S.C. § 1377

The Marine Mammal Protection Act of 1972 (MMPA)[56] prohibits, with very narrow exceptions, the "taking"[57] of marine mammals in the U.S. waters and by U.S. citizens on the high seas as well as the importation of marine mammals[58] and marine mammal products.[59]

The MMPA was enacted after an increase in concern from the scientific community and the U.S. public that certain species of marine mammal populations were rapidly declining as a result of human activities. Through the National Marine Fisheries Service, the Department of Commerce is responsible for the protection of whales, dolphins, porpoises, seals, and seal lines. Through the U.S. FWS, the Department of Interior is responsible for the protection of walrus, manatees, otters, and polar bears. The protection of marine mammals in captivity is the regulation by the Animal and Plant Health Inspection Service, a division of the Department of Agriculture.

The Act was the first federal legislation to provide a complete federal program that replaced state-run programs that had attempted to address living marine resources at the state level. It also directed the protection of complete population stocks, species, and subspecies; a significant change from a prior stance where enforcement was not subspecies specific. Additionally, it shifted the burden from a regulating agency to the "resource user" to require that a proposed taking of a living marine resource would not adversely affect the resource or the ecosystem. Further, the MMPA was the catalyst that directed federal agencies to engage in international arrangements regarding the research and conservation of all marine mammals.[60] It is important to note a few of the MMPA's exceptions to the moratorium of the taking of marine mammals in the U.S. waters. The MMPA does not generally apply to Alaska natives who live on the Alaskan coast, properly permitted scientific research and take that is deemed incidental to commercial fishing and other nonfishing activities, and marine mammals that are utilized for public display at licensed institutions.[61]

The Endangered Species Act of 1973—16 U.S.C. §§ 1531-1544

The Endangered Species Act (ESA) protects any species, as well as their ecosystem, that is endangered or threatened with extinction through a prohibition that prevents any person from "taking[62] any (endangered) species within the United States or the territorial sea of the United States."[63] The ESA was enacted to prevent various species of fish, wildlife, and plants in the United States from becoming "extinct as a consequence of economic growth and development," with Congress specifically stating that "species of fish, wildlife, and plants are of esthetic, ecological, educational, historical, recreational, and scientific value to the Nation and its people."[64] Through the ESA, the United States pledged to conserve,[65] to the extent practicable, the various species of fish or wildlife and plants facing extinction, pursuant to

1. migratory bird treaties with Canada and Mexico;
2. the Migratory and Endangered Bird Treaty with Japan;
3. the Convention on Nature Protection and Wildlife Preservation in the Western Hemisphere;
4. the International Convention for the Northwest Atlantic Fisheries;
5. the International Convention for the High Seas Fisheries of the North Pacific Ocean;
6. the Convention on International Trade in Endangered Species of Wild Fauna and Flora; and
7. other international agreements; and
8. encouraging the States and other interested parties, through Federal financial assistance and a system of incentives, to develop and maintain conservation programs which meet national and international standards is a key to meeting the Nation's international commitments and to better safeguarding, for the benefit of all citizens, the Nation's heritage in fish, wildlife, and plants.[66]

All federal agencies are charged with enforcing the ESA. However, the lead agencies for enforcement are the Department of Interior, through the U.S. FWS, and for marine species, the Department of Commerce, through the National Marine Fisheries Service.

Illegal Immigration[67]

The Department of Homeland Security (DHS) is charged with enforcing the laws of the United States regarding immigration.[68] On land, a substantial amount of this responsibility is fulfilled by the U.S. Immigration and Customs Enforcement (ICE). In the maritime domain, this responsibility is shouldered by the USCG as well as Customs and Border Protection (CBP). The DOD can assist with migration operations in the form of initial migrant reception, transportation, housing, and the support services associated with those tasks. The USCG and CBP have statutory authority to engage in law enforcement activities including interdiction and repatriation.

Immigration and Nationality Act

Passed in 1952, the INA summarizes the U.S. immigration laws. In the maritime domain, smuggling ventures, particularly from Haiti and the Bahamas, increase in number every year. These ventures involve a high risk of danger, including death, and are often conducted without regard to the safety of those onboard. There are numerous substantive laws that prohibit the illegal entry of, and facilitation of, illegal entry in to the United States.

Improper Entry by Alien 8 U.S.C. § 1325 (2010)

8 U.S.C. § 1325 criminalizes the conduct of any alien who enters or attempts to enter the United States at any time or place other than as designated by immigration officers, eludes examination or inspection by immigration officers, or attempts to enter or obtains entry to the United States by a willfully false or misleading representation or the willful concealment of a material fact.[69] For the first commission of any offense, the alien shall be fined, or imprisoned not more than 6 months, or both, and for subsequent commissions of the offense, the alien shall be fined, or imprisoned not more than 2 years, or both.[70]

Bringing in and Harboring Certain Aliens 8 U.S.C. § 1324

8 U.S.C. § 1324 criminalizes the conduct of any person who

1. knowing that a person is an alien, brings to or attempts to bring to the United States in any manner whatsoever such person at a place other than a designated port of entry or place other than as designated by the Commissioner, regardless of whether such alien has received prior official authorization to come to, enter, or reside in the United States and regardless of any future official action which may be taken with respect to such alien;
2. knowing or in reckless disregard of the fact that an alien has come to, entered, or remains in the United States in violation of law, transports, or moves or attempts to transport or move such alien within the United States by means of transportation or otherwise, in furtherance of such violation of law;
3. knowing or in reckless disregard of the fact that an alien has come to, entered, or remains in the United States in violation of law, conceals, harbors, or shields from detection, or attempts to conceal, harbor, or shield from detection, such alien in any place, including any building or any means of transportation;
4. encourages or induces an alien to come to, enter, or reside in the United States, knowing or in reckless disregard of the fact that such coming to, entry, or residence is or will be in violation of law;

   or
5. (I) engages in any conspiracy to commit any of the preceding acts,

   or

   (II) aids or abets the commission of any of the preceding acts.

8 U.S.C. § 1324 carries both civil and criminal penalties including fines and imprisonment up to 20 years, or both, and as much as life in prison if a violation results in the death of any person.

Reentry of Removed Aliens 8 U.S.C. § 1326

8 U.S.C. § 1326 prohibits the attempted entry into the United States of any alien who has been previously removed from the United States by a final order of removal. The purpose of this statute is to deter reentry after deportation and to provide varied maximum terms of imprisonment. 8 U.S.C. § 1326 states, in part, that any alien who

1. has been denied admission, excluded, deported, or removed or has departed the United States while an order of exclusion, deportation, or removal is outstanding, and thereafter
2. enters, attempts to enter, or is at any time found in, the United States, unless
    a. prior to his reembarkation at a place outside the United States or his application for admission from foreign contiguous territory, the Attorney General has expressly consented to such alien's reapplying for admission; or
    b. with respect to an alien previously denied admission and removed, unless such alien shall establish that he was not required to obtain such advance consent under this chapter or any prior Act,

shall be fined under title 18, or imprisoned not more than 2 years, or both. The criminal penalties are wide ranging. In the case of any alien

1. whose removal[71] was subsequent to a conviction for commission of three or more misdemeanors involving drugs, crimes against the person, or both, or a felony (other than an aggravated felony), such alien shall be fined under title 18, imprisoned not more than 10 years, or both;
2. whose removal was subsequent to a conviction for commission of an aggravated felony, such alien shall be fined under such title, imprisoned not more than 20 years, or both;
3. who has been excluded from the United States pursuant to section 1225(c) of this title because the alien was excludable under section 1182(a)(3)(B) of this title, or who has been removed from the United States pursuant to the provisions of subchapter V, and who thereafter, without the permission of the Attorney General, enters the United States, or attempts to do so, shall be fined under title 18 and imprisoned for a period of 10 years, which sentence shall not run concurrently with any other sentence; or
4. who was removed from the United States pursuant to section 1231(a)(4)(B) of this title who thereafter, without the permission of the Attorney General, enters, attempts to enter, or is at any time found in, the United States (unless the Attorney General has expressly consented to such alien's reentry) shall be fined under title 18, imprisoned for not more than 10 years, or both.

Any alien previously deported who enters, attempts to enter, or is at any time found in, the United States (unless the Attorney General has expressly consented to such alien's reentry) shall be incarcerated for the remainder of any prior sentence of imprisonment which was pending at the time of deportation without any reduction for parole or supervised release.[72] Additionally, the alien shall be subject to such other penalties relating to the reentry of deported aliens as may be available under this section or any other provision of law.

Aiding or Assisting Certain Aliens to Enter 8 U.S.C. § 1327

8 U.S.C. § 1327 provides for civil fines or imprisonment, or both, for any person or persons who conspire to allow any alien who is inadmissible for entry in to the United States. 8 U.S.C. § 1327 states:

> Any person who knowingly aids or assists any alien inadmissible under section 1182(a)(2)(a)(2) (insofar as an alien inadmissible under such section has been convicted of an aggravated felony) or 1182(a)(3) (other than subparagraph (E) thereof) of this title to enter the United States, or who connives or conspires with any person or persons to allow, procure, or permit any such alien to enter the United States, shall be fined under title 18, or imprisoned not more than 10 years, or both.

Criminal Sanctions for Failure to Heave to, Obstruction of Boarding, or Providing False Information 18 U.S.C. § 2237

18 U.S.C. § 2237 prohibits the master, operator, or person in charge of a vessel of the United States, or a vessel subject to the jurisdiction of the United States, to knowingly fail to obey an order by an authorized Federal law enforcement officer to heave to that vessel.[73] This statute is often utilized to prosecute noncompliant vessels who refuse to heave to during a counterdrug boarding, smuggling venture, or during a fisheries enforcement boarding. This statute also criminalizes any person or vessel that forcibly resists, opposes, prevents, impedes, intimidates, or interferes with a boarding or other law enforcement action authorized by any Federal law or to resist a lawful arrest, or who provides materially false information to a Federal law enforcement officer during a boarding of a vessel regarding the vessel's destination, origin, ownership, registration, nationality, cargo, or crew.[74] Whoever knowingly commits a violation, that individual shall be fined or imprisoned for not more than 5 years or both.[75]

Summary

There are a number of key International Conventions and the U.S. laws and regulations which govern the response of government agencies to TCOs, drug traffickers, illegal fishing, and other illicit activity. How the International Conventions are enforced globally varies. Whether the response involves an at-sea boarding or a port State control examination, authority is derived from these international treaties and domestic laws.

End Notes

1. 'A Constitution for the Oceans,' Remarks by Tommy T.B. Koh, of Singapore, President of the Third United Nations Conference on the Law of the Sea, available at http://www.un.org/depts/los/convention_agreements/texts/koh_english.pdf, accessed July 11, 2015.
2. *See* Oceans & Law of the Sea United Nations, United Nations Convention on the Law of the Sea of 10 December 1982 Overview and full text, at http://www.un.org/depts/los/convention_agreements/convention_overview_convention.htm, accessed July 11, 2015 (emphasis added).
3. *See* Oceans & Law of the Sea United Nations, United Nations Convention on the Law of the Sea of 10 December 1982 Overview and full text, at http://www.un.org/depts/los/convention_agreements/convention_overview_convention.htm, accessed July 11, 2015.
4. U.S. President Reagan's 'United States Ocean Policy, March 10, 1983, provides in part, that the "United States is prepared to accept and act in accordance with the balance of interests relating to traditional uses of the oceans—such as navigation and overflight."
5. *See* United Nations Treaty Collection, Chapter VI, Narcotic Drugs and Psychotropic Substances, "19. United Nations Convention against Illicit Traffic in Narcotic Drugs and Psychotropic Substances," at https://treaties.un.org/pages/viewdetails.aspx?src=treaty&mtdsg_no=vi-19&chapter=6&lang=en, accessed September 11, 2015.
6. *See* Report of the Judge Advocate General of the United States Coast Guard Presented to the American Bar Association, Chicago, IL, July 2015, available at https://www.uscg.mil/legal/Home_doc/ABA_Report.pdf, accessed September 9, 2015.
7. Vessels in international waters are not subject to the jurisdiction of any nation other than the flag State. However, under international law, a warship, military aircraft, or other duly authorized ship or aircraft may approach any vessel in international waters to verify its nationality. *Mariana Flora*, 24 US 1, 11 Wheat. 43–44 (1826). An example of questions that could be asked by an approaching vessel include inquiries about the nationality of the vessel and crew, the type of catch or cargo onboard, the vessel's next and last port of call, and the purpose of the vessel's voyage. These questions do not constitute custodial interrogation under the U.S. law. *United States v. Rioseco*, 845 F.2d 299, 302–03 (11th Cir. 1988) (finding no evidence that the USCG deliberately used routine preboarding questions to obtain information that was prejudicial to the defendant rather than for the usual routine purpose). Answers to Right of Approach questions can be used to establish reasonable suspicion to further investigate the vessel's intentions.
8. A "submersible vessel" means any vessel that is capable of operating completely below the surface of the water, including both manned and unmanned watercraft. 46 U.S.C. § 70502.
9. A "semi-submersible vessel" means any watercraft constructed or adapted to be capable of operating with most of its hull and bulk under the surface of the water, including both manned and unmanned watercraft. 46 U.S.C. § 70502.
10. 18 U.S.C. § 2285, Sec. 101.
11. Brian Wilson, Submersibles and Transnational Criminal Organizations (2011). Ocean & Coastal Law Journal, Vol. 17, p. 1, 2011. available at SSRN: http://ssrn.com/abstract=2019496 or http://dx.doi.org/10.2139/ssrn.2019496, accessed September 9, 2015 (the discussion of the DTVIA and SPSS-type platforms is excerpted with permission of the author).
12. Ibid.
13. 18 U.S.C. § 2285
14. 18 U.S.C. § 2285, Sec. 101.
15. Wilson, Submersibles and Transnational Criminal Organizations (2011). Ocean & Coastal Law Journal.
16. Ibid.
17. *See* 2014 National Drug Control Strategy, The White House, available at https://www.whitehouse.gov/ondcp/national-drug-control-strategy, accessed September 11, 2015.
18. In re Barracuda Tanker Corp., 281 F. Supp. 228, 229 (S.D.N.Y. 1968).

19. American Academy of Sciences, Oil in the Sea III, 2003, cited by http://www.marinedefenders.com/oilpollutionfacts/sources.ph, accessed on 22 July 2015.
20. Includes the Merchant Shipping (Prevention of Oil Pollution) Regulations 1996 and the Merchant Shipping (Implementation of Shipping Source Pollution Directive) Regulations 2009.
21. Section 142 of the MSA 1995
22. Parl. Deb., *supra note* 13, col. 127WH, accessed from: http://www.loc.gov/law/help/marpol-convention/uk.php
23. Press release, Commission Vice President in charge of transport, (2007).
24. OECD (2002), *OECD Environmental Performance Reviews: United Kingdom 2002*, OECD Publishing, Paris.
25. *See* The Paris MOU on Port State Control, Port State Control: Adjusting Course 2014 Annual Report *available at* https://www.parismou.org/publications-category/annual-reports
26. Ibid.
27. https://www.amsa.gov.au/environment/legislation-and-prevention/prosecutions/oil/table.asp
28. Marine Orders 93, 94, 95, 96, and 97 likewise require compliance with the associated MARPOL annex.
29. Sub-Committee on Flag State Implementation, 14th session, Agenda item 7, FSI 14/INF.8, correct as of 18 April 2005.
30. Ibid.
31. *See* The Tokyo MOU on Port State Control, Annual Report on Port State Control in the Asia-Pacific Region (2014) *available at* http://www.tokyo-mou.org/doc/Ann14/index.html#/0; The Indian Ocean MOU on Port State Control, 2014 Annual Report *available at* http://www.iomou.org/armain.htm
32. *See* The Tokyo MOU on Port State Control, Annual Report on Port State Control in the Asia-Pacific Region (2014) *available at* http://www.tokyo-mou.org/doc/Ann14/index.html#/0; The Indian Ocean MOU on Port State Control, 2014 Annual Report *available at* http://www.iomou.org/armain.htm
33. Act No 136 of 1970.
34. Ibid.
35. Japan Coast Guard Act, art. 5(11).
36. OECD (2002), *OECD Environmental Performance Reviews: Japan 2002*, p. 241, OECD Publishing, Paris. DOI: http://dx.doi.org/10.1787/9789264175334-en
37. Coast Guard Proceedings of the Merchant Marine Council, Vol 24, No 4, April 1968.
38. See H.S. Bang, The Int'l Journal of Marine and Coastal Law 23 (2008) 715-759.
39. (*MAR. TRANSP. COMM., ORG. FOR ECON. CO-OPERATION & DEV., COST SAVINGS* STEMMING FROM NON-COMPLIANCE WITH INTERNATIONAL ENVIRONMENTAL REGULATIONS IN THE MARITIME SECTOR 4 (2003) [hereinafter COST SAVINGS] *available at* http://www.oecd.org/sti/transport/maritimetransport/2496757.pdf)
40. The official size of the United States Exclusive Economic Zone is 3.36 million square nautical miles. If every country claimed the maximum EEZ allowed by international law, the United States EEZ would constitute 10% of the world's EEZ. The United States EEZ has approximately 95,000 miles of coastline and 14 National Marine Sanctuaries..
41. 16 U.S.C. § 1801(a)(12) (2010)
42. 16 U.S.C. §§ 1801-1883 (2010).
43. 16 U.S.C. §§ 1801-1883
44. 16 U.S.C. § 1851, Sec. 302. The eight councils are the North Pacific, Western Pacific, Pacific, Gulf of Mexico, South Atlantic, Mid-Atlantic, New England, and the Caribbean Council.
45. 16 U.S.C. § 1851, Sec. 302.

46. A fishery management plan is required, among other provisions, to contain the conservation and management measures, applicable to foreign fishing and fishing by vessels of the United States, which are (A) necessary and appropriate for the conservation and management of the fishery to prevent overfishing and rebuild overfished stocks, and to protect, restore, and promote the long-term health and stability of the fishery. 16 U.S.C. § 153, Sec. 303. Contents of Fishery Management Plans..
47. NOAA Fisheries, Sustainable Fisheries, Councils, Regional Fishery Management Councils, available at http://www.nmfs.noaa.gov/sfa/management/councils/index.html (last visited July 22, 2015).
48. 16 U.S.C. § 1859 (2010). Civil penalties can include written warnings, summary settlement tickets, Notices of Violation and Assessment (NOVA), forfeiture of seized property including catch, vessel, and equipment, and permit sanctions.
49. 16 U.S.C. §1860 (2010). *See Gulf of Maine Trawlers v. United States*, 674 F.Supp.927 (D.Me.1987); *Jensen v. United States*, 743 F.Supp. 1091 (D.N.J. 1990).
50. The term "fish or wildlife" means any wild animal, whether alive or dead, including without limitation any wild mammal, bird, reptile, amphibian, fish, mollusk, crustacean, arthropod, coelenterate, or other invertebrate, whether or not bred, hatched, or born in captivity, and includes any part, product, egg or offspring thereof. 16 U.S.C. § 3371.
51. The terms "plant" and "plants" mean any wild member of the plant kingdom, including roots, seeds, and other parts thereof (but excluding common food crops and cultivars) which is indigenous to any State and which is either (A) listed on an appendix to the Convention on International Trade in Endangered Species of Wild Fauna and Flora, or (B) listed pursuant to any State law that provides for the conservation of species threatened with extinction. 16 U.S.C. § 3371. The Lacey Act exempts "scientific specimens of plant genetic material (including roots, seeds, germplasm, parts, or products thereof) that will be used for laboratory or field research from the definition of 'plant' unless they are an endangered or threatened species under the Endangered Species Act, or pursuant to any State law that provides for the conservation of species that are indigenous to the State and are threatened with extinction, or they are specifically listed in connection with the Lacey Act as being prohibited.".
52. 16 U.S.C. § 3371.
53. Drift nets are utilized during commercial fishing and can often be multiple miles long. They often do not discriminate catch, and therefore capture anything in its path including sea turtles, porpoises, seals, and sea lions. There are varying international definitions of "drift net." One proposed definition by the EC is as follows, "Drift net means any gillnet held on the sea surface or at a certain distance below it by floating devices, drifting with the current either independently or with the boat to which it may be attached. It may be equipped with devices aiming to stabilize the net and/or to limit its drifting." available at http://www.nmfs.noaa.gov/ia/iuu/driftnet_reports/2011_driftnet_report.pdf (last visited July 22, 2015). "Ghost nets" are what environmentalists call drift nets that are cut, lost, or set adrift by commercial vessels that continue to catch anything in its path for long periods of time.
54. The Agreement for the Implementation of the Provisions of the United Nations Convention on the Law of the Sea of December 10, 1982 Relating to the Conservation and Management of Straddling Fish Stocks and Highly Migratory Fish Stocks, page 2. UNFSA was adopted on August 4, 1995, opened for signature on December 4, 1995, remained open for signature until December 4, 1996, with 59 States and entities signing the Agreement.
55. There are currently 17 RFMOs, some of which have overlapping geographic areas.
56. 16 U.S.C. § 1377 (2012).
57. The term "take" means to harass, hunt, capture, or kill, or attempt to harass, hunt, capture, or kill any marine mammal. 16 U.S.C. § 1377, Sec. 3 (2012).
58. "Marine mammal" means any mammal which (A) is morphologically adapted to the marine environment or (B) primarily inhabits the marine environment (such as the polar bear); and, includes any part of any such marine mammal, including its raw, dressed, or dyed fur or skin. 16 U.S.C. § 1377, Sec. 3 (2012).

59. The term "marine mammal product" means any item of merchandise which consists, or is composed in whole or in part, of any marine mammal. 16 U.S.C. § 1377, Sec. 3 (2012).
60. 16 U.S.C. §1377, Sec. 2 (2012).
61. 16 U.S.C. §1377, Sec. 101 (2012).
62. The term 'take' means to harass, harm, pursue, hunt, shoot, wound, kill, trap, capture, or collect, or to attempt to engage in any such conduct. 16 U.S.C. § 1538 Sec. 3 (2012).
63. 16 U.S.C. §1538(a)(1)(B).
64. 16 U.S.C. §1540 Sec. 2 (a) (2012).
65. ESA states that the" terms "conserve," "conserving," and "conservation" mean to use and the use of all methods and procedures which are necessary to bring any endangered species or threatened species to the point at which the measures provided pursuant to this Act are no longer necessary. Such methods and procedures include, but are not limited to, all activities associated with scientific resources management such as research, census, law enforcement, habitat acquisition and maintenance, propagation, live trapping, and transplantation, and, in the extraordinary case where population pressures within a given ecosystem cannot be otherwise relieved, may include regulated taking." 16 U.S.C. § 1540 Sec. 3 (2012).
66. 16 U.S.C. §1540 Sec. 2 (a) (2012).
67. Not all international agencies and media organizations agree that the terms "migrant" or "refugee" are appropriate, proper terms to utilize when discussing immigration issues and the migration of people. For international discourse on the use of the term "migrant," *see* The battle over the words used to describe migrants, at http://www.bbc.com/news/magazine-34061097?post_id=1454757634854405_1454757624854406, accessed September 9, 2015.
68. *See* 6 U.S.C. §101B, Homeland Security Act of 2002, Pub. L. No. 107-296, 116 Stat. 2135 (2002) (codified primarily at 6 U.S.C. §§ 101-557).
69. An "alien" is "any person not a citizen or national of the United States." 8 U.S.C. §1101 Sec. 101 (3).
70. 8 U.S.C. § 1325. The civil penalty shall be at least $50 and not more than $250 for each such entry (or attempted entry); or twice the amount in the case of an alien who has been previously subject to a civil penalty under this subsection. Civil penalties under this subsection are in addition to, and not in lieu of, any criminal or other civil penalties that may be imposed. *See* Sec. (b) Improper time or place; civil penalties.
71. The term "removal" includes any agreement in which an alien stipulates to removal during (or not during) a criminal trial under either Federal or State law. *See* 8 U.S.C. § 1326 Sec. (b).
72. 8 U.S.C. § 1326 Sec. (c) Reentry of alien deported prior to completion of term of imprisonment.
73. Heave to" means to cause a vessel to slow, come to a stop, or adjust its course or speed to account for the weather conditions and sea state to facilitate a law enforcement boarding." *See* 18 U.S.C. § 2237 Sec. (e).
74. 18 U.S.C. § 2237 (a) (2).
75. 18 U.S.C. § 2237 (b) (1).

Index

Note: Page numbers followed by "f" indicate figures, "t" indicate tables and "b" indicate boxes.

D

J

K

L

U

CPSIA information can be obtained
at www.ICGtesting.com
Printed in the USA
FSHW01n0311280918
52466FS